12th International Conference on Natural Language Processing (ICON-2015)

Trivandrum, India
11 – 14 December 2015

ISBN: 978-1-5108-3787-4

12th International Conference on Natural Language Processing

Proceedings of the Conference

11-14 December 2015
IIITM-Kerala, Trivandrum, India

Preface

Research in Natural Language Processing (NLP) has taken a noticeable leap in the recent years. Tremendous growth of information on the web and its easy access has stimulated large interest in the field. India with multiple languages and continuous growth of Indian language content on the web makes a fertile ground for NLP research. Moreover, industry is keenly interested in obtaining NLP technology for mass use. The internet search companies are increasingly aware of the large market for processing languages other than English. For example, search capability is needed for content in Indian and other languages. There is also a need for searching content in multiple languages, and making the retrieved documents available in the language of the user. As a result, a strong need is being felt for machine translation to handle this large instantaneous use. Information Extraction, Question Answering Systems and Sentiment Analysis are also showing up as other business opportunities.

These needs have resulted in two welcome trends. First, there is much wider student interest in getting into NLP at both postgraduate and undergraduate levels. Many students interested in computing technology are getting interested in natural language technology, and those interested in pursuing computing research are joining NLP research. Second, the research community in academic institutions and the government funding agencies in India have joined hands to launch consortia projects to develop NLP products. Each consortium project is a multi-institutional endeavour working with a common software framework, common language standards, and common technology engines for all the different languages covered in the consortium. As a result, it has already led to development of basic tools for multiple languages which are inter-operable for machine translation, cross lingual search, hand writing recognition and OCR.

In this backdrop of increased student interest, greater funding and most importantly, common standards and interoperable tools, there has been a spurt in research in NLP on Indian languages whose effects we have just begun to see. A great number of submissions reflecting good research is a heartening matter. There is an increasing realization to take advantage of features common to Indian languages in machine learning. It is a delight to see that such features are not just specific to Indian languages but to a large number of languages of the world, hitherto ignored. The insights so gained are furthering our linguistic understanding and will help in technology development for hopefully all languages of the world.

For machine learning and other purposes, linguistically annotated corpora using the common standards have become available for multiple Indian languages. They have been used for the development of basic technologies for several languages. Larger set of corpora are expected to be prepared in near future.

This volume contains papers selected for presentation in technical sessions of ICON-2015 and short communications selected for poster presentation. We are thankful to our excellent team of reviewers from all over the globe who deserve full credit for the hard work of reviewing the high quality submissions with rich technical content. From 134 submissions, 56 papers were selected, 31 for full presentation and 25 for poster presentation, representing a variety of new and interesting developments, covering a wide spectrum of NLP areas and core linguistics.

We are deeply grateful to *Yuji Matsumoto, Nara Institute of Science and Technology (NAIST), Japan* for giving the keynote lecture at ICON. We would also like to thank the members of the Advisory Committee and Programme Committee for their support and co-operation.

We thank Sudip Kumar Naskar, Chair, Student Paper Competition and Manish Shrivastava and Amitav Das, Chairs, NLP Tools Contest for taking the responsibilities of the events.

We convey our thanks to P V S Ram Babu, G Srinivas Rao, G Namratha and A Lakshmi Narayana, International Institute of Information Technology (IIIT), Hyderabad for their dedicated efforts in successfully handling the ICON Secretariat. We also thank IIIT Hyderabad team of Peri Bhaskararao, Vasudeva Varma, Soma Paul, Radhika Mamidi, Manish Shrivastava, B Yegnanarayana, Suryakanth V Gangashetty and Anil Kumar Vuppala. We heart-fully express our gratitude to Rajeev R R, Maya Moneykumar, VRCLC team members, Research Scholars and student volunteers for their timely help with sincere dedication to make this conference a success.

We also thank all those who came forward to help us in this task.

Finally, we thank all the researchers who responded to our call for papers and all the participants of ICON-2015, without whose overwhelming response the conference would not have been a success.

December 2015
Trivandrum

Dipti Misra Sharma
Rajeev Sangal
Elizabeth Sherly

Advisory Committee:

Aravind K Joshi, University of Pennsylvania, USA (Chair)

Conference General Chair:

Rajeev Sangal, IIT (BHU), Varanasi, India

Programme Committee:

Elizabeth Sherly, IIITM-Kerala, Trivandrum, India (Chair)
Dipti Misra Sharma, IIIT Hyderabad, India (Co-Chair)

Tools Contest Chairs:

Manish Shrivastava, IIIT Hyderabad, India
Amitav Das, NIIT University, Rajasthan, India

Organizing Committee:

Rajeev R R, IIITM-K, Trivandrum, India (Chair)

Organized by

International Institute of Information Technology, Hyderabad

Natural Language Processing Association, India

IIITM-Kerala, Trivandrum

LDC-IL, CIIL Mysore

Sponsors

Microsoft Research, India

Kerala State Council for Science, Technology & Environment

Referees

We gratefully acknowledge the excellent quality of refereeing we received from the reviewers. We thank them all for being precise and fair in their assessment and for reviewing the papers in time.

A Kumaran
A R Balamurali
Abhijit Mishra
Aditi Sharan
Aditya Joshi
Ajit Kumar
Alok Parlikar
Amba Kulkarni
Amitava Das
Anandaswarup Vadapalli
Anil Kumar Singh
Anil Kumar Vuppala
Anil Thakur
Aniruddha Tammewar
Anoop Kunchukuttan
Anupam Jamatia
Anupam Mondal
Aravind Ganapathiraju
Ashwini Vaidya
Asif Ekbal
Ayushi Dalmia
Ayushi Pandey
B Bajibabu
Balaji Jagan
Bharat Ram Ambati
Bharathi Raja Asoka Chakravarthi
Bhaskararao Peri
Bhuvana Narasimhan
Bira Chandra Singh
Bjorn Gamback
Bonnie Webber
Braja Gopal Patra
Brijesh Bhatt
C V Jawahar
Debasis Ganguly
Deepak Padmanabhan
Dhananjaya Gowda
Dipankar Das
Dipti Misra Sharma
Dwijen Rudrapal
Elizabeth Sherly
Enrique Flores
Fei Xia
Ganesh Katrapati
Gautam Mantena
Geethanjali Rakshit
Girish Palshikar
Gurpreet Singh Lehal
Harikrishna K V
Hema A Murthy

Jim Maddock
Joakim Nivre
Jyoti Pareek
Jyoti Pawar
K V Subbarao
Kalika Bali
Kamal Garg
Keh-Yih Su
Kishorjit Nongmeikapam
Kunal Chakma
Lars Bungum
Litton Kurisinkel
Maaz Anwar
Maite Giménez
Malhar Kulkarni
Manish Shrivastava
Matthias Huck
Monojit Choudhury
Mounika K V
N Vasudevan
Neha Prabhugaonkar
Nicoletta Calzolari
Nikhil Pattisapu
Nikhilesh Bhatnagar
Niladri Chatterjee
Niladri Sekhar Dash
Owen Rambow
Paolo Rosso
Parminder Singh
Parth Gupta
Partha Talukdar
Pattabhi Rao
Pawan Goyal
Pranaw Kumar
Prateek Bhatia
Preethi Raghavan
Priya Radhakrishnan
Pruthwik Mishra
Pushpak Bhattacharyya
Radhika Mamidi
Rafiya Begum
Rajeev R R
Rajeev Sangal
Rajesh Bhatt
Rakesh Balabantaray
Raksha Sharma
Ranjani Parthasarathi
Ratish Surendran
Raveesh Motlani
Riyaz Ahmad Bhat

Royal Sequeira
Sachin Pawar
Samar Husain
Sandipan Dandapat
Sanjukta Ghosh
Santanu Pal
Satarupa Guha
Shashi Narayan
Shruti Rijhwani
Silpa Kanneganti
Sivaji Bandyopadhyay
Sivanand Achanta
Sobha L
Soma Paul
Somnath Banerjee
Sopan Kolte
Srinivas Bangalore
Sriram Venkatapathy
Subhash Chandra
Sudip Kumar Naskar
Sunayana Sitaram
Suryakanth V Gangashetty
Sutanu Chakraborti
Swapnil Chaudhari
Tapabrata Mondal
Tejas Godambe
Thamar Solorio
Thoudam Doren Singh
Umamaheswari E
Vandan Mujadia
Vasudeva Varma
Vigneshwaran Muralidaran
Vijaysundar Ram
Vinay Kumar Mittal
Vineet Chaitanya
Vishal Goyal

Table of Contents

Conference Program

Saturday, December 12, 2015 (continued)

+ 11:00-13:05 Technical Session II: WSD and Lexicon

Word Sense Disambiguation in Hindi Language Using Hyperspace Analogue to Language and Fuzzy C-Means Clustering
Devendra K. Tayal, Leena Ahuja and Shreya Chhabra

Using Word Embeddings for Bilingual Unsupervised WSD
Sudha Bhingardive, Dhirendra Singh, Rudramurthy V and Pushpak Bhattacharyya

Compositionality in Bangla Compound Verbs and their Processing in the Mental Lexicon
Tirthankar Dasgupta, Manjira Sinha and Anupam Basu

IndoWordNet Dictionary: An Online Multilingual Dictionary using IndoWordNet
Hanumant Redkar, Sandhya Singh, Nilesh Joshi, Anupam Ghosh and Pushpak Bhattacharyya

+ 13:05-14:00 Lunch

+ 14:00-15:30 Poster and Demo Session:

Let Sense Bags Do Talking: Cross Lingual Word Semantic Similarity for English and Hindi
Apurva Nagvenkar, Jyoti Pawar and Pushpak Bhattacharyya

A temporal expression recognition system for medical documents by
Naman Gupta, Aditya Joshi and Pushpak Bhattacharyya

An unsupervised EM method to infer time variation in sense probabilities
Martin Emms and Arun Jayapal

Solving Data Sparsity by Morphology Injection in Factored SMT
Sreelekha S, Piyush Dungarwal, Pushpak Bhattacharyya and Malathi D

Authorship Attribution in Bengali Language
Shanta Phani, Shibamouli Lahiri and Arindam Biswas

TransChat: Cross-Lingual Instant Messaging for Indian Languages
Diptesh Kanojia, Shehzaad Dhuliawala, Abhijit Mishra, Naman Gupta and Pushpak Bhattacharyya

A Study on Divergence in Malayalam and Tamil Language in Machine Translation Perceptive
Jisha P Jayan and Elizabeth Sherly

Automatic conversion of Indian Language Morphological Processors into Grammatical Framework (GF)
Harsha Vardhan Grandhi and Soma Paul

Logistic Regression for Automatic Lexical Level Morphological Paradigm Selection for Konkani Nouns
Shilpa Desai, Jyoti Pawar and Pushpak Bhattacharyya

Ruchi: Rating Individual Food Items in Restaurant Reviews
Burusothman Ahiladas, Paraneetharan Saravanaperumal, Sanjith Balachandran, Thamayanthy Sripalan and Surangika Ranathunga

Dependency Extraction for Knowledge-based Domain Classification
Lokesh Kumar Sharma and Namita Mittal

An Approach to Collective Entity Linking
Ashish Kulkarni, Kanika Agarwal, pararth Shah, Sunny Raj Rathod and Ganesh Ramakrishnan

Development of Speech corpora for different Speech Recognition tasks in Malayalam language
Cini Kurian

+ 15:30-16:00 Tea Break

+ 16:00-17:40 Technical Session III: Emerging Areas

POS Tagging of Hindi-English Code Mixed Text from Social Media: Some Machine Learning Experiments
Royal Sequiera, Monojit Choudhury and Kalika Bali

Automated Analysis of Bangla Poetry for Classification and Poet Identification
Geetanjali Rakshit, Anupam Ghosh, Pushpak Bhattacharyya and Gholamreza Haffari

Sentence Boundary Detection for Social Media Text
Dwijen Rudrapal, Anupam Jamatia, Kunal Chakma, Amitava Das and Björn Gambäck

Mood Classification of Hindi Songs based on Lyrics
Braja Gopal Patra, Dipankar Das and Sivaji Bandyopadhyay

+ 11:00-13:05 Technical Session V:Statistical Machine Translation

Augmenting Pivot based SMT with word segmentation
Rohit More, Anoop Kunchukuttan, Pushpak Bhattacharyya and Raj Dabre

Using Multilingual Topic Models for Improved Alignment in English-Hindi MT
Diptesh Kanojia, Aditya Joshi, Pushpak Bhattacharyya and Mark James Carman

Triangulation of Reordering Tables: An Advancement Over Phrase Table Triangulation in Pivot-Based SMT
Deepak Patil, Harshad Chavan and Pushpak Bhattacharyya

Post-editing a chapter of a specialized textbook into 7 languages: importance of terminological proximity with English for productivity
Ritesh Shah, Christian Boitet, Pushpak Bhattacharyya, Mithun Padmakumar, Leonardo Zilio, Ruslan Kalitvianski, Mohammad Nasiruddin, Mutsuko Tomokiyo and Sandra Castellanos Páez

Generating Translation Corpora in Indic Languages:Cultivating Bilingual Texts for Cross Lingual Fertilization
Niladri Sekhar Dash, Arulmozi Selvraj and Mazhar Hussain

+ 11:00-13:05 Technical Session VI: NLP Tools Contest

+ 13:20-14:20 Lunch

+ 14:00-15:30 Technical Session VII: Machine Translation

Translation Quality and Effort: Options versus Post-editing
Donald Sturgeon and John S. Y. Lee

Investigating the potential of post-ordering SMT output to improve translation quality
Pratik Mehta, Anoop Kunchukuttan and Pushpak Bhattacharyya

Applying Sanskrit Concepts for Reordering in MT
Akshar Bharati, , Prajna Jha, Soma Paul and Dipti M Sharma

+ 14:00-15:30 Technical Session VIII: Dialog System and Question

Dialogue Act Recognition for Text-based Sinhala
Sudheera Palihakkara, Dammina Sahabandu, Ahsan Shamsudeen, Chamika Bandara and Surangika Ranathunga

A Semi Supervised Dialog Act Tagging for Telugu
Suman Dowlagar and Radhika Mamidi

Ranking Model with a Reduced Feature Set for an Automated Question Generation System
Manisha Satish Divate and Ambuja Salgaonkar

+ 15:30-16:00 Tea Break

+ 16:00-17:30 Technical Session IX: Speech Processing

Natural Language Processing for Solving Simple Word Problems
Sowmya S Sundaram and Deepak Khemani

Analysis of Influence of L2 English Speakers' Fluency on Occurrence and Duration of Sentence-medial Pauses in English Readout Speech
Shambhu Nath Saha and Shyamal Kr. Das Mandal

Acoustic Correlates of Voicing and Gemination in Bangla
Aanusha Ghosh

+ 17:30-18:00 Valedictory Function

Keynote Lecture

on

Scientific Paper Analysis

Yuji Matsumoto
Nara Institute of Science and Technology (NAIST, Japan)
<matsu@is.naist.jp>

Rapid increase of scientific documents causes difficulty in acquiring up-to-date information even by experts. Through deepening the text and document analysis technologies and automatic construction of knowledge bases necessary for document understanding, this project aims to develop foundations of content understanding of large scale technical documents and structural similarity analysis at various levels of contents and documents. In collaboration with the experts in Bio-science, Material Science, Neuroscience, Law, and Artificial Intelligence, we aim to develop an integrated environment for content-based document retrieval, summarization and knowledge discovery by aggregating the contents from large scale documents, and survey generation by inter-document relation analysis.

1

D S Sharma, R Sangal and E Sherly. Proc. of the 12th Intl. Conference on Natural Language Processing, page 1,
Trivandrum, India. December 2015. ©2015 NLP Association of India (NLPAI)

Addressing Class Imbalance in Grammatical Error Detection with Evaluation Metric Optimization

Anoop Kunchukuttan, Pushpak Bhattacharyya
Center for Indian Language Technology
Department of Computer Science and Engineering
Indian Institute of Technology Bombay
{anoopk,pb}@cse.iitb.ac.in

Abstract

We address the problem of class imbalance in *supervised* grammatical error detection (GED) for non-native speaker text, which is the result of the low proportion of erroneous examples compared to a large number of error-free examples. Most learning algorithms maximize *accuracy* which is not a suitable objective for such imbalanced data. For GED, most systems address this issue by tuning hyperparameters to maximize metrics like F_β. Instead, we show that learning classifiers that directly learn model parameters by optimizing evaluation metrics like F_1 and F_2 score deliver better performance on these metrics as compared to traditional sampling and cost-sensitive learning solutions for addressing class imbalance. Optimizing these metrics is useful in recall-oriented grammar error detection scenarios. We also show that there are inherent difficulties in optimizing precision-oriented evaluation metrics like $F_{0.5}$. We establish this through a systematic evaluation on multiple datasets and different GED tasks.

1 Introduction

The task of *grammatical error detection* (GED) and *grammatical error correction* (GEC) refers to the identification and repair of grammatical errors in text generated by speakers of a language (native/non-native). Many techniques, rule-based as well as machine learning based, have been proposed for addressing this task. A common and successful method for building *grammatical error detection* (GED) systems is to apply *supervised learning* on annotated learner corpora. For instance, the problem of noun number error detection can be formulated as a task of classifying if

Task	Errors	Tokens	Error Rate
Article	6658	234,695	2.84%
Noun Number	3379	245,026	1.38%
Preposition*	1955	123,419	1.58%

Table 1: Error rates for GED tasks (NUCLE)
* statistics for 10 most frequent prepositions

the head noun of a noun phrase has the `correct` or `incorrect` grammatical number. As opposed to rule-based methods, classification methods can easily incorporate complex and arbitrary evidence as features. Some of the best performing systems for the most frequent grammatical errors, *viz.* noun number, article and preposition errors, are classification systems (Ng et al., 2013).

However, a major problem in learning classifiers from an annotated learner corpus is the very low **error rate** (number of errors per token) in the corpus (Chodorow et al., 2012). For instance, the error rates are less than 3% for noun-number, article and preposition errors in the NUCLE annotated learner corpus (Dahlmeier et al., 2013) as shown in Table 1. Such low error rates (less than 5%) have been observed across various learner corpora (see Table 2) *viz.* the NUCLE corpus (Dahlmeier et al., 2013), HOO12 corpus (Dale et al., 2012) and NICT-JLE corpus (Izumi et al., 2004). Thus, learning classifiers for GEC/GED from annotated learner corpora is a case of learning a classifier from an **imbalanced dataset** *i.e.* a dataset where the class ratios are highly skewed (He and Garcia, 2009). In contrast to many imbalanced problems studied in datamining literature, GED tasks are characterized by large and sparse features spaces and very high imbalance ratios.

Since it is easy to achieve high accuracy by simply assigning all training examples to the majority class, *accuracy* as the optimization objective performs poorly for classification on imbal-

D S Sharma, R Sangal and E Sherly. Proc. of the 12th Intl. Conference on Natural Language Processing, pages 2–10,
Trivandrum, India. December 2015. ©2015 NLP Association of India (NLPAI)

Corpus	Tokens	Errors	%Error Rate
NUCLE	1,161,567	46,597	3.82
HOO12	374,680	8,432[‡]	2.25[‡]
NICT-JLE	169,662	14,407	8.49

Table 2: Errors statistics for learner corpora
[‡] articles and prepositions errors only

anced datasets. Moreover, accuracy is not the right evaluation metric for GED. Non-native language learners require a GED system with a **high precision** so that they are not misguided by wrong error notifications. On the other hand, professional copy-editors and language instructors will require a **high recall** system that helps improve productivity and quality of service by identifying all potential errors that need review, even at the cost of flagging some spurious errors. Hence, a precision oriented optimization objective like $F_{0.5}$ and a recall oriented objective like F_2 would be appropriate for non-native speakers and copy-editors respectively. *In this paper, we explore the hypothesis that by directly optimizing the desired evaluation metric, we can satisfy the requirements of asymmetric misclassification cost and customization of the recall/precision trade-off.*

The following are the contributions of our work:

- Sampling and example-weighting methods have been traditionally applied to overcome this limitation. We systematically investigate different solutions to the class imbalance problem for three GED tasks (noun number, article and preposition) over multiple annotated learner corpora. We compare the following sampling methods over a range of sampling ratios: *random undersampling, Synthetic Minority Over-sampling Technique (SMOTE) and example weighting.* We analyze and present experimental results to demonstrate the limitations of these traditional methods in addressing class imbalance.

- As an alternative to sampling methods, we propose that a GED classifier be learnt by directly optimizing the evaluation metrics, typically F_1, F_2 or $F_{0.5}$. For copy-editors, F_2 is a suitable evaluation measure which addresses the need for high recall in GED. We use the performance measure optimization framework proposed by Joachims (2005) for optimizing these metrics. For the three GED

tasks under consideration, we show that optimizing the F_2 metric of the `incorrect` class gives better performance compared to sampling methods.

- We also show that evaluation metric optimization, as well as sampling methods, are not suitable for improving precision. While evaluation metric optimization helps improve recall and obtain a reasonable precision-recall trade-off, improving precision remains a challenge.

The rest of the paper is organized as follows. Section 2 describes the limitations of sampling methods, motivates the use of evaluation metrics optimization for imbalanced data problems, and the use of F_2 as an evaluation metric for GED. Sections 3 and 4 discuss the related work and the learning algorithm used for directly optimizing evaluation metrics. Section 5 explains classifiers for the GED tasks under consideration, while Section 6 describes our experimental setup. We analyze results in Section 7. Section 8 summarizes our contributions and describes possible future directions.

2 Motivation

There are many GED applications where users do not consider false positive and false negative errors as equally damaging. To copy-editors, false negative errors are costlier than false positive errors. They would not mind evaluating a few false alarms, but cannot afford to miss genuine errors since that would affect the quality of service. They would prefer the GED system to err on the side of higher recall. Similarly, translators using computer-aided translation systems would prefer to have most errors pointed out. Even an automatic post-editing system for MT would prefer to have most errors identified since alternatives can then be evaluated for these potential errors in a post-editing stage.

We hypothesize that by directly optimizing the desired evaluation metric, we can satisfy the requirements of asymmetric loss and customization of the recall/precision trade-off. For a GED system designed to help copy-editors, F_2 would be a reasonable choice as an optimization objective since it is biased towards recall. Similarly, $F_{0.5}$ would be a reasonable choice for a GED system designed for language learners. Our choice of

$\beta = 0.5, 2$ follows the conventional choices mentioned in literature for evaluating precision and recall bias.

Traditionally, sampling and example-weighting have been the most common methods to handle class imbalance. **Sampling** involves either *undersampling* the `correct` examples or *oversampling* the `incorrect` examples in the training set (Van Hulse et al., 2007; Domingos, 1999). In **example-weighting**, misclassification costs are associated with the training examples, with higher misclassification costs for wrongly classifying `incorrect` examples (Zadrozny et al., 2003). In theory, example-weighting and sampling techniques can be shown to be equivalent (Zadrozny et al., 2003), and in the rest of the paper we use *sampling* to refer to both. However, sampling methods have a few limitations which direct optimization of the performance metrics does not suffer from:

- Even the choice of sampling ratio is arbitrary and its effect on the evaluation metrics is not obvious. A validation set may be used to select the appropriate ratio which maximizes the evaluation metric, at the cost of setting aside some valuable training data for tuning. On the other hand, while optimizing an evaluation metric, it naturally induces a loss function.

- A high degree of undersampling is required to negate the effect of the very low error rate in GED tasks. However, this results in a drastic reduction in the examples available for training. Random undersampling has been reported to work reasonably on some datasets with a dense feature space and a small number of features (Van Hulse et al., 2007). In contrast, the classification problems for GED results are characterized by large and sparse feature spaces leading to a loss of many features due to undersampling. Optimizing evaluation metrics directly does not incur this loss since data is not sampled prior to learning.

- Oversampling with repetition of `incorrect` class instances generally does not improve classification performance and results in overfitting. Informed oversampling through introduction of synthetic instances belonging to the minority class (SMOTE) by interpolation of minority class instances in the training set has shown good improvement in many applications (Chawla et al., 2002). For large feature spaces, the generation of synthetic examples can be computationally expensive since it involves a k-nearest neighbourhood search. Optimizing evaluation metrics directly does not incur this computational overhead.

3 Related Work

The most common methods to handle **imbalanced datasets** in GED involve undersampling the `correct` instances (Dahlmeier et al., 2012; Putra and Szabo, 2013; Kunchukuttan et al., 2013) or oversampling the `incorrect` instances (Xing et al., 2013). Rozovskaya et al. (2012) propose an *error inflation* method for preposition error correction, where a fraction of the correct prepositions are marked as incorrect prepositions and these new "erroneous" instances are distributed among different possible erroneous prepositions. This method is similar to the *Meta-Cost* (Domingos, 1999) approach of re-labelling examples in the training set according to a cost function. Some whole-sentence correction approaches (Kunchukuttan et al., 2014; Junczys-Dowmunt and Grundkiewicz, 2014; Dahlmeier and Ng, 2012) are tuned to maximize the F_β scores.

In all the work mentioned above, the systems maximize F_β by tuning only the "hyperparameters" like sampling threshold, features weights for scores of underlying components —classifier (Dahlmeier and Ng, 2012) or SMT component scores (Kunchukuttan et al., 2014; Junczys-Dowmunt and Grundkiewicz, 2014) —on a tuning dataset using *approximate* methods like MERT (Och, 2003), PRO (Hopkins and May, 2011) and grid search. In contrast, we optimize all the model parameters *exactly and efficiently* to maximize F_β.

4 Optimizing Performance Measures

A loss function like the induced F_β loss is non-decomposable *i.e.* it cannot be expressed as the sum of losses over individual instances. We use the max-margin formulation proposed by Joachims (2005) for *exactly* optimizing such non-decomposable loss functions which can be computed from the contingency table[1]. It is applicable only to binary classification problems.

The training loss is described in terms of a loss function (Δ) which measures the discrepancy between the expected output vector ($\bar{\mathbf{y}}$) and observed output vector ($\bar{\mathbf{y}}'$) on training data of size m:

$$\Delta : (y_1...y_i...y_m) \times (y_1'...y_i'...y_m') \to \mathbb{R} \quad (1)$$

For a decomposable loss functions like 0-1 loss, hinge loss, *etc.* we can express the loss as:

$$\Delta(\mathbf{y}, \bar{\mathbf{y}}) = \sum_{i=1}^{m} \Delta'(y_i, y_i') \quad (2)$$

where, Δ' is the loss function for a single instance:

$$\Delta' : y \times y' \to \mathbb{R} \quad (3)$$

In the max-margin framework, a decomposable loss function (hinge loss in the example below) can be minimized by solving the following objective function for support vector machines (SVM):

$$\min \frac{1}{2}\mathbf{w}.\mathbf{w} + C \sum_{i=1}^{n} \xi_i \quad (4)$$

$$s.t : \bigvee_{i=1}^{n} : y_i[\mathbf{w}.\mathbf{x_i}] \geq 1 - \xi_i \quad (5)$$

Here, $\xi_i = 1 - y_i[\mathbf{w}.\mathbf{x_i}]$ is an upper bound on the loss (Δ') for the ith training instance.

However, non-decomposable loss functions cannot be modeled in this framework since the constraint, and hence the loss, is defined per instance. We need a framework to represent the problem in terms of loss over the entire training set (*i.e.* the observed and expected label vector) using a custom loss function. The *StructSVM* framework (Tsochantaridis et al., 2005) provides the ability to define custom loss functions over arbitrary output structures like vectors, trees, etc. Joachims (2005) framed the binary classification problem with non-decomposable loss functions as a structured prediction problem, where the entire training set becomes a single instance. The input ($\bar{\mathbf{x}}$) is a tuple of the original features vectors ($\mathbf{x_i}$) and output is the label vector ($\bar{\mathbf{y}}$). The training objective can be represented as:

$$\min \frac{1}{2}\mathbf{w}.\mathbf{w} + C\xi \quad (6)$$

---

[1] http://en.wikipedia.org/wiki/
Confusion_matrix

Noun Number	
O: It was great to see the **excitements** on the child's face.	
C: It was great to see the **excitement** on the child's face.	
Article	*Preposition*
O: I want to buy pen.	Keep the pen **in** the table.
C: I want to buy **a** pen.	Keep the pen **on** the table.
O: original,	*C: corrected*

Table 3: Examples of grammatical errors

O: original, C: corrected

subject to the following constraints

$$\forall \bar{\mathbf{y}}' \in \mathcal{Y} \backslash \bar{\mathbf{y}} : \langle \mathbf{w}, \delta\Psi(\bar{\mathbf{x}}, \bar{\mathbf{y}}') \rangle \geq \Delta(\bar{\mathbf{y}}, \bar{\mathbf{y}}') - \xi \quad (7)$$

where,

$$\delta\Psi(\bar{\mathbf{x}}, \bar{\mathbf{y}}') = \Psi(\bar{\mathbf{x}}, \bar{\mathbf{y}}) - \Psi(\bar{\mathbf{x}}, \bar{\mathbf{y}}') \quad (8)$$

$$\Psi(\bar{\mathbf{x}}, \bar{\mathbf{y}}') = \sum_{i=1}^{m} y_i'\mathbf{x_i} \quad (9)$$

Thus any label vector of the training set ($\bar{\mathbf{y}}'$) other than the expected label vector ($\bar{\mathbf{y}}$) would incur a loss upper bounded by:

$$\xi = \Delta(\bar{\mathbf{y}}, \bar{\mathbf{y}}') + \Psi(\bar{\mathbf{x}}, \bar{\mathbf{y}}') - \Psi(\bar{\mathbf{x}}, \bar{\mathbf{y}}) \quad (10)$$

where, Δ is a custom loss function between the expected and observed label vectors.

The number of constraints is exponential in m, since there are $2^m - 1$ possible values of $\bar{\mathbf{y}}'$. However, the above optimization problem can be solved efficiently in a polynomial number of iterations using an iterative, cutting plane algorithm. The efficiency of the overall algorithm depends on the efficiency of finding the most violated constraint, *i.e.* finding the $\bar{\mathbf{y}}'$ which maximizes Equation 10. This *loss-augmented inference problem* can be solved in polynomial time for binary classification problems involving loss functions which can be computed from the contingency table *e.g.* F_β, precision, recall loss.

5 Grammatical Error Detection Classifiers

The GED tasks and the classifiers under study are described in this section.

5.1 Tasks

We consider the following three GED tasks: Noun Number (NN), Article (Art) and Preposition (Prep)

ARTICLE and NOUN NUMBER features
Head Noun
Is the noun capitalized?
Is the noun an acronym?
Is the noun a named entity?
Is the noun a (i) mass noun, (ii)*pluralia tantum*?
Observed number of the noun
POS of the noun
Start letter of noun ‡
Suffixes of the noun (length 1-4) ‡
Noun Phrase (NP)
Does the NP have: (i) article (ii) demonstrative (iii) quantifier?
What (i) article (ii) demonstrative (iii) quantifier does the NP have?
Number of tokens in the NP
Start letter of the word to the right of article ‡
Contextual
(i)Token (ii) POS (iii) Chunk tag in ± 2 word-window around head noun
(i)Token (ii) POS (iii) Chunk tags in ± 2 word-window around article ‡
Are there words indicating plurality in the context of the noun?
Is the noun a part of a list of nouns?
Grammatical Number of majority of nouns in noun list
Sentence
The first two words of the sentence and their POS tags
Has the noun been referenced earlier in the sentence?
PREPOSITION features
Contextual
(i) Token (ii) POS tag in ± 4 word-window around preposition
2-4 grams of (i) Token (ii) POS tag around preposition
‡: *features used only for articles*

Table 4: Feature set for various GED tasks

error detection. A few examples of these errors are shown in Table 3.

Each is a binary classification task which labels an instance as grammatically `correct` (*negative*) or `incorrect` (*positive*). The training instances for each task are defined as follows. For **noun number**, each noun phrase is an instance. For **articles**, each noun phrase containing the articles $\{a, an, the, \phi\}$ is an instance. For **preposition**, we consider only preposition deletion and substitution errors. We consider only the ten most frequent prepositions as instances: $\{on, from, for, of, about, to, at, in, with, by\}$ (Rozovskaya and Roth, 2010). The top 10 prepositions account for 78% of all prepositions in the NUCLE corpus and 81% of all the preposition errors. The feature sets for the GED tasks are shown in Table 4.

5.2 Directly optimizing evaluation metrics

We directly optimize F_β using the support vector method for optimizing performance measures (**SVM-Perf**) proposed by Joachims (2005). We chose this method since it can *exactly* and *efficiently* optimize non-decomposable evaluation metrics which can be computed from the contingency table *e.g.* F_β. We train different classifiers corresponding to $\beta = 0.5, 1, 2$.

5.3 Sampling Methods

Sampled datasets were created from the original training set using three sampling methods. In **random undersampling** (Van Hulse et al., 2007), the `correct` instances are undersampled at random and all `incorrect` instances are retained in the training set. In **SMOTE** (Chawla et al., 2002), `incorrect` class examples are oversampled by generating synthetic examples for every `incorrect` instance using linear interpolation with one of its five nearest incorrect neighbours. In **cost-sensitive learning** (Zadrozny et al., 2003), misclassifying `incorrect` instances incurs a higher cost as compared to misclassifying `correct` instances.

For each sampling method, sampled datasets were created using different representative sampling ratios ($p = 0.3, 0.5, 1.0$) which span the entire range. The sampling ratio (p) refers to the ratio of `incorrect` to `correct` examples in the sampled dataset. For cost-senstive learning, the corresponding misclassification cost ratio (J) can be computed as $J = pR$, where R is the ratio of `correct` to `incorrect` instances in training set. An SVM is trained with hinge loss on each of these sampled datasets.

6 Experimental Setup

We tested our GED systems on three annotated learner corpora: NUCLE (Dahlmeier et al., 2013), HOO11 (Dale and Kilgarriff, 2011) and HOO12 (Dale et al., 2012) shared task corpora. For the HOO12 dataset, noun number error detection was not done since the dataset did not have these annotations.

For hinge loss, the classifiers were trained using the *SVMLight* package (Joachims, b). For other loss functions, classifiers were trained using the *SVM-Perf* package (Joachims, a) with extensions to optimize recall, precision and F_β. We used a linear kernel for all our experiments.The evaluation was done using Precision, Recall, $F_{0.5}$, F_1 and F_2 metrics. The average scores over a 5-fold cross-validation are reported.

7 Results and Discussion

7.1 Limitations of sampling methods

Figure 1 shows the F_2 scores of sampling methods for different GED tasks on the NUCLE dataset as a function of the sampling ratio. We can see

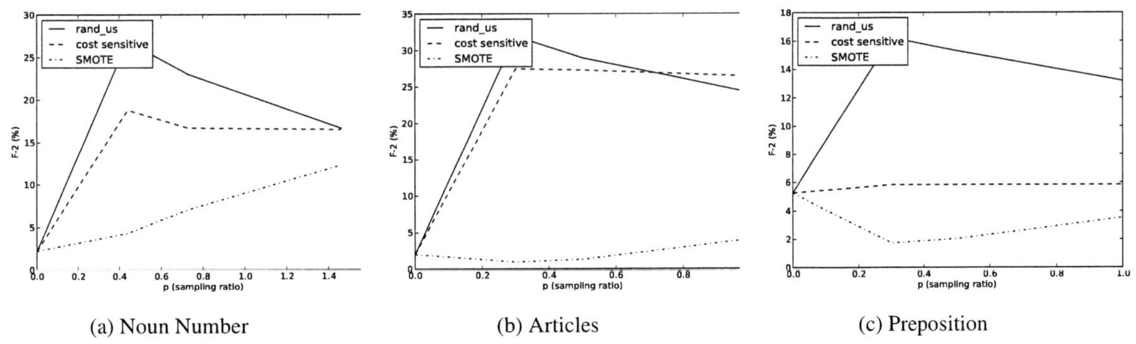

(a) Noun Number   (b) Articles   (c) Preposition

Figure 1: Comparison of sampling methods on NUCLE dataset (scores in %)

Dataset	Method	Noun Number			Article			Preposition		
		$F_{0.5}$	F_1	F_2	$F_{0.5}$	F_1	F_2	$F_{0.5}$	F_1	F_2
NUCLE	Hinge Loss	7.80	3.42	2.19	6.92	3.07	1.98	**15.37**	7.85	5.27
	Random Undersampling (p=0.3)	11.01	15.62	26.89	14.57	20.01	**31.94**	6.75	9.53	16.23
	Cost-Sensitive (p=0.3)	10.46	13.43	18.79	**18.58**	22.15	27.43	13.53	8.14	5.82
	SMOTE (p=1.0)	**18.91**	14.74	12.27	10.50	5.78	4.00	10.52	5.28	3.52
	SVM-Perf $F_{0.5}$	14.93	19.17	26.82	17.74	22.34	30.17	6.39	9.41	17.84
	SVM-Perf F_1	15.72	**19.92**	27.24	17.95	**22.65**	30.72	6.60	**9.70**	**18.28**
	SVM-Perf F_2	13.72	18.43	**28.08**	18.02	22.65	30.51	6.55	9.63	18.15
HOO-11	Hinge Loss	**18.48**	**14.15**	11.64	**35.55**	**29.87**	25.85	**28.90**	16.92	12.22
	Random Undersampling (p=0.3)	3.55	5.36	10.98	14.64	19.54	29.42	9.90	11.96	15.20
	Cost-Sensitive (p=0.3)	**18.48**	**14.15**	11.64	33.88	29.49	26.23	**28.90**	16.92	12.22
	SMOTE (p=1.0)	**18.48**	**14.15**	11.64	34.28	29.64	26.19	**28.90**	16.92	12.22
	SVM-Perf $F_{0.5}$	4.42	6.45	11.98	25.86	27.89	30.44	26.67	**17.69**	13.32
	SVM-Perf F_1	4.42	6.45	11.98	24.06	28.12	33.88	24.84	17.19	13.21
	SVM-Perf F_2	4.70	6.96	**13.42**	18.58	24.01	**34.05**	12.69	14.39	**16.81**
HOO-12	Hinge Loss				7.66	3.74	2.47	**17.63**	10.14	7.12
	Random Undersampling (p=0.3)				10.11	13.75	21.50	12.26	15.91	22.66
	Cost-Sensitive (p=0.3)				**14.66**	**16.79**	19.65	17.58	11.47	8.51
	SMOTE (p=1.0)				7.28	3.90	2.66	12.74	6.83	4.68
	SVM-Perf $F_{0.5}$				11.37	15.05	**22.29**	12.79	**17.01**	**25.42**
	SVM-Perf F_1				11.69	15.22	21.83	10.84	15.11	24.91
	SVM-Perf F_2				11.94	15.48	22.02	9.48	13.80	25.32

Table 5: Comparison of SVM-Perf with best sampling methods (scores in %)

that *the scores vary sharply with sampling ratio*, making the choice of the right sampling ratio extremely important. Undersampling techniques show a sharp increase in recall with increasing sample ratios (up to 20%), but a sharp drop in precision with increase in sampling ratio (halving the precision in some cases). Thus, the methodology does not offer much in terms of achieving a good precision-recall trade-off. The drastic variation indicates that the bias introduced by the sampling ratio is driving the classifier's decision and the training data's role is made irrelevant due to sampling loss.

In general, we can observe a trend that *undersampling and cost-sensitive techniques perform best at low sampling ratios (p=0.3), whereas SMOTE performs best at higher sampling ratios* (p=1.0). This is a consequence of the high imbalance ratio for GED tasks. However, there is no sampling method that is uniformly best across tasks and evaluation metrics. *Empirical cross-validation is the only way to determine the best sampling method and configuration for a particular task.*

7.2 SVM-Perf vs. sampling methods

Table 5 shows F_1, F_2 and $F_{0.5}$ evaluation for various SVM-Perf classifiers (optimized for F_β=0.5,1,2) and compares them with the classic hinge loss classifier and the best undersampling, oversampling and cost-sensitive learning methods on three datasets.

For the F_2 evaluation metric, optimizing F_2 is clearly better than the sampling techniques in all but one out of 8 cases (NUCLE, Art). Even in this case, the performance of F_β optimization is comparable to the best sampling method (96% of the undersampling score). Improvements up to 15% in F_2 score over the best sampling techniques have been observed. For instance, on the HOO11 dataset, the F_2 scores improve by about 15%, 15% and 10% over the best sampling methods for the NN, Art and Prep tasks respectively. Using F_2 optimization, the precision is generally higher than that of the best performing sampling technique. Only in 3 cases, F_2 optimization gives slightly lower F_2 scores than F_1 or $F_{0.5}$ optimizations ($\approx 1\%$ lesser). *A GED system designed to achieve high recall can thus benefit from optimizing the F_2 metric.*

F_1 optimization gives the best F_1 score on the NUCLE dataset for all tasks, and on some tasks on other datasets. For instance, the F_1 scores improve by 27.52%, 2.26% and 1.78% over the best sampling methods for the NN, Art and Prep tasks respectively on the NUCLE dataset. Only on the NN task for the HOO-11 dataset, the sampling methods vastly outperform F_1 optimization. On the remaining tasks, the performance is comparable to the best performing sampling method. *In most cases, we can conclude that F_1 optimization would yield a good F_1 score.*

Finally, none of the F_β optimizers perform well for $F_{0.5}$ as the evaluation metric. The precision/recall analysis in the next section explains this issue.

7.3 Precision, Recall and Accuracy Analysis

Table 6 shows the accuracy, precision and recall for the classic hinge loss classifier and the best undersampling, oversampling, cost-sensitive and SVM-Perf classifiers on the NUCLE dataset. Other datasets also show similar trends.

Undersampling methods achieve higher recall (more than 70% for all tasks with $p = 1.0$), which can be attributed to the strong inductive bias that alters the class prior in favour of the minority class. But there is a substantial reduction in precision and accuracy. The classic SVM with no sampling achieves the highest precision for all tasks (more than 40% for all tasks), while SMOTE also shows higher precision (between 25-32%). But the recall is as low as 5%. The SVM-Perf classifier maintains a comparatively high precision ($\approx 15\%$, except preposition GED task) as well recall (be-

tween 35-45%), while the accuracy drop compared to the classic hinge is comparatively less.

We also investigated if SVM-Perf is effective in obtaining high precision or recall by directly optimizing precision and recall respectively (see Table 7 for results). Optimizing recall significantly increases the recall over F_β optimization, with recall of more than 50% achieved on all tasks. However, optimizing precision does not show much improvement over the F_β optimization and is clearly far worse than the precision obtained with the baseline SVM. Precision loss can be represented as $FP/(FP + TP)$. We can see that $FP = 0$ can easily be achieved by assigning all examples to the correct class, since FN does not affect the precision. This loss function does not provide a sufficient bias for increasing precision. This also explains why optimizing F_1, F_2 are more effective than optimizing $F_{0.5}$ which is precision oriented.

8   Conclusion and Future work

We have shown on multiple GED tasks and datasets that optimizing F_1 and F_2 outperforms sampling for these evaluation metrics, while maintaining accuracy and precision above what is achieved through sampling methods. Directly optimizing evaluation metrics scores over sampling since: (i) the optimization objective can incorporate precision requirements and needs no empirical determination of hyper-parameters, and (ii) no data loss/corruption due to sampling.

It is beneficial to use F_2 optimization to learn GED classifiers designed for recall-oriented usecases like copyediting. The gains are largely due to improvement in recall, and we show the inherent difficulties in optimizing a precision-oriented metric. Future directions of work include improving precision and direct optimization of evaluation metrics for grammatical error **correction**.

A natural extension is to apply this method to error detection in native speaker text and machine translation output. Our method also has wider applicability to other problems in NLP which encounter the imbalanced dataset problem *e.g.* sarcasm detection, sentiment thwarting detection, WSD, NER, *etc.*

References

Nitesh V. Chawla, Kevin W. Bowyer, Lawrence O. Hall, and W. Philip Kegelmeyer. 2002. SMOTE:

Method	Noun Number			Article			Preposition		
	A	P	R	A	P	R	A	P	R
Hinge Loss	**98.54**	**54.29**	1.77	**97.50**	**42.39**	1.60	**98.41**	**42.91**	4.32
Random Undersampling (p=0.3)	91.79	9.20	**51.88**	89.44	12.33	**53.06**	90.92	5.65	30.54
Cost-Sensitive(p=0.3)	95.16	9.11	25.63	94.29	16.78	32.62	98.27	24.26	4.89
SMOTE (p=1.0)	98.16	25.00	11.07	97.34	24.15	3.32	98.38	31.46	2.88
SVM-Perf $F_{0.5}$	95.46	13.02	36.67	93.17	15.60	39.40	86.60	5.26	44.46
SVM-Perf F_1	95.72	13.79	36.22	93.16	15.77	40.30	87.01	5.44	**44.63**
SVM-Perf F_2	94.39	11.72	43.19	93.26	15.86	39.68	86.97	5.40	44.24

Table 6: NUCLE dataset: Comparison of Accuracy (A), Precision (P), Recall (R) (scores in %)

Method	Noun Number		Article		Preposition	
	Precision	Recall	Precision	Recall	Precision	Recall
SVM-Perf Precision	12.60	39.92	15.97	39.26	7.52	0.45
SVM-Perf Recall	3.93	63.16	7.35	56.37	4.02	52.76

Table 7: NUCLE dataset: Optimizing Precision and Recall (scores in %)

Synthetic Minority Over-sampling Technique. *Journal of Artificial Intelligence Research*, 16(1).

Martin Chodorow, Markus Dickinson, Ross Israel, and Joel R Tetreault. 2012. Problems in evaluating grammatical error detection systems. In *COLING*, pages 611–628. Citeseer.

Daniel Dahlmeier and Hwee Tou Ng. 2012. A beam-search decoder for grammatical error correction. In *Proceedings of the 2012 Joint Conference on Empirical Methods in Natural Language Processing and Computational Natural Language Learning*.

Daniel Dahlmeier, Hwee Tou Ng, and Eric Jun Feng Ng. 2012. NUS at the HOO 2012 Shared Task. In *Proceedings of the Seventh Workshop on Building Educational Applications Using NLP*.

Daniel Dahlmeier, Hwee Tou Ng, and Siew Mei Wu. 2013. Building a Large Annotated Corpus of Learner English: The NUS Corpus of Learner English. In *Proceedings of the 8th Workshop on Innovative Use of NLP for Building Educational Applications*.

Robert Dale and Adam Kilgarriff. 2011. Helping our own: The HOO 2011 pilot shared task. In *Proceedings of the 13th European Workshop on Natural Language Generation*.

Robert Dale, Ilya Anisimoff, and George Narroway. 2012. HOO 2012: A report on the preposition and determiner error correction shared task. In *Proceedings of the Seventh Workshop on Building Educational Applications Using NLP*.

Pedro Domingos. 1999. Metacost: A general method for making classifiers cost-sensitive. In *Proceedings of the fifth ACM SIGKDD international conference on Knowledge Discovery and Data Mining*.

Haibo He and Edwardo A Garcia. 2009. Learning from imbalanced data. *IEEE Transactions on Knowledge and Data Engineering*, 21(9).

Mark Hopkins and Jonathan May. 2011. Tuning as ranking. In *Proceedings of the Conference on Empirical Methods in Natural Language Processing*, pages 1352–1362. Association for Computational Linguistics.

Emi Izumi, Kiyotaka Uchimoto, and Hitoshi Isahara. 2004. The NICT JLE Corpus: Exploiting the Language Learners Speech Database for Research and Education. *International Journal of the Computer, the Internet and Management*.

Thorsten Joachims. Svm-perf: Support vector machine for multivariate performance measures. http://www.cs.cornell.edu/People/tj/svm_light/svm_perf.html/.

Thorsten Joachims. Svmlight: Support vector machine. http://svmlight.joachims.org/.

Thorsten Joachims. 2005. A Support Vector Method for Multivariate Performance Measures. In *Proceedings of the 22nd International Conference on Machine Learning*.

Marcin Junczys-Dowmunt and Roman Grundkiewicz. 2014. The AMU System in the CoNLL-2014 Shared Task: Grammatical Error Correction by Data-Intensive and Feature-Rich Statistical Machine Translation. In *Proceedings of the Eighteenth Conference on Computational Natural Language Learning: Shared Task*.

Anoop Kunchukuttan, Ritesh Shah, and Pushpak Bhattacharyya. 2013. IITB System for CoNLL 2013 Shared Task: A Hybrid Approach to Grammatical Error Correction. In *Proceedings of the Seventeenth Conference on Computational Natural Language Learning: Shared Task*.

Anoop Kunchukuttan, Sriram Chaudhury, and Pushpak Bhattacharyya. 2014. Tuning a Grammar Correction System for Increased Precision. In *Proceedings of the Eighteenth Conference on Computational Natural Language Learning: Shared Task*.

Hwee Tou Ng, Siew Mei Wu, Yuanbin Wu, Christian Hadiwinoto, and Joel Tetreault. 2013. The CoNLL-2013 Shared Task on Grammatical Error Correction. In *Proceedings of the Seventeenth Conference on Computational Natural Language Learning: Shared Task*.

Franz Josef Och. 2003. Minimum error rate training in statistical machine translation. In *Proceedings of the 41st Annual Meeting on Association for Computational Linguistics-Volume 1*.

Desmond Darma Putra and Lili Szabo. 2013. UdS at CoNLL 2013 Shared Task. In *Proceedings of the Seventeenth Conference on Computational Natural Language Learning: Shared Task*.

Alla Rozovskaya and Dan Roth. 2010. Generating confusion sets for context-sensitive error correction. In *Proceedings of the 2010 Conference on Empirical Methods in Natural Language Processing*.

Alla Rozovskaya, Mark Sammons, and Dan Roth. 2012. The UI system in the HOO 2012 shared task on error correction. In *Proceedings of the Seventh Workshop on Building Educational Applications Using NLP*.

Ioannis Tsochantaridis, Thorsten Joachims, Thomas Hofmann, and Yasemin Altun. 2005. Large margin methods for structured and interdependent output variables. In *Journal of Machine Learning Research*.

Jason Van Hulse, Taghi M Khoshgoftaar, and Amri Napolitano. 2007. Experimental perspectives on learning from imbalanced data. In *Proceedings of the 24th International Conference on Machine learning*.

Junwen Xing, Longyue Wang, Derek F. Wong, Lidia S. Chao, and Xiaodong Zeng. 2013. UM-Checker: A Hybrid System for English Grammatical Error Correction. In *Proceedings of the Seventeenth Conference on Computational Natural Language Learning: Shared Task*.

Bianca Zadrozny, John Langford, and Naoki Abe. 2003. Cost-sensitive learning by cost-proportionate example weighting. In *Third IEEE International Conference on Data Mining*.

Words are not Equal: Graded Weighting Model for building Composite Document Vectors

Pranjal Singh
B.Tech.-M.Tech. Dual Degree
Computer Science & Engineering
Indian Institute of Technology Kanpur
`pranjals16@gmail.com`

Amitabha Mukerjee
Professor
Computer Science & Engineering
Indian Institute of Technology Kanpur
`amit@cse.iitk.ac.in`

Abstract

Despite the success of distributional semantics, composing phrases from word vectors remains an important challenge. Several methods have been tried for benchmark tasks such as sentiment classification, including word vector averaging, matrix-vector approaches based on parsing, and on-the-fly learning of paragraph vectors. Most models usually omit stop words from the composition. Instead of such an yes-no decision, we consider several graded schemes where words are weighted according to their discriminatory relevance with respect to its use in the document (e.g., idf). Some of these methods (particularly tf-idf) are seen to result in a significant improvement in performance over prior state of the art. Further, combining such approaches into an ensemble based on alternate classifiers such as the RNN model, results in an 1.6% performance improvement on the standard IMDB movie review dataset, and a 7.01% improvement on Amazon product reviews. Since these are language free models and can be obtained in an unsupervised manner, they are of interest also for under-resourced languages such as Hindi as well and many more languages. We demonstrate the language free aspects by showing a gain of 12% for two review datasets over earlier results, and also release a new larger dataset for future testing (Singh, 2015).

1 Introduction

Language representation is a very crucial aspect to perform various NLP tasks and has been looked into great detail in recent times. Language representation models have fallen into broadly two categories: ones which require hand-trained language databases such as treebanks (e.g., (Socher et al., 2013)) and ones which are language agnostic and work on raw corpora (e.g., LDA, BOW, Skip-Gram, NLM, etc.). Liu (2015) compare various language agnostic models for topic modeling.

Language independent models such as LDA and BOW have been quite effective since long time. Variants of BOW such as tf-idf had changed the perception of researchers towards these models when they were proved effective in various NLP tasks. LDA was able to model inter and intra documental statistical and relational structure quite well overcoming the drawbacks of BOW. But the semantic and syntactical dependencies were still ignored. After the introduction of neural language vector models, NLP saw a huge diversion in representation of words and documents. For indi-

Method	IMDB	Amazon	Hindi
RNNLM (Baseline)	86.45	90.03	78.84
Paragraph Vector (Le and Mikolov, 2014)	92.58	91.30	74.57
Averaged Vector	88.42	88.52	79.62
Weighted Average Vector	89.56	88.63	85.90
Composite Document Vector	93.91	92.17	90.30

Table 1: Comparison of accuracies on 3 Datasets (IMDB, Amazon Electronics Review and Hindi Movie Reviews (IITB)) for various types of document composition models. The state of the art for these tasks are: IMDB: 92.58% (Le and Mikolov, 2014); Amazon:85.90% (Dredze et al., 2008), Hindi:79.0% (Bakliwal et al., 2012).

D S Sharma, R Sangal and E Sherly. Proc. of the 12th Intl. Conference on Natural Language Processing, pages 11–19,
Trivandrum, India. December 2015. ©2015 NLP Association of India (NLPAI)

vidual words, vectors are obtained via distributional learning, the mechanisms for which varies from document-term matrix factorization (Landauer and Dumais, 1997), various forms of deep learning (Collobert et al., 2011; Turian et al., 2010; Socher et al., 2013), optimizing models to explain co-occurrence constraints (Mikolov et al., 2013b; Pennington et al., 2014), etc. Once the word vectors have been assigned, similarity between words can be captured via cosine distances. The same models have been extended ((Le and Mikolov, 2014)) with new variables to build vector models for sentences and documents. These models include the essence of individual words as well as their relative order in terms of sentence vector which was earlier absent in word vectors. The advantage of these approaches is that they can capture both the syntactic and the semantic similarity between words/documents in terms of their projections onto a high-dimensional vector space; further, it seems that one can tune the privileging of syntax over semantics by using local as opposed to large contexts (Huang et al., 2012).

Some grammarians have been trying to find whether sentence meaning accrues by combining word meanings, or whether words gain their meanings based on the context they appear in (Matilal, 2001). (Turney et al., 2010) give a detailed overview of various vector space models and their composition. A surprising event in Information Theory has higher information content than an expected event (Shanon, 1948). The same happens when we give weights to word vectors. We give more weight to events which evoke surprise and less weight to events which are expected. The most popular weighting concept in this domain is the idea of tf-idf which we have utilized in this work (Refer Table 1).

In this work, we focus on a graded approach to assessing the importance of each word in a compositional models. Graded models such as tf-idf have long been used in NLP, but they do not seem to have been used in word vector composition tasks yet. The intuition is that in discrete cutoff functions, while simple, raise questions regarding threshold (what constitutes a stop word), and do not degrade performance gradually (Fig. 1).

We claim that the document vectors in hand is a much better representation of each document than doing it separately. This can be justified by the fact that we now incorporate contribution of

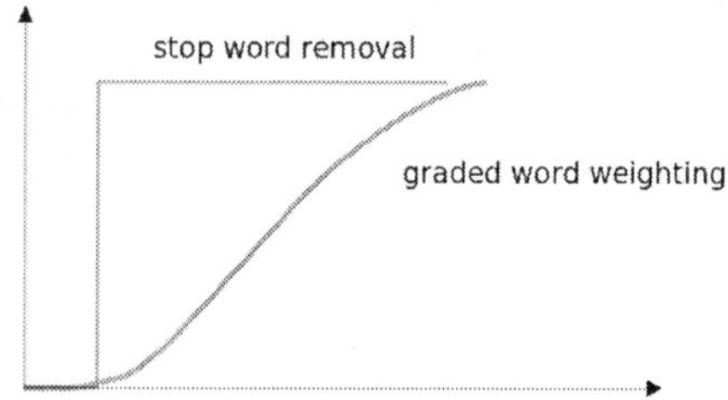

Figure 1: Intuition behind the proposed approach is that graded mechanisms for word combination may do better than discrete models that simply reject stop words and treat all other words equally(e.g. averaging methods).

each word as per its importance as well as well as that of document without ignoring tf-idf representation which performs considerably well in tasks such as retrieval. Hence, we call this as composite document vector representation. We then go a step ahead to build an ensemble of our model and recurrent neural network, which essentially has the properties of a generative model, to achieve state-of-the-art result on IMDB movie review dataset (94.19%) and on Amazon electronics reviews dataset with a significant improvement over previous best. The world class results in English clearly indicate the efficacy of our approach and improvements in Hindi depict the deficiency in other models which were used earlier.

2   Related Work

2.1   Neural Language Model

Language modeling problem involved using frequency counts of n-grams for so many years but it ignores a large number of n-grams which are not seen while training leading to data sparsity and over-fitting of training data. Also these n-gram models along with BOW suffers from the curse of dimensionality. Neural Networks tend to overcome the drawbacks of n-gram models because they can model continuous variables or distributed representation, which is a necessity if we would like to find better generalizations over the highly discrete word sequences (Bengio et al., 2003). Neural language models were introduced by Bengio et al., 2001 (revised in 2003(Bengio et al., 2003)). They build a mapping C from each word i of the vocabulary V to a feature vector $C(i) \in \mathbb{R}^m$, m is the number of features; a probability function g over words expressed with

C; and finally learn the word vector and parameters of probability function. Morin(2005) proposed a hierarchical model to speed up the training cost by clustering similar words before computing their probability in order to only have to do one computation per word cluster at the output layer of the NN. Le(2011) combined neural networks with n-gram language models in a unified approach. They cluster words to structure the output vocabulary. Mikolov(2010) achieved the best reduction in perplexity by using recurrent neural network which uses the the current input as well as the output of the previous iteration. Mikolov(2011) present several modifications of the original recurrent neural network language model (RNN LM). The present approaches that lead to more than 15 times speedup for both training and testing phases. Collobert(2011) show the use of semi-supervised learning using deep neural networks to perform at the state-of-the-art of various NLP tasks. Wang(2014) propose a word vector neural-network model, which takes both sentiment and semantic information into account. This word vector expression model learns word semantics and sentiment at the same time as well as fuses unsupervised contextual information and sentence level supervised labels. Neelakantan(2014) took word vector models to next level where they proposed multiple embeddings per word. The problem that still remains in hand is that either these models are computationally expensive or they have failed to generalize properly. We, therefore, adopt skipgram model (Mikolov et al., 2013b), details about which have been discussed in next section, because deep network model of Collobert et al.(2008) takes too much time for training (skipgram reduces computational complexity from O(V) to O(log V) (Morin and Bengio, 2005)).

2.2 Sentiment Analysis

Majority of the existing work in this field is in English (Pang and Lee, 2008). Medagoda(2013) surveys sentiment analysis in non-English languages while (Sharma et al., 2014) give a summary of work done in Hindi in the field of opinion mining. There have been heuristic based and machine learning based models used in this domain. Heuristic based methods, in general, classify text sentiments on the basis of total number of derived positive or negative sentiment oriented features. But these models rely heavily on human engineered features which, in general, is a domain and language dependent task. Several groups have attempted to improve the situation by modeling the composition of words into larger contexts (Le and Mikolov, 2014; Socher et al., 2013; Johnson and Zhang, 2014; Baroni et al., 2014).

Pang(2004) achieved an accuracy of 87.2% (Pang et al. 2004) on a dataset that discarded objective sentences and used text categorization techniques on the subjective sentences. Le(2014) use paragraph vector model and obtain 92.6% accuracy on IMDB movie review dataset. More difficult challenges involve short texts with nonstandard vocabularies,as in twitter. Here, some authors focus on building extensive feature sets (e.g. Mohammad et al.(2013); F-score 89.14).

However, most of the work on sentiment analysis in Hindi has not attempted to form richer compositional analyses. For the type of corpora used here, the best results, obtained by combining a sentiment lexicon with hand-crafted rules (e.g. modeling negation and "but" phrases), reach an accuracy of 80% (Mittal et al., 2013). Joshi(2010) compared three approaches: In-language sentiment analysis, Machine Translation and Resource Based Sentiment Analysis. By using WordNet linking, words in English SentiWordNet were replaced by equivalent Hindi words to get H-SWN. The final accuracy achieved by them is 78.1%. Bakliwal(2012) traversed the WordNet ontology to antonyms and synonyms to identify polarity shifts in the word space. Further improvements were achieved by using a partial stemmer (there is no good stemmer / morphological analyzer for Hindi), and focusing on adjective/adverbs (seed words given to the system); their final accuracy was 79.0% for the product review dataset. Mukherjee et al. (2012) presented the inclusion of discourse markers in a bag-of-words model and how it improved the sentiment classification accuracy by 2-4%.

Many approaches seek to improve their performance by combining POS-tags and even parse tree structures into the models for higher accuracies in specific tasks (Socher et al., 2013). One problem in this approach is that of combining the word vectors to build document vectors because of issues in merging parse trees. Also these models are language dependent and computationally very expensive.

3 Method

The algorithms and data structures used in this thesis have been introduced and discussed below.

3.1 Distributed Representation

Mikolov et al. (2013b) proposed two neural network models for building word vectors from large unlabeled corpora; Continuous Bag of Words(CBOW) and Skip-Gram. In the CBOW model, the context is the input, and one tries to learn a vector for the central word; in Skip grams, the input is the target word and one tries to guess the set of contexts. We have adopted skipgram model to build vector representations for words as it performs better with larger vocabulary.

Each current word acts as an input to a log-linear classifier with continuous projection layer, and predict words within a certain range before and after the current word. The objective is to maximize the probability of the context given a word within a language model:

$$p(c|w;\theta) = \frac{\exp^{v_c \cdot v_w}}{\sum_{c' \in C} \exp^{v_c \cdot v_w}}$$

where v_c and $v_w \in R^d$ are vector representations for context c and word w respectively. C is the set of all available contexts. The parameters θ are v_{c_i}, v_{w_i} for $w \in V$, $c \in C$, $i \in 1, ..., d$ (a total of $|C| \times |V| \times d$ parameters).

This distributed representation of sentences and documents (Le and Mikolov, 2014) modifies word2vec (Skip-Gram) algorithm to unsupervised learning of continuous representations for larger blocks of text, such as sentences, paragraphs or entire documents. The algorithm represents each document by a dense vector which is later trained and tuned to predict words in the document. In this framework, every paragraph is mapped to a unique vector and id, represented by a matrix D, which is a column matrix. Every word is mapped to a unique vector and word vectors are concatenated or averaged to predict the context, i.e., the next word.
The paragraph vector is shared across all contexts generated from the same paragraph but not across paragraphs. The word vector matrix W, however, is shared across paragraphs. i.e., the vector for "good" is the same for all paragraphs. The paragraph vector represents the missing information from the current context and can act as a memory of the topic of the paragraph. The advantage of using paragraph vectors is that they inherit the property of word vectors, i.e., the semantics of the words. In addition, they also take into consideration a small context around each word which is in close resemblance to the n-gram model with a large n. This property is crucial because the n-gram model preserves a lot of information of the sentence/paragraph, which includes the word order also. This model also performs better than the Bag-of-Words model which would create a very high-dimensional representation that has very poor generalization.

Our model incorporates property of document vector as well as property of word vectors to build an enhanced representation of documents without ignoring the properties of tf-idf representation.

3.2 Semantic Composition

The Principle of Compositionality is that meaning of a complex expression is determined by the meaning of its parts or constituents and the rules which guide this combination. It is also known as *Frege's Principle*. In our case, the constituents are word vectors and the expression in hand is the sentence/document vector. For example,

The movie is funny and the screenplay is good

Composition	Accuracy
Multiplication	50.30
Average	88.42
Idf Graded Weighted Average	**89.56**

Table 2: Results of Vector Composition with different Operations

Analyzing the results from Table 2, we observed that when we deal with large number of features, there is a presence of large number of *zeros* and presence of a single zero in a feature will make that features contribution zero in the final vector, which happens in our case and thus multiplicative composition fails.
We, therefore, adopt both simple and idf weighted average methods in our work. The advantage with addition is that, it doesnot increase the dimension of the vector and captures high level semantics with ease. In fact, (Zou et al., 2013) have used simple average to construct phrase vectors which they have later used to find phrase level similarity using cosine distance.
(Mikolov et al., 2013c) showed that relations between words are reflected to a large extent in the

offsets between their vector embeddings. They also use additive composition to reflect semantic dependencies.

$$queen - king \approx woman - man$$

(Blacoe and Lapata, 2012) clearly show that vectors of Neural Language Model and Distributed Model when used with additive composition outperform those with multiplicative composition in Paraphrase Classification task. DM vectors outperform by nearly giving accuracy difference of 6%. They also perform very well on Phrase similarity tasks.

We, therefore, propose graded weighting schema for better composition of vectors which is described below.

3.2.1 Graded Weighting

We describe two approaches to incorporate graded weighting into word vectors for building document vectors. Let v_{w_i} be the vector representation of the ith word. Then document vector v_{d_i} for i^{th} document is:

$$v_{d_i} = \begin{cases} 0 & w_k \in stopwords \\ \sum_{w_k \in d_i} v_{w_k} & w_k \notin stopwords \end{cases}$$

The above equation is 0-1 step-function which ignores contribution of all stop words. Now we propose another schema which weighs the contribution of each word while building document vector with a graded approach. We define $idf(t, d) = \log(\frac{|D|}{df(t)})$ where t is the term, d is the document and other notations are same as in previous subsection. The new document vector representation considering this graded schema is:

$$v_{d_i} = \begin{cases} 0 & idf(w_k, d_i) \leq \delta \\ \sum_{w_k \in d_i} idf(w_k, d_i).v_{w_k} & otherwise \end{cases}$$

where δ is a pre-defined threshold below which the word has no importance and above which the *idf* terms gives importance to that particular word.

Till date, everyone has ignored how to effectively use vector composition techniques and as a result, this area has seen very less attention. But we have successfully used *idf* values to give weights to word vectors and hence obtain much better sentence/document vectors. The advantage of this model is that once we obtain *idf* values from training corpus, we can directly use it with test corpus without any additional computation. The results

(see 4.3) obtained by using this technique clearly demonstrate how effective it is for tasks such as sentiment analysis.

3.3 Composite Representation

This experiment redefined document representation in NLP used for sentiment classification. It has the property of including both syntactic and semantic properties of a piece of text. The limitations of skip-gram word vectors have been fulfilled by document vectors and hence we achieve state-of-the-art results on IMDB movie review dataset as well as amazon electronics review dataset.

We first generated n-dimensional word vectors by training skip-gram model on the datasets. We then assigned weights to word vectors for each document to create document vectors. This now acts as a feature set for that particular document. We then created *tf-idf* vectors for each document. This can be seen as a vector representation of that particular document. We then concatenated these document vectors with document vectors obtained after training the desired dataset separately with the model proposed in (Le and Mikolov, 2014). Discrimination weighted vectors give a great boost to classification accuracies on various datasets and hence justifies our claim.

3.4 Dimensionality Reduction

Dimensionality Reduction is the process of reducing the number of random variables in such a way that the remaining variables effectively reproduce most of the variability of the dataset. The reason for using such techniques is because of the *curse of dimensionality* which is a phenomena that occurs in high-dimension but doesn't occur in low-dimension.

Table 3 summarizes how feature selection has improved classification accuracy on the 700 Movie review dataset. With ANOVA-F, we selected around 4k features but with PCA, this number was just 50. So, the low accuracy with PCA can be attributed to the fact that we may have lost some important features in low dimension. Also, PCA cannot work with size of dimension d >*size of learning set*. This sharp decrease in accuracy in both cases happens because ANOVA-F selects features with larger variance across group and thus reduces noise to a larger extent whereas PCA reduces angular variance which is not effective in this case due to the distribution of data points in high-dimensional space.

Method	Feature Selection	Accuracy
Document Vector + tfidf	None	74.57
	PCA(n=50)	76.33
	ANOVA-F	88.07
Weighted Word Vector + tfidf	None	76.43
	ANOVA-F	90.37
	PCA(n=50)	78.61

Table 3: Accuracies on our newly released 700-Movie Review Dataset

This newly released dataset is much larger than previous standard dataset and very less focused towards sentiment of the review.

4 Experiment

In this section, we describe the experiments and analyze the results.

4.1 Datasets

We have used 3 datasets for experiments in Hindi and 5 for English. All the datasets including our self created Hindi dataset are described below.

We experimented on two Hindi review datasets. One is the Product Review dataset (LTG, IIIT Hyderabad) containing 350 Positive reviews and 350 Negative reviews. The other is a Movie Review dataset (CFILT, IIT Bombay) containing 127 Positive reviews and 125 Negative reviews. Each review is around 1-2 sentences long and the sentences are mainly focused on sentiment, either positive or negative.

Our 700-Movie Review Corpus in Hindi contains movie reviews from websites such as *Dainik Jagran* and *Navbharat Times*. The movie reviews are longer than the previous corpus and contains subjects other than sentiment. There are in total 697 movie reviews from both the websites. The statistics compiled is described below.

For experiments in English, we trained on IMDB movie review dataset (Maas et al.(2013)) which consists of 25,000 positive and 25,000 negative reviews. It also contains an additional 50,000 unlabeled documents for unsupervised learning.

Positive Reviews	356
Negative Reviews	341
Total Reviews	697
29.7 sentences per document	
494.6 words per document	

Table 4: Statistics of Movie Reviews of the 700-Movie Reviews Dataset

The Trip Advisor Review dataset contains around 240K reviews (206MB) from hotel domain. Reviews with overall rating $>=3$ were annotated as positive and those with overall rating <3 were annotated as negative. The dataset was split into 80-20 ratio for training and testing purpose.

We also took amazon reviews for our experiments. Reviews with overall rating $>=3$ were annotated as positive and those with overall rating <3 were annotated as negative. The dataset was split into 80-20 ratio for training and testing purpose. There were 3 review datasets: Electronics dataset consists of 1,241,778 reviews, Watches Dataset consists of 68,356 reviews and MP3 Dataset consists of 31,000 reviews.

4.2 SkipGram or CBOW

We present an interesting experiment to demonstrate that skipgram indeed performs better than CBOW. SkipGram model tends to predict a context given a word whereas CBOW model predicts a word given a context. It seems intuitive and also from observation (Mikolov et al., 2013a) that SkipGram will perform better on semantic tasks and CBOW on syntactic tasks. We now try to evaluate how they differ on classification accuracies on the two datasets: *Watches* and *MP3*. Figure 2 show that skipgram outperforms CBOW on sentiment classification task. It can be justified by the fact that sentiment inclination of a document is more oriented towards semantics of that document rather than just syntax and our results clearly demonstrate this fact.

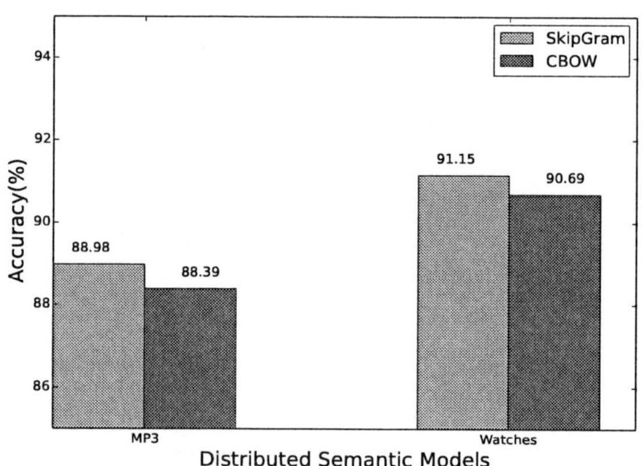

Figure 2: Variation of Accuracy with skipgram and cbow on Watches and MP3 Datasets.

4.3 Results

Method	Accuracy
Maas et al.(2011)	88.89
NBSVM-bi (Wang & Manning, 2012)	91.22
NBSVM-uni (Wang & Manning, 2012)	88.29
SVM-uni (Wang & Manning, 2012)	89.16
Paragraph Vector (Le and Mikolov(2014))	92.58
Weighted WordVector+Wiki(Our Method)	88.60
Weighted WordVector+TfIdf(Our Method)	90.67
Composite Document Vector	**93.91**

Table 5: Results on IMDB Movie Review Dataset

Table 5 summarizes the results obtained by others and by us on the IMDB movie review dataset. We have gone above the previous best (Le and Mikolov, 2014) by a margin of 1.33% using discrimination weighting. The main contributor for improvement in results is our new document vector which overcomes the weaknesses of BOW and document vectors taken separately.

Method	Weight	Accuracy(1)	Accuracy(2)
0-1 Weighting	0	93.84	93.06
	1	**93.91**	**93.18**
	2	**93.89**	93.17
	2.5	93.87	93.16
Graded idf Weighting	2.8	93.86	93.16
	3	93.86	**93.22**
	4	93.83	93.12
	5	93.75	93.03

Table 6: Results on IMDB Movie Reviews using Various Weighting Techniques(Composite Document Vector);Accuracy(2) is when we exclude tf-idf features

Tables 6 demonstrate the effectiveness of our proposed graded weighting technique. Without *tf-idf* features, our proposed method performs better in the graded idf weighting case and when we include *tf-idf* features, 0-1 weighting perform better than idf graded technique and both perform better than the previous state-of-the-art. We see that with larger weights there is a decrease in accuracy and that is because we are now filtering out more words which are important while building document vector. Table 7 is a further improvement in results once we incorporate predictions of RNNLM and Composite document vector model together(voting ensemble). Here, we first trained a *RNNLM* and then obtained predictions on test reviews in terms of probability. We trained Linear SVM classifier using new Document Vectors and then obtained predictions on test reviews. We then merged these two predictions using a voting based approach to obtain final classification.

Method	Accuracy
Composite Document Vector	93.91
Composite Document Vector + RNNLM (Our Method)	**94.19**

Table 7: Results on IMDB Movie Review Dataset

Table 8 presents result of experiment conducted on famous Amazon electronics review dataset (Leskovec and Krevl, 2014). Our vector averaging method alone has beaten previous best by 3.3%.

Features	Accuracy
(Dredze et al., 2008)	85.90
Max Entropy (Dredze et al., 2008)	83.79
WordVector Averaging(Our Method)	88.63
Composite Document Vector (Our Method)	92.17
Composite Document Vector + RNNLM	**92.91**

Table 8: Results on Amazon Electronics Review Dataset

Features	Accuracy(1)	Accuracy(2)
WordVector Averaging	78.0	79.62
WordVector+tf-idf	90.73	89.52
WordVector+tf-idf without stop words	91.14	89.97
Weighted WordVector	89.71	85.90
Weighted WordVector+tfidf	**92.89**	**90.30**

Table 9: Accuracies for Product Review and Movie Review Datasets.

Table 9 represents the results using five different techniques for feature set construction. We see that there is a slight improvement in accuracy on both datasets once we remove stop-words but the major breakthrough occurs once we used weighted averaging technique for construction of document vectors from word vectors.

Experiment	Features	Accuracy
In-language with SVM (Joshi et al., 2010)	tfidf	78.14
MT Based with SVM (Joshi et al., 2010)	tfidf	65.96
Improved HindiSWN (Bakliwal et al., 2012)	Adj. & Adv. presence	79.0
WordVector Averaging	word vector	78.0
Word Vector Averaging	word vector+tfidf	89.97
Weighted Word Vector with SVM (Our method)	tfidf+weighted word vector	**90.30**

Table 10: Comparison of Approaches: Movie Review Dataset

Experiment	Features	Accuracy
Subjective Lexicon (Bakliwal et al., 2012)	Simple Scoring	79.03
Hindi-SWN Baseline (Arora et al., 2013)	Adj. & Adv. presence	69.30
Word Vector with SVM	word vector+tfidf	91.14
Weighted Word Vector with SVM (Our method)	tfidf+weighted word vector	**92.89**

Table 11: Comparison of Approaches: Product Review Dataset

Table 10 and 11 compares our best method with other methods which have performed well using techniques such as tf-idf, subjective lexicon, etc.

5 Conclusion

In this work we present an early experiment on the possibilities of distributional semantic models (word vectors) for low-resource, highly inflected languages such as Hindi. What is interesting is that our word vector averaging method along with tf-idf results in improvements of accuracy compared to existing state-of-the art methods for sentiment analysis in Hindi (from 80.2% to 90.3% on IITB Movie Review Dataset). Also from Table 1, we can see that paragraph vector proposed by (Le and Mikolov, 2014) doesn't perform well owing to the fact that the Hindi dataset just contains single sentences highlighting the weakness of this model. The size of the corpus is also small to learn paragraph vectors. Thus, our model overcomes these weaknesses with a better document representation. We observe that pruning high-frequency stop words improves the accuracy by around 0.45%. This is most likely because such words tend to occur in most of the documents and don't contribute to sentiment. For example, the word फिल्म(Film) occurs in 139/252 documents in Movie Reviews(55.16%) and has little effect on sentiment. Similarly words such as सिद्धार्थ(Siddharth) occur in 2/252 documents in Movie Reviews(0.79%). These words don't provide much information.

We also see that when number of features accumulate to a large number than there are few redundant features creating noise in the representation of the text. We tried to reduce this noise by using feature variance techniques. The large increase in accuracy(around 11%) justifies our claim.

Before concluding, we return to the unexpectedly high improvement in accuracy achieved. One possibility we considered is that when the skip-grams are learned from the entire review corpus, it

incorporates some knowledge of the test data. But this seems unlikely since the difference in including this vs not including it, is not too significant. The best explanation may be that the earlier methods, which were all in some sense based on a sentiWordnet, and at that one that was initially translated from English, were essentially very weak. This is also clear in an analysis from (Bakliwal et al., 2012), which shows intern-annotator agreement on sentiment words are very poor (70%) - i.e. about 30% of these words have poor human agreement. Compared to this, the word vector model provides considerable power underlining the claim that distributional semantics is a topic worth exploring for Indian languages.

Our experiments on new dataset and existing datasets show that our method is competitive with existing methods including state-of-the-art. This new concept of document vectors can overcome the weaknesses of existing models which were either deficient in capturing syntactic or semantic properties of text. These models failed to incorporate contribution of each word while we have tapped this area and hence achieved state-of-the art results. The ensemble of RNNLM and Composite Document Vector has beaten state-of-the-art by a significant margin and has opened this area for future research. These models have the advantage that they don't require parsing at any step neither do they require a lot of heavy pre-processing. These tasks require a lot of extra effort and they slow the progress a lot.

6 Future Work

Distributional semantics approaches remain relatively under-explored for Indian languages, and our results suggest that there may be substantial benefits to exploring these approaches for Indian languages. While this work has focused on sentiment classification, it may also improve a range of tasks from verbal analogy tests to ontology learning, as has been reported for other languages. For future work, we can explore various compositional models - a) weighted average - where weights are determined based on cosine distances in vector space; b) weighted multiplicative models. Identifying morphological variants would be another direction to explore for better accuracy. With regard to sentiment analysis, the idea of aspect-based models (or part-based sentiment analysis), which looks into constituents in a document and classify their sentiment polarity separately, remains to be explored in Hindi.

In English, our Composite document vectors has led open a new area to look at where there can be many possible ensembles which may improve our work. Also, we could incorporate multiple word vectors here as well to distinguish between polysemous words. Another interesting and open area is to look at *Region of Importance* in NLP where we filter out sentiment oriented sentences and phrases from a unfocused corpus which contains text from various domains. The code and parameters are available at *github* for future research.

References

Akshat Bakliwal, Piyush Arora, and Vasudeva Varma. 2012. Hindi subjective lexicon: A lexical resource for hindi adjective polarity classification. In *Proceedings of the Eighth International Conference on Language Resources and Evaluation (LREC-2012)*. European Language Resources Association (ELRA).

Marco Baroni, Raffaela Bernardi, and Roberto Zamparelli. 2014. Frege in space: A program of compositional distributional semantics. *Linguistic Issues in Language Technology*, 9.

Yoshua Bengio, Réjean Ducharme, Pascal Vincent, and Christian Janvin. 2003. A neural probabilistic language model. *The Journal of Machine Learning Research*, 3:1137–1155.

William Blacoe and Mirella Lapata. 2012. A comparison of vector-based representations for semantic composition. In *Proceedings of the 2012 Joint Conference on Empirical Methods in Natural Language Processing and Computational Natural Language Learning*, pages 546–556. Association for Computational Linguistics.

Ronan Collobert, Jason Weston, Léon Bottou, Michael Karlen, Koray Kavukcuoglu, and Pavel Kuksa. 2011. Natural language processing (almost) from scratch. *The Journal of Machine Learning Research*, 12:2493–2537.

Mark Dredze, Koby Crammer, and Fernando Pereira. 2008. Confidence-weighted linear classification. In *Proceedings of the 25th international conference on Machine learning*, pages 264–271. ACM.

Eric H. Huang, Richard Socher, Christopher D. Manning, and Andrew Y. Ng. 2012. Improving Word Representations via Global Context and Multiple Word Prototypes. In *Annual Meeting of the Association for Computational Linguistics (ACL)*.

Rie Johnson and Tong Zhang. 2014. Effective use of word order for text categorization with convolutional neural networks. *arXiv preprint arXiv:1412.1058*.

Aditya Joshi, AR Balamurali, and Pushpak Bhattacharyya. 2010. A fall-back strategy for sentiment analysis in hindi: a case study.

Thomas K Landauer and Susan T Dumais. 1997. A solution to plato's problem: The latent semantic analysis theory of acquisition, induction, and representation of knowledge. *Psychological review*, 104(2):211.

Quoc V Le and Tomas Mikolov. 2014. Distributed representations of sentences and documents. *arXiv preprint arXiv:1405.4053*.

Hai-Son Le, Ilya Oparin, Alexandre Allauzen, J Gauvain, and François Yvon. 2011. Structured output layer neural network language model. In *Acoustics, Speech and Signal Processing (ICASSP), 2011 IEEE International Conference on*, pages 5524–5527. IEEE.

Jure Leskovec and Andrej Krevl. 2014. SNAP Datasets: Stanford large network dataset collection. http://snap.stanford.edu/data.

Yang Liu, Zhiyuan Liu, Tat-Seng Chua, and Maosong Sun. 2015. Topical word embeddings.

B. K. Matilal. 2001. *The Word and The World India's contribution to the study of language*. Oxford Paperback, Delhi.

Nishantha Medagoda, Subana Shanmuganathan, and Jacqueline Whalley. 2013. A comparative analysis of opinion mining and sentiment classification in non-english languages. In *Advances in ICT for Emerging Regions (ICTer), 2013 International Conference on*, pages 144–148. IEEE.

Tomas Mikolov, Martin Karafiát, Lukas Burget, Jan Cernockỳ, and Sanjeev Khudanpur. 2010. Recurrent neural network based language model. In *INTERSPEECH 2010, 11th Annual Conference of the International Speech Communication Association, Makuhari, Chiba, Japan, September 26-30, 2010*, pages 1045–1048.

Tomas Mikolov, Stefan Kombrink, Lukas Burget, Jan H Cernocky, and Sanjeev Khudanpur. 2011. Extensions of recurrent neural network language model. In *Acoustics, Speech and Signal Processing (ICASSP), 2011 IEEE International Conference on*, pages 5528–5531. IEEE.

Tomas Mikolov, Kai Chen, Greg Corrado, and Jeffrey Dean. 2013a. Efficient estimation of word representations in vector space. *arXiv preprint arXiv:1301.3781*.

Tomas Mikolov, Ilya Sutskever, Kai Chen, Greg S Corrado, and Jeff Dean. 2013b. Distributed representations of words and phrases and their compositionality. In *Advances in Neural Information Processing Systems*, pages 3111–3119.

Tomas Mikolov, Wen-tau Yih, and Geoffrey Zweig. 2013c. Linguistic regularities in continuous space word representations. In *HLT-NAACL*, pages 746–751.

Namita Mittal, Basant Agarwal, Garvit Chouhan, Nitin Bania, and Prateek Pareek. 2013. Sentiment analysis of hindi review based on negation and discourse relation. In *proceedings of International Joint Conference on Natural Language Processing*, pages 45–50.

Frederic Morin and Yoshua Bengio. 2005. Hierarchical probabilistic neural network language model. In *Proceedings of the international workshop on artificial intelligence and statistics*, pages 246–252. Citeseer.

Arvind Neelakantan, Jeevan Shankar, Alexandre Passos, and Andrew McCallum. 2014. Efficient nonparametric estimation of multiple embeddings per word in vector space. In *Proceedings of EMNLP*.

Bo Pang and Lillian Lee. 2004. A sentimental education: Sentiment analysis using subjectivity summarization based on minimum cuts. In *Proceedings of the 42nd annual meeting on Association for Computational Linguistics*, page 271. Association for Computational Linguistics.

Bo Pang and Lillian Lee. 2008. Opinion mining and sentiment analysis. *Found. Trends Inf. Retr.*, 2(1-2):1–135, January.

Jeffrey Pennington, Richard Socher, and Christopher Manning. 2014. Glove: Global vectors for word representation. In *Proceedings of the 2014 Conference on Empirical Methods in Natural Language Processing (EMNLP)*, pages 1532–1543. Association for Computational Linguistics.

Richa Sharma, Shweta Nigam, and Rekha Jain. 2014. Opinion mining in hindi language: A survey. *arXiv preprint arXiv:1404.4935*.

Pranjal Singh. 2015. Decompositional semantics for document embedding. `http://www.cse.iitk.ac.in/users/grounded-lang/spranjal/`.

Richard Socher, Alex Perelygin, Jean Y Wu, Jason Chuang, Christopher D Manning, Andrew Y Ng, and Christopher Potts. 2013. Recursive deep models for semantic compositionality over a sentiment treebank. In *Proceedings of the conference on empirical methods in natural language processing (EMNLP)*, volume 1631, page 1642. Citeseer.

Joseph Turian, Lev Ratinov, and Yoshua Bengio. 2010. Word representations: A simple and general method for semi-supervised learning. In *Proceedings of the 48th Annual Meeting of the Association for Computational Linguistics*, ACL '10, pages 384–394, Stroudsburg, PA, USA. Association for Computational Linguistics.

Peter D Turney, Patrick Pantel, et al. 2010. From frequency to meaning: Vector space models of semantics. *Journal of artificial intelligence research*, 37(1):141–188.

Gang Wang, Jianshan Sun, Jian Ma, Kaiquan Xu, and Jibao Gu. 2014. Sentiment classification: The contribution of ensemble learning. *Decision support systems*, 57:77–93.

Will Y Zou, Richard Socher, Daniel M Cer, and Christopher D Manning. 2013. Bilingual word embeddings for phrase-based machine translation. In *EMNLP*, pages 1393–1398.

Online Adspace Posts' Category Classification

Dhawal Joharapurkar
Manipal Institute of Technology
dmjan21@gmail.com

Vaishak Salin
Microsoft India Pvt. Ltd.
vaishak93@gmail.com

Vishal Krishna
Microsoft India Pvt. Ltd.
viscrisn@gmail.com

Abstract

Online adspaces require the seller/buyer to select a category to post their advertisements. This practice not only causes hindrance to legitimate users while posting their advertisements, but, also deter the user experience as they will see a lot of non-categorized ads due to human error or spam. Classifying advertisements posted on an online adspace can help in spam detection, better information propagation which in turn enhances user experience.

Craigslist is a prevalent platform for local classified advertisements. In this paper, we present a classification system for an online advertisement space such as Craigslist. We show the performance of our algorithm with three standard classifiers, *viz.*, Support Vector Machine, Random Forest, and Multinomial Naive Bayes. An accuracy of 84% was achieved with the SVM.

1 Introduction

With the advent of online adspaces, there are several hundred advertisements that get posted every second and such an influx of unstructured information is a rich source of data. Classification of advertisements into categories based on the text of the advertisement, a simple but rather useful technique is presented in this paper along with its implications.

Craigslist is an online place with local classifieds and forums which are community moderated, and largely free, on commodities like jobs, housing, goods, services, romance, local activities, advice, etc. There are different sub-domains of Craigslist, for each country they operate in. Each country has listings organized by sections which

	users	Countries	posts/month
Craigslist	500M+	70+	80M+
Ebay	300M+	40	50M+

Table 1: Craigslist vs Ebay

are then further subdivided into categories. We chose Craigslist as they have made some of their data publicly available is one of the largest online adspaces currently operating as shown by the statistics in the table below. However, this method can be applied to any online adpsace.

As the table indicates, Craigslist is a more data rich source of advertisements. One reason for this is that Craigslist doesn't limit itself to goods only whereas other e-commerce websites do.

We use supervised learning techniques to classify a Craigslist post into different categories. We use text mining techniques like text normalization(Sproat et al., 2001) and term frequency inverse document frequency for preparing the data for classification. We tested several classification techniques and tabulated the results obtained using various assessment methods. SVM(Joachims, 1998) with a linear kernel yields the best result with an accuracy of 84% on the test data.

An online adspace such as Craigslist could use a recommender system that predicts the category under which the post must be filed while a user is posting an advertisement, using our classifier in an online setting. This sort of recommendation system is a very nifty way of improving the user experience for a site which sees on an average an excess of 80 million advertisements posted per month.

Our Contribution: We propose a classifier wherein, when a user is posting an advertisement on an online adspace such as Craigslist, a recom-

21

D S Sharma, R Sangal and E Sherly. Proc. of the 12th Intl. Conference on Natural Language Processing, pages 20–28,
Trivandrum, India. December 2015. ©2015 NLP Association of India (NLPAI)

mendation is made to the user to select the category for the advertisement to be displayed in. In the case that the user doesn't select it, the post will be displayed in the predicted category by default.

2 Motivation

Recommendations can be made in an online setting wherein the text from the description of the advertisement is used to create feature vectors and fed into a classifier which predicts the category of the post. Based on this categorization, a recommendation is made to the user. This elementary step reduces the work of the user having to manually select the category to post his/her advertisement to. The category predicted can also be helpful in preventing the user from spamming the adspace by placing totally irrelevant ads to a particular category. This in turn enhances the user experience of the people browsing the advertisements listed.

Specifically, given the city, section and heading of a Craigslist post, we have to predict the category under which it should be posted.

3 Related Work

To our knowledge, there has been no work done in detecting spam (wrongly located advertisements) on online advertisement spaces. However, there has been some work in prediction of the price of an object using the title and the textual description of the advertisement by fitting a Naive Bayes classifier. (Elridge)

We chose to build such a classifier on Craigslist data as Fuxman et al. (Fuxman et al., 2009) have showed Craigslist to be a data source to improve classification accuracy in cases where a simple algorithm can outperform a sophisticated algorithm if it is provided with more training data.

4 Data

The dataset is a subset of the data generated on the Craigslist sites for a set of sixteen different cities (such as New York, Mumbai, etc.). The dataset has records from four sections forsale, housing, community and services and a total of sixteen categories from those sections. The categories are: activities, appliances, artists, automotive, cellphones, childcare, general, household-services, housing, photography, real-estate, shared, temporary, therapeutic, video-games and wanted-

housing. Each category belongs to only one section. This data was made publicly available.

The first line in the dataset is an integer N. N lines follow, each line being a valid JSON object. The following fields of raw data, given in JSON:

- city (string, ASCII) : The city for which this Craigslist post was made

- section (string, ASCII) : for-sale / housing / community / services

- heading (string, UTF-8) : The heading of the post

A sample record looks as follows:

{"city": "singapore", "section": "for-sale", "heading": "Panasonic ,2doors fridge(238L)($220 with delivery+1mth warranty)"}

A total of approximately 20,000 records were made available, proportionally represented across these sections, categories and cities. The format of training data is the same as input format but with an additional field category, the category in which the post was made. A separate test dataset of 15,370 records was also provided, which we have used to test our final model on.

5 Experimental Setup

In our work, we have used scikit-learn(Pedregosa et al., 2011) (formerly scikits.learn) which is an open source machine learning library for the Python programming language. It features various classification, regression and clustering algorithms such as support vector machines, logistic regression, naive Bayes, random forests, gradient boosting, kmeans clustering and DBSCAN, etc. It is designed to interoperate with the Python numerical and scientific library SciPy (Jones et al., 2001).

5.1 Preprocessing of Data

Most category based ads have similar words. For example, words like BHK, wooden flooring, etc occur in house advertisements; MB, GB, camera, appear in cellphone advertisements.

One major feature of advertisements which are usually considered spam is the presence of lot of special characters. Most spam advertisements

	Accuracy	F1	Precision	Recall
SVM	0.81	0.82	0.83	0.82
Random Forest	0.73	0.75	0.76	0.75
Multinomial NB	0.68	0.74	0.75	0.74

Table 2: Baseline Performance of Algorithms

have several special characters more than legi
mate advertisements.

Feature generation: We remove all the spec
characters from the data as these arent rea
helpful from a lexical perspective, but use
count of these characters as a feature.

Normalization: We treat all numbers t
occur equally as these usually represent the pr
or quantity of the product, which doesnt rea
help us decide the category of an advertisem
We normalize it by using the word numbr for ;
digit or number that occurs.

5.2 Creation of Classifier

The preprocessed data is then used to the create
feature matrix. We use the bag of words model
and then apply tf-idf (Salton and Yang, 1973) to
generate feature vectors for each advertisement.

The feature matrix is sent to the classifier whose
parameters have been optimized by the Grid-
SearchCV module present in sklearn.(Pedregosa
et al., 2011)

6 Evaluations and Results

Baseline results: The baseline results are calculated with the default/standard classifiers with no
parameter optimizations done. The scores are averaged over 3-fold cross validation.

Results: After tweaking the parameters of
the classifier using GridSearchCV our results improved and have been listed in Table 3.

From the confusion matrix, it is evident that the
class labelled "therapeutic" was the best classified class with more than 1400 of the 1600 data
points being correctly classified as "therapeutic".

	Accuracy	F1	Precision	Recall
SVM	0.84	0.84	0.85	0.84
Random Forest	0.75	0.77	0.77	0.77
Multinomial NB	0.68	0.77	0.77	0.78

Table 3: Performance of Algorithms after Parameter Tweaking

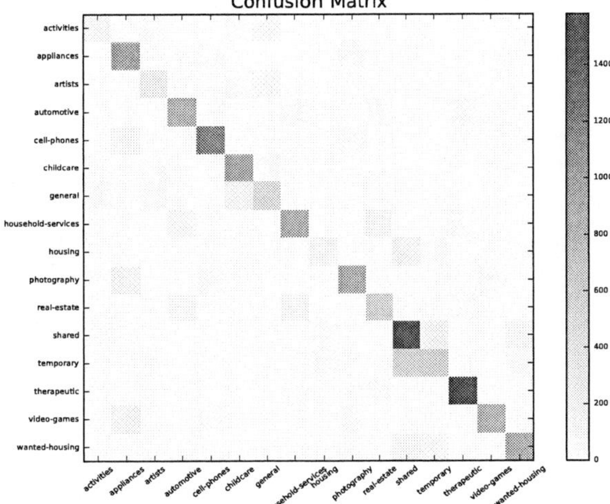

Figure 1: Confusion Matrix

This is an important result as it is well known that
advertisements which fall under this category are
most likely spam when found in other categories.
Hence, classification on the text of the advertisement can help detect spam and block it out. We
can also note for example, appliances get confused
with cell phones and video games which is an interesting finding since the two are semantically
closer than, say, housing.

Another stark importance of such a system is
the amount of man hours saved. With 80M posts
coming in every month, let us say a user spends
about 30 seconds selecting the section and category of the advertisement. That is approximately a
whopping 666,000+ man hours saved each month.

7 Conclusion

In this paper, we present a classifier for online adspaces, which classifies an advertisement
amongst 16 categories. If an advertisement is ac-
curately classified in its correct class, it helps increase the reach of the advertisement as it is displayed to the people looking in the particular section and is not classified as spam. In this work,

we have used the Craigslist data which is publicly available, and, very rich in terms of categories and datapoints. Our classifier secures an mean accuracy of 84% when tested using cross-validation.

8 Future Work

We look to improve this work in two ways. First, we would like to expand the current classifier to be a multi-class classifier. This would help classify ads which can belong to more than one category, thereby it would result in the advertisement being displayed in more than one category and hence reach more "prospective" buyers. As an alternative, it would be interesting to treat this as a multi-label classification problem, wherein each item can be labelled with more than one category. This allows us to tag each advertisement with classes which are related.

Secondly, we would want to explore and implement better feature engineering. The section-category tags of posts follow a hierarchy. Being able to incorporate this hierarchy as features would, we believe, significantly improve our feature vectors. Using such a classifier in setting where advertisements can comprise a code-mixed dataset like on Indian online adspaces such as Olx, Junglee, etc., can will benefit from learning features from such data.

References

Ariel Fuxman, Anitha Kannan, Andrew B Goldberg, Rakesh Agrawal, Panayiotis Tsaparas, and John Shafer. 2009. Improving classification accuracy using automatically extracted training data. In *Proceedings of the 15th ACM SIGKDD international conference on Knowledge discovery and data mining*, pages 1145–1154. ACM.

Thorsten Joachims. 1998. *Text categorization with support vector machines: Learning with many relevant features*. Springer.

Eric Jones, Travis Oliphant, Pearu Peterson, et al. 2001–. SciPy: Open source scientific tools for Python. [Online; accessed 2015-08-22].

F. Pedregosa, G. Varoquaux, A. Gramfort, V. Michel, B. Thirion, O. Grisel, M. Blondel, P. Prettenhofer, R. Weiss, V. Dubourg, J. Vanderplas, A. Passos, D. Cournapeau, M. Brucher, M. Perrot, and E. Duchesnay. 2011. Scikit-learn: Machine learning in Python. *Journal of Machine Learning Research*, 12:2825–2830.

Gerard Salton and Chung-Shu Yang. 1973. On the specification of term values in automatic indexing. *Journal of documentation*, 29(4):351–372.

Richard Sproat, Alan W Black, Stanley Chen, Shankar Kumar, Mari Ostendorf, and Christopher Richards. 2001. Normalization of non-standard words. *Computer Speech & Language*, 15(3):287–333.

Noun Phrase Chunking for Marathi using Distant Supervision

Sachin Pawar[1,2]   Nitin Ramrakhiyani[1]   Girish K. Palshikar[1]
Pushpak Bhattacharyya[2]   Swapnil Hingmire[1,3]
{sachin7.p, nitin.ramrakhiyani, gk.palshikar}@tcs.com
pb@cse.iitb.ac.in, swapnil.hingmire@tcs.com
[1]Systems Research Lab, Tata Consultancy Services Ltd., Pune, India
[2]Department of CSE, IIT Bombay, Mumbai, India
[3]Department of CSE, IIT Madras, Chennai, India

Abstract

Information Extraction from Indian languages requires effective shallow parsing, especially identification of "meaningful" noun phrases. Particularly, for an agglutinative and free word order language like Marathi, this problem is quite challenging. We model this task of extracting noun phrases as a sequence labelling problem. A Distant Supervision framework is used to automatically create a large labelled data for training the sequence labelling model. The framework exploits a set of heuristic rules based on corpus statistics for the automatic labelling. Our approach puts together the benefits of heuristic rules, a large unlabelled corpus as well as supervised learning to model complex underlying characteristics of noun phrase occurrences. In comparison to a simple English-like chunking baseline and a publicly available Marathi Shallow Parser, our method demonstrates a better performance.

1   Introduction

One of the key steps of a Natural Language Processing (NLP) pipeline is chunking or shallow parsing. It allows the system to identify building blocks of a sentence namely phrases. Further, the identification of phrases is of importance to applications in information extraction, text summarization and event detection. In English, the task of chunking is relatively simple as compared to other steps of the NLP pipeline. Given the Parts-Of-Speech (POS) tags of the sentence tokens, it is a matter of using rules based on the POS tags (Abney, 1992) to extract the chunks with high confidence. State of the art papers on Noun Phrase (NP) chunking in English (Sun et al., 2008), (Shen and Sarkar, 2005), (McDonald et al., 2005) report results of more than 94% F-measure.

However, the scenario is different for many Indian languages. Their suffix agglutinative and free word order nature makes it challenging to identify the correct phrases. In this paper, we focus on the problem of identifying noun phrases from Marathi, a highly agglutinative Indian language. Marathi is spoken by more than 70 million people worldwide [1] and it exhibits a large web presence in terms of e-newspapers, Marathi Wikipedia, blogs, social network banter and much more. There are various motivations for the problem and the most important one being the lack of domain specific information extraction systems in Indian Languages. The problem also poses challenges in terms of NLP resource-poor nature of Indian languages and a complex suffix agglutination scheme in Marathi. Keeping these challenges in sight, we propose the use of distantly supervised approach for the task.

The task of identifying meaningful noun phrases in Marathi becomes challenging due to another fact that two different noun phrases can be written adjacently in a sentence. Such noun phrases are individually meaningful but their concatenation is not. Hence, it is important to correctly identify the boundaries of such noun phrases. We propose to model the task of identifying noun phrases as a sequence labelling task where the labelled data is generated automatically by using a set of heuristic rules. Moreover, these rules are not based on deep linguistic knowledge but are devised using corpus statistics.

In the next section, related work on Indian Language shallow parsing is presented. Section 3 describes a simple baseline for noun phrase identification for Marathi. Thereafter in Section 4, the distant supervision based sequence labelling approach is described in detail. This is followed by

---

[1]https://en.wikipedia.org/wiki/
Marathi_language (accessed 11-AUG-2015)

D S Sharma, R Sangal and E Sherly. Proc. of the 12th Intl. Conference on Natural Language Processing, pages 29–38,
Trivandrum, India. December 2015. ©2015 NLP Association of India (NLPAI)

a description of the corpus, experiments and evaluation results.

2 Related Work

This section describes relevant work in the field of shallow parsing and chunking in Indian languages. The work is presented based on a categorization into papers and tool sets.

Starting with the path setting paper on parsing of free word order languages (Bharati and Sangal, 1993), there have been multiple contributions to parsing of Indian Languages. A national symposium on modelling and shallow parsing of Indian languages held at IIT Bombay in April 2006 (MSPIL, 2006) brought together Indian NLP researchers to discuss on problems in Indian language NLP. Investigations in shallow parsing and morphological analysis in Bengali, Kannada, Telugu and Tamil were presented.

Also in 2006, a machine learning contest on POS tagging and chunking for Indian languages (NLPAI and IIIT-H, 2006) was organized which lead to release of POS tagged data (20K words) in Hindi, Bengali and Telugu and Chunk tagged data in Hindi. The participating systems employed various supervised machine learning methods to perform POS tagging and chunking for the three languages. The team from IIT Bombay (Dalal et al., 2006), trained a Maximum Entropy Markov Model (MEMM) from the training data to develop a chunker in Hindi and then evaluated it on test data. Their chunker was able to achieve an F1-measure of 82.4% on test data. In the entry by the team from IIT Madras (Awasthi et al., 2006), apart from a HMM based POS tagger, a chunker was developed by training a linear chain CRF using the MALLET toolkit. It achieved an overall F1-measure of 89.69% (with reference POS tags) and 79.58% (with the generated POS tags). Another system from Jadavpur University (Bandyopadhay et al., 2006) contributed a rule-based chunker for Bengali which comprised of a two stage approach - chunk boundary identification and chunk labelling. On an unannotated test set, the chunker reported an accuracy of 81.61%. The system from Microsoft Research India (Baskaran, 2006), comprised of a chunker for Hindi. It was developed by training a HMM and using probability models of certain contextual features. The system reported an F1-measure of 76% on the test set. The team from IIIT Hyderabad developed a chunker

(Himashu and Anirudh, 2006) by training Conditional Random Fields (CRFs) and then evaluating on the test data. Their chunker performed at an F1-measure of 90.89%.

A more formal effort lead to the organization of the IJCAI workshop on Shallow Parsing for South Asian Languages and an associated contest (Bharati and Mannem, 2007), which brought out multiple contributions in POS tagging and shallow parsing of Hindi, Bengali and Telugu. Chunk data for Bengali and Telugu was also made available, however data of no other languages were introduced. In total, a set of 20,000 words for training, 5000 words for validation and 5000 words for testing were provided for all three languages. A listing of major contributions for the chunking task is presented as follows. A rule based system was proposed by Ekbal et al. (2007), where the linguistic rules worked well for Hindi (80.63% accurate) and Bengali (71.65% accurate). A Maximum Entropy Model based approach (Dandapat, 2007) worked well for Hindi (74.92% accurate) and Bengali (80.59% accurate). It used contextual POS tags as features than the context words. In another submission (Pattabhi et al., 2007), the technique involved a Transformation-Based Learning (TBL) for chunking and reported to have moderate results for Hindi and Bengali. The technique proposed in (Sastry et al., 2007) was tried at learning chunk pattern templates based on four chunking parameters. It used the CKY algorithm to get the best chunk sequence for a sentence. The results were moderate for all the three languages. Rao and Yarowsky (Rao and Yarowsky, 2007), observed that punctuations in the sentence act as roadblocks to learning clear syntactic patterns and hence they tried to drop them, leading to a rise in accuracy. However, they reported results on a different Naive Bayes based system. The system that came close second to the winner was by Agrawal (2007). It divided the chunking task into three stages - boundary labelling (BL), chunk boundary detection using labels from first stage and finally re-prediction of chunk labels. For Bengali and Telugu, their system performed almost at par with the the best system's accuracy. The system that performed the best on all three languages was proposed by PVS and Karthik (2007) which used HMMs for chunk boundary detection and CRFs for chunk labelling. They reached chunking accuracies of 82.74%, 80.97% and 80.95% for

Bengali, Hindi and Telugu respectively.

Apart from the two major exercises above, there has been a constant stream of work being published in the area. One of the older and primary effort was by Singh et al. (2005), where a HMM based chunk boundary identification system was developed by training it on a corpus of 1,50,000 words. The chunk label identification was rule based and the combined system was tested on a corpus of manually POS tagged 20,000 words leading to an accuracy of 91.7%. A more recent work on Malayalam shallow parsing (Nair and Peter, 2011) proposes a morpheme based augmented transition network for chunking and is reported to achieve good results on a small dataset used in the paper. Another important contribution by Gahlot et al. (2009) is an analysis paper on use of sequential learning algorithms for POS-tagging and shallow parsing in Hindi. The paper compares Maximum Entropy models, CRFs and SVMs on datasets of various sizes leading to conclusive arguments about the performance of the chosen systems. An important contribution is by Gune et al. (2010), where development of a Marathi shallow parser is explored using a sequence classifier with novel features from a rich morphological analyser. The resulting shallow parser shows a high accuracy of 97% on the moderate dataset (20K words) used in the paper.

On the tools front, there are various tool sets for shallow parsing in Indian languages which are available for public download. The most important and foremost ones being the shallow parsers provided by Language Technology Research Centre at IIIT-H (2015). The available shallow parsers are for languages - Hindi, Punjabi, Urdu, Bengali, Tamil, Telugu, Kannada, Malayalam and Marathi. We use this LTRC IIIT-H provided Marathi shallow parser as one of our baselines. Another set of shallow parsing tools are available from the CALTS, School of Humanities at University of Hyderabad (2015). They are focused on another set of languages namely Assamese, Bodo, Dogri, Gujarati, Hindi, Kashmiri, Konkani, Maithili, Manipuri, Nepali, Odia and Santali.

3 A Simple Baseline Approach

We define a noun phrase as a contiguous "meaningful" sequence of adjective (optional) followed by nouns. Here, we consider both types nouns: proper nouns and common nouns. Our definition also stresses on the "meaningfulness" of the sequence of nouns to be identified as a "valid" noun phrase.

Our observation is that extraction of such noun phrases is quite straight-forward in English and requires application of a simple regular expression on POS tagged text. In English, boundaries of such noun phrases are explicitly marked by prepositions, punctuations, determiners and verbs. Consider the sentence: `Ajay met Sachin Tendulkar in Mumbai.` Here, it can be observed that there are 3 "valid" noun phrases: `Ajay`, `Sachin Tendulkar` and `Mumbai`, which are perfectly separated by the verb `met` and the preposition `in`. There is no other way of writing this sentence in English such that any of the two noun phrases are written adjacently to each other. Hence, it is straight-forward in English to extract such noun phrases by writing a simple rule / regular expression. However, such a simple rule does not work for Indian languages like Marathi. Marathi has a free word order and is also highly agglutinative. In Marathi, the same sentence will be written as अजय सचिन तेंडुलकरला मुंबईमध्ये भेटला. Here, the first four words are nouns and hence the English-like phrase extraction rule will extract only one noun sequence (अजय सचिन तेंडुलकरला मुंबईमध्ये) which is not "meaningful".

We propose a simple baseline approach to extract "meaningful" noun phrases in Marathi which is a modification of the English-like phrase extraction rule. In Marathi, unlike English prepositions are not separate words but they are written as suffixes of the nouns. Hence, it is essential to remove suffixes attached to the words and write them as a separate token. This process of removing suffixes and identifying rootword for each word, is called as *Stemming*. After stemming, the above sentence becomes : अजय सचिन तेंडुलकर ला मुंबई मध्ये भेट ला. Now, if we extract all the consecutive nouns, we get 2 sequences : अजय सचिन तेंडुलकर and मुंबई. Here, the second sequence is a "valid" noun phrase but the first one is not.

Computationally, to use this baseline method it is necessary to apply stemming and POS tagging on a sentence to produce a sequence as follows:
अजय/NNP सचिन/NNP तेंडुलकर/NNP ला/SUF मुंबई/NNP मध्ये/SUF भेट/VM ला/SUF ./SYM
Then the following regular expression is applied for extraction of noun phrases.

(<word>/JJ)?(<word>/NNP?)*(<word>/NNP?)

This proposed baseline approach is quite efficient and effective. But unlike English, in Marathi all contiguous sequences of nouns (without any suffixes attached to these nouns) need not yield a "meaningful" noun phrase. This is because, in Marathi it is perfectly syntactical to have multiple consecutive noun phrases without any explicit (prepositions, verbs, punctuations etc.) or implicit (e.g. suffixes attached to words, change of POS from NN to NNP and vice versa) boundary markers.

4 Distantly supervised sequential labelling approach

"Distant supervision" is a learning paradigm in which a labelled training set is constructed automatically using some heuristics or rules. The resulting labelled data may have some noisy / incorrect labels but it is expected that majority of the automatically obtained labels are correct. Since it is possible to create a large labelled dataset (much larger than manually labelled data), majority correct labels will hopefully reduce the effect of a smaller number of noisy labels in the training set.

For any distant supervision based algorithm, there are two essential requirements - i) Large pool of unlabelled data and ii) Heuristic rules to obtain noisy labels. Distant supervision has been successfully used for the problem of Relation Extraction (Mintz et al., 2009). Semantic database like FreeBase (Bollacker et al., 2008) is used to get a list of entity pairs following any particular relation. Also, a large number of unlabelled sentences are used which can be easily obtained by crawling the Web. The labelling heuristic used here is: If two entities participate in a relation, any sentence that contains both of them might express that relation. For example, Freebase contains entity pair `<M. Night Shyamalan, The Sixth Sense>` for the relation ID /film/director/film, hence both of the following sentences are considered to be positive examples for that relation:

1. `M. Night Shyamalan` gained `international recognition` when he wrote and directed 1999's `The Sixth Sense`.

2. `The Sixth Sense` is a 1999 American supernatural thriller drama film written and directed by `M. Night Shyamalan`.

Though this assumption is expected to be true for majority of the sentences, it may introduce few noisy labels. For example, following sentence contains both the entities but does not express the desired relation.

1. `The Sixth Sense`, a supernatural thriller film, was written by `M. Night Shyamalan`.

4.1 Motivation

It is difficult to obtain labelled data where valid noun phrases are marked, because such a manual task is time consuming and effort intensive. In order to build a phrase identifier for Marathi, without spending manual efforts on creation of labelled data, we propose to use the learning paradigm of "Distant Supervision". Unlabelled data is easily available in this case, which is the first essential requirement of the distant supervision paradigm. We label sentences from a large unlabelled Marathi corpus with POS tags using a CRF-based POS tagger. We also check whether any suffixes are attached to the words and split such words into root word followed by suffixes as separate tokens [2]. The baseline method explained in the previous section, is then applied on all of these sentences to extract "candidate" noun phrases. As we have already described, this baseline method fails when two different noun phrases occur adjacent to each other. In order to devise some effective rules to create labelled data automatically, we take help of these candidate phrases. Based on corpus statistics (described in Section 4.2), we split some of the candidate phrases and keep other candidate phrases intact. In order to simplify the splitting decision, we assume that there will be at most one split point, i.e. any candidate phrase consists of at most two different consecutive noun phrases. After analysing a lot of Marathi sentences, we observed that this is a reasonable assumption to make because it is very rare to have more than 2 consecutive noun phrases.

4.2 Corpus Statistics

Various statistics of words and phrases are computed by using a large unlabelled corpus. These statistics are used in order to devise rules for distant supervision.

4.2.1 Phrase Counts:

We extract all the candidate phrases from the corpus using the first baseline method. For each candidate phrase, we note the number of times it oc-

---

[2]Marathi Stemmer by CFILT, IIT Bombay is used

curs in the corpus. Any candidate phrase which occurs more than 2 times in the corpus is likely to be a "valid" phrase.

4.2.2 Word Statistics:

Some useful statistics of words are computed using the list of "valid" noun phrases. For each word w, following counts are noted:

1. *Start_Count* : Number of times w occurs as a first word in a "valid" phrase with multiple words (E.g. बेकारी in the phrase बेकारी भत्ता)

2. *Unitary_Count* : Number of times w occurs as the only word in a "valid" phrase (E.g. पक्ष in the phrase पक्ष)

3. *Continuation_Count* : Number of times w is NOT the first or last word in a "valid" phrase with more than 2 words (E.g. क्रिकेट in the phrase भारतीय क्रिकेट संघ)

4. *End_Count* : Number of times w occurs as a last word in a "valid" phrase with multiple words (E.g. भत्ता in the phrase बेकारी भत्ता)

For each word, its most frequent category (out of *Start*, *End*, *Unitary* and *Continuation*) is stored in the structure *WordType*. Four different sets of words are defined : *Start_Words*, *Unitary_Words*, *Continuation_Words* and *End_Words*. If any word w occurs n times overall in the "valid" phrases and its *Start_Count* is at least $0.1 * n$, then the word w is added to the set *Start_Words*. The other three sets *Unitary_Words*, *Continuation_Words* and *End_Words* are similarly populated corresponding to the counts *Unitary_Count*, *Continuation_Count* and *End_Count*, respectively. One special set of words, *Unitary_Only_Words* is defined which contains all those words in *Unitary_Words* which are not present in any of the other 3 sets. Table 1 shows all these corpus statistics for some of the representative words.

4.3 Rules for Distant Supervision

With the help of the output of first baseline method and the corpus statistics, we devise heuristic rules for creating labelled data. For each candidate phrase p generated by the baseline method, following rules are applied sequentially.

4.3.1 Rule 1 (W1)

If p has only one word, then it is trivially correct. All the remaining rules are applied for only multi-word candidate phrases.

4.3.2 Rule 2 (AdjNoun)

If p has exactly two words such that the first word is an adjective and the second word in a noun, then p is a correct phrase.

4.3.3 Rule 3 (C3)

If p has corpus count of 3 or more, then it is very likely to be correct. But in order to make this rule more precise, some more constraints are applied to p. If the first word of p is in the set *Unitary_Words* but not in the set *Start_Words* or if the last word of p is in the set *Unitary_Words* but not in the set *Last_Words*, then then p is likely to be incorrect. Hence, excluding such phrases, this rule assumes all other candidate phrases with corpus count of at least 3 to be correct phrases.

4.3.4 Rule 4 (C2C2)

All the rules till now checked whether the candidate phrase as a whole is correct. This rule tries to estimate whether to split any candidate phrase into two consecutive meaningful phrases. If there are n words in a candidate phrase, then there are $(n-1)$ potential splits. Algorithm 1 *Split_Check* is used to determine whether any given split is valid or not. Algorithm 2 describes this rule in detail. In simple words, this rule splits a candidate phrase only if its sub-phrases are "valid" and each of the sub-phrase has been observed at least twice in the corpus.

Algorithm 1: *Split_Check* (checking validity of a split)

Data: Candidate phrase p, Split Index i, Corpus Statistics (as explained in Table 1)
Result: Whether splitting p at i is "valid"

1   $L_1 := i^{th}$ word of p; /* Last word of first sub-phrase */
2   $F_2 := (i+1)^{st}$ word of p ; /* First word of second sub-phrase */
3   **if** L_1 *or* F_2 *are unseen words* **then return** *FALSE*;
4   **if** $L_1 \in$ Continuation_Words **then return** *FALSE*;
5   **if** $F_2 \in$ Continuation_Words **then return** *FALSE*;
6   **if** $i = 1$ **and** $L_1 \notin$ Unitary_Words **then return** *FALSE*;
7   **if** $i = len(p) - 1$ **and** $F_2 \notin$ Unitary_Words **then return** *FALSE*;
8   **if** $L_1 \in$ Start_Words **then return** *FALSE*;
9   **if** $F_2 \in$ End_Words **then return** *FALSE*;
10   **return** *TRUE*;

4.3.5 Rule 5

Similar to Rule 4, this rule also tries to estimate whether any candidate phrase can be split into two consecutive meaningful phrases. But unlike Rule

Word	Corpus Count	Start Count	End Count	Unitary Count	Continuation Count	Member of Sets	Word Type
लोकसभा *loksabhaa* Loksabha	640	**331**	7	**293**	9	*Start_Words* *Unitary_Words*	*Start*
गांधी *gandhee* Gandhi	567	16	**482**	48	21	*End_Words*	*End*
स्वयंसेवक *swayamsevak* volunteer	61	0	4	**16**	**41**	*End_Words* *Continuation_Words*	*Continuation*
तंत्रज्ञान *TanTradnyan* technology	302	8	**102**	179	13	*End_Words* *Unitary_Words*	*End*
निर्णय *nirNay* decision	2200	164	130	**1892**	14	*Unitary_Words* *Unitary_Only_Words*	*Unitary*

Table 1: Examples of various corpus statistics generated. Specific counts more than 10% of the total counts are shown in **bold**.

Algorithm 2: Rule 4 for splitting a candidate phrase using corpus counts

```
Data: Candidate phrase p, Corpus Statistics (as
      explained in Table 1)
Result: Two "valid" sub-phrases OR FALSE if no
      "valid" sub-phrases are found
1  i := 1;
2  while i < length(p) do
3      if Split_Check(p,i) = FALSE then continue;
4      i := i + 1;
5      p₁ := p[1 : i] ;  /* First sub-phrase */
6      p₂ := p[i + 1 : length(p)] ;      /* Second
       sub-phrase */
7      if CourpusCount(p₁) < 2 then continue;
8      if CourpusCount(p₂) < 2 then continue;
9      return (p₁, p₂);
10 end
11 return FALSE;
```

Algorithm 4: Rule 6 Unitary Split

```
Data: Candidate phrase p, Corpus Statistics (as
      explained in Table 1)
Result: Two "valid" sub-phrases OR FALSE if no
      "valid" sub-phrases are found
1  p₁ := p[1] ;          /* First word of p */
2  p₂ := p[2 : length(p)] ;  /* Remaining words
   of p */
3  if p₁.POS = NN and p₁ ∈ Unitary_Only_Words
   then return (p₁, p₂);
4  p₂ := p[lenght(p)] ;   /* Last word of p */
5  p₁ := p[1 : lenght(p) − 1] ;        /* Remaining
   words of p */
6  if p₂.POS = NN and p₂ ∈ Unitary_Only_Words
   then return (p₁, p₂);
7  return FALSE;
```

4 which uses corpus counts, this rule uses properties of the words at split boundary. Algorithm 3 explains this rule in detail.

4.3.6 Rule 6 (UnitarySplit)

Like rules 4 and 5, this rule also checks whether a candidate phrase can be split. This rule handles the specific case of a single common noun (NOT proper noun) adjacent to other meaningful phrase. It does not check the validity of a split by using the algorithm *Split_Check* (Algorithm 1) but uses a stricter check to validate "Unitary" nature of such single common nouns. The detailed explanation is provided in the Algorithm 4.

4.3.7 Rule 7 (W2*)

This is the default rule applied on those candidate phrases for which none of the earlier rule is satisfied. In other words, rules 1 to 3 are not able to identify these phrase as "valid" phrases as a whole. Also, rules 4 to 6 are not able to identify a "valid" split to produce two consecutive meaningful phrases. This rule assumes that all such phrases are "valid" and keeps them intact without any split.

4.4 Estimated Accuracy of Rules

All the rules explained in the Section 4.3 are applied on a large unlabelled corpus (approximately 200,000 sentences) and labelled data is automatically produced. These automatically labelled sentences are further used to train a sequence classifier (CRF in our case) so that it can be used to extract proper noun phrases from any unseen sentence. Automatically obtained phrase labels may contain some noise. In order to get an estimate of accuracy of the labels, for each rule we collected random sample of 100 candidate phrases. These samples were manually verified to get an estimate of accuracy of each rule which are shown in the

```
Algorithm 3: Rule 5 for splitting a candidate phrase using word properties
─────────────────────────────────────────────────────────────────────────
    Data: Candidate phrase p, Corpus Statistics (as explained in Table 1)
    Result: Two "valid" sub-phrases OR FALSE if no "valid" sub-phrases are found
 1  i := 1;
 2  while i < length(p) do
 3  │   if Split_Check(p,i) = FALSE then continue;
 4  │   i := i + 1;
 5  │   p₁ := p[1 : i] ;                                      /* First sub-phrase */
 6  │   p₂ := p[i + 1 : length(p)] ;                          /* Second sub-phrase */
 7  │   L₁ := iᵗʰ word of p ;                         /* Last word of first sub-phrase */
 8  │   F₂ := (i + 1)ˢᵗ word of p ;                  /* First word of second sub-phrase */
 9  │   if length(p₁) = 1 and length(p₂) = 1 then
10  │   │   if L₁ ∈ Unitary_Words and F₂ ∈ Unitary_Words and L₁.POS ≠ F₂.POS then return (p₁, p₂);
11  │   │   if WordType[L₁] = Unitary and WordType[F₂] = Unitary then return (p₁, p₂)
12  │   end
13  │   if length(p₁) = 1 and length(p₂) > 1 then
14  │   │   if L₁ ∈ Unitary_Words and F₂ ∈ Start_Words and L₁.POS ≠ F₂.POS then return (p₁, p₂);
15  │   │   if WordType[L₁] = Unitary and WordType[F₂] = Start then return (p₁, p₂);
16  │   end
17  │   if length(p₁) > 1 and length(p₂) = 1 then
18  │   │   if L₁ ∈ End_Words and F₂ ∈ Unitary_Words and L₁.POS ≠ F₂.POS then return (p₁, p₂);
19  │   │   if WordType[L₁] = End and WordType[F₂] = Unitary then return (p₁, p₂);
20  │   end
21  │   if length(p₁) > 1 and length(p₂) > 1 then
22  │   │   if L₁ ∈ End_Words and F₂ ∈ Start_Words and L₁.POS ≠ F₂.POS then return (p₁, p₂);
23  │   │   if WordType[L₁] = End and WordType[F₂] = Start then return (p₁, p₂);
24  │   end
25  end
26  return FALSE;
```

Table 2. Higher the number of phases labelled by a rule, higher is its *Support* and lower the number of estimated errors, higher is its *Confidence*.

Rule	#Candidate Phrases Labelled	#Errors in Random Sample of 100
Rule 1 (W1)	632735	0
Rule 2 (AdjNoun)	56133	0
Rule 3 (C3)	56401	4
Rule 4 (C2C2)	22883	16
Rule 5 (ValidSplit)	2158	32
Rule 6 (UnitarySplit)	23948	51
Rule 7 (W2*)	102387	36

Table 2: Estimated Accuracy of the Rules used for Distant Supervision

Here, it is to be noted that "Error" is rule specific. For a non-splitting rule like rule 3, an error will occur when it keeps an incorrect candidate phrase intact which should have been split. However, for a splitting rule like rule 4, an error will occur when it splits a "valid" phrase which should not have been split. It can be observed that rule 6 (UnitarySplit) is the least accurate rule, but we still use it because we believe that the noise introduced by it can be overcome by the sequence classifier because of other better performing rules having more coverage.

4.5 Sequence Labelling

The intuition behind learning a sequence labelling model is that such a statistical model can implicitly learn several more complex rules to identify meaningful noun phrases. We use Conditional Random Fields (CRF) (Lafferty et al., 2001) for sequence labelling. In this section, we describe how the labelled data is automatically created for training CRF model and what are the various features used by the CRF model.

4.5.1 Creation of Training Data for CRF

Our unlabelled corpus contains around 200,000 sentences. Approximately 55,000 sentences have at least two candidate phrases labelled by any of the rules from rule 1 to rule 6. These sentences are used for training sequence labelling model using CRF. Table 3 shows some examples of candidate phrases labelled by the rules. We are using the BIO labelling scheme which assigns one of the three different labels to each sequence element (word or suffix in our case) as follows:
B: First word in a phrase is labelled as **B**.
I: All subsequent words except the first word in a phrase are labelled as **I**.
O: All other words or suffixes which do not belong to any phrase are labelled as **O**.

Rule	Labelled Phrases
Rule 1 (W1)	संधी/B बातमी/B
Rule 2 (AdjNoun)	अपेक्षित/B बदल/I मराठी/B माणूस/I
Rule 3 (C3)	परिवहन/B विभाग/I भारतीय/B क्रिकेट/I संघ/I
Rule 4 (C2C2)	आरोप/B भाजप/B तपशील/B कामगार/B आयुक्त/I
Rule 5 (ValidSplit)	कार्यभार/B प्रभारी/B अधिकारी/I मालक/B राहुल/B लिमये/I
Rule 6 (UnitarySplit)	प्रयत्न/B फायर/B ब्रिगेड/I घोषणा/B सरकार/B
Rule 7 (W2*)	शास्त्रशुद्ध/B प्रशिक्षण/I विनायक/B कम्प्युटर्स/I

Table 3: Examples of automatically labelled candidate phrases using distant supervision rules

4.5.2 Features used by the CRF classifier

In general, there are two types of features used in a CRF model : unigram and bigram. Unigram features are combination of some property of the sequence w.r.t. the *current* token and the *current* label. Bigram features are combination of some property of the sequence w.r.t. the *current* token, *current* label and *previous* label. For every i^{th} token (word or suffix) in a sequence, following classes of unigram features are generated.

1. Lexical Features: Word or suffix at the positions $i, (i-1)$ and $(i+1)$. If current word belongs to any candidate phrase, then the words preceding and succeeding that candidate phrase are also considered as features. If the current word does not belong to any candidate phrase, then values of these features are "NA".

2. POS Tag Features: POS tags of words at the positions $i, (i-1), (i-2), (i+1)$ and $(i+2)$. If current word belongs to any candidate phrase, then the POS tags of the words preceding and succeeding that candidate phrase are also considered as features. If the current word does not belong to any candidate phrase, then values of these features are "NA".

Similary, for every i^{th} token (word or suffix) in a sequence, following classes of bigram features are generated.

1. Edge Features: Combination of labels at positions i and $(i-1)$.

2. POS Tag Edge Features: Combination of POS tag at position i and labels at positions i and $(i-1)$.

5 Experiments and Evaluation

5.1 In-house POS Tagger

We developed an in-house POS tagger by training a CRF on the NLTK(Bird et al., 2009) Indian languages POS-tagged corpus for Marathi. Features like prefixes, suffixes, rootwords and dictionary categories of the tokens were used while training. The POS tagger was evaluated based on a 80-20 train-test split of the NLTK data and the accuracy of 91.08% was obtained.

5.2 Corpus

As described earlier, distant supervision allows creation of large amount of training data through heuristics. However, the first requirement is a large corpus of Marathi text on which such heuristics can be applied. We considered the Marathi FIRE Corpus (Palchowdhury et al., 2013) which has crawled archives of a Marathi Newspaper (Maharashtra Times [3]) for 4 years starting from 2004 to 2007. We used all the articles of year 2004 for the task. After a trivial preprocessing we were able to extract all the text sentences from the files for compiling the corpus. The corpus comprises of about 200,000 sentences.

5.3 Evaluation using Test Dataset

We created a test dataset of 100 sentences and manually identified all the "valid" noun phrases in them. Apart from the baseline approach using English-like phrase extraction rule, we also consider two other baselines: i) the LTRC IIIT-H provided Marathi Shallow Parser and ii) Applying Heuristic rules (defined in the section 4.3) directly on the sentences of test dataset. We evaluated all the baseline methods and our distantly supervised CRF by applying them on this test dataset. For each method, the gold-standard set of noun phrases was used to evaluate the set of noun phrases extracted by that method by computing the following:

True Positives (TP) : Number of extracted phrases which are also present in the set of gold-standard phrases.

False Positives (FP) : Number of extracted phrases which are not present in the set of gold-standard phrases.

False Negatives (FN) : Number of gold-standard phrases which are not extracted.

[3]http://maharashtratimes.indiatimes.com/

Method	P (%)	R (%)	F1 (%)
IIITH Shallow Parser	83.38	88.68	85.95
Baseline 1 (English-like rule)	88.89	85.07	86.94
Baseline 2 (Heuristic Rules)	87.43	89.72	88.56
Distantly supervised CRF	88.31	89.14	**88.72**

Table 4: Comparative performance of various methods on a test dataset of 100 labelled sentences

The overall performance of any method is then measured in terms of *Precision* (P), *Recall* (R) and *F-measure* (F) as follows:

$$P = \frac{TP}{(TP+FP)}, R = \frac{TP}{(TP+FN)}, F = \frac{2PR}{(P+R)}$$

Table 4 shows the comparative performance of all the methods and it can be observed that our method outperforms all the baselines. Also, the performance improvement of distantly supervised CRF over the heuristic rules is not very significant. We plan to carry out more detailed analysis of this phenomenon in future, by experimenting with additional features in the CRF model.

5.4 Analysis

After analyzing the error cases, we found that one of the major reasons for the errors was the lack of sufficient corpus statistics for some of the words (especially proper nouns). Consider the following sentence from our test dataset : गेल्या आठवड्यात चंदाबाबू लायन्स क्लबच्या एका मेळाव्यास संबोधित करण्यासाठी अहमदाबादेसही जाऊन आले (Chandababu had been to Ahmedabad last week for addressing a gathering of the Lions Club.) Here, all the methods (IIIT-H Shallow parser, baseline methods as well as our method using CRF) incorrectly identify the phrase चंदाबाबू लायन्स क्लब as a single "meaningful" noun phrase. Ideally, चंदाबाबू and लायन्स क्लब are two separate phrases. Here, both the words चंदाबाबू and लायन्स are proper nouns and they occur rarely in the corpus, resulting in unreliable corpus statistics for these words.

However, most of the common nouns have significant presence in the corpus producing reliable corpus statistics for these words. As our method is heavily dependent on the corpus statistics, such cases involving frequent words are handled correctly. Consider following sentence from our test dataset: देशभरातून लाखो भाविक दर्शनासाठी तिथे जात असतात (From across the country, lacs of devotees keep going there for the auspicious sight). Here, the noun phrases extracted by the IIIT-H Shallow Parser are देशभरातून and लाखो भाविक दर्शनासाठी whereas our method correctly identifies 3 noun phrases : देशभर, लाखो भाविक and दर्शन. Here, both the words लाखो भाविक and दर्शन have reliable corpus statistics and hence our method correctly splits the candidate phrase लाखो भाविक दर्शन producing "meaningful" noun phrases.

6 Conclusion and Future Work

We highlighted an important problem of extraction of "meaningful" noun phrases from Marathi sentences. We propose a distant supervision based sequence labelling approach for addressing this problem. A novel set of rules based on corpus statistics are devised for automatically creating a large labelled data. This data is used for training a CRF model. Most other approaches to chunking for Indian languages are supervised and need large corpus of labelled training data. The main advantage of our work is that it does not need manually created labelled training data, and hence can be used for resource-scarce Indian languages. Our approach not only reduces the efforts for creation of labelled data but also demonstrate better accuracy than the existing approaches.

As our rules for distant supervision are based on corpus statistics and not on deep linguistic knowledge, they can be easily ported to other Indian languages. In future, we would like to take our work further on these lines. We also plan to extend our framework to a full-scale chunking tool for Marathi, not just noun phrases. Additionally based on this work, we plan to build a generic Information Extraction engine for Marathi and later for other Indian languages.

References

Steven P Abney. 1992. *Parsing by chunks*. Springer.

Himanshu Agrawal. 2007. POS tagging and chunking for Indian languages. In *IJCAI Workshop On Shallow Parsing for South Asian Languages (SPSAL)*.

Pranjal Awasthi, Delip Rao, and Balaraman Ravindran. 2006. Part of speech tagging and chunking with HMM and CRF. In *NLPAI Machine Learning Contest*.

Sivaji Bandyopadhay, Asif Ekbal, and Debasish Halder. 2006. HMM based POS tagger and rule-based chunker for bengali. In *Sixth International Conference on Advances In Pattern Recognition*, pages 384–390. World Scientific.

Sankaran Baskaran. 2006. Hindi POS tagging and chunking. In *NLPAI Machine Learning Contest*.

Akshar Bharati and Prashanth R Mannem. 2007. Introduction to shallow parsing contest on South Asian languages. In *IJCAI Workshop On Shallow Parsing for South Asian Languages (SPSAL)*, pages 1–8. Citeseer.

Akshar Bharati and Rajeev Sangal. 1993. Parsing free word order languages in the paninian framework. In *ACL*, pages 105–111. ACL.

Steven Bird, Ewan Klein, and Edward Loper. 2009. *Natural language processing with Python.* ” O'Reilly Media, Inc.”.

Kurt Bollacker, Colin Evans, Praveen Paritosh, Tim Sturge, and Jamie Taylor. 2008. Freebase: a collaboratively created graph database for structuring human knowledge. In *ACM SIGMOD international conference on Management of data*, pages 1247–1250. ACM.

Aniket Dalal, Kumar Nagaraj, Uma Sawant, and Sandeep Shelke. 2006. Hindi part-of-speech tagging and chunking: A maximum entropy approach. In *NLPAI Machine Learning Contest*.

Sandipan Dandapat. 2007. Part of specch tagging and chunking with maximum entropy model. In *IJCAI Workshop On Shallow Parsing for South Asian Languages (SPSAL)*, pages 29–32.

Asif Ekbal, S Mondal, and Sivaji Bandyopadhyay. 2007. POS tagging using HMM and rule-based chunking. In *IJCAI Workshop On Shallow Parsing for South Asian Languages (SPSAL)*, pages 25–28.

Himanshu Gahlot, Awaghad Ashish Krishnarao, and DS Kushwaha. 2009. Shallow parsing for hindi-an extensive analysis of sequential learning algorithms using a large annotated corpus. In *Advance Computing Conference, 2009. IACC 2009. IEEE International*, pages 1158–1163. IEEE.

Harshada Gune, Mugdha Bapat, Mitesh M Khapra, and Pushpak Bhattacharyya. 2010. Verbs are where all the action lies: experiences of shallow parsing of a morphologically rich language. In *COLING : Posters*, pages 347–355. ACL.

Agarwal Himashu and Amni Anirudh. 2006. Part of Speech Tagging and Chunking with Conditional Random Fields. In *NLPAI Machine Learning Contest*.

LTRC IIIT-H. 2015. Language technology research centre, IIIT-H. [Online; accessed 20-August-2015].

John Lafferty, Andrew McCallum, and Fernando CN Pereira. 2001. Conditional random fields: Probabilistic models for segmenting and labeling sequence data. In *Proceedings of the Eighteenth International Conference on Machine Learning*.

Ryan McDonald, Koby Crammer, and Fernando Pereira. 2005. Flexible text segmentation with structured multilabel classification. In *HLT-EMNLP*, pages 987–994. ACL.

Mike Mintz, Steven Bills, Rion Snow, and Dan Jurafsky. 2009. Distant supervision for relation extraction without labeled data. In *ACL-IJCNLP, Volume 2*, pages 1003–1011. ACL.

MSPIL. 2006. Modelling and shallow parsing of Indian languages. [Online; accessed 20-August-2015].

Latha R Nair and S David Peter. 2011. Shallow parser for malayalam language using finite state cascades. In *Biomedical Engineering and Informatics (BMEI)*, volume 3, pages 1264–1267. IEEE.

NLPAI and IIIT-H. 2006. NLPAI contest on POS tagging and shallow parsing of Indian languages. [Online; accessed 20-August-2015].

University of Hyderabad. 2015. Calts lab, school of humanities, university of hyderabad. [Online; accessed 20-August-2015].

Sauparna Palchowdhury, Prasenjit Majumder, Dipasree Pal, Ayan Bandyopadhyay, and Mandar Mitra. 2013. Overview of FIRE 2011. In *Multilingual Information Access in South Asian Languages*, pages 1–12. Springer.

RK Pattabhi, T Rao, R Vijay Sundar Ram, R Vijayakrishna, and L Sobha. 2007. A text chunker and hybrid POS tagger for Indian languages. In *IJCAI Workshop On Shallow Parsing for South Asian Languages (SPSAL)*.

Avinesh PVS and G Karthik. 2007. Part-of-speech tagging and chunking using conditional random fields and transformation based learning. *Shallow Parsing for South Asian Languages*, 21.

Delip Rao and David Yarowsky. 2007. Part of speech tagging and shallow parsing of Indian languages. *Shallow Parsing for South Asian Languages*, page 17.

GM Ravi Sastry, Sourish Chaudhuri, and P Nagender Reddy. 2007. An HMM based part-of-speech tagger and statistical chunker for 3 Indian languages. In *IJCAI Workshop On Shallow Parsing for South Asian Languages (SPSAL)*.

Hong Shen and Anoop Sarkar. 2005. *Voting between multiple data representations for text chunking*. Springer.

Akshay Singh, Sushma Bendre, and Rajeev Sangal. 2005. HMM based chunker for Hindi. In *IJCNLP*.

Xu Sun, Louis-Philippe Morency, Daisuke Okanohara, and Jun'ichi Tsujii. 2008. Modeling latent-dynamic in shallow parsing: a latent conditional model with improved inference. In *COLING-Volume 1*, pages 841–848. ACL.

Self-Organizing Maps for Classification of a Multi-Labeled Corpus

Lars Bungum and **Björn Gambäck**
Department of Computer and Information Science
Norwegian University of Science and Technology
Sem Sælands vei 7–9, 7094 Trondheim, Norway
`{larsbun,gamback}@idi.ntnu.no`

Abstract

A Self-Organizing Map was used to classify the Reuters Corpus, by assigning a label to each of the documents that cluster to a specific node in the Self-Organizing Map. The predicted label is based on the most frequent label among the training documents attributed to that particular node. Experiments were carried out on different grid sizes (node numbers) to determine their influence on classification results. Informative visualizations of the resulting Self-Organizing Maps are demonstrated. We argue that the Self-Organizing Map is well suited to classify a document collection in which many documents simultaneously belong to several categories.

1 Introduction

Categorization of a text corpus in which each article is attributed with a set of categories (labels), is a classical *supervised* classification task. Most supervised classification methods learn parameters from a training set of labeled instances, and use the learned model to score test instances. The Self-Organizing Map (SOM) is in contrast an *unsupervised* technique, clustering similar training instances together, without knowledge of their categories. The resulting maps display visually identifiable, but non-delimited, clusters. In this way, the SOM algorithm makes underlying similarities in high-dimensional space visible in lower dimensions. Through a two-step methodology, the labels of a training corpus associate with areas of the map; areas that in turn can be used to classify previously unseen documents.

The Reuters Corpus (Lewis et al., 2004) consists of text documents with a varying amount of labels attributed to them. Sebastiani (2002) notes a fundamental distinction between the *single-label*

and *multi-label* classification tasks. In the former, only one label is attributed to each document, whereas any number can be attributed to the documents in the latter. Most research has gone into the single-label problem, as this will generalize to multi-label classification, by transforming the problem to a sequence of binary classification problems. This however, rests on the assumption that the categories are stochastically independent, that is, that the label of a document does not depend on the whether the document also has another label.

Another key problem in document classification relates to vectorization, how a group of documents is converted into a vector-based feature representation. The way documents are represented, and often the cut-off point in deriving TFIDF or ngram statistics, will result in different amounts of features. Documents can in principle be vectorized to any dimensionality, in its simplest form counts of occurrences of a given set of words.

A number of experiments were conducted on two different portions of the Reuters Corpus, the Top 10 and Full set of categories, respectively. While this follows a tradition of SOM-based classification, we offer more details on the implementation, the vectorization, and the parameters for creating the map. Self-Organizing Maps of different sizes were used to evaluate the importance of the number of nodes in SOM classification. The cost of computing the maps increase with the size of their topologies, posing the research question: Can this be justified with classifier performance?

We demonstrate that the method elucidates similarities between labels as well as between documents, and argue that the reduction of the multi-label classification of the corpus into a cascade of binary classification problems under the assumption that the categories are stochastically independent is not plausible.

D S Sharma, R Sangal and E Sherly. Proc. of the 12th Intl. Conference on Natural Language Processing, pages 39–48,
Trivandrum, India. December 2015. ©2015 NLP Association of India (NLPAI)

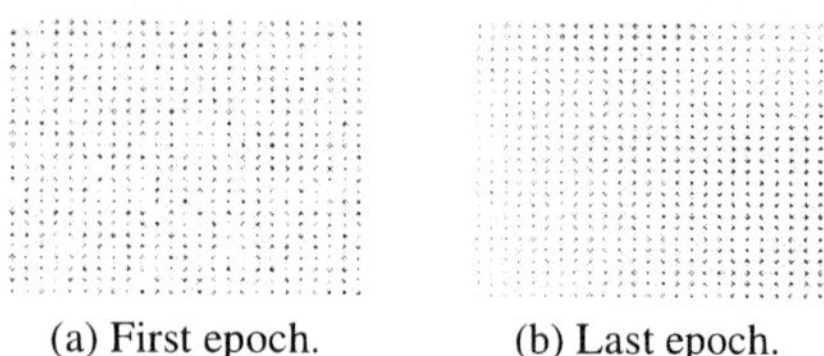

Figure 1: RGB color coding of a SOM.

---

1. Initialize nodes in the 2-dimensional topology.
2. (a) Sample all vectorized documents from the training material in succession.
   (b) Find the closest match in the node layout.
   (c) Update this matching node and its neighbors to be closer to the sample.
3. Reduce learning rate and/or neighborhood size.
4. Return to Step 2 until end of all epochs.

Figure 2: SOM algorithm.

Section 2 discusses related work and presents some background on the SOM algorithm and using them as a classification device, while Section 3 describes the Reuters Corpus and Section 4 goes through the applied methodology. Section 5 presents the experimental results, that are further discussed in Section 6. Section 7 concludes and looks forward.

2 Self-Organizing Maps

Self-Organizing Maps (Kohonen, 1982) is a Cluster Analysis Algorithm with roots in Artificial Neural Networks, also termed Kohonen Neural Networks, as discussed by Lo et al. (1991). A SOM functions on nodes organized according to a given topology (usually 2-dimensional). The nodes are made up by vectors of some higher dimensionality, directly comparable to vectors representing training samples. The properties of the nodes are gradually changed during a pre-defined number of epochs, making the nodes more similar to the training samples. Changing one data point (node) will also affect its neighboring nodes, in a fashion inspired by biological systems in which neurons with similar functions organize in the same areas.

This process is illustrated in Figure 1, where 25x25 nodes are represented as vectors with three dimensions, each with values between 0 and 1. The training samples consist of a set of fixed colors, encoded as RGB (red, green, and blue) values. After the end of training, the grid has "self-organized" into areas of similar colors. This is accomplished by comparing each training sample to each node, according to a *distance metric*, and drawing the closest node ("the winner") and its neighborhood towards the training sample. The samples are processed serially, and this is repeated for *n* epochs, as outlined in Figure 2.

Samples can be of any dimensionality; the higher the dimensionality, the more computationally costly will each comparison be. The resulting map will group (self-organize) similar high-dimensional vectors together, that can be visually inspected in the original topology, a low-dimensional space. Hence a feat of cartography in the landscape of documents is achieved, not only because documents are found in the same areas on the map, but also because the distances between nodes are visible with color shadings or contour plots. In this way differences in high-dimensional space become apparent in lower dimensions, creating a dimensionality reduction.

Hyötyniemi (1996) used a SOM to extract features for document representation, based on the clustering of character trigrams, arguing that this would account better for linguistic features.

Eyassu and Gambäck (2005) and Asker et al. (2009) used Self-Organizing Maps to classify Amharic news text. Categorized by experts, each document in the training corpus was associated with a query. A merged query and document matrix (i.e., the vector representation of the collection) was used for training the SOM. They report using many epochs (up to 20,000) and achieved classification accuracies in line with comparable methods such as Latent Semantic Indexing (Deerwester et al., 1990).

In order to use the SOM for a supervised classification task, consisting of a training and test corpus, it is necessary to establish a mechanism by which to ascribe a label to each of the test samples, i.e., what class membership (label) to *predict* for the sample in question. During classification, a test sample will be compared to the 2-dimensional grid to find its *winning node*, just like in training.

Going from a winning node to a prediction requires attribution of labels to individual nodes. One way to choose the label to be attributed by a node is to assign the test sample all categories found in the node. Saarikoski (2009) and Saarikoski et al. (2011) suggested another straightforward method by which the label prediction is taken as the most frequent label, i.e., is selected

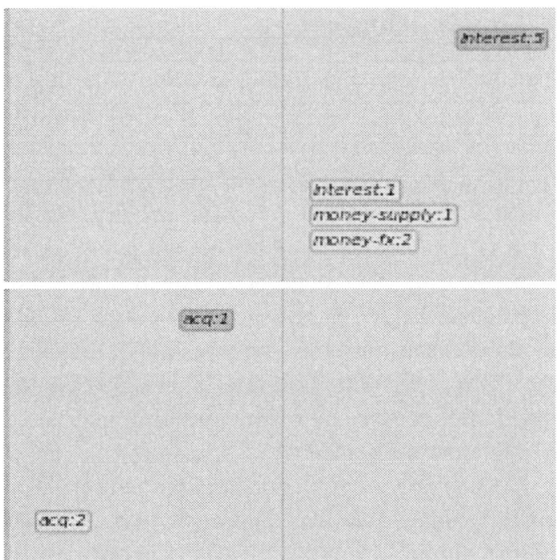

Figure 3: Example of SOM clustering with majority voting. Yellow labels from training corpus, magenta labels from test corpus.

by majority vote of the class labels of all training samples that had this node as winner. In the last run of the SOM, the Best-Matching Unit (BMU) of each training sample in the final epoch is recorded.

For empty nodes, being no sample's BMU, the next closest n nodes (the BMUs being the closest) are investigated for training samples until a non-empty node is found. The prediction is made according to the most frequent label of this node.

This process is illustrated with Figure 3, where each square represents a node (so a 2x2 SOM). Two of the four nodes have documents attaching to them. The yellow labels are from the training corpus, and the magenta from test samples. The SOM classifies test documents correctly, if their labels match that attributed to them by the node.

In the bottom-left node, both matching training samples (2 in yellow) had the label *acq* (acquisitions), which would be the prediction of this node. The one test sample (1 in magenta) that had this node as its BMU was also labeled *acq*, i.e., a correct prediction.

For the top-right node, the figure shows that the four training samples were split between *money-fx* (2), *money-supply* (1) and *interest* (1). By majority voting, the predicted label of the node becomes *money-fx*. However, the five test samples were all labeled *interest*, and all of them would thus be falsely classified (as *money-fx*).

3 Data

The Reuters Corpus (Lewis et al., 2004) has been used extensively for text classification research. For easier comparison of results, several ways of processing the corpus have been established. Those pertain to the corpus subsets, and a specific split of it into training and test sets called the ModApté split (Lewis, 1997).

A further much used split means dividing the ModApté into either the ten most frequent categories, the categories with at least one positive training and one test example (90), or the categories with at least one training example (115).

The split with the 90 categories with at least one positive training and test example is somewhat confusingly called AptéMod by Yang and Liu (1999), while Debole and Sebastiani (2004) refer to it as the *R(90)* subset of the ModApté split. Elsewhere, the R(90) split with 10,789 documents is also called ModApté (Yang et al., 2009; Chen et al., 2004; Saarikoski et al., 2011).

The Natural Language Toolkit (NLTK) interface (Loper and Bird, 2002) to the Reuters Corpus provides the AptéMod split as comprised by 7,769 training examples and 3,019 test instances. The category frequencies are $[9160, 1173, 255, 91, 52, 27, 9, 7, 5, 3, 2, 1, 0, 2, 1]$, i.e., 9,160 documents with just one category, 1,173 with two, etc. A plot of the log-frequency of categories is shown in Figure 4.

The NLTK interface provides a data structure where the raw text and categories are indexed on filenames. This was used in the present work, and the documents were transformed into a matrix of TF-IDF values, i.e., the product of the Term Frequency (the occurrence of the term in the document) and the Inverse Document Frequency (the log of the number of documents containing this term). A term can be any n-gram.

The corpus is comprised of text documents with 0 to 15 different category labels. The five most frequent labels of the 90 categories in the ModApté split have the following counts: $[3923, 2292, 374, 326, 309]$, totalling 7,224 of the 9,160 documents. The skewed distribution means that accuracy on the entire corpus is not always a good measure of classifier performance, as the performance on less frequent categories may drown in the larger categories. The distinction between micro- and macroaveraging mitigates this.

The *microaverage* averages over the categories

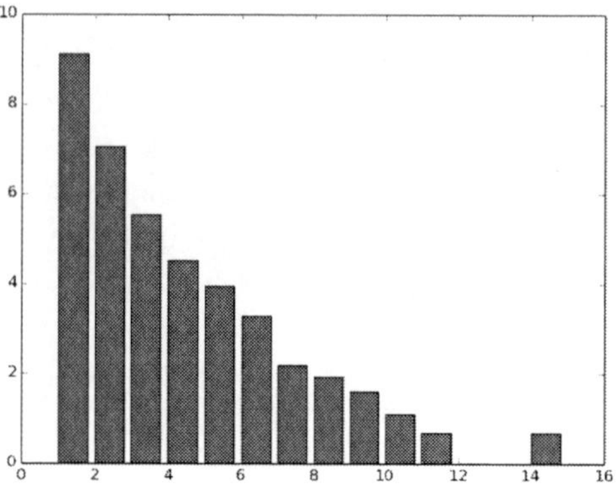

Figure 4: Log-frequencies of categories in the Reuters Corpus. Log of 0 set to 0.

to be classified within an experiment counting all correct predictions in one pool and dividing by the number of classified documents. This is expressed in Equation 1 where c denotes the number of correctly classified documents and n the total number of documents.

$$Microaverage = \frac{c}{n} \qquad (1)$$

This measure will be skewed towards larger classes: Consider a classifier that classifies one large category with 90 documents 100% correctly, whereas 10 other classes with one document each were all wrong. That would give a microaverage of 90%, even though most categories were completely wrong.

The *macroaverage* is a measure that is weighted with relative size, expressed formally in Equation 2 where c_j and n_j are the number of correctly classified documents belonging to class j and the total number of documents in that class, resp.

$$Macroaverage = \frac{\sum \frac{c_j}{n_j}}{|Classes|} \qquad (2)$$

In the same way as for accuracy, micro- and macroaverages can be calculated for precision, recall and F-score. However, when the classification problem is framed as a *one-of* classification, i. e., when all documents in the test set belong to exactly one class, the microaveraged F-score will be the same as the accuracy, because the number of false positives and false negatives will always be the same. If a document is classified with a label it does not have, it will be a false positive in that class, but also a false negative in the class it correctly belongs to (Manning et al., 2008).

4 Implementation

The Self-Organizing Map algorithm was implemented in MPI (mpi4py)[1] and Python, and run on a Portable Batch System (PBS)[2] scheduler. A quadratic layout of nodes was used for the experiments. Samples were processed serially, but for each sample, the vector comparisons and updating of nodes were done in parallel. The availability of large-scale High-Performance Computing (HPC), facilitated feasibility of the "on-line" version of the SOM algorithm. "On-line" as weights are updated after processing of each training sample, as formulated in Figure 2.

Methods for reducing computational cost include using a two-step approach (i. e., a SOM on the output of another SOM) (Kohonen et al., 1996), or formulating a "batch-SOM" algorithm. These methods contrast the "on-line" version by updating all node weights in one operation per epoch. See Lawrence et al. (1999) and Patel et al. (2015) for parallel batch-SOM implementations. Fort et al. (2002) compared the approaches and noted some problems with the batch formulation, e. g., initialization sensitivity, while it had advantages in terms of speed and efficiency.

In the on-line formulation, vector comparisons and updates are run per training sample, increasing linearly with the number of training samples. In turn, the vector comparisons increase with the number of nodes in the grid. Vector comparisons are costly, and therefore lend themselves well to parallelization. Hence, the parallel on-line implementation used in these experiments is sensitive to a large amount of training samples, but well equipped to handle large SOM topologies.

Each experiment in Section 5 was defined in a configuration file, where parameters such as the size of the grid, the number of iterations, the learning rate and the size of the initial neighborhood radius were specified, as well as details about the vectorization of training data. The neighborhood surrounding each BMU was defined by a diminishing-by-epoch radius, with a configurable initial size. The radius was reduced by exponential decay, as was the learning rate, i. e., the degree to which Best-Matching Units were updated to be similar to training samples.

The vectorization of documents was done with scikit-learn (Pedregosa et al., 2011), offering

---

[1] http://mpi4py.scipy.org/
[2] Both OpenPBS and PBS Professional were used.

38

a large selection of convenient vectorizers that swiftly transform test documents into the same vector form as the training corpus. In these experiments, the TFIDF transformer was used for vectorization. Similarly the library offers a number of metrics for vector comparison, such as Euclidean, Hamming or Chebichev distances. An Euclidean distance metric was used for all the following experiments. The implementation was fully modular with regard to the choice of these methods.

5 Experiments

Two rounds of experiments were carried out. The first experiments were conducted with the same vectorization parameters on five different grid sizes; 8x8, 16x16, 32x32, 64x64, and 128x128 (i.e., from 64 to 16,384 nodes) on the Top 10 categories of the Reuters Corpus, comparing execution times for grid configurations with increasing numbers of parallel processes. The second round of experiments was done on the entire `AptéMod` split (90 categories), investigating the effect on classification performance of varying grid sizes by the same amount. In both rounds of experiments, the SOM was configured with an initial learning rate of 0.10 and an initial neighborhood radius of a quarter of the grid dimension.

In order to focus experiments on the *one-of* classification problem, the training and test corpora were limited to documents with only one category when classifying the Top 10 categories. When using majority voting for prediction, the method would not benefit from the added information that some documents have more classes, as less frequent classes in each node could be voted down. Using documents restricted to one label could therefore bring about better separation in the Self-Organizing Map.

5.1 Top 10 Categories

In these experiments, the documents were limited to those belonging to the Top 10 categories. Documents were vectorized into 33,120 dimensions. Each vector consists of the TFIDF values for the ngrams ranging from 1 to 7, with a cut-off frequency of 5 (i.e., ignoring dictionary terms with a frequency below this threshold). The number of documents labeled with these categories are listed in Table 1.

The first experiments are summarized in Table 2. While we did not exhaustively experiment

Category name	Num. train	Num test
earn	2840	1083
acq	1596	696
money-fx	222	87
crude	253	121
trade	250	76
interest	191	81
ship	108	36
sugar	97	25
coffee	90	22
grain	41	10

Table 1: Number of training/test samples in Top 10 categories of the AptéMod restricted to documents with only one category.

Grid size	8x8	16x16	32x32	64x64	128x128
Microavg.	0.80	0.89	**0.89**	0.85	0.80
Macroavg.	0.52	0.79	**0.82**	0.78	0.75
Processes	8	64	256	1024	2048
Hours	0.5	1	2	4.5	11.5

Table 2: Classification scores for Reuters Corpus (Top 10 categories) across grid sizes.

with the optimal number of parallel processes for all experiments — i.e., finding the sweet spot beyond which new processes do not mean a speed-up due to overhead costs — we did one experiment on creating the same SOM (identical parameters) with a different amount of nodes processes in use on the High-Performance Computing (HPC) grid. The experiment compared creating a SOM with a 16x16 node grid, computed with 64 processes over 4 nodes (the same as in Table 2), to running it all on just one node, with parallel 16 processes. The former (64 parallel processes) took 1 hour to complete vs. 4 hours when running on only one node (16 processes).

5.2 All Categories

The second group of experiments was conducted on all (90) categories, summarized in Table 3.

Grid size	8x8	16x16	32x32	64x64	128x128
Microavg.	0.65	0.75	**0.78**	0.77	0.76
Macroavg.	0.07	0.13	0.25	0.25	**0.30**

Table 3: Classification scores for Reuters Corpus (all categories).

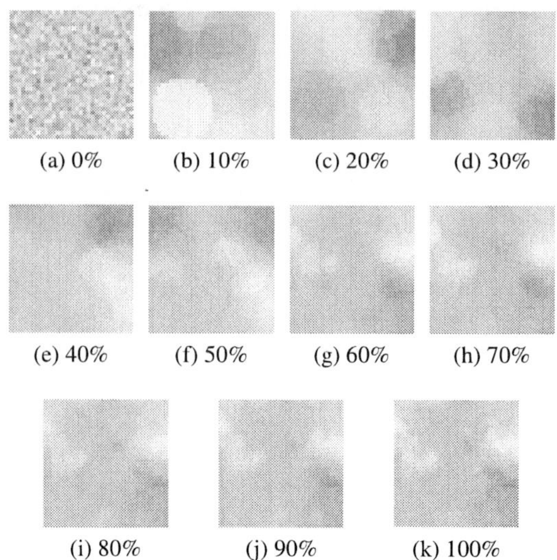

(a) 0% (b) 10% (c) 20% (d) 30%

(e) 40% (f) 50% (g) 60% (h) 70%

(i) 80% (j) 90% (k) 100%

Figure 5: Development of SOM Top 10 categories vectorized with 33,120 dimensions, 32x32 grid and 100 iterations.

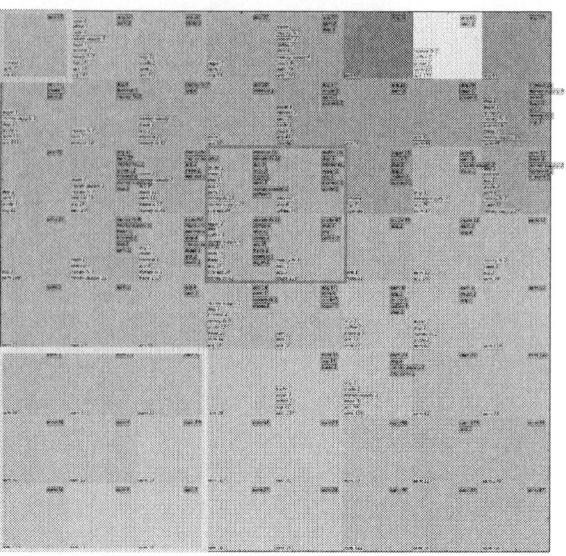

Figure 6: Annotated SOM with grid size 8x8 of the Top 10 categories, with highlighted excerpts. Training samples yellow, test samples magenta.

In these experiments, documents were vectorized into 19,092 dimensions. Each vector was comprised by TF-IDF values for ngrams ranging from 1 to 7, with a cut-off frequency of 10. While documents both in training and test sets could have multiple labels, each label was treated individually when predicting and scoring, as a series of single-label classification problems.

5.3 Visualization of SOM Development

Figure 5 shows the development of a Self-Organizing Map with a grid size of 32x32 from the experiments on the Top 10 categories. During the first iteration steps, the radius of the initial neighborhood is clearly visible before the grid self-organizes into a map. Each node is represented by a vector with the same dimensionality as the vectorized documents; these node vectors were reduced to four dimensions using Principal Component Analysis (PCA) (Jolliffe, 1986).

The four values were then used to encode a color in the Matplotlib library (Hunter, 2007), displaying each node as a color grading. The library accepts vectors of both three and four dimensions to create colors, so in order to retain more of the variance in the original node vectors, the vectors were reduced to four dimensions. Similarity in colors visualize similarity between vectors in the same area. Document labels verify that these areas represent texts belonging to the same categories.

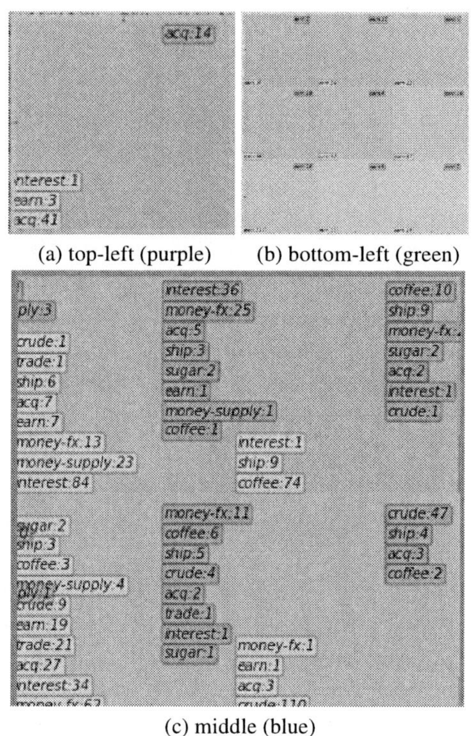

Figure 7: Excerpts from Figure 6 showing how document categories cluster.

5.4 Visualization of Resulting SOMs

Figure 6 shows a completed Self-Organizing Map annotated with the categories of the training (yel-

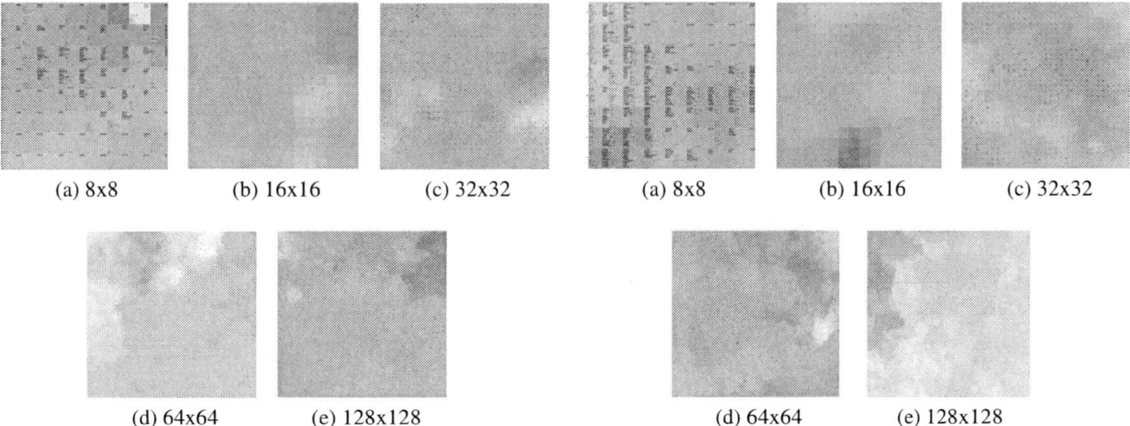

(a) 8x8   (b) 16x16   (c) 32x32

(d) 64x64   (e) 128x128

Figure 8: Various size SOMs, Top 10 categories.

(a) 8x8   (b) 16x16   (c) 32x32

(d) 64x64   (e) 128x128

Figure 9: Various size SOMs, all categories.

low) and the test (magenta) samples.

The 8x8 map is used for illustration here since it is easier to show the contents of grid cells in this format. As the number of nodes grows larger, it is difficult to fit the areas in one frame.

Three excerpts of the 8x8 SOM of Figure 6 are detailed in Figure 7. Starting with Figure 7a, the cell in the top left corner of the map has three training corpus labels attaching to it, *acq* (41 documents), *earn* (3) and *interest* (1); and 14 documents from the test corpus, all with the category *acq*. Majority voting among the training samples assigns the category *acq* to the node and hence ensures that all of the test samples are labeled correctly.

In Figure 7b, all documents — both from the training and test corpora — have the label *earn*, so classification is straight-forward (and correct).

Finally, the four nodes in Figure 7c have attracted documents with multiple labels. The figure shows four cells, each representing a node in the SOM. The yellow training labels are sorted in decreasing order from the left bottom up, and the magenta test labels in decreasing order from the left top corner of the cell.

The labels with the highest frequency both in the training and test corpora match all four cells in Figure 7c (*interest*, *coffee*, *money-fx* and *crude*). Thus, these labels from the training corpus are the predictions for each node, and the set of correctly predicted test samples, respectively.

In addition to the most frequent labels, the lists in Figure 7c share many other members, indicating that the clustered documents have more properties in common.

The final maps for the Top 10 category and all category runs are shown in Figures 8 and 9. In the larger maps there are fewer categories attaching to each node, both from training and test corpus. As can be seen from the results in Tables 2 and 3, macroaveraged F-scores increase as the grid sizes increase. With fewer categories per node, smaller categories have a better chance of being the majority category of a node, enabling the SOM to predict that node.

Figure 8d shows a SOM with grid size 64x64. On the left side of the picture, a light green area is visible. The green area is populated by documents labeled *crude*, going into an area labeled *earn* as the area turns gray in the vertical direction. Likewise, in the middle of the figure, areas populated by *interest* neighbor areas labeled *money-supply*. The map images are too large to include, and hence left out from the present paper.

Figure 10 complements the information of the color shadings. The heatmap shows the amount of documents attached to each node (having the node as their BMU). This number is not visible from the color gradings of the map Visualization, and offers insight into the relative size of these areas. The Unified Distance Matrix (UDM) shows the differences between the nodes on the map. The UDM is computed by taking the average distance between each node and its immediate neighbors in 2D space. High distances between nodes are shown as peaks in Figure 10b, and low areas represent clusters of similar vectors. Comparing Figures 8d and 10a, the flat area on the UDM reflects the large area in the bottom right corner in the same gray shading.

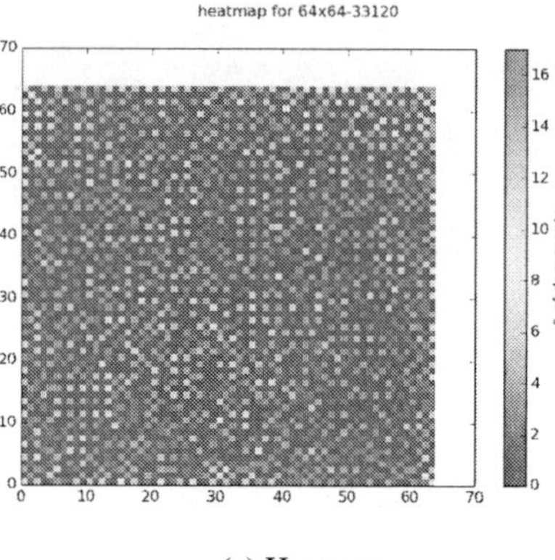

(a) Heatmap

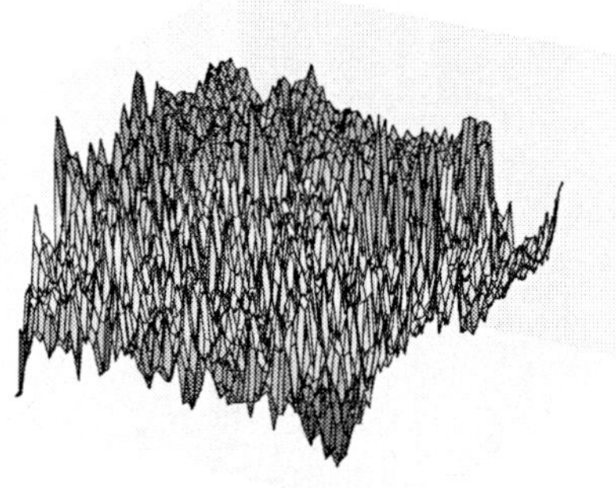

(b) Unified Distance Matrix

Figure 10: Heatmap and Unified Distance Matrix of SOM with grid size 64x64. Top 10 categories.

6 Discussion and Related Work

Using the unsupervised Self-Organizing Map approach we observe relations between categories, both through clusters of documents belonging to similar categories being placed next to each other on the map, and also in terms of some nodes in the SOM attracting separate documents with thematically adjacent labels as their Best-Matching Unit, such as *money-fx* and *interest*. This could be a reflection of these documents being in a thematical intersection between topics, or outright belonging to both.

Wermter and Hung (2002) integrated the SOM with WordNet-based (Miller, 1995) semantic networks for doing classification on the Reuters Corpus. Documents were represented by *significance vectors*, i. e., the degree to which the documents belong to certain preassigned topics, that were in turn calculated from the importance of words in each category.

Saarikoski (2009) performed several experiments on using Self-Organizing Maps for In-

formation Retrieval and document classification (Saarikoski et al., 2011), comparing the algorithm to other machine learning techniques. While they explained how the SOM was applied to the problem, some factors that affect classification performance were unaccounted for, such as the parameters for the SOM creation, notable grid size and learning rate. Restricting the classification to the Top 10 categories (by frequency) their best experiments had micro- and macroaverages of 93.2% and 83.5%, respectively.

Interestingly, Saarikoski et al. (2011) report that a Naïve Bayes classifier outscored all other methods on the data (95.2% and 90.4%), results that also significantly beat the findings of Dumais et al. (1998), who reported only 81.5% accuracy for the Naïve Bayes method. This discrepancy is likely due to a difference in scoring, as Dumais et al. (1998) reported break-even scores (motivated by comparability with other research), as opposed to Saarikoski et al. (2011) that gave true accuracy scores without any adjustment for precision-recall trade-off. The break-even point is where the precision is equal to recall, the point at which false positive and negative mis-classifications are done at the same rate.

Saarikoski et al. (2011) noticed how the costly training of SOMs is followed by cheap testing of new instances when doing classification, and suggested using multiple maps for multi-label classification, or alternatively using the three nearest labels for a new instance. This would, however, assume that all documents should have the same amount of labels in multi-label classification, which clearly is not the case in general. Still, it is possible to equip each node with a notion of label distribution, among its BMU training samples, possibly within a region (neighborhood) of the BMU.

While we did not see an increase in the *one-of* classification when the Self-Organizing Map topologies went above 32x32 nodes, it is likely that the multi-label problem benefits from a larger amount of nodes, offering finer granularity.

7 Conclusion and Future Work

In this paper we have used a parallel implementation of an "on-line" Self-Organizing Map algorithm on a well-researched classification task. Expanding the analysis offered in comparable research, we have explored how the grid size of the

SOM affects classification performance. We observe that classification performance increases up to the size of 32x32 nodes, and then deteriorates for the vectorizations used in the experiments. The paper offers extensive details on the parameters used to create the SOMs.

Using the Self-Organizing Map analysis, we observe underlying relations between documents, visible in 2D space, although represented with high-dimensional vectors. In the Self-Organizing Maps, similarities between *labels* as well as similarities between individual documents are visible. We therefore argue that the simplification of the *multi-label* classification task to a cascade of binary classification tasks is not plausible for the Reuters Corpus, because of the presence of relations between labels.

Further research into the multi-label problem and its relation to large-topology Self-Organizing Maps is prudent, given the findings of the present work. Devising a fair evaluation scheme for measuring the accuracy of SOM classifiers that attribute many labels to each document instance as a multi-label problem, is still an open question. Similarly, it is also an open question which method to use to decide how many labels to attribute to a new training instance. It is a natural next step to run more experiments on attributing several labels to documents in one operation and comparing that to running a series of binary classifications, as in the experiments presented in this paper.

Having implemented the Self-Organizing Map algorithm in a highly modular fashion, we would also like to experiment with both a) using different vectorizers and b) applying different distances metrics, in order to investigate their impact on classification results. Wermter and Hung (2002) reported good results on integrating other knowledge sources in vectorization, calling for a systematic comparison to purely data-driven vector transformers, and to hybrids between knowledge- and data-driven vectorizers.

Acknowledgments

The research leading to these results has been funded by Norwegian University of Science and Technology (NTNU), and by the Norwegian Research Council (NFR) and the Czech Ministry of Education, Youth and Sports (MŠMT) through the Norwegian Financial Mechanism 2009–2014 under Contract no. MSMT-28477/2014.

References

Lars Asker, Atelach Alemu Argaw, Björn Gambäck, Samuel Eyassu Asfeha, and Lemma Nigussie Habte. 2009. Classifying Amharic webnews. *Information Retrieval*, 12(3):416–435.

Junli Chen, Xuezhong Zhou, and Zhaohui Wu. 2004. A multi-label Chinese text categorization system based on boosting algorithm. In *Proceedings of the Fourth International Conference on Computer and Information Technology*, pages 1153–1158, Washington, DC, USA. IEEE Computer Society.

Franca Debole and Fabrizio Sebastiani. 2004. An analysis of the relative hardness of Reuters-21578 subsets. *Journal of the American Society for Information Science and Technology*, 56:971–974.

Scott Deerwester, Susan T. Dumais, George W. Furnas, Thomas K. Landauer, and Richard Harshman. 1990. Indexing by latent semantic analysis. *Journal of the American Society for Information Science*, 41(6):391–407.

Susan Dumais, John Platt, Mehran Sahami, and David Heckerman. 1998. Inductive learning algorithms and representations for text categorization. In *Proceedings of the 7th International Conference on Information and Knowledge Management*, pages 148–155. ACM Press.

Samuel Eyassu and Björn Gambäck. 2005. Classifying Amharic news text using Self-Organizing Maps. In *Proceedings of the 43rd Annual Meeting of the Association for Computational Linguistics*, Ann Arbor, Michigan, June. ACL. Workshop on Computational Approaches to Semitic Languages.

Jean-Claude Fort, Patrick Letrémy, and Marie Cottrell. 2002. Advantages and drawbacks of the Batch Kohonen algorithm. In Michel Verleysen, editor, *Proceedings of the 10th European Symposium on Artificial Neural Networks*, pages 223–230, Bruges, Belgium.

John D. Hunter. 2007. Matplotlib: A 2D graphics environment. *Computing in Science & Engineering*, 9(3):90–95.

Heikki Hyötyniemi. 1996. Text document classification with self-organizing maps. In J. Alander, T. Honkela, and M. Jakobsson, editors, *Proceedings of 7th Finnish Artificial Intelligence Conference*, pages 64–72, Vaasa, Finland.

Ian T. Jolliffe. 1986. *Principal Component Analysis*. Springer Verlag, New York, NY, USA.

Teuvo Kohonen, Samuel Kaski, Krista Lagus, and Timo Honkela. 1996. Very large two-level SOM for the browsing of newsgroups. In C. von der Malsburg, W. von Seelen, J. C. Vorbrüggen, and B. Sendhoff, editors, *Proceedings of ICANN96, International Conference on Artificial Neural Networks*, Lecture Notes in Computer Science, vol. 1112, pages 269–274. Springer, Berlin, July.

Teuvo Kohonen. 1982. Self-organized formation of topologically correct feature maps. *Biological Cybernetics*, 43(1):59–69.

Richard D. Lawrence, George S. Almasi, and Holly E. Rushmeier. 1999. A scalable parallel algorithm for self-organizing maps with applications to sparse data mining problems. *Data Mining and Knowledge Discovery*, 3(2):171–195.

David D. Lewis, Yiming Yang, Tony G. Rose, and Fan Li. 2004. RCV1: A new benchmark collection for text categorization research. *Journal of Machine Learning Research*, 5:361–397, December.

David D. Lewis. 1997. Reuters-21578 text categorization test collection.
`http://www.daviddlewis.com/`
`resources/testcollections/`
`reuters21578/`.

Zhen-Ping Lo, Masahiro Fujita, and Behnam Bavarian. 1991. Analysis of neighborhood interaction in Kohonen neural networks. In *Proceedings of the Fifth International Parallel Processing Symposium*, pages 246–249. IEEE.

Edward Loper and Steven Bird. 2002. NLTK: The natural language toolkit. In *Proceedings of the ACL-02 Workshop on Effective Tools and Methodologies for Teaching Natural Language Processing and Computational Linguistics - Volume 1*, ETMTNLP '02, pages 63–70, Stroudsburg, PA, USA. Association for Computational Linguistics.

Christopher D. Manning, Prabhakar Raghavan, and Hinrich Schütze. 2008. *Introduction to Information Retrieval*. Cambridge University Press, New York, NY, USA.

George A. Miller. 1995. WordNet: A lexical database for English. *Communications of the ACM*, 38(11):39–41, November.

Bhavik Patel, Anurag Jajoo, Yash Tibrewal, and Amit Joshi. 2015. An efficient parallel algorithm for self-organizing maps using MPI-OpenMP based cluster. *International Journal of Computer Applications*, IJCA Proceedings on International Conference on Advanced Computing and Communication Techniques for High Performance Applications(2):5–9, February.

Fabian Pedregosa, Gaël Varoquaux, Alexandre Gramfort, Vincent Michel, Bertrand Thirion, Olivier Grisel, Mathieu Blondel, Peter Prettenhofer, Ron Weiss, Vincent Dubourg, Jake Vanderplas, Alexandre Passos, David Cournapeau, Matthieu Brucher, Matthieu Perrot, and Édouard Duchesnay. 2011. Scikit-learn: Machine learning in Python. *Journal of Machine Learning Research*, 12(1):2825–2830.

Jyri Saarikoski, Jorma Laurikkala, Kalervo Järvelin, and Martti Juhola. 2011. Self-organising maps in document classification: A comparison with six machine learning methods. In Andrej Dobnikar, Uroš Lotric, and Branko Šter, editors, *Adaptive and Natural Computing Algorithms: 10th International Conference, ICANNGA 2011, Ljubljana, Slovenia, April 14-16, 2011, Proceedings, Part I*, volume 6593 of *Lecture Notes in Computer Science*, pages 260–269. Springer.

Jyri Saarikoski. 2009. A study on the use of self-organised maps in information retrieval. *Journal of Documentation*, 65(2):304–322.

Fabrizio Sebastiani. 2002. Machine learning in automated text categorization. *ACM Computing Surveys*, 34(1):1–47, March.

Stefan Wermter and Chihli Hung. 2002. Self-organizing classification on the Reuters news corpus. In *Proceedings of the 19th International Conference on Computational Linguistics - Volume 1*, COLING '02, pages 1–7, Stroudsburg, PA, USA. Association for Computational Linguistics.

Yiming Yang and Xin Liu. 1999. A re-examination of text categorization methods. In *Proceedings of the 22nd Annual International ACM SIGIR Conference on Research and Development in Information Retrieval*, SIGIR '99, pages 42–49, New York, NY, USA. ACM.

Shuang-Hong Yang, Hongyuan Zha, and Bao-Gang Hu. 2009. Dirichlet-Bernoulli alignment: A generative model for multi-class multi-label multi-instance corpora. In Y. Bengio, D. Schuurmans, J.D. Lafferty, C.K.I. Williams, and A. Culotta, editors, *Advances in Neural Information Processing Systems 22*, pages 2143–2150. Curran Associates, Inc.

Word Sense Disambiguation in Hindi Language Using Hyperspace Analogue to Language and Fuzzy C-Means Clustering

Devendra K. Tayal
Associate Professor
IGDTUW,
Delhi-110006

Leena Ahuja
Ex-Student
IGDTUW,
Delhi-110006

Shreya Chhabra
Ex-Student
IGDTUW,
Delhi-110006

Abstract

The problem of Word Sense Disambiguation (WSD) can be defined as the task of assigning the most appropriate sense to the polysemous word within a given context. Many supervised, unsupervised and semi-supervised approaches have been devised to deal with this problem, particularly, for the English language. However, this is not the case for Hindi language, where not much work has been done. In this paper, a new approach has been developed to perform disambiguation in Hindi language. For training the system, the text in Hindi language is converted into Hyperspace Analogue to Language (HAL) vectors, thereby, mapping each word into a high-dimensional space. We also deal with the fuzziness involved in disambiguation of words. We apply Fuzzy C-Means Clustering algorithm to form clusters denoting the various contexts in which the polysemous word may occur. The test data is then mapped into the high dimensional space created during the training phase. We test our approach on the corpus created using Hindi news articles and Wikipedia. We compare our approach with other significant approaches available in the literature and the experimental results indicate that our approach outperforms all the previous works done for Hindi Language.

1. Introduction:

Words in a language may carry more than one sense. Human beings can easily decipher the context in which the word is being used in a sentence. However, the same cannot be said for the machines. Various applications like speech processing, text processing, search engines, etc, in order to function properly, need to figure out the sense of the word. Thus there is a need for word sense disambiguation for correctly interpreting the meaning of a sentence written in natural language.

Given a word and its possible senses, as defined in a knowledge base, the problem of Word Sense Disambiguation (WSD) can be defined as the process of identifying which sense of a word (i.e. meaning) is used in a sentence, when the word has multiple meanings. It was first formulated as a distinct computational task during the early days of machine translation in the 1940s, making it one of the oldest problems in computational linguistics.

Warren Weaver (1949), in his famous 1949 memorandum on translation, first introduced the problem in a computational context. Early researchers understood the significance and difficulty of WSD well. Since then there have been various approaches for handling the problem of Word Sense Disambiguation. Majorly, WSD can be done using Knowledge Based Approaches (Navigli, 2009), Machine Based Approaches (Navigli, 2009) and Hybrid Approach (Navigli, 2009). Knowledge-based methods rely primarily on dictionaries, thesauri, and lexical knowledge bases, without using any corpus evidence. Lesk Algorithm (1986) is a classical approach based on Knowledge bases.

D S Sharma, R Sangal and E Sherly. Proc. of the 12th Intl. Conference on Natural Language Processing, pages 49–58,
Trivandrum, India. December 2015. ©2015 NLP Association of India (NLPAI)

Semi-supervised or minimally supervised methods make use of a secondary source of knowledge such as a small annotated corpus as seed data in a bootstrapping process, or a word-aligned bilingual corpus. Yarowsky Algorithm (1995) is based on this approach. Supervised methods make use of sense-annotated corpora to train from while unsupervised methods (Schütze, 1998) are based on the assumption that similar senses occur in similar contexts, and thus senses can be induced from text by clustering word occurrences using some measure of similarity of context.

Although much work is available for WSD in English language, but for Hindi language very few research works have been contributed.

Sinha, Reddy and Bhattacharya (2012) did a statistical approach towards Word Sense Disambiguation in Hindi. In their work, a set of context words are selected using the surrounding window and for each sense w of a word, a semantic bag is created by referring to the Hindi WordNet® (hypernymy, hyponymy and meronymy). They claim that sense of the word that has the maximum overlap between the context bag and the semantic bag is the correct sense. But, their system does not detect the underlying similarity in presence of morphological variations. Kumari and Singh (2013) used genetic algorithm to perform word sense disambiguation on Hindi nouns. Genetic algorithm is a heuristic search algorithm used to find approximate solutions to optimization and search problems using techniques inspired by evolutionary biology. But in their work, the recall values associated with the algorithm depend upon the genetic parameters chosen for evaluation and therefore is not universally applicable. Yadav and Vishwakarma (2013) use association rules to first mine the itemsets depending upon the context of the ambiguous word and then mine the association rule corresponding to the most frequent itemset.

Tomar *et al.* (2013) use the technique of PLSA for making 'k' clusters representing the senses or the different contexts of the word. The clusters are then further enriched using the Hindi WordNet®. The cluster with which the maximum similarity score (cosine distance) is obtained gives the correct sense of the ambiguous word. The performance of their work varies linearly with the amount of training data used. In (2013), Jain, Yadav and Tayal used graph based approach for Word Sense Disambiguation in Hindi Text. Here, to construct a graph for the sentence each sense of the ambiguous word is taken as a source node and all the paths which connect the sense to other words present in the sentence are added. The importance of nodes in the constructed graph is identified using node neighbor based measures and graph clustering based measures. This method disambiguates all open class words and disambiguates all the words present in the sentence simultaneously.

In (2005) , Hao Chen, Tingting He, Donghong Ji and Changqin Quan used an unsupervised approach, for disambiguating words in Chinese Language, where contexts that include ambiguous words are converted into vectors by means of a second-order context method, and these context vectors are then clustered by the k-means clustering algorithm and lastly, the ambiguous words can be disambiguated after a similarity calculation process is completed. But, the K-means clustering limits the word to belong to only one cluster and hence also limits the accuracy of Word Sense Disambiguation. After going through the literature survey, we found that all the methodologies for WSD used till date do not take into account the fuzziness involved in disambiguation of the words.

In this paper, we develop an approach whereby we first train our system taking Hindi newspaper and Wikipedia articles as input and use Hyperspace Analogue to Language model to convert Hindi words into vectors, representing points in the high dimensional Hyperspace.

Fuzzy C-Means Clustering is then applied to get the clusters where each word may belong to more than one cluster with an associated membership value. The words belonging to one context are grouped together in a cluster. The polysemous words belong to more than one cluster, each cluster corresponding to the possible sense of that word. Once the training of the system is complete, the test data containing the polysemous word is processed using Hyperspace Analogue to Language (HAL) model to map the polysemous word of the test data as a point in the hyperspace created in the training phase. Then, Euclidean Distance is calculated between this point and all the cluster centers and the nearest cluster corresponds to the sense of the polysemous word used in the test data. And similar computation can be easily performed for each polysemous word of the test data in order to determine the correct sense of that word.

We tested our approach using Netbeans IDE to develop a Hyperspace Analogue to Language (HAL) Model and MATLAB for construction of fuzzy clusters and finding the nearest cluster. The results obtained were compared with all of the previous approaches and our approach shows the best results.

The remainder of the paper is organized as follows: Section 2 provides a review of Hyperspace Analogue to Language, Fuzzy Logic and Fuzzy C-Means Clustering Algorithm. Section 3 describes the specifics of the proposed algorithm to carry out word sense disambiguation. Section 4 illustrates the application of the proposed approach on a small data set. Section 5 describes the experimental results obtained for our approach and the compares it with already existing techniques for Word Sense Disambiguation for Hindi language. Finally, the last section concludes the paper, and makes some suggestions for future work.

2 Preliminaries:
2.1 Hyperspace Analogue to Language (HAL):

Hyperspace Analogue to Language is a numeric method developed by Kevin Lund and Curt Burgess (1996) for analyzing text. It does so by running a sliding window of fixed length across a text, calculating a matrix of word co-occurrence values along the way. The basic premise that the work relies on is that words with similar meanings repeatedly occur closely (also known as co-occurrence).

Given a N word vocabulary, the HAL space is a N × N matrix constructed by moving a window of length l over the corpus by one word increments. Given two words W1 and W2, whose distance within the window is d, the weight of association between them is computed by $l - d + 1$. After traversing the corpus, an accumulated co-occurrence matrix for all the words in a target vocabulary is produced. HAL is direction sensitive: the co-occurrence information for words preceding each word and co-occurrence information for words following each word are recorded separately by row and column vectors.

2.1.1 Illustration:
Consider the following piece of Hindi Text:
"भारत की राजधानी दिल्ली है। दिल्ली मे अनेक वर्ग के लोग है।"

HAL Matrix constructed is as follows:

	भारत	राजधानी	दिल्ली	वर्ग	लोग
भारत	-	-	-	-	-
राजधानी	4	-	-	-	-
दिल्ली	4	8	-	-	-
वर्ग	-	-	4	-	-
लोग	-	-	1	4	-

Taking a window of size 6, we consider all the words that are lying before and after the focus word but within the context window. For example, consider the word ""लोग". The distance between "वर्ग" and "लोग" in the sentence given above is 3. So the value of the cell(लोग, वर्ग) = 6-3+1=4.

2.2 Fuzzy Logic:

Fuzzy logic (2005) is a form of many-valued logic; it deals with reasoning that is approximate rather than fixed and exact. Compared to traditional binary sets (where variables may take on true or false values), fuzzy logic variables may have a truth value that ranges in degree between 0 and 1. Fuzzy logic has been extended to handle the concept of partial truth, where the truth value may range between completely true and completely false (1999). The term fuzzy logic was introduced with the 1965 proposal of fuzzy set theory by Lotfi A. Zadeh (1965). Fuzzy logic has been applied to many fields, from control theory to artificial intelligence.

2.3 Fuzzy C-Means Clustering:

Data clustering is the process of dividing data elements into classes or clusters so that items in the same class are as similar as possible, and items in different classes are as dissimilar as possible. Depending on the nature of the data and the purpose for which clustering is being used, different measures of similarity may be used to place items into classes, where the similarity measure controls how the clusters are formed. Some examples of measures that can be used as in clustering include distance, connectivity, and intensity.

In hard clustering, data is divided into distinct clusters, where each data element belongs to exactly one cluster. In fuzzy clustering (also referred to as soft clustering), data elements can belong to more than one cluster, and associated with each element is a set of membership levels. These indicate the strength of the association between that data element and a particular cluster. Fuzzy clustering is a process of assigning these membership levels, and then using them to assign data elements to one or more clusters. Thus, points on the edge of a cluster, may be *in the cluster* to a lesser degree than points in the center of cluster. In (Ross, 2004), Fuzzy C-Means (FCM) is described as a method of clustering which allows one piece of data to belong to two or more clusters. It is based on minimization of the following objective function:

$$J_m = \sum_{i=1}^{N} \sum_{j=1}^{C} u_{ij}^m \ || \ x_i - c_j||^2 \qquad \ldots\ldots\ldots 1$$

where m is any real number greater than 1, u_{ij} is the degree of membership of x_i in the cluster j, x_i is the ith of d-dimensional measured data, c_j is the d-dimension center of the cluster, and $||*||$ is any norm expressing the similarity between any measured data and the center. Fuzzy partitioning is carried out through an iterative optimization of the objective function shown above, with the update of membership u_{ij} and the cluster centers c_j by:

$$u_{ij} = \frac{1}{\sum_{k=1}^{C} \left(\frac{||x_i - c_j||}{||x_i - c_k||} \right)^{\frac{2}{m-1}}} \qquad \ldots\ldots\ldots 2$$

$$c_j = \frac{\sum_{i=1}^{N} u_{ij}^m . x_i}{\sum_{i=1}^{N} u_{ij}^m} \qquad \ldots\ldots\ldots 3$$

3. Proposed Approach:

The disambiguation process can be divided into two phases- Training Phase and Testing Phase.

3.1 Training Phase

The Training Phase involves the use of Hyperspace Analogue to Language model and Fuzzy C-Means Clustering Algorithm to cluster the words in the Q-dimensional space where Q is the number of significant words in the training document. Each cluster denotes the context in which the ambiguous word may occur. Here, a word can belong to more than one cluster, and associated with each word is a set of membership levels. More the membership value, more the word belongs to that cluster. The flow chart of the Training Phase is shown below:

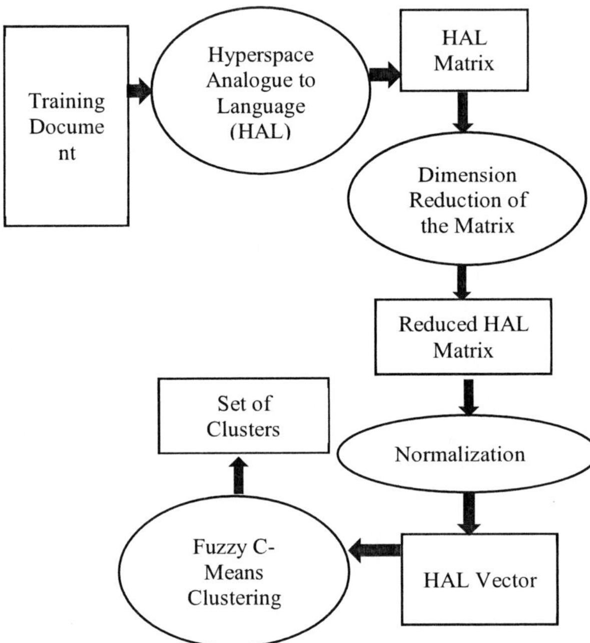

Figure 1: Training Phase

3.1.1 Training Document:

A set of documents were selected for the purpose of collecting words and then building the clusters of those words based on their co-occurrences.

Documents used for training included articles from Hindi newspapers, magazines and Wikipedia.

3.1.2 Hyperspace Analogue to Language:

In this phase, the training documents are processed as per the Hyperspace Analogue to Language Model. The algorithm for HAL (Lund and Burgess, 1998) calculates HAL matrix containing entries corresponding to all the unique words occurred during the training of the system. The matrix so generated is a N × N matrix where N is the total number of unique words in the training document set.

3.1.3 Dimension Reduction of the Matrix:

As mentioned previously, the training document is a collection of the words, taken from a source such as news articles, Wikipedia and magazines. Some words are significant during the process of disambiguation while the other words that are not significant with respect to disambiguation

process are called as the stop words like की है, की,और,यहाँ,पर,को,था,यह,थे,का,जिसकी,हुई,थी etc. Since the words are not significant with respect to our disambiguation process, we can remove the rows and columns corresponding to these words from Hyperspace Analogue to Language (HAL) Matrix that helps in reducing the dimensionality of the Hyperspace Analogue to Language (HAL) space and further mathematical processing of the stop words. This reduction process reduces the N × N dimensional HAL matrix into Q × Q dimensional HAL matrix where Q is the number of significant words in the training document which are used for the disambiguation process.

3.1.4 Normalization:

The reduced HAL matrix is then normalized to get the HAL vector corresponding to each significant word.

In order to represent a Word as a Point in Q dimensional space, we consider each word as a concept:

Concept $C = < W_{cp_1}, W_{cp_2}, W_{cp_3}, \ldots\ldots W_{cp_Q}>$

where p_1, $p_2 \ldots p_n$ are called dimensions of C, each corresponding to a unique word that forms a dimension of the hyperspace and W_{cp_i}, denotes the weight of p_i in the vector representation of C. In order to calculate weights, we normalize the values in the HAL matrix.

Normalization Formula:

$$W_{c_i p_j} = \frac{W_{c_i p_j} + W_{c_j p_i}}{\sqrt{\sum_{k=1}^{Q} W_{c_i p_k}{}^2 + W_{c_k p_i}{}^2}} \qquad \ldots\ldots\ldots 4$$

Since we need to consider the correlation between two given words irrespective of the order in which those words appeared, we consider both $W_{c_i p_j}$ and $W_{c_j p_i}$.

Therefore, by constructing a HAL space from training document, concepts are represented as weighted vectors in the high dimensional space, whereby each word in the vocabulary of the corpus gives rise to an axis in the corresponding semantic space.

3.1.5 Fuzzy C-Means Clustering

The HAL vectors for Q words generated in the previous step represent Q points in the Q-dimensional space. These vectors are then fed in as the input to the module implementing Fuzzy C-Means Clustering algorithm. The output of the Fuzzy Clustering module is a set of fuzzy clusters each representing a context of the ambiguous word. As is the nature of fuzzy clusters, a word may belong to one or more clusters with different membership values.

3.2 Testing Phase

This phase describes the disambiguation of the senses of the target ambiguous word in the test data. The flow diagram shown below describes the process:

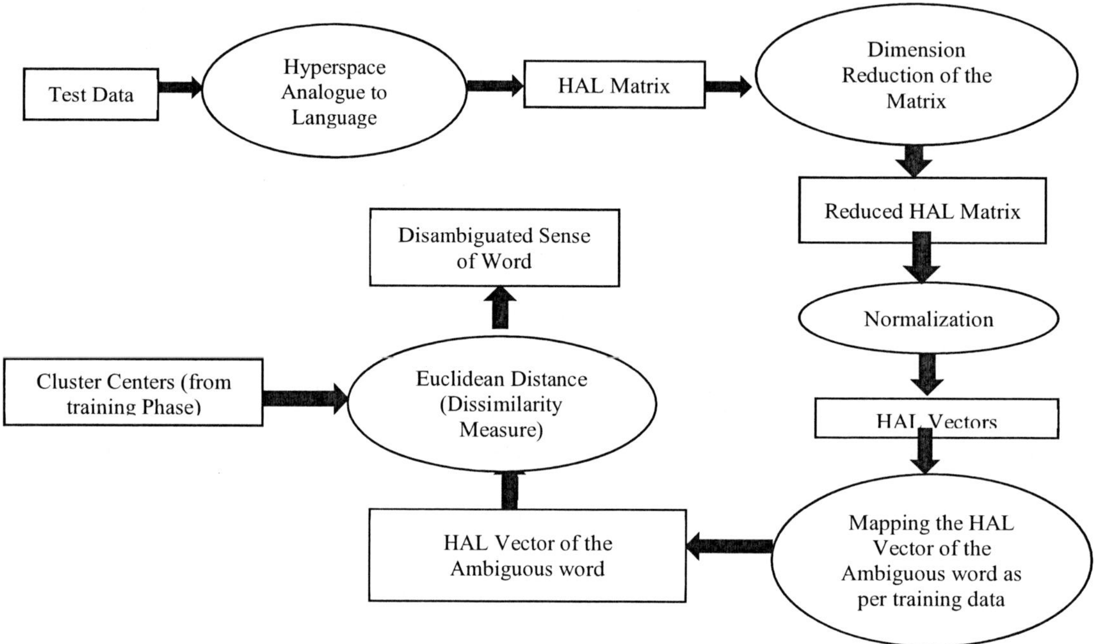

Figure 2 Testing Phase

Given the test data, we apply HAL Model to get the M × M HAL Matrix where M is the number of unique words in the test data. The rows and columns in the HAL matrix correspond to the word in the test data. Dimension reduction and Normalization process is applied in the manner similar to the training phase to get the HAL vectors of the words in the test data.

In order to apply dissimilarity measure for disambiguation process in the Q-dimensional Hyperspace, we need to map the M-dimensional HAL vector of the target ambiguous word to the Q-dimensional vector in the Hyperspace generated in the training phase.

The mapping process involves initializing the Q-dimensional HAL vector of the ambiguous word to all zeros and then finding the common words in the training document and the test data. The weights corresponding to the common words are extracted from the M-dimensional HAL vector of the test data and then these weights are substituted in the Q-dimensional HAL vector of the test data with respect to the indexes of the words generated in the training phase. Hence, we get the Q-dimensional HAL vector of the target ambiguous word with respect to the test data containing weights for common words and zeros for the other dimensions.

In order to disambiguate the correct sense of the target ambiguous word, Euclidean distance between target word's HAL vector and centers of the clusters generated in the previous phase are calculated one by one as follows:

$$d(p,q) = d(q,p)$$
$$= \sqrt{(q_1 - p_1)^2 + (q_2 - p_2)^2 + \cdots + (q_Q - p_Q)^2}$$
$$= \sqrt{\sum_{i=1}^{n} (q_i - p_i)^2}$$

……………5

The one with the minimum distance is then chosen to be the most related cluster and hence that corresponds to the most related sense.

4. Illustrative Example

The following example illustrates the proposed technique for disambiguation for the polysemous word '**तीर**'.

The word **तीर**' can have different senses as follows:

- धातु आदि का बना वह पतला लम्बा हथियार जो धनुष द्वारा चलाया जाता है (Arrow)

- नदी या जलाशय का किनारा (Bank of River)

The training data for the above mentioned ambiguous word can be found in the Appendix. Training Data consists of total 91 words. After removing the stop words we get 63 base words:
धनुष, प्रयुक्त, वाला, अस्त्र, तीर, अग्र, भाग, नुकीला, सर्वप्रथम, उल्लेख , ऋग्वेद, संहिता, मिलता, इषुकृत्, इषुकार, सिद्ध, दिनों, निर्माण-कार्य, व्यवस्थित, व्यवसाय, ऋग्वेदकालीन, लोहार, केवल, लोहे, काम , तैयार, बनाता, शेष,
बाण, निर्मातानिकाय, भीषण, बाढ़, भूस्खलन, तबाही, सबक, उत्तरा खंड, सरकार, राज्य, नदियों, नई, इमारतें,

बनाने, पूरी, रोक, लगा, दी, आपदा, प्रभावित, लोगों, वित्तीय, मदद, देने , उबरने, अल्पकालिक, दीर्घकालिक, कदम, उठाने, वास्ते, पुनर्निर्माण, पुनर्वास, प्राधिकरण, फैसला .

Using these base words, we form a HAL matrix of dimensions 63×63 using the window of size 10. Normalization is carried out over the HAL Matrix to get the HAL vectors corresponding to each unique word. This was developed in the code written in Java language using the NetBeans Platform. Fuzzy C-Means Clustering is then applied to the generated HAL Vectors. Two clusters have been generated using code written in the Matlab. The following snippet shows the minimization of the objective function (using Equation 1) in the process of generating the clusters.

```
Iteration count = 1, obj. fcn = 68.610140
Iteration count = 2, obj. fcn = 55.431179
Iteration count = 3, obj. fcn = 55.283578
Iteration count = 4, obj. fcn = 55.253781
Iteration count = 5, obj. fcn = 55.245683
Iteration count = 6, obj. fcn = 55.243071
Iteration count = 7, obj. fcn = 55.242142
Iteration count = 8, obj. fcn = 55.241794
Iteration count = 9, obj. fcn = 55.241660
Iteration count = 10, obj. fcn = 55.241608
Iteration count = 11, obj. fcn = 55.241587
Iteration count = 12, obj. fcn = 55.241579
```

Figure 3: Minimization of the objective function in fuzzy clustering

Once we get the clusters, we consider the test data.

Refer to Appendix for test data used in this case.

The HAL vector (63 dimensional) is then obtained for the ambiguous word तीर. Euclidean distance between the Test Vector and the two cluster centers are calculated. The following snapshot shows the two values.

```
calc_dist =

    0.9333
    0.9337
```

Cluster 2 is hence obtained as the target sense of the ambiguous word which means that the word 'तीर' here is correctly disambiguated as 'Arrow'.

5. Results and Discussions

Since there is no standard corpus available for Hindi language, we created our own corpus by selecting relevant articles from Hindi Wikipedia as well as Hindi language newspapers viz Dainik Jagran, Nav Bharat Times etc.

The training data used consists of 3753 words in total. A collection of polysemous words was made and training data was collected depicting the different contexts in which the word was used. The formula for accuracy is given as follows:

$$Accuracy = \frac{Number\ of\ correctly\ disambiguated\ words}{Total\ number\ of\ ambiguous\ occurrences}$$

When the proposed technique for disambiguation of Hindi Text was applied on the corpus, we found an efficiency of nearly 79.16%. Our technique, therefore, performs better than all the previously used approaches used for performing word sense disambiguation in Hindi language. It can be noted that all the methodologies used till date do not take into account the fuzziness involved in disambiguation of the words. In this paper, we use the concept of Fuzzy C-Means Clustering to overcome this major drawback of the previous approaches.

The following table shows the comparative efficiency of our technique with the previous techniques available in the literature that have been used in Word Sense Disambiguation in the Hindi language with their comparative accuracies. Thus, we conclude that the results obtained from our approach are better than all the other approaches that currently exist in the Hindi language and this is what makes it more promising.

S.No.	Technique Used	Author	Year	Accuracy
1.	Probabilistic Latent Semantic Analysis for Unsupervised Word Sense Disambiguation	Gaurav S Tomar, Manmeet Singh, Shishir Rai, Atul Kumar, Ratna Sanyal, Sudip Sanyal[2]	2013	74.12%
2.	Lesk Algorithm	Manish Sinha ,Mahesh Kumar, Reddy .R ,Pushpak Bhattacharyya , Prabhakar Pandey ,Laxmi Kashyap [9]	2012	Varies from 40-70%
3.	Association Rules	Preeti Yadav, Sandeep Vishwakarma[13]	2013	72%
4.	A Graph Based Approach to Word Sense Disambiguation for Hindi Language	Sandeep Kumar Vishwakarma, Chanchal Kumar Vishwakarma[16]	2013	65.17%

6. Conclusion:

In this work, we have proposed a new approach for Hindi Word Sense Disambiguation which incorporates fuzzy measures. We found that unlike the previous unsupervised approaches which discard contexts into which an ambiguous word may fall, the current approach retains the fuzziness associated with the ambiguity, thereby, giving better results. Moreover, the technique proposed by us is not language specific; it can be extended to other languages as well. As is evident from the results obtained by the use of HAL that the context knowledge in context specific WSD is very important and that world knowledge from the surrounding words plays a very important role in revealing the actual sense of the word in the given context.

Thus, the above mentioned advantages make our approach particularly promising. This approach can be extended in the future to include semantic relations from sources like Wikipedia and Wordnet in the enrichment of clusters that will lead to better accuracy for disambiguating a polysemous word.

References:

1. Cao G, Song D and Bruza PD "Fuzzy C-means clustering on a high dimensional semantic space" In Proceedings of the 6th Asia Pacific Web Conference (APWeb'04),LNCS 3007, 2004, pp. 907-911.

2. Gaurav S Tomar, Manmeet Singh, Shishir Rai, Atul Kumar, Ratna Sanyal, Sudip Sanyal "Probabilistic Latent Semantic Analysis for Unsupervised Word Sense Disambiguation", IJCSI International Journal of Computer Science Issues, Vol. 10, Issue 5, No 2, September 2013

3. Hao Chen, Tingting He, Donghong Ji and Changqin Quan, "An Unsupervised Approach to Chinese Word Sense Disambigua-tion Based on Hownet",Computational Linguistics and Chinese Language Processing Vol. 10, No. 4, December 2005, pp. 473-482 473

4. Hindi Wordnet from Center for Indian Language Technology Solutions, IIT Bombay, Mumbai, India http://www.cfilt.iitb.ac.in/wordnet/webhwn/

5. Jain, A; Yadav, S. ; Tayal, D. , "Measuring context-meaning for open class words in Hindi language" Contemporary Computing (IC3), 2013 Sixth International Conference, 2013, 118 - 123

6. Kwang H. Lee , "First Course on Fuzzy Theory and Applications",Springer-Verlag Berlin Heidelberg 2005

7. Lesk, M. (1986). Automatic sense disambiguation using machine readable dictionaries: how to tell a pine cone from an ice cream cone. In SIGDOC '86: Proceedings of the 5th annual international conference on Systems documentation, pages 24-26, New York, NY, USA. ACM.

8. Lund and Burgess, "Producing high-dimensional semantic spaces from lexical co-occurrence" Behavior Research Methods, Instruments, & Computers 1996, 28 (2), 203-208

9. Manish Sinha, Mahesh Kumar Reddy, R Pushpak Bhattacharyya ,Prabhakar Pandey, Laxmi Kashyap " Hindi Word Sense Disambiguation" International Journal of Computer Technology and Electronics Engineering (IJCTEE) Volume 2, Issue 2,2012

10. Michael Sussna," Word Sense Disambiguation for Free-text Indexing Using a Massive Semantic Network" Proceedings of the second conference on Information and knowledge management, New York, 1993, 67-74

11. Navigli, R..Word sense disambiguation: A survey. ACM Comput. Surv. 41, 2, Article 10,February 2009

12. Novák, V., Perfilieva, I. and Močkoř, J. *Mathematical principles of fuzzy logic* "Dodrecht: Kluwer Academic, 1999

13. Preeti Yadav, Sandeep Vishwakarma "Mining Association Rules Based Approach to Word SenseDisambiguation for Hindi Language" International Journal of Emerging Technology and Advanced Engineering Volume 3, Issue 5, May 2013

14. Rada Mihalcea, Using Wikipedia for Automatic Word Sense Disambiguation, in Proceedings of the North American Chapter of

the Association for Computational Linguistics (NAACL 2007), Rochester, April 2007

15. Sabnam Kumari "Optimized Word Sense Disambiguation in Hindi using Genetic Algorithm" International Journal of Re-search in Computer andCommunication Technology, Vol 2, Issue 7, July-2013

16. Sandeep Kumar Vishwakarma, Chanchal Kumar Vishwakarma, "A Graph Based Approach to Word Sense Disambiguation for Hindi Language", International Journal of Scientific Research Engineering & Technology (IJSRET) Volume 1 Issue5, August 2012, 313-318.

17. Schütze, H. "Automatic word sense discrimination" Computational Linguistics, 1998, 97–123.

18. Shaul Markovitch, Ariel Raviv, "Concept-Based Approach to Word-Sense Disambiguation" In *Proceedings of the Twenty-Sixth AAAI Conference on Artificial Intelligence*, 807-813 Toronto, Canada, 2012.

19. Song D and Bruza PD "Discovering information flow using a high dimensional conceptual space" Proceedings of the 24th Annual International Conference on Research and Development in Information Retrieval (SIGIR'01), 2001,327-333.

20. Timothy J.Ross, Fuzzy Logic with Engineering Applications, 2004, John Wiley & Sons Ltd PP:369-386

21. Weaver, Warren "Translation" Locke, W.N.; Booth, A.D. Machine Translation of Languages: Fourteen Essays. Cambridge, MA: MIT Press , 1949

22. Yarowsky "Unsupervised word sense disambiguation rivaling supervised methods"

Proc. of the 33rd Annual Meeting of the Association for Computational Linguistics, 1995

23. Zadeh, L.A. "Fuzzy sets", *Information and Control* Volume 8, Issue 3, 338–353, June 1965

Appendix:

Training Data*: "*धनुष के साथ प्रयुक्त होने वाला एक अस्त्र तीर है जिसका अग्र भाग नुकीला होता है| तीर का सर्वप्रथम उल्लेख ऋग्वेद संहिता में मिलता है| इषुकृत् और इषुकार शब्दों का प्रयोग सिद्ध करता है कि उन दिनों तीर निर्माण-कार्य व्यवस्थित व्यवसाय था ऋग्वेदकालीन लोहार केवल लोहे का काम ही नहीं करता था, तीर भी तैयार करता था| तीर का अग्र भाग लोहार बनाता था और शेष बाण-निर्मातानिकाय बनाता था| *"

Translation: Arrow (तीर) is a pointed instrument used with the bow. Tracing the history, its first mention was in 'Rigved'.The use of words 'ishukrit' and 'ishukar' signifies that the people in those days were involved in the business of Arrow(तीर(making. The pointed front part of the arrow(तीर) was manufactured by Ironsmith while the rest was made by other specialized manufacturer.

"भीषण बाढ़ और भूस्खलन से तबाही से सबक लेते हुए उत्तराखंड सरकार ने राज्य में नदियों के तीर नई इमारतें बनाने पर पूरी तरह रोक लगा दी है| सरकार ने आपदा प्रभावित लोगों को वित्तीय मदद देने और आपदा से उबरने के लिए सभी अल्पकालिक एवं दीर्घकालिक कदम उठाने के वास्ते पुनर्निर्माण एवं पुनर्वास प्राधिकरण बनाने का भी फैसला किया है|

Translation: The Government of Uttarakhand has banned the construction of new buildings due to heavy floods and landslide in the region. The Government has also decided to take all kinds of steps that includes providing financial help to disaster prone people to overcome the big loss.

Test Data :अग्निपुराण में तीर के निर्माण का वर्णन है | यह लोहे या बाँस से बनता है | बाँस सोने के रंग का और उत्तम कोटि के रेशोंवाला होना चाहिए | तीर के पुच्छभाग पर पंख होते हैं | उसपर तेल लगा रहना चाहिए, ताकि उपयोग में सुविधा हो | इसकी नोक पर स्वर्ण भी जड़ा होता है | प्राचीन काल मे युद्ध के समय धनुष से तीर चलाकर शत्रु का वध किया जाता था

Translation: The art of arrow (तीर) making is described in 'Agnipuran'. It mentions that the arrow(तीर) is made up of either iron or the wood. The material used should be a good quality golden coloured wood. Feather like structure is attached to the end of the arrow(तीर). Proper oiling of the arrow should be done to enable ease of use. The pointed front end of the arrow also has small amount of gold attached to it. In past, Bow and arrow were used during war times to kill the enemy

Using Word Embeddings for Bilingual Unsupervised WSD

Sudha Bhingardive   Dhirendra Singh   Rudramurthy V   Pushpak Bhattacharyya

Department of Computer Science and Engineering,
Indian Institute of Technology Bombay.
{sudha,dhirendra,rudra,pb}@cse.iitb.ac.in

Abstract

Unsupervised Word Sense Disambiguation (WSD) is one of the challenging problems in natural language processing. Recently, an unsupervised bilingual WSD approach has been proposed. This approach uses context aware EM formulation for estimating the sense distribution by using the co-occurrence counts of cross-linked words in comparable corpora. WordNet-based similarity measures are used for approximating the co-occurrence counts. In this paper, we explore the feasibility of the use of Word Embeddings for approximating these counts, which is an extension to the existing approach. We evaluated our approach for Hindi-Marathi language pair, on Health domain. On using the combination of Word Embeddings and WordNet-based similarity measures, we observed 8.5% and 2.5% improvement in the F-score of verbs and adjectives respectively for Marathi and 7% improvement in the F-score of adjectives for Hindi. The experiments show that the combination of Word Embeddings and WordNet-based similarity measures is a reasonable approximation for the bilingual WSD.

1   Introduction

One of the well known research area in the field of Natural Language Processing (NLP) is the word sense disambiguation. Over the years, various WSD algorithms are proposed. These algorithms come under two broad categories, *viz.,* Knowledge based and Machine Learning based. Knowledge based approaches rely on various lexical knowledge resources like machine readable dictionaries, ontologies, WordNets *etc*. Machine learning based approaches are further classified as supervised, semi-supervised and unsupervised. Supervised WSD approaches (Lee et al., 2004; Ng and Lee, 1996) always perform better because of the availability of the sense-annotated data. However, the cost of creation of the sense-annotated data limits their applicability to only a few resource rich languages. On the other hand, semi-supervised approaches (Yarowsky, 1995; Khapra et al., 2010) provide a fine balance in terms of resource requirements and accuracy, but they still rely on some amount of sense-annotated data. Therefore, despite of the less accuracy, much focus is given for unsupervised WSD algorithms (Diab and Resnik, 2002; Kaji and Morimoto, 2002; Mihalcea et al., 2004; Jean, 2004; Khapra et al., 2011). These algorithms do not need any sense-annotated data for the disambiguation. Moreover, they make use of lexical knowledge resources or comparable/parallel corpora for training the algorithm (Kaji and Morimoto, 2002; Diab and Resnik, 2002; Specia et al., 2005; Lefever and Hoste, 2010; Khapra et al., 2011).

Khapra et al. (2011) have shown that how two resource deprived languages can help each other in WSD without using any sense-annotated data in either of the languages. Here, the intuition is that, the sense distribution remains same across languages when the comparable corpora is provided. They used the Expectation Maximization (EM) based formulation for estimating the sense distribution of words. Further, Bhingardive et al. (2013) extended this approach and hypothesized that, the co-occurrence sense distribution also remains same across languages, given the comparable corpora. Since, the co-occurrence counts require a large corpora, they approximate the co-occurrence counts using WordNet-based similarity measures. An improvement of 17% - 35% in the F-Score of verbs was observed while the F-Score was comparable for other POS categories.

In this paper, we propose to explore the use of

55

D S Sharma, R Sangal and E Sherly. Proc. of the 12th Intl. Conference on Natural Language Processing, pages 59–64,
Trivandrum, India. December 2015. ©2015 NLP Association of India (NLPAI)

distributional similarity measures as an approximation to the co-occurrence counts in Bhingardive et al. (2013) approach. We used the cosine distance between the word embeddings of the words as a similarity measure. These word embeddings are obtained from a large monolingual corpus.

The roadmap of the paper is as follows. Section 2 covers the background work on Bilingual EM Our extension of the Bilingual EM using distributional similarity is explained in Section 3. Section 4 gives detail about the experimental setup. Results are presented in section 5. Section 6 covers discussion on the results. Related work is given in section 7. Conclusion and future work are presented in section 8.

2 Bilingual EM using WordNet-based Similarity

Bhingardive et al. (2013) extended the bilingual EM approach (Khapra et al., 2011) and observed that adding contextual information further helps in the disambiguation process. Original bilingual EM approach estimates the sense distribution in one language by using the raw counts of the cross-linked words from the other language using EM algorithm. Bhingardive et al. (2013) modified this approach by replacing the raw counts of the words with the co-occurrence counts of the target word and the context words. They approximated the co-occurrence counts by using WordNet based similarity measures to avoid the data sparsity. The modified EM formulation with context information is as follows:

E-Step:

$$P(S_k^{L_1}|u,a) = \frac{\sum\limits_{v,b} P(\pi_{L_2}(S_k^{L_1})|v,b) \cdot simi(v,b)}{\sum\limits_{S_i^{L_1}} \sum\limits_{x,b} P(\pi_{L_2}(S_i^{L_1})|x,b) \cdot simi(x,b)}$$

$$where, S_i^{L_1}, S_k^{L_1} \in synsets_{L_1}(u)$$
$$a \in context(u)$$
$$v \in crosslinks_{L_2}(u, S_k^{L_1})$$
$$b \in crosslinks_{L_2}(a)$$
$$x \in crosslinks_{L_2}(u, S_i^{L_1})$$

Here, u is the target word to be disambiguated, a is the context word, $\pi_{L_2}(S_k^{L_1})$ means the linked synset of the sense $S_k^{L_1}$ in L_2. $simi(x,b)$ is the WordNet based similarity over all senses of words

x and b. $crosslinks_{L_2}(u, S_j^{L_1})$ is the set of possible translations of the word 'u' from language L_1 to L_2 in the sense $S_j^{L_1}$. $crosslinks_{L_2}(a)$ is the set of all possible translations of the word 'a' from L_1 to L_2 in all its senses.

M-Step:

$$P(S_j^{L_2}|v,b) = \frac{\sum\limits_{u,a} P(\pi_{L_1}(S_j^{L_2})|u,a) \cdot simi(u,a)}{\sum\limits_{S_i^{L_2}} \sum\limits_{y,b} P(\pi_{L_1}(S_i^{L_2})|y,a) \cdot simi(y,a)}$$

$$where, S_i^{L_2}, S_j^{L_2} \in synsets_{L_2}(v)$$
$$b \in context(v)$$
$$u \in crosslinks_{L_1}(v, S_j^{L_2})$$
$$a \in crosslinks_{L_1}(b)$$
$$y \in crosslinks_{L_1}(v, S_i^{L_2})$$

where, $simi(y,a)$ is the WordNet based similarity over all senses of words y and a.

Here, given a target word and its context in one language, the probability of various senses of the target word is calculated in that particular context using their cross-links information from other language. Synset aligned multilingual dictionary (Mohanty et al., 2008) is used to find the cross-links of the target word and its context words in other language. The probability of the sense of the target word given its context is estimated by the modified EM formulation as mentioned earlier. The maximum similarity over all senses of the target word is chosen as the sense of the target word. In this way, given the bilingual comparable corpora and the synset aligned dictionary, context aware EM formulation is used to estimate the sense distributions in both the languages.

3 Our approach: Bilingual EM using Distributional Similarity

Continuous word embeddings have recently gained popularity in various NLP tasks like POS Tagging, Named Entity Recognition, Semantic Role Labeling, Sentiment Analysis, *etc.* (Collobert et al., 2011; Tang et al., 2014). Word embeddings have shown to capture the syntactic and semantic information about a word. In our approach, we look forward to use these word embeddings for the bilingual WSD and compare the results with the existing approaches.

WSD Algorithm	HIN-HEALTH				
	NOUN	**ADV**	**ADJ**	**VERB**	**Overall**
EM-C-DistSimi+WnSimi	59.32	68.98	63.18	60.02	**60.94**
EM-C-DistSimi	59.59	69.20	**63.87**	55.73	61.09
EM-C-WnSimi	59.82	67.80	56.66	**60.38**	59.63
EM	**60.68**	67.48	55.54	25.29	58.16
WFS	53.49	**73.24**	55.16	38.64	54.46
RB	32.52	45.08	35.42	17.93	33.31

Table 1: Comparison(F-Score) of our approach (EM-C-DistSimi-WnSimi and EM-C-DistSimi) with other WSD algorithms on Hindi-Health domain

WSD Algorithm	MAR-HEALTH				
	NOUN	**ADV**	**ADJ**	**VERB**	**Overall**
EM-C-DistSimi+WnSimi	62.75	61.19	**56.22**	**60.99**	**61.30**
EM-C-DistSimi	63.09	61.82	55.60	43.69	58.92
EM-C-WnSimi	62.90	62.54	53.63	52.49	59.77
EM	**63.88**	58.88	55.71	35.60	58.03
WFS	59.35	**67.32**	38.12	34.91	52.57
RB	33.83	38.76	37.68	18.49	32.45

Table 2: Comparison(F-Score) of our approach (EM-C-DistSimi-WnSimi and EM-C-DistSimi) with other WSD algorithms on Marathi-Health domain

Our formulation is based on Bhingardive et al. (2013) formulation, where we use distributional similarity measures along with WordNet based similarity measures for finding the sense distribution. As shown previously, in E-step and M-step, $simi(v, b)$, $simi(x, b)$, $simi(u, a)$ and $simi(y, a)$ are computed as the distributional similarities (cosine distance) calculated from the large untagged text.

4 Experimental setup

In this section, we describe various datasets used in our experiments. We discuss how we obtained word embeddings and evaluated their quality.

4.1 Datasets used for WSD

In our experiments, we used the same corpus as used by Khapra et al. (2011) . This corpus is publicly available[1] for Health domain.

4.2 Training Word Embeddings

The word embeddings were obtained using *word2vec*[2] tool (Mikolov et al., 2013). This tool provides two broad techniques for creating word embeddings : Continuous Bag of Words (CBOW) and Skip-gram models. CBOW model predicts the current word based on the surrounding context whereas, the Skip-gram model tries to maximize the probability of seeing the context word given the word under consideration (Mikolov et al., 2013).

We have used the most widely used hyperparameter settings for training word embeddings. The Skip-gram model is used with 300 dimensions along with the window size equal to 5 (i.e. $w = 5$).

Word Embeddings for Hindi

For obtaining the word embeddings for Hindi, we used Bojar et al. (2014) corpus. This corpus contains around 812.6 million words along with POS and lemma information. We have trained the word embeddings using the lemmatized version of the corpus.

Word Embeddings for Marathi

Marathi corpus was collected from various resources like Web & Wikipedia dumps[3], Leipzig corpus[4] , Newspaper corpus from Maharashtra Times [5] & e-Sakal, [6] *etc*. This corpus contains

---

[1] http://www.cfilt.iitb.ac.in/wsd/annotated_corpus/
[2] https://code.google.com/p/word2vec/
[3] http://ufal.mff.cuni.cz/ majlis/w2c/download.html
[4] http://corpora.uni-leipzig.de/
[5] http://maharashtratimes.indiatimes.com/
[6] http://online4.esakal.com/

approximately 26.3 million words. Marathi word embeddings are trained on this corpus using the same parameters as used for Hindi.

4.3 Evaluating the quality of Word Embeddings

For evaluating the quality of both Hindi and Marathi word embeddings, we have created a *similarity word pair* dataset by translating the standard similarity word pair dataset (Finkelstein et al., 2001) available for English. Three annotators were instructed to give the score for each word-pair based on the semantic similarity and relatedness. The scale was chosen between 0 - 10. The least similar word-pair was given a score of 0, while the most similar word-pair was given a score of 10. We calculated the average inter-annotator agreement using Spearman's correlation coefficient. The embeddings giving the best Pearson's correlation coefficient was used in our experiments.

4.4 WSD Experiments

We performed WSD experiments on all content words. The entire sentence was considered as the context for the word to be disambiguated. Experiments are performed on Hindi-Marathi health domain corpus.

The F-Score of the following WSD algorithms are reported.

Random Baseline [RB]

This algorithm assigns the senses randomly to the words to be disambiguated.

Wordnet First Sense [WFS]

WFS baseline assigns the first listed sense in the WordNet to the word irrespective of its context.

Basic EM [EM]

This is basic EM approach by Khapra et al., (2011) which estimates the sense probability of a word in one language by using the raw counts of its cross-linked words in another language.

EM-C-WnSimi

This is an extended EM approach where Bhingardive et al. (2013) modified the basic EM formulation by adding the contextual information and using the WordNet based similarity for approximating the co-occurrence counts.

EM-C-DistSimi

This is our approach where we modify the formulation of Bhingardive et al. (2013) using the distributional similarity measure for estimating the sense distributions.

EM-C-DistSimi-WnSimi

This is also our approach where we use combination of distributional and WordNet similarity for estimating the sense distributions.

5 Results

In this section, we discuss our results and compare it with other WSD approaches. Table 1 and Table 2 show the results of our approach on Hindi-Health and Marathi-Health domain respectively. Results are given in terms of F-score. EM-C-DitSimi-WnSimi and EM-C-DistSimi achieves better result as compared to EM-C-WnSimi and EM. Using EM-C-DistSimi-WnSimi approach, verb accuracy increases at the level 8.5% for Marathi and for Hindi, it is very close to the existing approaches. The adjective accuracy also improved by 7% for Hindi and 2.5% for Marathi. Results for noun and adverb are observed very close to the existing approaches. The overall F-Score obtained is comparable. The results show that word embeddings can be used as an approximation along with WordNet-Based similarity measures for bilingual WSD.

6 Discussion

6.1 Poor performance for verbs using Word Embeddings

It has been observed that if we use only distributional measure (EM-C-DistSimi) as an approximation then we get significant performance except for verbs. We believe the reason that the word embeddings of verbs fail to capture the semantic information resulting in poor performance. Therefore, the word embeddings of verb fails in finding out relevant context words and choose its correct sense. But if we use the combination of distributional similarity and wordnet similarity then we get better results for the same.

6.2 Misleading contexts

In our approach, we consider the entire sentence as the context for performing WSD. As a result, we end up choosing many context words which causes topic drift. The approach needs to be careful while selecting the context words for the disambiguation task.

7 Related work

Recently, several unsupervised WSD algorithms have been proposed. McCarthy et. al (2004) used distributional methods for finding the context clues for unsupervised most frequent sense detection. They have shown that MFS can be detected without the need of any sense tagged corpora. Only untagged text is used for finding the predominant senses of words. Parallel or comparable corpora have also been explored for unsuperwised WSD (Diab and Resnik, 2002; Kaji and Morimoto, 2002; Mihalcea et al., 2004; Jean, 2004; Khapra et al., 2011). Chen et. al (2014) have presented a unified model which focused on creating sense representations using word embeddings and used the same for the disambiguation purpose.

8 Conclusion and Future Work

We explored the usefulness of word embeddings from a bilingual WSD perspective. We used the distributional similarity measure as an approximation to the co-occurrence counts in bilingual EM Context based WSD. We found that the word embeddings along with wordnet similarity measure are a reasonable approximation to the simple co-occurrence counts. We also observed that the word embeddings for verbs fail to capture the relevant semantic information. Much focus is needed on getting the good quality word embeddings for verbs. We would also like to explore the strategies for choosing the most informative context words for disambiguation depending on the POS category of the word.

References

Sudha Bhingardive, Samiulla Shaikh, and Pushpak Bhattacharyya. 2013. Neighbors help: Bilingual unsupervised wsd using context. In *ACL (2)*, pages 538–542. The Association for Computer Linguistics.

Ondrej Bojar, Vojtěch Diatka, Pavel Rychlý, Pavel Stranak, Vit Suchomel, Aleš Tamchyna, and Daniel Zeman. 2014. Hindencorp - hindi-english and hindi-only corpus for machine translation. In Nicoletta Calzolari (Conference Chair), Khalid Choukri, Thierry Declerck, Hrafn Loftsson, Bente Maegaard, Joseph Mariani, Asuncion Moreno, Jan Odijk, and Stelios Piperidis, editors, *Proceedings of the Ninth International Conference on Language Resources and Evaluation (LREC'14)*, Reykjavik, Iceland, may. European Language Resources Association (ELRA).

Xinxiong Chen, Zhiyuan Liu, and Maosong Sun. 2014. A unified model for word sense representation and disambiguation. In *Proceedings of the 2014 Conference on Empirical Methods in Natural Language Processing (EMNLP)*, pages 1025–1035. Association for Computational Linguistics.

Ronan Collobert, Jason Weston, Léon Bottou, Michael Karlen, Koray Kavukcuoglu, and Pavel Kuksa. 2011. Natural language processing (almost) from scratch. *J. Mach. Learn. Res.*, 12:2493–2537, November.

Mona Diab and Philip Resnik. 2002. An unsupervised method for word sense tagging using parallel corpora. In *Proceedings of the 40th Annual Meeting on Association for Computational Linguistics*, ACL '02, pages 255–262, Morristown, NJ, USA. Association for Computational Linguistics.

Lev Finkelstein, Evgeniy Gabrilovich, Yossi Matias, Ehud Rivlin, Zach Solan, Gadi Wolfman, and Eytan Ruppin. 2001. Placing search in context: The concept revisited. *ACM Trans. Inf. Syst.*

Véronis Jean. 2004. Hyperlex: Lexical cartography for information retrieval. In *Computer Speech and Language*, pages 18(3):223–252.

Hiroyuki Kaji and Yasutsugu Morimoto. 2002. Unsupervised word sense disambiguation using bilingual comparable corpora. In *Proceedings of the 19th international conference on Computational linguistics - Volume 1*, COLING '02, pages 1–7, Stroudsburg, PA, USA. Association for Computational Linguistics.

Mitesh M. Khapra, Anup Kulkarni, Saurabh Sohoney, and Pushpak Bhattacharyya. 2010. All words domain adapted wsd: Finding a middle ground between supervision and unsupervision. In Jan Hajic, Sandra Carberry, and Stephen Clark, editors, *ACL*, pages 1532–1541. The Association for Computer Linguistics.

Mitesh M Khapra, Salil Joshi, and Pushpak Bhattacharyya. 2011. It takes two to tango: A bilingual unsupervised approach for estimating sense distributions using expectation maximization. In *Proceedings of 5th International Joint Conference on Natural Language Processing*, pages 695–704, Chiang Mai, Thailand, November. Asian Federation of Natural Language Processing.

K. Yoong Lee, Hwee T. Ng, and Tee K. Chia. 2004. Supervised word sense disambiguation with support vector machines and multiple knowledge sources. In *Proceedings of Senseval-3: Third International Workshop on the Evaluation of Systems for the Semantic Analysis of Text*, pages 137–140.

Els Lefever and Veronique Hoste. 2010. Semeval-2010 task 3: cross-lingual word sense disambiguation. In Katrin Erk and Carlo Strapparava, editors, *SemEval 2010 : 5th International workshop on Semantic Evaluation : proceedings of the workshop*, pages 15–20. ACL.

Diana Mccarthy, Rob Koeling, Julie Weeds, and John Carroll. 2004. Finding predominant word senses in untagged text. In *In Proceedings of the 42nd Annual Meeting of the Association for Computational Linguistics*, pages 280–287.

Rada Mihalcea, Paul Tarau, and Elizabeth Figa. 2004. Pagerank on semantic networks, with application to word sense disambiguation. In *COLING*.

Tomas Mikolov, Kai Chen, Greg Corrado, and Jeffrey Dean. 2013. Efficient estimation of word representations in vector space. *arXiv preprint arXiv:1301.3781*.

Rajat Mohanty, Pushpak Bhattacharyya, Prabhakar Pande, Shraddha Kalele, Mitesh Khapra, and Aditya Sharma. 2008. Synset based multilingual dictionary: Insights, applications and challenges. In *Global Wordnet Conference*.

Hwee Tou Ng and Hian Beng Lee. 1996. Integrating multiple knowledge sources to disambiguate word sense: an exemplar-based approach. In *Proceedings of the 34th annual meeting on Association for Computational Linguistics*, pages 40–47, Morristown, NJ, USA. ACL.

Lucia Specia, Maria Das Graças, Volpe Nunes, and Mark Stevenson. 2005. Exploiting parallel texts to produce a multilingual sense tagged corpus for word sense disambiguation. In *In Proceedings of RANLP-05, Borovets*, pages 525–531.

Duyu Tang, Furu Wei, Nan Yang, Ming Zhou, Ting Liu, and Bing Qin. 2014. Learning sentiment-specific word embedding for twitter sentiment classification. In *Proceedings of the 52nd Annual Meeting of the Association for Computational Linguistics (Volume 1: Long Papers)*, pages 1555–1565. Association for Computational Linguistics.

David Yarowsky. 1995. Unsupervised word sense disambiguation rivaling supervised methods. In *Proceedings of the 33rd Annual Meeting on Association for Computational Linguistics*, ACL '95, pages 189–196, Stroudsburg, PA, USA. Association for Computational Linguistics.

Compositionality in Bangla Compound Verbs and their Processing in the Mental Lexicon

Tirthankar Dasgupta[1]
TCS Innovation Lab,
New Delhi
`iamirthan-`
`kar@gmail.com`

Manjira Sinha[1]
Xerox Research Center India, Bangalore
`Manjira87@gmail.com`

Anupam Basu
Department of Computer Science and Engineering,
IIT Kharagpur
`anupambas@gmail.com`

Abstract

We conduct a cross-modal priming experiment to determine the mental representation and access strategies for compound verbs (CV) in Bangla. Analysis of reaction time indicates that compositionality among CVs triggers priming effects for both the constituent verbs. On the other hand non-compositional CVs exhibit priming only for the polar verb. Thus, compositional CVs are decomposed into their constituent verbs during processing. On the other hand, non-compositional verb phrases are represented and accessed as a whole in the minds of a Bangla speaker. The reaction time data thus collected are used to evaluate our vector space model for compositionality judgment.

1 Introduction

The term compositionality refers to the idea that the meaning of a complex expression is derived from (i) its structure and (ii) the meanings of its constituents (refer to (Fodor and Pylyshyn, 1988) for details). Compound verbs (henceforth CV) in Bangla are known to exhibit continuum of compositionality. Thus, some of them are compositional (khete bashA "sit to eat"), some are non-compositional (jAliye mArA "to irritate") and some in between (ghure berAno "loitering").

There is a considerable linguistic debate on whether CVs are considered as two distinct words connected by some syntagmatic rule or whether

Work done during the tenure at IIT Kharagpur.

they form a single lexical unit (Paul, 2010; Chakrabarti et al., 2008; Butt, 1995) and whether semantic compositionality plays any role deciding the above. These linguistically and computationally challenging issues play an important role in developing lexical resources like WordNet (Fellbaum, 2010).

Since, none of the linguistic arguments and computational approaches has so far led to any consensus, we here for the first time performed a series of psycholinguistic experiments on Bangla compound verbs to study and model how the *mental lexicon*(ML), organize and process such complex expressions. The term mental lexicon refers to the storage of words in the human mind (Aitchison, 2005). A clear understanding of the structure and processing mechanism of CVs in the ML may provide us insight about how to represent and process CVs in computational lexicons. Further, the reaction time of the subjects for recognizing various lexical items under appropriate conditioning may lead us to develop more robust computational models of automatic identification of CVs.

A plethora of works have been done to explore the representation and processing of words in the mental lexicon (refer to Seidenberg, 2012 to get a detail account of it). Attempts have also been made to study the processing of Bangla derivationally suffixed morphologically complex words (Dasgupta et al., 2010; Dasgupta et al., 2012, 2014) and Bangla compound words (Dasgupta et al., 2015). However, to the best of our knowledge

[1] *D S Sharma, R Sangal and E Sherly. Proc. of the 12th Intl. Conference on Natural Language Processing*, pages 65–70, Trivandrum, India. December 2015. ©2015 NLP Association of India (NLPAI)

no such prior attempts have been made to psycho-linguistically analyze the representation and processing of the Bangla compound verbs.

Based on the above discussion, the objective of this paper is to explore the semantic compositionality in Bangla CVs and its role in the possible organization and processing of CVs in the ML. Accordingly, we first use empirical techniques to collect user judgment of compositionality for Bangla CVs. Next, we perform the cross modal priming experiment to understand the processing of CVs ML. We found that Bangla CV exhibit continuum of compositionality. Highly compositional verb phrases V_1V_2 trigger significant priming effect for both its constituent verbs V_1 and V_2. On the other hand, non-compositional verb sequences exhibit priming effect only for V_1. These observations together imply that the mental lexicon decomposes compositional verb sequences into their constituent verbs and recognize separately during processing. On the other hand non-compositional verb sequences are organized and accessed as a whole. Based on the dataset collected from the above experiments, we further develop a vector space model to compute semantic compositionality in a verb sequence. The predicted values are compared with the human judgment scores and the priming experiment results where a significant correlation is found.

2 Compositionality Judgments

We could not find any Bangla CV dataset publicly available and annotated in terms of compositionality. Thus, we choose 300 verb sequences and presented them to 36 native Bangla speakers. Similar to the work discussed in (Reddy et al., 2011), we request each subject to give compositionality score of the verb sequences by asking a) how literal the verb phrase is in a given context and b) how literal the constituent verbs are. Subjects were asked to rate the compositionality under 1-10 point scale, 10 being highly compositional and 1 for non-compositional. In order to validate the user annotated data, we compute the inter-annotator agreement using the Fleiss Kappa measure (Fleiss et al., 1981). We found an agreement of κ= 0.68.

3 The Priming Experiment

Priming effects are observed because of the way our brain is supposed to function. Presentation of a stimulus (say a word P) activates a group of neurons (often called a functional web) in the brain.

When another stimulus (say word T) is then presented to the individual within a short duration, the recognition of T is faster if the functional web of T shares a lot of neurons with that of P. This fast reaction time to recognize a stimulus due to the prior exposure to a functionally related stimulus is known as priming (Tulving et al., 1982). Thus, through priming experiments, we can identify word pairs whose functional webs have a stronger overlap, which in turn reveals how brain organizes the words in the mental lexicon (See (Pulvermüller, 2003; Spivey et al., 2012) for a detailed account of such phenomena and different types of priming techniques).

Experiment design: We conduct the cross-modal repetition priming experiments as described in (Marslen-Wilson et al., 1994). Here, a subject gets an audio stimulus (called prime (P)) of a verb sequence V1V2 and immediately at the offset of the spoken prime, gets a visual representation of the target (T) word V1. The same audio stimulus is presented to the subject after a random number of trials with the target V2. Based on the auditory prime and the visual target probe, the subjects are asked to decide whether the visually presented target V1 or V2 is a valid word in the language. The above experiment is also repeated with the same target words but with different auditory inputs called the controls(C). The control verb sequences do not have any relatedness with the targets. For example, "kheye felo" (complete eating) and "khAOyA" (to eat) or "kheye felo" and "felo" (to drop) are P-T pairs, for which the corresponding C-T pair could be "niye jAO" (take away) and "khAOyA" (to eat). The time taken by a subject to complete the lexical decision task after the visual presentation of the target is defined as the response time (RT). For both the experiments, RTs of all the targets were recorded and analyzed to observe priming effects.

Materials: The 300 verb pairs as discussed in section 2, are grouped into two classes *highly compositional* (C1) and *non-compositional* (C2). We randomly choose 30 V_1V_2 pairs from each class as primes. For each prime, we have two targets V_1 and V_2, which makes 120 P-T pairs. Consequently, 120 C-T and 240 fillers (or non-words) have been chosen to restrict the subjects to apply any strategic guess during the experiment. Overall, we have collected RTs for 480 word pairs in one experiment. A set of 10 P-T and C-T pairs were also collected for a practice session before the true experiments. However, the RTs of these practice pairs are not included in any analysis.

The experiment was conducted using the DMDX software tool that plays the auditory stimulus and then showed the visual probe for 200ms. Corresponding to each visual probe, subjects had 3000ms to perform the lexical decision after which the system presents the next audio stimulus. The subject performs the decision task by pressing either the "K'" key for a VALID word and "S'" for INVALID word. The system automatically records the RT, which in this case is the time between the onset of the visual probe and clicking of one of the buttons by the subject. The experiments were conducted on 36 native Bangla speakers; 29 of them have a graduate degree and 7 hold a post graduate degree. The age of the subjects varies between 25 to 35 years.

Results: The RTs with extreme values (>2000ms) and those for incorrect lexical decisions (about 3.2%) were excluded from the data. The raw RTs for all correct responses were inversely transformed (Ratcliff, 1993) and entered into a mixed-design analysis of variance with two factors: priming (primed and unprimed), and condition (C1, C2). In the subject's analysis (F1), condition and priming were treated as repeated measures. In the items analysis (F2), priming is treated as repeated factor and condition as independent factor. Table 1 summarizes the mean RTs for the prime (P) and control (C) sets of the V1 and V2 for the two classes.

Class	Example	Avg. Comp	Avg RT	
			$V_1(P,C)$	$V_2(P,C)$
C1	*khete basA* (sit to eat)	8.8	666,688	661, 696
C2	*kheye felA* (to eat)	2.3	657,679	687, 659

Table 1: Average compositionality and RTs for the different word classes

There was a strong main effect of priming with faster RTs to primed (667ms for V_1 and 687ms for V_2) than unprimed (679ms and 659ms) targets, $F_1(1, 36)= 47.60$, $p<.01$; $F_2(1, 60)=26.00$, $p<0.01$. There was a main effect of condition $F_1(1, 30)=11.69$, $p<0.01$, $F_2(1,60) =3.51$, $p<0.01$, and a significant condition by priming interaction, indicating that priming effects varied across conditions. Thus, we have observed that when V_1 is presented as target, significant priming occurred for words belonging to both C_1 and C_2. These results are statistically significant according to the 2-way ANOVA test. On the other hand, when V_2 is presented as target with the same prime stimulus V_1V_2, priming is observed only in C2. This result indicates that, compositional verb sequences exhibits priming for both the constituent verbs V_1 and V_2 whereas, non-compositional verb sequences (C1) exhibit priming only with V_1. This may be accounted for by the fact that non-compositional verb sequences derive their meaning mainly from the meaning of its first constituent verb V_1, thus, priming occurs only with V_1. On the other hand, as semantic compositionality between verb sequences increases, both the constituent verbs (V_1 and V_2) plays role in determining the meaning of the whole expression. Thus, both the constituent verbs exhibit priming behavior when preceded by the prime V_1+V_2. The above observations together imply that:

Compositional verb sequences are in general represented in terms of their constituent verbs in the mental lexicon; lexical access and comprehension is facilitated through decomposition of the surface forms into the corresponding constituent verbs. On the other hand non compositional verb sequences are represented and accessed as a whole.

4 Computational Model

Based on the collected data, we now try to develop a vector space model of semantic compositionality to predict the organization and processing of verb phrases in the mental lexicon. We evaluate our model with the data collected from our human judgment compositionality score and the cross-modal priming experiments.

In our vector space model we represent a word's meaning in an n-dimensional space. Here, meaning of individual words is represented in terms of its co-occurrences observed in a large corpus. These co-occurrences are stored in a vector format acquired from a corpus following the different procedures as suggested in the literature (refer to (Mitchell and Lapata, 2008) for a detailed overview).

We have considered the lemmatized context words around the target word in a window of size 200 as the co-occurrences. For the purpose of lemmatization, we have used a Bangla morphological analyzer having an accuracy of around

95%. A Bangla corpus of 33 million words is already available[2]. The corpus contains document from different domain like literature, tourism, news and personal blogs. The top 10000 frequent content words from the corpus are used for the feature co-occurrences. To measure similarity between two vectors, cosine similarity (*sim*) is used. We have used the raw co-occurrence frequency as the values of the constructed vector.

Given a CV W_3 with the constituents W_1 and W_2, the compositionality score S_3 of W_3 is computed as $S_3 = f(S_1, S_2)$. Where, S_1 and S_2 are the literality scores of W_1 and W_2 respectively and f is the semantic compositionality function defined in Column 1 of Table 1. S_1 and S_2 are computed as

$$S_1 = sim(v_1, v_3) \text{ and}$$
$$S_2 = sim(v_2, v_3).$$

Where, v_1, v_2 and v_3 be the co-occurrence vectors of W_1, W_2 and W_3 respectively and *sim* is the cosine similarity between two vectors computed as:

$$sim(v_1, v_2) = \frac{v_1 . v_2}{|v_1||v_2|}$$

The primary idea behind the constituent based compositionality model is the fact that if a constituent word is used literally in a given verb sequence it is possible that the verb sequence and its constituent share common co-occurrences.

We compare the compositionality score S_3 of all the five composition functions namely, *f1, f2, f3, f4, and f5* with the human annotated compositionality score. The constant parameters (α, β, γ) for all the five models have been computed using list square linear regression technique. We perform a 6 folded cross validation over the test data. The performance of the individual models is reported in Table 2 below. We can observe that the composition functions *f1* and *f5* are better predictor of phrase based compositionality than the other models.

#	F	ρ, R^2	(α, β, γ)
1	$\alpha\, v_1 + \beta v_2 = v_3$	0.73, 0.80	0.02, 0.40
2	$\gamma v_1 v_2 = v_3$	0.40, 0.71	0.32
3	$\alpha v_1 + \beta v_2 + \gamma(v_1 . v_2) = v_3$	0.43, 0.77	0.01, 0.41, 0.33
4	$\alpha v_1 = v_3$	0.30, 0.55	0.12
5	$\beta v_2 = v_3$	0.75, 0.89	0.73

Table 2: Correlation between the human judgment compositionality and the predicted S3 by each of the composition function along with the goodness of fit.

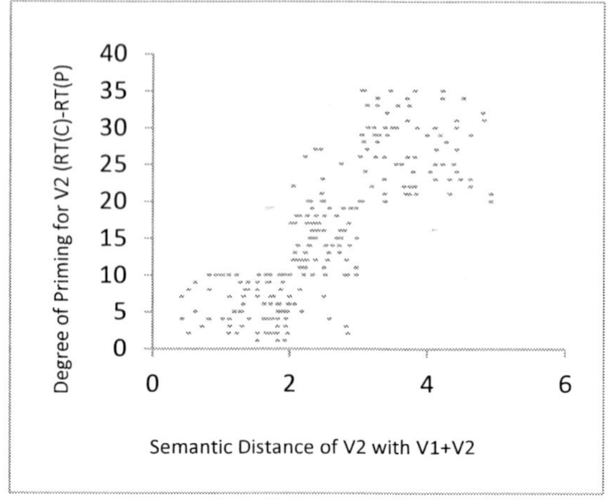

Figure 1: Change in degree of priming of V_1 with respect to the semantic distance of V_1 and V_1+V_2

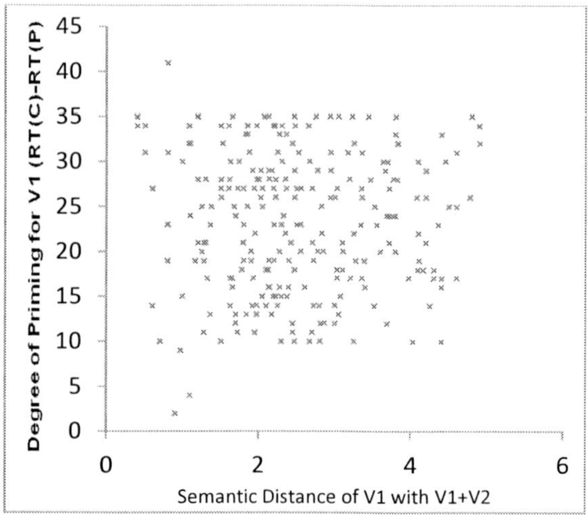

Figure 2: Change in degree of priming of V_2 with respect to the semantic distance of V_2 and V_1+V_2

In the final phase of our work, we have compared the phrase level compositionality score S_3 and the literality scores S_1 and S_2 with the priming behavior of targets V_1 and V_2. The correlation results are reported in Table 3. We observe S_3 has got a high correlation with the priming behavior of the second constituent verb V_2. On the other hand, weak correlation exists between S_3 and V_1. The observations are quite expected, as priming behavior in V_1 is observed irrespective of the semantic compositionality of the phrase V_1V_2,

---

[2] www.cel.iitkgp.ernet.in

whereas, priming behavior in V_2 changes as compositionality in V_1V_2 changes. This is also reflected in Figure 1 and Figure 2 respectively.

Similar observations are found for S1 and S2. Overall, the results in Table 3 are in agreement with that of Table 1: compositional verb phrases exhibit priming for both its constituents whereas non-compositional verb phrases shows priming only to its first constituent verb (V1).

	V_1	V_2
S_3	0.04	0.78
S_1	0.73	0.01
S_2	0.12	0.74

Table 3: Correlation between priming in V1 and V2 and the computed cosine similarity scores (S1, S2).

5 General Discussion and Conclusion

In this paper we have presented some preliminary psycholinguistic experiments to identify the role of compositionality in the representation and processing of Bangla compound verbs in the mental lexicon. In order to do so, we first computed the user judgment of compositionality score. We found that there is a continuum of compositionality between Bangla compound verbs. Next, we employ the cross-modal repetition priming experiment over a set of Bangla compound verbs. Our initial results show that non-compositional verb sequences exhibit priming only with V_2. On the other hand compositional verb sequences exhibit priming with both the constituent verbs V_1 and V_2. These observations together lead us to believe that mental representation and access of compound verbs in Bangla typically depends on the compositionality of the constituent verbs. Compositional verb phrases are accessed via decomposition of the phrase into its constituent verbs whereas non-compositional phrases are accessed as a whole.

In the next phase of our work, we try to develop a vector space model of semantic compositionality to predict the organization and processing of verb phrases in the mental lexicon. We evaluate our model with the data collected from our human judgment compositionality score and the cross-modal priming experiments. Comparing the models output with that of the empirically collected data, we claim that the proposed vector space model correctly predicts the semantic compositionality of Bangla verb sequences and their possible organization and processing in the mental lexicon. However, it would be premature to conclude anything concrete based only on the current experimental results. We also observe that several other factors including usage frequency and verb ordering affect the overall word recognition time and access mechanisms. Each of these factor calls for rigorous experimentation for understanding the exact nature of their interdependencies that we intend to perform in future.

Acknowledgement

We are thankful to all the participants who actively helped us to conduct the psycholinguistic experiments. We are also thankful to TCS Innovation Lab, Delhi for funding us to travel and attend the conference.

Reference

Aitchison, J. (2005). *Words in the mind: An introduction to the mental lexicon.* Taylor & Francis.

Butt, M. (1995). *The structure of complex predicates in Urdu.* Center for the Study of Language and Inf.

Chakrabarti, D., Mandalia, H., Priya, R., Sarma, V., and Bhattacharyya, P. (2008). Hindi compound verbs and their automatic extraction. In *International Conference on Computational Linguistics*, pages 27–30.

Fellbaum, C. (2010). Wordnet. *Theory and Applications of Ontology: Computer Applications*, pages 231–243.

Fleiss, J. L., Levin, B., and Paik, M. C. (1981). The measurement of interrater agreement. *Statistical methods for rates and proportions*, 2:212–236.

Fodor, J. A. and Pylyshyn, Z. W. (1988). Connectionism and cognitive architecture: A critical analysis. *Cognition*, 28(1):3–71.

Marslen-Wilson, W., Tyler, L., Waksler, R., and Older, L. (1994). Morphology and meaning in the english mental lexicon. *Psychological Review*, 101(1):3.

Mitchell, J. and Lapata, M. (2008). Vector-based models of semantic composition. *proceedings of ACL-08: HLT*, pages 236–244.

Paul, S. (2010). Representing compound verbs in indo wordnet. In *Golbal Wordnet Conference*, pages 84–91.

Pulvermüller, F. (2003). *The neuroscience of language: on brain circuits of words and serial order.* Cambridge University Press.

Ratcliff, R. (1993). Methods for dealing with reaction time outliers. *Psychological bulletin*, 114(3):510.

Reddy, S., McCarthy, D., and Manandhar, S. (2011). An empirical study on compositionality in compound nouns. In *Proceedings of IJCNLP*.

Spivey, M. J., Joanisse, M., and McRae, K. (2012). *The cambridge handbook of psycholinguistics*. Cambridge University Press.

Tulving, E., Schacter, D. L., and Stark, H. A. (1982). Priming effects in word-fragment completion are independent of recognition memory. *Journal of experimental psychology: learning, memory, and cognition*, 8(4):336–342.

Seidenberg, M. S. (2012). Computational models of reading. *The Cambridge handbook of psycholinguistics*, page 186.

Dasgupta, T., Choudhury, M., Bali, K. and Basu, A. (2010). *Mental representation and access of polymorphemic words in bangla: Evidence from cross-modal priming experiments*. International conference on natural language processing (ICON). pp. 58-67.

Dasgupta T., Sinha M., Basu A. (2012). "*Computational Models to understand the Access and Representation of Bangla Polymorphemic Words in the Mental Lexicon*". International Conference on Computational Linguistics (COLING), 2012, pp-235-244.

Dasgupta T., Sinha M., Basu A. (2014), "*Computational Modeling of Morphological Effects in Bangla Visual Word Recognition*", Journal of Psycholinguistic Research (JOPR), Springer, 2015.

Dasgupta T., Sinha M., Basu A. (2015). *Computational Models of the Lexical Representation of Bangla Compound Words in the Mental Lexicon*", Journal of Psycholinguistic Research (JOPR), Springer, 2015

IndoWordNet Dictionary:
An Online Multilingual Dictionary using IndoWordNet

Hanumant Redkar
Center for Indian Language Technology,
Indian Institute of Technology Bombay, India
hanumantredkar@gmail.com

Sandhya Singh
Center for Indian Language Technology,
Indian Institute of Technology Bombay, India
sandhya.singh@gmail.com

Nilesh Joshi
Center for Indian Language Technology,
Indian Institute of Technology Bombay, India
joshinilesh60@gmail.com

Anupam Ghosh
Center for Indian Language Technology,
Indian Institute of Technology Bombay, India
anupam.ghsh@gmail.com

Pushpak Bhattacharyya
Department of Computer Science and Engineering,
Indian Institute of Technology Bombay, India
pushpakbh@gmail.com

Abstract

India is a country with diverse culture, language and varied heritage. Due to this, it is very rich in languages and their dialects. Being a multilingual society, a dictionary in multiple languages becomes its need and one of the major resources to support a language. There are dictionaries for many Indian languages, but very few are available in multiple languages. WordNet is one of the most prominent lexical resources in the field of Natural Language Processing. IndoWordNet is an integrated multilingual WordNet for Indian languages. These WordNet resources are used by researchers to experiment and resolve the issues in multilinguality through computation. However, there are few cases where WordNet is used by the non-researchers or general public. This paper focuses on providing an online interface – *IndoWordNet Dictionary* to non-researchers as well as researchers. It is developed to render multilingual WordNet information of 19 Indian languages in a dictionary format. The WordNet information is rendered in multiple views such as: sense based, thesaurus based, word usage based and language based. English WordNet information is also rendered using this interface. The IndoWordNet dictionary will help users to know meanings of a word in multiple Indian languages.

1 Introduction

Language is a constituent element of civilization. In a country like India, diversity is its primary aspect. This leads to varied languages and their dialects. There are numerous languages in India which belong to different language families. These language families are Indo-Aryan, Dravidian, Sino-Tibetan, Tibeto-Burman and Austro-Asiatic. The major ones are the Indo-Aryan, spoken by the northern to western part of India and Dravidian, spoken by southern part of India. The Eighth Schedule of the Indian Constitution lists 22 languages, which have been referred to as scheduled languages and given recognition, status and official encouragement.

A *Dictionary* can be called as a resource dealing with the individual words of a language along with

D S Sharma, R Sangal and E Sherly. Proc. of the 12th Intl. Conference on Natural Language Processing, pages 71–78,
Trivandrum, India. December 2015. ©2015 NLP Association of India (NLPAI)

its orthography, pronunciation, usage, synonyms, derivation, history, etymology, *etc.* arranged in an order for convenience of referencing the words. Various criterions used for classifying this resource are - density of entries, number of languages involved, nature of entries, degree of concentration on strictly lexical data, axis of time, arrangement of entries, purpose, prospective user, *etc.* Some of the common types of dictionaries are[1]-

- **Encyclopedia:** Single or multi-volume publication that contains accumulated and authoritative knowledge on a subject arranged alphabetically. *E.g.* Britannica encyclopedia.
- **Thesaurus:** Thesaurus is a dictionary that lists words in groups of synonyms and related concepts.
- **Etymological Dictionary:** An etymological dictionary discusses the etymology/origin of the words listed. It is the product of research in historical linguistics.
- **Dialect Dictionary:** These dictionaries deal with the words of a particular geographical region or social group which are non standard.
- **Specialized Dictionary:** These dictionaries covers relatively restricted set of phenomena.
- **Bilingual or Multilingual Dictionary:** These are linguistic dictionaries in two or more languages.
- **Reverse Dictionary**: These dictionaries are based on the concept/idea/definition to words.
- **Learner's Dictionary:** These dictionaries are meant for foreign students/tourists to learn the usage of the word in language.
- **Phonetic Dictionary**: These dictionaries help in searching the words by the way they sound.
- **Visual Dictionary**: These dictionaries use pictures to illustrate the meaning of words.

WordNet is a lexical resource composed of synsets and semantic relations. Synsets are sets of synonyms. They are linked by semantic relations like hypernymy, meronymy, *etc.* and lexical relations like antonymy, gradation, *etc.* (Miller et al., 1990; Fellbaum, 1998). IndoWordNet[2] is a linked structure of WordNets of 19 different Indian languages from Indo-Aryan, Dravidian and Sino-Tibetan families (Bhattacharyya, 2010). Other popular multilingual WordNets are: EuroWordNet,

which is a linked WordNet for European languages (Vossen, 1999) and BalkaNet, which is a linked WordNet for Balkan Languages (Christodoulakis, 2002). The most innovative aspect of WordNets is that lexical information is organized in terms of meaning; *i.e.*, a synset contains words of the same part-of-speech which have approximately the same meaning. Thus, it is synonymy that functions as the essential principle in the construction of WordNets (Vincze et al., 2008). This feature of WordNet is most important for the dictionary construction.

IndoWordNet is used in the field of Natural Language Processing tasks like Machine Translation, Information Retrieval, Information Extraction, *etc.* But, not much has been explored to use this resource beyond research labs. In this paper, we present an interface – *IndoWordNet Dictionary* (*IWN Dictionary*) in the form of multilingual online dictionary which uses IndoWordNet as a resource. The primary focus of this interface is to provide synset information in a systematic and classified manner which is rendered in multiple views.

The rest of the paper is organized as follows: Section 2 justifies the need of IndoWordNet Dictionary. Section 3 details the IndoWordNet Dictionary, its components, followed by its design and layout. Section 4 gives the features of the dictionary. Section 5 lists its limitations. Finally, the conclusion, scope and enhancements to the IWN Dictionary are presented.

2   Need for IndoWordNet Dictionary

Our work on developing IWN Dictionary interface is motivated from various available online resources. To name some: `langtolang.com`[3] which includes cross-lingual references across 47 non-Indian languages, `wordreference.com`[4] which includes 17 non-Indian languages, and others being `logosdictionary.org`[5] and `xobodo.org`[6] which has multiple languages including some Indian languages. But, all these resources render not more than two languages at a given instance.

Further survey is done, which reveals that Mohanty et al. (2008) had developed a tool for multilingual dictionary development process to

---

[1] http://www.ciil-ebooks.net/html/lexico/link5.htm
[2] http://www.cfilt.iitb.ac.in/indowordnet/
[3] http://www.langtolang.com/
[4] http://www.wordreference.com
[5] http://www.logosdictionary.org/
[6] http://www.xobdo.org/

create and link the synset based lexical resource for machine translation purpose. The aim was to simplify the process of synset creation and to link it with different Indian language WordNets. The tool was mainly used by lexicographers involved in the process of creating various Indian language WordNets. Also, Sinha et al. (2006) who have designed a browsable bilingual interface for viewing WordNet information in two languages, Hindi and Marathi. The input to this browser is a search word in any of the two languages and the output is the search result for both the languages. The primary usage of this interface is to help users get the semantic information of the search string in both Hindi and Marathi. However, Sarma et al. (2012) built a multilingual dictionary considering three languages, *viz.*, Assamese, Bodo and Hindi. The dictionary interface allows searching between Hindi-Assamese and Hindi-Bodo language pairs at a time.

All these interfaces mentioned above could display the meanings in at most two languages with the lexical information available in the WordNet at a time. Hence, we have developed a web based interface to render multilingual WordNet information in a dictionary format. This interface is developed keeping in mind the general public, apart from researchers.

Following points justify the need of online multilingual dictionary in today's time:

- To know or understand other languages.
- To find the meaning of a word in multiple languages on a single platform.
- To understand other languages with the help of a pivot language (referring one of the known languages).
- To understand synonymous words in input language as well as in another languages.
- To understand additional information like part-of-speech, gender, etc. in input as well as other different languages.
- To understand the semantic variations in different languages.
- To fulfil the social need of bridging the communication gap.
- To understand the script of various languages.
- To understand a local language when relocated to that area.

- To improve on one's own language vocabulary.
- To address social and educational needs.

3 IndoWordNet Multilingual Dictionary

3.1 What is IndoWordNet Dictionary?

IndoWordNet Dictionary[7] or *IWN Dictionary* is an online interface to render multilingual IndoWordNet information in the dictionary format. It allows user to view the results in multiple formats as per the need. Also, user can view the result in multiple languages simultaneously. The look and feel of the IWN Dictionary is kept same as a traditional dictionary keeping in mind the user adaptability. So far, it renders WordNet information of 19 Indian languages. These languages are: Assamese, Bodo, Bengali, Gujarati, Hindi, Kannada, Kashmiri, Konkani, Maithili, Malayalam, Manipuri, Marathi, Nepali, Odia, Punjabi, Sanskrit, Tamil, Telugu and Urdu. The WordNet information is also rendered in English. The English WordNet information is taken from Princeton University[8] website. All these WordNets are imported into IndoWordNet database structure (Prabhu, et al., 2012) using DB Import tool developed under the Indradhanush WordNet Project[9]. The work is still going on to include other non-Indian languages and storing them in the World WordNet Database Structure (WWDS) proposed by Redkar et al. (2015).

3.2 Modules of IWN Dictionary

The IWN Dictionary has two major modules: *IWN Dictionary Search Module* and *IWN Dictionary Display Module*. Figure 1 shows the block diagram of the IWN Dictionary.

3.2.1 IWN Dictionary Search Module

The main function of the IWN Dictionary Search module is to process the input word in the form which can be used to search the database and retrieve relevant information. Its function is divided into three sub modules, which involves analyzing a

---

word, database lookup and multilingual data extraction.

Each of these sub modules are described in detail below –

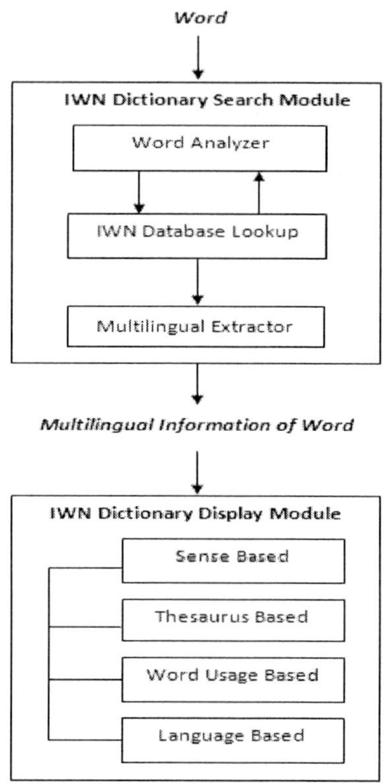

Figure 1. Block diagram of IWN Dictionary.

Word Analyzer

Word Analyzer analyses and processes the input word. It checks whether it is in its root form. If it is in root form then it is directly passed on to the IWN Database Lookup module, else it will be processed to find the closest possible word in the database. The concept of human mediated lemmatizer is adopted from the work of Bhattacharyya et al., (2014) to find the closest possible words of an input word. Here, the trie data structure is created out of the vocabulary in the input language and this structure is navigated to find the match between the input word and an entry in trie. Accordingly, the closest possible word(s) is populated and given for the next module for the database lookup.

IWN Database Lookup

In IWN Database Lookup module, the word received from Word Analyzer is searched in the IWN database and the corresponding synset ids of all the senses of a word are sent to the Multilingual Extractor engine for further processing. If the word is not found in the database then the control is sent back to the Word Analyzer module to look for other similar or closest words.

Multilingual Extractor

The basic task of Multilingual Extractor module is to take the input synset ids and extract synset information of all the languages available in the IWN database. This extracted synset information, *i.e.,* the multilingual senses of an input word are then sent to the IWN Dictionary Display module for rendering information in the dictionary format.

3.2.2   IWN Dictionary Display Module

The IWN Dictionary Display module takes the extracted multilingual senses of a given word and renders it in the traditional dictionary format. Here, the multilingual IndoWordNet data can be rendered using different views. This is an important module of an IWN Dictionary which renders and ranks information based on the user response and statistics. Here, *IWN Click-Based-Rendering Algorithm* is used to rank most frequently used senses using this interface. The basic task of this algorithm is to record and maintain the number of user clicks on a sense being viewed and accordingly rank the sense in the output interface. Similarly, this algorithm is applied to all the other views available for this IWN Dictionary.

The different views in IWN Dictionary are:

- **Sense Based view:** All the meanings of an input word are displayed with respect to the senses available in the IWN database. Here, each sense is shown in a different card, where user can click or unclick to get the corresponding senses in other languages.

- **Thesaurus Based view:** In thesaurus based view, synonymous words in each language are rendered. Here, user can click on any of the words in the list to go to see other senses of that word.

- **Word Usage Based view:** In word usage based view, usage of an input word with respect to the languages is rendered. Here, the examples of a synset from IWN database are rendered.

- **Language Based view:** In language based view, meaning of a word is rendered with respect to the language. Here, for each sense of a word, the meaning in all the languages is rendered in a horizontal tabbed format or a card format.

Apart from these views, transliteration information is displayed for each of these views. The transliteration information is seen once a user hovers on any of the content in the dictionary. For now, we have used transliteration into a roman script using the Indic NLP Library[10] developed by Kunchukuttan et al. (2015). However, we are in the process to implement transliteration in all the Indian languages, so that anyone can read other language in their chosen *transliteration language*.

3.3 Design and Layout of IWN Dictionary

The IWN Dictionary is designed keeping in mind, its simplicity and usability; more importantly, the user friendliness of the system. The frontend is designed and developed with PHP, CSS, JavaScript, etc. and at the backend, MySQL database is used. The IWN Dictionary data is retrieved from IndoWordNet database using IndoWordNet APIs (Prabhugaonkar et al., 2012).

The basic input parameters of this dictionary are; input language, search string, phonetic transliteration, keyboard and different views selector. Figure 2, figure 3, figure 4 and figure 5 shows sample screen shots of the IWN Multilingual Dictionary Interface with different views. In all these views, initial information is always shown in the source language. This initial information is rendered on the horizontal tab in the card format. User can click on plus or minus button to expand or collapse to see the details in each card respectively. Also, user can check the checkbox next to each Language in *sense based view*, *thesaurus based*

view and *word usage based view* to see information in the checked language.

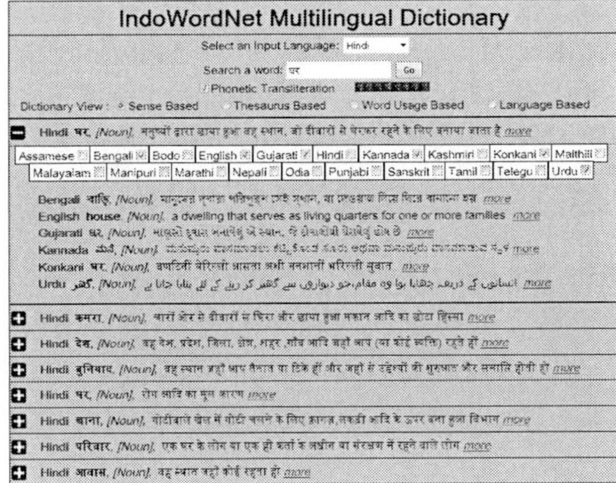

Figure 2. IndoWordNet Multilingual Dictionary showing multiple languages with sense based view.

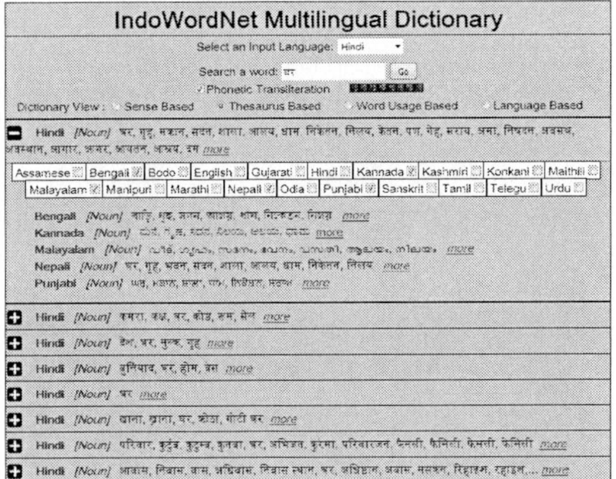

Figure 3. IndoWordNet Multilingual Dictionary showing multiple languages with thesaurus based view.

In figure 3, we can see that the source language is Hindi and the target languages are Bengali, Kannada, Malayalam, Nepali and Punjabi. Here, *thesaurus based view* is enabled; Hence, the IWN Dictionary renders synonymous words in the form of thesaurus. On clicking hyperlink *more*, user can see the meaning of these words. Also, user can click on any of the words in the list which displays the multilingual senses of that particular word.

---

[10] http://anoopkunchukuttan.github.io/indic_nlp_library/

In figure 4, we can see that the source language is Hindi and the target languages are English, Gujarati, Hindi, Kannada, Nepali and Odia. Here, *word usage based view* is enabled; hence, the IWN Dictionary renders usage of a word by showing the example sentences in a synset from IWN database.

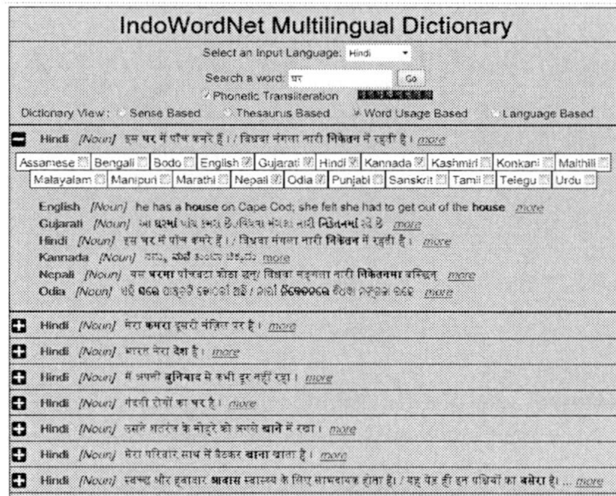

Figure 4. IndoWordNet Multilingual Dictionary showing multiple languages with word usage based view.

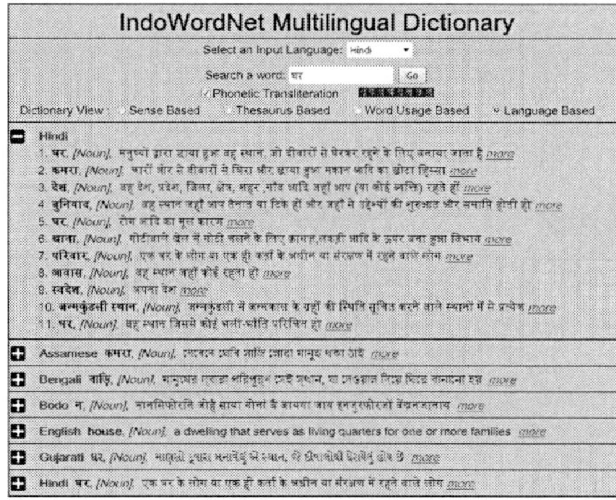

Figure 5. IndoWordNet Multilingual Dictionary showing multiple languages with language based view.

In figure 5, we can see that the source language is Hindi and in the target languages initially, the information is rendered in Hindi, However, the user can click on any of the horizontal bars to see all senses in each language. Here, *language based view* is enabled.

The procedure to use this IWN multilingual dictionary is as follows:

- User selects an input language.
- User types-in a word. To input a word, he can enable phonetic transliteration or use onscreen keyboard.
- User selects the Dictionary View. By default, *sense based view* is enabled and information is rendered sense wise.
- User clicks on the button GO.
- The meanings of an input word are displayed in horizontal tabbed format.
- User can toggle between different views by clicking on sense based, thesaurus based, language based, word usage based radio buttons.
- User can click on *more* to get additional information under each of these views.
- The transliterated information is provided under each of these views. User has to click on checkbox 'view transliteration' for this purpose; this is available under the hyper link *more*. However, user sees transliteration of each language on mouse *hover* in the roman script.

4 Features of IWN Dictionary

The salient features of IndoWordNet Dictionary are as follows:

- Renders information in multiple languages at a time.
- Different views to display the information: *sense based, thesaurus based, word usage based, language based.*
- Transliteration feature available which can help in effective reading.
- Can assist language translation task where multilinguality is primary concern.
- Can be referred for educational and social needs.
- Automatic word suggestion is assisted.
- Similar / closest word suggestion is assisted.
- Usage analysis and statistics available.
- Provides statistics such as most frequently searched word with respect to the selected language, input language searched, *etc.*

5   Limitations of IWN Dictionary

- It is a concept based dictionary, *i.e.,* for all the synonymous words, it will show only one gloss or a concept definition.
- Based entirely on WordNet as a backend resource, which is an ongoing development resource so issues/errors in WordNet data will also be propagated.
- Issues of WordNet can be its limitations like, word spellings, word senses, word relations, *etc.,* as found in corpus used for creating WordNet.
- Since the development of WordNet in all mentioned languages is not at the same pace, at times we may not get the meaning in a language if it does not exist in the database.
- The availability of words and their meanings depend upon how much the WordNet data is available.
- Features such as pronunciation, sound, pictures, domain, origin of a word, *etc.* are not incorporated due to unavailability of the same in the IndoWordNet.

6   Conclusion

In this paper, we have presented an online interface *viz. IWN Dictionary*. The IWN Dictionary renders IndoWordNet information in a systematic and classified manner, providing the look and feel of a traditional dictionary. There are various views; such as *sense based, thesaurus based, word usage based, language based* to view the IndoWordNet information. Transliteration feature is also provided in this interface for user readability. Rendering is done based on the user response and usage.

7   Future Scope and Enhancements

In future, we plan to expand this interface by including morph analyzer to process inflected input word. The ontological details along with semantic and lexical relations can be incorporated in the dictionary interface. Further, there can be a feature to link IndoWordNet dictionary to other available dictionaries along with the foreign language WordNets using WWDS. The features like picture, pronunciation, domain, source of a word, glossary, *etc.* can be implemented in the future versions. The transliteration feature to effectively read in one's native language can be implemented in this interface.

Acknowledgments

We graciously thank all the members of CFILT[11] Lab, IIT Bombay for providing necessary help and guidance needed for the development of *IndoWordNet Dictionary*. Further, we sincerely thank the members of IndoWordNet community and the users of IndoWordNet resource.

References

Anoop Kunchukuttan, Ratish Puduppully, Pushpak Bhattacharyya, *Brahmi-Net: A transliteration and script conversion system for languages of the Indian subcontinent*, Conference of the North American Chapter of the Association for Computational Linguistics (NAACL 2105) - Human Language Technologies: System Demonstrations. 2015

Christiane Fellbaum, (ed.) 1998, *WordNet: An Electronic Lexical Database*. The MIT Press.

Christodoulakis, Dimitris N. 2002. *BalkaNet: A Multilingual Semantic Network for Balkan Languages*. EUROPRIX Summer School, Salzburg Austria, September, 2002.

George Miller, R., Fellbaum, C., Gross, D., Miller, K. J. 1990. *Introduction to wordnet: An on-line lexical database*. International journal of lexicography, OUP. (pp. 3.4: 235-244).

Hanumant Redkar, Sudha Bhingardive, Diptesh Kanojia, and Pushpak Bhattacharyya. 2015. *World WordNet Database Structure: An Efficient Schema for Storing Information of WordNets of the World*. In Twenty-Ninth AAAI Conference on Artificial Intelligence, Austin, Texas.

Manish Sinha, Mahesh Reddy and Pushpak Bhattacharyya. 2006. *An Approach towards Construction and Application of Multilingual Indo-WordNet*. 3rd Global Wordnet Conference (GWC 06), Jeju Island, Korea, January, 2006.

Neha R Prabhugaonkar, Apurva S Nagvenkar, Ramdas N Karmali. 2012. *IndoWordNet Application Programming Interfaces*. COLING2012, Mumbai, India.

---

[11] http://www.cfilt.iitb.ac.in/

Pushpak Bhattacharyya. 2010. *IndoWordNet*. In the Proceedings of Lexical Resources Engineering Conference (LREC), Malta.

Pushpak Bhattacharyya, Ankit Bahuguna, Lavita Talukdar, and Bornali Phukan. . 2014 *Facilitating Multi-Lingual Sense Annotation: Human Mediated Lemmatizer*. In Global WordNet Conference, 2014.

Piek Vossen, (ed.) 1999. *EuroWordNet: A Multilingual Database with Lexical Semantic Networks for European languages*. Kluwer Academic Publishers, Dordrecht.

Rajat Mohanty, Pushpak Bhattacharyya, Prabhakar Pande, Shraddha Kalele, Mitesh Khapra and Aditya Sharma. 2008. *Synset based multilingual dictionary: Insights, applications and challenges*. Global WordNet Conference, Hungary, January 22-25.

Shikhar Sarma, Kr Sarma Dibyajyoti, Biswajit Brahma, Mayashree Mahanta, Himadri Bharali, and Utpal Saikia. 2012. *Building Multilingual Lexical Resources Using Wordnets: Structure, Design and Implementation*. 24th International Conference on Computational Linguistics. 2012.

Venkatesh Prabhu, Shilpa Desai, Hanumant Redkar, Neha Prabhugaonkar, Apurva Nagvenkar, Ramdas, Karmali. 2012. *An Efficient Database Design for IndoWordNet Development Using Hybrid Approach*. COLING 2012, Mumbai, India. p 229.

Veronika Vincze, György Szarvas, and János Csirik. 2008. *Why are wordnets important*. Proc. of 2nd ECC, Malta, WSEAS Press (2008): 316-322.

Let Sense Bags Do Talking: Cross Lingual Word Semantic Similarity for English and Hindi

Apurva Nagvenkar
DCST, Goa University
apurv.nagvenkar@gmail.com

Jyoti Pawar
DCST, Goa University
jyotidpawar@gmail.com

Pushpak Bhattacharyya
CSE, IIT Bombay
pb@cse.iitb.ac.in

Abstract

Cross Lingual Word Semantic (CLWS) similarity is defined as a task to find the semantic similarity between two words across languages. Semantic similarity has been very popular in computing the similarity between two words in same language. CLWS similarity will prove to be very effective in the area of Cross Lingual Information Retrieval, Machine Translation, Cross Lingual Word Sense Disambiguation, etc.

In this paper, we discuss a system that is developed to compute CLWS similarity of words between two languages, where one language is treated as resourceful and other is resource scarce. The system is developed using WordNet. The intuition behind this system is that, two words are semantically similar if their senses are similar to each other. The system is tested for English and Hindi with the accuracy 60.5% precision@1 and 72.91% precision@3.

1 Introduction

Word Semantic Similarity between two words is represented by the similarity between concepts associated with it. It plays a vital role in Natural Language Processing (NLP) and Information Retrieval (IR). In NLP (Sinha and Mihalcea, 2007), it is widely used in Word Sense Disambiguation, Question Answering system, Machine Translation (MT) etc. In IR (Hliaoutakis et al., 2006) it can be used in Image Retrieval, Multimodal Document Retrieval, Query Expansions etc.

The goal of CLWS Similarity is to measure the semantic similarity between the two words across languages. In this paper, we have proposed a system that computes CLWS similarity between two languages i.e. Language L_s and L_t, where L_s is treated as resourceful language and L_t is treated as resource scarce language. Given two words in language L_s and L_t the CLWS Similarity engine will analyze which two concepts of the word from L_s and L_t are similar. Let m & n be the number of concepts for the word in L_s & L_t respectively then, the output will generate a sorted list of all the possible combination of concepts (i.e. $m * n$ sorted list) ordered by their similarity score and the topmost combination of the concepts from L_s and L_t are similar to each other. The system is developed and tested for the English and Hindi language where English is L_s and Hindi is L_t.

1.1 Semantic Similarity

Lot of research effort has been devoted to design semantic similarity measures having monolingual as parameter. WordNet has been widely adopted in semantic similarity measures for English due its large hierarchical organization of synsets. Monolingual semantic similarity can be computed using Edge Counting and Information Content (IC). Edge counting is path based approach which makes use of knowledge bases. It measures the similarity by computing shortest distance from two concepts and the distance is nothing but a IS-A hierarchy. There are different path based measures such as Path Length Measure, Leacock and Chodorow Measure (Leacock and Chodorow, 1998), Wu & Palmer Measure (Wu and Palmer, 1994). IC is probabilistic based approach which makes use of corpus. It computes the negative logarithm of the probability of the occurrence of the concept in a large corpus. The different IC approaches are Resnik Measure (Resnik, 1995), Jiang Conrath Measure (Jiang and Conrath, 1997), Lin Measure (Lin, 1998), etc.

75

D S Sharma, R Sangal and E Sherly. Proc. of the 12th Intl. Conference on Natural Language Processing, pages 79–83,
Trivandrum, India. December 2015. ©2015 NLP Association of India (NLPAI)

2   The Proposed Idea

The aim of our work is to design a CLWS similarity engine that computes similarity between two words across languages. So, given a word in English and Hindi the system will analyze which two synsets of the words are similar by making use of WordNet.

To obtain CLWS similarity we follow the following steps.

1. Given a word W_{EN} and W_{HN} and its senses must be present in their respective WordNets i.e. English and Hindi WordNet.

2. Let $S_{EN} = \{s_{EN}^1, s_{EN}^2 ... s_{EN}^m\}$ & $S_{HN} = \{s_{HN}^1, s_{HN}^2 ... s_{HN}^n\}$ be the set sense bags. The sense bags are obtained from its synset constituents i.e. content words from concept, examples, synonyms and hypernym (depth=1). We make sure that the words in sense bag must be present in the WordNet.

3. S_{HN} Hindi sense bags must be translated to resourceful language i.e. English. The translations are obtained by making use of bilingual dictionary or GIZA++ (Och and Ney, 2003) aligner that identifies the word alignment considering a parallel corpus.

We say that two words are semantically similar if

1. W_{EN} is compared with s_{EN}^i and s_{HN}^j then their score must be similar. i.e. $CLWS_w(W_{EN}, s_{EN}^i) \approx CLWS_w^{tr}(W_{EN}, s_{HN}^j)$ this is further explained in section 3.1.

2. If they have similar sense bags. i.e. $CLWS_s(s_{EN}^i, s_{HN}^j) \approx 1$ & $CLWS_s^{weight}(w_{EN}, s_{EN}^i, s_{HN}^j) \approx 1$ this is further explained in section 3.2.1 and section 3.2.2.

3   CLWS Similarity Measures

Following are the different measures that are used to compute CLWS similarity score.

3.1   Measure 1: Word to Sense Bag Similarity Measure

In this measure, the source word W_{EN} is compared with the words present in the sense bag using monolingual similarity function i.e. equation (1). Where the parameters w_1 & w_2 are the words from the source (English) language and the parameter τ is the approach viz. obtained from either edge counting or information content.

$$sim(w_1, w_2, \tau) \tag{1}$$

3.1.1   Source Word to Source Sense Bag Similarity Measure

The source word i.e. W_{EN} is compared with the words present in the source sense bag s_{EN}^i i.e. $s_{EN}^i = (ew_1, ew_2, .., ew_p)$. So, W_{EN} is compared with the first word ew_1 from s_{EN}^i using monolingual similarity function i.e. $sim(W_{EN}, ew_1, \tau)$ the same procedure is applied for the other words from the source sense bag and we obtain the following measure.

$$CLWS_w(W_{EN}, s_{EN}^i) = \frac{1}{p} \sum_{k}^{p} sim(W_{EN}, ew_k, \tau) \tag{2}$$

3.1.2   Source Word to Target Sense Bag Similarity Measure

Here, the source word i.e. W_{EN} is compared with the words present in the target (Hindi) sense bag s_{HN}^j i.e. $s_{HN}^j = (hw_1, hw_2, .., hw_q)$. So, W_{EN} is compared with the first word hw_1 from s_{HN}^j. In this case, hw_1 is replaced with its translation. If a word has more than one translation then maximum score between the translations is considered to be the winner candidate (equation (3)). The same procedure is applied for the other words from the target sense bag and we obtain the equation (4) for this measure.

$$sim_{tr}(W_{EN}, hw_j, \tau) = \max_{k=1}^{l} sim\left(W_{EN}, ew_k^{tr}, \tau\right)$$
$$where\ hw_j = (ew_1^{tr}, ew_2^{tr}, .., ew_l^{tr}) \tag{3}$$

$$CLWS_w^{tr}(W_{EN}, s_{HN}^j) = \frac{1}{q} \sum_{k=1}^{q} sim_{tr}(W_{EN}, hw_k, \tau) \tag{4}$$

We say that, two (source and target) sense bags are similar to each other if they are related to the source word.

$$score_1 = 1 - \mid CLWS_w(W_{EN}, s_{EN}^i)$$
$$- CLWS_w^{tr}(W_{EN}, s_{HN}^j) \mid \tag{5}$$

3.2   Sense Bag to Sense Bag Similarity Measure

In this measure, the source sense bag s_{EN}^i is compared with target sense bag s_{HN}^j.

3.2.1 Measure 2: Sense Bag to Sense Bag Similarity without weight

In this measure, every word from $s_{EN}{}^i$ is compared with all the words from $s_{HN}{}^j$. For example, the first word ew_1 is compared with all the words from $S_{HN}{}^j$ using equation (3) and the maximum score is retrieved. The same process is continued for the remaining words present in the source sense bag to get equation (6).

$$CLWS_s(s_{EN}{}^i, s_{HN}{}^j)$$
$$= \frac{1}{p} \sum_{k=1}^{p} \left(\max_{l=1}^{q} sim_{tr}(ew_k, hw_l, \tau) \right) \quad (6)$$

$$score_2 = CLWS_s(s_{EN}{}^i, s_{HN}{}^j) \quad (7)$$

3.2.2 Measure 3: Sense Bag to Sense Bag Similarity with weight

This is similar to the above measure (Section 3.2.1) but at every iteration the weights are assigned to the words that are compared. Every word from both the sense bags is assigned with a weight viz. obtained by comparing it with the source word i.e. W_{EN}, by using equation(1) & (3). This weight depicts how closely the words from sense bags are related to W_{EN}.

$$CLWS_s{}^{weight}(w_{EN}, s_{EN}{}^i, s_{HN}{}^j) =$$
$$\frac{1}{p} \sum_{k=1}^{p} sim(w_{EN}, ew_k, \tau)$$
$$\times \max_{l=1}^{q} \left(sim_{tr}(w_{EN}, hw_l, \tau) \times sim_{tr}(ew_k, hw_l, \tau) \right) \quad (8)$$

$$score_3 = CLWS_s{}^{weight}(w_{EN}, s_{EN}{}^i, s_{HN}{}^j) \quad (9)$$

3.3 Measure 4: Incorporating Monolingual Corpus

To check the frequency of a sense we compare the sense bag to a large monolingual corpora. A context bag (CB_{EN}), is obtained for a word W_{EN} by using word2vec[1] toolkit (Mikolov et al., 2013). CB_{EN} is compared with all the sense bags of S_{EN} (using Sense Bag to Sense Bag Similarity with weight since, it gives higher accuracy than others, refer section 5.3). This method will assign a similarity score to all the sense bags. The sense bag with most frequent usage will be assigned with high value than the sense bag with low frequent usage. This score is further multiplied with the similarity score obtained from $s_{EN}{}^i$ and $s_{HN}{}^j$.

$$score_4 = CLWS_s{}^{weight}(w_{EN}, s_{EN}{}^i, CB_{EN})$$
$$\times CLWS_s{}^{weight}(w_{EN}, s_{EN}{}^i, s_{HN}{}^j) \quad (10)$$

4 Resources and Dataset Used

Princeton WordNet (Miller et al., 1990) has 117791 synsets and 147478 words whereas, Hindi WordNet (Bhattacharyya, 2010) has 38782 synsets and 99435 words in its inventory. These wordNets are used to derive sense bags for each language. We have used publicly available pre-trained word embeddings for English which are trained on Google News dataset[2] (about 100 billion words). These word embeddings are available for around 3 million words and phrases. We also make use of ILCI parallel corpus[3] to obtain the word alignment of Hindi with respect to English for translating Hindi word to English. The size of ILCI corpus contains 50,000 parallel sentences.

To check the performance of our system we need to evaluate it against human judgment. Currently, synset linking task is carried out at CFILT[4], this task is carried out manually where the word-pairs (Hindi-English) across the languages having the similar senses are linked together. We take 2000 word pairs for development. Figure 1 shows the number of occurrences of degree of polysemy for English and Hindi words as well as the word pairs (i.e. the product of degree of polysemy for English and Hindi word) that are used in development of the system.

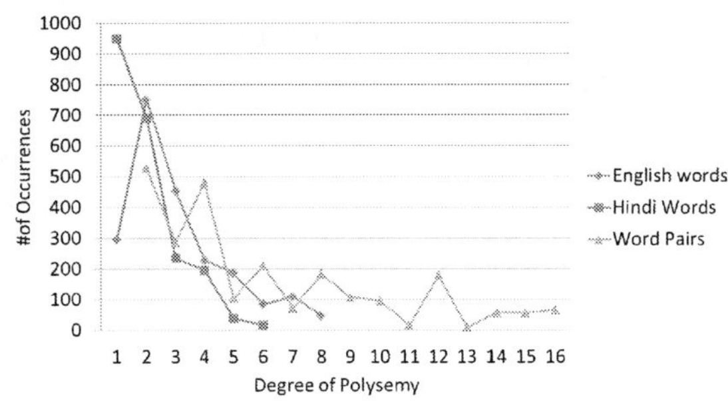

Figure 1: degree of polysemy v/s #of occurrences

[1]https://code.google.com/p/word2vec/

[2]Downloaded from https://code.google.com/p/word2vec/

[3]Downloaded from http://tdil-dc.in/

[4]http://www.cfilt.iitb.ac.in/

5 Experimental Results

For system evaluation we take 80% of word pairs for training and 20% of word pairs for testing. The system is evaluated for all the measures described above. To get the best possible accuracy we have to set following parameters at training:

- α - threshold value that will decide the size of sense bag

- τ - the monolingual similarity measures like PATH, JCN, LIN, WUP, etc.

5.1 The Baseline system

To date, there is no work carried out in computing the CLWS similarity for English and Hindi word pairs. So we define our own baseline system. The synsets in English and Hindi WordNet are organized based on their most frequent sense usage. As a baseline we say that given a word pair their most frequent sense is similar to each other. The baseline system makes an assumption by considering most frequent sense for both the word pairs. So, given a word in English and Hindi their most frequent sense are similar to each other.

5.2 The size of sense bag

The IC measures the specificity of the concept (Pedersen, 2010). The general concepts are assigned low value and specific concepts are assigned high value. In this scenario, we measure the specificity of the word instead of concept i.e. $IC(w) = -log(P(w))$. The IC value is computed for every word present in the sense bag. The size of sense bag depends on the IC threshold i.e. α. The sense bag will contain only those words with $IC(w) \geq \alpha$. Figure 2 shows how the size of the sense bag affects the performance of the system. In this, figure the α value is iterated from 0 to 13. When $\alpha = 0$ the sense bag will contain all the words but as α value increases to t it will contain only those word whose $IC(w) \geq t$. The system reported best performance when the size of sense bag was 6.

5.3 Results

The system is also evaluated by making use of bilingual dictionary and GIZA++ for word alignment. The reason behind this is that many of the under resource languages may not have well defined bilingual dictionary and therefore we used unsupervised approach i.e. word alignment.

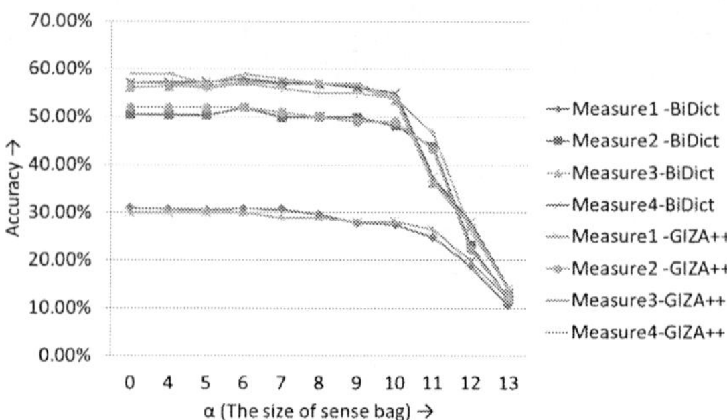

Figure 2: Accuracy of the CLWS Similarity when α value iterated from 0 to 13.

After training the CLWS similarity system, parameters were assigned with values α=6.0 and τ=RES.

Baseline	Precision					
	42%					
	Bilingual Dictionary			GIZA++		
	P@1	P@2	P@3	P@1	P@2	P@3
Measure1	25.5%	34.38%	45.0%	22.7%	28.21%	36.97%
Measure2	51.0%	64.91%	72.91%	42.2%	56.78%	63.44%
Measure3	58.5%	65.26%	73.3%	47.34%	56.78%	64.70%
Measure4	60.5%	65.26%	72.91%	52.65%	59.64%	69.74%

Table 1: Accuracy of CLWS Similarity measures computed from test dataset of 400 word pairs.

Table 1 contains the accuracy in terms of precision of the system computed from test dataset i.e. 400 word pairs. Form the table it is very clear that the system outperforms baseline system in most of the cases. The system performs best for Measure 4 with precision 60.5% .

6 Conclusion and Future Work

In this paper we presented several measures that are used to achieve the CLWS similarity. The main objective is to compute CLWS similarity for settings in which one language has many resources and the other is resource scarce. The system is tested for English-Hindi language pair and demonstrates which approach is better over the other. The accuracy of the system is further enhanced by making use of large monolingual corpora and Word2vec toolkit. We achieve 60.5% precision@1 and 72.91% precision@3 for English and Hindi word pairs.

In future we will like to implement the CLWS similarity for other resource scarce languages. CLWS similarity models are very much required for resource scarce languages but we need to think about the ways to reduce dependency of existing resources by making use of mathematical modeling.

References

Pushpak Bhattacharyya. 2010. Indowordnet. In Nicoletta Calzolari, Khalid Choukri, Bente Maegaard, Joseph Mariani, Jan Odijk, Stelios Piperidis, Mike Rosner, and Daniel Tapias, editors, *LREC*. European Language Resources Association.

Angelos Hliaoutakis, Giannis Varelas, Epimeneidis Voutsakis, Euripides G. M. Petrakis, and Evangelos Milios. 2006. Information retrieval by semantic similarity. In *Intern. Journal on Semantic Web and Information Systems (IJSWIS), 3(3):5573, July/Sept. 2006. Special Issue of Multimedia Semantics.*

J.J. Jiang and D.W. Conrath. 1997. Semantic similarity based on corpus statistics and lexical taxonomy. In *Proc. of the Int'l. Conf. on Research in Computational Linguistics*, pages 19–33.

C. Leacock and M. Chodorow. 1998. Combining local context and wordnet similarity for word sense identification. In Christiane Fellfaum, editor, *MIT Press*, pages 265–283, Cambridge, Massachusetts.

Dekang Lin. 1998. An information-theoretic definition of similarity. In *Proceedings of the Fifteenth International Conference on Machine Learning*, ICML '98, pages 296–304, San Francisco, CA, USA. Morgan Kaufmann Publishers Inc.

Tomas Mikolov, Kai Chen, Greg Corrado, and Jeffrey Dean. 2013. Efficient estimation of word representations in vector space. *CoRR*, abs/1301.3781.

George A. Miller, Richard Beckwith, Christiane Fellbaum, Derek Gross, and Katherine Miller. 1990. Wordnet: An on-line lexical database. *International Journal of Lexicography*, 3:235–244.

Franz Josef Och and Hermann Ney. 2003. A systematic comparison of various statistical alignment models. *Computational Linguistics*, 29(1):19–51.

Ted Pedersen. 2010. Information content measures of semantic similarity perform better without sense-tagged text. In *Human Language Technologies: The 2010 Annual Conference of the North American Chapter of the Association for Computational Linguistics*, HLT '10, pages 329–332, Stroudsburg, PA, USA. Association for Computational Linguistics.

Philip Resnik. 1995. Using information content to evaluate semantic similarity in a taxonomy. In *Proceedings of the 14th International Joint Conference on Artificial Intelligence - Volume 1*, IJCAI'95, pages 448–453, San Francisco, CA, USA. Morgan Kaufmann Publishers Inc.

Ravi Sinha and Rada Mihalcea. 2007. Unsupervised graph-basedword sense disambiguation using measures of word semantic similarity. In *Proceedings of the International Conference on Semantic Computing*, ICSC '07, pages 363–369, Washington, DC, USA. IEEE Computer Society.

Zhibiao Wu and Martha Palmer. 1994. Verbs semantics and lexical selection. In *Proceedings of the 32Nd Annual Meeting on Association for Computational Linguistics*, ACL '94, pages 133–138, Stroudsburg, PA, USA. Association for Computational Linguistics.

A temporal expression recognition system for medical documents by taking help of news domain corpora

Naman Gupta[1]   Aditya Joshi[1,2,3]
Pushpak Bhattacharyya[1]
[1]IIT Bombay, India, [2]Monash University, Australia
[3]IITB-Monash Research Academy, India
`{adityaj,pb}@cse.iitb.ac.in`
`namanbbps@gmail.com`

Abstract

A bottleneck for medical domain Temporal Expression Recognition (TER) is the availability of data. An open-domain TER system may not be able to capture domain-specific expressions, while domain-specific TER may be cumbersome to implement. We present a novel neural network based medical TER system that uses corpora from news and medical domains. Thus, it serves as a middle ground between an open-domain and a domain-specific TER. We show that our system outperforms state-of-art open-domain baselines, and gets close to domain-specific skylines. Thus, our system proves to be a promising alternative for domain specific TER for domains where data may be limited.

1 Introduction

Temporal Expression Recognition (TER) is the process of locating phrases that denote temporal information. Temporal expressions may be an expressed point in time, a duration or a frequency (Wikipedia, 2014). These expressions can be used in information extraction and question-answering to (a) answer time-specific queries, (b) arrange information in a chronological manner, etc. Early work in TER considers it as a part of named entity recognition (Bikel et al., 1999). TER, as a separate task, was introduced as Temporal Expression Recognition and Normalization (TERN). TER in general domain has been widely studied. Rule-based methods for specific domains were adopted by popular systems like Heideltime (Strötgen and Gertz, 2010), SUTime (Chang and Manning, 2012), MayoTime (Sohn et al., 2013). The rules were regular expressions over word or tokens. Supervised Classifiers like SVM, CRF using linguistic features have been explored (Adafre and de Rijke, 2005; Bethard, 2013). Joint inference-based classifiers like Markov Logic have also been reported (UzZaman and Allen, 2010). Medical domain TER (Sun et al., 2013; Bethard et al., 2015) has resulted in alternate methods and systems for detecting and normalizing temporal expressions. Our system uses a neural network based architecture which has hitherto not been used for TER. In addition, we also deal with a specific situation: In-domain data being difficult to obtain. Research in TER mostly deals with news domain text, arguably because of availability of large corpora and abundance of temporal expressions in news documents. In recent times, TER has also been applied to other domains like medical. Approaches for medical domain TER in the past have been either rule-based (Sohn et al., 2013; Jindal and Roth, 2013), statistical (Xu et al., 2013; Roberts et al., 2013) or hybrid (Lin et al., 2013).

However, a bottleneck for medical domain TER is the **availability of data**. Medical documents such as discharge summaries are of classified nature, and also must be de-identified (*i.e.*, anonymized) before being used. **Our paper is motivated by this limitation**. An open-domain TER system (*i.e.*, a TER not learned from medical domain data) may not be able to capture domain-specific expressions (for example, Latin acronyms like *bid, tid* that are used in medical documents). On the other hand, a domain-specific TER system is time-consuming to construct[1].We address the question:

Can a TER system that uses documents of two domains serve as a middle ground between an open-domain and a domain-specific TER, in case domain-specific data is difficult to obtain ?

The novelty of our work lies in: (a) A simple yet effective neural network based architecture for

---

[1]This holds irrespective of whether it is rule-based or statistical.

D S Sharma, R Sangal and E Sherly. Proc. of the 12th Intl. Conference on Natural Language Processing, pages 84–88,
Trivandrum, India. December 2015. ©2015 NLP Association of India (NLPAI)

TER, (b) Use of a combination of open-domain and domain-specific data. Thus, **our TER system combines information from medical and news domain, to perform TER of medical documents.** In the rest of the paper, we refer to news as out-of-domain corpora, and medical documents as in-domain corpora.

2 Our System: Neural Network based TER

In the past, TER has been modeled either as a sequence labeling (Bethard, 2013) or a classification task (Tissot et al., 2015). We choose the latter design. Our model takes as input a word and outputs the most probable tag. We have used 9 tags, namely *B-DATE, B-DURATION, B-FREQUENCY, B-TIME, I-DATE, I-DURATION, I-FREQUENCY, I-TIME and O*. For a temporal expression, B,I,O indicate beginning, inside and outside respectively.

Our three-layer neural network model is shown in Figure 1. It makes use of vector representation of words. Mikolov et al. (2013) proposed a computationally efficient method for learning distributed word representation such that words with similar meanings will map to similar vectors. We use the same approach for learning word vectors using word2vec (https://code.google.com/p/word2vec/). Table 1 shows nearest neighbors for four sample words that are commonly used as temporal expressions. We then create a *lookup table* $LT \in \mathbb{R}^{|C| \times d}$ to store a d-dimensional representation of every word in vocabulary C.

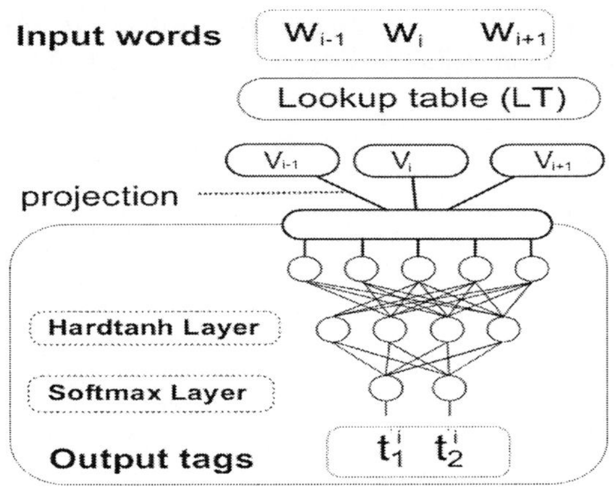

Figure 1: Our Neural network-based architecture

A neural network is trained with a word as a data unit. First, the size of a context window

w_s is chosen. The word along with its context words forms a n-gram sequence S represented as $\{W_{i-1}, W_i, W_{i+1}\}$ in the network. Every word W_i is mapped to its corresponding word vector V_i using lookup table LT. Word vectors V_i's are projected onto the input layer. In order to preserve word order, projection concatenates the word vectors into single vector $X \in \mathbb{R}^{|w_s * d|}$ which are passed to non-linear *hardtanh* layer.

After applying the $hardtanh$ transformation, we get the H as the output of the hidden layer

$$H = hardtanh(W_1^T X + b_1) \qquad (1)$$

We then transform the output of the hidden layer using a *softmax* layer.

$$O = W_2^T H + b_2 \qquad (2)$$

The output layer $O \in \mathbb{R}^t$ has the dimensionality of number of tags t. Errors on cost are back propagated into the network using back-propagation algorithm (Russell and Norvig, 1967) to generate probability distribution over output tags t_1^i, t_2^i.

qd	postop	admission	tuesday
tid	post-operative	transfer	sunday
qid	post-op	discharge	saturday
qday	hospital	admit	monday
qam	day	preoperative	march
daily	life	0/0/0	august
qhs	number	report	thursday
q0s	post-day	summary	january

Table 1: Nearest neighbors for sample temporal expressions

3 Experimental Setup

We evaluate our systems in three settings: (1) **Overlap**, where overlapping spans are considered as match, (2) **Exact**, where precise matches are counted, and (3) **Partial**, where full credit is awarded for exact match, and half credit for overlapping match. All the systems (baseline, skyline and our system) are tested on a publicly available dataset from the i2b2 2012 Temporal Relation Challenge (Sun et al., 2013). This is a benchmark dataset, and consists of 120 discharge summaries from Partners Healthcare and Beth Israel Deaconess Medical Center.

Type	Sentences	Tokens	Vocabulary
Medical	20,125	481,601	12,142
News	24.445	717,698	30,527

Table 2: Statistics of the datasets

	Overlap			Partial			Exact		
	P	**R**	**F**	**P**	**R**	**F**	**P**	**R**	**F**
BL - SUTime (RB)	73.53	74.78	**74.15**	62.75	63.82	**63.28**	51.97	52.86	**52.41**
BL - Heideltime (RB)	79.92	56.43	**66.15**	72.10	50.91	**59.68**	64.28	45.38	**53.20**
BL - ClearTk (ST)	44.36	19.34	**26.94**	34.41	15.05	**20.95**	24.46	10.77	**14.95**
SL-Rule	87.91	92.25	**90.02**	79.86	83.98	**81.87**	71.81	75.71	**73.71**
SL-Stat	95.13	83.74	**89.07**	89.11	78.46	**83.45**	83.09	73.19	**77.83**
Our System: News	86.18	77.36	**81.53**	74.28	66.70	**70.29**	62.39	56.04	**59.04**
Our System: News + Medical	81.37	86.98	**84.08**	73.19	78.10	**75.57**	65.02	69.23	**67.06**

Table 3: Comparison of our system with baseline (BL-*) and skyline (SL-*) systems

3.1 Datasets

The datasets used for training word vectors were created as follows. The statistics are shown in Table 2.

1. **In-domain dataset**: Medical discharge summaries are collected from i2b2. The documents are pre-processed by removing markup tags and irrelevant information in the form of document numbers and codes.

2. **Out-of-domain dataset**: Out-of-domain word vectors are learned from Timebank, AQUAINT (Pustejovsky et al., 2003), and TE-3 silver dataset (UzZaman et al., 2012)

3.2 Baseline: Open-domain TER

Rule-based temporal taggers like Heideltime (Strötgen and Gertz, 2010) and SUTime (Chang and Manning, 2012) and Statistical tagger like ClearTk[2] were developed as a part of TempEval-2,3 challenges for news text. They are our baselines: BL-SUTime, BL-Heideltime, and BL-ClearTk.

3.3 Skyline: Medical TER

State-of-art rule-based (Sohn et al., 2013) and a statistical (Roberts et al., 2013) medical domain TER systems are chosen as skylines. These system (indicated by SL-Rule and SL-Stat respectively) were developed as a part of i2b2 2012 challenge, and trained on medical data. We call them as skyline because the availability of medical data itself is the best situation for medical TER.

---

[2]https://code.google.com/p/cleartk/
wiki/ClearTKTimeML

4 Results

We now compare our results of our system with the existing systems, and then describe how proportion of in-domain data impacts the performance. Finally, we discuss a detailed error analysis.

4.1 Comparative performance against baseline and skyline

Table 3 compares the performance of the baseline (**BL-***) (first three rows) and skyline (**SL-***) approaches (next two rows) with our system, for overlap, partial and exact matches. For our system, we experiment with two settings: (1) Word vectors trained on out-of-domain dataset (indicated by **Our System: News**), and (2) Word vectors trained on both datasets (indicated by **Our System: News + Medical**). In case of overlap match, the best performance of baseline systems is 74.15% in case of BL-SUTime. When neural network architecture is used **even in absence of any in-domain data**, the F-score increases to 81.53%. This value rises to 84.08% when a combination of medical and news domain is used.

SL-Rule and SL-Stat were created for medical TER. In case of our premise, medical data is difficult to obtain. Our system shows that by mixing out-of-domain (news) data with in-domain (medical) data, we can get close to the skyline performance. This degradation in performance is likely to be because of the small size of medical domain corpora available for training word vectors. It must be noted that while our dataset has 12,142 (as shown in Table 2) unique tokens, the corresponding value is usually much higher. For example, the pre-trained vectors trained on Google

News dataset had a vocabulary size of 300K[3].

4.2 Impact of proportion of in-domain data

Availability of in-domain data is restricted for medical documents as compared to news text. To find how our system peforms if a combination of in-domain and out-of-domain data is to be used, we conduct experiments by incrementally adding in-domain data to learn word vectors. Figure 2 plots the F-score against the percentage of total in-domain data used during training. 10 on the X-axis indicates that 10% of the total available medical domain data (along with the complete news data) was used during training. For all three kinds of matches, the F-score stabilizes beyond 40% (which is 5K sentences). There is a dip in performance for all three matches when 10% medical data is used. This may be due to dilution of word vectors, since only a small portion of a new domain has been added to the training set.

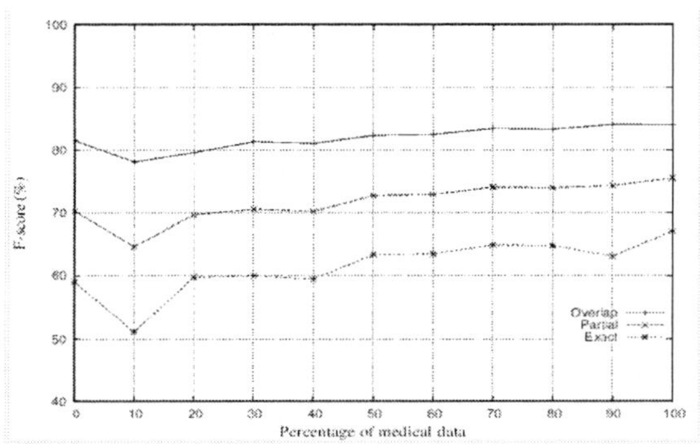

Figure 2: Performance of our system on addition of in-domain data

4.3 Error Analysis

We manually labeled 468 erroneous instances into one out of 11 broad categories. The distribution of these errors is shown in Figure 3.

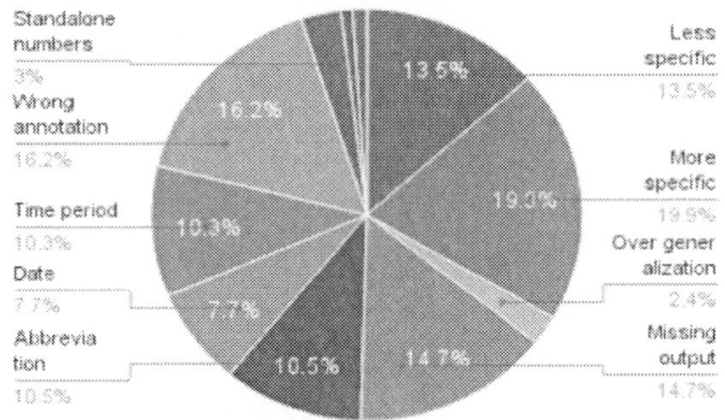

Figure 3: Distribution of errors made by our system

[3]https://code.google.com/p/word2vec/

'More specific' errors form 19.9% of total errors. This means that our system could extract temporal expressions that were more specific than the annotations. For example, our system tags *'one day prior to admission'* when only *'one day'* was expected. 16.2% of our errors arise due to wrong annotations. 'More specific' output is acceptable. 'Wrong annotations' are the ones where a second manual check revealed that the labels were disputable. Thus, **36% errors do not directly point to deficiencies in the system**.

'Less specific' errors (13.5%) are when our system leaves out a part of the temporal expression. 10.3% of errors are related to time periods and frequency-related words like *'daily'*. Overgeneralization errors are said to occur when an extracted time expression contains some non-time-related words. Medical domain text is fraught with abbreviations (such as q.i.d.) leading to 10.5% errors, and peculiar date formats (for example, 12-20 as a date indicates 20th December) leading to 7.7% errors. 'Special' words are related to seasons and events like Halloween. Standalone numbers indicate situations like the '2' in 'see you at 2'. The 'Others' category includes errors due to garbled characters, relative days ('tomorrow'), ordinal numbers and WSD errors (two senses of 'may' can be derived out of 'this may', in absence of capitalized 'M')

5 Conclusion & Future Work

We presented a simple yet effective three-layer neural network based TER system for medical domain. Our system used out-of-domain news text to extract temporal expressions from medical documents. Our system, without any in-domain data at all, improves the F-score by 7% over three baseline systems, and to a greater degree when in-domain data is used. With a dataset of 5K medical domain sentences, we obtain a good performance . Our error analysis showed that the top three kinds of errors are: 'More specific output', 'Wrong annotations' and 'Missing output'. We, thus, show that our TER system can act as a middle ground between an open-domain and a domain-specific TER, in situations where in-domain data is difficult to obtain. A possible future work is to model TER as a sequence labeling task while still using a neural network based system.

References

Sisay Fissaha Adafre and Maarten de Rijke. 2005. Feature engineering and post-processing for temporal expression recognition using conditional random fields. In *Proceedings of the ACL Workshop on Feature Engineering for Machine Learning in Natural Language Processing*, pages 9–16. Association for Computational Linguistics.

Steven Bethard, Leon Derczynski, James Pustejovsky, and Marc Verhagen. 2015. Semeval-2015 task 6: Clinical tempeval. In *Proceedings of the 9th International Workshop on Semantic Evaluation (SemEval 2015). Association for Computational Linguistics.*

Steven Bethard. 2013. Cleartk-timeml: A minimalist approach to tempeval 2013. In *Second Joint Conference on Lexical and Computational Semantics (* SEM)*, volume 2, pages 10–14.

Daniel M. Bikel, Richard Schwartz, and Ralph M. Weischedel. 1999. An algorithm that learns whats in a name. *Mach. Learn.*, 34(1-3):211–231, feb.

Angel X Chang and Christopher D Manning. 2012. Sutime: A library for recognizing and normalizing time expressions. In *LREC*, pages 3735–3740.

Prateek Jindal and Dan Roth. 2013. Extraction of events and temporal expressions from clinical narratives. *Journal of biomedical informatics*, 46:S13–S19.

Yu-Kai Lin, Hsinchun Chen, and Randall A Brown. 2013. Medtime: A temporal information extraction system for clinical narratives. *Journal of biomedical informatics*, 46:S20–S28.

Tomas Mikolov, Kai Chen, Greg Corrado, and Jeffrey Dean. 2013. Efficient estimation of word representations in vector space. *CoRR*, abs/1301.3781.

James Pustejovsky, Patrick Hanks, Roser Sauri, Andrew See, Robert Gaizauskas, Andrea Setzer, Dragomir Radev, Beth Sundheim, David Day, Lisa Ferro, et al. 2003. The timebank corpus. In *Corpus linguistics*, volume 2003, page 40.

Kirk Roberts, Bryan Rink, and Sanda M Harabagiu. 2013. A flexible framework for recognizing events, temporal expressions, and temporal relations in clinical text. *Journal of the American Medical Informatics Association*, 20(5):867–875.

S Russell and P Norvig. 1967. The most popular method for learning in multilayer networks is called back-propagation. *Artif. Intel. Mod. Approach*, pages 201–218.

Sunghwan Sohn, Kavishwar B Wagholikar, Dingcheng Li, Siddhartha R Jonnalagadda, Cui Tao, Ravikumar Komandur Elayavilli, and Hongfang Liu. 2013. Comprehensive temporal information detection from clinical text: medical events, time, and tlink identification. *Journal of the American Medical Informatics Association*, 20(5):836–842.

Jannik Strötgen and Michael Gertz. 2010. Heideltime: High quality rule-based extraction and normalization of temporal expressions. In *Proceedings of the 5th International Workshop on Semantic Evaluation*, pages 321–324. Association for Computational Linguistics.

Weiyi Sun, Anna Rumshisky, and Ozlem Uzuner. 2013. Evaluating temporal relations in clinical text: 2012 i2b2 challenge. *Journal of the American Medical Informatics Association*, 20(5):806–813.

Hegler Tissot, Cel Franc H dos Santos, Genevieve Gorrell, Angus Roberts, Leon Derczynski, and Marcos Didonet Del Fabro. 2015. Ufprsheffield: Contrasting rule-based and support vector machine approaches to time expression identification in clinical tempeval.

Naushad UzZaman and James F Allen. 2010. Trips and trios system for tempeval-2: Extracting temporal information from text. In *Proceedings of the 5th International Workshop on Semantic Evaluation*, pages 276–283. Association for Computational Linguistics.

Naushad UzZaman, Hector Llorens, James Allen, Leon Derczynski, Marc Verhagen, and James Pustejovsky. 2012. Tempeval-3: Evaluating events, time expressions, and temporal relations. *arXiv preprint arXiv:1206.5333*.

Wikipedia. 2014. Temporal expressions — wikipedia, the free encyclopedia. [Online; accessed 12-June-2015].

Yan Xu, Yining Wang, Tianren Liu, Junichi Tsujii, I Eric, and Chao Chang. 2013. An end-to-end system to identify temporal relation in discharge summaries: 2012 i2b2 challenge. *Journal of the American Medical Informatics Association*, 20(5):849–858.

An unsupervised EM method to infer time variation in sense probabilities

Martin Emms
Dept of Computer Science
Trinity College, Dublin
Ireland
`martin.emms@cs.tcd.ie`

Arun Jayapal
Dept of Computer Science
Trinity College, Dublin
Ireland
`jayapala@cs.tcd.ie`

Abstract

The inventory of senses for a given word changes over time – *tweet* has gained the 'Twitter post' sense only relatively recently and this paper addresses the problem of the computational detection of such change. We propose a generative model which conditions context words on a target expression's sense and conditions the sense choice on the *time* of writing. We develop an EM algorithm to estimate the parameters from raw time-stamped n-gram data with no sense annotation. We are able to demonstrate the inference of parameters which plausibly reflect the objective dynamics of sense use frequencies, in particular the emergence of a new sense.

1 Introduction

Many words are ambiguous so that a simple count of a word frequency is really a sum of several word-*sense* frequencies. It is also the case that over time the inventory of senses possessed by a word *changes* and there must be a point in time where a given sense first came into use: the 'Twitter post' sense of *tweet* is an example of a relatively recent new arrival. Fig 1 summarises the

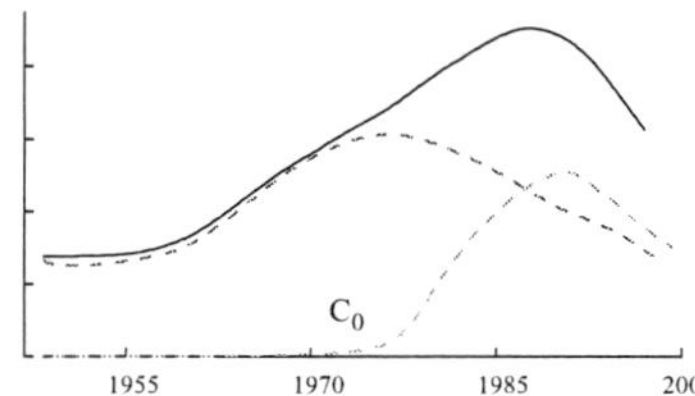

Figure 1: Word frequency (solid line) and sense frequencies (dashed lines).

situation abstractly, with the solid black-line a plot of simple word frequency over time (as might easily be produced the Google n-gram viewer), and

the dashed lines a hypothetical decomposition into two senses, with one of the senses first emerging around 1970. Essentially the aim of the paper is to propose a method which can carry out this kind of decomposition and then use it to detect the time of emergence of a novel sense: we have marked this point C_0 in the sense plot.

As lexical information is central to so many NLP tasks, means to automatically identify *changes* to the required information could be useful. For example, if an SMT system trained from aligned corpora from particular times is to be applied to text from different times it could be of use to know whether there have been sense changes, perhaps identifying which occurrences can be anticipated to be poorly translated. Overlooking this is perhaps what underlies the following case of poor translation fron English to Tamil via Google translate:

S1. With Clara, however, his brow cleared, and he was gay again (from 'sons and lovers' by D.H. Lawrence 1931:)

T1. கிளாரா ஆயினும் அவரது புருவம் அகற்றப்படும் மற்றும் அவர் மீண்டும் ஓரினச்சேர்க்கையாளர்

L1. Kiḷārā, āyinum, avaratu puruvam akaṟṟappaṭum, maṟṟum avar mīṇṭum ōriṇaccērkkaiyāḷar

The English original, S1, comes from 1931, at which time *gay* simply meant 'happy'. In recent decades it has overwhelmingly gained the sense 'homosexual'. T1 and L1 are the Tamil translation and its transliteration where the word is translated as *ōriṇaccērkkaiyāḷar*, which has the 'homosexual' sense.

We will propose a relatively simple probabilistic model which conditions words in a target's context on that target's sense and conditions senses on times, which incorporates an independence assumption that the context words are independent of time given the target's sense. We use the Google n-gram data set (Michel et al., 2011) which provides time-stamped data but *no* sense information and develop an EM algorithm to estimate

85

D S Sharma, R Sangal and E Sherly. Proc. of the 12th Intl. Conference on Natural Language Processing, pages 89–94,
Trivandrum, India. December 2015. ©2015 NLP Association of India (NLPAI)

the model's parameters in an unsupervised fashion from this data. We will show that the algorithm is able to provide an accurate date of sense emergence (true positives), and also to detect the absence of sense emergence when appropriate (true negatives). We make some points also concerning the difficulties in the evaluation of such a sense-emergence system.

2 A model with time-dependent senses

It is intuitive that the distribution of words in the context of given target word is not independent of the sense of that target and this leads to approaches to unsupervised word-sense disambiguation which seek to model that dependency (Manning and Schütze, 2003). These approaches also include a *prior* on the different senses. We essentially generalise this by having a *succession of priors*, one for each time period.

To make this more precise, assume a data item d represents a particular occurrence of a target expression T, and let $\vec{W}$ be the sequence of words in a window around T and let Y be its time-stamp. Suppose there are k different senses of T, modeled with a discrete variable S. A *complete* data item is to be thought of as providing values for Y, S and $\vec{W}$; raw data will be *incomplete* concerning S, the sense. $p(Y, S, \vec{W})$ may factorised as $p(Y)p(S|Y)p(\vec{W}|S, Y)$ without loss of generality. We then make some independence assumptions: (i) that conditioned on S the words $\vec{W}$ are independent of Y, so $p(\vec{W}|S, Y) = p(\vec{W}|S)$ and (ii) that conditioned on S the words are independent of each other, so $p(\vec{W}|S) = \prod_i(p(\vec{W}_i|S))$. This gives equation (1):

$$p(Y, S, \vec{W}) = p(Y) \times p(S|Y) \times \prod_i p(W_i|S) \quad (1)$$

The term $p(S|Y)$ directly models the fact that a sense's likelihood can vary over time, possibly having zero probability on some early range of times and thus representing the non-availability of that sense of target T at those times. Assumption (i) reflects a plausible idea that given a concept being conveyed, the expected accompanying vocabulary is at least substantially time-independent. It also drastically reduces the number of parameters to be estimated. The parameters of the model in (1) have to be estimated from data in which the values of the sense variable S are not given. We tackle this unsupervised estimation problem via

an EM procedure (Dempster et al., 1977), though Gibbs sampling could be an alternative. We iterate between an E and an M step, as follows[1]:

(E) for each data item d and each possible value s of S, determine the conditional probability of $S = s$ given Y^d and $\vec{W}^d$, under current parameters – call this $\gamma^d(s)$.

(M) use the $\gamma^d(s)$ values to derive new estimates of parameters via the update formulae

$$P(S = s|Y = y) = \frac{\sum_{d:Y^d=y}[\gamma^d(s)]}{\sum_{d:Y^d=y}[1]}$$

$$P(w|S = s) = \frac{\sum_d(\gamma^d(s) \times \#(w, \vec{W}^d))}{\sum_d(\gamma^d(s) \times length(\vec{W}^d))}$$

2.1 Evaluation possibilities

As others have noted, the evaluation of the inferred sense dynamics produced by such a system is a challenge: large-scale, sense-labelled, diachronic corpora to serve as a gold-standard do not exist (Cook et al., 2014). So without doing large scale manual annotation, the full detail of the inferred sense dynamics cannot be straightforwardly evaluated.

However, concerning just the times of sense *emergence* (the point C_0 in Fig.1) the prospects are somewhat better. First of all, for *recent* lexical innovations, native speakers are often confident that they can judge that it is indeed recent (see section 4). A speaker's intuition that a sense emerged recently could serve as prima facie evidence against a system verdict outcome which finds no such recent emergence.

In pursuit of more objectivity and to consider innovations that are less recent, it is natural to consider dictionaries. For a given form/meaning pairing, an historically oriented dictionary (eg. the Oxford English Dictionary (OED)) will strive to include the very earliest citation that has been discovered – call this D_0^c. We will use D_0^c as a *lower* bound on the true emergence date C_0, which seems reasonable. The results section 3 will show a couple of examples wherre D_0^c is considerably earlier than C_0, the time at which which the use steadily starts to grow in use. Form/meaning pairings also make it into dictionaries at some particular time, so close inspection of a succession of dictionaries, though labour intensive, can give a

---

[1] $P(Y)$ is not estimated can be easily shown not to be needed for the other estimates.

date of its first inclusion – call this D_0^i. Some researchers have attempted this (see section 4), though in what follows we will not.

There is a further option to establish an emergence date for a novel sense of a target T. If there are words which it is intuitive to expect in the vicinity of T in the novel sense, and not in other senses, then one would expect the probability of seeing these words in T's context to start to climb at a particular time. For example, *mouse* has come to have a sense referring to a computer pointing device, in which usage it is intuitive to expect words like *click*, *button*, *pointer* and *drag* in it's context. For any word w and target T let us define $track_T(w)$ to be the sequence of its per-year probabilities of occurrence in the context of T. If when $track_{mouse}(w)$ is plotted for the above words, they all show a sharp increase at the *same* time point, this is good evidence that this is the emergence time of the novel sense. In the results section 3 we will use such 'tracks'-based dates as a target against which to compare any apparent inflection point of an inferred $P(S|Y)$ parameter – the righthand plot in Figure 2(a) is an example.

3   Experiments

The experiments reported here use the Google 5-gram dataset (Michel et al., 2011). This is a data set released by Google giving per-year counts of 5-grams in their digitized books holdings. From the entire 5-gram data-set it is possible to pull for a given target word T, a corpus of time-stamped 5-grams (with counts) containing T. As a diachronic corpus this data set has size and time range advantages. For example, prior work (Emms, 2013; Emms and Jayapal, 2014) used text snippets from search results obtained using Google's date specific search facility, giving a time range of 1990-2013 and about *100* examples per year. The 5-gram data reaches far further back with a far larger amount of data per year (see Table 1). For example for the target *mouse* there is on average over *15000* 5-gram entries featuring it per year. Its largest seeming disadvantage is that each 5-gram for a target gives a context of no more than 4 words.

Each line of the Google 5-gram data gives a year-specific *count* for the particular 5-gram. The EM presentation in section 2 assumed data items represented *single* target occurrences. In using the 5-gram data we effectively treat each 5-gram data entry as representing n separate tokens of T con-

tributing to no other 5-gram counts: the data set makes it impossible to know to what extent any original token of T has contributed to several different 5-gram counts. This involves changing the M step to

$$P(S = s|Y = y) = \frac{\sum_{d:Y^d=y}[\gamma^d(s) \times n^d]}{\sum_{d:Y^d=y}[n^d]}$$
$$P(w|S = s) = \frac{\sum_d(\gamma^d(s) \times n^d \times \#(w, \vec{W}^d))}{\sum_d(\gamma^d(s) \times n^d \times length(\vec{W}^d))}$$

Concerning initialisation, for an experiment on a target T having a corpus of occurrences *corp*, we initialise $P(w|S)$ to $(1 - \lambda)P_{corp} + \lambda P_{ran}$, where P_{corp} are the word probabilities in *corp*, P_{ran} is a random word distribution and λ is a mixing proportion, here set to 10^{-5}. Also initially the per-year sense distributions $P(S|Y)$ values are set to the same as each other. These start values thus are very far from representing the senses as being drastically different to each other or having any time variation at all.

Two sets of targets where chosen, a first set {*strike, mouse, boot, compile, surf* } of words known to exhibit sense emergence and a second set { *ostensible, present* } of words where there is not an expectation of an emergent sense. The two sets together give both positive and negative tests for the algorithm. Table 1 lists these words and for the first set gives an indication of the emergent senses. The next two columns give two kinds of reference dating information for the emergence of these senses. The 'OED-first' column gives the first citation date according to the OED, a lower bound for any inferred emergence date. The 'tracks date' gives an emergence date that is apparent from the 'tracks' plots for words that are intuitively associated with the emergent sense (see section 2.1). The final 'EM date' column is the emergence date inferred when the EM algorithm was run.

Figure 2(a-d) depicts various aspects of the outcomes on some of the test items. The leftmost plot in (a-c) shows the EM-inferred $P(S|Y)$ parameters for different targets T, and the rightmost plot shows some $tracks_T(w)$ plots (see section 2.1), for some words thought especially associated with the novel sensse – these track the probabilities of these words in the n-grams for the target and are the basis for the 'tracks date' column in Table 1.

mouse Figure 2(a): the algorithm was run for 3 sense variants on data from 1950 to 2010, and in the lefthand plot the blue line, for $P(S = 1|Y)$,

Target	Years	Lines	New sense	OED-first	tracks date	EM date	within 10%
mouse	1950-2008	910k	computer pointing devince	1965	1983	1982	yes
surf	1950-2008	183k	exploring internet	1992	1994	1993	yes
boot	1920-2008	1286k	computer start up	1980	1980	1983	yes
compile	1950-2008	689k	transform to machine code	1952	1966	1966	yes
strike	1800-2008	5053k	industrial action	1810	1880	1866	yes
ostensible	1800-2008	130k	NA	–	–	none	–
present	1850-2008	56333k	NA	–	–	none	–

Table 1: The test items, their new senses and dating information – see text for explanation of columns

shows an emergent sense, departing from near zero first around 1983. The righthand plot 'tracks' plots also show a sharp increase around 1983.

We wrote an *inflection* function which applied to an inferred $P(S|Y)$ parameter returns the date, if any, at which the sense probability starts to depart from, and continues to climb from, zero and the 'EM date' column of Table 1 gives the inflection points obtained on a particular inferred $P(S|Y)$ parameter for each test item. For *mouse*, the EM-based emergence date is later than the OED first citation date, and very close to the tracks-based date. This illustrates why simply taking the OED first citation date as a gold standard would be a mistake. The OED first citation comes from a research paper in 1965, but the mouse computer peripheral only became popular considerably later and it is not unexpected that the date at which this use of the term *mouse* departed and continued to climb from zero is substantially later. For all the test items, the 'within 10%' column indicates the agreement between the EM- and tracks-based dates.

Also in Fig. 2(a-c), the box below shows for the apparently emerging sense S, the top 30 words when ranked according to the ratio of $P(w|S)$ to $P_{corp}(w)$ (call this $gist(S)$). For the *mouse* case, $gist(S = 1)$ seems mostly consistent with the 'pointing device' sense.

surf Figure 2(b). EM was run on data from 1950 to 2010, for 5 senses. In the lefthand plot the green line, for $P(S = 3|Y)$, is an emergent sense, appearing to depart from near zero first around 1993. The 'tracks' plots to the right seem to increase around around 1994. The OED first citation date of 1992 is consistent with both. The 'gist' words for $S = 3$ also seem mostly consistent the 'internet exploration' sense.

strike Figure 2(c): EM was run on data from 1800 to 2008, for 3 senses, a far longer time span than the preceding cases. In the left-hand plot, the blue line, for $P(S = 1|Y)$, is an emergent sense, appearing to depart from near zero first around 1865. The tracks plot for words intuitively associated with the industrial action sense indicate an increase from around 1880. Both of these are consistent with the OED first citation date of 1820. The 'gist' words for $S = 1$ seem consistent with $S = 1$ representing the 'industrial action' sense. For space reasons, the *boot* and *compile* outcomes are not shown in Fig.2, but analogous outcomes were obtained, summarised in Table 1.

ostensible and **present** Figure 2(d) shows the plots of the inferred $P(S|Y)$ distributions. Neither shows an emerging sense, in line with expectations.

The number of senses sought in the EM runs for the different target items varied somewhat (between 3 and 5). This is somewhat to be expected as the extent of ambiguity probably varies for the different target items and in some cases where an emergence was less clear with n senses, it became clearer with $n + 1$ senses.

The procedure was implemented in C++. To obtain the code or data see `www.scss.tcd.ie/ Martin.Emms/SenseDynamics`. As an indication of exection time, for a data-set of approximately 900k lines a single EM iteration takes 8.01 seconds.

4   Prior Work

In this section we review some related work on novel sense detection. Wijaya and Yeniterzi (2011) did make some analyses on the Google n-gram data in relation to indicators of sense change, seeking to apply ideas from *LDA* (Blei et al., 2003). It is not however a concrete proposal for novel sense detection and to suit the LDA perspective they artificially concatenate a year's worth of n-grams to create a single document.

In a number of papers (Lau et al., 2012; Cook et al., 2013; Cook et al., 2014) have applied a

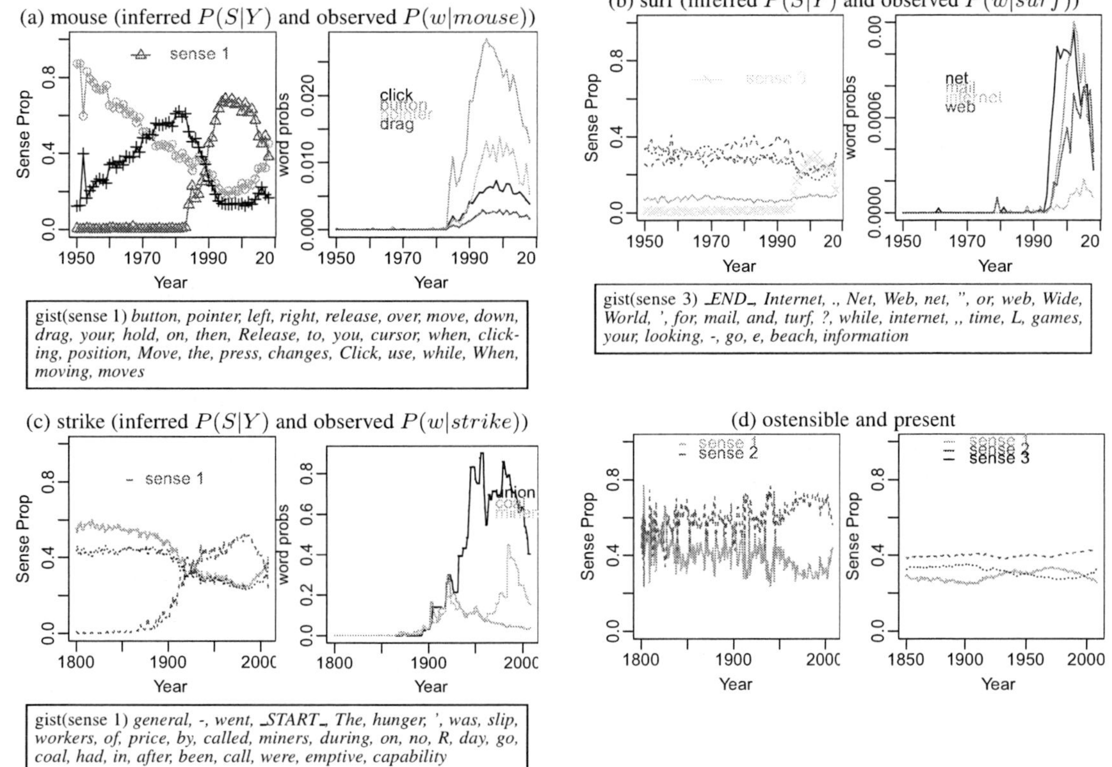

gist(sense 1) *button, pointer, left, right, release, over, move, down, drag, your, hold, on, then, Release, to, you, cursor, when, clicking, position, Move, the, press, changes, Click, use, while, When, moving, moves*

gist(sense 3) *_END_, Internet, ., Net, Web, net, ", or, web, Wide, World, ', for, mail, and, turf, ?, while, internet, ,, time, L, games, your, looking, -, go, e, beach, information*

gist(sense 1) *general, -, went, _START_, The, hunger, ', was, slip, workers, of, price, by, called, miners, during, on, no, R, day, go, coal, had, in, after, been, call, were, emptive, capability*

Figure 2: For (a-c), lefthand plot shows EM-inferred values for $P(S|Y)$, with the sense number S of an apparent emergent sense labelled; the righthand plot show probability 'tracks' for some words intuitively associated with the emergent sense (see text for further details). $gist(S)$ in the boxes is the top-30 as ranked by $P(w|S)/P_{corp}(w)$; (d) shows inferred $P(S|Y)$ for items with no sense emergence

pre-existing word sense induction (WSI) system to novel sense detection. They draw on ideas from *LDA*, treating each context of n words as generated from n topics, and define a target's *sense* to be the most frequent *topic* amongst the context words. A striking difference to our model is that their model essentially has no parameters referring to time. They therefore take time-stamped data and pool it to train a time-unaware system, then assign target expressions their most probable sense, and finally inspect the pattern of assigned senses and the time stamps. As data, rather than a real year-by-year diachronic corpus, they worked with data representing two time *periods*, T_1 and T_2. Presumabaly in the ideal case, if a sense S truly emerged between T_1 and T_2 it should assign sense S only to items from T_2. Their approach to evaluation uses dictionary inclusion dates (ie., D_0^i see section 2.1), so refers to senses which came to be included in dictionaries between the investigated time periods. Relative to a set of distractor expressions not thought to exhibit sense emergence

their system has some success in distinguishing between true cases and the distractors in so far as when items are ranked by the ratio $p_2 : p_1$ of their inferred sense frequencies in the periods T_2 and T_1, the neologisms tend to be more highly ranked than the distractors.

Mitra et al. (2014) have also presented work on sense emergence. Their data set is a dependency-parsed version of the Google 5-grams, whose time-line they divide into eras containing equal amounts of data. They do not propose a probabilistic model but instead have a distance-based clustering system. On each era's data they perform a clustering of occurrences, and then propose ways to relate the clusters for era T_1, $\{s_1^{T_1}, \ldots s_m^{T_1}\}$ to the clusters of a later era T_2, $\{s_1^{T_2}, \ldots s_n^{T_2}\}$: if a T_2 cluster, $s_i^{T_2}$, relates to no T_1 cluster, this is counted as evidence of the emergence of a sense between T_1 and T_2. For evaluation purposes they considered the inferred emergences between the eras 1909-1953 and 2002-2005, verifying not by reference to dictionaries but by reference to the intuitions of one of the authors. Some of the examples given in the paper (eg. organ-related use of *donation*) seem plausible, others are noted as true emergences though the OED would suggest otherwise (eg. an assailant sense of *thug*).

5 Conclusions

We have proposed a relatively simple generative model, one which assumes that *given* the target's sense, the context words are independent of time – the $P(w|S)$ parameter – and that for each time, there is a prior for each sense – the $P(S|Y)$ parameter. Together this models the way the context words for a given target *do* vary over time, through the sum $\sum_S [p(S|Y)p(\vec{W}|S)]$. We have proposed an EM procedure for the estimation of the parameters of such a model and how this can be applied to Google n-gram data, which gives counts for time-stamped n-grams, and we have shown that intuitive values for the $P(S|Y)$ parameters can be obtained.

The approach is in several respects simpler than some related work discussed in section 4. To emphasize this further, the algorithm used raw rather than lemmatized words and used a data-set with no syntactic annotation. It also lacks any inherent constraint to keep $P(S|Y_1)$ and $P(S|Y_2)$ close when Y_1 and Y_2 are close and its striking that the inferred $P(S|Y)$ come out as relatively smooth functions of time. Nonetheless a direction of future work could be to consider modeling such a smoothness constraint.

Section 4 mentioned the LDA-based model of (Lau et al., 2012; Cook et al., 2013; Cook et al., 2014) and it would certainly be of interest to seek to apply their algorithms to the data we have considered and conversely, our algorithms to their data. Also the work of Mitra et al. (2014) suggests a line of development in which we adapt our approach to first estimate separate models on data belonging to eras and then similarly attempt to relate the obtained collections of word distributions.

Acknowledgments

This research is supported by Science Foundation Ireland through the CNGL Programme (Grant 12/CE/I2267) in the ADAPT Centre (www.adaptcentre.ie) at Trinity College Dublin.

References

David M. Blei, Andrew Y. Ng, and Michael I. Jordan. 2003. Latent dirichlet allocation. In *Journal of Machine Learning Research*, volume 3, pages 993–1022,, March.

Paul Cook, Jey Han Lau, Michael Rundell, Diana McCarthy, , and Timothy Baldwin. 2013. A lexicographic appraisal of an automatic approach for detecting new word senses. In *Proceedings of eLex 2013*.

Paul Cook, Jey Han Lau, Diana McCarthy, and Timothy Baldwin. 2014. Novel word-sense identification. In *Proceedings of COLING 2014, the 25th International Conference on Computational Linguistics*, page 1624–1635. ACL, August.

A.P. Dempster, N.M. Laird, and D.B. Rubin. 1977. Maximum likelihood from incomplete data via the em algorithm. *J. Royal Statistical Society*, B 39:1–38.

Martin Emms and Arun Jayapal. 2014. Detecting change and emergence for multiword expressions. In *Proceedings of the 10th Workshop on Multiword Expressions (MWE)*, pages 89–93, Gothenburg, Sweden. Association for Computational Linguistics.

Martin Emms. 2013. Dynamic EM in neologism evolution. In Hujun Yin, Ke Tang, Yang Gao, Frank Klawonn, Minho Lee, Thomas Weise, Bin Li, and Xin Yao, editors, *Proceedings of IDEAL 2013*, volume 8206 of *Lecture Notes in Computer Science*, pages 286–293. Springer.

Jey Han Lau, Paul Cook, Diana McCarthy, David Newman, and Timothy Baldwin. 2012. Word sense induction for novel sense detection. In *Proceedings of the 13th Conference of the European Chapter of the Association for Computational Linguistics (EACL 2012)*, pages 591–601, Avignon, France, April.

Christopher Manning and Hinrich Schütze, 2003. *Foundations of Statistical Language Processing*, chapter Word Sense Disambiguation, pages 229–264. MIT Press, 6 edition.

Jean-Baptiste Michel, Yuan Kui Shen, Aviva Presser Aiden, Adrian Veres, Matthew K. Gray, The Google Books Team, Joseph P. Pickett, Dale Hoiberg, Dan Clancy, Peter Norvig, Jon Orwant, Steven Pinker, Martin A. Nowak, and Erez Lieberman Aiden. 2011. Quantitative analysis of culture using millions of digitized books. *Science*, 331(6014):176–182.

Sunny Mitra, Ritwik Mitra, Martin Riedl, Chris Biemann, Animesh Mukherjee, and Pawan Goyal. 2014. That's sick dude!: Automatic identification of word sense change across different timescales. In *Proceedings of the 52nd Annual Meeting of the Association for Computational Linguistics*, page 1020–1029. Association for Computational Linguistics, June.

Derry Tanti Wijaya and Reyyan Yeniterzi. 2011. Understanding semantic change of words over centuries. In *Proceedings of the 2011 International Workshop on DETecting and Exploiting Cultural diversiTy on the Social Web*, DETECT '11, pages 35–40, New York, NY, USA. ACM.

Solving Data Sparsity by Morphology Injection in Factored SMT

Sreelekha S
IIT Bombay
India

Piyush Dungarwal
IIT Bombay
India

Pushpak Bhattacharyya
IIT Bombay
India

Malathi D
SRM University
India

{sreelekha,piyushdd,pb}@cse.iitb.ac.in

{malathi.d}@ktr.srmuniv.ac.in

Abstract

SMT approaches face the problem of data sparsity while translating into a morphologically rich language. It is very unlikely for a parallel corpus to contain all morphological forms of words. We propose a solution to generate these unseen morphological forms and inject them into original training corpora. We observe that morphology injection improves the quality of translation in terms of both adequacy and fluency. We verify this with the experiments on two morphologically rich languages: Hindi and Marathi, while translating from English.

1 Introduction

Statistical translation models which translate into a morphologically rich language face two challenging tasks: 1. correct choice of inflection, and 2. data sparsity. To understand the severity of these two problems, consider an example of verb morphology in Hindi[1]. Hindi verbs are inflected based on gender, number, person, tense, aspect, and modality. Gender can be masculine or non-masculine (2). Number can be singular or plural (2). Person can be first, second or third (3). Tense can be present or non-present (2). Aspect can be simple, progressive or perfect (3). Modality can be due to shall, will, can, etc. (9). Thus, for a single root verb in Hindi, we have in total 648 (2*2*3*2*3*9) inflected forms. It is very unlikely for a Hindi corpus to have all inflected forms of each verb. Also, lesser the corpus size of morphologically richer language, more severe the problem of sparsity.

Using factored models helps in solving the problem of correct inflectional choice. But solving the sparsity problem is more challenging task. In this paper, we propose a simple and effective solution of enriching the input corpora with various morphological forms of words. We perform experiments with factored models (Koehn and Hoang, 2007) as well as unfactored models, i.e., phrase-based models (Koehn, Och and Marcu, 2003) while translating from English to Hindi and English to Marathi. Results show that morphology injection performs very well in order to solve the sparsity problem.

The rest of the paper is organized as follows: We present related work in Section 2. Then, we study the basics of factored translation models in Section 3. We also describe a general factored model for handling morphology. Then, we discuss the sparsity problem and the morphology generation, in general in Section 4, and in context of Hindi and Marathi in Section 5. Section 6 draws conclusion and points to future work.

2 Related work

Substantial volume of work has been done in the field of translation into morphologically rich languages. The source language can be enriched with grammatical features (Avramidis and Koehn, 2008) or standard translation model can be appended with *synthetic phrases* (Chahuneau et al., 2013). Also, previous work has been done in order to solve the verb morphology in English to Hindi SMT (Gandhe et al., 2011).

Although past work focuses on studying complexity (Tamchyna and Bojar, 2013) and solving morphology using factored translation models (Ramanathan et al., 2009), the problem of data sparsity is not addressed, to the best of our knowledge.

3 Factored translation models

Factored translation models can be seen as the combination of several components (language

---

[1]Hindi and Marathi are morphologically rich languages compared to English. They are widely spoken in Indian sub-continent.

D S Sharma, R Sangal and E Sherly. Proc. of the 12th Intl. Conference on Natural Language Processing, pages 95–99,
Trivandrum, India. December 2015. ©2015 NLP Association of India (NLPAI)

model, reordering model, translation steps, generation steps). These components define one or more feature functions that are combined in a log-linear model (Koehn and Hoang, 2007):

$$p(e|f) = \frac{1}{Z} exp \sum_{i=1}^{n} \lambda_i h_i(e, f)$$

Each h_i is a feature function for a component of the translation, and the λ_i values are weights for the feature functions. Z is a normalization constant.

Factored models treat each word in the corpus as vector of tokens. These tokens can provide extra linguistic information about the word. This information can be used to generate more accurate inflections compared to other unfactored models.

3.1 Factored model for handling morphology

Note that our goal is to solve the sparsity problem while translating to morphologically rich languages. Figure 1 shows a basic factored model for translation from morphologically poor language to rich language. On the source side we have: Surface word, root word, and set of factors S that affect the inflection of the word on the target side. On the target side, we have: Surface word, root word, and suffix (can be any inflection). The model has single translation (T0) and generation step (G0).

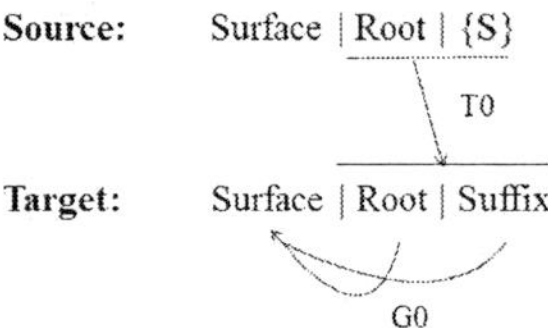

Figure 1: Factored model setup to handle inflections

4 Problem of Data Sparsity and Morphology Generation

A simple and effective solution to the sparsity problem is to generate the unseen morphological forms of words and inject them into original model. Note that, we also need to generate factors that affect the inflections of the newly generated morphological forms. For example, for the factored model described in Section 3.1, we need to generate new *Source root|{S}* → *Target surface word|Target root|suffix* pairs.

But then the question remains: *How do we generate these new morphological forms?* Here is the general procedure that can be adopted while translating from language X to Y:

1. We identify the factor set (S) that affects the inflections of words in language Y

2. We learn which inflection the target word will have for a particular combination of factors in S on the source side

3. We generate the surface word from the root word and inflection in language Y

In Section 5, we discuss the problem of data sparsity and morphology generation in detail, in context of Hindi and Marathi, while translating from English..

5 Morphology Generation

Hindi and Marathi are morphologically rich languages compared to English. They show morphological inflections on nouns and verbs. Before studying actual generation of various word forms, we present the factored model setup that is used for our experiments.

5.1 Factored model setup

Noun inflections in Hindi are affected by the number and case of the noun only (Singh et al., 2010). So, in this case, the set S, as in Section 3.1, consists of number and case. Number can be *singular* or *plural* and case can be *direct* or *oblique*. Example of factors and mapping steps are shown in Figure 2.

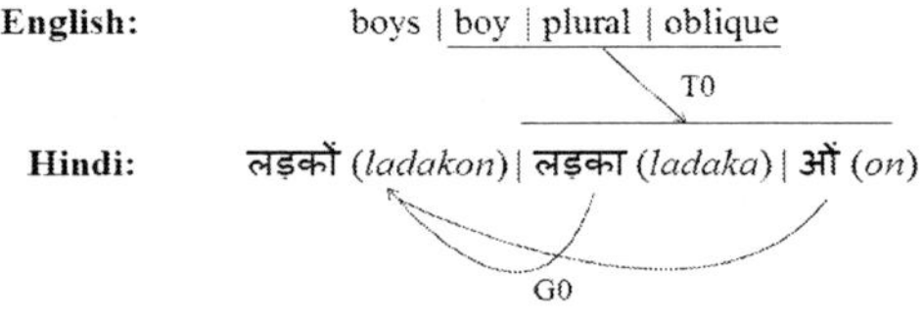

Figure 2: Factored model setup to handle nominal inflections

Similarly, verb inflections in Hindi are affected by gender, number, person, tense, aspect, and modality (Singh and Sarma, 2011). As it is difficult to extract gender from English verbs, we do not use it as a factor on English side. We just replicate English verbs for each gender inflection on

Hindi side. Hence, set S, as in Section 3.1, consists of number, person, tense, aspect, and modality only.

We build similar factored model for Marathi nouns and verbs. But, Marathi is morphologically more complex than Hindi, as multiple suffixes can be attached with Marathi root nouns and root verbs. But, still we can generate one-suffix word forms of Marathi nouns and verbs.

5.2 Building word-form dictionary

Word-form dictionary is a list consisting of all inflected forms of root words. Figure 3 shows a pipeline to generate new morphological forms for an English-Hindi/Marathi word pair. The pipeline needs the information about suffix classification based on the factors that affect those inflections. With the help of such classification, we create a list of the form: *Source root|Source S factors → Target root|Target suffix* by extracting source-target noun/verb pairs from the training corpus.

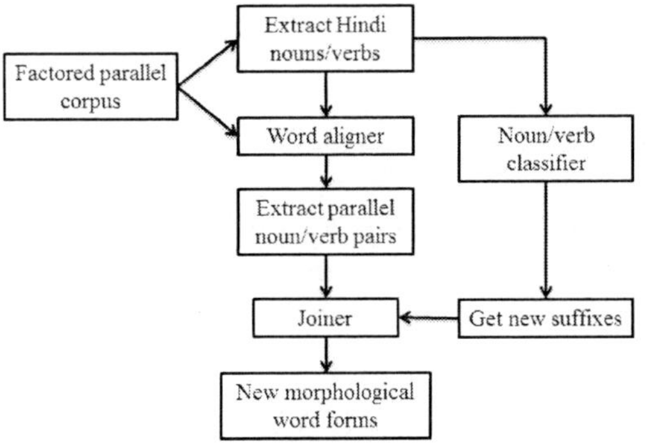

Figure 3: Pipeline to generate new morphological forms for an English-Hindi/Marathi noun/verb pair

Next step is to create a *Target surface word* from the new list of *Target root|Target suffix*. We build a joiner (reverse morphological) tool in target language, which merges root word and suffix to give target surface word. The joiner uses the ending of the root noun/verb and the class to which the suffix belongs as features. The final word-form list, thus generated, is augmented to original training data. Table 1 shows four morphological forms of *boy-लड़का (ladakaa)* noun pair. Similarly different morphological forms are created for Hindi verbs and Marathi nouns and verbs.

We also learn a factored model which combines factors on both nouns and verbs. We build word-

English root|Number|Case	Hindi surface|Root|Suffix
boy|singular|direct	लड़का (ladakaa)|लड़का (ladakaa)|null
boy|singular|oblique	लड़के (ladake)|लड़का (ladakaa)|ए (e)
boy|plural|direct	लड़के (ladake)|लड़का (ladakaa)|ए (e)
boy|plural|oblique	लड़कों (ladakon)|लड़का (ladakaa)|ओं (on)

Table 1: New morphological forms of boy-लड़का (ladakaa) noun pair

form dictionaries separately for nouns and verbs and augment training data with both. Note that, factor normalization[2] on each word is required to maintain same number of factors.

We also create a word-form dictionary for phrase-based model. We follow the same procedure as described above, but we remove all factors from source and target words except the surface form.

5.3 Experiments and Evaluation

We performed experiments on ILCI (Indian Languages Corpora Initiative) En-Hi and En-Mr data set. Domain of the corpus is health and tourism. We used 44,586 sentence pairs for training and 2,974 sentence pairs for testing. Word-form dictionary was created using the Hindi and Marathi word lexicon. It consisted of 182,544 noun forms and 310,392 verb forms of Hindi and 9,869 noun forms and 101,621 verb forms of Marathi.

Moses toolkit[3] was used for training and decoding. Language model was trained on the target side corpus with *IRSTLM*[4].

For our experiments, We compared the translation outputs of: Phrase-based (unfactored) model (**Phr**), basic factored model (**Fact**) as in Section 5.1, phrase-based model trained on the corpus augmented with word-form dictionary (**Phr'**), and factored model trained on the corpus augmented with the word-form dictionary (**Fact'**).

We use *Stanford POS tagger*[5] (Toutanova et al., 2003) and *Stanford's typed dependencies* (De Marneffe et al., 2008) to extract the factors that affect the inflections (number, person, tense, etc.) from English sentence.

5.3.1 Automatic evaluation

The translation systems were evaluated by BLEU score (Papineni et al., 2002). Also, as the reduc-

---

[2]To use *null* when particular word can not have that factor
[3]http://www.statmt.org/moses/
[4]https://hlt.fbk.eu/technologies/irstlm-irst-language-modelling-toolkit
[5]http://nlp.stanford.edu/software/tagger.shtml

Morph. problem	Model	BLEU		# OOV		% OOV reduction		Adequacy		Fluency	
		En-Hi	En-Mr	En-Hi	En-Mr	En-Hi	En-Mr	En-Hi	En-Mr	En-Hi	En-Mr
Noun	*Fact*	22.30	8.84	2,030	1,399	**14.33**	**2.14**	3.62	2.52	3.65	2.20
	Fact'	22.41	8.85	1,739	1,369			3.73	2.55	3.66	2.23
Verb	*Fact*	23.23	9.02	1,141	1,772	**14.11**	**4.35**	3.85	2.67	3.86	2.26
	Fact'	23.26	9.02	980	1,695			3.91	2.73	3.91	2.30
Noun & Verb	*Fact*	20.93	7.55	2,193	3,137	**14.87**	**5.56**	3.89	2.69	3.92	2.28
	Fact'	21.03	7.58	1,867	2,963			4.17	2.77	4.06	2.34
Noun & Verb	*Phr*	22.87	9.27	813	1,572	**7.38**	**2.27**	4.07	2.70	3.90	2.24
	Phr'	22.89	9.28	753	1,537			4.12	2.72	3.92	2.25

Table 2: Automatic and Subjective evaluation of the translation systems

tion in number of unknowns in the translation output indicates better handling of data sparsity, we counted the number of OOV words in the translation outputs. Table 2 shows the evaluation scores and numbers.

From the evaluation scores, it is very evident that *Fact'/Phr'* outperforms *Fact/Phr* while solving any morphology problem in both Hindi and Marathi. But, improvements in *En-Mr* systems are very low. This is due to the small size of word-form dictionaries that are used for injection. % reduction in OOV shows that, morphology injection is more effective with factored models than with the phrase-based model. Also, improvements shown by BLEU are less compared to % reduction in OOV.

Why BLEU improvement is low?

One possible reason is ambiguity in lexical choice. Word-form dictionary may have word forms of multiple Hindi or Marathi root words for a single parallel English root word. Hence, many times the translation of the English word may not match the reference used for BLEU evaluation, even though it may be very similar in the meaning. Table 3 shows the number of OOVs that are actually translated after morphology injection and number of translated OOVs that match with the reference. We see that matches with the reference are very less compared to the actual number of OOVs translated. Thus, BLEU score cannot truly reflect the usefulness of morphology injection.

5.3.2 Subjective evaluation

As BLEU evaluation with only single reference is not a true measure of evaluating our method, we also performed human evaluation. We found out that *Fact'/Phr'* systems really have better outputs compared to *Fact/Phr* systems, in terms of both, adequacy and fluency.

For evaluation, randomly chosen 50 translation

Morph. problem	En-Hi		En-Mr	
	#OOV translated	#Ref. Matches	#OOV translated	#Ref. Matches
Noun (*fact*)	291	105	30	5
Verb (*fact*)	436	77	77	0
Noun & Verb (*fact*)	601	137	174	20
Noun & Verb (*phr*)	124	21	35	7

Table 3: Counts of total OOVs translated after morphology injection and the matches with the reference used for BLEU evaluation

outputs from each system were manually given adequacy and fluency scores. The scores were given on the scale of 1 to 5 going from worst to best, respectively. Table 2 shows average scores for each system. We observe upto **7%** improvement in adequacy and upto **3%** improvement in fluency.

6 Conclusion

SMT approaches suffer due to data sparsity while translating into a morphologically rich language. We solve this problem by enriching the original data with the missing morphological forms of words. Morphology injection performs very well and improves the translation quality. We observe huge reduction in number of OOVs and improvement in adequacy and fluency of the translation outputs. This method is more effective when used with factored models than the phrase-based models.

Though the approach of solving data sparsity seems simple, the morphology generation may be painful for target languages which are morphologically too complex. A possible future work is to generalize the approach of morphology generation and verify the effectiveness of morphology injection on morphologically complex languages.

Acknowledgments

This work is funded by Department of Science and Technology, Govt. of India under Women Scientist Scheme- WOS-A with the project code- SR/WOS-A/ET-1075/2014.

References

Avramidis, Eleftherios, and Philipp Koehn. 2008. *Enriching Morphologically Poor Languages for Statistical Machine Translation*. ACL.

Chahuneau, Victor, Eva Schlinger, Noah A. Smith, and Chris Dyer. 2013. *Translating into Morphologically Rich Languages with Synthetic Phrases*. Proceedings of the 2013 Conference on Empirical Methods in Natural Language Processing. Association for Computational Linguistics.

De Marneffe, Marie-Catherine, and Christopher D. Manning. 2008. *Stanford typed dependencies manual*. URL http://nlp. stanford. edu/software/dependencies manual. pdf (2008).

Gandhe, Ankur, Rashmi Gangadharaiah, Karthik Visweswariah, and Ananthakrishnan Ramanathan. 2011. *Handling verb phrase morphology in highly inflected Indian languages for Machine Translation*. IJCNLP.

Koehn, Philipp, Franz Josef Och, and Daniel Marcu. 2007. *Statistical phrase-based translation*. Proceedings of the 2003 Conference of the North American Chapter of the Association for Computational Linguistics on Human Language Technology-Volume 1. Association for Computational Linguistics.

Koehn, Philipp and Hieu Hoang. 2007. *Factored Translation Models*. EMNLP-CoNLL.

Papineni, Kishore, Salim Roukos, Todd Ward, and Wei-Jing Zhu. 2002. *BLEU: a method for automatic evaluation of machine translation*. Proceedings of the 40th annual meeting on association for computational linguistics. Association for Computational Linguistics.

Ramanathan, Ananthakrishnan, Hansraj Choudhary, Avishek Ghosh, and Pushpak Bhattacharyya. 2009. *Case markers and morphology: addressing the crux of the fluency problem in English-Hindi SMT*. Proceedings of the Joint Conference of the 47th Annual Meeting of the ACL and the 4th International Joint Conference on Natural Language Processing of the AFNLP: Volume 2-Volume 2. Association for Computational Linguistics.

Singh, Smriti, Vaijayanthi M. Sarma, and Stefan Müller. 2010. *Hindi Noun Inflection and Distributed Morphology*. Université Paris Diderot, Paris 7, France. Stefan Müller (Editor) CSLI Publications http://csli-publications. stanford. edu (2006): 307.

Singh, Smriti, Vaijayanthi M. Sarma. 2011. *Verbal Inflection in Hindi: A Distributed Morphology Approach*. PACLIC.

Tamchyna, Aleš, and Ondřej Bojar. 2013. *No free lunch in factored phrase-based machine translation*. Computational Linguistics and Intelligent Text Processing. Springer Berlin Heidelberg. 210-223.

Toutanova, Kristina, Dan Klein, Christopher D. Manning, and Yoram Singer 2003. *Feature-rich part-of-speech tagging with a cyclic dependency network*. Proceedings of the 2003 Conference of the North American Chapter of the Association for Computational Linguistics on Human Language Technology-Volume 1. Association for Computational Linguistics.

Authorship Attribution in Bengali Language

Shanta Phani
Information Technology
IIEST, Shibpur
Howrah 711103, West Bengal, India
shantaphani@gmail.com

Shibamouli Lahiri
Computer Science and Engineering
University of Michigan
Ann Arbor, MI 48109
lahiri@umich.edu

Arindam Biswas
Information Technology
IIEST, Shibpur
Howrah 711103, West Bengal, India
abiswas@it.iiests.ac.in

Abstract

We describe Authorship Attribution of Bengali literary text. Our contributions include a new corpus of 3,000 passages written by three Bengali authors, an end-to-end system for authorship classification based on character n-grams, feature selection for authorship attribution, feature ranking and analysis, and learning curve to assess the relationship between amount of training data and test accuracy. We achieve state-of-the-art results on held-out dataset, thus indicating that lexical n-gram features are unarguably the best discriminators for authorship attribution of Bengali literary text.

1 Introduction

Authorship Attribution is a long-standing and well-studied problem in Natural Language Processing where the goal is to classify documents (often short passages) according to their authorship. Different flavors of the problem treat it as either "closed-class" (train and test authors come from the same set), or "open-class" (test authors may be different from train authors). A related variant is Authorship Verification, where the goal is to verify if a given document/passage has been written by a particular author via, e.g., binary classification.

Although Authoship Attribution in English has received a lot of attention since the pioneering study of Mosteller and Wallace (1963) on the disputed *Federalist Papers*, equivalent work in Bengali – one of the most widely spoken South Asian languages – has spawned only three strands of research till date (Das and Mitra, 2011; Chakraborty, 2012; Jana, 2015). Part of the reason behind this lack of research progress in Bengali Authorship Attribution is a shortage of adequate corpora and tools, which has only very recently started to change (Mukhopadhyay et al., 2012).

In this paper, our contributions are as follows:

- **Corpus**: a new corpus of 3,000 literary passages in Bengali written by three eminent Bengali authors (Section 3).

- **Authorship Attribution System**: a classification system based on character bigrams that achieves 98% accuracy on held-out data (Section 4).

- **Feature Selection**: six types of lexical n-gram features, and selection of the best-performing combination on an independent development set (Section 5).

- **Learning Curve**: how the performance on held-out data changes as the number of training instances varies (Section 6).

- **Feature Ranking**: most discriminative lexical features by Information Gain (Section 7).

- **Feature Analysis**: frequency analysis of discriminative features, grouped by authors (Section 7).

We would like to mention that there are many different ways in which our Authorship Attribution system could potentially improve or be extended (more powerful learning algorithms; syntactic, semantic and discourse features; etc). However, given that we already achieved impressive accuracy values on held-out data (Section 6), such improvements would necessarily be incremental, unless new corpora are introduced that warrant different feature sets and/or classifiers.

2 Related Work

A general overview of the topic of Authorship Attribution has been given in the surveys by Juola (2006), Stamatatos (2009), and Koppel et al. (2009). Unsurprisingly, there are many recent studies in English Authorship Attribution. Seroussi et al. (2012) showed that author-topic model outperforms LDA for Authorship Attribution tasks with many authors. They came up with a combination of LDA and author-topic model (DADT – disjoint author-document-topic model) that outperforms the vanilla author-topic model

96

D S Sharma, R Sangal and E Sherly. Proc. of the 12th Intl. Conference on Natural Language Processing, pages 100–105,
Trivandrum, India. December 2015. ©2015 NLP Association of India (NLPAI)

Author		Overall	Train	Test	Development
Rabindranath	Mean #words	221.18 (26.08)	215.28 (27.21)	228.60 (23.73)	225.56 (23.09)
	Mean #characters	3232.61 (385.44)	3139.87 (405.12)	3352.16 (339.98)	3298.53 (338.50)
Sarat Chandra	Mean #words	188.99 (29.57)	186.18 (30.29)	192.49 (30.05)	191.12 (26.97)
	Mean #characters	2661.23 (421.84)	2628.64 (432.10)	2695.18 (423.85)	2692.47 (393.02)
Bankim Chandra	Mean #words	841.05 (256.86)	832.38 (250.32)	846.44 (261.31)	853.01 (264.55)
	Mean #characters	13259.56 (4188.04)	13153.46 (4083.46)	13325.55 (4284.03)	13405.75 (4290.50)

Table 1: Corpus statistics. Values in parentheses are standard deviations. Mean and standard deviation are taken across passages.

and an SVM baseline. Seroussi et al. (2014) further showed state-of-the-art performance on PAN 11, blog, IMDB, and court judgment datasets.

As we discussed in Section 1, Authorship Attribution in Bengali is a relatively new problem. Among the three studies we found, Chakraborty (2012) performed a ten-fold cross-validation on three classes (Rabindranath, Sarat Chandra, others) with 150 documents in each, and showed that SVM outperforms decision tree and neural network classifiers. The best accuracy was 84%. An earlier study by Das and Mitra (2011) also worked with three authors – Rabindranath, Bankim Chandra, and Sukanta Bhattacharya. They had 36 documents in total. Unigram and bigram features were rich enough to yield high classification accuracy (90% for unigrams, 100% for bigrams). However, their dataset was not very large to draw reliable conclusions. Further, the authors they experimented with had very different styles, unlike our (more difficult) case where two of the authors often had similar styles in their prose (Rabindranath and Sarat Chandra).

Jana (2015) looked into Sister Nivedita's influence on Jagadish Chandra Bose's writings. He notes that "The results reveal a distinct change in Bose's writing style after his meeting with Nivedita. This is reflected in his changing pattern of usage of these three stylistic features. Bose slowly moved back towards his original style of writing after Nivedita's death, but his later works still carried Nivedita's influence." This study, while interesting, is not directly comparable to ours, because it did not perform any classification experiments. Among other recent studies in Authorship Attribution in Indian languages, Nagaprasad et al. (2015) worked on 300 Telugu news articles written by 12 authors. SVM was used on word and character n-grams. It was observed that F-score and accuracy decrease as size of training data decreases, and/or the number of authors increases.

Bobicev et al. (2013) looked into Authorship Attribution in health forums. In their 30-class classification problem, orthographic features performed well, and Naive Bayes was shown to perform better than KNN. The best accuracy was close to 90%.

Bogdanova and Lazaridou (2014) experimented with cross-language Authorship Attribution. They designed cross-language features (sentiment, emotional, POS frequency, perceptual, average sentence length), and posited that Machine Translation could be used as a starting point to cross-language Authorship Attribution. Using six authors' English books and their Spanish translations, they obtained 79% accuracy with KNN. The best pairwise accuracy was 95%. Nasir et al. (2014) framed Authorship Attribution as semi-supervised anomaly detection via multiple kernel learning. They learned *author regions* from the feature space by representing the optimal solution as a linear mixture of multiple kernel functions.

Luyckx and Daelemans (2008) introduced the important problem of *Authorship Verification*. To model realistic situations, they experimented with 145 authors and limited training data (student essays on Artificial Life). They showed that Authorship Verification is much harder than Authorship Attribution, and that more authors and less training data led to decreased performance. Memory-based learning (e.g., KNN) was shown to be robust in this scenario. An interesting study was presented by van Cranenburgh (2012), where he focused on *content words* rather than *function words*, and showed that tree kernels on fragments of constituency parse trees provide information complementary to a baseline trigram model for Authorship Attribution. Literary texts from five authors were used, and the best (combined) accuracy reached almost 98%.

Sarawgi et al. (2011) attempted to remove *topic bias* for identifying gender-specific stylistic markers. They used deep syntactic patterns with PCFG, shallow patterns with token-level language models, morphological patterns with character-level language models, and bag of words (BoW) with MaxEnt classifier. Per-gender accuracy reached 100% using morphological features on blog data. On paper data, BoW features also reached 100% per-author accuracy for both male and female authors.

3 Corpus

In this work, we focused on Authorship Attribution of Bengali *literary text*, in keeping with prior studies(Das and Mitra, 2011; Chakraborty, 2012; Jana, 2015). Note that with the emergence of social media, it would be completely valid to pursue this problem on news articles, tweets, Facebook posts, online forum threads, blog entries, or other social media outlets. However, the problems with such data are: (a) they are less clean than literary text, leading to a lot of surface variation, and (b) the number of authors is essentially unbounded, thereby rendering the problem more difficult and lowering accuracy values (Layton et al., 2010; Schwartz et al., 2013).

We chose three eminent Bengali authors for our study, and extracted 1000 passages from the works of each author. The authors are:

1. **Rabindranath Tagore** (1861-1941)

2. **Sarat Chandra Chattopadhyay** (1876-1938)

3. **Bankim Chandra Chattopadhyay** (1838-1894)

Note that all three are male authors, and lived during the golden age of Bengali Renaissance, thus their writing styles could often be very similar – echoing the premises of the original Mosteller and Wallace study (1963). Besides, these authors have an extensive repertoire of works (novels, essays, poetry, songs, dramas, short stories, reviews, letters, critiques, etc) that have been completely digitized for researchers to leverage (Mukhopadhyay et al., 2012).[1]

We sampled 1,000 random passages for each author as follows. We first removed poetry and songs because they are not uniformly distributed across all three authors. Thereafter, we merged the remaining prose in a single large file, and sampled 25 random fragments for each passage (25K fragments in total). We have taken necessary care to ensure that passage contents were *disjoint*.

The above procedure yielded a balanced corpus of passages for the three authors. The corpus is realistic, because it embodies the *fragmentary* nature of realistic authorship attribution scenarios where all too often texts are not recovered in their entirety. Furthermore, it sidesteps the problem of unequal sample lengths (e.g., by having whole documents or books as samples). Our corpus statistics are shown in Table 1. Note that the corpus has been divided into (balanced) train, test, and development sets, with 1,500 samples in the train set, and 750 samples in the test and development sets. Table 1 shows that passages from Bankim Chandra are the longest (on average), followed by Rabindranath and Sarat Chandra. The reason is the former's usage of complex and formal language constructs in his writings which typically led to longer and more intricate fragments.

4 Authorship Attribution System

We   pose   the problem as one of supervised classification. With three classes, our accuracy on held-out data reaches 98%.[2] In accordance with previous research, we found that the best results are obtained from *most frequent lexical n-grams*. Among the features we experimented with are:

- **Stop words**: 355 Bengali stop words.[3]

- **Uni, bi, and trigrams**: Word n-grams (n = 1, 2, 3) that are most frequent on the complete dataset.

- **Character bi and trigrams**: Character n-grams (n = 2, 3) that are most frequent on the complete dataset. Whitespace characters were ignored.

We have tried three feature representations on the above categories – binary (presence/absence), tf, and tfidf. While it may seem that such shallow features are not enough to capture the variability and complexity of individual authors, as we shall see in Section 6, the impressive performance values we obtained dispel such doubts.

We used three classifiers from Weka (Hall et al., 2009) – Naive Bayes (NB), SVM SMO, and J48 decision tree – to test their performance on the development set. As shown in Table 2, J48 performs significantly worse than NB and SMO across the board, whereas NB and SMO perform close to each other. We chose NB as our final classifier. This decision is guided by the fact that NB is simpler to conceptualize and implement, and faster to train than SMO.

Note further from Table 2 that word unigrams give the best performance. However, as we shall see in Section 5, best values are obtained from character bigrams (tf), so our final system consists of 300 most frequent character bigrams (tf) as features on Naive Bayes classifier.

5 Feature Selection

As we see from Table 2, best numbers are in the region of stop words, word unigrams, character bigrams, and character trigrams. It is therefore instructive to look into what performance benefit we can achieve by varying the number of features in these categories, along with their representation (binary/tf/tfidf). The results are shown in Figure 1. We observed that the best development accuracy of 97.87% was obtained for 300 character bigrams (tf) feature combination, so we used that combination for our final system.

Note from Figure 1 that in almost all cases, increasing the number of features led to improved performance on the development set. However, overfitting is clearly visible for character bigrams and trigrams beyond a certain number of features (around 300). This observation offers a completely organic feature selection strategy – cut off where the development accuracy dips for the first time. Note also that the features were ordered by Information Gain, so e.g. the *top k* n-grams are the most discriminative *k* n-grams within the most frequent.

---

[1]The complete works of these three authors are available from http://www.nltr.org/.

[2]A random baseline would achieve only 33% on the same data.

[3]Available at http://www.isical.ac.in/~fire/data/stopwords_list_ben.txt.

Feature Representation	Feature Category	J48	NB	SMO
Binary (Presence/Absense)	Stop words	89.73	96.40	96.00
	Word unigrams	92.80	**97.60**	98.40
	Word bigrams	67.87	73.47	73.87
	Word trigrams	36.80	40.00	40.00
	Character bigrams	84.53	96.40	96.40
	Character trigrams	79.60	93.07	92.27
Tf (Term Frequency)	Stop words	92.93	95.73	97.60
	Word unigrams	94.93	97.47	98.80
	Word bigrams	69.20	74.13	74.40
	Word trigrams	36.80	39.07	40.67
	Character bigrams	90.93	97.33	98.67
	Character trigrams	85.07	94.27	96.93
Tfidf (Term Frequency Inverse Document Frequency)	Stop words	92.53	95.87	97.73
	Word unigrams	**95.20**	**97.60**	**98.93**
	Word bigrams	65.87	74.13	74.00
	Word trigrams	36.80	40.00	40.67
	Character bigrams	91.47	97.33	98.40
	Character trigrams	85.07	94.93	97.93

Table 2: Percentage accuracy of three classifiers when trained on the training set and tested on the development set. For each category of feature, 500 most frequent were used. For stop words, there were 355. Best number in each column is boldfaced.

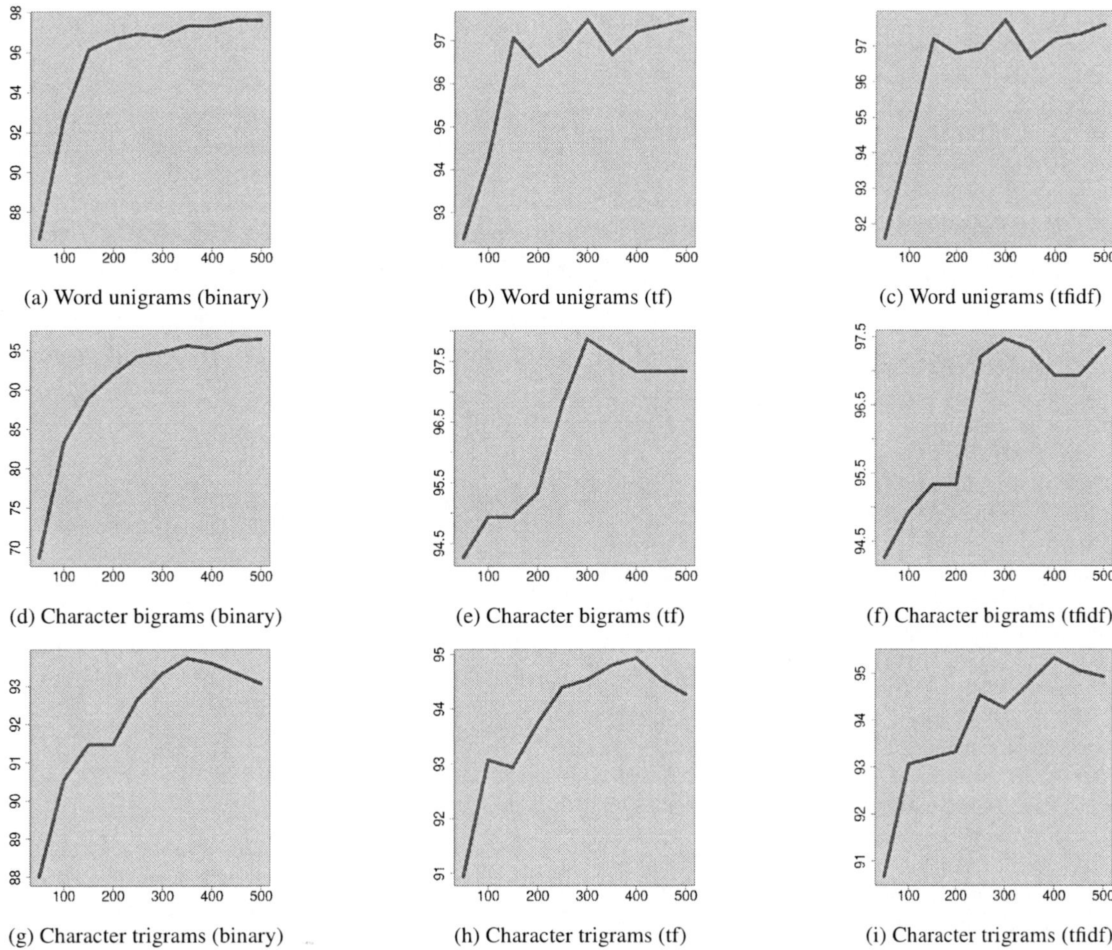

(a) Word unigrams (binary)

(b) Word unigrams (tf)

(c) Word unigrams (tfidf)

(d) Character bigrams (binary)

(e) Character bigrams (tf)

(f) Character bigrams (tfidf)

(g) Character trigrams (binary)

(h) Character trigrams (tf)

(i) Character trigrams (tfidf)

Figure 1: Impact of number of features on accuracy. X-axis is Number of Features, and Y-axis is Percentage Accuracy on the development set (can be viewed in grayscale).

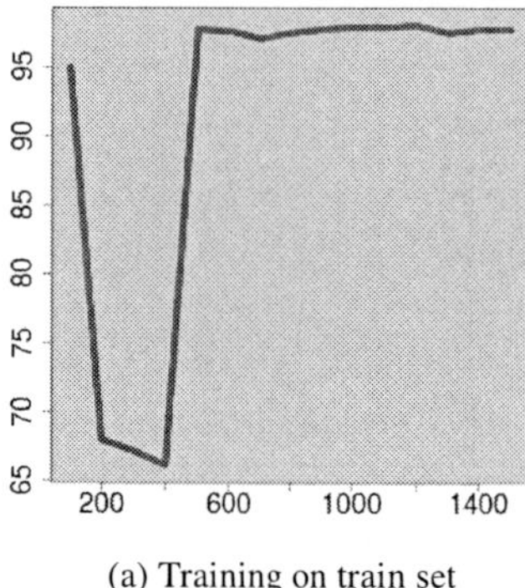
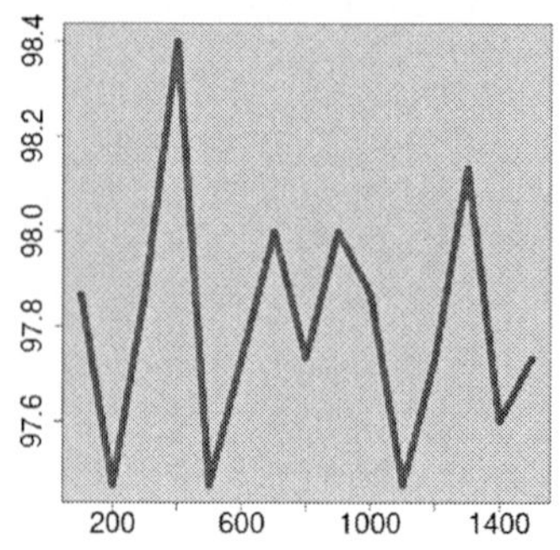

(a) Training on train set   (b) Training on train + development set

Figure 2: Learning curves. X-axis is Number of Training Samples, and Y-axis is Percentage Accuracy on the **test set** (can be viewed in grayscale).

6 Learning Curve

With the feature set and classifier now optimized on the development data, we re-trained the model on train set (1,500 instances) and train + development set (2,250 instances), and measured accuracy on the **test set** that was untouched so far. In both cases, we obtained 97.73% test accuracy – thereby showing the viability of our approach on completely untouched held-out data. To be noted is the fact that this high test accuracy is similar to the high development accuracy we obtained in Section 5. This is because our samples were drawn from the same *universe* of authors. Furthermore, our test accuracy is superior to the state-of-the-art (84% reported by Chakraborty (2012)), and more reliable because we worked with a much larger sample of passages than (Chakraborty, 2012) and (Das and Mitra, 2011), and because we followed a more rigorous experimental paradigm by splitting our data into three parts and selecting the model on the development set.

We next asked the following question: *Can we reduce the amount of training data, and still get the same (or better) performance?* To answer this question, we plotted two learning curves, shown in Figure 2. Figure 2a shows the case when we train on the training data only, and test on the test data. Figure 2b shows the case when we train on training + development data, and test on the test data. In both cases, we varied the number of training samples from 100 to 1,500 in steps of 100.[4]

We empirically observed that the best test accuracy of 98.4% was obtained for 200 training instances + the development set (the first spike in Figure 2b). In general, the performance almost always stayed within a tight band between 95 and 99%, thus indicating the validity of our approach, and (relative) insensitivity to the number of training examples. We would like to recommend that 500 training examples should be good enough for practical applications.

---

[4]For Figure 2b, the development set part was fixed; only the training samples were varied.

7 Feature Ranking

We next investigated the most discriminative features among Bengali stop words. The top 20 stop words are shown in Table 3, ordered by their Information Gain (IG) on the training set. Note that apart from pronouns such as তা, এ, কে, and যে, we also obtained do-verbs such as করি, করিয়া, and করিতে in the top ranks. This is an interesting finding.

Further, we show the term frequency of the features in the last three columns of Table 3, grouped by authors. Note that in all cases, Bankim Chandra's passages contain many more of the stop words, indicating that the passages are longer and more complex (as mentioned in Section 3). Among Rabindranath and Sarat Chandra, the variations are less systematic. Sometimes Sarat Chandra has more occurrences of a particular word, sometimes Rabindranath.

8 Conclusion

We presented the first large-scale study of Authorship Attribution in Bengali. As part of our study, we constructed a corpus of 3,000 literary passages from three eminent Bengali authors. On our balanced dataset, we performed classification experiments, and reached state-of-the-art test accuracy of 98% using character bigrams (tf) as features and Naive Bayes classifier. We further showed how performance varied on held-out data as the number of features and the number of training samples were altered. In most cases, we obtained a range of accuracy values between 95 and 99%. We analyzed the most discriminative features (stop words) and showed that the passages from one of our authors (Bankim Chandra) was longer and more complex than others. To the best of our knowledge, our study is the first reliable attempt at Authorship Attribution in Bengali, especially because prior studies had very limited training and test data. As future work, we would like to extend our approach to other forms

100

Rank	Word	PhTr	Meaning	IG	F_R	F_S	F_B
1	ই	/ee/	–	0.898	9249	8572	42637
2	করি	/kori/	I do	0.864	2268	2398	14174
3	তা	/taa/	then/that	0.852	4899	3815	17559
4	এ	/ay/	this/these	0.851	5595	4537	18624
5	কে	/kay/	who	0.843	4640	3186	14045
6	না	/naa/	no	0.828	4442	4321	19162
7	যা	/jaa/	that/which	0.792	2035	1778	10172
8	কি	/ki/	what	0.776	2152	3085	9912
9	যে	/jay/	that/which	0.762	2779	1946	10074
10	বা	/baa/	or	0.748	4446	4361	16436
11	পর	/por/	after/other	0.677	1332	1323	6738
12	তাহা	/taahaa/	that	0.672	1364	1402	6634
13	জন	/jon/	person/people	0.660	958	646	4657
14	করিয়া	/koria/	having done	0.657	1031	1245	5306
15	ও	/o/	and/also	0.639	2294	2408	8669
16	এই	/ey/	this	0.629	1055	752	4441
17	নাই	/naai/	no/not	0.601	413	425	3157
18	করিতে	/koritey/	to do	0.600	461	380	3215
19	হইতে	/hoitey/	to be	0.578	502	343	2989
20	সে	/shay/	he/she	0.578	2812	2128	7028

Table 3: Feature ranking of most discriminative Bengali stop words (by Information Gain). PhTr = phonetic transcription (approximate); IG = information gain (on training set); F_R, F_S, and F_B denote term frequency of the feature in the training set for Rabindranath, Sarat Chandra and Bankim Chandra, respectively.

of text, such as blogs, news articles, tweets, and online forum threads.

References

Victoria Bobicev, Marina Sokolova, Khaled El Emam, and Stan Matwin. 2013. Authorship Attribution in Health Forums. In *Proceedings of the International Conference Recent Advances in Natural Language Processing RANLP 2013*, pages 74–82. INCOMA Ltd. Shoumen, Bulgaria.

Dasha Bogdanova and Angeliki Lazaridou. 2014. Cross-Language Authorship Attribution. In *Proceedings of the Ninth International Conference on Language Resources and Evaluation (LREC-2014)*. European Language Resources Association (ELRA).

Tanmoy Chakraborty. 2012. Authorship Identification Using Stylometry Analysis in Bengali Literature. *CoRR*, abs/1208.6268.

Suprabhat Das and Pabitra Mitra. 2011. Author Identification in Bengali Literary Works. In Sergei O. Kuznetsov, Deba P. Mandal, Malay K. Kundu, and Sankar K. Pal, editors, *Pattern Recognition and Machine Intelligence*, volume 6744 of *Lecture Notes in Computer Science*, pages 220–226. Springer Berlin Heidelberg.

Mark Hall, Eibe Frank, Geoffrey Holmes, Bernhard Pfahringer, Peter Reutemann, and Ian H. Witten. 2009. The WEKA Data Mining Software: An Update. *SIGKDD Explor. Newsl.*, 11(1):10–18, November.

Siladitya Jana. 2015. Sister Nivedita's influence on J. C. Bose's writings. *Journal of the Association for Information Science and Technology*, 66(3):645–650.

Patrick Juola. 2006. Authorship Attribution. *Found. Trends Inf. Retr.*, 1(3):233–334, December.

Moshe Koppel, Jonathan Schler, and Shlomo Argamon. 2009. Computational methods in authorship attribution. *J. Am. Soc. Inf. Sci. Technol.*, 60(1):9–26, January.

Robert Layton, Paul Watters, and Richard Dazeley. 2010. Authorship Attribution for Twitter in 140 characters or less. In *Cybercrime and Trustworthy Computing Workshop (CTC), 2010 Second*, pages 1–8, July.

Kim Luyckx and Walter Daelemans. 2008. Authorship Attribution and Verification with Many Authors and Limited Data. In *Proceedings of the 22nd International Conference on Computational Linguistics (Coling 2008)*, pages 513–520, Manchester, UK, August. Coling 2008 Organizing Committee.

Frederick Mosteller and David L. Wallace. 1963. Inference In An Authorship Problem: A comparative study of discrimination methods applied to the authorship of the disputed Federalist papers. *Journal of the American Statistical Association*, 58(302):275–309.

Sibansu Mukhopadhyay, Tirthankar Dasgupta, and Anupam Basu. 2012. Development of an Online Repository of Bangla Literary Texts and its Ontological Representation for Advance Search Options. In *Workshop on Indian Language and Data: Resources and Evaluation Workshop Programme*, page 93. Citeseer.

S. Nagaprasad, T. Raghunadha Reddy, P. Vijayapal Reddy, A. Vinaya Babu, and B. VishnuVardhan. 2015. Empirical Evaluations Using Character and Word N-Grams on Authorship Attribution for Telugu Text. In Durbadal Mandal, Rajib Kar, Swagatam Das, and Bijaya Ketan Panigrahi, editors, *Intelligent Computing and Applications*, volume 343 of *Advances in Intelligent Systems and Computing*, pages 613–623. Springer India.

A. Jamal Nasir, Nico Görnitz, and Ulf Brefeld. 2014. An Off-the-shelf Approach to Authorship Attribution. In *Proceedings of COLING 2014, the 25th International Conference on Computational Linguistics: Technical Papers*, pages 895–904. Dublin City University and Association for Computational Linguistics.

Ruchita Sarawgi, Kailash Gajulapalli, and Yejin Choi. 2011. Gender Attribution: Tracing Stylometric Evidence Beyond Topic and Genre. In *Proceedings of the Fifteenth Conference on Computational Natural Language Learning*, pages 78–86, Portland, Oregon, USA, June. Association for Computational Linguistics.

Roy Schwartz, Oren Tsur, Ari Rappoport, and Moshe Koppel. 2013. Authorship Attribution of Micro-Messages. In *Proceedings of the 2013 Conference on Empirical Methods in Natural Language Processing*, pages 1880–1891. Association for Computational Linguistics.

Yanir Seroussi, Fabian Bohnert, and Ingrid Zukerman. 2012. Authorship Attribution with Author-aware Topic Models. In *Proceedings of the 50th Annual Meeting of the Association for Computational Linguistics (Volume 2: Short Papers)*, pages 264–269, Jeju Island, Korea, July. Association for Computational Linguistics.

Yanir Seroussi, Ingrid Zukerman, and Fabian Bohnert. 2014. Authorship Attribution with Topic Models. *Volume 40, Issue 2 - June 2014*, pages 269–310.

Efstathios Stamatatos. 2009. A survey of modern authorship attribution methods. *J. Am. Soc. Inf. Sci. Technol.*, 60(3):538–556, March.

Andreas van Cranenburgh. 2012. Literary authorship attribution with phrase-structure fragments. In *Proceedings of the NAACL-HLT 2012 Workshop on Computational Linguistics for Literature*, pages 59–63, Montréal, Canada, June. Association for Computational Linguistics.

TransChat: Cross-Lingual Instant Messaging for Indian Languages

Diptesh Kanojia[1]   Shehzaad Dhuliawala[1]   Abhijit Mishra[1]
Naman Gupta[2]   Pushpak Bhattacharyya[1]
[1]Center for Indian Language Technology, CSE Department
[1]IIT Bombay, India, [2]Yahoo Labs, Japan
[1]{diptesh,shehzaadzd,abhijitmishra,pb}@cse.iitb.ac.in
[2]naman.bbps@gmail.com

Abstract

We present *TransChat*[1], an open source, cross platform, Indian language Instant Messaging (IM) application that facilitates cross lingual textual communication over English and multiple Indian Languages. The application is a client-server IM architecture based chat system with multiple *Statistical Machine Translation (SMT)* engines working towards efficient translation and transmission of messages. *TransChat* allows users to select their preferred language and internally, selects appropriate translation engine based on the input configuration. For translation quality enhancement, necessary pre- and post-processing steps are applied on the input and output chat-texts. We demonstrate the efficacy of *TransChat* through a series of qualitative evaluations that test- (a) The usability of the system (b) The quality of the translation output. In a multilingual country like India, such applications can help overcome language barrier in domains like tourism, agriculture and health.

1 Introduction

In a multilingual country like India which has around 22 official languages spoken across 29 states by more than one billion people, it often becomes quite difficult for a non-speaker of a particular language to communicate with peers following the same language. Be it a non-Indian tourist visiting India for the first time or a farmer from Punjab trying to get tips from a Tamil speak-

ing professor on modern agricultural tools and techniques, communication is often hindered by *language barrier*. This problem has been recognized and well-studied by computational linguists as a result of which a large number of automatic translation systems have been proposed and modified in the last 30 years. Some of the notable Indian Language translation systems include Anglabharati (Sinha et al., 1995), Anusaraka (Padmanathrao, 2009), Sampark (Anthes, 2010) and Sata-Anuvaadak[2] (Kunchukuttan et al., 2014). Popular organizations like Google and Microsoft also provide translation solutions for Indian languages through Google- and Bing- Translation systems. Stymne (2011) demonstrate techniques for replacement of unknown words and data cleaning for Haitian Creole SMS translation, which can be utilized in a chat scenario. But even after so many years of MT research, one can still claim that these systems have not been able to attract a lot of users. This can be attributed to factors like- (a) poor user experience in terms of UI design, (b) systems being highly computational-resource intensive and slow in terms of response time, and (c) bad quality translation output. Moreover, the current MT interfaces do not provide a natural environment to attract more number of users to use the system in an effective way. As Flournoy and Callison-Burch (2000) point out, a successful translation application is one that can *reconcile overly optimistic user expectations with the limited capabilities of current MT technologies*. We believe, a chat application like *TransChat* bridges the current web programming paradigms with MT to provide users a powerful yet natural mode of communication.

---

[1]http://www.cfilt.iitb.ac.in/transchat/

[2]http://www.cfilt.iitb.ac.in/indic-translator

102

D S Sharma, R Sangal and E Sherly. Proc. of the 12th Intl. Conference on Natural Language Processing, pages 106–111,
Trivandrum, India. December 2015. ©2015 NLP Association of India (NLPAI)

Our work is motivated by the following factors,

- The ever-increasing usage of hand-held devices and Instant messaging provides us a rich platform to float our application. We can expect a large number of users to download and use it.

- Unavailability of cross lingual instant messaging applications for Indian languages motivates us to build and open-source our application that can be modified by developers as per the needs.

There are several challenges in building such an application. Some of them are,

1. IM users often abbreviate text (especially when the input language is English) to save time. (*e.g.* *"Hw r u?"* instead of *"How are you?"*). A translation system is often built on top of human-crafted rules (RBMT) or by automatically learning patterns from examples (EBMT) or by memorizing pattens(SMT). In all of these cases, the systems require the input text to be grammatically correct, thereby, making it necessary to deal with ungrammatical input text

2. To provide a rich *User Experience*, the basic requirement of an IM system is that it should transmit messages with ease and speed. Hence, language processing modules should be light-weight in order not to incur delay.

We try to handle these challenges by making use of appropriate language processing modules. The novelty of our work is three fold:

- Our system is scalable, *i.e.*, it allows large number of concurrent user access.

- It handles ungrammatical input through fast efficient text normalization and spell checking.

- We have tried to build a flexible system, *i.e* it can work with multiple translation engines built using different Machine Translation toolkits.

In the following sections we describe the system architecture, UI design and evaluation methodologies.

2 System Architecture

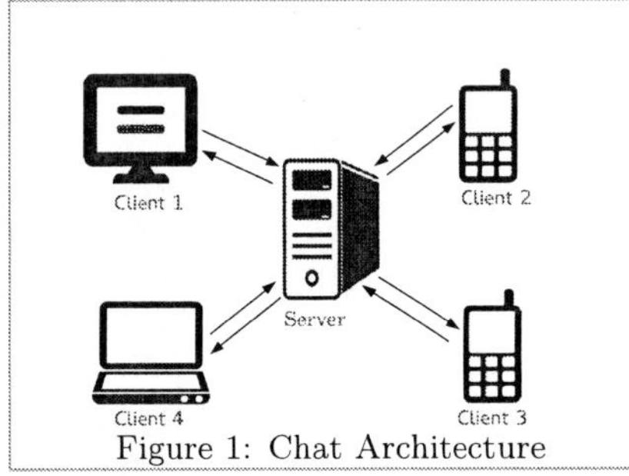

Figure 1: Chat Architecture

Figure 1 shows the system architecture of *TransChat*. Our system consists of a highly scalable chat server ejabberd[3] based on *Extensible Messaging and Presence Protocol(XMPP)*[4] protocol.

It is extensible via modules, which can provide support for additional capabilities such as saving offline messages, connecting with IRC channels, or a user database which makes use of user's vCards. It handles the chat requests, users and message transactions from one user to another.

We build our chat client using publicly available Smack library APIs[5] , which is easily portable to Android devices, thus, providing cross device integration for our chat system.

A user logs in to the server with their respective chat client and gets an option to select a language for his chats. The user then sends a message which is transferred via XMPP protocol to the server where it's processed and then shown to the user at the other end.

Figure 2 shows in detail the processes through which a message passes. The message is processed using the following techniques described in sections 2.1, 2.2, 2.3, and 2.5

2.1 Compression

While chatting, users often express their emotions/mood by stressing over a few characters in the word. For example, usage of words like *thankssss, hellpppp, sryy, byeeee, wowww, goood* corresponds the person being *obliged, needy, apologetic, emotional, amazed,* etc.

As far as we know, it is unlikely for an English word to contain the same character con-

---

[3]https://www.process-one.net/en/ejabberd/
[4]http://xmpp.org/xmpp-protocols/
[5]https://www.igniterealtime.org/projects/smack/

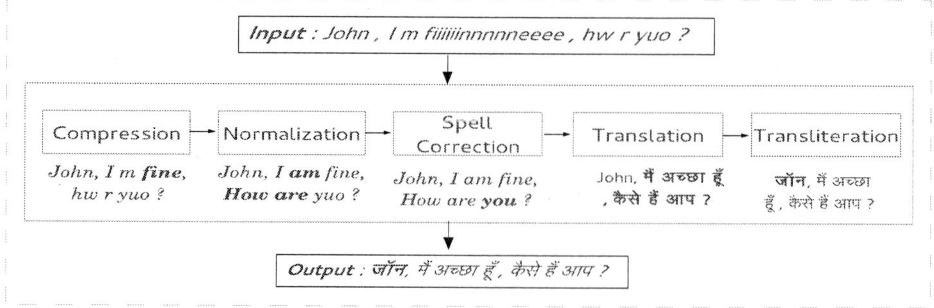

Figure 2: Server Side Processing of *TransChat*

Input Sentence	Output Sentence
I feeellll soooooo gooood	I feel so good
I m veryyyy happyyyyy	I m very happy

Table 1: Sample output of Compression module

secutively for three or more times. We, hence, compress all the repeated windows of character length greater than two, to two characters. For example "pleeeeeeeaaaaaaassseeee"is converted to "pleeaassee".

Each window now contains two characters of the same alphabet in cases of repetition. Let n be the number of windows, obtained from the previous step. Since average length of English word (Mayzner, 1965) is approximately 4.9 , we apply brute force search over 2^n possibilities to select a valid dictionary word. If none of the combinations form a valid English word, the compressed form is used for *normalization.*

Table 1 contains sanitized sample output from our compression module for further processing.

2.2 Normalization

Text Message Normalization is the process of translating ad-hoc abbreviations, typographical errors, phonetic substitution and ungrammatical structures used in text messaging (SMS and Chatting) to plain English. Use of such language (often referred as Chatting Language) induces noise which poses additional processing challenges. While dictionary lookup based methods[6] are popular for Normalization, they can not make use of context and domain knowledge. For example, *yr* can have multiple translations like *year, your.*

We tackle this by implementing a normal-

izationsystem[7](Raghunathan and Krawczyk, 2009) as a Phrase Based Machine Translation System, that learns normalization patterns from a large number of training examples. We use Moses (Koehn et al., 2007), a statistical machine translation system that allows training of translation models.

Training process requires a Language Model of the target language and a parallel corpora containing aligned un-normalized and normalized word pairs. Our language model consists of 15000 English words taken from the web.

Parallel corpora was collected from the following sources :

1. Stanford Normalization Corpora which consists of 9122 pair of un-normalized and normalized words / phrases.

2. The above corpora, however, lacks acronyms and short hand texts like *2mrw, l8r, b4* which are frequently used in chatting. We collected additional data through crowd-sourcing involving peers from CFILT lab[8]. They were asked to enter commonly used chatting sentences/acronyms and their normalized versions. We collected 215 pairs unnormalized to normalized word/phrase mappings.

3. Dictionary of Internet slang words was extracted from `http://www.noslang.com`.

Table 2 contains input and normalized output from our module.

---

[6]`http://www.lingo2word.com`

[7]Normalization Model: `http://www.cfilt.iitb.ac.in/Normalization.rar`

[8]`http://www.cfilt.iitb.ac.in`

Input Sentence	Output Sentence
shd v go 2 ur house	should we go to your house
u r awesm	you are awesome
hw do u knw	how do you know

Table 2: Sample output of Normalization module

2.3 Spell Checking

Users often make spelling mistakes while chatting. A spell checker makes sure that a valid English word is sent to the Translation system and for such a word, a valid output is produced. We take this problem into account and introduce a spell checker as a *pre-processing* module before the sentence is sent for translation. We have used the JAVA API of Jazzy spell checker[9] for handling spelling mistakes.

An example of correction provided by the Spell Checker module is given below:-

Input: *Today is* **mnday**
Output: *Today is* **monday**

Please note that, our current system performs compression, normalization and spell-checking if the input language is English. If the user selects one of the available Indian Languages as the input language, the input text bypasses these stages and is fed to the translation system directly. We, however, plan to include such modules for Indian Languages in future.

If the input language is not English, the user can type the text in the form of Romanized script, which will get transliterated to indic-script with the help of Google's transliteration API. The user can also input the text directly using an in-script keyboard (available in Windows and Android platforms), in which case the transliteration has to be switched off.

2.4 Translation

Translation system is a plug-able module that provides translation between two language pairs. Currently *TransChat* is designed for translation between English to five Indian languages namely, Hindi, Gujarati, Punjabi, Marathi and Malayalam. Translations between these languages are carried out using Statistical Phrase Based Machine Translation

paradigm, powered by the Sata-Anuvadak[10] system.

2.5 Transliteration

There is a high probability that a chat will contain many Named Entities and Out of Vocabulary (OOV) words. Such words are not parts of the training corpora of a translation system, and thus do not get translated. For such words, we use Google Transliteration API[11] as a *post processing step*, so that the output comes out in the desired script. Table 3 contains the sample output from our Transliteration module.

3 User Interface

We designed the interface using HTML, CSS, JavaScript and JSP on the front end as a wrapper on our system based on Tomcat web server. We have used Bootstrap[12] and Semantic UI[13] CSS frameworks for the beautification of our interface. The design of our system is simple and sends the chat message using socket to the chat server and receives the response from the server, and shown on the interface.

We use a similar interface for the mobile version of our applications. We have used Web-View class in Android, and Windows applications, and UIWebView for iOS. Figure 3 shows a screen-shot of the interface.

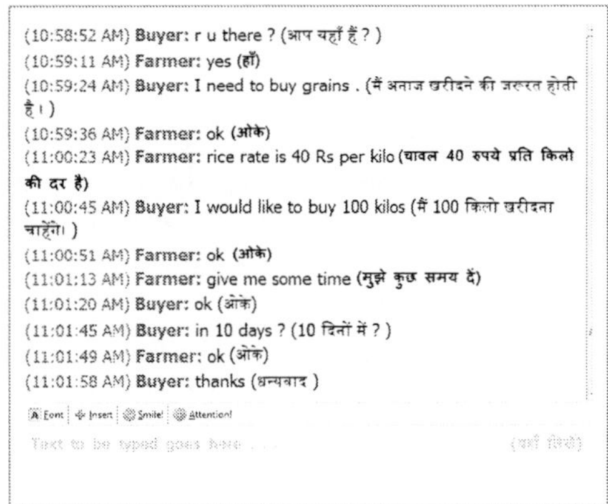

Figure 3: Chat Screenshot

---

[9] http://sourceforge.net/projects/jazzy/

[10] http://www.cfilt.iitb.ac.in/static/download.html
[11] https://developers.google.com/transliterate/
[12] http://getbootstrap.com/
[13] http://semantic-ui.com/

	Input Sentence	Output Sentence
Example 1	Putin अमेरिका आए थे । (Putin amerika aaye the) (Putin visited America)	पुतिन अमेरिका आए थे । (Putin amerika aaye the) (Putin visited America)
Example 2	Telangana भारत का नया राज्य है (telangaana bhaarat ka nayaa rajya hai) (Telangana is a new state of India)	तेलंगाना भारत का नया राज्य है । (telangaana bhaarat ka nayaa rajya hai) (Telangana is a new state of India)

Table 3: Sample output of Transliteration module

	BLEU (Google)	BLEU (SATA)	BLEU Bing	METEOR (Google)	METEOR (SATA)	METEOR (Bing)
Hindi	0.1991	0.1757	0.0497	0.2323	0.1529	0.2217
Marathi	0.088	0.0185	NA	0.1478	0.0843	NA
Punjabi	0.2277	0.0481	NA	0.2084	0.0902	NA
Gujarati	0.0446	0.0511	NA	0.1354	0.1255	NA
Malayalam	0.0612	0.0084	NA	0.1259	0.0666	NA

Table 4: Evaluation Statistics on Normalized input

	P1	P2	P3
P1	1		
P2	.63	1	
P3	.67	.61	1

Table 6: Inter Annotator Agreement for User experience evaluation

4 Evaluation Details

We do a two fold evaluation of our system that ensures the following

- Good user experience in terms of (a) using the system and (b) acceptable translation quality etc.

- The pre- and post-processing steps employed helped enhance the quality of translated chat.

We study the first point qualitatively by employing three human users who are asked to use the system by giving 20 messages each. They have to eventually assign three scores to the system, *Usability score, Fluency score of the chat output* and *Adequacy score of the chat output*. Fluency indicates the grammatical correctness where as adequacy indicates how appropriate the machine translation is, when it comes to semantic transfer. We then compute the average Inter Annotator Agreement (IAA) between their scores. Table 6 presents the results. We have obtained a substantial IAA via Fliess' Kappa evaluation.

To justify the second point, we input the un-normalized chat messages to three different translators *viz.* Google, Bing and Sata-

Anuvaadak. We then obtain the BLEU (Papineni et al., 2002) and METEOR (Denkowski and Lavie, 2014) translation scores. We then compute the evaluation scores after applying the pre- and post-processing steps explained in section 2. Table 4 and 5 present the scores for processed and un-processed inputs. As we can see, applying pre- and post-processing steps help us achieve better evaluation scores.

We observe a slight inconsistency between BLEU and METEOR scores for some cases. BLEU has been shown to be less effective for systems involving Indian Languages due to *language divergence, free-word order* and *morphological richness* (Ananthakrishnan et al., 2007). On the other hand, our METEOR module has been modified to support stemming, paraphrasing and lemmatization (Dungarwal et al., 2014) for Indian Languages, tackling such nuances to some extent. This may have accounted for the score differences.

5 Conclusion and Future Work

In today's era of short messaging and chatting, there is a great need to make available a multilingual chat system where users can interact despite the language barrier. We present such an Indian language IM application that facilitates cross lingual text based communication. Our success in developing such an application for English to Indian languages is a small step in providing people with easy access to such a chat system. We plan to make efforts towards improving this application to enable chatting in all Indian languages via a

	BLEU (Google)	BLEU (SATA)	BLEU (Bing)	METEOR (Google)	METEOR (SATA)	METEOR (Bing)
Hindi	0.0306	0.0091	0.0413	0.0688	0.053	0.0778
Marathi	0.0046	0.0045	NA	0.0396	0.0487	NA
Punjabi	0.0196	0.0038	NA	0.0464	0.0235	NA
Gujrati	0.0446	0.0109	NA	0.1354	0.06	NA
Malyalam	0.0089	0.0168	NA	0.0358	0.1045	NA

Table 5: Evaluation Statistics on Unnormalized input

common interface. We also plan to inculcate Word Suggestions based on corpora statistics, as they are being typed, so that the user is presented with better lexical choices as a sentence is being formed. We can also perform emotional analysis of the chat messages and introduce linguistic improvements such as euphemism for sensitive dialogues.

Such an application can have a huge impact on communication, especially in the rural and semi-urban areas, along with enabling people to understand each other.

6 Acknowledgment

We would like to thank CFILT, IIT Bombay for granting us the computational resources, and annotation of our experiments. We would also like to thank Avneesh Kumar, who helped us setup the experiment in its initial phase.

References

R Ananthakrishnan, Pushpak Bhattacharyya, M Sasikumar, and Ritesh M Shah. 2007. Some issues in automatic evaluation of english-hindi mt: More blues for bleu. *ICON*.

Gary Anthes. 2010. Automated translation of indian languages. *Communications of the ACM*, 53(1):24–26.

Michael Denkowski and Alon Lavie. 2014. Meteor universal: Language specific translation evaluation for any target language. In *Proceedings of the EACL 2014 Workshop on Statistical Machine Translation*.

Piyush Dungarwal, Rajen Chatterjee, Abhijit Mishra, Anoop Kunchukuttan, Ritesh Shah, and Pushpak Bhattacharyya. 2014. The iit bombay hindi english translation system at wmt 2014. *ACL 2014*, page 90.

Raymond S Flournoy and Christopher Callison-Burch. 2000. Reconciling user expectations and translation technology to create a useful real-world application. In *Proceedings of the 22nd International Conference on Translating and the Computer*, pages 16–17.

Philipp Koehn, Hieu Hoang, Alexandra Birch, Chris Callison-Burch, Marcello Federico, Nicola Bertoldi, Brooke Cowan, Wade Shen, Christine Moran, Richard Zens, Chris Dyer, Ondřej Bojar, Alexandra Constantin, and Evan Herbst. 2007. Moses: Open source toolkit for statistical machine translation. In *Proceedings of the 45th Annual Meeting of the ACL on Interactive Poster and Demonstration Sessions*, ACL '07, pages 177–180, Stroudsburg, PA, USA. Association for Computational Linguistics.

Anoop Kunchukuttan, Abhijit Mishra, Rajen Chatterjee, Ritesh Shah, and Pushpak Bhattacharyya. 2014. Sata-anuvadak: Tackling multiway translation of indian languages.

S. Mayzner. 1965. *Tables of Single-letter and Digram Frequency Counts for Various Word-length and Letter-position Combinations*. Psychonomic monograph supplements. Psychonomic Press.

Anantpur Amba Padmanathrao. 2009. Anusaaraka: An approach for mt taking insights from the indian grammatical tradition.

Kishore Papineni, Salim Roukos, Todd Ward, and Wei-Jing Zhu. 2002. Bleu: a method for automatic evaluation of machine translation. In *Proceedings of the 40th annual meeting on association for computational linguistics*, pages 311–318. Association for Computational Linguistics.

Karthik Raghunathan and Stefan Krawczyk. 2009. Cs224n: Investigating sms text normalization using statistical machine translation. *Department of Computer Science, Stanford University*.

RMK Sinha, K Sivaraman, A Agrawal, R Jain, R Srivastava, and A Jain. 1995. Anglabharti: a multilingual machine aided translation project on translation from english to indian languages. In *Systems, Man and Cybernetics, 1995. Intelligent Systems for the 21st Century., IEEE International Conference on*, volume 2, pages 1609–1614. IEEE.

Sara Stymne. 2011. Spell checking techniques for replacement of unknown words and data cleaning for haitian creole sms translation. In *Proceedings of the Sixth Workshop on Statistical Machine Translation*, WMT '11, pages 470–477, Stroudsburg, PA, USA. Association for Computational Linguistics.

A Database of Infant Cry Sounds
to Study the Likely Cause of Cry

Shivam Sharma[1], Shubham Asthana[2], V. K. Mittal[3]
[1,2,3]Indian Institute of Information Technology, Chittoor District, India
[1]shivam.sharma@iiits.in, [2]asthana.shubham@gmail.com and [3]vkmittal@iiits.in

Abstract

Infant cry is a mode of communication, for interacting and drawing attention. The infants cry due to physiological, emotional or some ailment reasons. Cry involves high pitch changes in the signal. In this paper we describe an 'Infant Cry Sounds Database' (ICSD), collected especially for the study of likely cause of an infant's cry. The database consists of infant cry sounds due to six causes: pain, discomfort, emotional need, ailment, environmental factors and hunger/thirst. The ground truth cause of cry is established with the help of two medical experts and parents of the infants. Preliminary analysis is carried out using the sound production features, the instantaneous fundamental frequency and frame energy derived from the cry acoustic signal, using auto correlation and linear prediction (LP) analysis. Spectrograms give the base reference. The infant cry sounds due to *pain* and *discomfort* are distinguished. The database should be helpful towards automated diagnosis of the causes of infant cry.

1   Introduction

Infant cry is an acoustic manipulation, that consists of different forms of vocalization, constrictive silence, coughing, choking and breaks (Neustein, 2010). Its analysis provides the information regarding health, disease, gender and emotions. In this way, infants communicate with their environment about what they feel. Infant cry falls in the most sensitive range of human auditory sensation (Jr et al., 2005).

First cry of an infant gives significant information to determine the APGAR count, a tool for the categorization of the new born baby as healthy, unhealthy or weak (Neustein, 2010). The time varying characteristics, limb movement and vocalization give insight to the transitional characteristics. Studies of physiological variables such as facial expression, muscular tonus, sleep and suction abilities were conducted to analyse the needs of an infant (Skogsdal et al., 1997). The study of infant cry has gained significance over the years, because of diverse applications.

Fundamental frequency and the first three formants of cry signals were studied earlier (Baeck and Souza, 2001); (Daga and Panditrao, 2011). Attempts were made to classify the cry signals on the basis of pain, sadness, fear and hunger etc. (Abdulaziz and Ahmad, 2010); (Mima and Arakawa, 2006). The pitch characteristics, aimed to classify the cry signals into categories: urgent, arousing, sick, distressing etc. (Zeskind and Marshall, 1988). A pitch detection algorithm was used to compute the instantaneous fundamental frequency (F_0) (Neustein, 2010). First three formants along with F_0 were used for the cry analysis (Hidayati et al., 2009). Cepstrum analysis was carried out for determining the F_0 and first three formants for cry (Chandralingam et al., 2012). A time domain cross-correlation pitch determination method gave details of every pitch epoch (Petroni et al., 1994).

Spectrographic analysis was carried out for characterizing pitch and harmonics (Neustein, 2010). Short-time energy, zero-crossing rate and LP coefficients were used for the analysis of the cry signals (Kuo, 2010). A cry is described by the duration and shape of the F_0 contour (Varallyay-Jr, 2007). Hyper-phonation was examined by

D S Sharma, R Sangal and E Sherly. Proc. of the 12th Intl. Conference on Natural Language Processing, pages 112–117,
Trivandrum, India. December 2015. ©2015 NLP Association of India (NLPAI)

mean, standard deviation and peak of the fundamental frequency (Zeskind and Marshall, 1988). In another study, segment density, segment length and pause length were used to examine the relationship between these parameters and gender of the baby (Varallyay, 2006). The frame-wise comparison of the mean F_0 gave insight into the analysis of cries of infants with different heart disorders (Chandralingam et al., 2012). This study also correlated disphonation to muscle *pain* or *discomfort*.

A different method to extract F_0 was proposed (Petroni et al., 1994). The F_0 for cry was observed to be between 200-500 Hz, with average F_0 320 Hz for male infant and 400 Hz for female infant (Daga and Panditrao, 2011). Typical characteristics were observed in the shape of power spectra of cry signals for hunger, sleepiness and discomfort (Mima and Arakawa, 2006). Cries of infants were divided into *normal* and *disorders* like Tetralogy of Fallot (TOF), Ventricular Septal Defect (VSD), Atrial Septal Defect (ASD), and Patent Ductus Arteriosus (PDA) (Chandralingam et al., 2012). Specific segments of cry signals showed similarity amongst infants with hearing disorders and normal infants. However, detailed study of an infant cry, in conjunction with likely causes as per expert medical opinion, is still required to be carried out in detail.

In this paper, an 'Infant Cry Sounds Database' *(IIIT-S ICSD)* is described in detail. The database consists of different categories of cries due to different reasons. The data of infant cry signals was recorded in a doctors cabin, where the infants were brought-in for routine check-up, vaccination trips or due to any ailment. Spectrographic study was carried for each case. Changes in the F_0 contour and harmonics were observed for cry causes. An effort is made for the classification of cry signals, based upon the spectrographic analysis and using signal processing methods. The analysed causes of each cry are compared with the ground truth determined as per doctors or parents.

This paper is organized as follows. Section II discusses details of the *IIIT-S ICSD*. Section III discusses signal processing methods for analysing the infant cry signals. Features of the Infant cry signals are discussed in Section IV. In Section V, the observations are made from the results of infant cry analysis. The paper is summarised in Section VI, along with the scope of future work.

Table 1: Template for naming files in IIIT-S ICSD

SPKR01_M_S1a_CRY07	
(a) Symbols	*(b) Interpretation*
SPKR#	The infant number (Ex: 01)
M/F	Sex of the infant (Ex: Male)
S#a	Session number and session subpart (Ex: 1a)
CRY#	Number of cries in the session being considered (Ex: 07)

2 The IIIT-S ICSD Cry

2.1 Data Collection

The data was collected from Pranaam hospital, Madinaguda, Hyderabad, under the supervision of Dr. Manish Gour (MBBS, DCH) and Dr Nizam (MBBS). The age group of infants was restricted between 3 months and 2 years. The cry signals of infants were collected during the regular check-up visits, the vaccination trips or any emotional need of attention. People present in the room were requested to maintain silence, so as to record the cry sample. Also the parents were advised not to comfort the baby for brief duration, to ensure the uninterrupted data collection. Along with data, the personal details noted include: infant name, parent name, parent profession, sex and age of the infant and predictive causes of the cry.

For the recording purpose, Roland R-09 Wave/MP3 recorder was used and was placed at 10-20 cm from the infant's mouth. Precautions were taken to avoid any unwanted noise or crosstalk. Sampling rate of 48 KHz, with 24 bit coding rate, was used for recording in stereo mode. There were no interruptions from the social environment during the data recording. The only unwanted noise that could overlap the cry sound may be from fan and air-conditioner. The ambient temperature during the recordings was 38°C, which was regulated by the air conditioner at 25°C.

2.2 Organization of the IIIT-S ICSD

The terminologies used in naming of the database files, given in *Table 1*, are described below:

- *Session*: The acoustic signal, right from the time an infant starts crying (including all inhalations and exhalations), until the infant becomes quiet, is a *session*.
- *Session subpart*: Each session consists of *subparts*, characterised by the contiguous set

Table 2: *Causes of Infant cry (in IIIT-S ICSD)*

(a) Cry Causes	(b) Description
1. Pain	Cry due to pain (caused by vaccination, physical hurt or internal pain)
2. Discomfort	Cry due to irritation caused by the external environment (e.g., the doctor opening baby's mouth to pour-in drops, or the vaccination)
3. Emotional Need	Cry when the baby wants to go back to parents arms
4. Ailment	Cries due to any ailments like cold, cough, fever
5. Environmental factors	Cry due to fear of the surroundings or change in environmental conditions.
6. Hunger/Thirst	Cry when the baby is hungry or thirsty

Table 3: *Summary of contents in IIIT-S ICSD*

Attributes	Values
Total # of files	76
Total # of speakers	33
Total # of session	76
Total # of cries in sessions	693
Average # of sessions per speaker	2.3
Average # of cries in each session	9.1
Total duration of all sessions	670.1 s
Average duration of each session	8.817 s

of signals, separated by some noise

- *Cry*: Each session subpart comprises of a number of cries, separated by some noise.

A two stage process was followed for data collection in the study. The first stage involved *raw data collection* at the hospital, and the second stage included *pre-processing*. The unwanted noise, in the raw data was removed using 'Wave-Surfer' tool, to render it cross-talk free. The cries were categorized as per the ground reality, i.e., the actual cause as per the doctor or parent. The main causes of cry that we came across, are described in *Table 2*, in columns (a) and (b).

The cry as combination of two or more causes is retained in a separate category. There was also a special case, when an infant cried by listening to another infant cry. Not many samples could be obtained for this cry due to *Domino effect*, but this is retained as another special category, for future study. The database consists of total 76 cry sound files, which can be categorised in 6 classes. The database summary is given in *Table 3*.

3 Signal Processing Methods

3.1 Short Time Fourier Transform

Short time Fourier Transform (STFT) (Oppenheim et al., 1989) is used to process the segments of the cry signals in the frequency domain. The data is divided into overlapping frames. The Fourier transform for each frame is given by:

$$X(\tau, \omega) = \sum_{n=-\infty}^{n=\infty} x[n]w[n-m]e^{-jwn} \qquad (1)$$

Where $x[n]$ is the signal and $w[n]$ is the window function. Here m is discrete and ω is continuous (Oppenheim et al., 1989). Magnitude of the STFT gives the *spectrogram*, i.e., $|X(\tau, \omega)|^2$. Spectrographic analysis basically represents the 3D spectral information obtained from the magnitude spectrum, for the short-time overlapped window segments. The *X-axis* represents time, *Y-axis* represents frequency, and the third dimension represents the log magnitude of the sinusoidal frequency components, which is converted to the proportional intensity.

3.2 Auto Correlation Analysis

The *auto correlation function* (Rabiner and Juang, 1993) reflects the similarity between a random sequence and the time-delayed same sequence. For the speech signal $x(n)$, the *correlation* function is defined as

$$r_x(m) = E[x(n)x(n+m)]$$

$$= \lim_{N \to \infty} \frac{1}{2N+1} \sum_{n=-N}^{n=N} x(n)x(n+m)$$

$$(2)$$

Where, $E[.]$ represents statistical expectations (Rabiner and Juang, 1993). Since speech production system can be regarded as stationary within short-time frames, the cry signal is divided into frames. The auto-correlation function is:

$$r'_x(m) = \frac{1}{2N+1} \sum_{n=-N}^{n=N} x(n)x(n+m) \qquad (3)$$

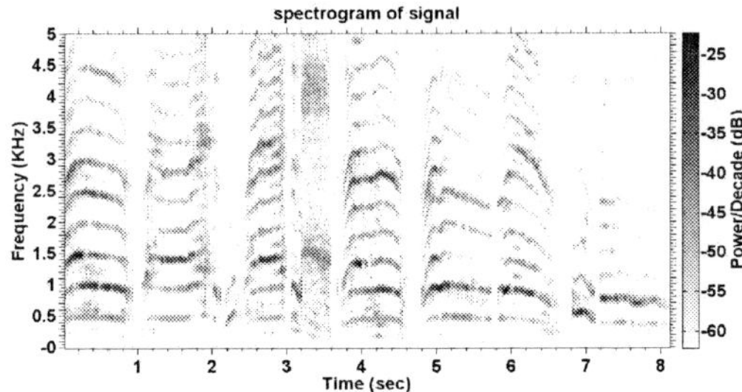

Figure 1: Spectrogram of *Pain Cry* of Infant #1

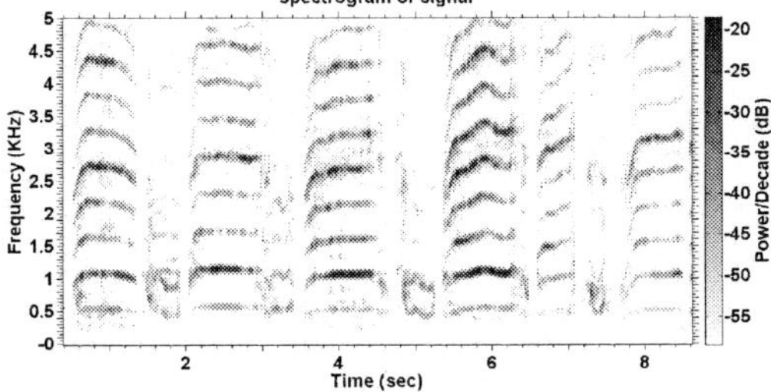

Figure 2: Spectrogram of *Discomfort Cry*, Infant #1

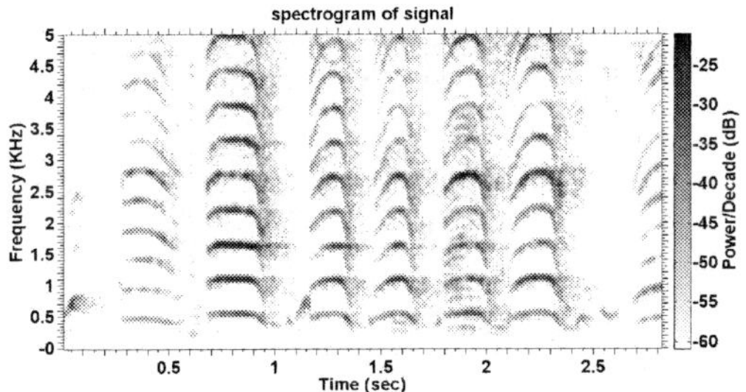

Figure 3: Spectrogram of *Pain Cry* of Infant #2

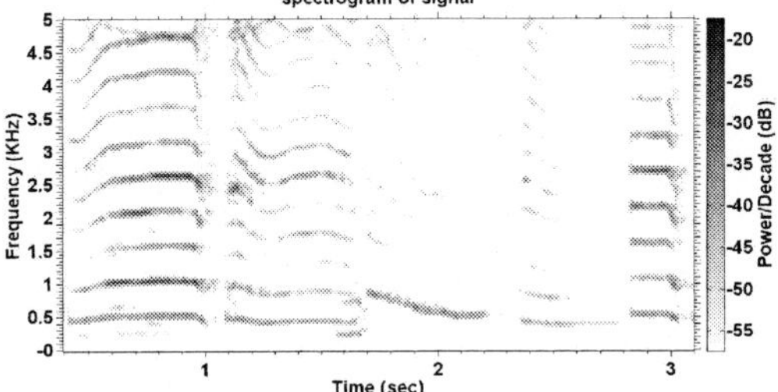

Figure 4: Spectrogram of *Discomfort Cry*, Infant #2

When $m = 0$, then (3) represents *short-term energy* of the signal (Shuyin et al., 2009). The pitch period information is more pronounced in auto-correlation, than in speech signal.

3.3 Linear prediction (LP) analysis

Speech signal is produced by the convolution of the excitation source and time-varying vocal tract system components. These components can be separated, using *LP analysis* (Makhoul, 1975). The prediction of current sample as a linear combination of past p samples forms the basis of LP analysis, where p is the order of prediction. The predicted sample is $\hat{s} = -\sum_{k=1}^{p} a_k s(n - k)$, where $a_k s$ are the *LP coefficients*. Here $s(n)$ is the *windowed speech* sequence, obtained by multiplying short-time speech frame with a Hamming window, i.e., $s(n) = x(n)w(n)$, where $w(n)$ is the windowing function. *The prediction error e(n)* can be computed by the difference between the actual sample $s(n)$ and the *predicted* samples $\hat{s}(n)$ (Rabiner and Juang, 1993). This is given by $e(n) = s(n) - \hat{s}(n)$, i.e., $e(n) = s(n) + \sum_{k=1}^{p} a_k s(n-k)$.

The LP coefficients are used to minimize the *prediction error e(n)*. The coefficients are computed using the *least squares* method, that minimizes the LP residual or *total prediction error* (Makhoul, 1975). In frequency domain, it can be represented as $E(z) = S(z) + \sum_{k=1}^{p} a_k S(z)z^{-k}$.

$$A(z) = \frac{E(z)}{S(z)} = 1 + \sum_{k=1}^{p} a_k z^{-k} \qquad (4)$$

The LP Spectrum *H(z)* can be obtained as,

$$H(z) = \frac{1}{1 + \sum_{k=1}^{p} a_k z^{-k}} = \frac{1}{A(z)} \qquad (5)$$

As *A(z)* is the reciprocal of *H(z)*, the LP residual is obtained by inverse filtering of the speech. The auto-correlation of LP residual can also give information about the pitch period.

4 Features explored

In this study, correlation between infant cry and the likely causes is examined using mainly the magnitude of short-time spectrogram and F_0. Spectrograms are used for obtaining the F_0 and harmonics as *Ground Truth*.

In this paper, F_0 is obtained by using two different methods to validate the results and the modified signal processing methods used. Autocorrelation and Linear Prediction analysis methods are used after modification, to detect peaks in the auto-correlation or LP residual. In both methods, the signal was divided into frames of 10 ms, with a shift of 6ms. The F_0 contour was smoothed further, using a binary mask derived using the signal energy for each frame. The results from auto-correlation and LP analysis are compared with the

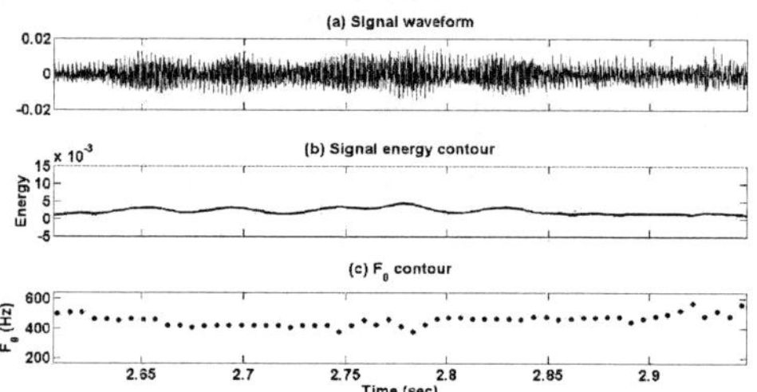

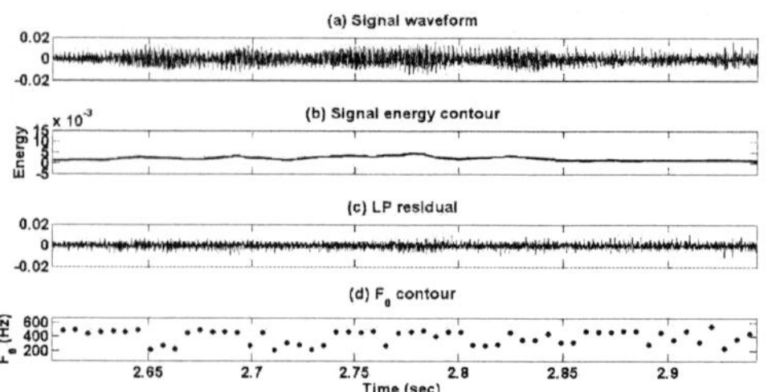

Figure 5: Illustration of (a) signal waveform, (b) signal energy contour and (c) F_0 contour of *Pain Cry* of infant #1 (using *auto-correlation*)

Figure 7: Illustration of (a) signal waveform, (b) signal energy contour, (c) LP residual and (d) F_0 contour of *Pain Cry* of infant #1 (using *LP analysis*)

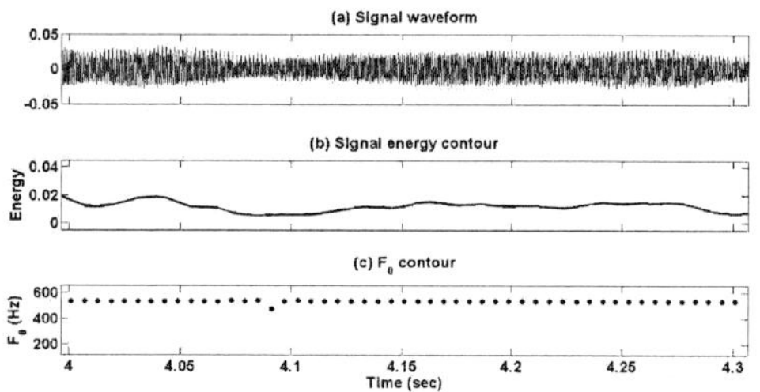

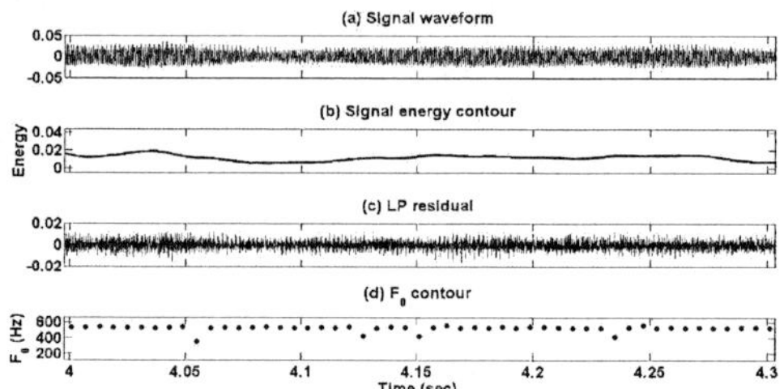

Figure 6: Illustration of (a) signal waveform, (b) signal energy contour and (c) F_0 contour of *Discomfort Cry* of infant #1 (using *auto-correlation*)

Figure 8: Illustration of (a) signal waveform, (b) signal energy contour, (c) LP residual and (d) F0 contour of *Discomfort Cry*, infant #1 *(LP analysis)*

ground truth, which is obtained using the spectrograms. Similar patterns of changes in the F_0 contours are observed for the cries due to similar causes, in particular for *pain cry* and *discomfort cry*.

5 Preliminary Analysis

The changes in F_0 contour and harmonics for infant cry signals were observed using the spectrograms. The spectrograms were plotted for cry signal frames of 30 ms with shift of 9ms, for the same infant, crying for different causes. The F_0 contours and harmonics of a *pain cry* (Fig. 1 and Fig. 3) indicate *cyclic changes* with larger fluctuations. These could be due to psychological conditions during *pain*. The shape of F_0 contour in the case of cries due to *discomfort* (Fig. 2 and Fig. 4) have relatively *flat* nature, with changes in F_0 at larger periods and having lesser fluctuations.

The F_0 contours derived using auto-correlation and LP analysis were observed in similar way. Similar to the observations from spectrograms, these F_0 contours show *cyclic* changes with larger fluctuations for cries due to *pain*, in Fig. 5 and Fig. 7. In the case of cries due to *discomfort*, the

F_0 contours are relatively *flat* in Fig. 6 and Fig. 8, with lesser fluctuations.

6 Summary and Conclusions

In the study of infant cry signals the database collection and collation plays a vital role, as the entire analysis depends upon it. Hence, in this paper emphasis is laid upon collection and organization of infant cry data, for the classification of infant cries according to different causes. The predictive reasons for infant cries were noted as per the inference by doctor and parents. Details of the IIIT-S ICSD database are also elaborated.

In this paper, the spectrographic analysis of the infant cry is carried out, by observing changes in the F_0 contour and harmonics, to determine the likely cause of the cry. Signal processing methods such as auto-correlation and linear prediction analysis are used after modification, in order to observe some particular patterns of infant cry. Possible leads, for association with any kind of ailment the infant is suffering from, are explored. The observations from spectrograms are similar to the changes in F_0 contours, derived using auto correlation and LP analysis, for cries due to same cause. The F_0 contours have *cyclic changes* with larger fluctuations for *pain cry*, and are relatively *flat* with lesser fluctuations for *discomfort cry*. The observations are consistent across different infant cries, and signal processing methods.

Further, we intend to utilize this database to examine the cry characteristics using other signal processing methods and carry out quantitative analysis in detail. This study would be helpful towards enabling the early diagnostics and medical care, if the reason of the infant cry due to a particular ailment is established early, especially where the reaction time could be critically important.

Acknowledgement

The authors are thankful to Dr. Manish Gour (M.B.B.S, DCH) and Dr. Nizam (M.B.B.S) of Pranaam Hospital, Madinaguda, Hyderabad and parents of the infants for supporting in collection of the cry samples needed for the study.

References

Y. Abdulaziz and S.M.S. Ahmad. 2010. Infant cry recognition system: A comparison of system performance based on mel frequency and linear prediction cepstral coefficients. In *Int. Conf. on Information Retrieval Knowledge Management, (CAMP)*, pages 260–263, March.

H.E. Baeck and M.N. Souza. 2001. Study of acoustic features of newborn cries that correlate with the context. In *Engineering in Medicine and Biology Society, 2001. Annual IEEE Int. Conf. of the 23rd Proceedings*, volume 3, pages 2174–2177.

S. Chandralingam, T. Anjaneyulu, and K. Satyanarayana. 2012. Estimation of fundamental and formant frequencies of infants cries; a study of infants with congenital heart disorder. In *Indian Journal of Computer Science and Engineering*, volume 3(4), pages 574–582.

Raina P. Daga and Anagha M. Panditrao. 2011. Article: Acoustical analysis of pain cries in neonates: Fundamental frequency. *IJCA Special Issue on Electronics, Information and Communication Engineering*, ICEICE(3):18–21, December. Full text available.

R. Hidayati, I.K.E. Purnama, and M.H. Purnomo. 2009. The extraction of acoustic features of infant cry for emotion detection based on pitch and formants. In *Int. Conf. onInstrumentation, Communications, Information Technology, and Biomedical Engineering (ICICI-BME)*, pages 1–5, Nov.

G. Varallyay Jr, Z. Benyo A. Illenyi, Z. Farkas, and G. Katona. 2005. The speech-chorus method at the analysis of the infant cry. In *Acoustic Review*, volume 6(2), page 915.

K. Kuo. 2010. Feature extraction and recognition of infant cries. In *IEEE Int. Conf. on Electro/Information Technology (EIT)*, pages 1–5, May.

J. Makhoul. 1975. Linear prediction: A tutorial review. *Proceedings of the IEEE*, 63(4):561–580, April.

Y. Mima and K. Arakawa. 2006. Cause estimation of younger babies' cries from the frequency analyses of the voice - classification of hunger, sleepiness, and discomfort. In *International Symposium on Intelligent Signal Processing and Communications, IS-PACS '06*, pages 29–32, Dec.

Amy Neustein, editor. 2010. *Advances in Speech Recognition: Mobile Environments, Call Centers and Clinics*. Springer, New York.

Alan V Oppenheim, Ronald W Schafer, John R Buck, and et al. 1989. *Discretetime signal processing*, volume 2. Prentice-hall Englewood Cliffs.

M. Petroni, M.E. Malowany, C.C. Johnston, and B.J. Stevens. 1994. A new, robust vocal fundamental frequency (f_0) determination method for the analysis of infant cries. In *Computer-Based Medical Systems, Proceedings IEEE Seventh Symposium*, pages 223–228, June.

Lawrence Rabiner and Biing-Hwang Juang. 1993. *Fundamentals of Speech Recognition*. Prentice-Hall, Inc., Upper Saddle River, NJ, USA.

Zhang Shuyin, Guo Ying, and Wang Buhong. 2009. Auto-correlation property of speech and its application in voice activity detection. In *First Int. Workshop on Education Technology and Computer Science, ETCS '09*, volume 3, pages 265–268, March.

Y Skogsdal, M Eriksson, and J Schollin. 1997. Analgesia in newborns given oral glucose. *Acta Pdiatrica*, 86(2):217–220.

Gyorgy Varallyay-Jr. 2007. The melody of crying. *Int. Journal of Pediatric Otorhinolaryngology*, pages 1699–1708.

Gyorgy Varallyay. 2006. Future prospects of the application of the infant cry in the medicine. In *Electrical Engineering*, volume 50(1-2), pages 47–62.

Philip Sanford Zeskind and Timothy R. Marshall. 1988. The relation between variations in pitch and maternal perceptions of infant crying. *Child Development*, 59(1):193–196.

Perplexed Bayes Classifier

Cohan Sujay Carlos
Aiaioo Labs
Bangalore
India
cohan@aiaioo.com

Abstract

Naive Bayes classifiers estimate posterior probabilities poorly (Zhang, 2004).

In this paper, we propose a modification to the Naive Bayes classification algorithm which improves the classifier's posterior probability estimates without affecting its performance.

Since the modification involves the use of the reciprocal of the *perplexity* of the class-conditional feature probabilities, we call the resulting classifier the *Perplexed Bayes* classifier.

We demonstrate that the modification results in better calibrated posterior probabilities on a gender categorization task.

1   Introduction

Probabilistic classifiers work by selecting the most probable *class* given the *features* of the data point being classified, as shown in Equation 1.

$$\arg\max_{c} P(C|F) \tag{1}$$

Bayesian classifiers transform $P(F|C)$ into $P(C|F)$ as shown in Equation 2.

$$P(C|F) = \frac{P(F|C) \times P(C)}{P(F)} \tag{2}$$

Naive Bayes classifiers additionally assume that the features f_1, f_2, f_3, etc. are all independent of one another, conditional on the class C, yielding the following equation.

$$P(F|C) = \prod_i P(f_i|C) \tag{3}$$

Equation 3 can be substituted into Equation 2 to obtain Equation 4.

$$P(C|F) = \frac{\left(\prod_i P(f_i|C)\right) \times P(C)}{P(F)} \tag{4}$$

The posterior probability estimates obtained using Equation 4 tend to be extreme as observed in Eyheramendy et al (2003).

Improving the posterior probability estimates of Naive Bayes classifiers might make them more useful for NLP (Nguyen and O'Connor, 1999).

In this paper, we present the *Perplexed Bayes* classification algorithm that produces better calibrated posterior probabilities than the Naive Bayes algorithm and operates with the same accuracy.

2   Related Work

The Naive Bayes classification algorithm is still commonly used as a baseline algorithm for many classification tasks (Rennie et al, 2003), and is reputed to perform surprisingly well (McCallum and Nigam, 1998; Rennie et al, 2003; Zhang, 2004) though the posterior probabilities might be estimated poorly (Eyheramendy et al, 2003; Rennie et al, 2003; Zhang, 2004).

Attempts to improve the Naive Bayes classifier have relied on augmentations to relax independence assumptions (Peng and Schuurmans, 2003; Peng et al, 2004), transformations to correct systemic errors (Rennie et al, 2003), the weighting of counts or probabilities (Zaidi et al, 2013; Frank et al, 2003; Webb and Pazzani, 2004) and the subsetting of features (Langley and Sage, 1994).

It has been proposed that one might use corrective sigmoid functions (Platt, 1999; Bennett, 2000; Niculescu-Mizil and Caruana, 2005; Caruana and Niculescu-Mizil, 2006)), isotonic regression (Zadrozny and Elkan, 2002), asymmetric distributions (Bennett, 2003) and binning (Zadrozny and Elkan, 2001; Bella et al, 2009) to obtain calibrated posterior probabilities (Rüping, 2006) from SVMs, decision trees and Naive Bayes classifiers.

D S Sharma, R Sangal and E Sherly. Proc. of the 12th Intl. Conference on Natural Language Processing, pages 118–123,
Trivandrum, India. December 2015. ©2015 NLP Association of India (NLPAI)

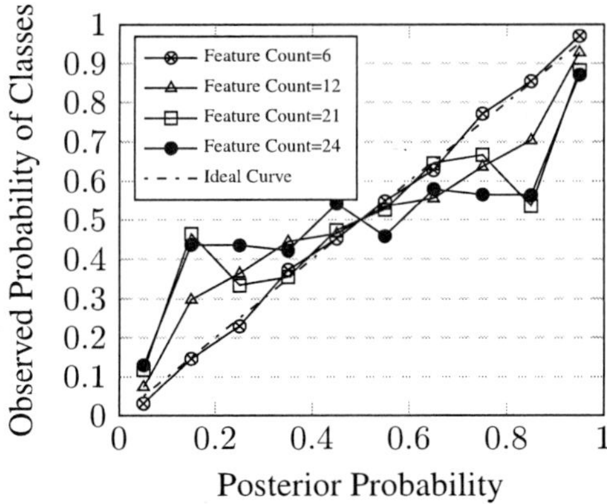

Figure 1: Reliability diagram for a Naive Bayes (NB) classifier.

Our approach is closer to that of Zaidi et al (2013) who used weighted class-conditional feature probabilities. One of the equations that Zaidi suggests could be used (but does not go on to explore) is identical to Equation 8 in this paper.

None of the previous studies has, to our knowledge, explored in detail, attempted to generalize, or developed a theoretical foundation for the approach that we describe in this paper.

3 Naive Bayes

In this section, we show that the posterior probabilities of the Naive Bayes classification algorithm are not well calibrated.

A Naive Bayes classifier's posterior probabilities were measured on a classification task (identifying the gender of names using the dataset described in Section 5) and a reliability diagram (Bröcker and Smith, 2007) plotted for different numbers of features used as shown in Figure 1.

A perfectly calibrated classifier's reliability diagram would show a straight line (like the ideal curve of Figure 1). As can be seen, the Naive Bayes classifier does not produce well-calibrated posterior probabilities, except for the feature count of 6. The calibration is seen to deteriorate as the number of features increases.

In the next section, we propose a modification to the Naive Bayes algorithm to attempt to solve the problem of poor posterior probability estimation.

4 Perplexed Bayes

The perplexity $PP(p_1, p_2, \ldots p_n)$ of a set of probabilities $\{p_1, p_2, \ldots, p_n\}$ is computed as shown in Equation 5.

$$PP = \frac{1}{(p_1 \times p_2 \times \ldots \times p_n)^{\frac{1}{n}}} \qquad (5)$$

So, the *reciprocal of the perplexity* of the probabilities is merely their *geometric mean* as shown in Equation 6.

$$PP^{-1} = (p_1 \times p_2 \times \ldots \times p_n)^{\frac{1}{n}} \qquad (6)$$

In the Perplexed Bayes classifier, we combine the class conditional feature probabilities using the geometric mean, as shown in Equation 7.

$$P(F|C) = \left(\prod_{1 \leq i \leq n} P(f_i|C) \right)^{\frac{1}{n}} \qquad (7)$$

So, the posterior probability equation can be written as shown in Equation 8, where n is the number of features, and N is the normalizer.

$$P(C|F) = \frac{\prod_i P(f_i|C)^{\frac{1}{n}} \times P(C)}{N} \qquad (8)$$

We call a classifier that uses the posterior probability equation in Equation 8 the fully *Perplexed Bayes* classifier.

4.1 Assumption

We can show that Equation 8 can be derived from Equation 2 if we assume that *the class C is independent of all features but one, and that none of the features is special* as shown in Equation 9, where $1 \leq i \leq n$.

$$P(C|f_1, f_2, \ldots f_n) = P(C|f_i) \qquad (9)$$

We can write Equation 9 in n different ways, as follows, because no feature is special.

$$\begin{aligned} P(C|f_1, f_2, \ldots f_n) &= P(C|f_1) \\ &= P(C|f_2) \\ &\vdots \\ &= P(C|f_n) \end{aligned} \qquad (10)$$

We show below that the assumption embodied in Equation 9 is sufficient for the derivation of Equation 8 (but we have not shown that it is also necessary).

4.2 Derivation

Multiplying together all the terms on both sides of Equation 10 we get Equation 11.

$$P(C|f_1, f_2, \ldots f_n)^n =$$
$$= \prod_{1 \leq i \leq n} P(C|f_i) \quad (11)$$

Inverting the terms on the right-hand side of Equation 11 using the Bayesian inversion equation (2), we get Equation 12.

$$P(C|F)^n = \left(\prod_{1 \leq i \leq n} \frac{P(f_i|C) \times P(C)}{P(f_i)} \right) \quad (12)$$

Since $P(C)$ and $P(F)$ are independent of i, we can write Equation 12 as Equation 13.

$$P(C|F)^n = \left(\prod_{1 \leq i \leq n} P(f_i|C) \right) \quad (13)$$
$$\times \frac{P(C)^n}{\prod_{1 \leq i \leq n} P(f_i)}$$

$$P(C|F) = \left(\prod_{1 \leq i \leq n} P(f_i|C) \right)^{\frac{1}{n}} \times \frac{P(C)}{N} \quad (14)$$

Finally, taking the nth root on both sides, we get Equation 14 (where N is the normalizer) and this is substantially the same as Equation 8.

So we have shown that the assumption that *the class C is independent of all features but one, and that none of the features is special* (written as Equation 10) can give us Equation 8.

It is interesting to note that Equation 15, representing the posterior probabilities of a classifier that uses the *arithmetic mean* instead of the *geometric mean*, can be derived by a similar sequence of steps from Equation 10 as well.

$$P(C|F) = \left(\sum_{1 \leq i \leq n} P(f_i|C) \right) \times \frac{P(C)}{n \times N} \quad (15)$$

4.3 Interpretation

It can be shown that the independence of classes and features $P(C|F) = P(C)$ is a direct result of Equation 10 as follows.

$$P(c_i) = \sum_F P(c_i, F) = \sum_F P(c_i|F)P(F)$$
$$(16)$$

But, since $P(c_i|F)$ is a constant m_i by reason of Equation 10, we get:

$$P(c_i) = m_i \times \sum_F P(F) \quad (17)$$

But, $\sum_F P(F) = 1$.
So, $P(c_i) = m_i = P(c_i|F)$ for all i.

So, it has been shown that Equation 10 implies that $P(C|F) = P(C)$ and therefore the features are independent of the classes.

Moreover, it can be seen that the constraints in Equation 10 are only constraints on the classes.

It follows that the features are not constrained in any way by Equation 10 and do not have to be class-conditionally independent of one other.

4.4 Generalization

It appears possible to model assumptions that fall between those of the Naive Bayes classifier and the fully Perplexed Bayes algorithm described above through the use of an *attenuation coefficient* k in the geometric mean as shown in Equation 18.

$$PP^{-k} = (p_1 \times p_2 \times \ldots \times p_n)^{\frac{k}{n}} \quad (18)$$

By plugging Equation 18 into Equation 2, we get the following posterior probablity equation.

$$P(C|F) = \left(\prod_{1 \leq i \leq n} P(f_i|C) \right)^{\frac{k}{n}} \times \frac{P(C)}{N'''} \quad (19)$$

The attenuation coefficient k ranges from 1 to n, where lower values correspond to more perplexity.

It may be noted that if we set $k = n$, Equation 19 becomes Equation 4 used in the Naive Bayes classifier.

On the other hand, if we set $k = 1$, Equation 18 becomes the same as Equation 8 used in the fully Perplexed Bayes classifier.

4.5 Approximation

It is possible to obtain the same accuracy as a Naive Bayes classifier and yet retain the excellent posterior probability characteristics of the Perplexed Bayes classifier using the approximation shown in Equation 20.

$$P(C|F) = \frac{\left(\left(\prod_i P(f_i|C)\right) \times P(C)\right)^{\frac{k}{n+1}}}{N''} \quad (20)$$

It can be seen from Equation 20 that the numerator is the $k/(n+1)$th root of the numerator of the posterior probability equation of the Naive Bayes classifier as shown in Equation 4.

So, the posterior probability approximation of Equation 20 provably makes classification decisions about data points in exactly the same way as Equation 4 because if a positive real number a/N' is greater than b/N', then a^k/N'' must also be greater than b^k/N'' where k, N' and N'' are constants.

5 Experimental Results

For our experiments, we used a collection of 7944 gender-labelled names with 2943 marked male and 5001 marked female.

The data set was randomized and then split into a training set consisting of the first 6354 names and a test set consisting of the remaining 1590 names[1].

In all experiments, the approximation in Equation 20 was used. Unless otherwise stated, for all experiments where the attenuation coefficient was automatically computed, it was chosen (through a binary search) so as to minimize the standard deviation of the normalized histogram of posterior probabilities on the training data.

5.1 Distribution Experiments

The curves of the standard deviation of normalized histogram counts of posterior probabilities plotted against feature counts in Figure 2 show that posterior probabilities are more evenly distributed in Perplexed Bayes classifiers than in Naive Bayes classifiers for higher feature counts.

5.2 Accuracy Experiments

It is to be expected that as the Perplexed Bayes classifier's confidence in its results increases, so would its accuracy. So, the accuracy of the classifier for different ranges of posterior probabilities was computed and is presented in Table 1. It can be seen from Table 1 that with higher thresholds, it is possible to obtain higher accuracies in the Perplexed Bayes classifier.

____

¹ The randomized collection of names used may be downloaded from http://www.aiaioo.com/downloads/namesfile.txt

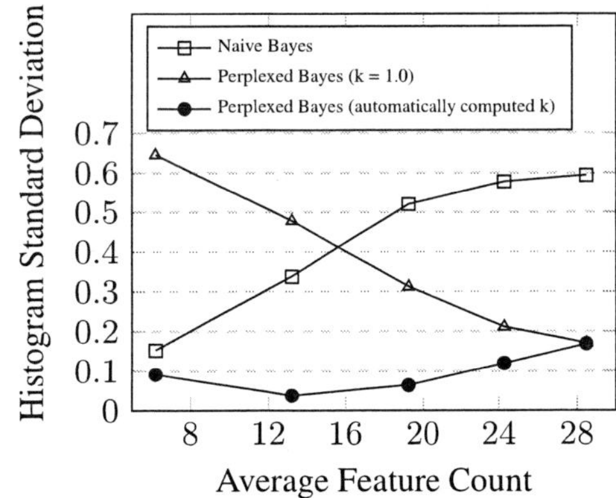

Figure 2: The standard deviation of the normalized histogram counts of the posterior probabilities plotted against the average number of features.

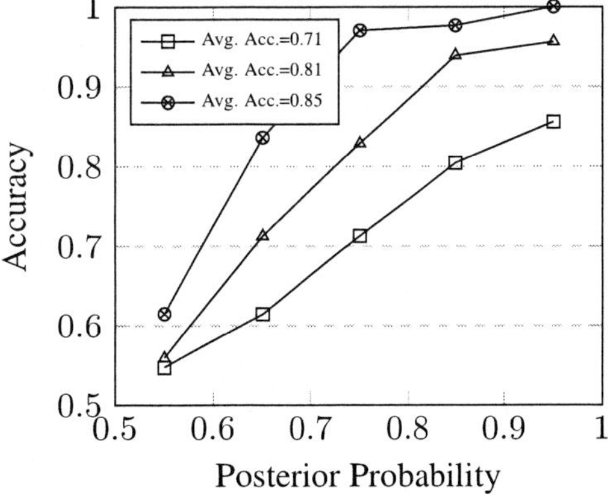

Figure 3: The accuracy of the Perplexed Bayes classifier against its posterior probability.

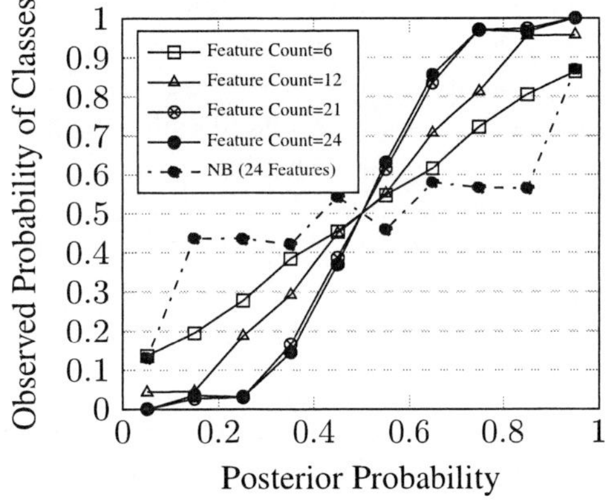

Figure 4: Reliability diagram for a Perplexed Bayes classifier with the *attenuation coefficient* optimized for flatness of the posterior probability histogram, alongside a Naive Bayes (NB) curve.

$P(C\|F)$	Points	PB Acc	Points	NB Acc
0.5-0.6	387	0.6149	26	0.5000
0.6-0.7	421	0.8361	22	0.3636
0.7-0.8	439	0.9703	26	0.5000
0.8-0.9	300	0.9766	42	0.5238
0.9-1.0	43	1.0000	1474	0.8792

Table 1: Perplexed and Naive Bayes classifier accuracies for different confidence intervals (average of 24.4 features, and overall accuracy of 0.85).

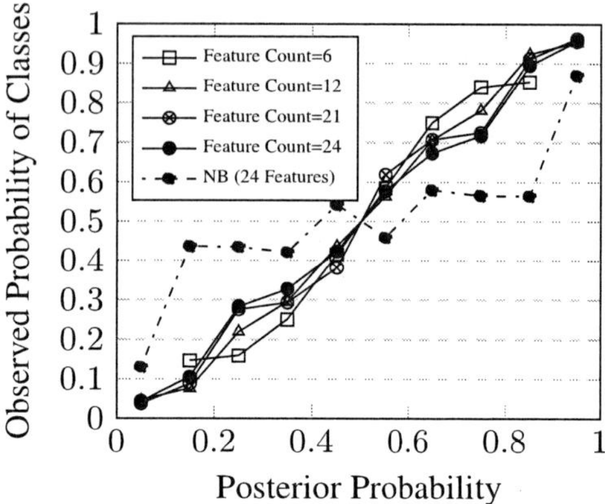

Figure 5: Reliability diagram for a Perplexed Bayes classifier with the *attenuation coefficient* optimized for good calibration a validation set, and a Naive Bayes (NB) curve for comparison.

In contrast, measurements for the Naive Bayes classifier, also shown in Table 1, indicate that 92.7% of the data points are classified with a confidence of above 0.9, and that the remaining data points are assigned to classes almost randomly, so the accuracy is not very sensitive to threshold changes between 0.5 and 0.9. Figure 3 shows an increase in the accuracy of classification with an increase in the posterior probability.

The reliability diagram for the Perplexed Bayes classifier with the Y-axis values representing the probability of a data point's real class equalling the class for which the classifier's posterior probability is plotted on the X-axis, is shown in Figure 4.

The reliability diagram in Figure 5 was obtained similarly using a Perplexed Bayes classifier where the attenuation coefficient was estimated so as to mimimize the Root Mean Square Error (RMSE) of the observed posterior probabilities from ideal values over a held-out validation set of data points.

The RMSEs of the observed posterior probabilities of Figure 5 were 0.069, 0.043, 0.049 and

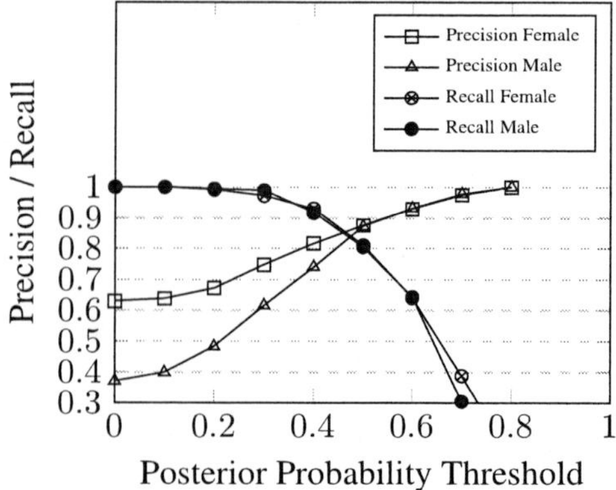

Figure 6: The precision and recall of the Perplexed Bayes classifier against decision thresholds.

0.064 for 6, 12, 21 and 24 features respectively, whereas the RMSEs for a Naive Bayes classifier were 0.016, 0.093, 0.173 and 0.164 (at accuracies of 71.5%, 81.5%, 85.7% and 84.5%), establishing that on this data set *the Perplexed Bayes classifier produced better calibrated posterior probabilities for higher feature counts than a Naive Bayes classifier of the same accuracy*.

5.3 Precision & Recall Experiments

The precision and recall of the Perplexed Bayes classifier plotted against confidence thresholds for the selection of one class over the others are as shown in Figure 6.

6 Conclusions

We have shown that it is possible to build a classifier (the Perplexed Bayes classifier) that makes classification decisions that are identical to those of a Naive Bayes classifier without assuming that the features used are class-conditionally independent, by combining the class-conditional feature probabilities into posterior probabilities using their geometric mean unlike the Naive Bayes classifier that takes their product, and that such a classifier incorporating an attenuation coefficient can produce better calibrated posterior probabilities on the given data set than a Naive Bayes classifier for higher feature counts.

7 Future Work

We should like to see if the mathematics used in the Perplexed Bayes classifier could be used to make improvements to Hidden Markov Models and in Probabilistic Graphical Models.

Acknowledgments

The author is grateful to Srivatsan Laxman for the assistance he willingly offered with matters related to probability theory and mathematics, to Sumukh Ghodke for his feedback, and to the reviewers for their helpful and very useful comments.

References

Alexandru Niculescu-Mizil and Rich Caruana. 2005. Predicting good probabilities with supervised learning. In *Proceedings of the 22nd international conference on Machine learning (ICML '05)*,625–632.

Andrew McCallum and Kamal Nigam. 1998. A comparison of event models for Naive Bayes text classification. *AAAI-98 workshop on learning for text categorization*,752:41–48.

Antonio Bella and Cèsar Ferri and José Hernández-Orallo and Marïa José Ramírez-Quintana. 2009. Similarity-binning Averaging: A Generalisation of Binning Calibration. In *Proceedings of the 10th International Conference on Intelligent Data Engineering and Automated Learning (IDEAL'09)*,341–349. Springer-Verlag.

Bianca Zadrozny and Charles Elkan. 2001. Obtaining calibrated probability estimates from decision trees and naive bayesian classiers. *ICML*, 609–616.

Bianca Zadrozny and Charles Elkan. 2002. Transforming classier scores into accurate multiclass probability estimates. *KDD*, 694–699.

Eibe Frank and Mark Hall and Bernhard Pfahringer. 2003. Locally Weighted Naive Bayes. In *Proceedings of the Nineteenth Conference on Uncertainty in Artificial Intelligence*, 249–256. Morgan Kaufmann Publishers Inc.

Fuchun Peng and Dale Schuurmans. 2003. Combining Naive Bayes and N-Gram Language Models for Text Classification. In *Proceedings ofThe 25th European Conference On Informmion Retrieval Research (ECIR03)*.

Fuchun Peng and Dale Schuurmans and Shaojun Wang. 2004. Augmenting Naive Bayes Classifiers with Statistical Language Models. *Information Retrieval*, 7(3-4):317–345. Springer.

Geoffrey I. Webb and Michael J. Pazzani. 1998. Adjusted probability naive Bayesian induction. In *Proceedings of the Eleventh Australian Joint Conference on Artificial Intelligence*, 285–295. Springer-Verlag.

Harry Zhang. 2004. The Optimality of Naive Bayes. In *Proceedings of the Seventeenth International Florida Artificial Intelligence Research Society Conference (FLAIRS 2004)*. AAAI Press.

Jason D. M. Rennie and Lawrence Shih and Jaime Teevan and David R. Karger. 2003. Tackling the Poor Assumptions of Naive Bayes Text Classifiers. In *Proceedings of the Twentieth International Conference on Machine Learning*, 20:616–623.

Jochen Bröcker and Leonard A. Smith. 2007. Increasing the Reliability of Reliability Diagrams. In *Weather and Forecasting*, 22:651661.

John C. Platt. 1999. Probabilistic outputs for support vector machines and comparisons to regularized likelihood methods. *Advances in Large Margin Classiers*, 61–74. MIT Press.

Khanh Nguyen, Brendan O'Connor. 2015. Posterior calibration and exploratory analysis for natural language processing models. *Proceedings of EMNLP 2015*.

Nayyar A. Zaidi and Jesús Cerquides and Mark J. Carman and Geoffrey I. Webb. 2013. Alleviating Naive Bayes Attribute Independence Assumption by Attribute Weighting. *Journal of Machine Learning Research*, 14(1):1947–1988. JMLR.org.

Pat Langley and Stephanie Sage. 1994. Induction of Selective Bayesian Classifiers. *Conference on Uncertainty in Artificial Intelligence*, 399–406. Morgan Kaufmann.

Paul N. Bennett. 2000. Assessing the calibration of naive Bayes posterior estimates. *Technical Report.* Carnegie Mellon University.

Paul N. Bennett. 2003. Using Asymmetric Distributions to Improve Text Classifier Probability Estimates. In *Proceedings of the 26th Annual International ACM SIGIR Conference on Research and Development in Informaion Retrieval (SIGIR '03)*, 111–118. ACM.

Rich Caruana and Alexandru Niculescu-Mizil. 2006. An Empirical Comparison of Supervised Learning Algorithms. In *Proceedings of the 23rd international conference on Machine learning (ICML '06)*,161–168. ACM.

Stefan Rüping. 2006. Robust Probabilistic Calibration. In *Proceedings of the 17th European Conference on Machine Learning*, 743–750. Springer.

Susana Eyheramendy and David D. Lewis and David Madigan. 2003. On the Naive Bayes Model for Text Categorization. In *9th International Workshop on Artificial Intelligence and Statistics*.

An Empirical Study of Diversity of Word Alignment and its Symmetrization Techniques for System Combination

Thoudam Doren Singh[†]

Department of Computer Science
National University of Singapore
13 Computing Drive
Singapore 117417
thoudam.doren@gmail.com

Abstract

The present work reports system combination task for the Chinese-English statistical machine translation systems. We focus on the strategy to build the candidate systems to enhance the gain of BLEU score by introducing diversity at the early stage of the system combination. One of the most effective strategies is to carry out system combination of the various systems with different word alignment algorithm. Our approach differs from previous work in one important aspect that we report on the diversity of the alignment refinement heuristics of word alignment techniques that are complementary to each other for the system combination. This approach could harness several word alignment possibilities and proved to be beneficial in generating consensus translation where the acting backbone which determines the word order is permitted to switch after each word. We carried out experiments on candidate systems of phrasal and hierarchical paradigms and system combination of both the paradigms as well. To our surprise, the combo systems using the various word alignments with various symmetrization techniques of both the MT paradigms show gain of 0.8 to 2.07 absolute BLEU score against the best candidates of the respective test sets.

1 Introduction

Machine translation outputs system combination based on confusion network decoding carried out has shown significant improvement in performance. The system combination task focused on core aspects of MT systems, i.e., decoding algorithm or alignment algorithm. The most prominent technique used in the system combination is consensus translation based on confusion network by rescoring using TER or METEOR. An

incremental alignment method to build confusion networks based on the TER algorithm (Rosti et al., 2008) yields significant improvement in BLEU score on the GALE test sets. Multi-objective optimization framework which supports heterogeneous information sources to improve alignment in machine translation system combination techniques has proven to be useful approach in Chinese-English data sets (Xia et al., 2013). We explore two approaches of system combination (a) using the word alignment and its different symmetrization method for both phrase based and hierarchical SMT paradigms to build candidate systems if they are complementary to each other for the system combination by sampling the outputs (b) using jointly trained HMM based SMT candidate systems together with MGIZA++ based best candidate systems for system combination for both phrase based and hierarchical SMT paradigms.

2 Related Work

A multiple string alignment algorithm is used to compute a single confusion network to generate a consensus hypothesis through majority voting by (Bangalore et al., 2001). There are other system combination techniques that uses TER (Snover et al., 2006) or ITG(Karakos et al., 2008) to align system outputs. The confusion network (Rosti et al., 2008) based system combination approach could improve the performance of the combined output. In this approach, one of the candidate system output which is acting as backbone determines the word order. The other candidate system outputs vote for insertion, deletion and substitution operations. Och and Ney (2003) and Koehn et al. (2003) used heuristics to merge the bidirectional GIZA++ alignments into a single alignment. Macherey and Och (2007) gave evidence that the systems to be combined should be of similar quality and need to be almost uncorrelated in order to be beneficial for system combination. The generation of diverse hypotheses from a single MT systems using traits

---
[†] Currently at the Department of Computer Science, University of Houston, Texas, USA. This work was carried out while the author was at NUS, Singapore.

D S Sharma, R Sangal and E Sherly. Proc. of the 12th Intl. Conference on Natural Language Processing, pages 124–129,
Trivandrum, India. December 2015. ©2015 NLP Association of India (NLPAI)

such as n-gram frequency, rule frequency, average output length and average rule length without making any algorithmic change have shown gain in BLEU score (Devlin and Matsoukas, 2012) using standard system combination technique. Xu and Rosti (2010) reported the combination of unsupervised (GIZA++ and HMM based aligner) and supervised (Inversion Transduction Grammar –ITG) classes of alignment algorithms and strategy to combine them to improve overall system performance. The ITG aligner (Haghighi et al., 2009) which is an extended work of original ITG Wu (1997) to handle block of words in addition to single words is used in their work.

3   Candidate Systems

In order to establish diverse baseline systems, we start our experiment by building various baseline systems to sort out the best candidate systems using the symmetrization method for Chinese-English language pair on FBIS domain. In total, we trained, tuned and tested 20 primary candidate systems. The Chinese sentences are segmented using the Chinese segmentation module of (Low et al., 2005). Out of the 20 primary candidates, 18 of them are built using MGIZA++. Two unsupervised Chinese-English SMT systems – one phrase based SMT (PBSMT) and one hierarchical phrase based SMT (HPBSMT) are also trained based on jointly trained HMM alignment. In the jointly trained HMM aligner (Liang et al., 2006), which is an extension of classical HMM based alignment (Vogel et al., 1996), two IBM Model 1s are trained jointly, one in each direction, for 2 iterations and these parameters are used to train two HMMs jointly for 2 iterations using Berkeley Aligner[1].

3.1   Word Alignment

In the present work, we focus on the alignment symmetrization heuristic rather than the individual alignments technique such as the MGIZA++, HMM or ITG. The baseline alignment model does not allow a source word to be aligned with more than one target word which is a birth defect of IBM models. To solve this problem, training from both directions (source-to-target and target-to-source) is performed and symmetrized the two alignments to increase the quality into an alignment matrix using various combination methods (Och and Ney, 2003; Koehn et al., 2003). Exper-

iments to find out the best word alignment method are conducted for the IWSLT'05 task by Koehn et al. (2005) using some of the symmetrization techniques. The various word alignment models and its different symmetrization methods that include *source-to-target*(srctotgt), *target-to-source*(tgttosrc), *union, intersection, grow, grow-diag, grow-diag-final, grow-diag-final-and, grow-final* of MGIZA++ are used to build the baseline candidate systems for the system combination task between Chinese-English language pair. These alignment heuristics are used in two different machine translation paradigms – phrase based and hierarchical. The MGIZA++ (Gao and Vogel, 2008), a multi-threaded and drop-in replacement version of GIZA++ (Och and Ney, 2003) which is a toolkit of the original IBM alignment models (Brown et al., 1993) implementation is used to built the above models. In the case of jointly trained HMM model, an EM-like algorithm to maximize the intuitive objective function that incorporates both data likelihood and a measure of agreement between models is derived to make the predictions of the models that agree at test time but also encourage agreement during training. Thus, the symmetrization is improved by explicitly modeling the agreement between the two alignments and optimizing it during the EM training (Liang et al., 2006) and implemented in Berkeley aligner.

3.2   Phrase Based SMT systems

In all the processes of training the PBSMT systems, all the parameters of the MT systems are kept the same except the parameter that generates phrase table from a specific alignment. We trained nine different Chinese-English PBSMT systems on the FBIS corpus using 220205 sentences up to length 85, which includes 8247326 English words. These translation models are built using statistical alignment toolkits, viz. MGIZA++ and Berkeley Aligner. The Berkeley aligner is used for jointly trained HMM alignment model (Liang et al., 2006). Standard training regimen is used - 5 iterations of model 1, 5 iterations of HMM, 3 iterations of Model 3, and 3 iterations of Model 4 for the MGIZA++ based models. All these systems are tuned using MTC13 data set of 1928 sentences. Hierarchical lexicalized reordering model (Galley and Manning, 2008) is used to improve non-local reordering and MBR (Kumar and Byrne, 2004) decoding is carried out to minimize expected loss of translation errors under loss functions to select a

---

[1] https://code.google.com/p/berkeleyaligner/

consensus translation on NIST Chinese-English test sets. Maximum phrase length is set to 7 for MGIZA++ based models and 5 for jointly trained HMM based models. A 5-gram interpolated with Knesyer Ney smoothing (Chen and Goodman, 1998) language model built using SRILM (Stolcke, 2002) is used. In our experiment, the Chinese-English SMT systems are decoded using Moses SMT toolkit[2] (Koehn et al., 2007). All the systems are evaluated on NIST 2002 /2003 /2004 /2005/ 2006 /2008 test sets using automatic scoring toolkit *mteval-v11b.pl* giving BLEU with four reference translations. Table 1 shows the BLEU scores of PBSMT and HPBSMT candidate systems.

3.3 Hierarchical Phrase Based SMT systems

Nine different baseline hierarchical phrase based statistical machine translation (HPBSMT) systems are trained, tuned and tested. In the process of building the HPBSMT systems; all the parameters and components of the MT systems are kept the same except the one that generates specific alignment. The hierarchical phrase based models (Chiang, 2005) of Chinese-English language pair arc built using thc Moscs SMT toolkit (Koehn et al., 2007) choosing the different alignment models using MGIZA++ and Berkeley aligner. To reduce the number of lexical items in the grammar, the maximum phrase length is set to 5 in the process of candidate MT systems training. Good Turing discounting is used for rule scoring to reduce actual counts. We carried out training for all the Chinese-English hierarchical phrase based SMT systems on the FBIS corpus of 220205 sentences up to length 85. The individual baseline candidate systems are tuned using MTC13 data set of 1928 sentences using minimum error rate training (Och, 2003) to optimize the feature weights and tested on NIST 2002 /2003 /2004 /2005 /2006 /2008 test sets with four reference translations. A 5-gram interpolated with Knesyer Ney smoothing language model built using SRILM (Stolcke, 2002) is used. The hierarchical phrase-based models are trained without the re-ordering model since most of the reordering behavior between the source and the target languages are expected to be captured by the synchronous grammar.

4   System combination of the Chinese-English SMT systems

The system combination of the candidate systems is carried out using MEMT3 (Heafield and Lavie, 2010). Alignment of outputs at the token level is carried out using a variant of METEOR (Denkowski and Lavie, 2010) aligner. This approach uses case-insensitive exact, stem, synonym and unigram paraphrase matched data for the alignment. Thereafter, a search space is defined on top of these alignments and a hypothesis starts with the first word of some sentences. The duplication in the output is prevented by ensuring that a hypothesis contains at most one word from each group of aligned words. Tuning and decoding is carried out using interpolated 5-gram language model with Kneyser-ney smoothing built using SRILM (Stolcke, 2002). A beam search with recombination is used since the search space is exponential in the sentence length. The language model log probability is used as a feature to bias translations towards fluency. Hypotheses to recombine are detected by hashing the search space state, feature state and hypothesis history up to a length requested by the features. The Best n+n combination (n+n combo hereafter) picks up the best n candidate system from PBSMT and best n candidate from HPBSMT systems. The outputs of the candidate systems are sampled and carried out the experiments choosing the best 3/4/5/6/7/8/9 candidate sets from each paradigm i.e., 3 from phrase based and 3 from hierarchical phrase based, 4 from phrase based and 4 from hierarchical phrase based and so on for NIST 2003, NIST 2004, NIST 2005, NIST 2006 and NIST 2008 test sets. The combo systems are tuned on NIST 2002 test set using Z-MERT (Zaidan, 2009). The result of the combo systems of each MT paradigm is shown by Table 2 for PBSMT and Table 3 for HPBSMT systems. All the baseline candidate systems and combo systems are evaluated in terms of BLEU metric (Papineni et al, 2002) with four reference translations on NIST test sets using standard MT evaluation toolkit mteval-v11b.pl. Table 6 shows BLEU scores of best candidates and the combo system of Berkeley Aligner and MGIZA++ based systems and gain in BLEU scores.

---

[2] http://www.statmt.org/moses/

[3] http://kheafield.com/code/memt/

| Symmetrization technique | NIST2002 | | NIST2003 | | NIST2004 | | NIST2005 | | NIST2006 | | NIST2008 | |
| | BLEU | | BLEU | | BLEU | | BLEU | | BLEU | | BLEU | |
	PB	HPB	PB	HPB	PB	HPB	PB	HPB	PB	HPB	PB	HPB
grow-diag-final-and	31.56	30.75	29.56	28.30	32.14	31.51	25.82	25.02	28.10	27.02	21.65	20.87
intersection	29.81	29.80	28.11	28.07	30.66	30.70	26.83	26.76	28.19	27.71	22.16	20.68
union	27.56	27.52	25.69	25.13	28.29	28.42	25.26	24.69	25.56	25.51	21.04	20.40
grow-diag-final	30.07	28.65	28.30	26.66	30.67	29.45	25.13	23.03	26.58	25.02	21.72	20.20
grow-diag	31.44	31.17	29.83	28.89	32.06	31.84	28.66	27.76	29.82	28.76	22.47	21.83
grow	30.68	30.17	28.89	28.10	31.50	31.23	27.81	27.09	29.12	28.62	22.53	21.48
srctotgt	29.67	28.09	27.58	25.77	29.80	28.82	26.83	25.44	27.22	25.67	21.89	19.79
tgttosrc	31.26	30.14	29.11	28.02	31.90	31.32	25.61	24.49	27.75	26.27	21.65	20.76
grow-final	30.11	28.50	28.42	26.56	30.60	29.28	24.89	23.12	26.66	25.01	21.20	20.49

Table 1: BLEU scores of different PB-SMT(PB) and HPB-SMT(HPB) systems keeping unknown words

Combo Systems	NIST2003 BLEU		NIST2004 BLEU		NIST2005 BLEU		NIST2006 BLEU		NIST2008 BLEU	
Best Candidate	29.83	Gain	32.14	Gain	28.66	Gain	29.82	Gain	22.53	Gain
Best 3 combo	29.75	-0.08	32.43	0.29	28.88*	0.22	29.75	-0.07	23.38	0.85
Best 4 combo	30.05	0.22	32.55	0.41	28.78	0.12	29.88	0.06	22.65	0.12
Best 5 combo	30.12	0.29	32.60	0.46	28.85	0.19	29.62	-0.2	23.83	1.3
Best 6 combo	30.43	0.6	32.69	0.55	29.08	0.42	30.25	0.43	24.24*	1.71
Best 7 combo	30.05	0.22	32.57	0.43	29.01	0.35	30.46	0.64	23.48	0.95
Best 8 combo	30.50	0.67	32.83	0.69	28.70	0.04	29.61	-0.21	23.37	0.84
All-systems-combo	30.33	0.5	32.76	0.62	29.01	0.35	30.09	0.27	24.43	1.9

Table 2: BLEU scores of System combination of different alignment PBSMT models

| Combo systems | NIST 2003 | | NIST 2004 | | NIST 2005 | | NIST 2006 | | NIST 2008 | |
	BLEU	Gain	BLEU	Gain	BLEU	Gain	BLEU	Gain	BLEU	Gain
Best Candidate	28.89	-	31.84	-	27.76	-	28.76	-	21.83	-
Best 3 combo	28.80	-0.09	31.76	-0.08	27.63	-0.13	28.76	0.0	22.21	0.38
Best 4 combo	29.18	0.29	31.91	0.07	27.94	0.18	29.35	0.59	21.91	0.08
Best 5 combo	29.28	0.39	32.43	0.59	27.98	0.22	29.37	0.61	22.93	1.10
Best 6 combo	29.45	0.56	32.38	0.54	27.90	0.14	29.45	0.69	22.93	1.10
Best 7 combo	29.31	0.42	32.38	0.54	28.09	0.33	29.65	0.89	23.57	1.74
Best 8 combo	29.33	0.44	32.18	0.34	27.55	-0.21	29.20	0.44	23.24	1.41
All-systems-combo	29.31	0.42	32.27	0.43	27.85	0.09	28.99	0.23	23.64	1.81

Table 3: System combination of different alignment models of HPBSMT and gain in BLEU

| Alignment Model | NIST2002 | NIST2003 | NIST2004 | NIST2005 | NIST2006 | NIST2008 |
	BLEU	BLEU	BLEU	BLEU	BLEU	BLEU
PBSMT- HMM	32.35	29.88	32.24	28.14	29.64	22.68
HPBSMT -HMM	31.73	29.53	31.82	27.91	29.03	21.91

Table 4: BLEU scores of jointly trained HMM candidate systems using Berkeley Aligner

Combo Systems	NIST2003 BLEU score		NIST2004 BLEU score		NIST2005 BLEU score		NIST2006 BLEU score		NIST2008 BLEU score	
Best Candidate	29.83	Gain	32.14	Gain	28.66	Gain	29.82	Gain	22.53	Gain
Best 3+3 combo	30.36	0.53	32.65	0.51	29.29	0.63	30.65	0.83	23.59	1.06
Best 4+4 combo	30.29	0.46	33.01	0.87	29.46	0.80	30.14	0.32	24.26	1.73
Best 5+5 combo	30.61	0.78	32.84	0.70	29.34	0.68	30.56	0.74	24.19	1.66
Best 6+6 combo	30.72	0.89	33.41	1.27	29.18	0.52	30.95	1.13	24.60	2.07
Best 7+7 combo	30.53	0.70	33.40	1.26	29.31	0.65	30.28	0.46	24.08	1.55
Best 8+8 combo	30.18	0.35	32.90	0.76	29.06	0.40	30.20	0.38	24.35	1.82
All-9+9-systems-combo	30.29	0.46	33.23	1.09	29.17	0.51	30.07	0.25	24.56	2.03

Table 5: System combination of MGIZA++ alignment models of PBSMT and Hierarchical PBSMT

Alignment Models	NIST02	NIST03	NIST04	NIST05	NIST06	NIST08
PBSMT- HMM	32.35	29.88	32.24	28.14	29.64	22.68
HPBSMT- HMM	31.73	29.53	31.82	27.91	29.03	21.91
Best-PBSMT-MGIZA++	31.56	29.83	32.14	28.66	29.82	22.53
Best-HPBSMT-MGIZA++	31.17	28.89	31.84	27.76	28.76	21.83
Combo of Four Systems	-	30.96	32.92	29.35	30.57	23.80
Gain in BLEU	-	1.08	0.68	0.69	0.75	1.12

Table 6: BLEU scores of best candidates and the combo system of Berkeley Aligner and MGIZA++

5   Discussion

We compare the best candidate systems performance against the combo system performance on NIST test sets and find out the gain in BLEU score. To our knowledge, our work is the first to report the extensive exploitation of the various alignment symmetrization heuristics for system combination. We carried out extensive experiments on Chinese-English language pair on specific domain and found that certain set of systems could improve output of the system combination. It is difficult to identify the right set of combinations of the candidate systems that shows the maximum gain in the BLEU score of the combined outputs unless we carry out all the possible system combination. The combination of all candidate systems does not always give the highest gain in BLEU score. The best 6+6 combo gives maximum gain in BLEU score as shown in Table no 5 against the combo systems of each paradigm for all the test sets except for NIST 2005 test set. The best 4+4 combo gives the maximum gain in BLEU score for NIST 2005 test set. The *grow-diag* alignment symmetrization method works best for HPBMST systems in terms of BLEU score of all the NIST test sets. The system combination of the PBSMT systems shows interesting characteristics of diversity. For example, there are two sets of NIST 2005 Best-3-system, viz. system combination of (*grow-diag*, *grow*, *intersection*) gives BLEU score 28.35 and system combination of (*grow-diag*, *grow*, *srctotgt*) results BLEU score of 28.88. This shows that *srctotgt* based system show higher degree of complementary behavior than *intersection* based system to *grow-diag* and *diag* based models though *intersection* and *srctotgt* systems give same BLEU scores.

6   Conclusion

The combo systems of PBSMT based candidate systems show gain in the range of 0.42 to 1.9 absolute BLEU score and combo systems of HPBSMT candidates show gain of 0.33 to 1.81 absolute BLEU score from the respective best candidates of the corresponding test sets. The overall gain of combo systems of both paradigms in the BLEU score from the best candidate systems of respective test set are in the range of 0.8 to 2.07 absolute. So, the outputs of the PBSMT and HPBSMT are complementary in system combination task of FBIS Chinese-English parallel corpora. The jointly trained HMM based PBSMT systems outperform the other candidates of MGIZA++ for NIST 2002, NIST 2003, NIST 2004 and NIST 2008 test sets. The combo systems of the four candidate systems using two aligner viz. MGIZA++ and Berkeley aligner and two MT paradigms show gain of BLEU score in the range of 0.68 to 1.12 from the best candidates of the respective test sets.

Acknowledgement

This work was supported by the grant under project "Research Collaboration between NUS and CSIDM: Phase 2 [R-252-100-372-490]". I thank Prof. Hwee Tou Ng of Dept of Computer Science, National University of Singapore.

References

Andreas Stolcke. 2002. SRILM – an extensible language modeling toolkit. *In Proceedings of the International Conference on Spoken Language Processing*, volume 2, pages 901–904.

Antti-Veikko I Rosti, Bing Zhang, Spyros Matsoukas, and Richard Schwartz. 2008. Incremental hypothesis alignment for building confusion networks with application to machine translation system combination. *In Proc. of WSMT*.

Aria Haghighi, John Blitzer, John DeNero and Dan Klein. 2009. Better word alignments with supervised ITG models. *In proceedings of the Joint Conference of the 47th Annual Meeting of the ACL and the 4th IJCNLP of the AFNLP*, pages 923-931, Suntec, Singapore.

Damianos Karakos, Jason Eisner, Sanjeev Khudanpur, Markus Dreyer. 2008. Machine Translation System Combination using ITG-based Alignments, *In Proceedings of ACL-08: HLT*, Short Papers (Companion Volume), pages 81–84, Columbus, Ohio, USA.

David Chiang. 2005. A Hierarchical Phrase-Based Model for Statistical Machine Translation, *Pro-*

ceedings of the 43rd Annual Meeting of the ACL, pages 263–270, Ann Arbor.

Dekai Wu, 1997. Stochastic inversion transduction grammars and bilingual parsing of parallel corpora. *Computational Linguistics*, 23(3).

Franz Josef Och, Hermann Ney. 2003 A Systematic Comparison of Various Statistical Alignment Models, *Computational Linguistics*, vol. 29, pages 19-51.

Franz Josef Och, Minimum error rate training in statistical machine translation, *Proceedings of the 41st Annual Meeting on Association for Computational Linguistics*, p.160-167, July 07-12, 2003, Sapporo, Japan.

Jacob Devlin and Spyros Matsoukas. 2012. Trait-Based Hypothesis Selection For Machine Translation, *In proceeding of the Conference of the North American Chapter of the Association for Computational Linguistics: Human Language Technologies*, pages 528–532, Montréal, Canada.

Jin Kiat Low, Hwee Tou Ng, and Wenyuan Guo. 2005. A maximum entropy approach to Chinese word segmentation. *In Proceedings of the 4th SIGHAN Workshop on Chinese Language Processing.*

Jinxi Xu and Antti-Veikko I. Rosti. 2010. Combining Unsupervised and Supervised Alignments for MT: An Empirical Study, *Proceedings of the 2010 Conference on Empirical Methods in Natural Language Processing*, pages 667–673, MIT, Massachusetts, USA, 9-11.

Kenneth Heafield, Alon Lavie. 2010. Combining Machine Translation Output with Open Source: The Carnegie Mellon Multi-Engine Machine Translation Scheme. *The Prague Bulletin of Mathematical Linguistics*, No. 93, pages 27–36, ISBN 978-80-904175-4-0. doi: 10.2478/v10108-010-0008-4..

Matthew Snover, Bonnie Dorr, Richard Schwartz, Linnea Micciulla, and John Makhoul. 2006. A Study of Translation Edit Rate with Targeted Human Annotation. *In Proceedings of Association for Machine Translation in the Americas.*

Michel Galley and Christopher D. Manning. 2008. A Simple and Effective Hierarchical Phrase Reordering Model, *In Proceedings of the Conference on Empirical Methods in Natural Language Processing*, pages 848–856, Honolulu.

Omar Zaidan. 2009. Z-MERT: A fully configurable open source tool for minimum error rate training of machine translation systems. *Prague Bulletin of Mathematical Linguistics*, 91:79-88.

Kishore Papineni, Salim Roukos, Todd Ward, and Wei-Jing Zhu. 2002. BLEU: a method for automatic evaluation of machine translation. *In Proceedings of 40th Annual Meeting of the Association for Computational Linguistics* (ACL), pages 311–318, Philadelphia, PA.

Percy Liang, Ben Taskar and Dan Klein. 2006. Alignment by agreement. *In proceedings of the Human Language Technology Conference of the North American Chapter of the ACL*, pages 104-111, New York.

Peter F. Brown, Vincent J. Della Pietra, Stephen, A. Della Pietra, and Robert L. Mercer. 1993. The mathematics of statistical machine translation: parameter estimation. *Computational Linguistics*,19(2):263–311.

Philipp Koehn, Franz Josef Och, Daniel Marcu, 2003. Statistical phrase based translation. *In proceedings of the Joint conference on HLT-NAACL*, Volume 1, Pages 48-54. Edmonton, Canada.

Philipp Koehn, Amittai Axelrod, Alexandra Birch Mayne, Chris Callison-Burch, Miles Osborne, David Talbot, 2005. Edinburgh System Description for the 2005 IWSLT Speech Translation Evaluation

Philipp Koehn, Hieu Hoang, Alexandra Birch, Chris Callison-Burch, Marcello Federico, Nicola Bertoldi, Brooke Cowan, Wade Shen, Christine Moran, Richard Zens, et al. 2007. Moses: Open source toolkit for statistical machine translation. *In Proc. of ACL:* Poster, pages 177–180.

Qin Gao and Stephan Vogel. 2008. Parallel Implementations of Word Alignment Tool, *Software Engineering, Testing, and Quality Assurance for Natural Language Processing*, pages 49-57, Columbus, Ohio, USA.

Shankar Kumar and William Byrne. 2004. Minimum Bayes-risk decoding for statistical machine translation, *In proceeding of HLT-NAACL*, pages 169-176, Boston, Massachusetts, USA.

Srinivas Bangalore, German Bordel, and Giuseppe Riccardi. 2001. Computing consensus translation from multiple machine translation systems. *In Automatic Speech Recognition and Understanding.*

Tian Xia, Zongcheng Ji, Shaodan Zhai, Yidong Chen, Qun Liu, Shaojun Wang. 2013. Improving Alignment of System Combination by Using Multi-objective Optimization, *Proceedings of the 2013 Conference on Empirical Methods in Natural Language Processing*, pages 535–544, Seattle, Washington, USA.

Stanley F. Chen and Joshua Goodman. 1998. An empirical study of smoothing techniques for language modeling. Technical Report TR-10-98, Harvard University Center for Research in Computing Technology.

Stephen Vogel, Hermann Ney and Christoph Tillmann. 1996. HMM-based Word Alignment in Statistical Translation. *In COLING '96: The 16th International Conference on Computational Linguistics*, pages 836-841, Copenhagen, Denmark.

Wolfgang Macherey, Franz Josef Och, 2007. An empirical study on computing consensus translation from multiple machine translation systems, *Proceedings of the 2007 joint conference on Empirical Methods in Natural Language Processing and Computational Natural Language Learning*, pages 986-995, Prague.

Domain Sentiment Matters: A Two Stage Sentiment Analyzer

Raksha Sharma and Pushpak Bhattacharyya
Dept. of Computer Science and Engineering
IIT Bombay, Mumbai, India
{raksha,pb}@cse.iitb.ac.in

Abstract

There are words that change its polarity from domain to domain. For example, the word *deadly* is of positive polarity in the cricket domain as in "Shane Warne is a 'deadly' leg spinner". However, 'I witnessed a deadly accident' carries negative polarity and going by the sentiment in cricket domain will be misleading. In addition to this, there exist *domain-specific* words, which have the same polarity across domains, but are used very frequently in a particular domain. For example, *blockbuster*, is specific to the movie domain. We combine such words as *Domain Dedicated Polar Words (DDPW)*.

A concise feature set made up of principal polarity clues makes the classifier less expensive in terms of time complexity and enhances the accuracy of classification. In this paper, we show that DDPW make such a concise feature set for sentiment analysis in a domain. Use of domain-dedicated polar words as features beats the state of art accuracies achieved independently with unigrams, adjectives or Universal Sentiment Lexicon (USL).

1 Introduction

The general approach of Sentiment Analysis (SA) is to summarize the semantic polarity (i.e., positive or negative) of sentences/documents by analysis of the orientation of the individual words (Riloff and Wiebe, 2003; Pang and Lee, 2004; Danescu-Niculescu-Mizil et al., 2009; Kim and Hovy, 2004; Takamura et al., 2005). In the real world, most sentiment analysis applications are domain oriented. All business organizations are interested in sentiment information about the product they deal with. For instance, an automobile organiza-

tion is concerned only about recognizing the sentiment information received for automobiles only. Therefore, a list of Domain Dedicated Polar Words (DDPW) can be proved as the best lexical resource for domain oriented sentiment analysis.

Most sentiment analysis applications rely on the Universal Sentiment Lexicons (USL) as a key feature along with additional features (Riloff and Wiebe, 2003). There are many USL resources like senti-word-net[1], subjectivity lexicon[2] by Wiebe and a list of positive and negative opinion words[3] by Liu. These lexicons contain only those words that are usual and have the same polarity across all the domains. These universal sentiment lexicons have the following problems:

- The words that have fluctuating polarity across domains, but have fixed polarity in a domain are strong candidate for the sentiment analysis in that domain. We call such words *chameleon words*. Consider the following example of *fluctuating polarity* phenomenon.

  1. *The cars steering was unpredictable while driving.* (-ve sentiment)
  2. *The story line of Palmetto was unpredictable.* (+ve sentiment)

  The word *unpredictable* bears *negative* polarity in the automobile domain, but it is *positive* in the movie domain. Hence, *unpredictable* assigns negative polarity to the first sentence and positive polarity to the second sentence. Due to the absence of *chameleon* words like *unpredictable*, the USL based classifier fails to determine the correct polarity of the sentences that contain chameleon words.

- On the other hand, consistency in use of a polar word in a particular domain, makes it a

---

[1]http://sentiwordnetisti.cnr.it/
[2]http://mpqa.cs.pitt.edu/
[3]http://www.cs.uic.edu/~liub/FBS/sentiment-analysis.html

126

D S Sharma, R Sangal and E Sherly. Proc. of the 12th Intl. Conference on Natural Language Processing, pages 130–137,
Trivandrum, India. December 2015. ©2015 NLP Association of India (NLPAI)

very strong candidate for sentiment analysis in that domain. Consider the following example of *fluctuating regularity (frequency of usage)* phenomenon.

1. *It's another summer **blockbuster** with plot points that are beyond unbelievable.* (+ve sentiment)
2. *The main Characters were **miscast*** (-ve sentiment)

The words *blockbuster* and *miscast* are used very frequently in the movie domain to express the opinion in comparison with other domains. The absenteeism of such strong polarity clues for a domain, makes the USL impoverished for sentiment analysis in a particular domain.

We combine the chameleon words and the domain specific regular words into a single unit: *Domain-Dedicated polar words (DDPW)*. The DDPW are missing from the USL, because of their fluctuating polarity and regularity across domains.

In this paper, we present sentiment analysis in a domain as a two stage process. Identification of domain-dedicated polar words prior to implementation of classification algorithms leads to less expensive and more efficient sentiment analysis system (Section 2). We examine the role of domain-dedicated polar words in three domains: movie, tourism and product. Our results show that use of domain-dedicated polar words as features either beats or equates the accuracy achieved independently with unigrams, adjectives or USL in all the three domains (Section 6). The two stage approach is depicted in the figure 1.

The first stage implements the Chi-Square[4] test on the difference in the counts of the word in positive and negative documents to detect domain-dedicated polar words. The second stage accomplishes the sentiment analysis task using the output of the first stage as features. We experimented with three standard classification algorithms: Neural Network (NN) classification, Logistic Regression (LR) classification and Support Vector Machine (SVM) classification. Accuracy figures (Section 6) substantiate the effectiveness of the *two stage sentiment analysis in a domain* in comparison with the single stage sentiment analysis that relies on standard features like, universal sentiment lexicons, adjectives or unigrams.

---

[4]http://math.hws.edu/ javamath/ryan/ChiSquare.html

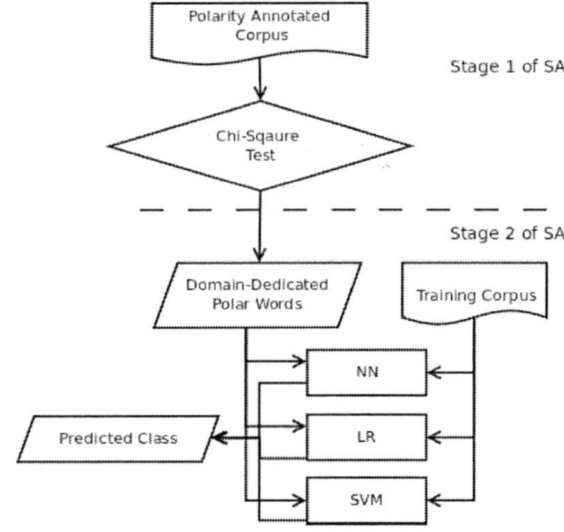

Figure 1: The two stage approach for SA in a domain

In this paper, we use subjectivity lexicon given by Wiebe as universal sentiment lexicon. Section 2 helps illustrate the reason behind improvement in accuracy with a very small feature set: domain-dedicated polar words. In section 3, we formulate the Chi-Square test to depict the generation of DDPW. Section 4 expands on the ML based classification algorithms that are used in stage-2. Section 5 and 6 illustrate the experimental set up and results respectively. Sections 7 and 8 discuss related work and conclusion.

2 Artifacts of Domain Significance in Sentiment Analysis

A feature is a piece of information that is potentially useful for prediction. Coming up with a big feature set increases the time complexity of the classifier. In addition to this, presence of irrelevant or redundant features misleads the classifier, hence, results in a poor accuracy. Pang et al. (2002) observed that the top 2633 unigrams are better features than unigrams or adjectives for sentiment classification of a document. They also proved that 'term presence' is more informative than 'term frequency' for sentiment prediction of a document.

A concise feature set made up of principal polarity clues makes the classifier less expensive in terms of time complexity and enhances the accuracy of classification. Our work falls in the same series, that is, identification of decisive components for sentiment analysis in a domain. As most of the applications of SA are domain specific, therefore, we can restrict ourselves to a domain for SA. For domain oriented sentiment analysis, we can come up with more prominent features, such as domain dedicated polar words. The following examples[5] from the movie domain help illustrate the problem we attempt to address.

juvenile, surreal, unpredictable, predictable, timeless, thrilling, well-made, well-written

The exemplified words are highly polar in the movie domain, but because of their fluctuating polarity and regularity in use are not included in most of the existing universal sentiment lexicons. We tested for the universal sentiment lexicon given by Wiebe and find 664 words that are not present in the USL, but are extracted as DDPW. The words shown in the example are a few of them. On the other hand, these features can be extracted as a subset of unigrams or adjectives from the input corpus, but at the cost of higher training time complexity and poor generalization in classification. Therefore, we define identification of domain-dedicated polar words as the foremost step (stage-1) for sentiment analysis in a domain.

In literature, Unigrams are considered as state-of-art features for sentiment classification, we are able to achieve the same level of accuracy with DDPW as features. However, instead of words, one uses word senses (synset ids in WordNets) as features, the accuracy improves dramatically. Balamurali et al. (2011) reported accuracy above 85% with $(sense + words)$ as features. However, accuracy accomplishment is a function of investment in annotation. This improvement is not significant enough to justify the cost of annotation.

However, the criterion of domain-dedication does not equally exist with all the polar words. There are words that have uniform polarity and regularity (frequency of usage) across domains. This phenomenon is considered implicitly by our proposed approach of DDPW extraction. Consequently, we are able to extract deterministic polar words that have uniform polarity and regularity across domains. Consider the following example from the movie domain.

enjoyable, entertaining, magnificent, impressive, irritating, awful, annoying, weakest

The significant occurrence of such deterministic polar words in a particular class (positive or negative) in the movie review corpus assures the satisfiability criterion of the Chi-Square test, hence, their extraction as DDPW in stage-1 of the proposed SA system.

3 Identification of Domain Dedicated Polar Words

The orientation of the polarity of a word and its frequency of usage vary from domain to domain. Such domain-dedicated polar words are the important clues for sentiment analysis in that domain. This section illustrates the stage-1 of the two-stage sentiment analysis approach that generates domain-dedicated polar words. We have performed an extensive evaluation of DDPW participation in sentiment analysis using three domains: movie, product and tourism.

3.1 Domain and Dataset

Providing polarity information about movie reviews is a very useful service (Turney, 2002). Its proof is the continuously growing popularity of the several film review websites[67]. For movie domain, we use 1000 positive and 1000 negative reviews[8]. Product reviews directly affect the business of e-commerce organizations. For product domain, we use 1000 positive and 1000 negative reviews (music instruments) from Amazon, used by Blitzer et al. (2007). The third domain is the tourism domain, a more accurate sentiment analysis in tourism domain can suggest a more accurate place for visit. We use 700 positive and 700 negative tourism reviews, used by Khapra et al. (2010) to train a word sense disambiguation system. In this paper, we report domain-dedicated words for the movie, product and tourism domain and show that these words are better features than universal sentiment lexicons, unigrams and adjectives for sentiment analysis in the respective domain.

3.2 Chi-Square Test

The Chi-Square test is a statistical test to identify the class (positive/negative) of the encountered word. We use Chi-Square test to extract domain-dedicated words from the corpus in stage-1 of the proposed sentiment analyzer. As Chi-square test

[5] All the examples reported in the paper are part of the output obtained through the Chi-Square test in stage-1.

[6] www.rottentomatoes.com

[7] www.imdb.com

[8] Available at: www.cs.cornell.edu/people/pabo/movie-review-data/(review corpus version 2.0).

requires values of two parameters, that are, expected count and observed count, we consider the arithmetic mean of the count in positive and negative files as expected count of the word in positive and negative classes, which is also a null hypothesis. The alternative hypothesis states that there is a statistically significant difference between the observed count and the mean value.

On the basis of the deviation of the observed count from the mean value (expected count), Chi-square test decides the polarity of a word for a particular domain to which documents belong. The statistically significant deviation resulted from the Chi-Square test shows that the word appears in a particular class of documents more frequently. This appearance is not by chance, rather, there is some reason behind its occurrence in that class of documents. The reason behind this significant deviation is the polarity orientation of the word that makes it a part of positive or negative documents more frequently. For example, *thought-provoking, superb, thrilling, tremendous* have positive polarity in the movie domain, so they would occur more frequently in the positive reviews rather than negative reviews (Sharma and Bhattacharyya, 2013). The Chi-Square test is formulated as follows:

$$X^2(W) = ((C_p - \mu)^2 + (C_n - \mu)^2)/\mu \quad (1)$$

Here, C_p is the count of a word W in the positive documents and C_n is the count in negative documents. μ represents an average of the word's count in positive and negative documents. μ is the expected count or null hypothesis, while C_p and C_n are the observed count of W. If the Chi-square test results in a value that is greater than the threshold value, then there is a significant difference between the expected and the observed. Since there is an inverse relation[9] between the Chi-Square value and the *probability of word given NULL hypothesis is true*, a high Chi-Square value indicates that the probability is very poor. Therefore, we reject NULL hypothesis, that is, we reject the uniform distribution of the word in positive and negative class. However, we assume that the word W belongs to a particular class (alternative hypothesis), either positive or negative.

To understand the identification of DDPW from the corpus, Consider the example of Chi-Square test performed for the word *unpredictable* in the movie domain. The count of the word *unpredictable* in positive (22) and negative files (10) are taken from the considered movie review corpus.

$$X^2(Unpredictable) = ((22-16)^2+(10-16)^2)/16 \quad (2)$$

The word *"unpredictable"* results in a Chi-Square value of 4.5, that is greater than 3.84 (Standard Threshold Value in Statistics). This relation implies that *P(Data|NULL-Hypothesis is true)* is less than 0.05 (5%) for the word *unpredictable*. Hence, reject NULL hypothesis and accept the alternative hypothesis, that is, the word *unpredictable* belongs to a particular class.

Bruce and Wiebe (1999) proved that 'adjectives' are the best candidate to adhere the polarity. They established a statistically significant correlation between sentence subjectivity and the presence of adjectives. At this stage, we also have considered adjectives[10] only as domain-dedicated words, but we believe that domain-dedicated words are not limited to adjective only. The same approach can be applied to find domain-dedicated words from other part of speeches.

4 Sentiment Classification in stage-2

The final class of the document is predicted in stage-2 of the proposed sentiment analysis system. Our utmost goal is to examine the behavior of SA system using a concise feature set: *Domain Dedicated Polar Words (DDPW)*, which are extracted as output of stage-1. For this purpose, we experimented with three machine learning based classification algorithms, that are, *Neural Network, Logistic Regression* and *SVM*.

4.1 Neural Network (NN)

Neural networks are able to produce a complex non linear hypothesis function for classification. Nowadays, NN has become "state-of-the-art" technique for many applications because of the fast computers that can solve a big network, (Yanagimoto et al., 2013; Hui, 2011). In our case also, the classification accuracy attained by Neural Network surpasses SVM and LR.

---

[9]The Chi-square score and probability table is given at http://faculty.southwest.tn.edu/jiwilliams/probab2.gif

[10]Bidirectional Standford POS tagger is used to find the part of speech of the word.

4.2 Logistic Regression (LR)

LR classifier is a non linear classifier. Non linearity is achieved through sigmoid function (equation 3) that estimates the probability of the document belonging to a class. If LR results in a probability value higher than 0.5, it implies that the document has more than 50% chance of being positive, else the document bears negative polarity. The Logistic (Sigmoid) function simulated by LR is as follows.

$$Hypothesis(X) = 1/(1 + e^{(-Theta' * X)}) \quad (3)$$

Here, X is the input feature vector of a document (Section 4), *Theta* is also a vector that contains the weights assigned to X.

4.3 Support Vector Machine (SVM)

The support vector machine (SVM) has been proven to be highly effective at traditional text categorization and sentiment classification (Joachims, 1998; Pang et al., 2002). SVM predicts the class of the document on the basis of a linear function, that is, z's score. LR takes a decision at z equals to zero, while SVM takes a decision at two boundaries: z equals to $+1$ and z equals to -1.

$$z = Theta' * X \quad (4)$$

5 Experimental Setup

For all the three observed domains: movie, product and tourism, we divide the data into five equal size folds, maintaining the balance of the negative and positive files in each fold. All the results reported in section 6 are the average five-fold cross validation results on the dataset.

In our work, we compare the performance of sentiment analysis system based on features, identified by Chi-Square test with the systems that are based on universal sentiment lexicon, Union of DDPW and USL, top-adjectives, adjectives and unigrams. Since training Logistic Regression is expensive with a large set of features, we considered only those unigrams that appear at least four times in the corpus. In the same way, top adjectives are chosen such that they appear at least five times in the corpus. These constants are chosen such that it satisfy both the conditions; it fetches maximum number of words which will be used as features and all those words occur frequently in the corpus.

Since all the three techniques, NN, LR, and SVM take input as a feature vector, each document is represented as a feature vector. Let $p_j(d)$ denotes the presence of feature j in the document d and n be the size of the feature set. Then, each document d is represented as a feature vector as shown here.

$$\vec{d} = (p_1(d), p_2(d), p_3(d), \ldots \ldots, p_n(d))$$

6 Results and Discussion

The table 1 shows the classification accuracies for the movie domain obtained with various feature sets and techniques separately. Accuracy is calculated as a fraction of total input documents that are correctly classified by the classifiers. The accuracies resulting from using only DDPW as features are shown in row (1) of table 1.

In literature, unigrams are considered as state-of-art features (Ng et al., 2006; Pang et al., 2002) for sentiment analysis, we also experimented with unigrams. Domain-dedicated words as features perform better than unigrams with all the three classification algorithms. At the same time, domain-dedicated words speed up the classification process with a small feature set of size 920. Since adjectives have been crucial clues in sentiment prediction (Hatzivassiloglou and Wiebe, 2000), we experimented with all the adjectives and top adjectives. We find that both the feature sets are not as effective as DDPW.

We experimented with a universal sentiment lexicon provided by Wiebi to capture more context in general. Such sentiment lexicons are good source of polar words with a compact size, but are independent of any domain. The absence of polar words from USL that are crucial for movie domain (e.g., blockbuster) causes accuracy to decline by 5% to 8%. On the other hand, inclusion of DDPW with the USL leads to a big increment in accuracy in comparison with USL only. Yet, the results shown in row (5) of table 1 are relatively poor: the feature set, consisting of 920 domain-dedicated polar words provide more information than the intersection of DDPW and USL.

Figure 2 shows the maximum classification accuracy obtained in the three domains using six feature sets. From figure 2, we can observe that DDPW outperform the accuracy obtained with the other features in the movie domain. In case of tourism domain, DDPW equate the accuracy obtained with unigrams, which is the highest accu-

	Features	Number of features	NN	LR	SVM
(1)	**DDPW**	**920**	**85.50**	**83.50**	**84.50**
(2)	Unigrams	18345	83.50	80.00	82.50
(3)	Adjectives	11151	83.00	82.75	80.25
(4)	Top-Adjectives	2500	82.50	82.00	81.50
(5)	DDPW ∪ USL	2220	81.50	81.75	81.75
(6)	USL	1946	76.50	75.50	76.00

Table 1: Average five-fold cross-validation accuracies, in percentage. Boldface: best performance achieved through NN, LR and SVM, for the given feature set

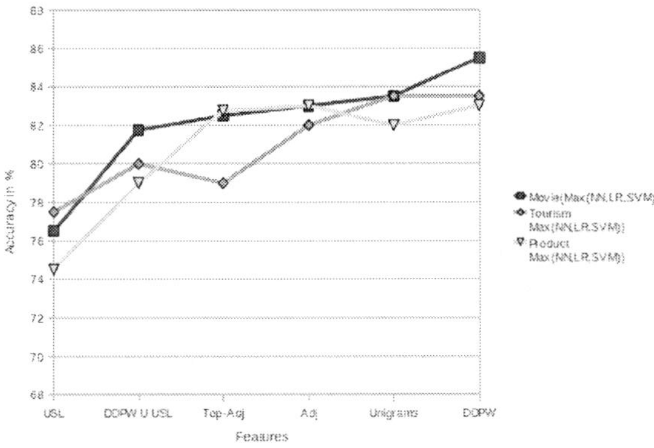

Figure 2: Sentiment classification accuracy in all three domains

racy for the tourism domain. For product domain, DDPW equate the accuracy obtained with adjectives, which is the highest accuracy for the product domain.

In terms of relative performance of classification techniques, Neural Network tends to perform the best, although the differences are not very large. As a whole, accuracy figures validate the prominence of identification of domain-dedicated polar words prior to the implementation of classification algorithm.

7 Related Work

Several works use the universal sentiment lexicons to decide whether a sentence expresses a sentiment (Riloff and Wiebe, 2003; Whitelaw et al., 2005; Mukherjee et al., 2012). Considering that the USL solely is not sufficient to achieve satisfactory performance, there are some more works that combine additional feature types for sentiment classification exist (Yu and Hatzivassiloglou, 2003; Kim and Hovy, 2004; McDonald et al., 2007; Melville et al., 2009; Ng et al., 2006).

Wiebe (2000), for the first time, worked in the area of sentiment lexicon. She focused on the problem of identifying subjective adjectives with the help of the corpus. She proposed an approach to find subjective adjectives based on the distributional similarity from the Lin (1998) thesaurus. Her approach was seeded by manually provided strong subjectivity clues. She used this new set of adjectives to find subjectivity in sentences, just by the presence of an adjective from the new set. However, the approach was unable to predict sentiment orientations of newly found subjective adjectives and sentences. Moreover, they did not take into account the domain-dedicated polar words and domain-dedicated sentiment analysis.

Pang et al. (2002) for the first time applied machine learning techniques for sentiment classification. They implemented Naive Bayes, maximum entropy classification, and support vector machines. They used frequency or the presence of unigrams or bigrams as features. In addition to this, they used combinations of unigrams and bigrams, unigrams and Part of Speech, unigrams and their position as features. They got the highest accuracy of 82.9% with SVM using a feature vector of size 16165. Besides this, they showed that simply using the 2633 most frequent unigrams are better choice. The feature vector made up of 2633 most frequent unigrams yielded performance comparable to that of using all unigrams (16165) from corpus. Our approach based on Chi-Square test identifies key features from unigrams and enhances the performance.

There are a few researchers who have worked for domain oriented sentiment analysis. The work of Qiu et al. (2009) exploited the relationship between sentiment words and product features. Their method begins with a seed set, then they extract product features that are modified by some sentiment word in the domain dependent corpus.

For example *zoom, flash, resolution* in the camera domain can be modified by *high, poor, nice,* respectively. The process was executed iteratively. The extraction rules are defined based on the relationships described in the dependency trees. They proposed that a feature should receive the same polarity throughout the review and the words extracted by the features will receive the polarity of the feature. However, the reviewer may associate polarity towards a feature with time. To understand this fact consider the following scenario.

> *When I purchased this camera, the battery was **good**, but now it is **disastrous**.*

The change in time changes the user's views for a feature in the same review.

8 Conclusion

In this paper, we propose that if we restrict the sentiment analysis task to a domain, then domain-dedicated polar words are the best features for sentiment prediction. For this purpose, we present the SA system as a two stage process, stage-1 identifies decisive words from a domain specific corpus for sentiment analysis in that domain. Stage-2 uses these words as features for classification task. Use of domain-dedicated polar words as features outperforms or equates the accuracies achieved independently with unigrams, adjectives, top-adjectives, Universal Sentiment Lexicon (USL) and union of USL and DDPW. Besides improvement in sentiment analysis, the research can be useful for creating writing aids for authors and in natural language generation.

References

A. R. Balamurali, Aditya Joshi, and Pushpak Bhattacharyya. 2011. Harnessing wordnet senses for supervised sentiment classification. In *Proceedings of the Conference on Empirical Methods in Natural Language Processing*, EMNLP '11, pages 1081–1091, Stroudsburg, PA, USA. Association for Computational Linguistics.

John Blitzer, Mark Dredze, and Fernando Pereira. 2007. Biographies, bollywood, boom-boxes and blenders: Domain adaptation for sentiment classification. In *ACL*, volume 7, pages 440–447. Citeseer.

Rebecca F. Bruce and Janyce M. Wiebe. 1999. Recognizing subjectivity: a case study in manual tagging. *Nat. Lang. Eng.*, 5(2):187–205, June.

Cristian Danescu-Niculescu-Mizil, Gueorgi Kossinets, Jon Kleinberg, and Lillian Lee. 2009. How opinions are received by online communities: A case study on amazon.com helpfulness votes. In *Proceedings of the 18th International Conference on World Wide Web*, WWW '09, pages 141–150, New York, NY, USA. ACM.

Vasileios Hatzivassiloglou and Janyce M. Wiebe. 2000. Effects of adjective orientation and gradability on sentence subjectivity. In *Proceedings of the 18th Conference on Computational Linguistics - Volume 1*, COLING '00, pages 299–305, Stroudsburg, PA, USA. Association for Computational Linguistics.

Wei Hui. 2011. A neural dynamic model based on activation diffusion and a micro-explanation for cognitive operations. In *Cognitive Informatics Cognitive Computing (ICCI*CC), 2011 10th IEEE International Conference on*, pages 397–404.

Thorsten Joachims. 1998. *Text categorization with support vector machines: Learning with many relevant features*. Springer.

Mitesh M Khapra, Sapan Shah, Piyush Kedia, and Pushpak Bhattacharyya. 2010. Domain-specific word sense disambiguation combining corpus based and wordnet based parameters. In *In 5th International Conference on Global Wordnet (GWC2010*. Citeseer.

Soo-Min Kim and Eduard Hovy. 2004. Determining the sentiment of opinions. In *Proceedings of the 20th international conference on Computational Linguistics*, page 1367. Association for Computational Linguistics.

Dekang Lin. 1998. Automatic retrieval and clustering of similar words. In *Proceedings of the 17th international conference on Computational linguistics - Volume 2*, COLING '98, pages 768–774, Stroudsburg, PA, USA. Association for Computational Linguistics.

Ryan McDonald, Kerry Hannan, Tyler Neylon, Mike Wells, and Jeff Reynar. 2007. Structured models for fine-to-coarse sentiment analysis. In *Annual Meeting-Association For Computational Linguistics*, page 432.

Prem Melville, Wojciech Gryc, and Richard D Lawrence. 2009. Sentiment analysis of blogs by combining lexical knowledge with text classification. In *Proceedings of the 15th ACM SIGKDD international conference on Knowledge discovery and data mining*, pages 1275–1284. ACM.

Subhabrata Mukherjee, Akshat Malu, Balamurali A.R., and Pushpak Bhattacharyya. 2012. Twisent: a multistage system for analyzing sentiment in twitter. In *Proceedings of the 21st ACM international conference on Information and knowledge management*, CIKM '12, pages 2531–2534, New York, NY, USA. ACM.

Vincent Ng, Sajib Dasgupta, and S. M. Niaz Arifin. 2006. Examining the role of linguistic knowledge sources in the automatic identification and classification of reviews. In *Proceedings of the COLING/ACL on Main Conference Poster Sessions*, COLING-ACL '06, pages 611–618, Stroudsburg, PA, USA. Association for Computational Linguistics.

Bo Pang and Lillian Lee. 2004. A sentimental education: Sentiment analysis using subjectivity summarization based on minimum cuts. In *Proceedings of the 42Nd Annual Meeting on Association for Computational Linguistics*, ACL '04, Stroudsburg, PA, USA. Association for Computational Linguistics.

Bo Pang, Lillian Lee, and Shivakumar Vaithyanathan. 2002. Thumbs up?: sentiment classification using machine learning techniques. In *Proceedings of the ACL-02 conference on Empirical methods in natural language processing-Volume 10*, pages 79–86. Association for Computational Linguistics.

Guang Qiu, Bing Liu, Jiajun Bu, and Chun Chen. 2009. Expanding domain sentiment lexicon through double propagation. In *Proceedings of the 21st international jont conference on Artifical intelligence*, pages 1199–1204.

Ellen Riloff and Janyce Wiebe. 2003. Learning extraction patterns for subjective expressions. In *Proceedings of the 2003 conference on Empirical methods in natural language processing*, EMNLP '03, pages 105–112, Stroudsburg, PA, USA. Association for Computational Linguistics.

Raksha Sharma and Pushpak Bhattacharyya. 2013. Detecting domain dedicated polar words. In *Proceedings of the Sixth International Joint Conference on Natural Language Processing*, pages 661–666, Nagoya, Japan, October. Asian Federation of Natural Language Processing.

Hiroya Takamura, Takashi Inui, and Manabu Okumura. 2005. Extracting semantic orientations of words using spin model. In *Proceedings of the 43rd Annual Meeting on Association for Computational Linguistics*, ACL '05, pages 133–140, Stroudsburg, PA, USA. Association for Computational Linguistics.

Peter D. Turney. 2002. Thumbs up or thumbs down?: semantic orientation applied to unsupervised classification of reviews. In *Proceedings of the 40th Annual Meeting on Association for Computational Linguistics*, ACL '02, pages 417–424, Stroudsburg, PA, USA. Association for Computational Linguistics.

Casey Whitelaw, Navendu Garg, and Shlomo Argamon. 2005. Using appraisal groups for sentiment analysis. In *Proceedings of the 14th ACM international conference on Information and knowledge management*, CIKM '05, pages 625–631, New York, NY, USA. ACM.

Janyce Wiebe. 2000. Learning subjective adjectives from corpora. In *Proceedings of the Seventeenth National Conference on Artificial Intelligence and Twelfth Conference on Innovative Applications of Artificial Intelligence*, pages 735–740. AAAI Press.

Hidekazu Yanagimoto, Mika Shimada, and Akane Yoshimura. 2013. Document similarity estimation for sentiment analysis using neural network. In *Computer and Information Science (ICIS), 2013 IEEE/ACIS 12th International Conference on*, pages 105–110.

Hong Yu and Vasileios Hatzivassiloglou. 2003. Towards answering opinion questions: separating facts from opinions and identifying the polarity of opinion sentences. In *Proceedings of the 2003 conference on Empirical methods in natural language processing*, EMNLP '03, pages 129–136, Stroudsburg, PA, USA. Association for Computational Linguistics.

Extracting Information from Indian First Names

Akshay Gulati
Dept. of Electronics&Comm.
Jamia Millia Islamia
New Delhi – 110025, India
akshaygulati@robot-maker.net

Abstract

First name of a person can tell important demographic and cultural information about that person. This paper proposes statistical models for extracting vital information that is gender, religion and name validity from Indian first names. Statistical models combine some classical features like n-grams and Levenshtein distance along with some self observed features like vowel score and religion belief. Rigorous evaluation of models has been performed through several machine learning algorithms to compare the accuracy, F-Measure, Kappa Static and RMS error. Experimental results give promising and favorable results which indicate that these models proposed can be directly used in other information extraction systems.

1 Introduction

Name validity, gender and religion of a person can be successfully predicted to a certain extent just by his first name. But, as there is no direct relationship between the first names and these entities an absolute prediction is impossible. Therefore, the proposed statistical models aim to develop an indirect relationship between the first names and these entities for extracting information from first names.

Theoretically, a first name is a proper noun, which means that a first name can be any sequence of alphabets. Therefore, absolute name validity is impossible as any sequence of alphabets is a valid first name. For practical purposes, this paper assumes that most of the Indian first names are the ones which have some historical/cultural/ethnic relevance and are not some arbitrary sequence of alphabets. Upon assuming this, statistical models proposed are constructed and are used with machine learning algorithms for training classifiers. The trained classifier can then be used for predicting the validity of a first name that is differentiating between a valid first name and an invalid first name.

Even absolute gender and religion predictions are impossible as there is no restriction on the naming process with regards to gender and religion. A person of any gender and any faith can identify himself/herself with any name of his/her choice. For example, a Hindu girl can name herself John without breaking any law. For practical purposes, such cases have been left out for construction of the statistical models proposed.

The models proposed along with the machine learning algorithms can find direct use in information extraction systems and real time applications such as:

   i.   Automatic field suggestions for form filling.
  ii.   Anomaly detection in pre-filled forms.
 iii.   Analyzing demographic and religious trends/sentiments from social media collected data based on first names.
 iv.   Filtering forms/application with respect to certain gender or religion.
  v.   Filtering spam/fake accounts on internet by name validity.

Other demographic information can also be extracted from Indian first name such as expected age group, caste of person and part of India (north/south/east/west). These topics have been left for future research purposes.

2 Data

The training and testing data used has been collected from public Indian name databases available on the internet.

D S Sharma, R Sangal and E Sherly. Proc. of the 12th Intl. Conference on Natural Language Processing, pages 138–143,
Trivandrum, India. December 2015. ©2015 NLP Association of India (NLPAI)

For name validity, the first names have been classified into 'Valid' and 'Invalid' classes. A total of 8970 first names are used in the training data out of which 7846 are valid first names. 650 are noisy words and 475 are completely random sequence of alphabets, together making invalid names.

For gender prediction, the first names have been classified into 'Male' and 'Female' classes. A total of 7846 first names are available in the training data out of which 4509 are male first names and 3337 are female.

For Religion prediction, the first names have been classified into 'Hinduism', 'Islamic' and 'Christian' classes. A total 7846 first names used in the training data out of which 3758 are 'Hinduism' first names, 3501 are 'Islamic' first names and 587 are 'Catholic' first names. The numbers are in proportion of diversity of first names of each religion in India. 'Sikhism' as class for prediction was not considered as many of its first names are common with 'Hinduism' and this causes ambiguity.

The dataset is available for download[1] and can be used for future research regrading Indian names with appropriate citations.

3 Content Models

Before applying machine learning algorithms it is important to convert the training data available into content models. These content models contain different features which have been developed or chosen after careful observation and evaluation of the training data.

3.1 Name Validity Models

This paper proposes four different name validity models for experiments. Each model contains two features for each first name in the training data. First feature is vowel score and is model independent. The second feature is the n-gram (Manning and Schütze, 1999) score for n = 1 or 2 or 3 or skipping bigrams, each for a different model. An n-gram model is a type of probabilistic language model for predicting the next item in such a sequence in the form of a $(n-1)$–order Markov model (Baum and Petrie, 1966).

Vowel score tells us the average vowel distance between the vowels in a first name and is normalized with respect to the length of first name. It is an important feature based on the observation that for any first name, occurrence of

vowels will be similar to all the other first names in the training data. As first names are sequences of letter with low vowel count averaging about 2-3 vowels per first name, the vowel score gives us a good idea of the vowel patterns in the first names in general. Therefore, any anomaly in the vowel occurrence will directly lead us to the result that the given first name is invalid. On the contrary, if there is no anomaly in vowel occurrence then other features like n-grams will be used.

Mathematically, the vowel score for a 'Name' is given by *VS(Name)*, where '*n*' is the length of the given first name and *Distance(i)* is the distance of the ith vowel from the $(i-1)^{th}$ vowel in the first name.

$$VS(Name) = \frac{\sum_{i=2}^{i=n}[Distance(i)]}{(No.\,of\,vowels)\,X\,(\,|Name|)}$$

Unigram is a n-gram where the size of token is 1. Unigrams help provide the probability of a token; it assumes the position of token to be independent of other tokens in the first name.

Mathematically, unigram score for a 'Name' is given by *U(Name)*, where '*Name_i*' is the ith token/letter of the given first name, '*n*' is the length of the given first name, *Token* is the set of the 26 alphabets and '$Token_j$' is the jth token/letter of the set *Token*.

$$U(Name) = \prod_{i=1}^{i=n} \frac{Count(Name_i)}{\sum_{j=1}^{j=26} Token_j}$$

Bigram is a n-gram where the size of token is 2. Bigrams help provide the conditional probability of a token given the preceding token has occurred.

Mathematically, bigram score for a 'Name' is given by *B(Name)*, where '$Name_i$' is the ith token/letter of the first name given that one start symbols (*) was added before each first name and an end symbol (#) was added after each first name before experiment, '*n*' is the length of given first name.

$$B(Name) = \prod_{i=2}^{i=n} \frac{Count(Name_{i-1}, Name_i)}{Count(Name_{i-1})}$$

Trigram is a n-gram where the size of token is 3. Trigrams help provide the conditional

[1] http://www.robot-maker.net/wp-content/uploads/2015/10/Indian_Unified_Names.txt

probability of a token given the preceding token has occurred.

Mathematically, trigram score for a 'Name' is given by $T(Name)$, where '$Name_i$' is the ith token/letter of the first name given that two start symbols (*) were added before each first name and an end symbol (#) was added after each first name before experiment, 'n' is the length of the given first name.

$$T(Name) = \prod_{i=3}^{i=n} \frac{Count(Name_{i-2}, Name_{i-1}, Name_i)}{Count(Name_{i-2}, Name_{i-1})}$$

Skipping Bigram (Xuedong *et al*, 1992) is a special n-gram where size of token is 2 and a condition that first character of a bigram can't be a vowel when the second character of bigram is a consonant. Skipping bigrams were used on careful observations of training data, it allows us to use only relevant bigrams and ignore the redundant ones.

Mathematically, the skipping bigram score is calculated by the same formula as for bigrams if only valid tokens are considered and invalid tokens are skipped.

3.2 Gender Prediction Models

This paper proposes four models for gender prediction. Each model contains two features for each first name in the training data, these features keep count of some specific tokens (listed below) which occur at the name endings for male and female first names respectively. The tokens are explained below, each for a different model.

Unigram model to keep count of all the unigrams (in training data) such that the only character of unigrams is the last character of the first name.

Bigram model to keep count of all the bigrams (in training data) such that the 2 characters of bigrams are the last two characters of the first name.

Trigram model to keep count of all the trigrams (in training data) such that the 3 characters of trigrams are the last 3 characters of the first name.

Vowel Bigram model to keep count of all the bigrams (in training data) such that the first character of bigram is the last vowel and the second character of bigrams is the last character of the first name.

3.3 Religion Prediction Model

This paper proposes one model for the religion prediction. The idea behind the design of religion prediction model is to calculate the similarity/closeness of a given first name with other first names of each religion in the training data. The concept of Levenshtein distance (Vladimir, 1966) is used to calculate the minimum edit distance between two first names. This model contains three features for each first name in the training data, these features are the Hinduism Belief, Islam Belief and Christianity Belief. These three features can be extracted from a single function *Belief(r)*.

Mathematically, belief for religion 'r' is given by *belief(r)*, where $Count(r,i)$ gives the total no. of first names of religion 'r' in training data with levenshtein distance equal to 'i' for the first name for which the features are being calculated and '*Depth*' is an experimentally chosen quantity whose value is to be taken equal to 3. '*Depth*' parameter sets maximum value of levenshtein distance for which *Belief(r)* will be calculated.

$$Belief(r) = \sum_{i=1}^{i=Depth} \frac{Count(r,i)}{i^2}$$

Mathematically, the Levenshtein distance between two strings 'a' and 'b' is given by $lev_{a,b}(|a|,|b|)$, where $1_{(a_i \neq b_i)}$ is the indicator function equal to 0 when $a_i = b_j$ and equal to 1 otherwise.

$$lev_{a,b}(i,j) = \begin{cases} \max(i,j) & if\ \min(i,j) = 0 \\ \min \begin{cases} lev_{a,b}(i-1,j) + 1 \\ lev_{a,b}(i,j-1) + 1 \\ lev_{a,b}(i-1,j-1) + 1_{(a_i \neq b_i)} \end{cases} & otherwise \end{cases}$$

4 Evaluation

The proposed statistical models are constructed in Python using the training data. Further, Weka (Hall *et al*, 2009) was used to apply various machine learning algorithms on the content models for training classifiers. Weka is an open source collection of machine learning algorithms. For all algorithms, 10 fold cross validation was done. Detailed results comprising of accuracy, F-Measure (Powers, 2011), Kappa Static and RMS error have been represented below in tabular form.

	LAD Tree	REP Tree	Random Forest	**Bagging**	Simple Cart
% Correct	96.3371	96.427	96.4607	**96.6854**	96.5843
% Incorrect	3.6629	3.573	3.5393	**3.3146**	3.4157
Precision	0.963	0.963	0.964	**0.966**	0.965
Recall	0.963	0.964	0.965	**0.967**	0.966
F-Measure	0.963	0.963	0.964	**0.966**	0.965
Kappa Static	0.8215	0.8223	0.8275	**0.8361**	0.8294
RMS Error	0.1639	0.1672	0.1637	**0.1596**	0.169

Table 1. Results of Unigram model for name validity

	LAD Tree	**REP Tree**	Random Forest	Bagging	Simple Cart
% Correct	98.1278	**98.1614**	97.7803	98.1502	98.0493
% Incorrect	1.8722	**1.8386**	2.2197	1.8498	1.9507
Precision	0.981	**0.982**	0.978	0.981	0.98
Recall	0.981	**0.982**	0.978	0.982	0.98
F-Measure	0.981	**0.982**	0.978	0.981	0.98
Kappa Static	0.9104	**0.9136**	0.8953	0.9125	0.9071
RMS Error	0.1224	**0.0286**	0.13	0.1196	0.0304

Table 2. Results of Bigram model for name validity

	LAD Tree	**REP Tree**	Random Forest	Bagging	Simple Cart
% Correct	96.1371	**96.4282**	95.7452	96.3722	96.4058
% Incorrect	3.8629	**3.5718**	4.2548	3.6278	3.5942
Precision	0.96	**0.963**	0.957	0.963	0.963
Recall	0.961	**0.964**	0.957	0.964	0.964
F-Measure	0.961	**0.964**	0.957	0.963	0.963
Kappa Static	0.8135	**0.8277**	0.7988	0.8252	0.8259
RMS Error	0.1693	**0.1703**	0.1795	0.166	0.1723

Table 3. Results of Trigram model for name validity

	LAD Tree	**REP Tree**	Random Forest	Bagging	Simple Cart
% Correct	97.8885	**97.9667**	97.5869	97.855	97.8773
% Incorrect	2.1115	**2.0333**	2.4131	2.145	2.1227
Precision	0.979	**0.979**	0.976	0.978	0.979
Recall	0.979	**0.98**	0.976	0.979	0.979
F-Measure	0.979	**0.98**	0.976	0.978	0.979
Kappa Static	0.9022	**0.9055**	0.8874	0.9	0.9016
RMS Error	0.1278	**0.1293**	0.1373	0.1278	0.1393

Table 4. Results of Skipping Bigram model for name validity

	LAD Tree	REP Tree	**Regression**	Bagging	Simple Cart
% Correct	75.2176	75.5163	**75.5683**	75.5553	75.5683
% Incorrect	24.7824	24.4837	**24.4317**	24.4447	24.4317
Precision	0.762	0.768	**0.768**	0.768	0.768
Recall	0.752	0.755	**0.756**	0.756	0.756
F-Measure	0.754	0.757	**0.757**	0.757	0.757
Kappa Static	0.5012	0.5089	**0.5097**	0.5095	0.5097
RMS Error	0.4095	0.4221	**0.4089**	0.4174	0.4222

Table 5. Results of Unigram model for gender prediction

	LAD Tree	REP Tree	**Regression**	Bagging	Simple Cart
% Correct	82.4823	82.7395	**83.0482**	82.7524	82.881
% Incorrect	17.5177	17.2605	**16.9518**	17.2476	17.119
Precision	0.826	0.829	**0.832**	0.829	0.83
Recall	0.825	0.827	**0.83**	0.828	0.829
F-Measure	0.825	0.828	**0.831**	0.828	0.829
Kappa Static	0.642	0.6476	**0.6546**	0.6477	0.6504
RMS Error	0.3625	0.3703	**0.358**	0.3668	0.3623

Table 6. Results of Bigram model for gender prediction

	LAD Tree	REP Tree	Regression	Bagging	Simple Cart
% Correct	**86.8424**	86.4201	86.8168	86.1001	86.1897
% Incorrect	**13.1576**	13.5799	13.1832	13.8999	13.8103
Precision	**0.868**	0.864	0.868	0.861	0.862
Recall	**0.868**	0.864	0.868	0.861	0.862
F-Measure	**0.868**	0.864	0.868	0.861	0.862
Kappa Static	**0.7303**	0.7221	0.73	0.7158	0.717
RMS Error	**0.3128**	0.3188	0.3072	0.3138	0.3197

Table 7. Results of Trigram model for gender prediction

	LAD Tree	REP Tree	Regression	**Bagging**	Simple Cart
% Correct	80.5624	81.7361	80.7558	**82.1488**	81.1815
% Incorrect	19.4376	18.2639	19.2442	**17.8512**	18.8185
Precision	0.813	0.824	0.814	**0.828**	0.817
Recall	0.806	0.817	0.808	**0.821**	0.812
F-Measure	0.807	0.818	0.809	**0.823**	0.813
Kappa Static	0.6081	0.6312	0.6114	**0.6395**	0.6193
RMS Error	0.3815	0.3658	0.3674	**0.3541**	0.3678

Table 8. Results of Vowel Bigram model for gender prediction

	J48	REP Tree	**Regression**	Bagging	Simple Cart
% Correct	82.2321	82.2704	**83.2908**	81.9388	82.1556
% Incorrect	17.7679	17.7296	**16.7092**	18.0612	17.8444
Precision	0.818	0.817	**0.829**	0.814	0.817
Recall	0.822	0.823	**0.833**	0.819	0.822
F-Measure	0.816	0.817	**0.826**	0.814	0.815
Kappa Static	0.6785	0.6795	**0.6963**	0.6739	0.6764
RMS Error	0.3044	0.3001	**0.289**	0.2937	0.3032

Table 9. Results of Religion Prediction model

5 Conclusion

The models proposed for different topics have performed well overall. The results have been tabulated and shown for comparison of the different types of models proposed.

i. From the results obtained, it can be seen that Bigram model has performed the best with accuracy of 98.1614% closely followed by the Skipping Bigram model, both using REP Tree algorithm.

ii. Due to sparse data the Trigram model has not performed well and its results are comparable to the Unigram model.

iii. For gender prediction, Trigram model has the best with the accuracy of 86.8424% with LAD Tree algorithm.

iv. Trigram model has outperformed other models not only because it is more detailed but also it has better chances for handling exception cases.

v. For religion prediction, the *belief(r)* has been proved to be an effective feature for calculating belief as the model has performed with an accuracy of 83.44%.using Regression algorithm.

In conclusion, the proposed models have been successfully tested through rigorous evaluations and have completed the objectives of the research. They can further be used in other research areas and real time applications as mention in the introduction.

Reference

L.E Baum and T. Petrie. 1966. *Statistical Inference for Probabilistic Functions of Finite State Markov Chains.* The Annals of Mathematical Statistics, Vol 37 (6): 1554–1563.

Christopher D. Manning and Hinrich Schütze. 1999. *Foundations of Statistical Natural Language Processing*, MIT Press: ISBN 0-262-13360-1 : 191-199.

Xuedong Huang, Fileno Alleva, Hsiao-wuen Hon, Mei-yuh Hwang and Ronald Rosenfeld. 1992. *The SPHINX-II Speech Recognition System: An Overview.* Computer, Speech and Language, Vol 7(1): 137-148.

Vladimir I. Levenshtein. 1966. *Binary codes capable of correcting deletions, insertions, and reversals.* Soviet Physics Doklad, Vol 10 (8): 707–710.

David M W Powers. 2011. *Evaluation: From Precision, Recall and F-Measure to ROC, Informedness, Markedness & Correlation.* Journal of Machine Learning Technologies, Vol 2 (1): 37–63.

Mark Hall, Eibe Frank, Geoffrey Holmes, Bernhard Pfahringer, Peter Reutemann, Ian H. Witten. 2009. *The WEKA Data Mining Software: An Update.* SIGKDD Explorations, Vol 11 (1).

punct - An Alternative Verb Semantic Ontology Representation

Kavitha Rajan
Language Technologies Research Centre
IIIT-Hyderabad
Gachiblowli. Telangana.
`kavitha@reseach.iiit.ac.in`

Abstract

The goal is to build a verb ontology based on Indian grammatical tradition. We propose here an ontological structure to represent verbs in a language, which can be adapted across languages. This is an ongoing work and presently the method has been applied to develop ontologically informed etymon in English.

1 Introduction

In an ontology based classification, the main criteria for class identification and membership are provided by extra-linguistic events or situations expressed by verb meanings (Lenci, 2010). Since ontology based classifications are concept dependent, they can be used as inter-lingual verb resources (Boas, 2005). The approach put forward here is an attempt to explore the feasibility of arriving at an ontological classification of verbs based on overlapping verb senses. This work is an extension of 'Understanding Verbs Based on Overlapping Verbs Senses (Rajan, 2013)'. In the prior work a new approach for inter-lingual ontological classification of verbs was put forward. This method looks into the inherent meaning of each verb and identifies seven meaning primitives. It is inspired by Conceptual Dependency(CD) theory (Schank, 1972; Schank, 1973; Schank, 1975) and the Indian grammatical traditional thinking of Niruktakāras: "all content words are either verbal roots (activities) or derived from verbal roots".

2 Why Verbs ?

According to Indian Grammatical Tradition, verbs occupy a central role in a language. Consider the following simple sentence (in Sanskrit):

```
devadattaH pacati
'Devadatta is cooking'.
```

According to Yāska (c.6th-5th centuries BCE); Nirukta (Sarup, 1920) 1.1:

> The principal meaning signified by the above utterance is the act of cooking - 'pacati' and not the subject - 'devadattaH' (who is predicted to be cooking).

In Pāṇini's derivational system, by means of which utterances (vākya) and their components are accounted for, items assigned the name dhātu 'verb, root' rank as core elements of utterances that are actually usable and serve as a starting point of derivation of such utterances. In the above sentence, cook 'pac' is called the dhātu (root verb) and hence the starting point of derivation. Pāṇiniyas, like Patañjali (second century BCE) unequivocally speak of the meaning of dhātvarthas (dhātu + artha) 'verb meanings' as kriyā 'act, action'.

In Sanskrit, verb is called 'kriyā' and kriyā stands for action or activity. But verb consists of both 'action(kriyā)' and 'state(bhāva)' verbs. The explanations put forward by grammarians in order to accomodate the concept of 'state' into the definition of verb, that is, transition from kriyā-based to bhāva-based definition is given in the following paragraphs.

Bhartṛhari is the first Pāṇiniya to formulate the technical definition of kriyā as given in Pāṇini's grammar.

According to Bhartṛhari (5th century CE):

> Every verb has 'sense of sequence' and 'state' in it. Hence, every verb projects a 'sense of happening', making this sense 'omnipresent' in all verbs.

Basic meaning of Sanskrit word bhāva is 'state, condition'. Word bhāva in P.2.3.37 (Joshi, 1991) is an instance of "a particular state or condition in which an item finds itself as a result of something happening, and also the happening, occurrence itself".

D S Sharma, R Sangal and E Sherly. Proc. of the 12th Intl. Conference on Natural Language Processing, pages 144–151,
Trivandrum, India. December 2015. ©2015 NLP Association of India (NLPAI)

So, we can use word 'bhāva' to mean 'happening'. We have already seen that 'sense of happening' is omnipresent in all verbs. That is, 'bhāva' is omnipresent or universal in all verbs.

From Indian grammatical tradition we have adopted the concept of *'universal verb'*. Our original contribution is that we have defined an 'ontological structure' to represent 'universal verb' and have used it to represent the 7 primary verb senses '(puncts[1])' which we have identified. The structure of bhāva and the identification of 7 puncts are explained in the next two sections.

The goal of this work is to classify *concept* 'verb/activity' and not the lexical category 'verb' across languages. Verbs belonging to specific languages are collected for this work but they represent 'concepts'. For example 'run' is a concept meaning 'to go quickly by moving the legs more rapidly than at a walk and in such a manner that for an instant in each step all or both feet are off the ground[2]'. Even if all languages do not have parts of speech they will surely have concepts like 'run', 'eat', etc.

3 Ontological Form of Happening

Structure of happening (see Figure 1) consists of two states: initial/state1 and final/state2, and the context within which the change in state occurs.

    'Context' consists of ontological attributes.
Ontological attributes are: space, location, time, manner, reason which in turn have sub-attributes.
The Sub-attributes of 'space' are :
direction - linear, curvilinear, down
'location' are: source, destination
'time' are: frequency, duration
'manner' are: mode, speed
'reason' are: purpose, cause, etc.

These are called ontological attributes as they are concepts and they can be represented across languages. To explain this point we have taken a sample verb 'run' in English and its Hindi counterparts 'bhāgana' and 'daudana' and shown the mapping in Table 1.

Table 1: Ontological attribute mapping among verbs in English and Hindi(Indian language)

English	Run	Hindi	dauḍanā	bhāganā
move / do	1	sthāna parivartan karanā / karanā	1	1
Direction(linear):	1	diśā(sidhā):	1	1
move along	1	sātha sātha sthāna parivartan karanā	1	1
Speed:	1	raftār:	1	1
fast	1	teja	1	1
Mode:	1	riti(praṇ āli):	1	1
putting one foot in front of the other allowing each foot to touch the ground before lifting up the next	1	ek paira ke Age dōsarā paira is tarah rakhana tāki ek paira jamīna par chūne ke bā da hi dūsarā chuye	1	1
Cause:	0	kāraṇa:	0	1
danger		āpatti		
fear		bhaya		
some reason	0	kuch kāraṇa	0	1

Happening or bhāva can be defined as change of state in a context. Bhāva has a formal structure and has been named 'punct' (Singh, 2001).

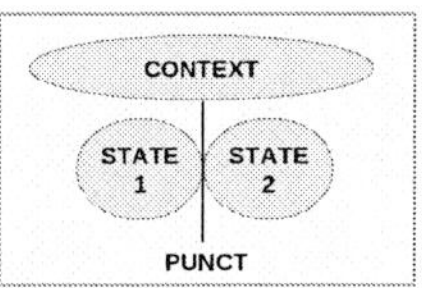

Figure 1: Structure of punct

The formal structure of bhāva/punct is:

$$\langle e1 | e2, C \rangle$$

where e1 stand for entity/state1, e2 for entity/state2, and C represents context / feature-space.

The formal structure is a recursive form as its context itself is made out of other formal structures. The two states in this structure are contiguous [3]. By adding a formal structure as form of contiguity, change transfers to two contiguous but different states and state transforms into combinatory context of happening. Every 'change of state' has a location, presence of force or absence of force, result, context and the context itself involves 'change of state' in some other context.

---

[1] an element held in Whitehead's philosophy of nature to be analogous to a point in a geometric system - Merriam Webster

[2] http://dictionary.reference.com/browse/run

[3] Take a verb 'cook - prepare a dish'. The initial and final states are related to each other.

4 The seven puncts

Two works WordNet (Miller, 1990) and Nirukta (Sarup, 1920) were influential in restricting the number of overlapping verb senses to 7. The WordNet has identified 8 common verbs (have, make, set, get, take, be, run, go). Let us take each verb and analyse it in detail and see how they were modified into 7 primitive verbs senses. The 7 senses are given names following the head word (Levin, 1993) style of nomenclature.

The verbs 'make', 'set', 'take' and 'get' are action verbs. Actions are done by an actor. These actions can take place only if an agent is involved in initiating them, 'My grandmother made a dress for me.', 'Catherine set a chair by the bed.', 'He took seven wickets in the second innings.', 'She got a cake for me.'. So the 'sense of agent' which is known as sense of 'doer' (Sanskrit, sādhya — sādhaka[4] bhāva) is common[5] and is also the primary verb sense in these four verbs. Since 'do-ing' sense is present in all 4 verbs. Here *'do'* is a head word (Levin, 1993) to represent all types of agent (both animate and in-animate) initiated actions.

The verb 'have/has' represents possession. Possession can be of three types 1) when a person himself obtains an object, like the verb 'take', 'He took seven wickets in the second innings.' 2) when the agent is the recipient of an object, like the verb 'get', 'I got a letter from him the other day.' and 3) possessing a quality, like the verb 'have', 'She has got blue eyes.'. Since, 'have', 'get' and 'take' have the verb sense 'possession' in common all the three verbs were grouped under the sense of *'have'* (Sanskrit, grāhya — grāhaka bhāva). As an agent should initiate the actions of transferring possessions in the verbs 'take' and 'get' they have possession as the secondary verb sense.

The verb 'be' represents state. Verbs like 'have', 'set' are state verbs. Sentence like - 'He has property. shows that the concerned person is in possession of some property. Having something in possession is a continuous 'state' until it is lost or given away. 'The village was set among olive groves on a hill.', shows the fixed position(state) of a village. The sense of state forms an integral part of the structure of verb. So, *'be (is)'* (Sanskrit, ādhāra — ādheya bhāva) is a primitive verb sense.

The verbs 'run' and 'go' have sense of 'movement' in the form of linear displacement in them. Verb 'make', 'My grandmother made a dress for me.', has movement in the form of change from initial(raw) to final(finished) state. Verb 'take' has movement in the form of change in the position of an object and its ownership, 'Someone must have sneaked in here and taken it.'. All the different types of movements or changes are together represented by the verb sense *'move'* (Sanskrit, pūrva — apara bhāva).

The verbs 'take' and 'get' have a sense of separation of a part from a whole. Both these verbs result in change in the location of objects being possessed or change in the initial and final states of the agent or recipient. Change in location means separation from the initial position, 'The Soviet forces took more than 30,000 Romanian prisoners and all their equipment.'. Change in state means adding or removing or modifying the existing state to a new one, 'Women have fought long and hard to get into positions that men hold within the leadership of the church.'. The verb sense *'cut'* (Sanskrit, amśa — amśi bhāva) is used to represent this.

The verbs 'make', 'take', 'set' and 'get' act on limited set of objects. 'Make' means to produce something, often using a particular substance or material[6]. But we can make only a restricted number of objects, 'Shall I make some coffee?'. In order to explain this sense of restriction or limitedness the verb sense *'cover'* (Sanskrit, āropya — āropaka bhāva) was included as a primitive verb sense.

One of the definitions of the verb 'make' is 'to bring into existence by shaping or changing material, combining parts, etc.[7]'. For this the doer needs to have knowledge as to how this process has to be done, 'She makes all her own clothes.'. Hence, the verb sense *'know'* (Sanskrit, jnāna — jnyeya bhāva) was included as a primitive verb sense.

Using the above mentioned method we have identified 7 mutually exclusive primitive verb senses (puncts) (see Table 2). Using such primitive verb senses and assuming that each verb has these senses we can analyze inherent meaning of different verbs. These seven[8] primitive senses are

---

[4]Category system followed in vaiśeṣika(system founded by sage kaṇāda circa 150 A.D). The 7 primitives are 7 such categories.

[5]If a sense is 'common', it means that it is found in many verbs. The identification process is explained in this section

[6]http://dictionary.cambridge.org/dictionary/british/make_1

[7]http://dictionary.reference.com/browse/make

[8]ṣat bhāva vikār of vārṣyāyaṇi(Sarup,1920) six types of bhāva are: origin, existence, modification, increase, decay, and destruction has influenced the identification of seven

also known as bhāva-s according to Indian grammatical tradition. This bhāva-s constitutes primitive meaning senses implicit in the meaning of each verb. Term bhāva means happening and this sense overlaps with all verbs. This is also a traditional Indian linguistic claim. These senses are mutually interwoven through their context. For example: The word 'cover' has the verb sense 'cover (wrap/wrapped)' as primary and 'move (before/after)' as secondary verb sense in it. Verbs can have senses ranging from one to all seven in them, but the 7 senses (know, move, do, have, is, cut, cover) are mutually exclusive and are logical structures (Refer Table 2).

The context (C) of each bhāva-s is made of:

C - [ontological: attributes (feature-space), bhāva (recursive), and any other information which can contribute to meaning disambiguation.]

5 Application

5.1 Annotation Process

Each verb can have all the seven meaning primitives in it. Overlap of verb meaning is illustrated best when meaning of a verb is explicated using another verb or verbs. On analysis, one can see that there is an order in which the verbs are used for explication. This order helps in finding the primary, secondary, tertiary, etc. meaning senses. The order can be found by using two methods. The methods are explained below using two verbs: *dance* and *confuse*.

Example 1:
First Method:

Verbs are mostly polysemous. We collect all the possible meanings of each verb from various resources like dictionaries. Then, we analyse each meaning and place them in different classes (cell in matrix) according to the order of the meaning primitives. The meaning primitives are identified by analysing the inherent meanings of the verbs by posing a series of questions.

Take verb 'dance'.

Step 1. If a verb is polysemous,

Verb 'dance' has two meanings. Meaning 1: (Of a person) move quickly and lightly

____
primitives / puncts in this work.

Table 2: puncts and explanations

Primitives (Elementary Bhāva-s/puncts)	Explanation
Know:Sense of knowing (Sanskrit, **jnāna—jnyeya** bhāva) (object of 'know' / the process involved in knowing that object)	Know/Knower Conceptualize, construct or transfer information between or within an animal. E.g. "forget" - to forget something one has to know about it. Forget is a process having state change from knowing to not knowing over a period of time. So,this particular verb has "knowing" as primary sense and change of state/"move" as secondary sense.
Move:Sense of Move /change /process (Sanskrit, **pūrva—apara** bhāva) (state at the beginning of a process / state at the end of the process)	Before/After Every process has a movement in it. The movement maybe a change of state or a change in location. E.g. "fall" - change of position from a higher state to lower state physically or in abstract sense. Actions like falling of leaves do not have a sense of agency, the fall happens on its own. So the word has the sense of 'pure movement'.
Do : Sense of agency (Sanskrit, **sādhya—sādhaka** bhāva) (something to be accomplished /accomplished)	Agent/Action A process which can be accomplished only with a doer. E.g. "cook" - has a sense of someone doing cooking. The process of cooking involves change of state from raw to cooked by a doer. So, it has 'doing' sense as primary and 'move' sense secondary to it.
Have : Sense of possession or having (Sanskrit, **grāhya—grāhaka** bhva) (something that is the object of grasping /to grasp)	Grip/Grasp Possessing, obtaining or transferring a quality or thing. E.g. "like" - To like something one must have prior 'knowledge' about it. Liking is something you "have or possess". Hence 'have' is primary sense and "knowing" is secondary sense.
Be : Sense of state of being (Sanskrit, **ādhāra—ādheya** bhāva) (location/attribute)	Locus/Locatee Continuously having or possessing a quality. E.g. - "confuse" (I am confused). It is a state and it is located in me. 'Be / is' is the primary state and to get confused you must know and have contradictory opinion about the object. So, sense of 'know' is secondary.
Cut : Sense of part and whole (Sanskrit, **amśa—amśi** bhāva) (part of an object or process/whole to which the part belongs)	Part/Whole Separation of a part from whole or joining of parts into a whole. Processes which causes pain. Processes which disrupt the normal state. E.g. - "break" It has a sense of a thing being divided into parts. 'Cut' sense is primary to it and breaking is 'done' by someone so has a sense of agency 'do' as the secondary sense.
Cover : Sense of ascribe and ascription (Sanskrit, **āropya—āropaka** bhāva) (to be attributed/the one to which it is attributed)	Wrap/Wrapped Processes which pertain to a specific object or category. It is like assigning a boundary. E.g. - "guarantee" - when you guarantee you are putting a kind of cover (ascription) on that object so it has 'cover' as primary sense and someone has to do it, and so has 'doing' as secondary sense.

143

Meaning 2: Move rhythmically to music, typically following a set sequence of steps

Step 2. Take one meaning at a time. Let us take verb 'dance' as in meaning 1.

Step 3. Take a simple sentence in which dance is used in the particular meaning.

'She danced happily into the room.'

Step 4. Instead of 'dance' substitute the meaning and rewrite the sentence.

She did + (move quickly and lightly) + happily into the room.

Step 5. Keep rewriting the sentence using primitives like 'do', 'move', 'have' etc.. so that you can re-write the entire sentence using them. While using primitives see in which order the primitives can be written too.

She DO+past + (MOVE) + quickly and lightly + happily + into the room.

Step 6. In this particular sentence, dance means a type of movement which is done by a person (doer). Hence, 'move' is primary meaning primitive and 'do' is secondary meaning primitive.

Hence we write it as : MOVE/DO

Second method is by nominalising verbs in a simple sentence. For example:

She danced into the room.

Step 1. She did the act of dancing into the room.

Step 2. She did the act of moving into the room dancing.

Step 3. She 'DO+past' (moving into the room) MOVE+ing as if dancing.

Hence we write it as : MOVE/DO

Example 2:
First method for verb 'confuse':
Confuse means 'Make (someone) bewildered or perplexed'

The flood of questions confused me.

Step 1. The flood of questions made me bewildered or perplexed.

Step 2. The flood of questions DID the process of creating bewilderment or perplexity in me.

Step 3. The flood of questions DO the act of creating a STATE of bewilder- ment or perplexity in me.

Step 4. The flood of questions DO the act of creating a 'STATE'of Inability to deal with or understand some- thing in me.

Step 5. The flood of questions DO the act of creating a 'IS' of Inability to deal with or KNOW about something in me.

Hence we write it as : IS/KNOW/DO

In this sentence 'confused' is a state. Confusion is always about some information / knowledge and so is about 'know'. This particular state occurs

only in an animate being and hence 'DOer' sense. the order is decided looking at the dependencies of the various senses. Confusion is a state and hence 'IS' is primary. The state is about an information so, 'KNOW' is secondary. This state occurs in an animate being and so 'DO'er sense is tertiary.

Second method for verb 'confuse'

You confuse me

Step 1. you create confusion in me

Step 2. You create confused (state of Knowledge) about something (object of knowledge)in me

Step 3. You 'DO' creation of Confused ('STATE' of 'KNOW' ledge) about something (object of 'KNOW'ledge) in me.

Hence we write it as : IS/KNOW/DO

In the last sentence 'do' is the tertiary sense, 'know' is the secondary sense and 'is' state of knowledge is the primary sense of verb 'confuse'.
Hence we write it as : IS/KNOW/DO

The annotation work consisted of identification of primary and secondary puncts and ontological attributes. Though almost all puncts can be found in every verb, presently we have restricted the identification to two. The verbs were grouped and represented in the form of a two-dimensional 7x7 matrix. The rows and the columns stand for the primary and secondary primitive senses respectively. All verbs in a row were grouped together and ontological attributes of 7 separate groups (7 rows) were identified. Ontological attributes consists of concepts like space, location, time, manner, etc.

Manual annotation was done first for all verbs (2500) in Sanskrit then for verbs in English (3750 - excluding all types of compounds). For Sanskrit, the verb list was collected from many sources. More than 3000 verbs including variations in accentuation were collected from various resources (Apte, 2008; Capeller, 1891; Kale, 1961; Bruno, 1922; Palsule, 1955; Palsule, 1961; Varma, 1953; Williams, 2008) and a new typed list was created in Devanagari script. List was created as such a complete list of Sanskrit verbs was not available online. The list was then annotated manually by one person and cross checked by three Sanskrit experts. For English, the verb list was created from various resources like - Levin's verb list (Levin, 1993) and verbs added to this list as extensions (Dang, 1998; Kipper, 2000; Korhonen, 2004). Meanings of all the verbs in English were obtained from various online dictionaries (Merriam Webster[9], Oxford[10], Dictionary.com[11], Cambridge Advanced Learners Dictionary[12]). The list was then manually annotated by the same person who had annotated the Sanskrit verbs and the annotation was cross-checked by three annotators.

5.2 Ontology Population: Using English and Sanskrit Verbs

Ideally meaning of a verb involves all seven layers of puncts. However, if we take two or three layers of primitive verb senses in a verb, they would be sufficient to identify meanings of most verbs. We took just the first two senses to demarcate meaning of verbs. The primary and secondary senses of all verbs in English and Sanskrit were identified. They were classified into a two-dimensional 7x7 matrix.

As mentioned in section 3, meaning of a verb also includes context which in turn includes ontological attributes[13]. The approach has similarities with work on use of clustering for finding verb semantics (Sun, 2009).

Ontological attributes[14] of a verb is the set of all 'meaning components (non-linguistic)' which can be used to define its meaning exhaustively and also help in distinguishing it from other verbs. Also, verbs very close in meaning, no matter how close they are, can be distinguished based on the differences in their meaning component set (even if they differ by one component, they differ in meaning). Thus, it is an ontological and computational resource of verbs. For example, 'Leave', 'depart' and 'abandon' are 3 verbs having 'move' sense as primary, cut sense as secondary, and do sense as tertiary. That means all the 3 verbs belong to the same cell / class. In order to differentiate between the 3 verbs in the same class, we identify the ontological attributes.

The process used for identifying ontological attributes is explained below. Collect all possible meanings of all three verbs. Isolate the meanings

---

[9]http://www.merriam-webster.com/

[10]http://oald8.oxfordlearnersdictionaries.com/

[11]dictionary.reference.com/browse/

[12]http://dictionary.cambridge.org/dictionary/british/

[13]Verbs with similar overlapping verb senses can be differentiated by the ontological attributes were concluded upon by introspection (looking at meanings of verbs in different resources) and based on the concept that there are no synonyms in languages.

[14]http://www.ei.sanken.osakau.ac.jp/main/documents/OnProperty.pdf

which have move as primary verb sense.

Table 3: Identification of ontological Attributes

Verb	Meaning	Ontological attributes
1) Leave	go away from, depart from permanently, go away from a place without taking (someone or something)	move away + from somewhere/ something/ someone + permanently/short time + accidentally/intentionally
2) Depart	Leave, especially in order to start a journey.	move away + from somewhere/ something/ someone + permanently/short time + intentionally
3) Abandon	Leave (a place or vehicle) empty or uninhabited, without intending to return	move away + from somewhere/ something/ someone + intentionally + permanently(forever)

From the above three meanings, we see that the meaning components similar in all three verbs are: direction - move away, source - from somewhere /something / someone, mode - intentionally. Meaning components which are different are: **duration** forever (abandon), for short time / permanently (leave, depart), **mode** - accidentally (leave). Using the method explained above ontological attributes were identified for motion verbs in English. The types and number of subtypes of motion verbs is given in Table 4.

6 Conclusion

Verbs can be searched based on its features and if the particular verb is absent in a language, verbs with neighbouring features can be searched. Feature space will be same across languages. That is, if we know the feature space of verb 'fall' in English, using the same feature space we can obtain the verb 'fall' in Hindi or Sanskrit or any other language. In a sentence if we can identify the feature space of a verb in a particular context[15] then it can be replaced by verb in another language which has similar feature space. Feature space of each verb will be unique. This method will help in resolving a major problem of translation which is identification and translation of verb in a sentence.

---

[15]A verb can have different meanings. Hence one verb will be placed in different cells in the punct matrix if it has more than one meaning and the feature space of verbs in different cells will be different. So if a verb has two meanings, the feature space of the two verbs will be different.

Acknowledgements

This work was done under the guidance of Prof. Navjyoti Singh, Center for Exact Humanities, IIIT-H and Dr. Dipti Misra Sharma, Language Technologies Research Center, IIIT-H. This work was done with the support of Chinmaya International foundation.

References

Anna Korhonen and Ted Briscoe. 2004. Extended Lexical-Semantic Classification of English Verbs. *Proceedings of the HLT/NAACL workshop on computational lexical semantics*, 38–45.

Lin Sun and Anna Korhonen. 2009. Improving Verb Clustering with Automatically Acquired Selectional Preferences. *Proceedings of the 2009 Conference on Empirical Methods in Natural Language Processing*, pages 638–647, Singapore, 6-7 August 2009.

Beth Levin. 1993. English Verb Classes and Alternation, A Preliminary Investigation. The University of Chicago Press.

Bruno Liebich. 1922. Materialien zum Dhatupatha. Winter C Heidelberg.

Carl Capeller. 1891. Sanskrit English Dictionary. (http://www.sanskrit-lexicon.uni-koeln.de/scans/MWScan/tamil/index.html), Online; accessed 2009 - 2010.

Gajanan B. Palsule. 1955. A Concordance of Sanskrit Dhātupāthas. *Deccan College Dissertation Series* Bhandarkar Oriental Research Institute, Poona.

Gajanan B. Palsule. 1961. The Sanskrit Dhātupāthas: A critical study. University of Poona, Pune.

George A. Miller and Richard Beckwith and Christiane Fellbaum and Derek Gross and Katherine Miller. 1990. WordNet: An on-line lexical database. *International Journal of Lexicography*, 3, 235–244.

Karin Kipper and Hoa Trang Dang and Martha Palmer. 2000. Class-Based Construction of a Verb Lexicon. *Proceedings of the Seventeenth National Conference on Artificial Intelligence and Twelfth Conference on Innovative Applications of Artificial Intelligence*, 691–696. AAAI Press.

Lakshman Sarup. 1920. The Nighantu and Nirukta: The Oldest Indian Treatise on Etymology, Philology and Semantics. *Computer Models of Thought and Language*. First Edition. Publisher: Motilal Banarsidass, New Delhi.

George A. Miller and Richard Beckwith and Christiane Fellbaum and Derek Gross and Katherine Miller. 1990. WordNet: An on-line lexical database. *International Journal of Lexicography*, 3, 235–244.

Monier M. Williams. 2008 revision. Sanskrit-English Dictionary. University Press, Oxford, 1964. (http://www.sanskrit-lexicon.uni-koeln.de/monier/), Online; accessed 2009 - 2010.

Moreshvar R. Kale. 1961. A higher Sanskrit grammar, for the use of schools and colleges. Motilal Banarsidass, New Delhi.

Siddheshwar Varma. 1953. *Vishveshvaranand indological Series*, 5. Hoshiarpur : Vishveshvaranand Institute.

Vaman S. Apte. 2008 revision. The Practical Sanskrit-English Dictionary. Poona, Prasad Prakashan, 1957 - 1959. (http://www.aa.tufs.ac.jp/ tjun/sktdic/), Online; accessed 2009 - 2010.

Alessandro Lenci 2010. Carving verb classes from corpora. Raffaele Simone and Francesca Masini, Word Classes Amsterdam Philadelphia: John Benjamins.

Hideyo Ogawa 2005. Process and Language: study of the Mahabhasya ad A1.3.1 bhuvadayo dhatavah. Motilal Banarsidass, Delhi, first edition.

Kavitha Rajan 2013. Understanding verbs based on overlapping verbs senses. In Proceedings of the ACL Student Research Workshop.August 4-9. Sofia,Bulgaria., pages 5966

Hans C. Boas 2005. From Theory to Practice: Frame Semantics and the Design of FrameNet. Semantisches Wissen im Lexikon. Langer, S. and Schnorbusch, D. Tübingen: Narr., pages 129-160.

Shivaram Dattatray Joshi and J.A.F. Roodbergen and Sahitya Akademi 1991. The Aṣṭādhyāyī of Pāṇini with Translation and Explanatory Notes.,v.7 Sahitya Akademi

Hoa Trang Dang and Martha Palmer and Joseph Rosenzweig 1998. Investigating regular sense extensions based on intersective Levin classes. Proceedings of the 36th Meeting of the ACL and the 17th COLING pages 293-299.

Roger C. Schank. October, 1972. Conceptual Dependency: A Theory of Natural Language Understanding. *Journal of Cognitive Psychology*, 3(4):552–631.

Roger C. Schank. 1973. Conceptualizations underlying natural language. *Computer Models of Thought and Language*. San Francisco: W.H. Freeman.

Roger C. Schank. 1975. The Primitive ACTs of Conceptual Dependency. *Proceedings of the 1975 workshop on Theoretical issues in natural language processing, TINLAP75*, 34–37.

Navjyoti Singh 2001. Comprehensive Schema of Entities: Vaiśeṣika Category System. *Science Philosophy Interface*, 5(2). 1–54.

Table 4: Feature-space of motion verbs consisting of ontological attribute set

Main Class of Ontological Attributes	Sub-Attributes		Sub-Sub-Attributes
Space	Direction (linear)	24	(backward, backwards, after, along, through, across, over, back — forth, side to side, forwards, forward, to, towards, from, in front, with, away, further away, behind, in , into, out of, up, upward)[prepositions]
	Direction (down)	1	(down) [prepositions]
	Direction (curvilinear)	3	(around, about, direction-less) [prepositions]
	Path	12	(circle, long way, along a path, direction-less, across a surface, straight line, winding course, zigzag course, long distance, over mountains / hills / forest, over difficult surface , in the direction you want it to move) [locations]
Location	Source	11	(observer, one side of something, position, point, somewhere, line, a fixed point, something, someone , a place , closed place) [locations]
	Object on which acted on	4	(something, someone, own body, group of people) [locations]
	Destination	17	(source of difficulty, source of anger, to somewhere, countryside, person, animal, goal, to a large area, destination, to previous place, to a particular place, to another place, speaker, location near / familiar to speaker, person being spoken to, point, position, lower value, direction-less) [locations]
	Relative position	1	(previous position) [locations]
	Place of action	9	[locations]
Time	Frequency	2	(repeatedly, continuously) [positions]
	Duration	4	(forever, short time , over a period of time, permanently) [adverbs]
Manner	Mode	100	(awkwardly, easily, closely, unwillingly, accidentally, intentionally, carrying load, smoothly, violently, noisily etc.) [adverbs]
	Speed	16	(quickly, very fast, regular(adj) step(v), easy and comfortable speed, very slowly, suddenly, slowly, fast, speed, swiftly, quick, more quickly than normal, very quickly, extremely quickly, moderately fast, rapidly) [adverbs]
Reason	Purpose	7	(hunting, make move, to go in a particular direction or have a particular result, or to allow or cause this, to get information secretly, try to catch or kill them, go where they go, to hold)
	Cause	5	((after)hitting a surface, force, by momentum / force of gravity by outside forces, rebound)
	Because	20	(strike, due to some reason, feeling tired / bored, tired, from danger , from fear, show annoyance, to start new journey, being frightened, playfully, due to injury / pain, for pleasure and relaxation, for pleasure, to escape, to look important, attract attention, old age, to show place to someone, make certain that they arrive safely or that they leave a place as a part of public celebration)
	Effect of(verb) action	1	((leave behind) pain)

SMT Errors Requiring Grammatical Knowledge for Prevention

Yukiko Sasaki Alam
Department of Digital Media
Hosei University
3-7-2 Kajino-cho, Koganei,
Tokyo, Japan
sasaki@hosei.ac.jp

Abstract

This paper introduces three types of Statistical Machine Translation (SMT) output errors that would require grammatical knowledge for prevention. The first type is due to words that are negative in meaning but not in form. Problems arise when the negative forms are obligatory in target languages. The second type of errors is derived from the rigidity of pattern phrases or correlatives which do not allow for intervening elements. The third type is caused by ellipses in input sentences which must be reinstated for output sentences when so required by rules of omission in target languages or the difference in Head-Complement order between source and target languages.

1 Introduction

Machine translation (MT) output errors are varied, and have been discussed and classified by many researchers. Flanagan (1994) classifies and ranks errors into three levels according to improvability and intelligibility. Elliot et al. (2004) identify fluency- and adequacy-related errors for automatic MT evaluation. Vilar et al. (2006) make a comprehensive classification of SMT output errors. Farrús et al. (2010) present a linguistic-based evaluation of a variety of SMT output errors. Popović and Burchardt (2011) attempt to provide methods for an automatic error analysis of MT output errors that overcome weaknesses of automatic evaluation metrics.

This paper introduces three particular types of errors made at the online English-to-Japanese translation on the Google Language Tools, a cutting-edge SMT system, and demonstrates that

grammatical knowledge is required for preventing such errors.

2 Negative in Meaning but Not in Form

There are several English determiners and adverbs that are negative in meaning but not in form, which are termed *negation-implying* words in this paper. Negation-implying determiners are *little* and *few*, whereas negation-implying adverbs include *little*, *seldom*, *rarely*, *scarcely*, *hardly* and *barely*. This discrepancy between meaning and form causes problems with translation into such languages as Japanese, the grammars of which require the explicit forms of negation.

2.1 Negation-implying determiners

The word *few* used as a determiner[1] as in *Few men* in (1a) below means "not many", emphasizing how small a number of people is.:

(1a) *Few people turned up for work.*

In Japanese, such an emphasis on scarcity is usually expressed both by a negation-implying determiner or adverb and the negative form of the predicate that follows it. (1a) could be roughly translated as the following:

(1b) *hotondo-no hito-ga   shokuba-ni*
almost-POSS[2] people-SUBJ[3] workplace-LOC[4]
araware-nakatta.
show-up NOT-DID

Notice that the predicate of the corresponding Japanese sentence is in the negative form.

Translation of an English sentence with such a negation-implying word into Japanese is problematic, because it requires additional tasks in-

---

[1] Determiners in English are located at the beginning of noun phrases. They include articles, demonstrative, quantifiers and possessives.

[2] *POSS* indicates the possessive marker.

[3] *SUBJ* denotes the subject marker.

[4] *LOC* stands for the locus marker indicating place, goal or point of time.

148

D S Sharma, R Sangal and E Sherly. Proc. of the 12th Intl. Conference on Natural Language Processing, pages 152–157,
Trivandrum, India. December 2015. ©2015 NLP Association of India (NLPAI)

cluding the recognizing of the relevant predicate and the changing of it into the negative form, let alone the identification of the part of speech of the word in question. Failure in carrying out such tasks leads to mistranslation. Take the following for instance:

(2a) *Few decisions will have as lasting an impact on your life as your choice of profession.*

The SMT system translates (2a) as a Japanese sentence that means:

(2b) A few decisions turn out to have a lasting impact on your life as the choice of profession.[5]

At this translation, the SMT system probably mistook *few* indicating "not many" for *a few* denoting "several". The resulting Japanese sentence does not convey the same importance on the rarity of such decisions as implied in the input sentence. The output sentence also fails to express the core meaning of the input sentence.

It is necessary to identify the part of speech of *few* in use, because it does not have a negative connotation when used in other parts of speech. It can be used as a pronoun, as illustrated below:

(3) *A lucky few will be able to enjoy the new low monthly payment.*

In addition, it can be used as an adjective, as below:

(4) *Read the first few pages.*

A tripartite distinction should be made in a noun phrase (NP) with *few*: (i) determiner in $_{NP}$[*few* ... noun],[6] (ii) pronoun in $_{NP}$[determiner ... *few*], and (iii) adjective in $_{NP}$[determiner ... *few* ... noun].

A similar word *little* is more problematic, because it can belong to the adverb category as well as the same parts of speech for *few*. Failure to recognize the negation-implying determiners is costly, because the output sentence could indicate an opposite meaning to that of the input sentence. Consider the following:

(5a) *This has received little attention since 1983.*

The SMT system in question translates (5a) as a Japanese sentence that means:

(5b) This has received almost attention since 1983.[7]

The meaning of the output is contrary to that of the input. This suggests that the SMT system requires grammatical knowledge for identifying the parts of speech for *few* and *little*, and, when used as a determiner, it needs to recognize the relevant predicate and transform it into the negative form of the equivalent of the target language.

2.2 Negation-implying adverbs

Adverbs such as *little*, *seldom*, *rarely*, *scarcely*, *hardly* and *barely* are negative in meaning but not in form. They seem to be treated by the SMT system better than the counterpart determiners, but a closer examination reveals that the treatment is indeed erratic.

As long as an input sentence with a negation-implying adverb is short and in the present tense, and the predicate is not a *be* verb, the SMT system in question generates an output with the negative form of the predicate, thus conveying the same emphasis on the rarity of the event. For instance, the sentence *It seldom works out that way* is translated as a sentence with the intended meaning,[8] only with a minor error of the wrong negative inflection of the predicate.

However, the translation of a short sentence fails, when the system is unable to identify the parts of speech of the adverb and the surrounding words, as illustrated below:

(6a) *The world will little note, nor long remember what we say here, but it can never forget what they did here.*[9]

The above sentence is translated as below:

(6b) The world will a short note, and also remember what we who are long say here, but it can never forget what they did here.[10]

The SMT system fails to identify the parts of speech of *little* and *note* in the initial clause, resulting in an ungrammatical output clause. It also fails to recognize that *long* is an adverb, and places the corresponding Japanese adjective immediately before *we*. That means that *long* modifies *we*. The negative conjunction *nor* is totally skipped, thus giving rise to the corresponding clause with the opposite meaning to the input clause

The SMT's treatment of the tense is puzzling for short sentences with a negation-implying adverb. It sometimes does not make a distinction between the present and past tenses. For instance, *He rarely eats red meat* and *He rarely ate red meat* are translated as the same Japanese sen-

---

[5] The output is "いくつかの決定は、職業の選択としてあなたの人生に影響を持続として持つことになります。".

[6] $_{NP}$[...] indicates that the phrase between brackets is a noun phrase.

[7] The output is "これは 1983 年以来、ほとんど注目されています。".

[8] The output is "それはほとんどそのようにうまくいくありません。".

[9] This is from the Gettysburg address by Abraham Lincoln.

[10] The output is "世界は少しノート、また長い私たちがここで言うことを覚えているだろうが、それは彼らがここで何をしたか忘れることはできません。".

tence in the present tense,[11] indicating that he rarely eats red meat. The treatment of the tense is correct sporadically, though.

Near perfect translations were produced when the predicates of sentences begin with *could hardly* or *can hardly*, and the verbs are not a *be* verb, as in:

(7) *She could hardly wait for her child coming back.*[12]
(8) *This fact can hardly be used to explain present patterns of crime.*[13]

The treatment of the tense is also correct in the two examples above.

With a *be* verb, however, even simpler input sentences in (9a) and (10a) than in (7) and (8) are translated as wrong output sentences, shown in (9b) and (10b):

(9a) *This was hardly surprising.*
(10a) *He was barely aware of the feeling.*

The above two sentences are respectively translated as Japanese sentences meaning:

(9b) This was something almost surprising.[14]
(10b) He was aware of almost every feeling.[15]

The resulting outputs convey opposite meanings to the English input sentences.[16]

We have seen that the SMT system in question is erratic in the treatment of negation-implying determiners and adverbs. For a comprehensive treatment, it must identify the part of speech of such a word, and, if it is used as a determiner or an adverb, find the predicate and change it into the negative form of the corresponding predicate.

3 Intervening Elements

It has been observed that when an English sentence consists of a pattern phrase containing an intervening element such as an adverb or a noun phrase (NP) of time, the SMT system in question generates incomprehensible Japanese outputs.

3.1 Adverbials causing discontinuous constituents

Adverbs and adverbial phrases (called hereafter *adverbials*) can be located at several positions of sentences. This mobility of adverbials often creates problems with translation by pattern matching. Take the following for instance:

(11a) *The government (may be paying incorrect subsidies to more than 1 million Americans for their health plans in the new federal insurance marketplace and)* [17] *has been unable <u>so far</u> to fix the errors.*

(11a) is roughly translated as below:

(11b) The government (can pay incorrect subsidies to more than 1 million Americans for its own health plans in the new federal insurance marketplace, and) has not so far been able to do it, in order to fix the errors.[18]

The SMT system in question fails to recognize the pattern phrase *unable to fix the errors*, because the phrase contains an adverbial *so far* between *unable* and *to fix the errors*.[19] Another example follows:

(12a) *Investments in the health systems of low-income countries have <u>long</u> been geared toward treating infectious disease, he said.*[20]

The sentence in (12a) is translated as a Japanese sentence roughly meaning:

(12b) Investments in the health systems of low-income countries are geared toward treating long infectious disease, he said.

The part of speech of *long* in the input sentence is an adverb meaning "for a long time", but in the output sentence, it is an adjective, resulting in a phrase denoting "a long disease". This error is probably due to the presence of *long* in the middle of the pattern phrase *have been geared*. With *long* taken off, (12a) is translated correctly by the SMT system in question.

To deal with adverbs and other unexpected interruptions such as interjections and rephrasing, a controlled skip parser was proposed (Yamada, 1996). The parser uses statistical information (N-

---

[11] The output is "彼はめったに赤肉を食べません".

[12] The output is "彼女はほとんど彼女の子供が戻ってくるのを待つことができませんでした。".

[13] The output is "この事実はほとんど犯罪の現在のパターンを説明するために使用することができません。".

[14] The output is "これはほとんど驚くべきことでした。".

[15] The output is "彼は感情のほとんどを知っていました。".

[16] It should be noted that when *barely* modifies a number as in *The industry employed barely 150,000 men*, it is translated as a word denoting "almost", and the output Japanese sentence is a little awkward, but intelligible. The output is "業界はほとんど 15 万人を採用します".

[17] The parentheses in the sentence indicate that the elements inside them are not targets for our discussion.

[18] The output is "政府は新たな連邦政府の保険市場で自分の健康の計画のために 100 万人以上のアメリカ人に誤った補助金を支払うことができ、エラーを修正するために、これまでできませんでした。".

[19] The present focus is on translation errors caused by the presence of an adverbial located inside a pattern phrase, and thus the other errors found in the Japanese output are not discussed here.

[20] The output is "低所得国の保健システムへの投資が長い感染性疾患の治療に向けられている、と彼は言いました。".

grams) to determine what to skip in newspaper articles. As far as the skipping of adverbs is concerned, it does not affect the meaning of the sentence when they are such adverbs as *so far* and *long* respectively in (11a) and (12a), but it would be detrimental if they are such adverbs as *little* and *hardly* in (6a) and (9a). A careful research would be conducted on the skipping of adverbials. The skipping of a constituent of an input sentence at machine translation (MT) should be a last resort.

A *to*-infinitive can be used either as an adverbial modifier as well as a nominal one. The following example shows that an adverbial use breaks a pattern.

(13a) *Exercise does more to bolster thinking than thinking does.*

(13a) is translated as a sentence roughly with the following meaning:

(13b) Exercise carries out than, in order to bolster thinking, than thinking.[21]

The Japanese word equivalent to *than* is followed by the object marker, indicating that *than* is interpreted as the object of the predicate, resulting in an intelligible output.

The removal of *to bolster thinking* from (13a) gives rise to a grammatical and comprehensible sentence. This demonstrates that the SMT system is able to handle the pattern phrase x (Subject) + verb + *more than* + y + *does*, but not one with an intervening element.

3.2 Elements intervening relative clauses and the heads

We have seen that the SMT system in question goes awry when an adverbial cuts into a pattern phrase. A similar error occurs when an element intervenes between usually adjacent elements such as a relative clause and the head noun phrase (NP). Take the following for instance:

(14) *"I want to marry Mii, but I can't do that," Marini said in a video posted online that attracted the attention of gaming blogs and online forums this week.*[22]

The SMT system is unable to recognize the head NP and the relative clause *a video ... that attracted ...* because of the intervening phrase *posted online* between. The removal of the inter-

vening phrase produces a fairly grammatical and intelligible output.[23]

In addition, the following relatively short and simple sentence is translated incorrectly for the same reason as above:

(15) *There were nine men that year who had run faster than 10.2 seconds.*[24]

Again, the SMT system is unable to recognize the relative clause and the head NP because of the presence of *last year* between them. It misinterprets *last year* as the head NP of the relative clause. Furthermore, *last year* is regarded as the subject NP of the predicate *were*. As a result, the output is an unintelligible sentence. The removal of *last year* from (15) produces a grammatical output,[25] recognizing the head NP and the relative clause.[26]

These examples indicate that the system in question needs grammatical knowledge to identify discontinuous constituencies and relations with unexpected intervening elements such as adverbials and NPs of time.

4 Omission and Recoverability

In languages, constituents of sentences which are predictable from context are often omitted. This omission, however, causes problems for machine translation (MT). An MT system must (i) detect if the sentence contains an ellipsis, and if it does and if the reinstatement is required by the target grammar, it must (ii) recover the word or phrase. Such reinstatement would require grammatical knowledge.

4.1 Verbal omissions

In (16a) below, the main predicate *changed* of the final clause is omitted because it is a repetition of the predicate of the immediately preceding clause. As the SMT system fails to recognize the omission, it mistook the auxiliary verb *have* for a regular verb denoting possession:

(16a) *Values have shifted, the population has changed, and the cities have too.*

---

[21] The output is "運動は思考よりも思考を強化するために、よりを行います。".

[22] The output is "「私はミイと結婚したいが、私はそれを行うことはできません、「マリーニは、ビデオが今週のゲームブログやオンラインフォーラムの注目を集め、オンラインを掲載で述べています。".

[23] The output is "「私はミイと結婚したいが、私はそれを行うことはできません、「マリーニは、今週のゲームブログやオンラインフォーラムの注目を集めたビデオの中で述べています。".

[24] The output is "9 男性はより速く 10.2 秒を実行していたその年がありました。".

[25] The output is "速い 10.2 秒よりも実行していた 9 人の男性がありました。".

[26] However, the verb *run* is translated as a Japanese word meaning "operate" instead of "move at a speed faster than a walk", probably because the frequency of the chosen meaning is higher on the SMT system in question.

The output roughly means:

> (16b) The numbers,[27] the population has been changed, has shifted, and[28] the cities possess too much.[29]

The sentence in (16a) is a flat one, conjoining three simple clauses. The SMT system fails to recognize the initial clause *Values have shifted* as a clause. It also fails to understand that the main verb of the final clause has been omitted. The word *too* is treated as the object NP of the verb *have*. The system does not have knowledge that *too* is an adverb, and that it cannot be the object of a verb. Nor does it have grammatical means of distinguishing *have* between uses of the auxiliary and the main verbs.

The following sentence in (17a) contains a relative clause in which both *did* and *did not* share the main verb phrase *watch television*. The system fails to identify the sharing, resulting in an unintelligible output roughly meaning (17b).

> (17a) *Conversely the difference between those who did and did not watch television widened.*[30]
>
> (17b) Conversely one conducted television, and difference from those who did not watch it widened.

It is difficult to imagine how such an output is produced. An MT system should be provided with grammatical knowledge for recognizing that the first *did* is not a verb meaning "conduct" or "perform", but is an auxiliary verb.

The omission of the repeated verb phrase poses problems for translation between head-initial languages in Verb-Object (VO) order and head-final languages in Object-Verb (OV) order. In VO languages like English, the object NP shared by two verbs can appear at the final position together with the second verb, creating the configuration of "Verb1 (=Head) and Verb2 (=Head) + Object (=Complement)". On the other hand, in OV languages like Japanese, the object NP should appear at the initial position of the verb phrase, generating the configuration of "Object (=Complement) + Verb1 (=Head) and Verb2 (=Head)". In (17a), the shared complement is the verb phrase *watch television*. (18a) is a partial phrase cut off from (17a) for the sake of discussion:

> (18a) *those who did and did not watch television*

The configuration showing the omission in (18a) is "AUX1 [31] (*did*=Head) and AUX2 (*did not*=Head) + Verb Phrase (*watch television*=Complement)". The Japanese configuration that corresponds to (18a) is "Verb Phrase (television watch=Complement) + AUX1 (PAST=Head) and AUX2 (NOT PAST=Head)". The grammatical output of (18a) is roughly as below:

> (18b) television-OBJ watch-PAST people and watch-NOT-PAST people

Notice that the verb phrase *watch television* is moved to the initial position. For a proper treatment of this type of omission, the system needs to identify the missing element (the verb phrase in this example), and move it to the appropriate place, according to the target language grammar.

4.2 Other problematic omissions

The omission of repeated verb phrases is fairly common and could be easy to handle, but repeated other categories can be omitted, too. Special measures should be taken for them when source and target languages differ much in grammars of omission. For instance, with recovered missing constituents, (18a) would look like the following:

> (18a') *those who <u>watched television</u> and <u>those who</u> did not watch television*

In (18a), *watched television* in (18a') is replaced with *did*, and the repeated phrase *those who* is omitted. A Japanese grammar of omission, however, does not permit such an omission, and therefore *those who* must be reinstated in translation into Japanese. It would be difficult to solve this type of problem by statistical means. It would need several rules of recognition and generation to bridge the gap in this regard between the two grammars.

Another example is an omission that takes place in an idiomatic phrase. English has the phrase *as* + adjective /adverb + *as* + x, which expresses a comparison in relation to the same degree. When the final part of the phrase is equivalent or similar in semantics to *as before*, it can be omitted, as follows:

> (19) *When she was running this whole show, and had her own money, she didn't need me <u>as much</u> from that standpoint.*[32]

---

[27] *Value* has at least two meanings: principles or standards of behavior and a numerical amount or number. The meaning of numbers is chosen in the output, probably because of the higher frequency stored at the SMT in question.

[28] Japanese uses different conjunctions for conjoining NPs and clauses. The conjunction used in the output is one for conjoining NPs, generating an awkward translation.

[29] The output is "値は、人口が変更された、シフトしている、と都市があまりにも持っています。".

[30] The output is "逆にテレビを行なったし、見なかった人との差が拡大しました。".

[31] *AUX* stands for auxiliary.

[32] The output is "彼女はこの番組全体を実行し、自分のお金を持っていたとき、彼女はその観点から、私は同じくらい必要はありませんでした。".

(20) *The journey from London to Bath took forty hours in 1720, but only half <u>as long</u> in 1770.*[33]

The output of (19) is unintelligible, because the object *me* of the verb *need* is translated as the subject. The phrase *as much* is regarded as an idiomatic phrase denoting the same, as in *I am sure she would do as much for me*. As a result, the clause *she didn't need me as much from that standpoint* is translated to mean "she from that standpoint I didn't need about the same". Probably the quality of translation would have been better by skipping the phrase *as much*.

The SMT system in question also fails to produce a comprehensible output of (20). The relevant portion in (20) to the topic of omission is *only half as long in 1770*. The adverb *only* is translated as a word meaning "unique", while the phrase *half as long* as a word meaning "half" followed by a stem denoting "long". The system cannot recognize the part of speech of *long*. An accumulation of these errors gives rise to an intelligible output. The removal of *as long*, however, generates a little ungrammatical but understandable Japanese sentence.[34] While looking for a general solution, it might be a realistic alternative to skip problematic words or phrases. But even for this approach, research would be required for identifying what to skip.

5   Conclusion

This paper has shown three types of English-to-Japanese SMT output errors, and demonstrated that the solution of these errors needs grammatical knowledge. The first type is caused by difference in negative implications of words in source and target languages. The second type of output errors is derived from the rigidity of pattern phrases. Adverbs and adverbial phrases can appear at one of several positions of sentences, resulting in discontinuous constituents. The inclusion of adverbials in pattern phrases would cause the proliferation of pattern phrases and probably be not a feasible solution. Skipping them could be an alternative, but the investigation of which one to skip and not to skip would require much research. The third type of errors concern the omission of the constituents of sentences. It is difficult for an SMT system to find a missing constituent, but the target grammar sometimes requires the reinstatement of the omitted element. The solution of these problems would need syntactic parsing and grammatical knowledge.

Reference

Bunt, H. and A Van Horck. 1996. *Discontinuous Constituency.* Mouton De Gruyter.

Condon, Sherri, Dan Parvaz, John Aberdeen, Christy Doran, Andrew Freeman, and Marwan Awad. Evaluation of Machine Translation Errors in English and Iraqi Arabic. *The MITRE Corporation.* 7 pages. 2010

Elliot, Debbie, Anthony Hartley, and Eric Atwell. A Fluency Error Categorization Scheme to Guide Automated Machine Translation Evaluation. *AMTA-2004.* 64-73, 2004.

Farrús, Mireia, Marta R. Costa-jussa, Jose B. Marino and Jose A. R. Fonollosa. Linguistic-based Evaluation Criteria to Identify Statistical Machine Translation Erros. *Annual Conference of the European Association for Machine Translation.* 167-173, 2010.

Farrús, Mireia, Marta R. Costa-jussa, Jose B. Marino, Marc Posh, Adolfo Hernandez, Carlos Henriquez, and Jose A. R. Fonollosa. Overcoming statistical machine translation limitations: error analysis and proposed solutions for the Catalan-Spanish language pair. *Language Resources and Evaluation* (Springer). Vol. 45 Issue 2. 181-,. 2011.

Flanagan, Mary A. Error classification for MT evaluation. *-1994.* 65-72, 1994.

Popović, Maja and Aljoscha Burchardt. From Human to Automatic Error Classification for Machine Translation Output. *Proceedings of the 15th Conference of the European Association for Machine Translation.* 265-272, 2011.

Stymne, Sara and Lars Ahrenberg. On the practice of error analysis for machine translation evaluation. *LREC.* 1785-1790. 2012.

Talbot, David, Hideto Kazawa, Hiroshi Ichikawa, Jason Katz-Brown, Mranz J. Och. A Lightweight Evaluation Framework for Machine Translation Reordering. *Proceedings of the 6th Workshop on Statistical Machine Translation.* 12-21. 2011.

Vilar, David, Jia Xu, Luis Fernaudo D'Haro, and Hermann Ney. Error Analysis of Statistical Machine Translation Output. *Proceedings of the LREC.* 697-702. 2006.

Yamada, Ken. 1996. A controlled Skip Parser. *Proceedings of the 2nd AMTA Conference.*

---

[33] The output is "バースへのロンドンからの旅は 1770 年に唯一の半分の長 1720 年 40 時間かかりました が、。".

[34] The output is "バースへのロンドンからの旅は、1720 年 40 時間かかりましたが、1770 年に半分だけ。".

Isolated Word Recognition System for Malayalam using Machine Learning

Maya Moneykumar
IIITM-K, Trivandrum
maya.moneykumar
@iiitmk.ac.in

Elizabeth Sherly
IIITM-K , Trivandrum
sherly@iiitmk.ac.in

Win Sam Varghese
IIITM-K , Trivandrum
sam.varghese
@iiitmk.ac.in

Abstract

Automatic Speech Recognition (ASR) has received greater level of acceptance as it creates speech recognition by the human machine interface. This paper focuses on developing a syllable based speech recognition system for Malayalam language. The proposed system consists of three different phases such as preprocessing, segmentation and classification. The preprocessing is performed for noise reduction, DC component removal, pre-emphasis and framing. The segmentation process implemented using Syllable Segmentation Algorithm segments the word utterances into syllables, that are inturn fed into the system for feature extraction. In the feature extraction step, we have proposed a novel approach by adding energy and zero crossing, along with MFCC features. The classification is done using Artificial Neural Network and is also compared with HMM classifier. Experiments are carried out with real-time utterances of 100 words, and obtained 96.4 % accuracy in ANN, which outperformed HMM.

1 Introduction

Automatic Speech Recognition (ASR) system, especially speech to text conversion is one of the most challenging tasks in nowadays. The ultimate aim of ASR is to understand spontaneous speech using a computer. However, a word-level identification, which is a complex task in itself is also a major chore in any ASR system. In this paper, a word-level identification is performed to make a computer identify the isolated words spoken by a person and to convert it into corresponding text. ASR is basically a pattern recognition problem which also involves a number of technologies and research areas like Signal Processing, Natural Language Processing, Statistics and Cognitive Science. Different factors like gender, emotional state, accent and pronunciation make speech recognition a complex task. The mode of articulation, nasality, pitch, volume, and speed variability in speech also make speech recognition a difficult task. Even when speech is recognized, the accuracy rate can be less due to various behaviors of speech, usage of words, higher variability, background noise and the linguistic features of language and speech. This can seriously affect the system performance. There exists works which attempt for speaker dependent and speaker independent recognition. Our attempt is to achieve Speaker independence, which is difficult to achieve because in order to recognize the speech patterns, these models should be trained with speech data of a large group of people.

Developing an efficient speech recognizer that can exhibit natural capabilities of every human possesses, along with language capability is much harder. As far as Malayalam language is considered, which has a rich set of vocabulary and the modern Malayalam alphabet has 15 vowel letters, 41 consonant letters, and a few other symbols. Malayalam is one of the richest languages in terms of number of alphabets and also one of the toughest languages while considering speech. This is because of the variations in pronunciation. Speech recognition in Malayalam language is still in its infancy stage and the dream of a system which can interact with the users in native language is still in its early stage. Hence, developing an efficient speech recognition system in Malayalam has great relevance. An isolated word identification system aims at identifying a spoken word from the trained vocabulary.

The work is explained in this paper in 6 sections. The first section is the abstract of the work. The second section gives an introduction where the

D S Sharma, R Sangal and E Sherly. Proc. of the 12th Intl. Conference on Natural Language Processing, pages 158–165,
Trivandrum, India. December 2015. ©2015 NLP Association of India (NLPAI)

problem and the relevance of the problem in the current scenario is explained. The third section gives a review of already existing methods and the comparative study about the advantages and disadvantages of the existing methods. The fourth section is the core part of this work which introduces the methodology adopted to solve the problem, and the implementation of the algorithm for the same. The results are analyzed in the fifth section which also contains a detailed study about the results obtained. The future scope of the work is included in the last section.

2 Literature Review

ASR technology, during the yesteryears has made advancement to a great extent and has reached the point where this facility is used in various fields by millions. Speech recognition works, in foreign languages, advanced a lot since 1920. The first work in speech recognition was the development of a toy named Radio Rex, a celluloid dog,which was developed in 1920. Even though researches were carried out since 1936, the first successful speech recognizer was developed in the year 1952 by David et.al, which could recognize digit utterances by a single speaker. The system used spectral energy and formant frequencies for recognition purpose. Another notable development in this field was the implementation of phoneme based speech recognizer in the year 1959. In 1960s Japan made their first leap into the field of speech recognition and developed a special purpose hardware to improve the computational speed of the then systems. They also developed a hardware phoneme recognizer in 1962 followed by a digit recognizer in 1963 (Nnamdi Okomba S et al. , 2015).

The ASR works were extended to the field of isolated word utterance recognition in 1970s, during which prominent works were carried out by Velichko and Zagoruyko in Russia , Itakura in United State and Cakoe and Chiba in Japan. Meantime, CMU also played their role in the ASR field. Several other systems such as HEARSAY II(1975), HARPY(1976), HWIM (1977) and KEAL (1977) were implemented during this period. A major shift in the ASR technology happened in 1980, where the template based approach got replaced by statistical modeling methods like Hidden Markov Model (HMM). Different international languages, including English, French and Pashto implemented speech recognition systems with HMM and proved successful. An automatic dictation system in French implemented using HMM gave an accuracy of 76.2%. A digit recognition system for English implemented using HMM gave an accuracy rate of 88%. It was in 1980s itself, that Support Vector Machine and Neural Network approach got popularity despite of its faded entry in the early 1950s. This period also witnessed the progress in speech recognition works carried out with continuous speech. ASR using Artificial Neural Networks (ANN) achieved excellent results in tasks such as voiced/unvoiced discrimination in 1989 as well as phoneme recognition and spoken digit recognition in 1989. Peeling and Moore applied Multi Layer Perceptron (MLP) to digit recognition and thereby obtained excellent results. Various foreign languages, including Malay, Indonesian and Arabic, later implemented ASR using ANN. The work carried out in Malay language using MLP considered utterances of 4 different speakers and obtained an accuracy of 95% in identifying words within the trained vocabulary (Ahmed et al., 2012; Sheila D Apte, 2012; Nnamdi Okomba S et al. , 2015).

Automatic Speech Recognition has tremendous potential in the Indian scenario, as well. Since common man depends on the internet and its services, they will be interacting with machines every time. In order to enjoy the benefits completely and to bridge the digital divide, the communication should happen in their local languages. Keeping this fact in mind, most of the Indian languages have worked and are still working with ASR tasks. Text- to speech conversion has been developed for the visually challenged section of society, for Indian languages such as Hindi, Bengali, Marathi, Tamil, Telugu and Malayalam. Isolated Word speech recognition system is built for most spoken Indian languages namely Telugu, Hindi, Urdu, Kannada, Marathi, Tamil, Malayalam, Bengali and Oriya using Hidden Markov Model tool kit (HTK). It works as text dependent speaker recognition mode. A notable work in Tamil - 'A syllable based isolated word recognizer for Tamil handling OOV words', uses a subword based continuous speech recognizer for word identification. Notable works were carried out during the period 2000 to 2005 in languages including Hindi, Tamil and Telugu. Some of the works include Speaker Independent Continuous speech recognizer for Hindi(2000), Speech recognizer for Specific Domain in Tamil (2001), Speech Recognition of Isolated Telugu Vowels Using Neural Networks (2003) and Digit Recognizer for Hindi (2006). Several other Indian languages like Punjabi, Marathi, Gujarathi, Assamese and Kannada successfully imprinted their footsteps in the field of ASR during early 2000s (Kurian Cini, and Kannan Balakrishnan. , 2012; Akila A and E. Chandra, 2013; Akila A and E. Chandra, 2014).

Eventhough Malayalam is still in the budding stage while considering ASR, there exist some noteworthy works and the significant one was from CDAC, Trivandrum where they developed a speech recognition system for visually impaired people. MFCC method was used as a front-end to extract acoustic features from the input signal and a hybrid model integrating rule based and statistical method was used to handle pronunciation variations in the dictionary. The system achieved word accuracy of 75%. A speaker independent continuous speech recognizer based on PLP Cepstral Coefficient, was also developed for Malayalam which employs Hidden Markov Model for pattern recognition. The system got trained with 21 male and female speakers and obtained a word accuracy of 89% when tested with continuous speech data. While considering LPC features for classification, Malayalam speech recognition system obtained an accuracy rate of 81.2%, which is indeed a notable work. Vimal Krishnan et.al developed a small vocabulary (5 words) speech recognition where Artificial neural network technique (ANN) is used for classification and recognition purpose and achieved a recognition rate of 89%. Raji Kumar et.al presented recognition of the isolated question words from the Malayalam speech query using DWT and ANN and recognition accuracy of 80% has been reported.

3 Methodology

The word identification system designed for Malayalam language uses a syllable based segmentation approach. Instead of training the system with independent words, we use syllable combinations for training and identification. This eliminates the problem of maintaining a large set of training data, as different words share common syllables as well as phone segments. New words can be added to the vocabulary without building new models for the existing syllables

and phonemes corresponding to the word. Here, we design a word identification system based on two popular classifier techniques which are Hidden Markov Model (HMM)and Artificial Neural Network (ANN). The various phases involved in speech recognition include data preparation, syllabification and classification. The general system architecture of the speech recognition system implemented in this work is given below.

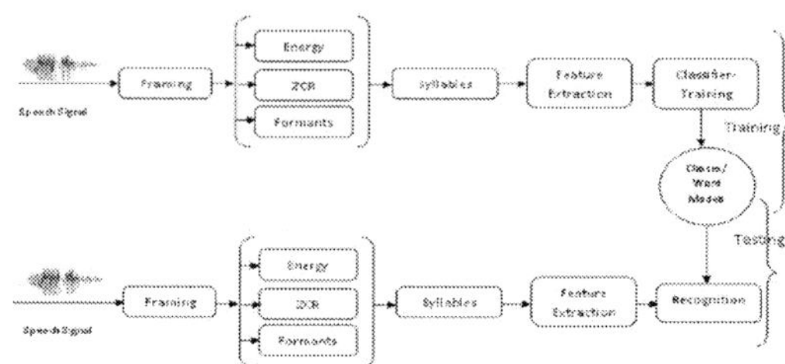

Figure 1: General System Architecture

3.1 Data Preparation

The work maintains a database of utterances which consists of a total of 100 words used in the agriculture domain. Multiple utterances of these words by 9 different speakers(6 male & 3 females) were recorded using an audio tool Audacity with a sampling frequency of 16000Hz. A speech corpus was in turn developed which consists of these audio files along with the syllable transcription.

In audio recording, a DC offset is an undesirable characteristic of a recording sound which occurs during sound capturing. The offset causes the center of the waveform to not be at 0, but at a higher value. This can cause two problems:

- Either the loudest part of the signal will be clipped prematurely, since the base of the waveform has been moved up

- Inaudible low frequency distortion will occur.

The signal, hence should undergo a DC component removal which is done as

$$x(n) = a(n)avg, \quad avg = mean(a); \quad (1)$$

where a is the speech signal

The pre-processing stage consists of noise

reduction and filtering. Pre-emphasis refers to a process designed to increase the magnitude of some (usually higher) frequencies with respect to the magnitude of other (usually lower) frequencies in order to improve the overall signal-to-noise ratio. In speech processing, a pre-emphasis is applied by high pass filtering the signal to smooth the spectrum to achieve a uniform energy distribution spectrum.

Pre-emphasis is done by applying the formula

$$y(n) = x(n) - 0.9955 * x(n-1) \qquad (2)$$

In speech processing, it is often advantageous to divide the signal into frames to achieve stationarity. A frame based analysis is essential for speech signal. Framing is the process of decomposing the speech signal into a series of overlapping/non-overlapping frames. The speech signal is stationary within windows of 20 to 30 ms duration and hence is divided into non-overlapping frames with a duration of 30 ms (Sheila D Apte, 2012) .

3.2 Syllabification & Feature Extraction

3.2.1 Syllabification

In this work, syllabification plays an important role and hence every recorded utterance which becomes the input to the system should eventually undergo syllabification. Instead of using commonly used approaches for syllabification including group delay method, we have developed a novel approach to syllabify utterances which make use of short time energy, zero crossing rate as well as formant frequencies. In syllabification, each and every utterance is segmented into respective syllables irrespective of the number of syllables it consist of. The Syllable Segmentation Algorithm introduced in this work is implemented using Matlab and has obtained an accuracy of 95%.

Syllable Segmentation Algorithm

The algorithm segments syllables, based on the concept that the energy measure for a vowel (voiced segment) is much higher than the silence part and the energy measure of the consonant(unvoiced segment) is lower than the voiced segment(vowel) but higher than the silence part. The zero crossing rate is higher for the silence part and lower for the voiced part of a signal.

Algorithm 1: Algorithm for Syllable Segmentation

Input: *Signal of Isolated Word utterance: I*
Output: *.wav files of Syllables*
1 *Signal Acquisition*
2 *Preprocessing*
3 *Apply a high pass filter and calculate ZCR*
4 *Apply low pass filter and calculate Energy*
5 *Calculate the formants F1 & F2*
6 *calculate the peaks*
7 *Calculate the Residual Energy*
8 *Find the approximate syllable boundaries using the calculated values.*
9 *Attenuate the syllables based on their energy to get the accurate syllable boundary.*
10 *Apply window function*
11 *Store the segmented syllables as wav files*

After obtaining the energy and ZCR values of frames, it is necessary to smooth the signal to find the energy and ZCR peaks. Smoothing means that we even out a signal, by mixing its elements with their neighbors. In order to obtain an accurate measure, we are considering two different energy calculations. The first one is the energy of the signal which is the short time energy and the second is the energy of the signal filtered with low pass filter with a cutoff frequency of 1100Hz. This energy calculation will help us in discarding the mis identified syllable boundaries.

The preprocessed signal then undergoes the syllabification process by detecting the syllable boundaries. Energy and Zero crossing

$$E = \sum_{n=0}^{N-1} s^2(n) \qquad (3)$$

and zero crossing rate as

$$Z = \sum_{n} |sgn(s(n)) - sgn(s(n-1))| \qquad (4)$$

where $sgn(s(n)) = 1, if s(n) \geq 0,$
$sgn(s(n)) = -1, if \quad s(n) < 0$

The syllable segmentation for a word with its speech signal is depicted below in Fig. 2.

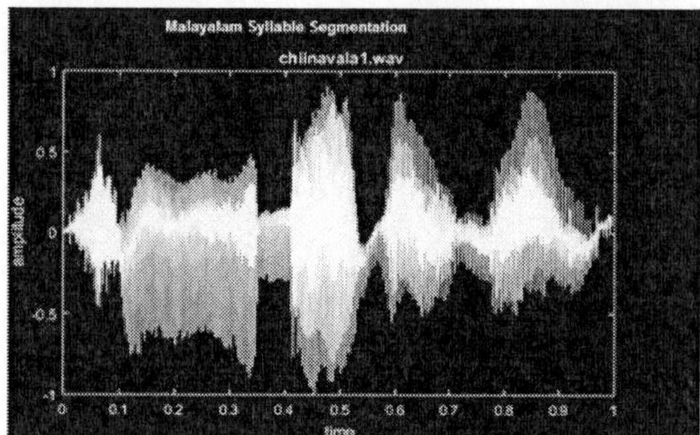

Signal representation for the utterance ചിനവള

Figure 2: Speech signal for utterance chiinavala

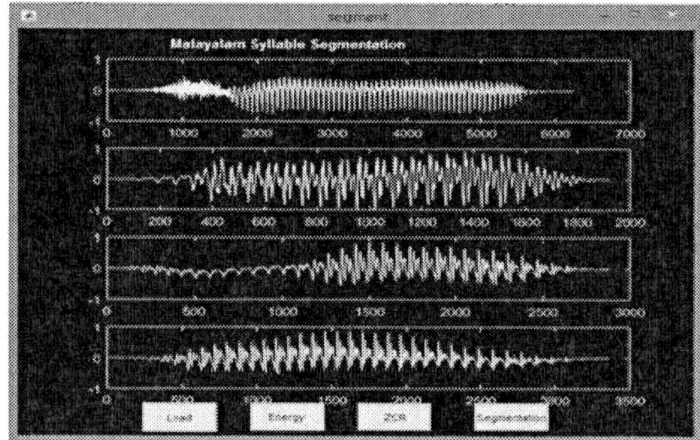

Figure 3: Result of Syllabification

3.2.2 Feature Extraction

The syllables which are stored as .wav files are then fed into the feature extraction process. The syllabified speech signal is divided into non-overlapping frames of 30 ms length by keeping in mind the concept that spectral evaluation are reliable in the case of a stationary signal and that a speech signal is stationary within a window of duration 20-30 ms. For the purpose of feature extraction, spectral analysis algorithm such as MFCC is used. Cepstral analysis has been widely used as the main analysis method for speech recognition. The mel-frequency cepstral coefficients (MFCC) appear to furnish a more efficient representation of speech spectra than other analysis methods. Human auditory system is assumed to process speech signal in a non-linear fashion. Lower frequency components of speech signal contain more information. The mel-frequency cepstrum (MFC) can be defined as the short-time power spectrum of a speech signal

which is calculated as the linear cosine transform of the log power spectrum. Conversion from normal frequency to mel-frequency is given by

$$m = 2595 log10(1 + (f = 700))(4.7) \quad (5)$$

where f indicates normal frequency and m is the corresponding mel-frequency. In order to improve the recognition accuracy, later two additional parameters, energy and zero crossing rate are also considered along with MFCC.

3.3 HMM Classification System

After preprocessing, syllabification and feature extraction, HMM is used to recognize the speech and training. The system is being trained using task grammar, acoustic models and lexical models using HTK toolkit.

For training, a 5 state HMM prototype model was created with the first and last non- emitting states. The main step in HMM training is defining a prototype model as a model structure. A train file is also created which will redirect HTK to the location where the feature vector files (mfcc files) are stored. Realigning the training data is done next where the word-to-phone mapping operation is performed. In this case, all pronunciations for each word is considered and then output the pronunciation that best matches the acoustic data. In order to recognize the word using phoneme combinations, triphone files are also generated (Pammi S. C and V. Keri., 2005).

The testing phase which is responsible for recognizing the utterances also follows the same set of steps till feature extraction, as in the training phase. The testing signals were also converted into a series of feature vectors. During the testing phase, recognition happens where the decoder compiles the recognition network using the task level word network. The word level transcriptions are constructed from the recognition network, as the next step.

3.3.1 ANN Based Speech Recognition System

The speech recognition system based on ANN was implemented using Multilayer Perceptron (MLP) which is a popular form of neural network. The input vectors are 12 MFCC values, along with two additional features energy and zero crossing rate. The architecture used for ANN based ASR is given below.

Table 1: ANN Architecture

No: of input neurons	60
No: of neurons in the hidden layer	100
No: of hidden layers	1
No: of output neurons	80
Activation function	Sigmoid

The system is trained using Backpropagation algorithm with learning rate 0.3 and number of epochs 200. The training and testing were performed with various scenarios. The system is trained only with MFCC and MFCC, along with energy and zero crossing. A notable greater performance is shown in later case.

4   Result & Discussions

The goal of this work was to design a speech recognition system for Malayalam. In order to identify a method which gives better recognition accuracy, we used two well known approaches which will solve pattern recognition problems. The system was trained with both Artificial Neural Network and Hidden Markov Model so that if a syllable is given, it will identify the class to which it belongs to. To test the performance of both ANN and HMM, various test data were given where the accuracy in recognizing words within the vocabulary and out of vocabulary words, by the same as well as different speakers. The test data is categorized as follows:

Exp	Test Data	Speaker
Test1	OOV	Same Speaker
Test2	OOV	Diff. Speaker same gender
Test3	within the vocabulary	Same Speaker
Test4	within the vocabulary	DIff. Speaker same gender
Test5	OOV	Diff. gender
Test6	within the vocabulary	Diff. gender

Table 2: Test Data Set

The system was provided a data set with a total of 564 instances out of which 70% of the data was taken for training and rest 30% for testing.

By comparing overall performance of both HMM and ANN, it was found that ANN outperformed HMM in almost all the test cases except for that of a different gender utterances. It was also found that the speech recognition system based on ANN performs better while adding more features other than the conventional MFCC features.

Given, are the results of recognition by both HMM and ANN, while using only MFCC features for training and testing.

Here, ANN has shown a better recognition accuracy in especially different speaker utterances and out of vocabulary utterances. But the performance of both HMM and ANN were not satisfactory in the case of different gender utterances, even though HMM showed slightly improved result.

Exp	HMM	ANN
Test1	87.5%	89.8%
Test2	62%	75%
Test3	91.67%	95.83%
Test4	93%	85.7%
Test5	79.17%	62.5%
Test6	80%	64.2%

Table 3: Results comparison HMM & ANN

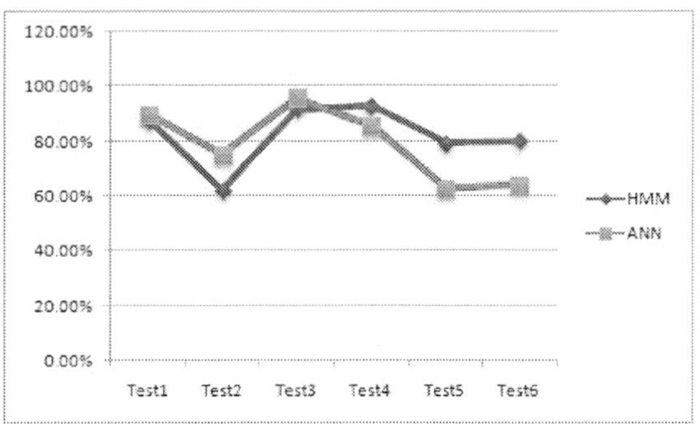

Figure 4: Results comparison HMM & ANN

In order to improve the performance rate, along

with the MFCC parameters, energy measure as well as zero crossing rate of the signal was also considered as attributes for ANN. This choice was proved correct by the recognition accuracy resulted. Given below, is the table and graph depicting the difference in performance by the system trained with ANN where the parameters selection alone is different. The total instances used for training and testing and also the test conditions were the same.

Exp	ANN (only mfcc)	ANN (mfcc,energy,zcr)
Test1	89.8.5%	95%
Test2	75%	81.25%
Test3	95.83%	99.2%
Test4	85.7%	96.4%
Test5	62.5%	62.5%
Test6	64.2%	65%

Table 4: ANN Results Comparison

Eventhough, addition of new parameters helped in improving recognition accuracy of Test 1 to Test 4, Test 5 and Test 6 didnt show any improvement. The system didnt successfully identify a different gender utterance.

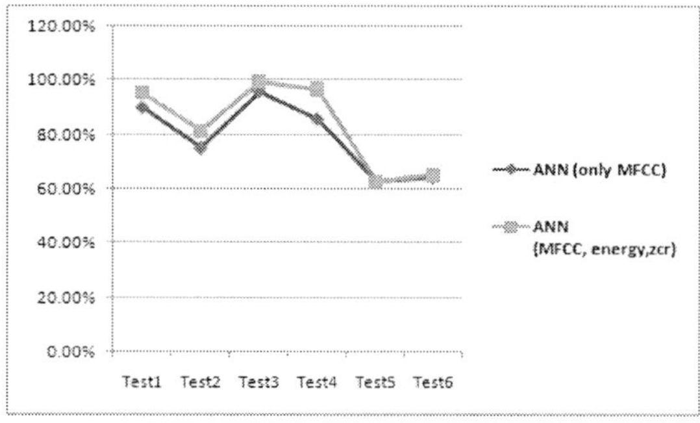

Figure 5: ANN Result Comparison

The diagram below depicts the overall performance comparison of the system performance.

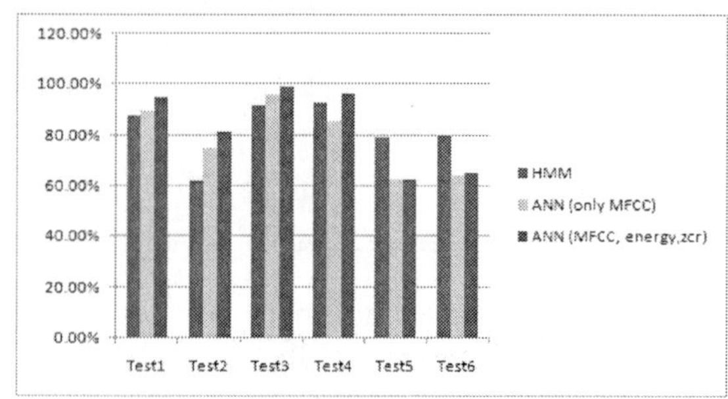

Figure 6: Overall Performance Comparison

5 Conclusion & Future Scope

This work addresses the problem of automatic speech recognition for isolated words in Malayalam language. A new algorithm was proposed with a feature set of formant frequencies, energy measure and zero crossing rate. An ANN based and HMM based models have been created and testing was performed words within the vocabulary and out of vocabulary. Based on performance evaluation, it is shown that Artificial Neural Network is well suited for speech recognition system of isolated words. However, the system performance is not satisfactory for gender specific.

5.1 Future Directions

In this research work, a speech recognition system with a moderate degree of accuracy is designed. The emphasis was on speech recognition for isolated words which finds applications in different areas where there is a man- machine interface. By considering the various factors, including noisy environment and gender specific, a deep leaning approach may be considered as future scope. The system shall also be extended for continuous speech recognition using syllable based approach. Attempts should be made to identify the features which will help the system identify utterances irrespective of the gender of the speaker.

References

. Ahmed, Irfan, Nasir Ahmad, Hazrat Ali, and Gulzar Ahmad. 2012. *The development of isolated words pashto automatic speech recognition system.*, In Automation and Computing (ICAC), 18th International Conference on IEEE, 1-4

. Al-Qatab Bassam AQ, and Raja N. Ainon. 1983. *Arabic speech recognition using hidden Markov model toolkit (HTK)..* In Information Technology (ITSim), International Symposium on IEEE, vol. 2, 557-562

. Kurian Cini, and Kannan Balakrishnan. 2012. *Continuous speech recognition system for Malayalam language using PLP cepstral coefficient.* Journal of Computing and Business Research, vol. 3.1

. Akila A and E. Chandra. 2013. *Isolated Tamil Word Speech Recognition System Using HTK.* International Journal of Computer Science , vol. 3.02, 30-38

. Akila A and E. Chandra. 2014. *Performance enhancement of syllable based Tamil speech recognition system using time normalization and rate of speech.* CSI Transactions on ICT , vol. 2.2, 77-84

. Khetri G. P., Padme S. L., Jain D. C., Fadewar H. S., Sontakke B. R., and Pawar V. P. 2012. *Automatic Speech Recognition for Marathi Isolated Words.* Application or Innovation in Engineering & Management (IJAIEM) , vol.1(3)

Resch Barbara 2003. *Automatic Speech Recognition with HTK.* Signal Processing and Speech Communication Laboratory. Inffeldgase. Austria , Disponible en Internet: http://www. igi. tugraz. at/lehre/CI .

Sheila D Apte 2012. *Speech and audio processing.* Wiley publication , Feb 2012

Sunny Sonia, S. David Peter, and K. Poulose Jacob 2013. *Performance of Different Classifiers in Speech Recognition.* International Journal of Research in Engineering and Technology , vol 2

Kurian Cini and Kannan Balakrishnan 2011. *Malayalam Isolated Digit Recognition using HMM and PLP cepstral coefficient.* International Journal of Advanced Information Technology (IJAIT) , vol 1.5

Kurian Cini and Kannan Balakrishnan 2011. *Malayalam Isolated Digit Recognition using HMM and PLP cepstral coefficient.* International Journal of Advanced Information Technology (IJAIT) , vol 1.5

Pammi S. C., and V. Keri 2005. *A package for automatic segmentation..*

Zegers Pablo 1998. *Speech recognition using neural networks.* Diss. University of Arizona

Gaikwad, Santosh K. Bharti W. Gawali and Pravin Yannawar 2010. *A review on speech recognition technique.* International Journal of Computer Applications , vol 10.3

Sunny Sonia, D. Peter, and K. Jacob 2013. *Combined Feature Extraction Techniques And Naive Bayes Classiffier For Speech Recognition.* CS & IT-CSCP

Jurafsky D. and Martin J 2000. *Speech and Language Processing: An Introduction to Natural Language Processing.* Computational Linguistics and Speech Recognition. Delhi, India , Pearson Education

Nnamdi Okomba S., Adegboye Mutiu Adesina, and Candidus O. Okwor. 2015. *Survey of Technical Progress in Speech Recognition by Machine over Few Years of Research.* IOSR Journal of Electronics and Communication Engineering   Vol 10, Issue 4, Ver. I (Jul - Aug .2015), PP 61-67

Judge a Book by its Cover: Conservative Focused Crawling under Resource Constraints

Shehzaad Dhuliawala   Arjun Atreya V
Ravi Kumar Yadav Pushpak Bhattacharyya
Center for Indian Language Technology, CSE Department
IIT Bombay, Mumbai, India,
{shehzaadzd, arjun, ravi, pb}@cse.iitb.ac.in

Abstract

In this paper, we propose a domain specific crawler that decides the domain relevance of a URL without downloading the page. In contrast, a focused crawler relies on the content of the page to make the same decision. To achieve this, we use a classifier model which harnesses features such as the page's URL and its parents' information to score a page. The classifier model is incrementally trained at each depth in order to learn the facets of the domain. Our approach modifies the focused crawler by circumventing the need for extra resource usage in terms of bandwidth. We test the performance of our approach on *Wikipedia* data. Our Conservative Focused Crawler (CFC) shows a performance equivalent to that of a focused crawler (skyline system) with an average resource usage reduction of $\approx 30\%$ across two domains *viz.*, *tourism* and *sports*.

1   Introduction

Crawling is a process of fetching documents iteratively from the web. While generic web search engines need to crawl and index a huge number of documents, there exist other search systems like enterprise search, domain search, patent search *etc.*, that concentrate on a particular section of the web. The crawling infrastructure required to process the entire web is huge and most small scale and academic organizations cannot afford them. Even though open source crawling frameworks help in crawling the web, resource constraints limit the number of documents being crawled. Most generic web crawlers employ a breadth-first approach for fetching documents from the web. A set of seed URLs which are manually fed to the crawler are processed in the first

depth and then the outlinks are processed for subsequent depths. This process continues for multiple depths to crawl more documents. Every document crawled needs to be processed before retrieval. Processing a document involves the following sequence of steps:

Fetching The process of downloading the document from the web. This is a bandwidth consuming task.

Parsing The process of extracting clean content from a web document. Parsing would also involve extracting outlinks, language, domain information and other meta information from the document. This is a CPU intensive task.

Indexing The process of storing the document in a searchable format. This is a memory intensive task.

In the context of crawling under resource constraints, it is important to carefully choose the appropriate outlinks to be crawled at each depth. Choosing the outlinks before actually fetching them involves taking a decision based on the outlink and its parents' characteristics (which are already fetched in the previous depths).

The organization of the paper is follows; in Section 2, we talk about related work. Section 3 describes the problem statement. Our approach is discussed in Section 4 while Section 5 details the experimental setup, 6 describes our skyline system. The analysis of the results obtained are discussed section 7. We conclude our work in section 8.

2   Related Work

(Chakrabarti et al., 1999) is the first work which talks about crawling a topic specific set of webpages. Classifying a document based on the URL and its content is discussed in (Kan, 2004). For the problem of classifying a document based on

D S Sharma, R Sangal and E Sherly. Proc. of the 12th Intl. Conference on Natural Language Processing, pages 166–171,
Trivandrum, India. December 2015. ©2015 NLP Association of India (NLPAI)

URL only, some of the features mentioned in this work is found to be useful. The closest work to our approach is by Aggarwal et al. (2001), which provides an idea about categorizing the domain of a URL while crawling but uses a simple weighted addition for scoring. This paper does not address the adaptability of the weights across domains.

Kan and Thi (2005) added URL features, component length, content, orthography, token sequence and precedence to model URL. The resulting features, used in supervised maximum entropy modeling, significantly improve over existing URL features. Baykan et al. (2009) showed that machine learning approach outperforms dictionary based approach for URL classification with n-grams as features.

Jamali et al. (2006) discusses use of link structure of web and content for focused crawler. They use a classifier to compute similarity of given web page to the topic. Qi and Davison (2009) describes multiple content based features that can be used for page classification in focused crawling. Priyatam et al. (2013) worked with URL based approach and tokenized them using n-grams to achieve high precision for Indian languages. The other works that use URL tokens as features for document classification are Shih and Karger (2004), Hernandez et al. (2012) and Anastacio et al. (2009).

3 Problem Statement

In this work, we address the problem of excess resource usage while classifying the document as in-domain or out-domain during crawling.

The formal problem statement is as follows:

Rank the URLs to be crawled in a given depth based on the URL and its parents' information gathered over previous depths.

4 Our Approach

We propose a light-weight focused crawler which selectively discards the out-domain URLs without fetching them. This is done by scoring and prioritizing the URLs to be crawled in each iteration. Our approach gives a set of in-domain URLs to be fetched at a given depth. As several links get rejected before the fetching stage, the cost of fetching them is averted.

Figure 1 describes the architecture of our proposed crawler. In a generic crawling pipeline, we integrate a classification module that assigns

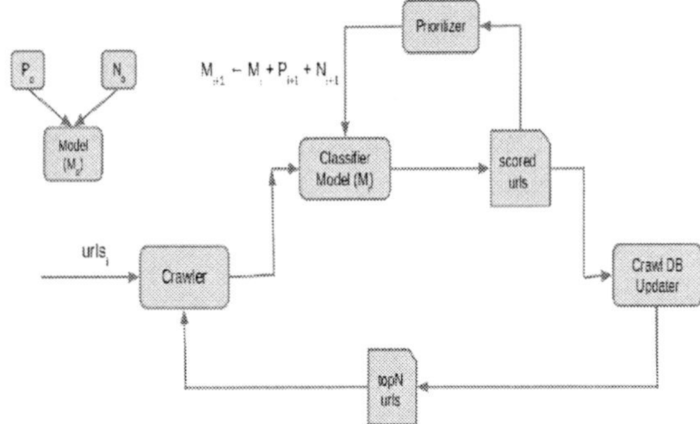

Figure 1: The system architecture

a confidence score to each outlink. The classification module uses the outlink's URL along with some features of the outlink's parents to decide the domain of the outlink. We prioritize the URLs based on these scores that would be fetched in the subsequent depths. The initial classification module is trained on a small set of outlinks. At every depth, the model is incrementally trained using the in-domain and out-domain outlinks encountered in that depth. As shown in figure 1, the initial model, M_0 is trained using a small set of initial *positive* and *negative* outlinks, P_0 and N_0. In depth $i + 1$, the model of the initial depth M_i is incrementally trained using $P_i + 1$ and $N_i + 1$.

4.1 Scoring

The process of assessing the confidence of an outlink pointing to an in-domain page involves the creation of a feature vector for every outlink. This feature vector is then fed to a binary classifier which then assigns a class(in-domain or out-domain) to the outlink along with a confidence score.

The scoring model incorporates four sets of tokens. These sets are called token pools. Two pools collate tokens of URLs and anchor texts linking to all the in-domain pages crawled till the current depth, while the other two pools comprise of tokens of URLs and anchor texts relating to out-domain pages. The pools also hold a weight for each token based on its frequency of occurrence.

In order to score every outlink the following features are used:

- The weighted overlap between the tokens in the outlink's URL with the *positive URL token pool*

- The weighted overlap between the tokens in

the outlink's anchor text with the *positive anchor text token pool*

- The weighted overlap between the tokens in the outlink's URL with the *negative URL token pool*

- The weighted overlap between the tokens in the outlink's anchor text with the *negative anchor text token pool*

- The weighted overlap between the tokens in the outlink's parents' URL with the *positive URL token pool*

- The weighted overlap between the tokens in the outlink's parents' URL with the *negative URL token pool*

- The average score of the outlink's parents

- The total number of in-domain parents

We use the concept of weighted overlap with pools over a *bag-of-words* approach is because the list of tokens relating to a domain is not exhaustive. These pools are updated at each depth with newer tokens discovered. A weighted overlap is chosen to accommodate for non-domain specific words. Tokens with no domain information would be present in equal amounts in both the negative and positive pools. Words which provide information about the domain and indicate that the outlink is in-domain would have a higher weight in the positive token pool.

4.2 Facets of a domain

A domain cannot be only categorized using a small exhaustive list of words. A domain often has several facets. Hence, trying to train a complete classifier for domain identification is often a huge task. For example, the domain *sports* may have sub-domains such as:

- Football

- Cricket

- Hockey

Quite obviously, the terms associated with the three above sub-domains of the domain of *sports* will not be the same. A classifier model which is trained using the terms of *Football* may be unable to recognize the terms of another sub-domain like *Cricket*. To overcome this we use an online classification model. The classification model is incrementally trained at every depth as newer outlinks are discovered. The online training is described in section 4.3.

4.3 Online Learning

Over multiple iterations the performance of the classifier may decrease as new tokens are encountered; online learning, in such a scenario, seems like a viable option (Priyatam et al., 2013). The incremental training aspect of the model manifests two major benefits. First, it allows for the initial set of training data to be relatively small (Zheng et al., 2013). Secondly, it prevents the accuracy from dipping over depths as new tokens are encountered.

Over the iterations, the size of the pools grow. The classifier uses the new training data to incrementally learn. There can be multiple combinations to create this training set. We selectively train our classifier with only a small fraction of the pages.

The risk of an incremental classifier, however, comes in the form of topic drift. A small amount of corruption in the training pool, can cause the classifier to accept several out-domain examples for training and hence decreasing the accuracy. As the model is further trained, it begins to assert its belief.

5 Experimental Setup

We customize the open source crawler, *Nutch 1.7* for our experimental setup.

We replace the scoring mechanism by our model. For the classifier we use an online Naive Bayes classifier. Given that we begin our crawl with a very small set of initial training data, we employ a Naive Bayes classifier.

5.1 Generating initial pools and training data

CFC requires a very small data set to initially train itself. The crawler starts with a single seed URL (The content page of the category). This crawler initially runs until it crawls 400 in-domain and 400 out-domain pages. This information is used to populate the initial set of pools and create the initial training file.

5.2 Crawling

We use Apache-Nutch-1.7 as the basic crawl frame work. The single seed URL for each of the domains is listed in table 2. The crawlers (CFC and Skyline) are instructed to fetch 100 in-domain URLs in every depth and the crawl is run for a total of 20 depths.

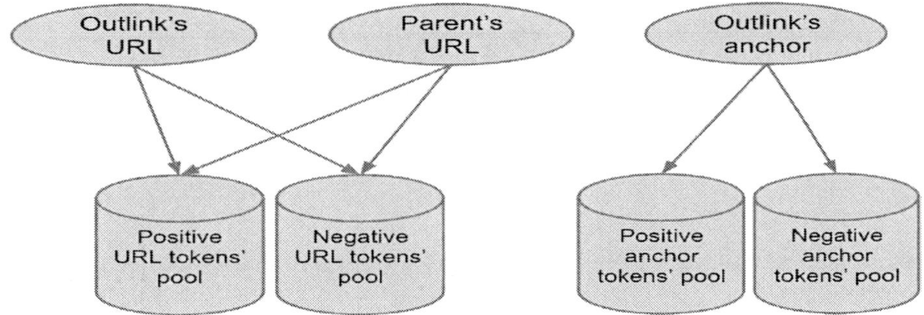

Figure 2: Scoring the token with the token pools

5.3 Data

We use English Wikipedia as our data set for experiments. Wikipedia was specifically chosen as pages are highly linked, so offering a highly connected web graph. Secondly, Wikipedia pages are category tagged. This allows for gold data to be effectively identified. In our experiments we aim to crawl over two topic domains: Indian Tourism and sports.

5.3.1 Preparing Gold Data

Each document in Wikipedia is associated with a set of categories. Each category represents a collection of documents belonging to a particular topic. A category may have one or more sub-categories resulting in a hierarchical structure.

For tourism we choose the category **Tourism in India**[1] and for sports we choose **Sports**[2]. Along with the chosen topic root categories, we choose the sub categories in their respective category trees.

The category lists obtained are further manually pruned to refine our gold category set.

6 Skyline

For a skyline, we use the idea behind a generic focused crawler. Here every page is downloaded before the crawler verifies its domain. The Skyline Crawler is built by inserting a domain identifier 6.1 into the pipeline of a generic crawler. The domain identifier downloads each page and asserts its domain. This is a bandwidth intensive process.

6.1 Domain Identifier

For the creation of our Skyline Crawler, we create a binary class, bag of words text classifier.

---

[1]https://en.wikipedia.org/wiki/Category:Tourism
[2]https://en.wikipedia.org/wiki/Category:Sports

Domain	Accuracy
Indian Tourism	95.4
Sports	94.8

Table 1: Domain Identifier accuracies

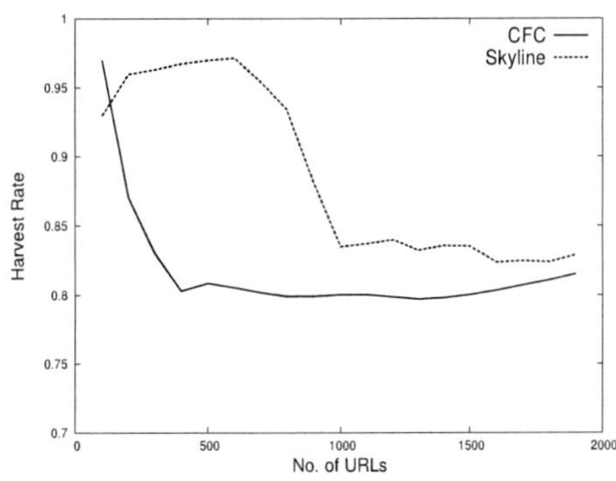

Figure 3: Harvest Rate: Indian Tourism

This classifier was trained over pre-crawled gold topic data. The classifier was trained using 1000 Wikipedia pages belonging to the required domain along with 1000 randomly selected general category documents. The classifier used was a C-SVC type SVM. The five-fold accuracies obtained by the classifiers for the domains of Indian Tourism and sports are described in table 1.

7 Results

7.1 Harvest-rate

This section discusses the performance of CFC when pitted against the Skyline crawler 6. We observe that CFC's performance is close to skyline accuracy.

The metric used to compare the crawlers performance is the *harvest-rate* obtained. (Li et al., 2008) defines *harvest rate* as:

Domain	Initial seed URL
Indian Tourism	https://en.wikipedia.org/wiki/Tourism_in_India
Sports	https://en.wikipedia.org/wiki/Sport

Table 2: Seed URLs

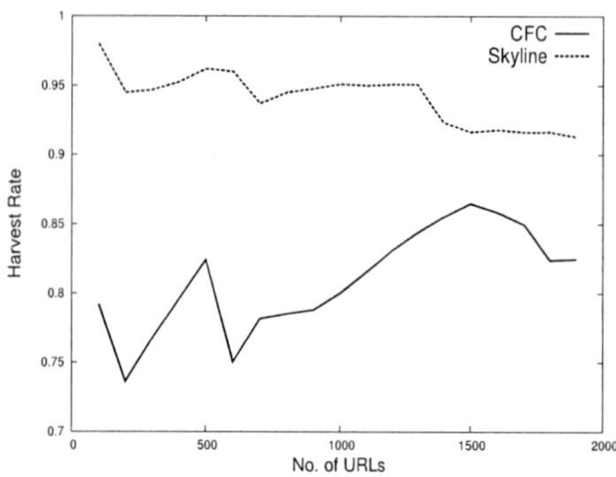

Figure 4: Harvest Rate: Sports

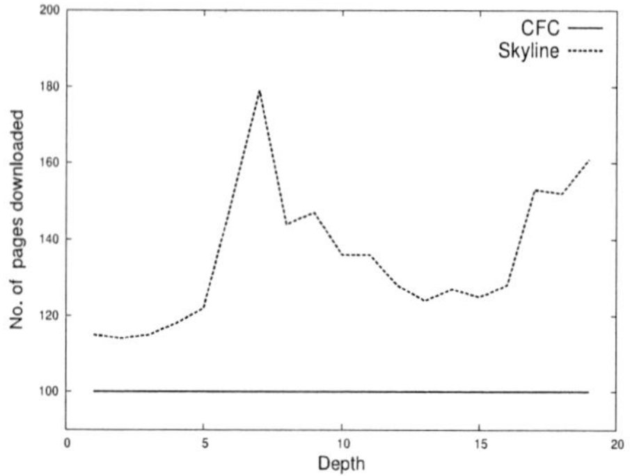

Figure 5: Resources: Indian Tourism

Crawler	Indian Tourism	Sports
CFC	0.82	0.82
Skyline	0.83	0.91

Table 3: harvest rate comparison

The harvest rate represents the fraction of web pages crawled that satisfy the crawling target R among the crawled pages P. If the harvest ratio is high, it means the focused crawler can crawl the relevant web pages effectively; otherwise, it means the focused crawler spends a lot of time eliminating irrelevant pages, and it may be better to use another crawler instead. Hence, a high harvest rate is a sign of a good crawling run."

The harvest rate for both *Indian tourism* and *sports* domain is depicted in figures 3 and 4. In figure 3, CFC starts with a very high harvest rate. However, this doesn't seem to be mirrored in figure 4. We feel this is just by chance as the harvest rate seems to soon stabilize. The graphs (figures 3 and 4) show that the Skyline outperforms CFC. However, as the number of URLs increase, the domain identifier is unable to maintain its high accuracy. A likely reason for this is that, over time, the domain identifier gets several pages of different facets of the domain which it hasn't been trained on. CFC, however, doesn't suffer from this dip as the online classifier model is constantly updated with new terms and tokens. Towards the end of the graphs, we notice that CFC and Skyline reach very close.

7.2 Resources

In this section we aim to compare CFC with the Skyline crawlers based on the amounts of resources required. Bandwidth (for fetching) is a major resource involved in crawling. All other resources like processing power (for parsing), memory (for indexing) depends on the number of pages fetched. Hence, we evaluate our crawling performance in terms of bandwidth usage.

The Skyline crawler requires an additional amount of internet bandwidth owing to the fact that it needs to download a page to determine the domain of the page. While CFC scores an outlink before the page is downloaded, only a fixed number of pages are downloaded at every depth. Downloading of extra pages increases the usage of bandwidth and also increases the time required for crawling.

Figures 5 and 6 show that the number of pages which need to judge the domain is much higher. The figures don't indicate any specific trend, however we notice that the average number of pages needed to be downloaded for **sports** is relatively higher than that for tourism. The maximum pages which needed to be downloaded in any depth is around 180 for each of the domains.

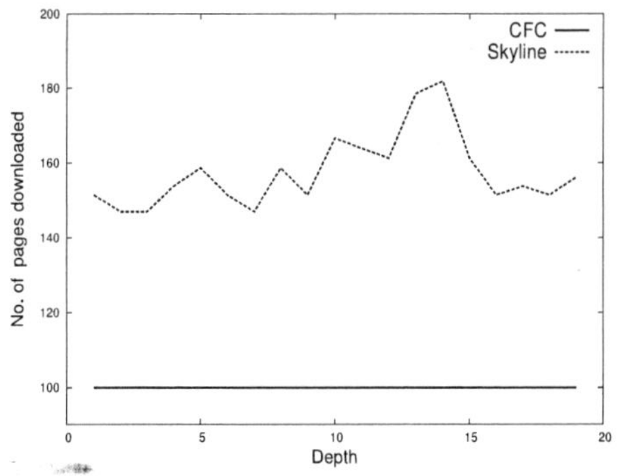

Figure 6: Resources: Sports

Crawler	Indian Tourism	Sports
CFC	137.4	157.5
Skyline	100	100

Table 4: Average pages downloaded

The metric indicating *number of pages downloaded* does not do complete justice when trying to judge the crawler on its resource usage. Several offline factors also do come into play. The Skyline crawler needs to train an SVM classifier on a huge number of documents. This clearly uses more computing power than training a Naive Bayes classifier on a few set of numeric features. The Skyline crawler also needs the huge set of in-domain documents which it can be trained upon.

8 Conclusion

In this paper, we developed a preemptive crawler that selectively picks a set of in-domain URLs to be crawled in each depth. Using the outlink's URL and its parent's information to determine a page's domain, yields results comparable to that of a fully fledged focused crawler. Our experimental results on *tourism* and *sports* domains validate reduced bandwidth usage of $\approx 30\%$. As a future work, we aim to evaluate our system on the open web which has a more complex web-graph as compared to *Wikipedia*.

References

Charu C Aggarwal, Fatima Al-Garawi, and Philip S Yu. 2001. Intelligent crawling on the world wide web with arbitrary predicates. In *Proceedings of the 10th international conference on World Wide Web*, pages 96–105. ACM.

Ivo Anastácio, Bruno Martins, and Pável Calado. 2009. Classifying documents according to locational relevance. In *Progress in Artificial Intelligence*, pages 598–609. Springer.

Eda Baykan, Monika Henzinger, Ludmila Marian, and Ingmar Weber. 2009. Purely url-based topic classification. In *Proceedings of the 18th international conference on World wide web*, pages 1109–1110. ACM.

Soumen Chakrabarti, Martin Van den Berg, and Byron Dom. 1999. Focused crawling: a new approach to topic-specific web resource discovery. *Computer Networks*, 31(11):1623–1640.

Inma Hernández, Carlos R Rivero, David Ruiz, and Rafael Corchuelo. 2012. A statistical approach to url-based web page clustering. In *Proceedings of the 21st international conference companion on World Wide Web*, pages 525–526. ACM.

Mohsen Jamali, Hassan Sayyadi, Babak Bagheri Hariri, and Hassan Abolhassani. 2006. A method for focused crawling using combination of link structure and content similarity. In *Proceedings of the 2006 IEEE/WIC/ACM International Conference on Web Intelligence*, pages 753–756. IEEE Computer Society.

Min-Yen Kan and Hoang Oanh Nguyen Thi. 2005. Fast webpage classification using url features. In *Proceedings of the 14th ACM international conference on Information and knowledge management*, pages 325–326. ACM.

Min-Yen Kan. 2004. Web page classification without the web page. In *Proceedings of the 13th international World Wide Web conference on Alternate track papers & posters*, pages 262–263. ACM.

Hang Li, Ting Liu, Wei-Ying Ma, Tetsuya Sakai, Kam-Fai Wong, and Guodong Zhou. 2008. *Information Retrieval Technology: 4th Asia Information Retrieval Symposium, AIRS 2008, Harbin, China, January 15-18, 2008, Revised Selected Papers*, volume 4993. Springer.

Pattisapu Nikhil Priyatam, Srinivasan Iyengar, Krish Perumal, and Vasudeva Varma. 2013. Dont use a lot when little will do: Genre identification using urls. *Research in Computing Science*, 70:207–218.

Xiaoguang Qi and Brian D Davison. 2009. Web page classification: Features and algorithms. *ACM Computing Surveys (CSUR)*, 41(2):12.

Lawrence Kai Shih and David R Karger. 2004. Using urls and table layout for web classification tasks. In *Proceedings of the 13th international conference on World Wide Web*, pages 193–202. ACM.

Jun Zheng, Furao Shen, Hongjun Fan, and Jinxi Zhao. 2013. An online incremental learning support vector machine for large-scale data. *Neural Computing and Applications*, 22(5):1023–1035.

Text Normalization and Unit Selection for a Memory Based Non Uniform Unit Selection TTS in Malayalam

Gokul P., Neethu Thomas, Crisil Thomas and Dr. Deepa P. Gopinath
College of Engineering Trivandrum
Trivandrum - 16
gokulpramesh@gmail.com, neetuthomas259@gmail.com
crisil971@gmail.com, deepapgopinath@gmail.com

Abstract

Text to speech synthesis system intended for any language, converts the given text in that language to corresponding speech. The major challenge in TTS system is to generate artificial speech which appears to be natural and intelligible. This is essential for visually impaired people to properly understand and comprehend the generated speech. This paper discuss about text normalization and unit selection for a memory based non-uniform unit selection concatenative speech synthesizer for Malayalam language.

1 Introduction

Text to speech synthesis systems(TTS) help users to interact with computer through speech. System with speech interaction is advantageous for physically challenged, especially visually impaired. Important challenge in speech synthesis is generating synthesized speech which is both intelligible and natural.

TTS systems synthesize speech by articulatory synthesis, formant synthesis or concatenative speech synthesis techniques, of which concatenative speech synthesis excels in performance. In concatenative speech synthesis, segments of speech waveform that are cut from recorded speech and stored in an inventory are concatenated to generate synthesized speech. Non-uniform unit selection involves selection of appropriate units of variable length for synthesizing speech. Non-uniform unit selection is the most popular technique in the current scenario. The selection of appropriate speech waveform for concatenation is the major concern within concatenative synthesis.

TTS systems attempts to synthesize speech which has the qualities of natural speech generated by humans. The best way to improve the quality of synthesized speech is to mimic the way humans generate speech. The process of mimicking human functionality requires a model of how humans store the language within their brain and how they retrieve appropriate units for speech production. A memory based model for Malayalam TTS can be developed based on Memory Prediction Framework, which is a theory of brain function.

This work attempts to implement the front end portions for a memory based Malayalam TTS. The TTS system deals with real world data, hence text preprocessing is an important challenge. The system attempts to mimic the functionality of human brain in generating speech. The system develops a memory model resembling memory organization of linguistic units within brain. The memory based model can be used in unit selection block for non-uniform unit selection concatenative speech synthesis.

Non-uniform unit selection concatenative speech synthesis is not reported for Malayalam language. The use of memory prediction framework for speech synthesis is a novel method in the realm of speech synthesis.

2 Text Normalization

A text to speech synthesis system requires handling of text input from various discourses. Preprocessing is required to convert non standard words of the language into units suitable for speech production. Numbers, abbreviations, acronyms, dates, phone numbers, etc. are examples of non standard words. Thus, one of the main components of a TTS system is the preprocessing part which does text normalization that transforms

D S Sharma, R Sangal and E Sherly. Proc. of the 12th Intl. Conference on Natural Language Processing, pages 172–177,
Trivandrum, India. December 2015. ©2015 NLP Association of India (NLPAI)

non standard text elements into their expanded form. This requires both linguistic and technical knowledge.

First step in text normalization module is input text tokenization, here the input text is converted into tokens based on the space between words. These tokens are then identified as standard or non standard words (NSW). An inventory of the non standard words must be stored to identify NSW in the given text. NSW includes acronyms, abbreviations, numbers, dates, currency, measurement units, etc. Examples are *12/5/15, Dr. prakash, 12.5 c. m.,* etc. These identified NSW are expanded to standard form. Period at the sentence boundary is identified.

The preprocessed text is used for selecting non uniform units from the database using memory based hierarchical model. The linguistic structure is unique for each language. Hence preprocessing module for Malayalam TTS need to be developed after analysing the linguistic features of language.

3   Memory based model

The memory model is based on Memory Prediction Framework (Hawkins and Blakeslee(2004)). Memory Prediction Framework is a theory of brain function. The organization of language possess a hierarchical tree structure with sentence at top node and syllable at lower node. Letters are combined to form syllables. Syllables are combined to form words. Words are combined with morphemes to form new word. Words and morphemes combine to form sentences or clauses.

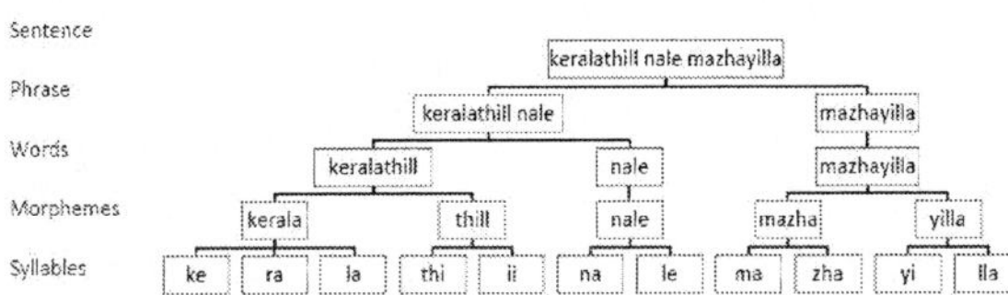

Figure 1: Hierarchical structure in language

Memory model exploits all properties of memory organization of language within brain. The model attempts to build a hierarchical text database that contains tokens of linguistic units at various levels from sentence to syllables. The unit selection algorithm selects the appropriate unit for concatenation from memory model for concatenative speech synthesis. The development of memory model requires a thorough study of morpho-logical and syllable structure of Malayalam language.

4   Morphological and Syllable structure of Malayalam

Morphological variations for words occur in Malayalam due to Inflections, Derivations and Word compounding(Shanavas(2015)).

As a general rule, the syllable structure in Malayalam can be schematized as (C)(C)(C)V(V)(C), where parenthesis indicates optionality(Mohanan(1989)). C stands for consonants and V for vowel. The basic syllable structure in Malyalam consist of a vowel and consonant. The syllabification rules are(Asher(1997))

- All intervocalic single and geminate consonants are assigned to following syllable

- Sequences of two homorganic oral plosives in which first unaspirated and second aspirated are treated in the same way as geminate consonant

- In other sequences of two consonants where both belong to P class(stops, oral, nasal), the two segments are assigned to different syllables.

- Where L(liquids or glides) as first segment followed by P or F(Fricatives), it is assigned to preceding syllable.

- Two-consonant clusters of the type PL,FL,LL are all assigned to following syllable with one exception, where in L_1L_2, L_1 is $/y/, /y/$ goes to preceding syllable.

In phonology, an allophone is one of a set of multiple possible spoken sounds used to pronounce a single phoneme. The allophonic variations has its impact mostly on syllables. If these variations are not considered, the synthesized speech will sound differently from original speech. A set of rules is to developed to account for this variability in Malayalam language.

5   Non- Uniform Unit Selection

Concatenative speech synthesis involves selecting optimal units from database and concatenation of these units to synthesize speech. Non-uniform unit selection involves selecting units which vary in length. The most appropriate units have to selected from the inventory to improve the quality of synthesized speech. The non-uniform unit selection algorithm formulated in this paper exploits the properties of brain in generating speech.

The unit selection algorithm maintains a top-down approach within the memory model. As we move down the hierarchy, sentences get unfolded into memory of sequences of phrases. In the next layer down, each phrase is unfolded into a memory sequence of words and so on. The best optimal unit will be selected while moving through the hierarchy. The algorithm is prioritized to select the longest unit if present in memory. In case of unavailability of longer units, the algorithm moves down the hierarchy to obtain shorter units.

6 Zipf's Law

The distribution of words in a corpus of any natural language is non uniform. The rank of a word (in terms of its frequency) in a given corpus of natural language utterances is approximately inversely proportional to its actual frequency, and so produces a hyperbolic distribution according to Zipf's law(K.(1949)). If the words of a sample text are ordered by decreasing frequency, the frequency of the kth word P(k), is given by

$$P(k) \propto k^{-\alpha} \qquad 1 < \alpha < 2 \qquad (1)$$

The memory based model replicates the memory organization within brain. Human brain memorizes only frequently repeating linguistic units. Such a system with limited size and efficiency is possible only if Malayalam language has certain units that would repeat more frequently compared with others. This assumption is evaluated using Zipf's law.

7 Methodology

7.1 Text Normalization

Non-standard words are identified and are then categorized into NSW with letters, numbers or combination of both. The NSW are converted to their standard form in the text normalization module.

In Malayalam language, conversion of number to text is not straight forward. For example in English the number "12,500" can be expanded to "twelve thousand and five hundred" by using a simple algorithm, because words like twelve, thousand, five, hundred, etc, are repeated in the text representation of numerals. But in Malayalam this does not occur, the same number is expanded in malayalam as "pantiiraayiratti anjnjuuR+". Thus here for Malayalam TTS complex algorithm is required for number conversion.

NSW with numbers is further classified into various subcategories which includes phone number, cardinal number, date and time. This is because a number "123" is pronounced as "nuuRRi irupatti muunn+", where as a phone number "9961..." is pronounced as "onpatu onpatu aaR+ onn+...". Due to this difference in the output text their classification is necessary, to generate the required output.

Finally acronyms and abbreviations are expanded and period at sentence boundary is identified eliminating all other periods denoting acronyms, abbreviations or ellipsis.

7.2 Identification of Linguistic Constructs for Building Memory model

The frequently repeating sentences, phrases, words, morphemes and syllables has to be identified for development of memory model. Sentences and words in each domain is identified by frequency analysis of text data in that domain. Phrases are obtained by ngram modelling of words.

N-grams are contiguous sequence of n items. The ngram modelling gives an idea of collocations which can be modelled for prediction of next word.

eg: nale mazha peyyum ennu thonnunnu

bigrams:(nale mazha), (mazha peyyum), (peyyum ennu), (ennu thonnunnu)

trigrams: (nale mazha peyyum),(mazha peyyum ennu),(peyyum ennu thonnunnu)

The morphemes are obtained after analysing the morphological structure of Malayalam language. The words containing morphemes are splitted into root word and morpheme. Both root word and morpheme are stored within memory model. In order to generate a new word we could combine root and morpheme from another word, if both are available in memory model. This would avoid the necessity syllable concatenation even if the required word is not present in memory.

The syllables are identified using automatic syllabification algorithm developed based rules for syllable formation in Malayalam(Asher(1997)). During syllabification the allophonic variations are also taken into account.

8 Results and Discussions

8.1 Text Normalization

Acronym expansion, abbreviation identification etc, was tested on the text corpus (including articles, newspapers) consisting of 90,000 sentences. Number to text conversion algorithm for Malayalam was successfully implemented.

A complex algorithm is implemented for number conversions considering the exceptions in case of Malayalam language. Initially, the algorithm classifies, the digits in the number based on their places in the string and separate conversion algorithm is adopted for digit at each place. For first and second place, the conversion is straight forward, even if the number of digit increases (eg : 12 is pronounced as "pantranTu" in 312 and in 1012), but complexity increases for numbers with higher places. Hence, rules are formulated for higher places considering exceptions, for example, if digit 1 is present at the third place in a four digit number it is pronounced as "orunnuuRRi" (eg : "aayiratti orunnuuRRi onn+" for 1101) and as "nuuRRi" (eg : "nuuRRi onn+" for 101) when at same place in a three digit number. And for numbers having fifth place the dictionary consisting of exceptions (such as "patinayyaayiram" for 15000) is used.

Acronym expansion and abbreviation identification was done by storing commonly occurring acronym. Period defining sentence boundary was identified after removing period defining acronym, abbreviation and ellipsis.

8.2 Verification of Possibility of memory model

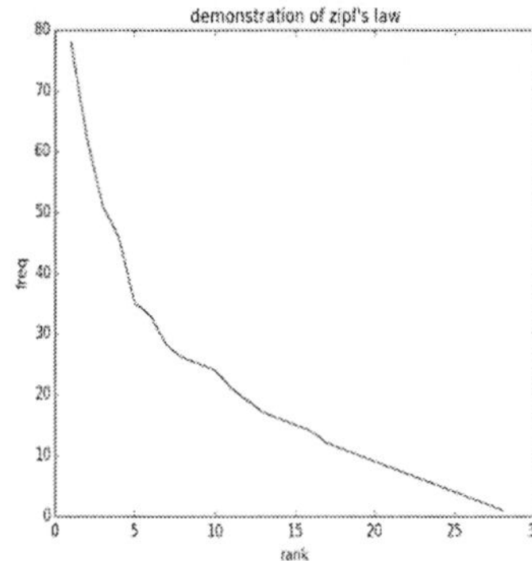

Figure 2: Zipf's law for Malayalam

The evaluation of Zipf's law is done over text database obtained from various online sites. Zipf's law is evaluated independently for each domain(news, literature, education, travel etc..) and for each writer. The hyperbolic graph obtained is found to follow the Zipf's law.

It is also observed that, not only words but phrases and whole sentences also follow Zipf's law. The significance of Zipf's law is that, a major portion of any speech corpus can be represented by the most frequently occurring constructs. Hence a memory model can be developed by storing frequently occurring constructs.

8.3 Development of Memory model

The memory model is developed by analysing 1000 Malayalam sentences taken from a collection of speech data prepared by IIIT-Hyderabad for various Indian languages(Kishore Prahallad(2012)). The development of memory model involved identification of frequently occurring constructs like sentences, phrases, words, morphemes, syllables. The memory model is a 8 layer structure with longer units at top. The model consisted of 10 sentences, 18 trigrams, 70 bigrams, 156 words, 78 morphemes and 670 syllables. The unit selection algorithm best suitable longest available unit for concatenation to synthesize speech.

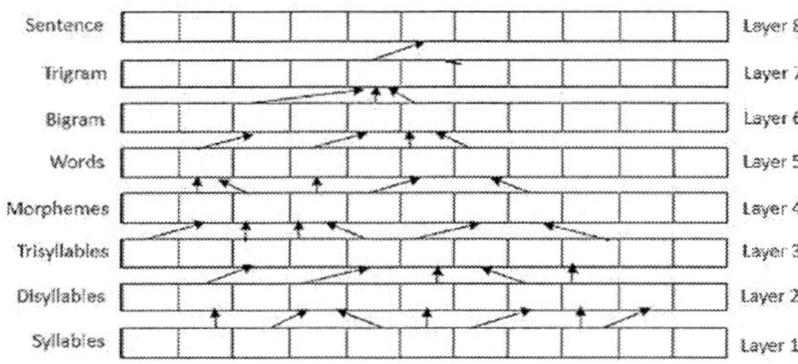

Figure 3: Memory model for Malayalam

9 Letter to sound rules

The rules to account for allophonic variation in Malayalam are[1]:

1. Allophonic variations for vowels

   (a) Case /u/

      If not word initial or word final and if preceding vowel (vowel in the preceding phoneme) is not /u/ then replace /u/

[1]The letter to sound rules were framed in a two day workshop of linguists, language experts, computational linguists and speech processing experts organized by SCERT (State Council for Education Research and Training), at Calicut University as a part of the programme to develop speech enabled systems for visually impaired.

with raised and retracted form of schwa eg:uTuppu

   (b) Case /a/

     If not in word final syllable and if succeeding consonant is palatal or alveolar or if preceding consonant is voiced stop or /ya/, /ra/, /Ra/, /la/ then replace /a/ with a special form of /a/ which is more similar to /e/ eg:balam

   (c) Case /i/

     If not word initial or word final then replace /e/ with raised and fronted form of shwa.

2. Palatalization of geminate velar plosives

If preceding phoneme is /i/, /e/ or /ya/ then replace /kka/ with its palatalized version(/k'k'/) eg:adik'k'uka

3. Case alveolar /n/

If not word initial and if preceding consonant or succeeding consonant is dental then replace with dental n eg:sandhi

Exceptions : perunnal, varumnal, malanad, somanadhan, karinizhal,vananira

4. Voicing of intervocalic plosives

If preceding phoneme is nasal sonorant then replace /ka, ca, ta, pa/ with a special form of /ga, ja, da, ba/ replace /Ta/ with /Da/

else if preceding phoneme is nonnasal sonorant and if succeeding phoneme is a vowel then replace /ka, cha, ta, pa/ with a special form of /ga, ja, da, ba/ replace /da/ with /Da/ eg: makan, apakadam

5. Consonant cluster with /h/

When in a consonant cluster with a nasal, /h/ is not pronounced, instead the consonant is geminated.

If succeeding phoneme or succeeding phoneme is nasal then replace /h/ with that nasal eg:brahmam, chihnam

6. Case /w/

   (a) If preceding phoneme is a consonant then replace /w/ with a special form, which is labiodental eg:varam

   (b) If preceding phoneme is anuswaram then replace /w/ with a special form of /w/ eg:swayamvaram

7. If preceding phoneme is a consonant and is succeeded by /a/ then replace /ya/ with a special form of /e/. eg:vyasanam

8. If not word initial or word final and if succeeding phoneme is not /m/ then replace /t/ with /l/ else if succeeding phoneme is /m/ then replace /t/ with $/l^p m/$ or $/t^m p/$ eg:athmavu

9. Post nasal stops converted to nasals

If not word initial or word final if succeeding phoneme is a consonant then replace it with corresponding nasal sound

10. If preceding phoneme is a consonant and is succeeded by /a/ then replace /ya/ with a special form of /e/ eg: nanni

11. If not word initial or word final and if succeeding phoneme is /k/ vargam then replace it with corresponding nasal eg:bhangi, sangeetham

12. For /n/ if preceding phoneme is /p/ then replace /p/ with a special form $/p^t/$ eg:swapnam

13. If preceding phoneme is /g/ then replace /p/ with a special form $/g^b/$. eg:yugmam

9.1 Evaluation

Front end developed consisting of text normalization and unit selection block was incorporated with waveform generation module and listening test was conducted. Listening tests involve preparing several samples of synthesized output from TTS system, randomizing the system sentence combinations and asking listeners to score each output audio. For DMOS evaluation based on semantically unpredictable sentences (SUS), 5 sentences were chosen and the evaluation was done with 6 subjects(Viswanathan and Viswanathan(2005)). The DMOS obtained must be unbiased. To ensure this the same listeners were not asked to participate in different tests. For DMOS we play randomly the natural sentences and synthesized sentences. An original file (sentence x) was played followed by a synthesised sentence (sentence y). All these sentences had different text. Headphones of reasonable quality was used for evaluation. Further, each listener was made to listen to a different set of sentences. The average DMOS score obtained is 3.7.

Sentence	DMOS
111000	3
naale skool avadiyaan+	3.5
aayiraM kollaM pazhakamulla nadiyaan+	4
keiralatile oru jillayaan+ tiruvanantapuraM	4
keiralappiravi navambeR 1	4

Table 1: Evaluation Results

10   Conclusion

Text to speech synthesis system finds its application for visually impaired people. Naturalness and intelligibility of the synthesized speech are necessary for a text to speech synthesis system.

The text processing module was developed for identifying the non standard words in Malayalam and to generate normalized text. Units selection for concatenation was performed using these normalized text.

To make the synthesized speech to appear similar to natural speech, we developed a model that mimics human brain in generating speech. Human brain maintains a hierarchical memory organization of language containing linguistic units. Brain uses non-uniform units stored within memory to generate speech. The memory based model also employs non-uniform unit selection algorithm.

The memory based model is developed by obtaining frequently occurring linguistic units in Malayalam Language. The evaluation of Zipf's law for Malayalam provided base for assumption that a few frequently repeating constructs could represent an entire language.

The model was incorporated to the unit selection block of non-uniform unit selection speech synthesizer. The average mean opinion score of 3.7 shows that the synthesized speech appears to be natural and intelligible. The memory model could be fine tuned by incremental learning by using a large text database.

References

Alfred V. Aho and Jeffrey D. Ullman. 1972. *The Theory of Parsing, Translation and Compiling*, volume 1. Prentice-Hall, Englewood Cliffs, NJ.

American Psychological Association. 1983. *Publications Manual*. American Psychological Association, Washington, DC.

Association for Computing Machinery. 1983. *Computing Reviews*, 24(11):503–512.

Ashok K. Chandra, Dexter C. Kozen, and Larry J. Stockmeyer. 1981. Alternation. *Journal of the Association for Computing Machinery*, 28(1):114–133.

Dan Gusfield. 1997. *Algorithms on Strings, Trees and Sequences*. Cambridge University Press, Cambridge, UK.

R Asher. Malayalam, 1997. Routledge.

Ramon Ferrer Cancho and Ricard V. Sole. Least effort and the origins of scaling in human language. *Proc. National Academy of Sciences of the United States of America*, 100:788–791, 2003.

Jeff Hawkins and Sandra Blakeslee. On intelligence, 2004. Times Books.

Haowen Jiang. Malayalam: a grammatical sketch and a text. *Department of Linguistics, Rice University*, 2010.

R D Johnston. Beyond intelligibility: the performance of text-to-speech synthesizers. *BT Technological Journal*, 1(2):100–111, 1996.

Zipf G. K. *Human Behavior and the Principle of Least Effort*. Cambridge, Massachusetts: Addison-Wesley, 1949.

Simon King. Degradation mos and word error rate for text to speech synthesis systems. *Private Communication*.

E.Naresh Kumar Kishore Prahallad. The iiit-h indic speech databases. *INTERSPEECH*, 2012.

Tara Mohanan. Syllable structure in malayalam. *Linguistic enquiry*, 20(4):589–625, 1989.

SK Saranya. Morphological analyzer for malayalam verbs. *Unpublished M. Tech Thesis, Amrita School of Engineering, Coimbatore*, 2008.

SA Shanavas. Structure of a computational laxicon of malayalam. 2015.

Catriona Tullo and James R Hurford. Modelling zipfian distributions in language,. *in Proc. of Language Evolution and Computation Work- shop at ESSLLI*, pages 62–75, 2003.

Mahesh Viswanathan and Madhubalan Viswanathan. Measuring speech quality for text-to-speech systems: development and assessment of a modified mean opinion score (mos)scale. *Computer Speech and Language*, 19(1):55–83, 2005.

Morphological Analyzer for Gujarati using Paradigm based approach with Knowledge based and Statistical Methods

Jatayu Baxi
Computer Engineering
Department
Dharmsinh Desai
University
Nadiad
jatayubaxi.ce@ddu.ac
.in

Pooja Patel
Computer Engineering
Department
Dharmsinh Desai
University
Nadiad
poopa-
tel2912@gmail.com

Brijesh Bhatt
Computer Engineering
Department
Dharmsinh Desai
University
Nadiad
brij.ce@ddu.ac.
in

Abstract

Morphological Analyzer is a tool which performs syntactic analysis of a word and finds root form of input inflected word form. Morph analyzer serves as a pre-processing tool for many NLP applications. Significant amount of work has been done in this area for many Indian languages but not much work has been reported for Gujarati language. We present Morph analyzer for Gujarati language. The Morph analyzer is developed using a hybrid approach that combines statistical, knowledge based and paradigm based approach. We present detailed study of different approaches. We demonstrate a significant improvement in overall accuracy and achieve 92.34% and 82.84% accuracy with knowledge based hybrid method and statistical hybrid method respectively.

1 Introduction to Morph Analyzer

Morphology is a branch of linguistics that carries out study of words, their internal structure and their meanings. A morpheme is the smallest grammatical unit in a language.

Developing an accurate Morph analyzer is a challenging task, particularly for highly inflectional and agglutinative language. In order to develop Morph analyzer for Gujarati, we studied inflections of Gujarati language and identified various grammatical paradigms. We have identified 8 paradigms for Noun , 3 paradigms for verb and 3 paradigms for Adjectives. Paradigm based approach suffers when a word falls into more than one paradigm because of common inflections. We reduce this problem by consulting knowledge base 'wordnet' and by performing corpus based statistical analysis of a word.

The rest of the paper is organized as follows: Section 2 discusses survey and comparison of existing approaches. Section 3 describes paradigm construction process and various paradigms. Section 4 discusses hybrid method used to build Morph analyzer for Gujarati and section 5 shows experiment and evaluation.

2 Related Work

Morphological analyzer has been a continuously evolving area of research. A lot of work has been done for English language. However it remains challenging task to develop Morph analyzer for highly agglutinative and inflectional languages

The first Morphological analyzer system is KIMMO(Karttunen, Lauri, 1983) which follows two level morphology approach. This approach is suitable for languages with less degree of inflection. For higher degree of inflection, the model does not perform well. Some unsupervised methods for developing Morph analyzer have also been tried. Hammarstorm and Borin,2003 presented survey based on various Unsupervised Learning Techniques for Morphological analyzer. The input to such algorithm is raw Natural Language text data. This approach requires large training corpus

D S Sharma, R Sangal and E Sherly. Proc. of the 12th Intl. Conference on Natural Language Processing, pages 178–182,
Trivandrum, India. December 2015. ©2015 NLP Association of India (NLPAI)

and hence in absence of sufficient corpus, the machine learning efficiency would be less. Niraj Aswani et al,2010 used unsupervised Method that takes both prefixes as well as suffixes into account. Given a corpus and a dictionary, this method can be used to obtain a set of suffix-replacement rules for deriving an inflected word's root form. This system is basically built for Hindi but some experiments are done on Gujarati language also. Akshar Bharti et al, 2001 presented an algorithm for unsupervised learning of morphological analysis and morphological generation for inflectionally rich languages. The method depends on variety of word forms present in the existing corpus.

Beesley, 2003 proposed concept of Finite state Morphology. and this approach was used to build Morphological analyzers for high inflectional languages, as language can be easily represented by Finite state machine. In this approach, XFST is used as an interface. It is an interface which gives access to finite state operations. The interface of XFST includes a lookup operation and generation operation. Hence this approach can be used for Generation and Analysis of Morphology.

Considerable amount of work has been done for the languages such as Hindi,Marathi,Tamil,Malayalam,Bangla also. Based on FST approach proposed by Bessley, (Akshar Bharti) proposed paradigm based approach for building Morphological analyzer. In this approach, the language expert provides different tables of word forms covering the words in the language. Set of roots covered by particular table have similar inflectional behaviour. This approach also requires dictionary with root of the word and the paradigm to which the root belongs. (Jyoti Pawar et al, 2012) discusses work in which the morphological analyzer for Konkani has been developed using FSA based approach with Word paradigm model. Unlike traditional method, they have sequenced morphemes. (Harshada Gune et al, 2010) developed paradigm based Finite state Morphological analyzer for Marathi.

(Rajendra Rajeev, 2011) developed Morphological analyzer using suffix stripping approach for Malayalam language. The finite state transducer is used to sequence the morphemes and to validate the ordering. In this system the Suffix stripping method with sandhi rules are used that does not require any lookup tables.

As far as work for Gujarati language is concerned (kashyap Popat et al, 2010) have developed lightweight stemmer for Gujarati language using hand crafted suffix rules. List of hand crafted Gujarati suffixes which contains the postpositions and the inflectional suffixes for nouns, adjectives and verbs are created for use in this approach.

(kartik Suba et al, 2011) developed Inflectional and derivational stemmer. The inflectional stemmer is built using hybrid approach and derivational stemmer is built using rule based approach. Four lists of suffixes which contain postpositions and inflectional suffixes respectively for nouns, verbs, adjectives and adverbs are created.

3 Paradigm Construction

Gujarati is morphologically rich language. Based on various grammatical features, single root may generate multiple word forms Words can be categorized into paradigms based on the similarity in grammatical features and word formation process. It is observed that for a particular grammatical feature there are some similarities in word formation process.

A Paradigm defines all word forms that can be generated from given stem along with grammatical feature set associated with each word form. For paradigm construction, sample corpus of inflected words is taken. A list is prepared for all possible suffixes from the sample data. The words which take similar set of suffixes are grouped into single paradigm. For example word સ્ત્રી(Stri) and છત્રી(chaatri) both take same inflection for plural transformation (સ્ત્રીઓ and છત્રીઓ) so we group them under single paradigm. For all the words belonging to same paradigm, the rule to form root word and set of possible suffixes to generate other word forms remains same.

Gujarati nouns inflect in gender and number and case. Gujarati has three genders and two numbers. Table 1 shows 7 paradigms identified for Gujarati noun. The first column shows paradigm ID, Second column shows suffix list which is used to detect this paradigm, third column shows one inflected word belonging to that paradigm and final column shows corresponding root word. We observe from table 1 that same suffix may belong to more than one paradigm.

Id	Suffix	Example	Root Word
1	ઓ, ી, ુ, ા ાઓ, ીઓ	છોકરાઓ (Chokrao)	છોકરું (Chokru)
2	ઓ, ી, ા	૦દિકરો (Dikro)	દિકરો (Dikro)
3	ઓ, ી, ુ, ા	કટકો (Katko)	કટકો (Katko)
4	ો	વાક્યો (Vaakyo)	વાક્ય (Vaaky)
5	ી, ીઓ	સ્ત્રીઓ (Strio)	સ્ત્રી (Stri)
6	ો, ા	મહિના (Mahina)	મહિનો (Mahino)
7	ો, ા	એકતા (Ekta)	એકતા (Ekta)

Table 1: Noun Paradigms

Id	Suffix	Example	Root Word
1	ો, ી, ુ	સારો (Saro)	સારું (Saru)
2	No Inflec-tion	સરસ (Saras)	સરસ (Saras)
3	ી	વ્યભિચારી (Vyabhichari)	વ્યભિચારી (Vyabhichari)

Table 2: Adjective Paradigms

Table 2 shows various paradigms for adjectives. Adjectives can be classified into variant and non-variant adjectives based on the inflections that they take. A non-variant adjective do not inflect with gender.

Gujarati verb inflect in gender, number, case and tense. Verb and adjective require gender agreement with Noun. Table 3 shows various paradigms for verb. We observe that unlike Hindi, Gujarati verbs inflect in gender for only past tense. For present and future tense, verb does not inflect with gender

4 Implementation

In this section we describe paradigm based, knowledge based and statistical approach. We also propose ways to merge these approaches.

Id	Suffix	Example	Root Word
1	આડે, આડી, આડશે, અડ્યા, એ, ઈશ, જો, ઓ, વું, તો, તી.	જમાડ્યું (Jamadyu)	જમ્યું (Jamvu)
2	આવવું, વ્યું, આવશે, આવ્યા, એ, ઈશ, જો, ઓ, વું, તો, તી.	કરશે (Karshe)	કર્યું (Karvu)
3	ધું, વ્યું, આવશે, આવ્યા, ય, જો, વ, વું, તો, તી, ુ	ખાધું (Khadhu)	ખાવું (Khavu)

Table 3: Verb Paradigms

4.1 Paradigm Based Method

We define paradigms for various part of speech for Gujarati language. Paradigm building methodology is covered in the next section in brief. Each paradigm consists of rules to obtain root word, various inflections possible with that paradigm and a representing word for that paradigm. An inflected word is given as an input to the system. The system checks suffix and determines one or more matching paradigm for input word. It is possible that the same rule is present in more than one paradigm. For each matched paradigm system applies rule to generate root word and gives root word as output.

It is possible that a single inflected word is mapped with more than one root word. So to eliminate this multiple output we incorporate two different methods knowledge based and statistical method.

4.2 Knowledge Based Method

Whenever an inflected word gives more than one Root word as an output using paradigm based method, We consult Gujarati Wordnet knowledge base and select best output. Gujarati wordnet contains around 81000 words in root form. Out of all multiple outputs, correct output is matched with wordnet and it is chosen as correct output. The success of this approach lies in the coverage of various root words in the dictionary.

4.3 Statistical Method

Statistical approach focuses on disambiguating multiple outputs based on heuristic developed on length of an inflected word and transformation process for generating root word. In this method we construct probability table which contains transformation rules along with its probability which is determined using set of training words. Snapshot of this table is shown in Table 4. For example if an inflected word ends with ીલ then according to Table 4 it has two possible transformations ીલ - > ુ + ઃ and ીલ -> ીલ. Training data suggests that probability of rule 2 is higher than rule 1 so in this case transformation 1 would be selected for root word generation.

Sr No	Suffix	Possible Trans-formation	Probability (%)
1	ીલ	ીલ - > ીલ	90.3
		ીલ- > ુ + ઃ	32.6
		ીલ- >No Suffix	2.36
2	ીલ	ીલ- > ીલ	82.36
		ીલ- > ુ + ઃ	12.28

Table 4: Statistical Method

5 Experiment Setup

For our experiment we have prepared Gold set of data which consists of 200 Nouns, 200 verbs and 100 Adjectives. Input to Morph analyzer is inflected word and Output is root word. We have root word information about this Gold data which is manually prepared by Linguists. We compare the result produce by our system with actual root word in the Gold data. Analysis of the result is based on factors like How many words are mapped to correct paradigm, How many words are not mapped to correct paradigm , How Many Words belongs to Multiple Paradigm, which category gives good result in the system. From these parameters we analyze accuracy of our system and analyze how various part of speech affects accuracy of the system.

We classify outputs into 2 different categories:

- Correct: Words for which only one output is generated which is correct output.
- Incorrect: Words for which one output is generated and which is incorrect.

Due to the fact that same rule can be part of multiple paradigms, for many words we get multiple outputs. For all those words we apply knowledge based and statistical methods for output enhancements and evaluate accuracy of the system after applying each of the above method.

6 Result Analysis

Simple rule based method has problem of multiple paradigm output. For the words giving multiple outputs we apply knowledge based method and statistical method for removing incorrect outputs. Table 5 and Table 6 summarize results obtained after applying knowledge based and statistical methods. Table 7 shows accuracy of both knowledge based and statistical methods. It can be seen that problem of multiple outputs in case of simple rule based technique can be handled by knowledge based and statistical methods.

POS	Correct	Incorrect	Accuracy
Noun	197	3	98.5
Verb	179	21	89.5
Adjective	89	11	89

Table 5: Results: Knowledge Based Method

POS	Correct	Incorrect	Accuracy
Noun	154	46	77
Verb	149	51	74.5
Adjective	97	3	97

Table 6: Results: Statistical Method

Following points were observed as a part of error analysis.

- For Rule based approach, same suffix rule may apply to different categories so number of words correctly classified is less and degree of multiple outputs is more.
- For Knowledge based method, the reason for error is that some words may not be present in wordnet dictionary so knowledge based approach fails to remove ambiguity from such words.

Approach	Accuracy (%)
Rule Based	58.26
Knowledge Based	92.34
Statistical	82.84

Table 7: Approach wise Accuracy

- Statistical Methods do not depend on any dictionary but they are probabilistic. So depend upon training data used, accuracy may vary.

7 Conclusion and Future Scope

In this paper we presented a Gujarati morphological analyzer. We choose paradigm based approach for our implementation and analyze results obtained for gold set of words. We incorporate two output enhancement methods knowledge based method and statistical methods. We prepared gold set of words and tested them with our system and analyzed results. We conclude that after removing multiple outputs system gives average accuracy of 92.34 for knowledge based method and 82.84 for statistical method. The limitation of current system is that it cannot handle derivational morphology.

References

M.F.Porter 1972. An algorithm for suffix stripping, volume 1. Program,14:130-137

Gulsen Eryigit and Adali Esref 2004. An affix stripping morphological analyzer for turkish, volume 1. IASTED International Multi- Conference on Artificial Intelligence and Applications,pages 299–304, Innsbruck, Austria.

Lauri Karttunen and Kenneth R. Beesley 2003. Finite State Morphology

Akshar Bharti Natural Language Processing - A Paninian Perspective

Harald Hammarstorm and Lars Borin 2004. Unsupervised learning of morphology, volume 1. Computational Linguistics June, 37:309–350, June 2011.

Jyoti Pawar Shilpa Desai and Pushpak Bhattacharya 2012. Automated paradigm selec-tion for fsa based konkani verb morphological analyzer, COLING 2012, Mumbai,India, 10-14 Dec, 2012.

Harshada Gune Mugdha Bapat and Pushpak Bhattacharyya 2010. A paradigm-based finite state morphological analyzer for marath, Workshop on South Asian and South East Asian NLP (part of COLING 2010), Beijing, China, August 2010.

Kashyap Popat Pratik Patel and Pushpak Bhattacharyya 2010. Hybrid stemmer for gujarati, International Conference on Computational Linguistics (COLING), pages 51–55, Beiging, August 2010.

Dipti Jiandani Kartik Suba and Pushpak Bhattacharyya 2011. Hybrid inflectional stemmer and rule-based derivational stemmer for gujarati, IJCNLP 2011 Workshop on Segmentation and Morphology for South Asian Languages, Chiang Mai,Thailand, November 2011.

Niraj Aswani and Robert Gaizauskas 2010. eveloping morphological analysers for south asian languages: Experimenting with the hindi and gujarati languages, Proceedings of the Seventh International Conference on Language Resources and Evaluation (LREC'10), Valletta,

Rajendran N Rajeev R and Elizabeth Sherly 2011. A suffix stripping based morph anal-yser for malayalam language, Dravidian Studies a Research Journal, pages 61–72.

George Cardona 1965. A Gujarati Reference Grammar

Colin Masica 1991. The Indo-Aryan Languages Malta, may 2010. European Language Resources Association (ELRA). ISBN 2-9517408-6-7.

W.S. Tisdall 1892. A Simplified Grammar of the Gujarati Language

Brijesh Bhatt, Dinesh Chauhan, Pushpak Bhattacharyya, C.K. Bhensdadia and Kirit Patel. 2012. Introduction to Gujarati Wordnet International Conference on Global Wordnets (GWC 2011),Matsue,Japan.

Karttunen, Lauri. 1983. KIMMO: A general morpholog-ical processor In: Linguistic Forum 22, (1983) 163–186

Nikhil Kanuparthi,Abhilash Inumella and Dipti Misra Sharma. 2012. Hindi Derivational Morpholog-ical Analyzer Proceedings of the Twelfth Meeting of the Special Interest Group on Computational Morphology and Phonology (SIGMORPHON2012) , pages 10–16

Akshar Bharti, Rajeev Sangal, S.M.Bendre, Pavan Kumar, Aishwarya 2001. Unsupervised improvement of Morphological Analyzer for inflectionally Rich Languages Proceedings of the Sixth Natural Language Processing Pacific Rim Symposium

Resolution of Pronominal Anaphora for Telugu Dialogues

Hemanth Reddy Jonnalagadda
IIIT Hyderabad
`hemanth.reddy`
`@research.iiit.ac.in`

Radhika Mamidi
IIIT Hyderabad
`radhika.mamidi`
`@iiit.ac.in`

Abstract

The challenge of anaphora resolution has been taken up from long time. However, most of the work did not include for dialogues. In this paper we discuss the types of pronouns and anaphora in Telugu language and make an attempt to build a rule based pronominal anaphora resolution algorithm for human to human conversations. The model mainly consists of two parts, creating a knowledge base with a set of pronouns along with its morphological information and designing an algorithm which uses this knowledge base to give an output. In this process we have worked on normal pronominal anaphora and suggested a set of rules applicable for Telugu dialogues. However, since there was no corpus for the Telugu language, we built a corpus and tested the algorithm on it. Results show that the suggested algorithm produced an output with an accuracy of 61.1%.

1 Introduction

Anaphora is the linguistic unit which refers to an entity that is previously mentioned in the same discourse. The word or phrase which it refers is called antecedent. The process of identifying the antecedent of an anaphora is called anaphora resolution. We find the importance of anaphora resolution in various NLP applications such as dialogue systems, text summarization, machine translation and so on. The pronouns in Telugu language carry much more information about the nouns than pronouns in English. Telugu is a morphologically rich and free word order language. The morphological richness of the language helps in building various NLP applications using simple parsing tools. Three types of anaphora are identified in Telugu language, they are normal pronominal anaphora, discourse deictic anaphora and one - anaphora which are discussed in detail in section 3. This paper concentrates mainly on normal pronominal anaphora. Many approaches have been proposed for anaphora resolution in discourse and in dialogues for different languages. This is the first attempt at anaphora resolution in Telugu dialogues.

2 Related work

Research has been going extensively in this area from past few decades. Many rule based, machine learning based and knowledge based systems have come up. One of the earliest work has been done by Hobbs (1976) on pronominal co-reference. Hirst (1981) has compared 5 different approaches and presented their strengths, weaknesses in resolving the anaphora. Lappin and Leass (1994) came up with salience feature based approach. Mitkov (1994a) came up with integrated anaphora resolution approach which relies on set of preferences and constraints. Robust knowledge poor pronoun resolution was developed by Mitkov (1998) which makes use of part-of-speech tagger and simple noun phrase rules. Strube and Eckert (1998) made an attempt to resolve discourse diectic anaphora in dialogues. et al., (2004) built an anaphora resolution method for multi person dialogues where they brought in semantic, syntactic and knowledge based techniques which were used in anaphora resolution.

Coming to the Indian languages, work has been done mostly on Hindi, Bengali, Tamil and Malayalam. Shobha and Patnaik (2002) came up with a rule based approach VASISTH which currently handles anaphora in Malayalam and Hindi languages. Shobha.L (2007) resolves pronominals in Tamil, in which they have adopted a probabilistic model. Praveen et al., (2013) built a hybrid approach for anaphora resolution in Hindi using dependency parser and decision tree classifier. A generic anaphora resolution engine using machine learning was developed for Indian languages by Shobha et al., (2014), they have tested the system on Bengali, Hindi and Tamil. In Telugu Chandramohan and Sadanandam (2014) implemented a rule based pronominal anaphora resolution system for discourse. The algorithm was tested on a limited set of data and an accuracy of 60.75% was obtained.

D S Sharma, R Sangal and E Sherly. Proc. of the 12th Intl. Conference on Natural Language Processing, pages 183–188,
Trivandrum, India. December 2015. ©2015 NLP Association of India (NLPAI)

3 Anaphora in the context of Telugu language

Telugu belongs to the Dravidian family of Indian languages. It is a free word order language. Two or more words undergoing some modifications to form a single compound word is called *sandhi*. It is very common in agglutinative languages. In Telugu an entire sentence can be expressed as a single word which can be seen in the following example where three words are combined to form a single word.
Example 1:
nuvvekkaDunnAvu - nuvvu + ekkaDa + unnAvu
(Where are you?)   you   where   present
These words cannot be analyzed by the NLP applications. To handle these cases there is a need for sandhi splitter which splits the word as shown above.

In Telugu, verbs are inflected with gender, number and person which give information about the subject,
Example 2:
The verb "vellu" can take all the below forms in Telugu. When subject is

male, sg, 3rd person	-	veltunnADu
female, sg, 3rd person	-	veltundi
neutral, pl, 3rd person	-	veltunnAru
neutral, sg, 1st person	-	veltunnAnu

3.1 Pronouns in Telugu

There are a wide variety of pronouns in Telugu. A pronoun can take different forms depending on gender, number, person, case and also on social relationships such as informal, formal, impolite, very polite etc.

This is illustrated below where all the pronouns refer to a male person relatively distant from the speaker.

vADu	-	3rd person, sg, male, impolite
atanu	-	3rd person, sg, male, neutral
Ayana	-	3rd person, sg, male, polite
vAru	-	3rd person, sg, male, very polite

There are 4 different types of pronouns in Telugu namely personal pronouns, demonstrative pronouns, reflexive pronouns and interrogative pronouns. The proposed algorithm works on all the above types of pronouns, excluding interrogative pronouns. In this paper we have classified these pronouns into two different categories and formed rules based on this.

Personal pronouns: Pronouns which map to human characters
Example 3:
"atanu" *(he)*, "Ame" *(she)*, "vADu" *(he)*, "tamaru" *(you)*, "adi" *(she)*, "nuvvu" *(you)*, "nEnu" *(me)* etc.
Non-personal pronouns: These pronouns map to the objects or animals
Example 4:
"adi" *(it)*, "avi" *(they)*, "vATiki" *(them)* etc.

3.2 Types of Anaphoras in Telugu Dialogues

Normal pronominal Anaphora: Where pronoun is referring to single word which is previously introduced in the context.
Example 5:
ramaNa: rAjA elA unnAvu? ninnu
    (Raja how present you)
    cUsi cAlA rojulayiMdi.
    (seen many days back)
(Ramana: How are you? It's been long time since I met you)
rAjA: nEnu bAgunnAnu, nuvvela unnAvu?
    (me good you_how present)
(Raja: I am fine. How are you?)

Discourse Diectic Anaphora: In this case, there is no single antecedent possible. The pronoun will be referring to multiple words in the previous sentence. This is illustrated in example 7 where the pronoun "adi" *(that)* is referring to the entire dialogue.
Example 6:
    rAmu: **rAju cAla mancivADu.**
    (Raju very good person.)
(Ramu: Raju is a very good person)
    ravi: **adi** nIku ela telusu?
    (that you how know)
(Ravi: How do you know that?)

One - Anaphora: It is the anaphoric noun phrase headed by the word one (okaTi in Telugu).
Example 7:
    rAju: nEnu kotta **baMDi** koMdAmani
    (I new bike buying)
    anukuMTunnAnu.
    (thinking.)
(Raju: I am thinking of buying a new bike)
    ravi: nAku **okaTi** kAvali.
    (I one need.)
(Ravi: I too need one.)

4 Anaphora Resolution

Our approach for anaphora resolution can be explained in three steps

- Parsing the dialogues
- Creating the knowledge base and
- Identifying the antecedent.

4.1 Parsing

We parse the dialogues one after the other using morph analyzer. In this process we store the speaker of each dialogue. The output of the morph analyzer is given as input to the POS tagger. The final output at this stage is in Shakti standard format (SSF). It is the highly readable representation for storing language analysis, an English and Telugu examples in SSF are given below.

```
children         NNS      <fs af='child,n,m,p,3,0,,' >
                            |    | | | | |
                            |    | | | | \
                          root  | | |pers |
                            |   | | |     case
                       category | number
                                |
                              gender
```

atanu   PRP   <fs af='atanu,pn,m,sg,3,d,0,0' name="atanu">

Initially we have implemented the system using only morph analyzer where POS tag of most of the pronouns, nouns and their features were not identified.
Example 8:
vATini
<fsaf='vATini,unk,,,,,,'poslcat="NM"name="vATini">

As we can see in this example, the category of this pronoun is shown as unknown and gender, number, person and case features are also null values.
The use of POS tagger in addition to the morph analyzer helped in obtaining POS tags for the nouns and pronouns which could not be tagged by the morph analyzer.

4.2 Knowledge Base

We stored all the pronouns which are tagged by POS tagger and not detected by the morph analyzer in a separate database file. Along with it we have also stored the gender, number, person and case features of these pronouns in the knowledge base. While running the anaphora resolution algorithm, if a pronoun falls in the above category then the information of that particular pronoun is obtained from the database file.
We have also stored the list of reflexive pronouns in the knowledge base as the algorithm consists of rules applicable only for reflexive pronouns.

4.3 Algorithm

We have implemented a rule based pronoun resolution algorithm. These rules were formed based on various pronouns and features obtained from the parsers. We have tried to concentrate more on 3rd person pronouns because it was relatively easy to identify the antecedents of 1st and 2nd person pronouns compared to 3rd person in human conversations. The system works on the rules explained below,

4.3.1 Personal pronouns

As mentioned in sec 3.1 personal pronouns should be referring to the human characters, these pronouns are mapped to the proper nouns or common nouns which tell about human identity.
Example 9:
"tammuDu" *(younger brother)*, "anna" *(elder brother)*, "akka" *(elder sister)*, "amma" *(mother)*, "DAktar" *(doctor)*, "tIcAr" *(teacher)*, etc.

1st person pronouns

1st person pronouns are mapped to the current speaker, if the root word of the pronoun is "mana" *(we)* then it will map to both speaker and listeners. Listeners are the speakers of previous and next dialogues.

Example 10:
amala: **nA**   pEru   amala.   nI   pEreMTi?
    (My name   Amala. You   name_what)
(Amala: My name is Amala. What's your name?)
sIta: nA   pEru   sIta.
    (My   name   Seetha.)
(Seetha: My name is Seetha.)
Example 11:
srInivAs: nAku   edayina   kottagA
    (I   something   new)
    nercukovAlani   uMdi.
    (learn   there.)
(Srinivas: I want to learn something new.)
gOpAl: kAni   **manaku**   vIlavvutuMdA?
    (but   us   feasible.)
(Gopal: But is it feasible for us?)

As we can see, in example 10 "nA" is referring to "amala" and in example 11 "manaku" which is a plural pronoun is referring both "srInivAs" and "gOpAl"

2nd Person pronouns

2nd person pronouns are mapped to the listener, if there is a previous dialogue then it will refer to the speaker of the previous dialogue. If there is no previous dialogue then it will be mapping to speaker of the next dialogue.

Example 12:
sIta: nA   pEru   sIta.
              (my   name   Seetha.)
(Seetha: My name is Seetha.)
amala: **nuvvu**   ekkaDa   caduvutunnAvu?
            (you   where   studying?)
(Amala: Where are you studying?)

Example 13:
amala: nA   pEru   amala.   **nI**
            (My   name   Amala   you)
            pEreMTi?
            name_what?
(Amala: My name is Amala. What's your name?)
sIta: nA   pEru   sIta.
              (my   name   Seetha)
(Seetha: My name is Seetha.)
"nuvvu" in example 12 and "nI" in example 13 are referring to the speakers of previous and next dialogues respectively.

3rd Person pronouns

We have tried to identify the antecedents based on gender, number, person features and a few rules. The step by step procedure and the rules are as follows,

1) While analyzing the parsed text word by word. If a possible antecedent is detected then it is stored along with its POS tag, gender, number and person.

    Example 14:
     ravi: **rAmuki** Dabbu   evaru   iccAru?
                (to_Ramu   money   who   gave)
    (Ravi: Who gave the money to Ramu?)
    rAju: gOpi   **ataniki**   Dabbu   iccADu.
          (Gopi   him   money   gave)
    (Raju: Gopi gave him the money)

All the nouns that appear before pronoun can be possible antecedents. Possible antecedents for the pronoun "ataniki" in example 14 are shown below with its morphological features,

rAmuki NNP   <fs af='rAmuki,unk,,,,,,,' poslcat="NM" name="rAmuki">
Dabbu NN   <fs af='Dabbu,n,,sg,,d,0,0'name="dabbu_2">
gOpi   NNP   <fs af='gOpi,n,,sg,,d,0,0' name="gOpi">

2) If a pronoun is detected then we will be extracting its gender, number and person features from the morph analyzer or through the preprocessing stage mentioned above.
    ataniki PRP   <fs af='atanu,pn,m,sg,3,,ki,ki' name="ataniki">

3) From the list of all possible antecedents, the antecedents which do not agree in gender, number and person features with the pronoun are removed from the list. Below constraints will be applied on the remaining antecedents.

    As we can see the noun "dabbu" agree in gender, number and person with the pronoun. Though the features of "rAmuki" and "gOpiki" are not identified by the morph analyzer, we have considered it as the possible antecedent.

4) Pronouns which come under the category of personal pronouns will be mapped to the proper nouns or the common nouns which tells about human identity. Some of these common nouns are given in example 9.

    As "Dabbu" cannot be referred by the personal pronouns, it is removed from the possible antecedent lists, we are left with "rAmuki", "gOpiki"

5) Reflexive pronouns will be referring the antecedents within the sentence. Example: "tanu" *(he/she)*,"tAmu" (they).
    Example 15:
    ravi: rAmuki Dabbu   evaru   iccAru?
              (to_Ramu   money   who   gave)
    (Ravi: Who gave the money to Ramu?)
    rAju: **gOpi   tana** Dabbu ataniki
              (Gopi   his   money   him)
              iccADu.
              (gave.)
    (Raju: Gopi gave his money to him.)

6) Whereas demonstrative pronouns will be referring to the antecedents outside the sentence. Example: "vADu" *(he)*, "Ame" *(she)*, etc.

    The referent in the Example 14 is a demonstrative pronoun, it should be referring the antecedent outside the sentence. So "gOpi" is removed from the list and we are left with only one possibility "rAmuki" which is the antecedent of the pronoun.

7) If more than one antecedent is left in the list, recently appeared one is preferred as its antecedent.

4.3.2 Non-personal Pronouns

We have applied the same procedure as mentioned above but the steps 4, 5, 6 will change because these pronouns will be mapping to the objects or animals. So, there is no possibility of reflexive pronouns.

Example 16:
gOpi: ravi nI **kukkalu** elA unnAyi?
     (Ravi your dogs how present)
     vATiki AhAram peTTAvA?
     (them foodkept?)
(Gopi: How are your dogs? Did you feed them?)
ravi: **avi** bAgunnAyi. **vATiki** AhAraM
     (they good them food)
     peTTAnu.
     (Kept.)
(Ravi: They are good. I fed them.)

5 Building the corpus

We have noted all the possible pronouns possible for Telugu and for each pronoun, we considered all the possible forms which it can take in different cases (Genitive, Nominative, Objective, and Dative).

The corpus consists of human to human conversations which has all the above pronouns excluding interrogative pronouns, as it is not part of our research currently.

The corpus consists of 108 human conversations, each conversation may contain around 2-8 dialogues. Total number of pronouns in the corpus are 509. About 40% of the corpus has been taken from online chat conversations and the remaining 60% of the conversations have been taken from telugu.webdunia.com and www.learningtelugu.org.

6 Results

Once we built the corpus, we have tagged all the pronouns in the corpus with its corresponding antecedents. This has been done manually. Corpus consists of all categories of pronouns mentioned in sec 3. The algorithm has been run on the entire corpus and we have compared the results with the tagged data.

We have analyzed the results based on the person of the referents. The accuracy of the system on different pronouns is shown in the below table,

	No. of pronouns	Pronouns unresolved	Pronouns wrongly resolved	Pronouns correctly resolved	Accuracy
1st person	138	11	14	113	81.88%
2nd Person	106	14	19	73	68.87%
3rd person	202	23	91	88	43.56%
Non personal pronouns	63	3	23	37	58.73%
Overall	509	51	147	311	61.10 %

7 Issues in Telugu

Corpus

Annotated text and annotated dialogues are not available for Telugu language. All the data is in printed books format and the text which is present in most of the Telugu websites is in image format which makes it difficult to extract.

Sandhi

This phenomenon makes it difficult for the parser to analyze the text. In such cases the algorithm is not able to identify the antecedent or the anaphora present in the sentence. The accuracy of the parsers will be less resulting in the low accuracy of the system which was dependent on these parsers.

Example 17:
ravi: ninna sIta inTiki vacindi.

(yesterday   seetha   home   came)
(Ravi: Yesterday, Seetha came to my home.)
rAju: AmeMdukocindi?
    Ame + eMduku + vacindi.
(she   why   came.)
(Raju: Why did she come?)
In example 17 Pronoun is a part of the compound word in such a case it becomes difficult to identify the anaphora/antecedent. Hence we require a good sandhi splitter for parsing the text.

Subject identification

Telugu is a free word order language. The morph analyzer which we are using is taking individual word as an input, so we are unable to get the case of the words and are unable to identify the subject. Identifying the subject of the sentence will improve the accuracy of 3rd person pronouns.
Example 18:
rAju: raviki   sIta   pustakaM   icindi.
    (to_Ravi   Seetha   book   gave)
    ataniki   pariksa   undanta.
    (he   exam   present.)
(Raju: Seetha gave the book to Ravi. He has an exam.)
In the above example, "sIta" is the subject of the first sentence and its gender is feminine which can be identified from the verb "icindi". As the algorithm is unable to identify the subject, the pronoun "ataniki" (male) is mapped to "sIta" (female).

Parsers

Morph analyzer and POS tagger used are giving lot of errors. These errors are carried forward affecting the overall accuracy of the anaphora resolution algorithm.

8   Future Work

In this paper we have concentrated mainly on normal pronominal anaphora. We would like to concentrate on cataphora in our future work as Telugu is a free word order language the possibility of occurrence of cataphoric reference is very high.

Work has been going on in dialogue systems in Telugu for tourism domain. We would like to add this anaphora resolution system into dialogue system.

We would like to work on 3rd person pronouns as it has very less accuracy.

Adding a good sandhi splitter to the system will improve the accuracy of the system.

References

Krishnamurti, Bhadriraju; J.P.L.Gwynn (1985). A Grammar of Modern Telugu. New Delhi: Oxford University Press.

http://web.cs.ucdavis.edu/~vemuri/Grammar/9.%20pronouns-1.pdf

Lappin & Leass (1994) Sh. Lappin, H. Leass - An algorithm for pronominal anaphora resolution. Computational Linguistics, 20(4), pp. 535-561.

Miriam Eckert & Michael Strube (1998). Discourse Deictic Anaphora in Dialogues. Institute for Research in Cognitive Science. University of Pennsylvania.

Mitkov R. (1998). Robust pronoun resolution with limited knowledge. In: 17th International Conference on Computational Linguistics (COLING''98/ACL''98), Montreal, Canada, pp. 869-875.

Hobbs,J. R. (1976). Pronoun Resolution, Research Report 76-1, Department of Computer Science, City College, New York

D. Chandra Mohan and M. Sadanandam (2014), Telugu Pronominal Anaphora Resolution. International Journal of Research and Applications

Daniel Jurafsky and James Martin (2009), Speech and Language Processing, Prentice-Hall.

Sobha.L and B.N.Patnaik, VASISTH (2002) - An anaphora resolution system for Hindi and Malayalam. In Proceedings of Symposium on Translation Support Systems.

Sobha.L and Vijay Sundar Ram (2014) - A Generic anaphora resolution engine for Indian languages. In the proceeding of COLING.

Sobha, L. (2007) Resolution of Pronominals in Tamil, Computing Theory and Application. The IEEE Computer Society Press, Los Alamitos, CA, pp. 475-79.

Praveen Dakwale, Vandan Mujadia, Dipti M. Sharma (2013). "A Hybrid Approach for Anaphora Resolution in Hindi." LTRC, IIIT-Hyderabad. India.

Prateek Jain, Manav R. Mittal, A Mukerjee and Achla M. Raina, 2004. "Anaphora Resolution in Multi-Person Dialogue", Strube, M. and Candy Sidner (ed.), Proceedings of the 5th SIGdial Workshop on Discourse and Dialogue.

Akshar Bharathi, Rajeev Sangal and Dipti Mishra (2007)   Shakti   Standard   Format.

A Study on Divergence in Malayalam and Tamil Language in Machine Translation Perceptive

Jisha P Jayan
Virtual Resource Centre for
Language Computing
IIITM-K,Trivandrum
`jisha.jayan@iiitmk.ac.in`

Elizabeth Sherly
Virtual Resource Centre for
Language Computing
IIITM-K,Trivandrum
`sherly@iiitmk.ac.in`

Abstract

Machine Translation has made significant achievements for the past decades. However, in many languages, the complexity with its rich inflection and agglutination poses many challenges, that forced for manual translation to make the corpus available. The divergence in lexical, syntactic and semantic in any pair of languages makes machine translation more difficult. And many systems still depend on rules heavily, that deteriates system performance. In this paper, a study on divergence in Malayalam-Tamil languages is attempted at source language analysis to make translation process easy. In Malayalam-Tamil pair, the divergence is more reported in lexical and structural level, that is been resolved by using bilingual dictionary and transfer grammar. The accuracy is increased to 65 percentage, which is promising.

Keywords- Translational divergence; semantic; syntactic; lexical;

1 Introduction

The problem with divergence in machine translation in a complex topic, which can be defined as the differences that occur in language with respect to the grammar. The divergence mainly occurs when these occur a translation from a source language to the target language. For any MT system, this topic is very crucial as to obtain an accurate translation, it is very much needed to resolve the nature of translational divergence. This divergence can be seen at different levels. Based on the complexity that occur in the specific translation, divergence affects the translation quality. Some translational divergences are universal in the sense that they occur across the languages while certain others are specific with respect to the language pair (Lavanya et al., 2005; Saboor and Khan, 2010). Hence, the divergence in the translation need to be studied both perspectives that is across the languages and language specific pair (Sinha, 2005).The most problematic area in translation is the lexicon and the role it plays in the act of creating deviations in sense and reference based on the context of its occurrence in texts (Dash, 2013).

Indian languages come under Indo-Aryan or Dravidian scripts. Though there are similarities in scripts, there are many issues and challenges in translation between languages such as lexical divergences, ambiguities, lexical mismatches, reordering, syntactic and semantic issues, structural changes etc. Human translators try to choose the correct wording by using knowledge from various sources, and the factors like phonology, orthography, morphology as well as knowledge of the person, and cultural differences influences the translation. Therefore, it is hard to get a translation of one person as same as other translator. MT is a complex and challenging research area because language translation itself is very difficult. While human processes language understanding and translation on many levels, but a machine processes data, with its linguistic form and structure, it is difficult to get the sense. This requires more of cognitive and intelligent systems in NLP, rather than considering MT development only in linguistic point of view. Many works have been performed based on linguistic and lexical level, but MT across the languages is a challenging task for several reasons like, the difference in the structure of source and target languages, ambiguity, multiword units like idioms, phrases and tense generation and many more. In this paper, we have considered two Dravidian languages Malayalam and Tamil and various challenges and issues in semantic and syntactical in both the languages are discussed.

185

D S Sharma, R Sangal and E Sherly. Proc. of the 12th Intl. Conference on Natural Language Processing, pages 189–196,
Trivandrum, India. December 2015. ©2015 NLP Association of India (NLPAI)

Malayalam and Tamil belong to Dravidian language family. Malayalam and Tamil are closely related to each other in grammar with a rich literary tradition. However, Malayalam is highly influenced by Sanskrit language at lexical, grammatical and phonemic levels where as Tamil is not. The Noun morphology is same in both the languages as the word may contain the root alone or root with suffixes attached to it. Agglutination is widely seen in Tamil and Malayalam. In both languages, the case markers are found to be attached to the nouns and pronouns. Post-positions are also seen to be attached to these. Morphology includes inflection, sandhi, and derivation. The Tamil verbs inflect for person, number and gender whereas Malayalam verbs do not. Hence the gender marking of the noun is not a relevant feature when Malayalam is considered.

Language divergence in most cases result in the ambiguities in translation. The divergence issue across a language is associated with many factors ranging from linguistic, cultural, and societal to psychological aspects of the languages. Syntactic and lexico-semantic divergence is the two board categories of divergence proposed by Dorr. Sentence level ambiguities are referred as syntactic while at the word level is semantic. A hybrid approach to develop the Malayalam to Tamil MT system comprising paradigm, rule and machine learning methods are proposed. The system deals with the analysis, transfer, and generation process. The issues being raised in the various stages in the development of the Machine Translation are discussed here. The next section deals with the related works carried out in this area. In section 3, various translational divergences are considered with respect to Malayalam and Tamil languages. Some other types of divergences found while translation are discussed in next section. Fifth sections give the methods for handling the divergence and finally the paper is concluded in section 6.

2 State of Art

Dorr (1994) gives a systematic solution to the problem of divergence derived from the formalization of two different information namely the linguistic ground on which the lexical and semantic divergence are based and the technique to solve these problems. The paper explains mainly seven types of divergence with examples with respect to English, Spanish and German. The paper focuses on Thematic, promotional, demotional, structural, conflational, categorical and lexical divergences. Barnett et al. (1994) divide distinctions between source and target languages into two categories mainly translation divergences and translation mismatches. The information conveyed in source and target language remain same while the structure of the sentence differ in translational divergence (1990). In definition of lexical-semantic representation and translation mappings is described. The paper discussed on the justification for distinguishing promotional and demotional divergence, the limits imposed on the range of repositioning possibilities, notion of full coverage in context of lexical selection and resolution of interacting divergence types. The paper concludes with a brief description of UNITRAN, a system for translation across a variety of languages, which accommodates the divergence types.

Nizar and Dorr (2002) proposed a novel approach to handle divergence in translation in a Generation-Heavy Hybrid Machine Translation (GHMT)system. Deep symmetric knowledge of source and target language is required for these approach. Various examples are illustrated to show the interaction between statistical and symbolic knowledge in GHMT system.

Dorr (1990) presented a mechanisms for mapping an underlying lexical-conceptual structure to a syntactic structure used by the UNITRAN. Also explains the ways to solve the problem of thematic divergences in machine translation. The solution is implemented in the bidirectional system for English, Spanish, and German. The two types of thematic divergence namely the reordering of arguments for a given predicate and reordering of predicates with respect to arguments or modifiers is explained. They presented three mechanisms to solve the thematic divergences with a set of general linking routines

Zhiwei (2006) describes different types of translation divergence in Machine Translation. Even though, translation divergence occurs at all phases of MT, the author concentrated on the translation divergence in the transfer phase. The translational divergence that are found in lexical selection in target language, in tense in thematic relation, in head-switch, in structure, in category, in conflation is described. The ambiguity with respect to syntactical, semantic and contextual that relate with the co-occurrence based approaches for the selection of translation equivalence. The author also suggests the use of feature vector to represent the co-occurrence cluster. The paper proposes some suggestions in Mt system.

Akeel and Mishra (2013) discussed about the language divergences and the ambiguities present in English to Arabic machine translation and the control methods used to resolve the same. the authors have implemented English to Arabic machine translation system using ANN and rule based approach. The proposed system is capable of handling conventional type of ambiguities like lexical and syntactic ambiguity and also structural divergences. The lexical ambiguities include category, homograph, transfer or translational, pronoun reference, gender and number. The word-order, agreement, tense and aspect are various structural divergence explained in the paper.

Dave et al. (2001) have studied the language divergence between English and Hindi. This paper also studied the implication of language divergence in machine translation using Universal Networking Language (UNL), introduced by united Nation University, to facilitate the transfer and exchange of information over the internet. The language divergence between these languages is considered as divergence between SOV and SVO classes of languages. Two criteria are considered for deciding the effectiveness of an interlingua. The first criteria is that the meaning conveyed by source text should be apparent from the interlingual representation. The next is a generator should be able to produce a target language sentence that a native speaker of that language accepts as natural. The use of lexical resources in constructing a semantically rich dictionary semi-automatically with an overview of major differences between English and Hindi is described. The syntactic and lexical-semantic divergences between Hindi and English from a computational linguistic perspective is explained.

Kulkarni et al. (2014) studied various divergence pattern that occurred between English and Marathi language pair translation. Their study involved the divergences based on lexico-sematic and syntactic. They further classified lexico-semantic divergence into thematic divergence, structural divergence, promotional and demotional divergence, conflational and inflational divergence, categorical divergence and lexical divergence. Syntactic divergence include constituent-order divergence, adjunction divergence, null-subject divergence and pleonastic divergences. They also focused on divergence that occurred in English and Marathi machine translation that are common. These include divergence found in replicative words, morphological gaps, determiner systems, honorific differences, word related divergences. All the translation divergences are explained with relevant examples.

Jayan et al. (2012) conducted a study to know the pattern of the source and target languages and the morphophonemic changes occurring during the translation of a sentence. The paper focused on the different types of divergence that occur among this language pair. The non-configurational nature of Malayalam is being explained with various examples. Author discusses the complexity of translational divergence among their language pair and provides a solution to classify and resolve the divergence problem. The paper gives a brief idea about the English Malayalam MAT system based on the Anglabharathi, which is an interlingua based approach.

Goyal and Sinha (2009) discusses the translation pattern between English-Sanskrit and Hindi - Sanskrit of various constructions to identify the divergence in these language pairs. Through this the authors come up with strategies to handle these situations and also with correct translations. The base of their classification of translation divergence is presented by Dorr (1994).

Sinha and Thakur (2005) studied different patterns of translation divergences both from Hindi to English and English to Hindi keeping in view the classification of translation divergence proposed by Dorr. They have observed that there are a number of areas in Hindi-English translation pair that fall under translation divergence but cannot be accounted for within the existing parameters of classification strategy.

Mishra and Mishra (2009) proposed a method to detect and implement the adaptation rules for the divergence in English to Sanskrit machine translation. The divergences in language between English and Sanskrit can be considered as representing the divergences between SVO (Subject - Verb - Object) and SOV (Subject - Object - Verb) classes of languages. The type of divergence detected is based on different aspects like linguistic to socio- and psycho-linguistic, role of conjunctions and particles, participle, gerunds and socio-cultural aspects. They have performed a novel method that uses rules and ANN technique to detect and implement the adaptation rules for the divergence in English to Sanskrit machine translation.

Gupta and Chatterjee (2003) presented adaptation for English-Hindi EBMT. They have discussed the issue of adaptation, in general, with special emphasis to divergence. Their work looks at adaptation of EBMT between English and Hindi. They have given special attention to the study of divergence by recognizing six different categories of divergence and providing schemes for identifying them

3 Translational Divergence

The divergence study is mainly dealt with languages. Divergence is a language dependent phenomenon and is not necessary that same set of divergences will occur across all the languages. Lexico-semantic translation divergences are accounted for by means of parameterization of the lexicon (Dorr, 1993). The reason behind divergence mainly lies with the incompatibility of a language with another, a common phenomenon for almost all natural languages. There are situations where a sentence in the source language needs to be translated in the target language in entirely different forms, making the task of both translations a difficult process.

3.1 Conflational and Inflational Divergence

Conflational divergence occurs when the sense conveyed by a single word is expressed by two or more words in one of the languages. The opposite case of conflational divergence is referred to by inflational divergence. The problem due to the lexical gap, an instance where there is an absence of a wordto express a specific concept of the source word in the target language during the translation process. Not all the words in one language have equivalent words in another language. In some cases a word in one language is to be expressed by a group of words or phrases in another. For examples:

വല *(vala)* : இணற்றை_முடும்_மரச்சட்டம் *(kiNaR-Rai_muuTum_maraccaTTam)*

പേട   *(peeta)* : பாலில்_செய்யப்படும்_இணிப்பு *(paalil_ceyyappaTum_inippu)*

കാല്‍വെള്ള *(kaal˜veLLa)*: பாதத்தின்_அடிப்பகுதி *(paattatin_aTippakuti)*

3.2 Lexical Divergence

This type of divergences arises mainly due to the lack of an exact lexical map for a word or construction in one language into another. Most of the conflational and inflational divergence overlap with lexical divergence.

3.3 Syntactic Ambiguity

A word may belong to more than one POS category, resulting in the syntactic ambiguity. This is a problem with the parsing resulting in the source language. There is a lack of one-to-one correspondence of parts of speech between two languages. For examples: can be INTF or PRP, can be NN or PSP, can be PSP or VM etc.

അവന്‍/PRP അത്രയും/QF ദൂരം/NN ബസില്‍/NN നിന്ന്‍/VM പോയി/VM ./SYM

(avan˜/PRP atrayuM/QF duuraM/NN basil˜/NN ninn/VM pooyi/VM ./SYM)

അവന്‍/PRP അവിടെ/NST നിന്ന്‍/PSP ഇപ്പോള്‍/RB ഇറങ്ങി/VM ./SYM

(avan˜/PRP aviTe/NST ninn/PSP ippooL˜/RB iRangngi/VM ./SYM)

In the first sentence, word "നിന്ന" refers to "stood" while in the second sentence the same word means "from". Another example

3.4 Null Subject Divergence

In Malayalam subject dropping can be seen frequently. But Tamil has restrictions in subject dropping. If the verb occurring in Tamil is an action at the end of a sentence, then subject dropping is not possible. But if it occurs in a statement, null subject construction is possible.

3.5 Agreement Divergence

Given two languages may have completely different structures. Malayalam is free-word order language while Tamil has SOV structure, so to identify the phrase performing the function of the subject in the sentence is a challenging process. Gender issues in translation are a subject that serves to point out the limitations of machine translation. The agreement between the subject and verb is one of the problematic issues in MT. The Tamil verbs depend on the PNG (Person Number Gender) information about nouns. Malayalam verbs do not depend on this information. Hence the gender marking of the noun is not a relevant feature when Malayalam is considered.

	Past	Present	Future
1st singular	வந்தேன் *(vandteen)*	வருகிறேன் *(varukiReen)*	வருவேன் *(varuveen)*
1st plural	வந்தோம் *(vandtoom)*	வருகிறோம் *(varukiRoom)*	வருவோம் *(varuvoom)*
2nd singular	வந்தாய் *(vandtaay)*	வருகிறாய் *(varukiRaay)*	வருவாய் *(varuvaay)*
2nd singular honorific	வந்தீர் *(vandtiir)*	வருகிறீர் *(varukiRiir)*	வருவீர் *(varuviir)*
2nd plural	வந்தீர்கள் *(vandtiirkaL)*	வருகிறீர்கள் *(varukiRiirkaL)*	வருவீர்கள் *(varuviirkaL)*
3rd singular male	வந்தான் *(vandtaan)*	வருகிறான் *(varukiRaan)*	வருவான் *(varuvaan)*
3rd singular female	வந்தாள் *(vandtaaL)*	வருகிறாள் *(varukiRaaL)*	வருவாள் *(varuvaaL)*
3rd singular honorific	வந்தார் *(vandtaar)*	வருகிறார் *(varukiRaar)*	வருவார் *(varuvaar)*
3rd plural	வந்தார்கள் *(vandtaarkaL)*	வருகிறார்கள் *(varukiRaarkaL)*	வருவார்கள் *(varuvaarkaL)*
3rd singular neutral	வந்தது *(vandtatu)*	வருகிறது *(varukiRawu)*	வரும் *(varum)*
3rd plural neutral	வந்தன *(vandtana)*	வருகின்றன *(varukinRana)*	வரும் *(varum)*

Table 1: Finite forms of verb vaa (வா)

From the above Table 1, for a single word "വരു ക "we have present tense "വരുന്നു", past tense "വ ന്നു" and future tense "വരും" in Malayalam, there have eleven forms for each tense in Tamil depending the agreement of a verb with the subject.

3.6 Semantic Divergence

Word Sense Disambiguation (WSD) or Lexical Ambiguity Resolution is a fundamental task, which processes to identify the sense of a word in a given sentence. Words can have more than one meaning and sometimes group of words or whole sentence may have more than one meaning in a language resulting in the ambiguities.Words having multiple meanings are called polysemy. Word disambiguation is another major challenge in translation where a same word can act differently based on the context. For examples:

രസം *(rasaM)* - അനുഭൂതി, കറി, ഇഷ്ടം, രുചി, അഭിരുചി, മെർക്കുറി

(anubhuuti, kaRi, ishTaM, ruci, abhiruci, mer˜kkuRi)

ലളിതമായ ചേരുവകൾ ചേർത്തുള്ള കുരുമുളക് രസം കഴിക്കുന്നത് ദഹനത്തെ സഹായിക്കും.

(laLitamaaya ceeruvakaL˜ceer˜ituLLa kurumuLak rasaM kazhikkunnat dahanatte sahaayikkuM.)

അവന് അടുത്തിടെയായി എന്നോട് അത്ര രസം ഇല്ല.

(avan˜aTuttuTeyaayi ennooT atra rasaM illa.)

The word in the above two sentences clearly distinguishes the difference in meanings respectively "curry" and "realization". Other examples:

നട *(naTa)* - ക്രിയ, നടക്കുക, പടി
  (kRIya , naTakkuka , paTi)

അടി *(aTi)* - ചുവടളവ്, പാദം, തല്ല്
  (cuvaTaLav , paadaM , tall)

വാനം *(vaanaM)* - മാനം, അഭിമാനം
  (maanaM , abhimaanaM)

ഉത്തരം *(uttaraM)* - മറുപടി, ചോദ്യോത്തരം, താങ്ങ്
  (maRupaTi, coodyoottaraM, taangng)

From the above examples here the word "ന s" can act as Noun as well as Verb depending on the context. This is applicable for both the languages. Thus the differences are either because of the absence of a concept or due to the differences at the level of identifying concepts. The case where there is an absence of a concept is comparatively easier to handle than the cases where the domains overlap with other domains.

Unless the correct meaning is captured, there are more chances for incorrect translation.

3.7 Structural Divergence

Both the languages have almost same grammatical structures. But there occurs some minor variations in the construction of the sentences

അവൻ ഇന്നലെ സിനിമയ്ക്ക് പോയി. ഞാനും.
(*avan˜innale sinimaykk pooyi. njaanuM.*)
அவன் நேற்று திரைப்படத்திந்கும் போனான். நானும் போனேன்.
(*avan ndeeRR tiraippTattindkum poonaan. ndaanum pooneen.*)

In the above example, in second sentence, its not necessary to specify "പോയി" *poyi* with "ഞാനും" *njaanuM* as its understood from the sentence construction. But in Tamil, this construction is not seen.

4 Other issues in Translation

4.1 Idiom Translation

An idiom can be defined as a phrase or sentence whose meaning is not specific from meaning of its individual units and that must be learnt as a whole unit. These are used in written as well as verbal communication, giving a stylistic way of delivering a message. While translating idioms from Malayalam to Tamil, some phrases can only be translated with correct sense, but some others can only be transliterated only.

മിന്നുന്നതെല്ലാം പൊന്നല്ല.
(*minnunnatellaaM ponnalla.*)
மின் நுவதெல்லாம் பொன்நல்ல
(*minnuvatellaam poonnalla.*)

In the above example, the correct translation is possible but in below example literal translation of the phrase gives an incorrect translation.

കൈയാല പുറത്തെ തേങ്ങ പോലെ.
(*kaiyaala puRatte teengnga poole.*)
மதில் மேல் பூனை பொல
(*matil meel puunai poola*)

4.2 Divergence in Copula Transfer

A copula is a verb or verb like word, capable of functioning as a main verb in a sentence. These are different from action verbs grammatically and semantically. In Malayalam, "ആക്" (aak) and "ഉണ്ട്" (uNT) functions as copula while Tamil lacks copula.

രാമന് സീതയെ ഇഷ്ടം ആണ്.

(*raaman siitaye ishTaM aaN.*)
இராமனுக்கு சீதையை பிடிக்கும்
(*iraamavukku ciitaiyai pitikkum*)

While translating from Malayalam to Tamil, copula is not needed as the translation without copula gives a meaningful sentence in Tamil .

4.3 Stylistic Variations

All languages have its own style. There are sentences in Malayalam for which direct translation in Tamil is not possible. There occur such sentences where many to one mappings can be seen from Malayalam to Tamil. The example below depicts this nature:

നീ എവിടെ പോകുന്നു.
(*nii eviTe pookunnu*)
നീ എങ്ങോട്ട് പോകുന്നു.
(*nii engngooTT pookunnu*)
நீ எந்க்கை போகிராய்
(*nii efkai pookiraay*)
നീ എവിടെയാണ് പോകുന്നത്.
(*nii eviTeyaaN pookunnu*)
நீ எந்க்கை போகிராய்
(*nii efkai pookiraay*)
നീ എങ്ങോട്ടാണ് പോകുന്നത്.
(*nii engngooTTaaN pookunnu*)
நீ எந்க்கை போகிராய்
(*nii efkai pookiraay*)

For the all four sentences shown above in Malayalam, there is only one equivalent translation in Tamil. In Malayalam, there is usages like "കാണുന്നുണ്ട്" (*kaaNunnuNT*) , "പോകുന്നുണ്ട്" (*pookunnuNT*). Tamil doesn't have these structure, which makes error in translation.

ഞാൻ നാളെ അവനെ കാണുന്നുണ്ട്.
(*njaan˜naaLe avane kaaNunnuNT.*)
நான் நாளை அவனை பார்ப்பேன்
(*ndaan ndaaLai avanee paarppeen.*)
நான் நாளை அவனை பார்க்கவிருக்கிறேன்
(*ndaan ndaaLai avanai paarkkavirukkiReen.*)

Other difference mostly found is the dropping of a word from a sentence in Tamil which is a must in Malayalam. In the examples given below, "ഒന്ന്" (onn) from first sentence and "ഒരു" (oru) from second sentence is droped. The following examples demonstrate this typical characteristics.

ഞാൻ ഒന്ന് പറഞ്ഞോട്ടെ.
(*njaan˜onn paRanjnjooTTe.*)
நான் சொல்லட்டுமா

(*ndaan collaTTumaa.*)
അവനെ ഒരു നോക്ക് കാണാൻ കൊതിയാകുന്നു.
(*avane oru nookk kaaNaan˘kotiyaakunnu.*)
அவனை பார்க்க ஆசைபடுகிறேன் .
(*avanai paarkka aacaipaTukikeen.*)

5   Handling Divergences

The divergence found in the MT system cannot
be handled completely by the system itself as
sometimes there may not be word meanings that
can be replaced exactly.   Various modules are
built for bridging the divergence encountered
while translating the text from Malayalam to
Tamil. The linguistics modules are very crucial
for any machine translation. A combination of
linguistic as well as statistical machine learning
techniques are used to build translation capability.
Various modules included in the MT system are
Malayalam morphological analyser which is a
paradigm based, parts of speech tagger and chunker statistical based, lexical transfer comprising
the bilingual dictionary, morphological generator
for Tamil with some additional minute modules.
The architecture of the system is based on the
analyse-transfer-generate.

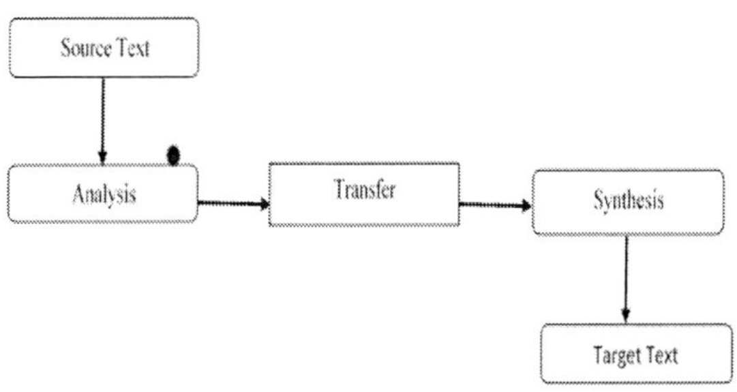

Figure 1: System Architecture

In the present study, the divergence issues are
solved at the analysis part only ie at the source
side. The analysis of the source language side
deals with different modules.   At each level
various grammatical rules are incorporated to get
a much better result. The Figure 2 depicts the
increase in the accuracy when certain rules are
applied.
The test was carried out for 100 sentences from
various domains, When rules are not given the
accuracy obtained ranges from 47-55%. At the
same time when certain rules were included in
different modules for rectifying the errors , the

accuracy increased to 53-65%. The divergences at
the lexical are solved using bilingual dictionary.
The structural transformations are carried out at
the Transfer grammar module.

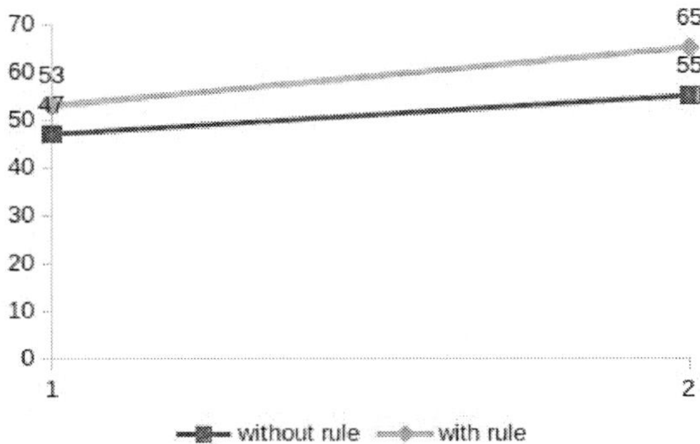

Figure 2: Accuracy Graph

The structural transformations are carried out at
the Transfer grammar module. The Lexical divergences are solved using bilingual dictionary.
Many rules are incorporated at various modules
for rectifying the errors occurring during the translation process.

6   Conclusion

Identifying the patterns of divergence in any languages is very crucial to obtain a quality machine
translation system. The translational divergence
requires combinations of manipulations both at
the lexical and structural level. Some important
types of divergence related to translation based
on Dorr's classification from Malayalam to Tamil
are discussed in this paper. Both manual and machine translation among this language pair is taken
in view. The divergence found can be semantic
or syntactic types. Various patterns of translation
divergence found at different phases of machine
translation is examined.

References

Abdus Saboor and Mohammad Abid Khan. 2010.
*Lexical-semantic divergence in Urdu-to-English Ex-
ample Based Machine Translation*, In Emerging
Technologies (ICET), 6th International Conference
on IEEE. 316-320

Bonnie J. Dorr. 1994. *Machine translation divergences: A formal description and proposed solution*,
Computational Linguistics , 20(4):597-633.

Bonnie J. Dorr. 1990. *A cross-linguistic approach to machine translation*, In Proceedings, Third International Conference on Theoretical and Methodological Issues in Machine Translation of Natural Languages, Linguistics Research Center, The University of Texas, Austin, Texas, 13-32.

Bonnie Dorr. 1993. *Machine Translation: A View from the Lexicon*, MIT press.

Bonnie Dorr. 1990. *Solving thematic divergences in machine translation*, In the *Proceedings of the 28th annual meeting on Association for Computational Linguistics* , Association for Computational Linguistics. 127-134.

Deepa Gupta and Niladri Chatterjee. 2003. *Identification of divergence for English to Hindi EBMT*, In *Proceeding of MT Summit-IX*, 141-148.

Feng Zhiwei,. 2006. *Translational divergence in Machine Translation*, Eafterm Symposium, Haikou.

James Barnett, Inderjeet Mani and Elaine Rich . 1994. *Reversible machine translation: What to do when the languages dont match up, Reversible Grammar in Natural Language Processing*, Springer US. 321-364

Jayan V, Sunil R, Sulochana Kurambath G and R Ravindra Kumar . 2012. *Divergence patterns in Machine Translation between Malayalam and English*, In *Proceedings of the International Conference on Advances in Computing*, Communications and Informatics. ACM. 788-794.

Marwan Akeel and R.B. Mishra. 2013. *Divergence and Ambiguity Control in an English to Arabic Machine Translation*, In the *International Journal of Engineering Research and Applications* , 3(6):1670-1679.

Niladri Sekhar Dash. 2013. *Linguistic Divergences in English to Bengali Translation*, INFOCOMP *International Journal of English Linguistics*, 3(1):31-40

Nizar Habash, Bonnie Dorr . 2002. *Handling translation divergences: Combining statistical and symbolic techniques in generation-heavy machine translation*, Springer Berlin Heidelberg.

Pawan Goyal and R. Mahesh K. Sinha . 2009. *Translation divergence in English-Sanskrit-Hindi language pairs*, In *Sanskrit Computational Linguistics*, Springer Berlin Heidelberg. 134-143.

Prahallad Lavanya, Prahallad Kishore, and Ganapa Thiraju Madhavi . 2005. *A simple approach for building transliteration editors for indian languages*, *Journal of Zhejiang University Science A* , 6(11):1354-1361.

R. Mahesh K. Sinha and Anil Thakur . 2005. *Translation Divergence in English-Hindi MT*, In the *Proceeding of EAMT Xth Annual Conference* , Budapest, Hungary. 30-31.

Shachi Dave, Jignashu Parikh and Pushpak Bhattacharyya . 2001. *Interlingua-based English-Hindi Machine Translation and Language Divergence, Machine Translation* , 16(4):251-304.

S. B Kulkarni, P.D. Deshmukh, M. M. Kazi and K. V. Kale . 2014. *Linguistic Divergence Patterns in English to Marathi Translation, International Journal of Computer Applications(0975 8887)*, 87(4):21-26.

R. Mahesh K. Sinha and Anil Thakur. 2005. *Translation Divergence in English-Hindi MT*, In the *Proceeding of EAMT Xth Annual Conference*, Budapest, Hungary. 245-254.

Vimal Mishra and R.B. Mishra. 2009. *Divergence patterns between English and Sanskrit machine translation*, INFOCOMP *Journal of Computer Science*, 8(3):62-71.

Automatic conversion of Indian Language Morphological Processors into Grammatical Framework (GF)

Harsha Vardhan Grandhi
LTRC
IIIT Hyderabad
`venkata.harshavardhan@research.`
`iiit.ac.in`

Soma Paul
LTRC
IIIT Hyderabad
`soma@iiit.ac.in`

Abstract

Grammatical framework (GF) is an open source software which supports semantic abstraction and linguistic generalization in terms of abstract syntax in a multi-lingual environment. This makes the software very suitable for automatic multi-lingual translation using abstract syntax which can be treated as a interlingua. As a first step towards building multi-Indian language translation system using GF platform, we aim to develop an automatic converter which will convert morphological processors available in various formats for Indian languages into GF format. In this paper we develop a deterministic automatic converter that converts LTtoolbox and ILMT morphological processors into GF format. Currently we have converted Hindi, Oriya and Tamil processors using our converter with 100% information preserved in the output. We will also report in this paper our effort of converting Sanskrit and Marathi LTtoolbox morphological processor into GF format.

1 Introduction

Many NLP resources have been developed for processing Indian languages in the last decade. A major consortium of Indian language - Indian language MT system (ILMT) has been successfully carried out for 9 language pairs. These systems mainly follow a transfer based approach. MT system from English to various Indian languages have also been developed through large projects. Morphological analyzers and generators have been developed as part of these projects as well as independently for many Indian languages. In this paper, we present an automatic converter that converts morphological processors that exist in different formats into one common format of Grammatical Framework. Grammatical framework (GF) is an open source software which supports semantic abstraction and linguistic generalization in terms of abstract syntax in a multi-lingual environment (Ranta Aarne, 2009). Abstract syntax can be viewed as an interlingua in the context of multi-lingual machine translation. Apart from abstract syntax there exists another module called concrete syntax in which the morphological specification and syntactic behavior of a language can be captured. The abstract syntax and concrete syntaxes of all languages that one wants to handle together can produce very good quality, especially for domain based MT systems. This is the motivation for converting morphological processors, that at present exist in different format for different Indian languages, into GF format so that good quality meaning driven multi-lingual MT can be accomplished.

Our morphological converter presently converts morph resources designed in Lttoolbox and ILMT morph framework into GF format. We have experimented with Hindi, Oriya, Tamil, Marathi and Sanskrit morphological processors. We have achieved 100% information preservation for the conversion of Hindi, Tamil and Oriya languages. Sanskrit and Marathi LTtoolbox resources are quite huge and we have encountered some issues in conversion which we will discuss in the paper.

The paper is divided into the following sections. In the next section, we will briefly introduce LTtoolbox, the structure of morph used in ILMT and functionalities required for representing morphological information in GF. Section 3 presents related work. Section 4 presents our approach of automatic conversion. In section 5, we will present the result of automatic conversion and analyze the results for Hindi, Oriya (Ithisree Jena and Dipti M. Sharma, 2011) and Sanskrit. We conclude the paper by presenting a critical review of our work

D S Sharma, R Sangal and E Sherly. Proc. of the 12th Intl. Conference on Natural Language Processing, pages 197–202,
Trivandrum, India. December 2015. ©2015 NLP Association of India (NLPAI)

and also insight into future work.

2 Frameworks

We will briefly discuss the architecture of the morphological processors of the three frameworks, Grammatical Framework, Lttoolbox and ILMT.

2.1 Grammatical Framework

GF is a development platform which allows linguists to build grammars (Ranta Aarne, 2009; Ranta Aarne, 2004). It uses paradigm approach in it's morph resource. Parameters and Operations are used as building blocks to create morph resource.

A **parameter** is a user-defined type which is used to model lexical features like number, gender etc.

```
param Number = Sg | Pl
```

Listing 1: " Example parameter "

Here, Number is a parameter representing the singularity/plurality of given word. Each parameter has a set of constructors, which represent possible values of that parameter. In this case, Number has two constructors namely Sg and Pl, which are declared as shown in the example above.

An **Operation** is a function which takes a lemma of the given word and generates a table consisting of all possible word forms. A table in operation consists of branches with constructors on the left and corresponding word forms on the right. Table is computed by pattern matching which returns the value from the first branch whose pattern matches the argument. (Ranta Aarne, 2003)
Ex:

```
oper regNoun : Str -> {s : Number => Str
    } = \dog -> {
        s = table {
                Sg => dog ;
                Pl => dog + "s"
        }
};
```

Listing 2: " Example Operation "

In the example shown above, the operation regNoun takes a String as an argument and returns a Number to String {s: Number => Str }. If the string dog is passed to the operation then it returns a paradigm stating that when the word is singular(Sg) , the operation returns the same word(i.e. dog), if it is plural(Pl) then it returns dogs.

2.2 Lttoolbox

Lttoolbox is an open source finite state toolkit used for lexical processing, morphological analysis and generation of words (Mikel L. Forcada et al., 2011). Like GF, Lttoolbox also uses the paradigm approach for creating morphological analyzer .

Morph resource in Lttoolbox has three important sections (i.e. for automatic conversion) namely symbol definition section, paradigm definition section and lexicon dictionary.

Symbols are used to define lexical categories, features and their values in the morph. These symbols are defined within **symbol definition** (sdef).

```
<sdef n="gen:m" c="masculine" />
```

Listing 3: "Example symbol definition"

In the above example, gen is the symbol for gender, m is the corresponding feature value.

Paradigm takes a lemma and generates all possible word forms. Each paradigm consists of several entries. Each entry has the data to create a word form for a given set of grammatical symbols. These paradigms of the grammar are defined within **paradigm definition** (pardef).

```
<pardef n="kAl/A__adj">
<e><p><l>e</l><r>A<s n="cat:adj"/><s n="
    case:o"/><s n="gen:m"/><s n="num:s
    "/></r></p></e>

</pardef>
```

Listing 4: " Example paradigm definition "

In the above example, the lemma in consideration is kAlA. For the given entry (e) , the word form kAle is generated for kAlA when the grammatical symbols are <cat=adj;case=o;gen=m;num=s>

2.3 ILMT

ILMT uses Computational Paninian Grammar (CPG) for analyzing language and combines it with machine learning. It is developed using both traditional rules-based and dictionary-based algorithms with statistical machine learning (Sampark, 2009).
ILMT morph resource has categories, features, feature_values and word_forms.
Each category with its name and its corresponding features are defined in a single file. Similarly, each feature along with its name and value are stored in a different file. Each category has its own paradigm file. A category can contain many words. Each word belonging to a category

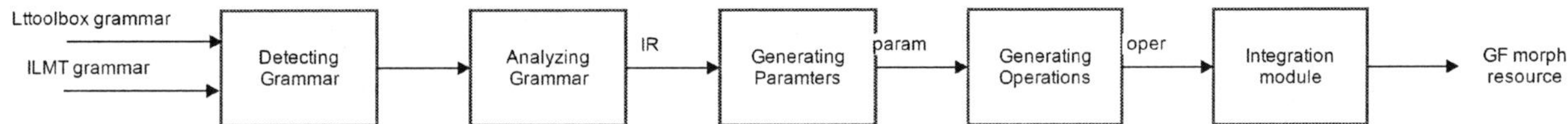

Figure 1: Module level Overview of our approach

is stored in its paradigm file with its root and all its forms. These word forms are listed in last varies first order. For example,

- Noun_m g_m case num means that Noun_m is a category depending on features g_m, case and num.
- case d o represents that case feature has values d and o. Similarly, g_m has value m. num has values s and p.
- Noun_m Gara, Gara, Gara, Gara, GaroM/-Garoz . means that the first word is the root form, and rest are its word forms in last varies fast order of category features(i.e, $<$m,d,s$>$, $<$m,d,p$>$, $<$m,o,s$>$, $<$m,o,p$>$).

3 Related Work

There's little work done on automatic resource sharing between frameworks. Some notable works include resource sharing between Apertium and Grammatical Framework (Gregoire and Ranta Aarne, 2014). In this paper, the author proposes an automatic approach to extract Apertium shallow-transfer rules from a GF bilingual grammar. The process of creating GF data from Lttoolbox grammar is done manually. They successfully created and tested the system with English-Spanish language pair. Also some work has been done to import Indian languages (Muhammad Humayoun and Ranta Aarne, 2011) into GF. However, this is manual process and it requires linguists. To the best of our knowledge, there exists no work addressing the automatic conversion from existing morph resources(ILMT/Lttoolbox) of Indian languages into GF.

4 Our Approach

In this section, we describe our approach of converting LTtoolbox and ILMT morph resources into GF morph resources. The steps of conversion is presented in the figure 1.

Our approach converts the morphological processors available either in XML or ILMT syntax format and converts them into Grammatical Framework. The key idea here is that Grammatical Framework is a programming language with a definite syntax and we need to transform the given morphological processors such that they adhere to Grammatical Framework's syntactic structure. This calls for the need to change morphological processors into non-ambiguous, permissible units which are supported by Grammatical Framework. Some examples of above mentioned challenges are as follows. Further details regarding these decisions are described in algorithms mentioned below.

- As already mentioned in above sections, Lttoolbox supports paradigms which depend on variable number of parameters whereas Grammatical Framework only supports dependence on pre-determined parameters. So we need to analyze all paradigms and their dependencies to find the specific occurrences and transform them into tabular syntax structure, supported by Grammatical Framework.

- Some attributes present in the source files (e.g. numeric attributes, duplicate attributes) cannot be transformed directly into GF e.g. parsarg = 0. We chose to modify the parameters to include the actual parameter value and other contextual information e.g. the parameter type, the paradigm name etc.

4.1 Detecting Grammar

In this step, we classify the user input as Lttoolbox or ILMT morph resource. This is a relatively simple step because of widely different syntaxes of both morph resources. We accomplish this using syntax-based heuristics.

4.2 Analyzing Grammar

In this step, we take the respective grammar, parse it and then convert into an intermediate representation (IR). The motivation behind this step is to reduce complexity for the following steps i.e Generating parameters and operations.

In the case of ILMT, the morph resource is present

across different sources. So we convert it into XML using the same structure as in Lttoolbox, to make the conversion process more generalized. Once we have the XML source, we will convert it into IR by using the algorithm shown in Algorithm.1.

Algorithm 1 " Algorithm for Analyze Grammar "

features = {} ▷ sdef - represents the set of all symbol definitions
for s ∈ sdef **do** ▷ s contains lexical features and lexical values
  features[s.lexical-feature].add(s.lexical-value)
paradigms = {} ▷ pardef - represents the set of paradigm definitions
for p ∈ pardef **do**
  root = p(n) ▷ root word
  for e ∈ p **do** ▷ e is an entry in paradigm definition ▷ e contains feature set and word form
    paradigms[root].add(e.feature-set,e.word-form)
return features,paradigms

In algorithm 1, we are converting symbol definitions and paradigm definitions into IR (i.e features and paradigms).

4.3 Generating Parameters

In this step, we use the features from IR to generate parameters and their constructors, using the algorithm shown in Algorithm 2. The function

---

Algorithm 2 " Algorithm for generating parameters "

for f ∈ features **do** ▷ features from IR ▷ f contains feature names and values
  buildParameters(f.name, f.value)

---

buildParameters generates GF syntax (parameters and corresponding constructors) for a given feature name and its values. For example calling the function buildParameters with arguments (Num,[num_s,num_p]) returns

```
Num = num_s | num_p;
```

Listing 5: " Example Parameter Syntax in GF "

4.4 Generating Operations

In this step, we use the IR (features, paradigms) to generate operations using the algorithm given in

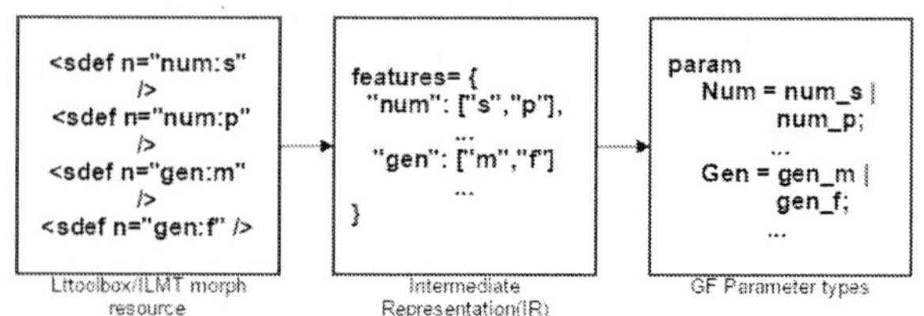

Figure 2: The entire process of generating parameters 1.Lttoolbox/ILMT morph as given by user 2.IR created in the previous step 3.GF morph resource parameters created in the present module.

Algorithm 3 " Algorithm for generating operations "

function   BUILDOPERATIONS(features, paradigms)
  for p ∈ paradigms **do**
    buildDecalaration(p,dependentFeatures)
      buildTable(features,p,dependentFeatures)
  return

Algorithm 3. The function buildOperations builds operations for each paradigm. As explained in the above section, each operation consists of declaration and description which are generated by buildDeclaration and buildTable respectively. To do this we need to keep track of all the features used for a paradigm. So we built a helper function which does this by iterating through all the entries in the paradigm.

For example, calling buildDeclaration with arguments (case,gen,num) produces the x1,,,,,,x8:Str -> Case => Gen => Num => Str (we used x1-x8 because each feature has two values, total possible values in table are 2x2x2 = 8).

The function buildTable recursively builds the table which is used to generate the possible word forms for a given lemma in GF, using the algorithm shown in Algorithm 4.

4.5 Code and Datasets

The entire code base has been written in Python. The description of datasets are shown in Table 1. Code and datasets are publicly available under open-source license.[1].

---

[1] https://github.com/harshavardhangsv/automaticMorphResourceConverter

Algorithm 4 " Algorithm for building table"
```
function BUILDTABLE(features,paradigm, de-
pendentfeatures)
    if dependentFeatures is empty then
        return
    for df ∈ dependentFeatures do
        for v ∈ features[df] do
            v => buildTable(features, paradigm,
rest(dependentFeatures))
                            ▷ rest(1,2,3) = 2,3
```

```
<pardef n="kAI/A__adj">
<e><p><l>A</l><r>A<s n="cat:adj"/><s n="case:d"/><s
n="gen:m"/><s n="num:s"/></r></p></e>
<e><p><l>l</l><r>A<s n="cat:adj"/><s n="case:d"/><s
n="gen:f"/><s n="num:s"/></r></p></e>
</pardef>
```

```
features = ["case":["case_d", "case_d"], "gen":
["gen_m","gen_f"], "num":["num_s","num_f"]];
paradigms = [
            (<case_d,gen_m,num:s>,"kAIA"),
            (<case_d,gen_f,num:s>,"kAIl"),
            ]
dependent_features = ["case","num","gen"]
```

```
kAIA_adj: (x1,,,,,,,,x8):Str -> {s: Case->Gen->Num}=\s ->  {
s= table -> {case_d => table{
    gen_m => table {
        num_s => "KAIA"
    };
    gen_f => table {
        num_s => "KALI'
    }..}
}
```

Figure 3: This figure explains the process of generating operations. 1.Lttool/ILMT morph resource given by user 2.variables state in IR form 3.GF syntax operations created from the buildTable

Dataset	# of paradigms	# of words
Hindi	57	26356
Tamil	254	34290
Oriya	45	2860
Bengali	148	5478

Table 1: Description of Datasets

5 Evaluation and Error Analysis

We measure the accuracy of the converter in the following way. The same text is given to both GF analyzer and the original source tool (LTtoolbox and ILMT). We verify that the output of GF analyzer and the original source tool is identical. Thus we ensure that information is faithfully transferred. We found that there is no loss of data for the chosen languages i.e Hindi, Oriya, Tamil and Bengali. This evaluation is repeated for various random news articles and 100% information was preserved in the output. However, we have come across with some problems in converting Sanskrit and Marathi morph resources. These problems are mainly caused due to presence of language-specific syntax which we had trouble in generalizing. Even though we had some troubles, we have found that, after analyzing files manually, our approach will still be able to make the automated conversion to around 65%.

6 Conclusion and Future Work

In this paper, we have explained the process of creating an automatic converter which deterministically converts morphological processor from different formats into GF format without any information loss for Hindi, Oriya and Tamil. We are presently working on other Indian languages such as Marathi, Sanskrit and Telugu. We have observed that if there exists any language specific morpho-syntactic information in the resource, conversion of such resources requires additional work. At present we are converting morph resources created in Lttoolbox and ILMT morph format.

In future we might come across a morphological processor developed in another framework. In order to bring the complete genericness into our tool, we want to modularize our system. We intend to develop a generic system that first asks the user about the format of their morphological processor and then activate the right module for the conversion. We hope that with our effort we will be able to offer a NLP resource to the community which will eradicate the barrier of framework differences.

References

Gregoire Dietrez and Ranta Aarne. 2014. *Sharing resources between free/open-source rule-based ma-*

chine translation systems: Grammatical Framework and Apertium. LREC.

Ithisree Jena, Dipti M. Sharma 2011. *Developing Oriya Morphological Analyzer Using Lt-Toolbox* . Communications in Computer and Information Science pp.124-129.

Mikel L. Forcada, Mireia Ginest-Rosell, Jacob Nordfalk, Jim ORegan, Sergio Ortiz-Rojas, Juan Antonio Prez-Ortiz, Felipe Snchez-Martnez, Gema Ramrez-Snchez and Francis M. Tyers 2011. *Apertium: a free/open-source platform for rule-based machine translation* . In Machine Translation: Volume 25, Issue 2 (2011), p. 127-144.

Muhammad Humayoun , Ranta Aarne 2011. *Developing Punjabi Morphology, Corpus and Lexicon* . Proceedings of the 24th Pacific Asia Conference on Language, Information and Computation.

Ranta Aarne 2003. *A revised version of the on-line GF tutorial, v1.0.*. In A. Beckmann and N. Preining, editors, ESSLLI Course Material I (2003).

Ranta Aarne 2004. *Grammatical Framework: A Type-Theoretical Grammar Formalism.* The Journal of Functional Programming 14(2) (2004) 145189.

Ranta Aarne 2009. *The GF Resource Grammar Library: A systematic presentation of the library from the linguistic point of view* . Linguistics in Language Technology, 2(2).

Ranta Aarne 2009. *Grammars as Software Libraries.* From Semantics to Computer Science, Cambridge University Press, Cambridge, pp. 281- 308.

Sampark: Machine Translation System among Indian languages 2009. http://tdildc.in/index.php?option=com_vertical &parentid=74, http://sampark.iiit.ac.in/.

Logistic Regression for Automatic Lexical Level Morphological Paradigm Selection for Konkani Nouns

Shilpa Desai
Department of Computer
Science and Technology
Goa University
sndesai@gmail.com

Jyoti Pawar
Department of Computer
Science and Technology
Goa University
jyotidpawar@gmail.com

Pushpak Bhattacharyya
Department of Computer
Science and Engineering
IIT-Patna
pb@cse.iitp.ac.in

Abstract

Automatic selection of morphological paradigm for a noun lemma is necessary to automate the task of building morphological analyzer for nouns with minimal human interventions. Morphological paradigms can be of two types namely surface level morphological paradigms and lexical level morphological paradigms. In this paper we present a method to automatically select lexical level morphological paradigms for Konkani nouns. Using the proposed concept of paradigm differentiating measure to generate a training data set we found that logistic regression can be used to automatically select lexical level morphological paradigms with an F-Score of 0.957.

1 Introduction

Morphological analysis is required for many NLP applications such as Spell Checkers, Text to Speech Systems, Rule Based Machine Translation, etc. Finite State Transducers (FSTs) are ideal for developing Morphological Analyzer for a language because they are computationally efficient, inherently bidirectional and can also be used for word generation. FST based Morphological Analyzers are based on word and paradigm model, wherein a word lemma is mapped to a corresponding Morphological Paradigm. A Morphological Paradigm is used to generate all possible word forms for a given word lemma. To develop a FST based Morphological Analyzer two resources namely Morphological Paradigm List and Morphological Lexicon are required. Morphological Paradigm List is prepared referring to grammar books, morphology related

linguistics thesis in Konkani and elaborate discussions with linguists. Lemmas[1] in the language are then mapped to appropriate Morphological Paradigms to create a Morphological Lexicon. Mapping of lemmas to Morphological Paradigms is time consuming when done manually.

Automating creation of Morphological Lexicon requires automatic mapping of lemmas to morphological paradigms. Morphological Paradigms can be defined at two level surface level and lexical level. At surface level two different morphological paradigms will generate a different Inflection Set for a given lemma whereas at lexical level two different morphological paradigms could generate same Inflection Set for a given lemma. Thus automatically choosing a correct morphological paradigm at the lexical level cannot be based on Suffix Evidence Value as in previous used methods (Carlos et al., 2009).

In this paper, we present the use of logistic regression for Automatic Lexical Level Paradigm Selection designed to facilitate the development of Morphological Lexicon. Here we propose the concept of *paradigm differentiating measure* (*pdm*) which has been used to map lemmas to Lexical Level Morphological Paradigms.

2 Related Work

Automatic mapping of word to a paradigm have been done earlier for other languages. An n-gram-based model has been developed (Sanchez et al., 2012; Linden and Tuovila, 2009) to select a single paradigm in cases where more than one paradigm generates the same set of word forms. These systems use POS information or some additional user in-

---

[1] Citation form of words

D S Sharma, R Sangal and E Sherly. Proc. of the 12th Intl. Conference on Natural Language Processing, pages 203–208,
Trivandrum, India. December 2015. ©2015 NLP Association of India (NLPAI)

put from native language speakers to map words to paradigms, instead of a corpus alone.

Lexicon acquisition methods (Carlos et al., 2009; Clement et al., 2004; Forsberg et al., 2006; Mohammed et al., 2012) exist for many languages that extract lemmas from a corpus and map them to morphological paradigms. Functional Morphology has been used to define morphology for languages like Swedish and Finnish, and tools based on Functional Morphology, namely Extract (Forsberg et al., 2006) which suggest new words for a lexicon and map them to paradigms, have been developed. To be able to use a tool like Extract, the morphology of the language has to be fitted into the Functional Morphology definition.

3 Terminology and Notations Used

Definition (Root, Stem, Base, Prefix and Suffix): A *Root* is the basic part of a lexeme[2] which cannot be further analyzed, using either inflectional or derivational morphology. *Root* is that part of word-form that remains when all derivational and inflectional affixes have been removed. A *Stem* is that part of the word form that remains when inflectional suffixes have been removed. A *Base* (b_i) is that part of the word form to which affixes of any kind can be added. It is a generic term which could refer to a *Root* or a *Stem*. A *Prefix* is a bound morpheme that is attached at the beginning of a *Base*. A *Suffix* $s_i \in \sum^*$ is a bound morpheme that is attached at the end of a *Base*.

Definition (Rule) An ordered 3-tuple (α, β, γ) is said to be a *Rule* used to convert a string x_i to a string y_i where $\alpha=$"ADD/DELETE" is an operation performed on input string x_i; $\beta=$position at which the operation specified in α is to be performed on string x_i; $\gamma=z_i$ is the argument for the operation to be performed.

Example: If $x_i=$धांवप$(dhaa.Nvapa)$[3] and *Rule*= ("DELETE", "END", "प(pa)") where $\alpha=$ "DELETE"; $\beta=$"END"; $\gamma=$"प(pa)" with respect to above Definition $y_i=$धांव$(dhaa.Nva)$.

Definition (Base Formation Rule (BFR)): An ordered n-tuple of *Rules*

which is used to convert lemma l_i to base b_i is said to be a *Base Formation Rule BFR*.

Example: If $l_i=$भास$(bhasa)$[4] and $BFR=$ (("DELETE", "END", "स(sa)"),("ADD", "END", "श(sha)")) with respect to above Definition $b_i=$भाश$(bhasha)$.

Definition (Morphological Paradigm): An ordered tuple $(\phi, \{(\psi_1, \omega_1, \gamma_1),...,(\psi_n, \omega_n, \gamma_n)\})$ where

- $\phi=p_i$, a unique identifier for the ith paradigm,

- $\psi_j=BFR$ the Base Formation Rule corresponding to the jth Base,

- $\omega_j = S_k$ a set of (suffix[5], grammatical feature) ordered pairs corresponding to the jth Base and

- $\gamma_j = $ A boolean flag which is set to 1 if corresponding suffixes uniquely identify the paradigm i.e. corresponding (ψ_j, ω_j) form the *paradigm differentiating measure*[6].

- n is the total number distinct bases for the paradigm,

is said to be a *Morphological Paradigm* which is used to generate the Inflectional Set i.e. all the inflectional word forms, for the input lemma.

Example: When the paradigm is given by

- $\phi=P11$,

- $\psi_1=$ (("DELETE", "END", "स(sa)"),("ADD", "END", "श(sha)")) is the BFR corresponding to the first Base.

- $\omega_1 = \{($ःॕ(e), singular oblique case), (ःॕक(eka), singular oblique accusative case), (ःॕकूच $(ekaUch)$, singular oblique accusative case with emphatic clitic), ... $\}$.

- $\gamma_1 = 1$

- $\psi_2=$ ("DELETE", "END", "∅") is the BFR corresponding to the second Base.

---

[2]Lexeme is the basic unit of meaning. It is an abstract unit of morphological analysis in linguistics, that roughly corresponds to a set of forms taken by a single word

[3]धांवप$(dhaa.Nvapa)$ $(to\ run)$

[4]भास$(bhasa)$ $(language)$

[5]Here suffix could be made up of more than one suffix concatenated with each other

[6]*paradigm differentiating measure* has been defined in the following subsection.

- $\omega_2 = \{($◌ो(o), plural direct case$)$, $($◌ोच (och), plural direct case with emphatic clitic$)$, ...$\}$

- $\gamma_2 = 0$

- n=2,

If the input lemma = भास(bhaasa), then the first Base is भाश(bhaasha) and the second Base is भास(bhaasa). The word forms generated by the above paradigm are as follows: {भाशे (bhaashe), भाशेक (bhaasheka), भाशेकूच (bhaashekaUch), ... भासो (bhaaso), भासोच (bhaasoch), ...}

Definition (Inflectional Set) A set $W_{p_i l_j}$ of all possible word forms generated by a Morphological Paradigm with p_i as paradigm identifier, for a lemma l_j is said to be the **Inflectional Set** for lemma l_j with respect to paradigm p_i.

Example: If $p_i{=}P10$, a verb Morphological Paradigm and $l_j{=}walk$ with respect to above Definition $W_{p_i l_j}{=}\{walk,\ walks,\ walking,\ walked\}$.

4   Types of Morphological Paradigms:

A Morphological Paradigm is used to generate the inflectional word forms for a given input lemma. At the Surface Level, a Morphological Paradigm generates a set of word forms which can be expressed in an abstract manner as $\{b_i.s_j$: where b_i is the Base; s_j is the Suffix$\}$. At the Lexical Level, a Morphological Paradigm generates a set of word forms which can be expressed in an abstract manner as $\{l_i{+}$grammatical features : where l_i is the lemma$\}$.

Example: If the input lemma $l_i{=}dance$, Word forms generated at Surface Level are $\{dancing,\ danced,\ dances,\ ...\}$ where $b_i{=}danc$. Word forms generated at Lexical Level are $\{dance + present\ continuous,\ dance + past\ perfect,\ dance + present,\ ...\}$.

Morphological Paradigms can differ from each other either at the Surface Level or at the Lexical Level

Surface Level difference between Morphological Paradigms: Two Morphological Paradigms are said to differ at surface level when they generate different set of word forms at the Surface Level for a given input lemma. Surface level difference implies that at least one of the following two conditions is true.

- $\exists$ at least one BFR that is not the same amongst them.

- $\exists$ at least one suffix which is not the same amongst them.

Lexical Level difference between Morphological Paradigms: Two distinct Morphological Paradigms are said to differ at lexical level when they generate same set of word forms at the Surface Level. Lexical level difference implies the following condition is true

- $\exists$ at least one word form which has different grammatical features in the two paradigms.

Each Morphological Paradigm is unique either at the Surface or Lexical level. We refer to the feature which makes the Morphological Paradigm unique as *paradigm differentiating measure* and is defined as follows

Definition (Paradigm Differentiating Measure) The ordered tuple $(\psi_j,\ \omega_j)$ with respect to Morphological Paradigm Definition above is called *paradigm differentiating measure* if it occurs only once across all possible paradigms.

Example 1: If set A and B represent two sets of word forms generated by two different paradigms p_1 and p_2 respectively which differ at the surface level, for a given lemma. Let set A and B be given as follows:

A= $\{\ (b_1.s_1,f_1),\quad (b_1.s_2,f_2),\quad (b_1.s_3,f_3),\ (b_1.s_4,f_4), (b_1.s_5,f_5)\}$

B= $\{\ (b_1.s_1,f_1),\quad (b_1.s_6,f_2),\quad (b_1.s_3,f_3),\ (b_1.s_4,f_4), (b_1.s_5,f_5)\}$

where b_j is a base obtained using ψ_j, s_j is the suffix obtained using ω_j and f_j is the corresponding grammatical feature.

From set A and B we observe that the word forms differ only at the second entry namely $(b_1.s_2,f_2) \in$ A and $(b_1.s_6,f_2) \in$ B hence the corresponding $(\psi_1,\ \omega_2)$ in p_1 and $(\psi_1,\ \omega_2)$ in p_2 are the *paradigm differentiating measure*.

Example 2: If set C and D represent two sets of word forms generated by two different paradigms p_1 and p_2 respectively which differ only at the lexical level, for a given lemma. Let set C and D be given as follows:

C= { $(b_1.s_1,f_1)$, $(b_1.s_1,f_2)$, $(b_1.s_3,f_3)$, $(b_1.s_4,f_4)$, $(b_1.s_5,f_5)$}
D= { $(b_1.s_1,f_1)$, $(b_1.s_3,f_2)$, $(b_1.s_3,f_3)$, $(b_1.s_4,f_4)$, $(b_1.s_5,f_5)$}

where b_j is a base obtained using ψ_j, s_j is the suffix obtained using ω_j and f_j is the corresponding grammatical feature.

From set C and D we observe that the word forms are same at surface level but corresponding grammatical features differ only at the second entry namely $(b_1.s_1,f_2) \in$ A and $(b_1.s_3,f_2) \in$ B hence the corresponding (ψ_1, ω_2) in p_1 and (ψ_1, ω_2) in p_2 are the *paradigm differentiating measure*.

5 Lexical Level Morphological Paradigm Selection for Konkani Nouns

A Konkani noun lemma can be mapped to more than one Morphological Paradigm. The noun Morphological Paradigms are such that they all differ from each other either at the surface level or at the lexical level. It is not possible to implement a Rule Based System to map noun lemmas to Morphological Paradigms due to ambiguity in paradigm selection presented next.

5.1 Ambiguity in Paradigm Selection for Konkani Nouns

Ambiguity in Paradigm Selection for Konkani Nouns exists due to the following reasons

1. Formative Suffix attachment: There is no known linguistic rule[7] to decide which Formative Suffix is to be attached to the Base to obtain the Inflectional Set. This gives rise to ambiguity in choosing the appropriate paradigm.

Example: When noun lemma does not end with a vowel as in case of the noun lemma पाल(*paala*)(*lizard*); then three possible formative suffixes could be attached which gives rise to three possible Stems namely पाला, पाली, पाले (*paalaa, paalI, paale*). Amongst these three possible Stems only पाली (*paalI*) is the correct choice. However no linguistic rule can be used to arrive at the correct stem thus causing an ambiguity in choosing a correct paradigm for the input noun lemma.

---

[7]Linguistic rule based on noun lemma ending characters alone in absence of knowledge of nouns grammatical gender

2. Multiple paradigm for single noun lemma: A single noun lemma could be mapped to more than one noun paradigm. This gives rise to another ambiguity is paradigm selection.

Example: For noun lemma मराठी(*maraThI*)(*marathi language or marathi speaking person*); the same lemma will map to two different paradigms for the two different senses namely *marathi language* and *marathi speaking person*. In such a case simply computing Suffix Evidence Value SEV is not enough to resolve ambiguity.

3. Lexical level differences in paradigms: Some paradigm differ only at lexical level and generate the same Inflectional Set at surface level. This is another ambiguity challenge faced for paradigm selection.

Example: For noun lemma पान(*paana*)(*leaf*); the same lemma will map to two different paradigms which are same at the surface level. This is because a single form in such paradigm have two different grammatical features as in case of पाना(*paanaa*) which could be *singular oblique form* or *direct plural form* which is a type of ambiguity.

5.2 Problem Statement

Given a set of noun lemmas $LX_N = \{l_i : i = 1$ to n, where n is number of lemmas which map to same surface level morphological paradigms}; a set of Lexical Noun Paradigm List $P_LN_L = \{(p_i, \{(BFR_j, s_l,g_l, pdm_l)\}) : p_i$ is the paradigm identifier, BFR_j is the Base Formation Rule, s_l is the stem formative suffix corresponding to the lth suffix group, g_l is the group identifier corresponding to the lth suffix group, pdm_l is the *paradigm differentiating measure* flag corresponding to the lth stem formative suffix, $i = 1$ to q, where q is number of noun paradigms in L, $j = 1$ to r, where r is number of Bases corresponding to the ith noun paradigm and $l = 1$ to s, where s is number of Noun Suffix Groups corresponding to the jth Base of i_{th} noun paradigms} and Lexical Training Data Set generate Lexical Level Noun Morphological Lexicon set $LX_{NM} = \{(l_i,p_j) : l_i \in LX_N$, and $p_j \in P_LN_L\}$

5.3 Design of Lexical Level Noun Morphological Paradigm Selection

A training data set is prepared for each Lexical Level Paradigm. The features used in the data set are listed in Table 1.

Table 1: Data Set Features for Lexical Level Paradigm Selection.

Name	Feature Description
PID	The paradigm identifier.
FreqDSF	Number of times the direct singular form of the noun occurs in the corpus
FreqSOF	Number of times the oblique singular form of the noun occurs in the corpus.
FreqPOF	Number of times the oblique plural form of the noun occurs in the corpus.

These features were chosen after observing that, in Konkani Lexical Level Paradigms, for one paradigm, the Direct Singular Form (DSF) and Direct Plural Form (DPF) are the same while for the other paradigm, Direct Plural Form (DPF) and Plural Oblique Form (POF) were the same. In general, these features correspond to those word forms that have multiple grammatical roles i.e. those word forms which cause ambiguity. The intuition behind choosing these features was that, if in one paradigm a particular word form has multiple grammatical roles, than its corresponding relative frequency should differ from the other paradigm where it has a single grammatical role.

Example: Let p_i and p_j be two paradigms which are same at surface level but differ at lexical level. Let l_i be the input lemma. In paradigm p_i, let the word form w_i have two grammatical roles as in case of Konkani word फातर(*phaatara*) (*stone*) which is both Direct Singular Form (DSF) and Direct Plural Form (DPF). In paradigm p_j, let the same word form w_i have only one grammatical role which is Direct Singular Form (DSF) and has a different form w_j for Direct Plural Form (DPF) which is also Plural Oblique Form (POF). Thus in the data set for paradigm p_i, frequency of DSF and POF will follow a different pattern when compared to frequency of DSF and POF in p_j.

To select appropriate machine learning model for the training data set various machine learning algorithms were tested on the training data set. The best performing model namely Logistic Regression was chosen as the learning model as it works well on numeric data, is simple and performed better than other machine learning classifiers as illustrated in Table 2. We created a training data set with 356 noun lemmas and assigned the paradigm identifier manually. This was used as a training model to pick lexical level paradigm for the input lemma. The algorithm for the Lexical Level Morphological Paradigm Selection is illustrated in Figure 1.

Algorithm: Lexical Level Morphological Paradigm Selection

Input: Noun lemma l_i, Lexical Training Data Set TDS, set of unique corpus words W_C, Lexical Noun Paradigm List ($P_L N_L$), Pruned Relevant paradigm set R_P, Surface Noun Paradigm List ($P_L N_S$)

Output: Relevant paradigm set with lexical paradigms R_P.

/ Select appropriate Lexical Level Paradigm */*
For each $p_i \in R_P$
   If $p_i \in P_L N_L$
     / Compute corresponding Feature Set FS for Lexical Level Paradigm*/*
     $FS = $ computeFeatureSet(l_i,W_C, p_i, $P_L N_S$)
     $R_{p_i} = $ applyLogisticRegression(TDS,FS)
     Replace p_i with R_{p_i} in R_P
   End If
End For

Figure 1: Algorithm: Lexical Level Morphological Paradigm Selection for Konkani Noun.

6 Experimental Results and Evaluation

The goal of the experiment was to identify a machine learning model to automatically assign lexical level morphological paradigms to noun lemmas. To choose the model for lexical level paradigm assignment, we ran various classification algorithms on our development data sets created with features listed in Table 1 using 10 fold cross validation to determine the best training model. The performance of machine learning classifiers on our data set are tabulated in Table 2. Here Precision, Recall and F-score are the weighted average values generated.

Table 2: Model Selection for Lexical Level Paradigm Selection.

Algorithm	Precision	Recall	F-Score
Bayesian Classifiers			
Naive Bayes	0.796	0.815	0.785
Bayes Net	0.787	0.806	0.79
Function Classifiers			
Logistic	0.94	0.941	0.94
Multilayer-Perceptron	0.821	0.834	0.822
RBFNetwork	0.806	0.82	0.79
SimpleLogistic	0.958	0.958	**0.957**
SMO	0.839	0.798	0.723
Instance-Based Classifiers			
B1	0.84	0.846	0.842
KStar	0.828	0.834	0.807
Ensemble Classifiers			
AdaBoost	0.915	0.916	0.912
Bagging	0.937	0.938	0.938
Random Sub Space	0.898	0.896	0.887
Decorate	0.952	0.952	0.951
Logit Boost	0.932	0.933	0.93
Rule-Based Classifiers			
PART Decision List	0.94	0.941	0.94
Ridor	0.94	0.941	0.94
ZeroR	0.61	0.781	0.685
Decision Tree Classifiers			
Random Forest	0.928	0.93	0.928
Logistic Model Tree	0.977	0.978	**0.977**
REPTree	0.936	0.935	0.936

Analyzing the performance of the various classifiers from Table 2, We observe that Logistic Regression based models namely SimpleLogistic and Logistic Model Tree outperform other models. Hence Logistic Regression was chosen as a training model to select relevant lexical level morphological paradigm.

7 Conclusion

In this paper we present a method to automatically select a lexical level morphological paradigm for a Konkani noun lemma. We define *paradigm differentiating measure* and use the same to select features and prepare the training data set. The data set thus created in used to identify logistic regression as an appropriate model to select lexical level morphological paradigms for Konkani nouns with an F-score of 0.957.

References

Carlos Sujay Cohan, Choudhury Monojit and Dandapat Sandipan. 2009. *Large-Coverage Root Lexicon Extraction for Hindi*. Proceedings of the 12th Conference of the European Chapter of the ACL (EACL 2009), Athens, Greece.

Clement Lionel, Sagot Benoit and Lang Bernard. 2004. *Morphology Based Automatic Acquisition of Large-coverage Lexica*. Proceedings of the Fourth International Conference on Language Resources and Evaluation (LREC'04), Lisbon, Portugal.

Markus Forsberg, Harald Hammarström and Aarne Ranta. 2006. *Morphological Lexicon Extraction from Raw Text Data*. Advances in Natural Language Processing, 5th International Conference on NLP, FinTAL 2006, Turku, Finland.

Lindén Krister and Tuovila Jussi. 2009. *Corpusbased paradigm selection for morphological entries*. Proceedings of NODALIDA 2009.

Attia Mohammed, Samih Younes, Shaalan Khaled and Genabith Josef. 2012. *The Floating Arabic Dictionary: An Automatic Method for Updating a Lexical Database through the Detection and Lemmatization of Unknown Words*. Proceedings of COLING 2012, Mumbai, India.

Vícor M. Sánchez-Cartagena, Miquel Esplá-Gomis, Felipe Sánchez-Martínez and Juan Antonio Pérez-Ortiz. 2012. *Choosing the correct paradigm for unknown words in rule-based machine translation systems*. Proceedings of the Third International Workshop on Cambridge University Free/Open-Source Rule-Based Machine Translation, Gothenburg, Sweden.

Ruchi: Rating Individual Food Items in Restaurant Reviews

**Burusothman Ahiladas, Paraneetharan Saravanaperumal, Sanjith Balachandran,
Thamayanthy Sripalan** and **Surangika Ranathunga**
Department of Computer Science and Engineering
University of Moratuwa, Katubedda 10400, Sri Lanka
{brusoth.10,parane.10,sanjith.10,thamayanthy.10,surangika}@cse.mrt.ac.lk

Abstract

Restaurant recommendation systems are capable of recommending restaurants based on various aspects such as location, facilities and price range. There exists some research that implements restaurant recommendation systems, as well as some famous online recommendation systems such as Yelp. However, automatically rating individual food items of a restaurant based on online customer reviews is an area that has not received much attention. This paper presents Ruchi, a system capable of rating individual food items in restaurants. Ruchi makes use of Named Entity Recognition (NER) techniques to identify food names in restaurant reviews. Typed dependency technique is used to identify opinions associated with different food names in a single sentence, thus it was possible to carry out entity-level sentiment analysis to rate individual food items instead of sentence-level sentiment analysis as done by previous research.

1 Introduction

Today, many factors affect a person's selection of a particular restaurant to dine in. People can find information on factors such as price, wifi and service from a restaurant's website and/or brochures. However, information about some important factors is not directly available. Ratings of individual dishes in restaurants is one such factor that is not directly available. Therefore it is common nowadays for people to rely on the reviews and ratings in restaurant review sites given by other customers. However, reading each customer review on restaurant review sites is time consuming, boring and exhaustive. This becomes more complex if someone wishes to search for a particular food item that he is interested in.

Existing restaurant recommendation systems such as Yelp do not have the facility to rate the individual food items of a restaurant. Moreover, as far as we are aware, existing research on restaurant recommendation systems has not focused on rating individual food items of restaurants, except for the work of Trevisiol et al. (2014).

This paper presents Ruchi (Ruchi means taste in Sinhala and Tamil, the two local languages in Sri Lanka), which is a system for rating individual food items (both food and beverages) in restaurants by automatically analyzing customer reviews. It combines the techniques of machine learning, natural language processing and information retrieval.

In order to rate and recommend individual food items, it was necessary to identify food names in customer reviews, and the customer opinions associated with them. Food names in reviews are identified using a trained NER model. For this purpose, a corpus[1] created from online customer reviews for restaurants was automatically annotated with food names extracted from various sources. As far as we are aware, this is the only freely available comprehensive corpus annotated with food names. Opinions related to these identified food items are extracted using a typed dependency parser. We then perform entity-level sentiment analysis to find the polarity of these opinions. Finally individual food items are rated based on the polarities of all the opinions received for each of these food items.

The rest of the paper is organized as follows. Next section discusses related work. Section three gives an overview of sentiment analysis. Section four discusses the data collection process. Section five discusses research and development work. Section six contains evaluation and discussion, and finally section seven concludes the paper.

---

[1] https://raw.githubusercontent.com/
brusoth09/Ruchi/master/res/review_train

D S Sharma, R Sangal and E Sherly. Proc. of the 12th Intl. Conference on Natural Language Processing, pages 209–214,
Trivandrum, India. December 2015. ©2015 NLP Association of India (NLPAI)

2 Related Work

Recommendation systems are available for many domains, including online business, specific products, restaurants and movies. As for restaurant recommendation systems, a very popular recommendation system is Yelp[2]. In Yelp, restaurant profiles are rated using a large data set with customer ratings and reviews. Yelp is capable of recommending the best restaurants, but not individual food items. Tripadvisor[3] also provides restaurant recommendations. It recommends a set of restaurants in a country that have famous food items, however these food items are not rated.

Snyder and Barzilay (2007) used the good grief algorithm to rate multiple aspects in restaurants. In their approach, each review is given a rating of 1 to 5 for five different aspects in a restaurant review: food, service, ambiance, value, and overall experience. But they did not rate the individual food items. Gupta et al. (2015) also discussed about sentiment based summarizing of restaurant reviews based on three aspects: food, ambiance and service.

As far as we are aware, the work by Trevisiol et al. (2014) is the only research that focused on rating individual food items using customer reviews. Their BuonAppetito system is capable of recommending personalized menus in a restaurant. In this system, a menu is considered to be comprised of food items. Food items are rated based on the customer opinions in the customer text reviews. The main difference between their approach and our approach is that they have carried out sentence-level sentiment analysis. In contrast, we carry out entity-level sentiment analysis. This is because one sentence of a review can contain more than one food item and associated opinions. For example, consider the sentence "Pizza was tasty but pasta was terrible". Here two food items are mentioned in one sentence - one has a positive opinion and the other one has a negative opinion. Therefore, if sentence-level sentiment analysis was performed, the overall review will be neutral. Despite the fact that we used a data set different to what was used by Trevisiol et al., we note that our recommendation system achieved a better precision and F1 measure than what was received by Trevisiol et al.

3 Sentiment Analysis

Sentiment analysis is a natural language processing technique that involves collecting and categorizing opinions (Liu, 2010). Sentiment analysis (or classification) can be done at different levels.

In document-level sentiment analysis, a whole opinion document is classified as a positive or negative sentiment (Liu, 2010; Liu, 2012). Document-level sentiment analysis assumes that each document expresses opinion on only one entity. More fine-grained analysis can be done using sentence-level sentiment analysis. In this level, each sentence is classified as positive, negative, or neutral. However, sentence-level sentiment analysis is not capable of handling cases where a single sentence contains opinions on multiple entities. Thus entity and aspect-level analysis can be done to obtain better insight to customer opinions. At aspect-level, opinions on multiple aspects (e.g. food, service, ambiance, value and overall experience aspects of the restaurant entity, or the size and color aspects of a mobile phone entity) are analyzed.

In this research, different food items could be considered as different aspects of the food entity in restaurants. Note that food is considered an entity here, rather than an aspect of a restaurant, as considered by Snyder and Barzilay (2007), and Gupta et al. (2015). However, we see that using the term aspect-level sentiment analysis is slightly misleading in our context, because in its true sense, a food item is not really an aspect of food, as opposed to color being an aspect of a mobile phone. Rather, in our context, we see a food item as a sub-entity of the food entity. Therefore in this paper, the term entity-level sentiment analysis is used.

4 Data Collection

Data collection had two aspects - collecting restaurant reviews and collecting food names.

Multiple sources for review collection were identified. These are Yelp, CityGrid[4] and tasty.lk[5]. One of the biggest issues with customer review system is opinion spam (Ott et al., 2013). Fake reviews can lead to false conclusions. We only used Yelp data source in our final system because Yelp has its very own spam filtering mechanism.

Food names were collected from the A-Z of Food and Drink dictionary published by Oxford

---

University (food Dictionary, 2015), food time-line (food list, 2015) and the Oregon State Glossary of food items (state food list, 2015).

5 Rating Individual Food Items in Restaurant Reviews

Figure 1 shows our overall approach for rating food items based on customer reviews. This has four main steps: extracting food names from customer reviews, associating opinions with each food name in a review, calculating the sentiment value for the given opinion, and finally rating the food item using all the sentiment scores recorded for it.

A NER system proceeded by a pre-processing step was used to extract food names from customer reviews. This NER system is particularly trained for food domain using our food list. Opinion word associated with each food item is determined using a typed dependency parser, and phrases that contain only one subject (i.e. a food item) are created. Sentiment analysis tool in the StanfordNLP toolkit is used for sentiment analysis. We used a modified version of Suresh et al. (2014)'s ranking algorithm for rating food items using the sentiment scores. Calculated ratings for the individual food items are finally saved in a persistent storage.

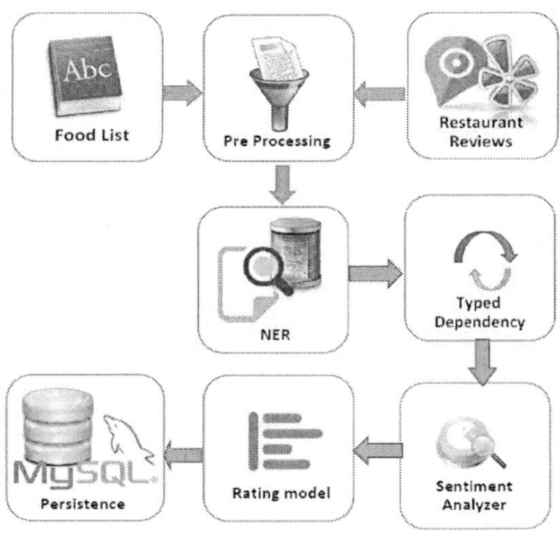

Figure 1: Overall system architecture

5.1 Pre-processing

In the pre-processing module, we focused on getting various data sources to a usable format for the NER module. Stemming, language detection, and symbol removing are these pre-processing steps.

5.2 Food Name Extraction

Named Entity Recognition (NER) was used for food name extraction. An NER model trained for the food name domain can be used to extract food names from sentences without explicitly searching for word tokens. POS tagging can be used to get the noun phrase from sentences, so that while training the NER, we can search only for noun phrases to tag food names.

Apache OpenNLP machine learning toolkit [6] was used for NER purpose. OpenNLP toolkit has NameFinder API for NER. It uses Maximum Entropy principle to classify entities using a pre-trained data model. Tokenized sentence should be given as input to NameFinder to predict categorized entities.

To make use of NER to identify food names in restaurant reviews, a corpus annotated with food names was required. Since such corpus was not available, we had to create one. We automated the process of creating a corpus by using the food names we collected from various sources. Figure 2 shows the process of creating this annotated corpus. We picked 150,000 reviews to create this corpus. From these reviews, about 300,000 sentences contained food names and thus got automatically annotated.

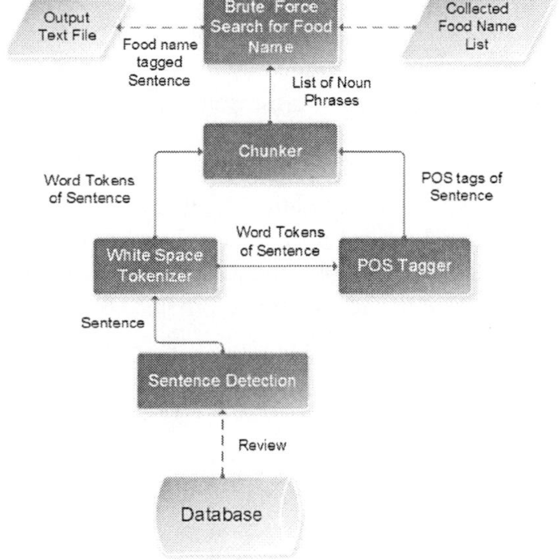

Figure 2: Process of creating the annotated corpus

First, each review was broken into its constituent sentences. Sentence detector in the

---

[6]https://opennlp.apache.org/

OpenNLP toolkit was used to break reviews into sentences using punctuation characters. Then, each of these sentences was tokenized and POS tagged. The whitespace tokenizer and the POS tagger (respectively) in the OpenNLP toolkit were used for these tasks. The POS annotated tokens were then sent to the chunker, which combines these tokens into syntactically correlated parts of words, such as noun groups and verb groups. This was required since some food items have more than one token. Finally, the noun groups are checked against the food name list we have prepared, and matching noun phrases are tagged with a unique tag ($< START : food >$ $food\_name < END >$) to identify food item names.

Now this annotated corpus could be used for NER. However, sometimes the output was just a part of the actual food name (e.g.: pepperoni pizza was identified when the actual name was Italian pepperoni pizza). This was because the dish names of most of the restaurants are not just the standard food names included in our food list.

A post-processing technique was used to eliminate this problem. This post-processing step is based on the observation that the common features (food names) come as noun phrases. So we first picked up the noun phrases from each sentence using POS tags and checked each phrase with our NER predicted food names. This process considers noun phrases around any food item as part of that food name. If a phrase contains the predicted name, then it will be considered as a food name. It is equally possible to apply this post-processing technique while annotating the corpus. However, we decided against it in order to make our corpus as general as possible, in order to use it for food name detection in a different type of application, say identifying food names in a supermarket context.

5.3 Sentiment Analysis

In our system, we are rating individual food items, therefore sentiment extraction is done at entity-level. Sentences may contain several subjects with different opinions. Stanford typed dependency representation (De Marneffe and Manning, 2008) is used to find the opinion associated with each food item in a sentence, and to create phrases that contain only one subject (i.e., a food name).

Many researchers have mentioned that opinion words are usually adjective or adverb. Gupta et al. (2015) have used two grammatical relations - amod and nsubj, to determine the noun that an adjective modifies. amod, short for adjectival modifier is any adjectival phrase that serves to modify the meaning of the noun phrase. nsubj, short for nominal subject is a noun phrase, which is the syntactic subject of a clause. In nsubj relation, there is a possibility that both words involved are nouns so we have to check for the presence of adjective in the relation. Other than these two grammatical relations, we also used advmod, which is the short form for adjectival modifier. This is because adverbs can also refer to opinion words.

First, opinion words are identified. Then other words that have grammatical relationship with food and opinion words are identified. After identifying all the words, we create opinion phrases containing only one subject.

Once the opinion phrases are identified, their sentiment orientation is determined by the sentiment analysis tool. Sentiment analysis tool in the StanfordNLP toolkit was used for this purpose. Sentiment analysis tool in the StanfordNLP toolkit uses deep learning technique. This technique uses a recursive neural sensor network to compute compositional vector representations for phrases of variable length and syntactic type. These representations will then be used as features to classify each phrase.

Other than the deep learning method in the StanfordNLP sentiment analysis tool, we also experimented with few other machine learning techniques (multilayer perceptron neural network, Support Vector Machine (SVM), PART, REPtree, Random Forest and J48) to determine the sentiment polarity of phrases. Since our system is for restaurants, restaurant reviews were used to train these algorithms. 1150 reviews were manually tagged according to Stanford Sentiment Treebank and were used to train the model.

StanfordNLP sentiment scores are: 4 - Very Positive, 3 - Positive, 2 - Neutral, 1 - Negative, 0 - Very Negative.

In the Treebank representation, training data structure is a binary tree. In the StanfordNLP sentiment analysis process, first the individual words are assigned a sentiment score. Then two words are combined and a single score is assigned to the combined words. This process continues combining word with word, phrase with word and phrase with phrase. Finally a sentiment score for the complete opinion phrase can be obtained.

5.4 Rating System

Rating system aims at scoring the food items in a restaurant based on customer reviews, using their sentiment weight. In order to rate a particular food item, sentiment weights assigned to it across all of the reviews should be considered.

In order to rate the food items using weak and strong positive and negative words, we first built a subjectivity lexicon. A subjectivity lexicon is a list of positive or negative opinion words. We created a master list that contains this subjectivity lexicon (each word in the lexicon has a sentiment weight), an intensifier word list (really, very, too, such etc.), and a negation word list (no, not etc.). We prepared the subjectivity lexicon from AFINN-111 word list[7] and the restaurant reviews that were not used to test the system. The POS tagged reviews are fed into our rating algorithm.

Our rating algorithm is an extension of Suresh et al. (2014)'s opinion score assignment algorithm. Suresh's algorithm focused on word-level scoring. However, in our approach, we focused on sentence-level scoring since word-level scoring mostly relies on sentiment weight of individual words and it fails to calculate rate for complex sentences. For example, if you consider the sentence "pizza was good, not service", this sentence has 2 opinion phrase and word-level score gives a wrong rating for pizza.

The rating algorithm takes polarity tagged phrases as input and provides a scoring value depending on the polarity of the phrase. If the word is POS tagged as an adverb or an adjective, it is considered as an opinion word. If the word appeared in a master list where all possible polarity words are classified according to sentiment weight, the score is calculated according to the sentiment weight of the word.

In the next step, if the opinion word is POS-tagged as a superlative sentiment, the score is increased or decreased by 2. If the opinion word is POS-tagged as comparative sentiment, the score is increased or decreased by 1. Words that modify the polarity (using negation word e.g. no) and intensifiers (e.g. too, very) are also considered for scoring the opinion word. Final score converges to

a value between 1 to 5 according to the sentiment score.

6 Results

Experiments were carried out to validate our (1) corpus creation process, (2) food name extraction, (3) sentiment analysis, and (4) the overall process.

Corpus creation process: In order to validate our corpus creation, a sample set of reviews containing 1000 sentences was randomly selected from the tagged corpus. Then these sentences were manually inspected to see how the tagging process has performed. This manual investigation identified 1898 occurrences of food names in these 1000 sentences. Out of these 1898 occurrences, 71.97% food names have been correctly tagged. It was noticed that sometimes only a part of a long food name was tagged.

Food name extraction: We used 1219 review sentences with manually tagged food names to evaluate the NER approaches. We achieved 63.2% precision, and 83.5% recall by using Maximum Entropy model technique of OpenNLP toolkit.

Sentiment analysis: We used 1150 sentiment sentences hand selected from restaurant reviews that included food names, and sentiments of each of these sentences were manually tagged. Our sentiment evaluation results obtained for different machine learning techniques are summarized in Table 1. However, after training the sentiment model for the restaurant context using the deep learning technique of StanfordNLP toolkit, we achieved 85.74109% accuracy, 82.9684% recall, 98.2708% precision and 89.9736% F1-measure. Deep learning technique is very promising. Therefore we used deep learning in our final system. For this experiment, our sentiment classification demonstrated an improvement of 6.7% over StanfordNLP baseline. We were able to achieve this because we used a trained model containing food item names.

Overall process: For the overall evaluation of the system, reviews were manually tagged with ratings. For each sentence in a review, all the food names and the corresponding opinion were tagged by human annotators. Whether the opinion rate is 1 to 5 (very negative to very positive) was also identified.

It is easy to judge whether an opinion of the sentence is positive or negative. However, deciding the opinion rate (score) can be somewhat subjec-

---

[7]http://www2.imm.dtu.dk/pubdb/views/
publication_details.php?id=6010

Table 1: Machine learning algorithm result for sentiment classification

Algorithm	precision	recall	F1
NeuralNetwork	0.8072	0.7867	0.7665
SVM(SMO)	0.7798	0.7205	0.6634
PART	0.8047	0.8014	0.7914
DecisionTable	0.8312	0.8161	0.8031
J48	0.8014	0.8047	0.7914
REPTree	0.8068	0.7941	0.7783
RandomForest	0.7520	0.7573	0.7492
RandomTree	0.7523	0.7573	0.7527
Naive Bayes	0.8222	0.8235	0.8226

tive. In order to validate our human tagged rating for sentence opinion rate, we carried out an inter-rater reliability (IRR) test. Each sentence was given to a primary human tagger (participant) and the secondary tagger (one of the authors). Final rate value was calculated using joint probability of agreement, and we received a joint probability of agreement value of 75%. Finally, all the results generated by our system are compared with the manually tagged result. Result of our final system is evaluated with respect to precision and F1 measure using 10-fold cross validation. The average precision of our recommendation system was 0.4177 and F1 measure was 0.4518.

7   Conclusion

This paper presented Ruchi, a system capable of rating individual food items. Ruchi makes use of NER for extracting the food item names from reviews, and typed dependency representation to identify the customer opinions. A corpus created from restaurant reviews was automatically tagged to be used in NER, using a list of food names compiled from various resources. This automated approach proved to be effective in creating a large corpus tagged with food names, as opposed to corpora manually tagged (Yasavur et al., 2013).

As for future work, we are planning to modify our system to be able to carry out time-based food rating. This feature will give the rating based on the reviews that were written within a preferred time period and avoid giving false rating to food items based on very old reviews.

References

Marie-Catherine De Marneffe and Christopher D Manning. 2008. Stanford typed dependencies manual. Technical report, Technical report, Stanford University.

Oxford food Dictionary. 2015. Oxford food dictionary. http://www.oxfordreference.com/view/10.1093/acref/9780192803511.001.0001/acref-9780192803511. Accessed: 2015-01-04.

Foodtimeline food list. 2015. Foodtimeline food list. http://www.foodtimeline.org/foodfaqindex.html. Accessed: 2015-01-04.

Abhishek Gupta, Tejaswi Tenneti, and Ankit Gupta. 2015. /sentiment based summarization of restaurant reviews. http://nlp.stanford.edu/courses/cs224n/2009/fp/9.pdf. Accessed: 2015-01-30.

Bing Liu. 2010. Sentiment analysis and subjectivity. *Handbook of natural language processing*, 2:627–666.

Bing Liu. 2012. Sentiment analysis and opinion mining. *Synthesis Lectures on Human Language Technologies*, 5(1):1–167.

Myle Ott, Claire Cardie, and Jeffrey T Hancock. 2013. Negative deceptive opinion spam. In *Proceedings of the Joint Human Language Technology/North American Chapter of the ACL Conference*, pages 497–501.

Benjamin Snyder and Regina Barzilay. 2007. Multiple aspect ranking using the good grief algorithm. In *Proceedings of the Joint Human Language Technology/North American Chapter of the ACL Conference*, pages 300–307.

Oregon state food list. 2015. Oregon state food list. http://health.oregonstate.edu/food/glossary/index.html. Accessed: 2015-01-04.

Vaishak Suresh, Syeda Roohi, Magdalini Eirinaki, and Iraklis Varlamis. 2014. Using social data for personalizing review rankings. In *Proceedings of the 6th Workshop on Recommender Systems and the Social Web*.

Michele Trevisiol, Luca Chiarandini, and Ricardo Baeza-Yates. 2014. Buon appetito: recommending personalized menus. In *Proceedings of the 25th ACM conference on Hypertext and social media*, pages 327–329. ACM.

Ugan Yasavur, Reza Amini, Christine L Lisetti, and Naphtali Rishe. 2013. Ontology-based named entity recognizer for behavioral health. In *27th International Conference of the Florida Artificial Intelligence Research Society (2013)*. AAAI press.

Dependency Extraction for Knowledge-based Domain Classification

Lokesh Kumar Sharma
Dept. of Computer Science & Engineering
Malaviya National Institute of Technology
Jaipur, Rajasthan, India
2013rcp9007@mnit.ac.in

Namita Mittal
Dept. of Computer Science & Engineering
Malaviya National Institute of Technology
Jaipur, Rajasthan, India
nmittal.cse@mnit.ac.in

Abstract

Question classification is an important part in Question Answering. It refers to classifying a given question into a category. This paper presents a learning based question classifier. The previous works in this field have used UIUC questions dataset for the classification purpose. In contrast to this, we use the Web-Questions dataset to build the classifier. The dataset consists of questions with the links to the Freebase pages on which the answers will be found. To extract the exact answer of a question from a Freebase page, it is very essential to know the domain of the answer as it narrows down the number of possible answer candidates. Proposed classifier will be very helpful in extracting answers from the Freebase. Classifier uses the questions' features to classify a question into the domain of the answer, given the link to the freebase page on which the answer can be found.

1 Introduction

Question classification refers to finding out the class to which a question belongs (Loni, 2011). In traditional question answering systems, the answers were extracted from the corpora. But more recent question answering systems use structured knowledge bases for extracting answers. One of the popular knowledge bases is the Freebase. Freebase is an online collection of structured data harvested from many sources. Freebase aims to create a global resource which allows people (and machines) to access common information more effectively. It was developed by the American software company Metaweb. It has over 39 million topics about real-world entities like people, places and

things. The freebase data is organized and stored in the form of a graph and each node in a graph has a unique id. The data is classified into one of the 71 domains like people, location, sports etc. The domains comprise of types and types comprise of properties. To extract an answer from the freebase we write MQL queries to query over Freebase (Yao et. al, 2014A, Yao et. al,2014B). For example: *"Who are the parents of Justin Bieber?"*. The MQL query to find out the answer will be The above MQL query, searches the freebase page with the id "/en/justin_bieber". The answer field /people/person/parents is left blank. The query returns the answer by filling in the answer fields. The /people is the domain which has /person as a type and this type has /parents as a property. It is shown in Fig. 1. If we do this manually by going to the freebase page named Justin Bieber, we have to scan through all the properties to find the answer. But by knowing the domain i.e. *people*, only the answers which fall under the *people* category are scanned. Hence number of possible answer candidates are

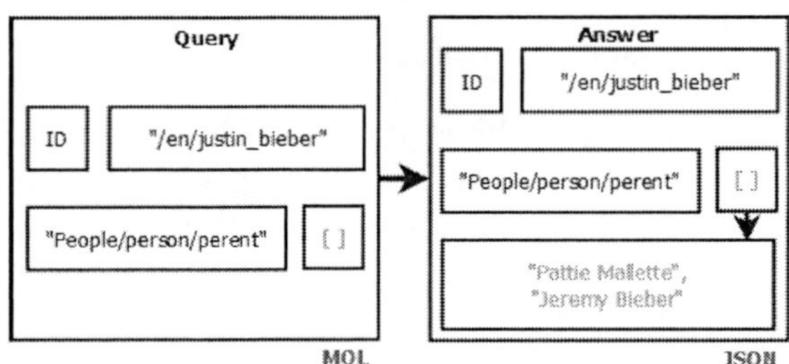

Figure 1: MQL query and answer from Freebase

reduced which considerably reduces our effort and time in finding the answer. In this approach, we build a learning based classifier which can classify a question into the domain of the answer. In case of multiple domains, we select the most suitable

D S Sharma, R Sangal and E Sherly. Proc. of the 12th Intl. Conference on Natural Language Processing, pages 215–218,
Trivandrum, India. December 2015. ©2015 NLP Association of India (NLPAI)

domain. We have assumed that only the common nouns can be the headwords of the questions. As a result, only ~50% of the questions have headwords present in them. We then use the feature set for these ~500 questions for training using a LIBSVM classifier. We get an accuracy of 76.565%.

2 Related Work

The previous works in this field have classified the UIUC dataset published by Li and Roth (2004). Li and Roth also defined a taxonomy with 6 course and 50 fine grained classes. They used four question features namely, (1) automatically acquired named entity categories, (2) word senses in Word-Net 1.7, (3) manually constructed word lists related to specific categories of interest, and (4) automatically generated semantically similar word lists. They obtained an accuracy of 92.5% for 6 coarse classes and 89.3% for 50 fine grained classes using a learning bases classification approach. Silva et al. (2011) used 5 features namely, (1) wh-word, (2) headword, (3) WordNet semantic feature, (4) N-grams and (5) word shape. They get an accuracy of 89.2% for coarse grained and 93.4% for fine grained classes, using learning based approach. Silva et al. (2011) obtained an accuracy of 90.8% on fine grained and 95.0% on coarse grained classes which is the highest accuracy reported on this dataset. They used a hybrid of the rule based and the learning based approach.

We use the before mentioned three features because they have contribute the most to the classification process in the previous works mentioned above. Thus we have a relatively smaller but rich feature set.

3 Proposed Approach

A question can be treated as a bag of features. These features then help us to map the question with a class. We have considered three features namely, the wh-tag, the similarities of the headword with the four domains (obtained using WordNet Similarity package) and the question unigrams as features. We use the WebQuestions dataset for training and testing the classifier. The WebQuestions dataset was created by the Stanford NLP group. It consists of 3,778 training examples and 2,032 test examples. On WebQuestions, each example contains three fields: utterance: natural

language utterance. TargetValue: The answer provided by AMT workers, given as a list of descriptions. url: Freebase page, where AMT workers found the answer. We use the training samples from the above dataset. We find out all the factoid questions (which have a single answer) from the dataset. There are about 2575 factoid questions out of 3778.

We find out the headwords of all the given questions. A headword is a word which the question is seeking (a noun). For example: *"Who are the parents of Justin Bieber?"* Here the word *parents* is the headword. Out of 2575 nearly 1303 questions have headwords present. We then use ~500 questions from these questions for the training of our classifier. We manually classify the questions by navigating to the url given with each question and searching for the answer. Then the domain of the answer is noted as the question class. All the questions fall into one of the four classes (domains) namely, people, location, government and sports. The classifier uses question features for training the dataset. In this approach, the question is treated as a bag of features. We use three features namely, the wh-tag, the similarities of the headword with the four domains (obtained using WordNet Similarity package) and the question unigrams as features.

3.1. Wh-word

A Wh-word is the word starting with *wh* with which the question begins. In our dataset it is one of *what, which, why, where* and *who*. If the wh-word is *who*, then the question has a high probability of falling into the *people* class. Similarly, for the wh-word being *where*, the question may fall in the *location* class.

3.2. Headword similarities with the four classes

A headword is a word the question is seeking. It plays an important role in classifying a question. For example if the headword is brother, the question is seeking for a person and will probably fall into the *people* class. This is because the word brother is semantically related to the class *people* more than the other three classes. Thus, we can use the similarities of the headword with the four classes as four separate features and take the active

Table I
Dependency tree's priority list

Parent	Direction	Priority List
S	Left	VP S FRAG SBAR ADJP
SBARQ	Left	SQ S SINV SBARQ FRAG
SQ	Left	NP VP SQ
NP	Right by position	NP NN NNP NNPS NNS NX
PP	Left	WNP NP WHADVP SBAR
WHNP	Left	NP
WHPP	Right	WHNP WHADVP NP SBAR

feature as the one corresponding to the class to which the headword is the most similar. To find out the similarities we make use of WordNet (Miller, 1995). WordNet is a large English lexicon in which meaningfully related words are connected via cognitive synonyms (synsets). The WordNet is a useful tool for word semantics analysis and has been widely used in question classification. We make use of the WordNet Similarity package to find out the similarities. For a pair of words, this package computes the length of the path to reach from one of the words to the other via the WordNet network. It then computes the similarity based on the path. The class which has the highest similarity with the headword is marked as an active feature. Starting from the root of the parse tree shown in

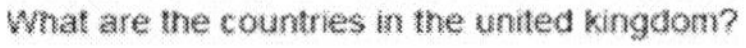

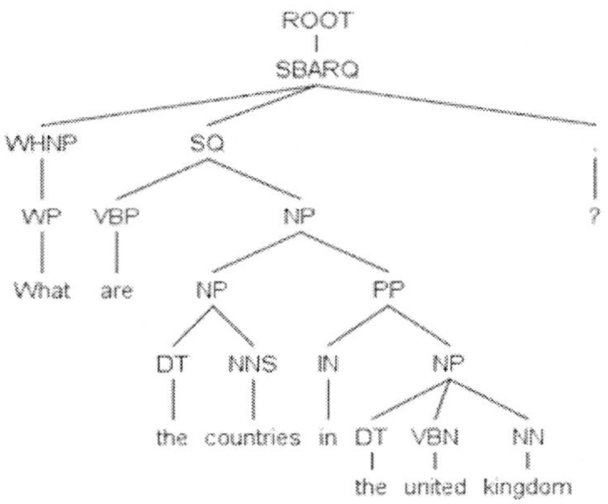

Figure 2: Parse tree traversal based on priority list

Fig. 2, the current node is matched with a parent. Depending upon the parent, all the child nodes of the current node are then compared with the corresponding priority list elements by the manner

specified by direction. If the direction of search is left by category then the algorithm starts from the leftmost child and check it against items in priority list and if it matches any, then the matched item will be returned as head. Otherwise if the algorithm reaches the end of the list and the child does not match with any of the items, it continues the same process with the next child. On the other hand, if the search direction is left by position, then the algorithm first starts checking the items in priority list and for each item it tries to match it with every child from left to right. The first matched item is considered as head. we applied the head rules starting from the root. The root of the tree is SBARQ. On matching it with the parent tag on table I, we get the rule comparing the children of SBARQ with the right hand side of the rule we get a match at SQ. We then match it with the table and get the rule NP matches the right hand side and in this way the procedure continued till we reach at NN and capital is returned as the headword. Apart from the head rules mentioned in table I, there are three more rules which have been used to find out the similarities are shown in table II. Thus, the question will fall into the class *government* as it has the highest similarity with the question headword. Hence we use the semantic meaning of the headword for classification.

Table II
Domain classes and their similarities

Classes	Similarity
Capital and People	0.1429
Capital and Location	0.2500
Capital and Government	0.3333
Capital and Sports	0.1111

headwords for some of the exceptions to the head rules. parse tree traversal shown in figure 2. By default the comparison is by category. They are:

1) When SBARQ has a WHXP child with at least two children, WHXP is returned.
2) After applying the first rule, if the resulting head is a WHNP containing an NP that ends with a possessive pronoun (POS), we return the NP as the head.
3) If the extracted headword is name, kind, type, part, genre or group, and its sibling node is a prepositional phrase PP, we use PP as the head and proceed with the algorithm.

After finding out the headword we use the Word-Net similarity package to find out the semantic similarity of the headword with the four classes.

3.3. N-grams

An *n*-gram is a contiguous sequence of *n* items from a given sequence of text or speech. We have considered the question unigrams as features because they are simple and contribute in the question classification process better than bigrams and trigrams. We have not used the proper nouns in the unigram feature set as the proper nouns cannot help in the classification process. Further we have also removed the stop words from the unigrams because of their triviality. For example for the question: *What is the capital of India?* The unigram feature set will be {(What,1),(capital,1)}. The Wh-word will also be a part of the unigrams.

4. Experimental Setup and Analysis

Out of 500 questions 379 questions are classified correctly shown in table III. The resultant ma-

TABLE III
CORRECT AND INCORRECT CLASSIFIED INSTANCES OUT OF 500

Correctly Classified	379	76.565%
In-Correctly Classified	116	23.434%

trix shown in table IV shows the accuracy of the classified questions. In the idea case the matrix should have all the non diagonal elements as 0. We

TABLE IV
RESULTANT MATRIX FOR FOUR CATEGORIES

A	B	C	D	CLASSIFIED AS
223	24	2	4	a = location
36	69	2	9	b = people
4	8	47	1	c = sports
12	11	3	40	d = government

see that the there is a discrepancy in the classification matrix. The discrepancy is maximum for the sports class. The discrepancy occurs because we have tried to classify the dataset using only a compact set of 312 features. To improve the accuracy, we can increase the number of features and the no of questions used for training. Also the domains under the freebase cannot be classified using the conventional classification techniques. We cannot always correctly classify the questions into their freebase domains by the question's features. Thus the classifier performs average as expected for the freebase domain classification as compared to the conventional classification using the taxonomy proposed by Li and Roth (2004).

5. Conclusion and Future Work

The accuracy obtained in classification is ~76% which can be improved by increasing the size of the feature set by adding more features like bigrams, N-grams, Word-Shapes, Question-Length, Hypernyms, Indirect-Hypernyms, Synonyms, Name Entities and Related-Words can be added to the feature set. The Wordnet similarity used in the project gives us the general similarity between two words. Hence a sense disambiguation technique can be used to improve the classification. Also we have worked on the domain classification, which is a new field of question classification. It will be helpful during answer extraction from the Freebase. We have ~312 features for each question, and the number of questions used is ~500. Thus with a comparatively compact dataset we have received an accuracy of 76% which is promising for any future work in this field.

References

Babak Loni, *"A Survey of State-of-the-Art Methods on Question Classication"*, Delft University of Technology, Tech. Rep, 2011.

João Silva, Luísa Coheur, Ana Cristina Mendes, Andreas Wichert, *"From symbolic to sub-symbolic information in question classification"*, 2011.

George A. Miller, *"WordNet: A Lexical Database for English"* Communications of the ACM Vol. 38, No. 11: 39-41, 1995.

Xin Li and Dan Roth, *"Learning Question Classifiers: The Role of Semantic Information"*, 2004.

Xuchen Yao and Benjamin Van Durme, *"Information Extraction over Structured Data: Question Answering with Freebase"*, Proceedings of ACL 2014.

Xuchen Yao, Jonathan Berant, Benjamin Van Durme, *"Freebase QA: Information Extraction or Semantic Parsing"*, Proceedings of ACL 2014.

An Approach to Collective Entity Linking

Ashish Kulkarni   **Kanika Agarwal**   **Pararth Shah**   **Sunny Raj Rathod**   **Ganesh Ramakrishnan**

Department of Computer Science
Indian Institute of Technology Bombay
Mumbai, India
{kulashish, kanika1712, pararthshah717, sunnyrajrathod} @gmail.com
ganesh@cse.iitb.ac.in

Abstract

Entity linking is the task of disambiguating entities in unstructured text by linking them to an entity in a catalog. Several collective entity linking approaches exist that attempt to collectively disambiguate all mentions in the text by leveraging both local mention-entity context and global entity-entity relatedness. However, the complexity of these models makes it unfeasible to employ exact inference techniques and jointly train the local and global feature weights. In this work we present a collective disambiguation model, that, under suitable assumptions makes efficient implementation of exact MAP inference possible. We also present an efficient approach to train the local and global features of this model and implement it in an interactive entity linking system. The system receives human feedback on a document collection and progressively trains the underlying disambiguation model.

1   Introduction

Search systems proposed today (Chakrabarti et al., 2006; Cheng et al., 2007; Kasneci et al., 2008; Li et al., 2010) are greatly enriched by recognizing and exploiting entities embedded in unstructured pages. In a typical system architecture (Cucerzan, 2007; Dill et al., 2003; Kulkarni et al., 2009; Milne and Witten, 2008) a spotter first identifies short token segments or "spots" as potential mentions of entities from its catalog. For our purposes, a catalog consists of a directed graph of categories, to which entity nodes are attached. Many entities may qualify for a given text segment, *e.g.*, both *Kernel trick* and *Linux Kernel* might qualify for the text segment "...Kernel...". In the second stage, a disambiguator assigns zero or more entities to

selected mentions, based on mention-entity coherence, as well as entity-entity similarity.

Some of the recent work (Zhou et al., 2010; Lin et al., 2012) shows that several mentions may have no associated sense in the catalog. This is referred to as the no-attachment (NA) problem (or NIL in the TAC-KBP challenge (McNamee, 2009)). The other, relatively lesser addressed challenge is that of multiple attachments (Kulkarni et al., 2014), where a mention might link to more than one entities from the catalog. This might often be a result of insufficient context and has been acknowledged by some of the recent entity disambiguation challenges[1].

We present an approach to collective disambiguation of several mentions by combining various mention-entity compatibility and entity-entity relatedness features. Also, unlike most of the prior work, we jointly learn the local and global feature weights. Our Markov network-based model, along with suitable assumptions, makes efficient learning possible. The model links mentions to zero or more entities, thus offering a natural solution to the problem of NAs and multiple attachments.

2   Prior Work

Earlier works (Dill et al., 2003; Bunescu and Pasca, 2006; Mihalcea and Csomai, 2007) on entity annotation focused on per-mention disambiguation. This involves selecting the best entity to assign to a mention, independent of the assignments to other mentions in the document. Wikify! (Mihalcea and Csomai, 2007) for instance, uses context overlap for disambiguation and combines it with a classifier model that exploits local and topical features. Cucerzan (Cucerzan, 2007) introduced the notion of agreement on categories of entities in addition to the local context overlap, in which the entity context comprised

---

[1] http://web-ngram.research.microsoft.com/ERD2014/

215

D S Sharma, R Sangal and E Sherly. Proc. of the 12th Intl. Conference on Natural Language Processing, pages 219–228,
Trivandrum, India. December 2015. ©2015 NLP Association of India (NLPAI)

out-links from and in-links to their corresponding Wikipedia documents. Milne *et al.* (Milne and Witten, 2008) formulated a "relatedness" measure of similarity between two entities from Wikipedia, based on their in-link overlap. Relatedness, in conjunction with the prior probability of occurrence of an entity, was then used to train a classifier model. Han *et al.* (Han and Zhao, 2009) leveraged the semantic information in Wikipedia to build a large-scale semantic network and developed a similarity measure to be used for disambiguation. Kulkarni *et al.* (Kulkarni et al., 2009) were the first to propose a general collective disambiguation approach, giving formulations for trade-off between mention-entity compatibility and coherence between entities. Several graph-based approaches (Hoffart et al., 2011; Fahrni and Strube, 2012) followed that cast the disambiguation problem as a problem of dense subgraph selection from a graph of mentions and candidate entities, making use of collective signals.

Most of these systems seem to prefer tagging conservatively. Some of them (Cucerzan, 2007; Hoffart et al., 2011) restrict their tagging to named entities, while others use a subset of entities from a background taxonomy such as TAP (Dill et al., 2003) or Wikipedia (Milne and Witten, 2008; Mihalcea and Csomai, 2007). Others (Kataria et al., 2011; Bhattacharya and Getoor, 2006) have proposed LDA-based generative models but focus only on person names. Some of the more recent systems (Kulkarni et al., 2009; Han et al., 2011) do perform aggressive spotting, aided by the anchor dictionary of Wikipedia entities and study the recall-precision tradeoff.

(Kulkarni et al., 2014) propose a joint disambiguation model based on a Markov network of entities as nodes and edges for their relatedness. Disambiguation is achieved by performing a MAP inference on this graph and it naturally handles the NA and multiple attachment cases. Unlike other approaches (Han and Sun, 2012; Ratinov et al., 2011), their graph models candidate entities with binary labels, instead of mentions with multiple labels. A suitable assumption on cliques and their potentials makes efficient computation of exact inference possible. However, it is not clear as to how the node and edge feature weights are set.

To the best of our knowledge, none of the graph-based models above have attempted to jointly learn the node and edge feature weights. While there is prior work (Wellner et al., 2004; Wick et al., 2009) that applied graphical models to the problem of information extraction and coreference resolution, exact inference and estimation is intractable in these models. Similar approaches have also been applied to the problem of entity disambiguation (Kulkarni et al., 2009; Han and Sun, 2012; Ratinov et al., 2011), but hardly anyone has attempted to jointly learn the feature weights.

2.1 Our Contributions

We leverage the disambiguation model of (Kulkarni et al., 2014) and propose an efficient approach to jointly learn the node and edge feature weights. We also develop an interactive active learning framework that progressively improves the model as more training data becomes available. We implemented our approach in an online annotation system[2] and used it to semi-automatically curate labeled data[3]. Our trained model performs better than several other systems including that of Kulkarni *et al.*

3 Preliminaries

We borrowed the features and the disambiguation model from the work described in Kulkarni *et al.* and present it in brief here. We first start with the problem definition.

3.1 Problem Definition

The primary goal of document annotation is to link entity mentions in an input document to entities in a catalog. Mentions (or "spots") are contiguous token sequences in a text, *e.g. Bush*, that can potentially link to an entity, *e.g. George Bush* in the catalog. Let $\mathcal{M}_d$ be the set of all mentions in a document d and $\mathcal{E}$ be the set of all entities in the catalog. Then, the entity linking problem is to find for each mention $m \in \mathcal{M}_d$, the set of entities $\hat{E}_m \subset \mathcal{E} \cup \{NA\}$ that it can link to.

As a first step, the input text d is processed by a "spotter" to identify the set $\mathcal{M}_d$ of mentions and the set of candidates $E_m \subset \mathcal{E}, \forall m \in \mathcal{M}_d$. $e_m \in E_m$ is called a candidate entity for spot m. The set $E_d = \cup_{m \in \mathcal{M}_d} E_m$ forms the candidate entities set for document d. This is then followed by a "disambiguation" phase that obtains from E_m, the set $\hat{E}_m$ of entities that the mention m can actually link to. When none of the entities in E_m

<hr>

[2]http://tinyurl.com/entitydisamb-demo
[3]http://tinyurl.com/entitydisamb-data

are valid, then $\hat{E}_m = \{NA\}$. Alternatively, more than one entities from E_m might get promoted to $\hat{E}_m$. Assuming *one sense per discourse* (Gale et al., 1992), an entity in the candidate set of more than one mentions, links (or does not link) to all those mentions.

3.2 Entity Catalog

A catalog is a structured knowledge base comprising categories with entities under them, along with their attributes and relations. Wikipedia has seen an extensive organic growth and covers entities spanning a vast set of domains. We report experimental results using the Wikipedia dump from May 2011, with approximately 4.4 million entities. For evaluation on ERD, we used as catalog, the snapshot of Freebase as provided in the challenge.

3.3 Features

We used three types of features - (1) Popularity-based features of an entity: Prior Sense Probability (Mihalcea and Csomai, 2007), In-Link Count, Out-Link Count; (2) Mention-Entity compatibility features (Kulkarni et al., 2009); (3) Entity-Entity relatedness features: Category-based Similarity (Cucerzan, 2007), In-link based Similarity (Milne and Witten, 2008), Out-link based Similarity, Contextual Similarity.

3.4 The Disambiguation Model

Having identified the set of candidate entities for each mention, a disambiguator attempts to link each mention to zero or more entities. The label of a candidate is a collective result of the interplay of local mention-entity and global entity-entity relatedness signals.

A *Markov Random Field* (MRF) is an undirected graphical model that captures local correlations between random variables (Taskar and Koller, 2001). A node is instantiated in the MRF

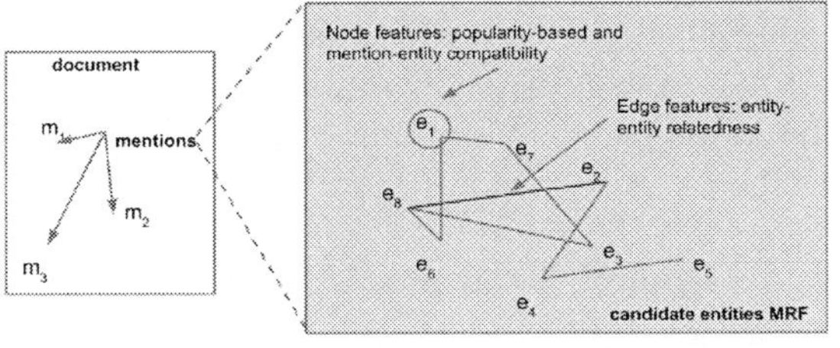

Figure 1: Candidate entities MRF model

graph for each possible entity mapping of each

mention instance in a document. Edges capture entity-entity relatedness. Let $\mathbf{x}_i$ be the node feature vector of candidate i and $\mathbf{x}_{ij}$ be the edge feature vector of the edge joining candidates i and j. Each candidate corresponds to a random variable that takes a binary label, $y_i \in \{0, 1\}$, based on whether or not it correctly disambiguates the underlying mention. Let C be the set of all cliques in the MRF and each clique $c \in C$ be associated with a clique potential $\phi_c(.)$. Cliques are restricted to nodes and edges and their potentials are parameterized by log-linear functions of feature vectors; *i.e.*, $log\ \phi_c(.) = \mathbf{w}_c \cdot \mathbf{x}_c$, where $\mathbf{x}_c$ is the feature vector of a clique and $\mathbf{w}_c$, the corresponding weight vector. The potentials are assumed to be submodular (Taskar et al., 2004), that is, they are associated with assignments where variables in a clique have the same label. Let $\mathbf{w}_0$ and $\mathbf{w}_1$ be the node feature weights influencing node labels 0 and 1 respectively and $\mathbf{w}_{00}$ and $\mathbf{w}_{11}$ be the associative edge weights influencing the connected nodes to take the same label. The probability of a complete graph labeling y is given by $P(y) = \frac{1}{Z} \prod_{c \in C} \phi_c(y_c)$, where Z is the partition function. Disambiguation is achieved by doing MAP inference on this graph.

$$L(y) = \arg\max_{y \in \mathcal{Y}} \sum_{i \in \mathcal{N}} log\ \phi_i(y_i) + \sum_{ij \in \mathcal{E}} log\ \phi_{ij}(y_{ij})$$

$$= \arg\min_{y \in \mathcal{Y}} -(\sum_{i \in \mathcal{N}} \mathbf{w}_0 \cdot \mathbf{x}_i(1 - y_i) + \mathbf{w}_1 \cdot \mathbf{x}_i y_i$$

$$+ \sum_{ij \in \mathcal{E}} \mathbf{w}_{00} \cdot \mathbf{x}_{ij}(1 - y_{ij}) + \mathbf{w}_{11} \cdot \mathbf{x}_{ij} y_{ij})$$

$$(1)$$

$\mathcal{N}$ is the set of nodes and $\mathcal{E}$ is the set of edges in the MRF, $y_i \in \{0, 1\}$ and $y_{ij} = y_i y_j$. For an MRF with binary labeled nodes and associative edge potentials, MAP inference can be computed exactly in polynomial time, by finding the min cut of an augmented flow graph (Boykov and Kolmogorov, 2004). The MRF is augmented by adding two special terminal nodes *source, s* and *sink, t* that correspond to the two labels 0/1. For each node i, we add terminal edges $s \rightarrow i$ with weight $\langle \mathbf{w}_0, \mathbf{x}_i \rangle$ and $i \rightarrow t$ with weight $\langle \mathbf{w}_1, \mathbf{x}_i \rangle$. For each neighborhood edge $i \rightarrow j$, we assign weight $\langle (\mathbf{w}_{00} + \mathbf{w}_{11}), \mathbf{x}_{ij} \rangle$. We also add weight $\langle \mathbf{w}_{00}, \mathbf{x}_{ij} \rangle$ to the edge $s \rightarrow i$ and $\langle \mathbf{w}_{11}, \mathbf{x}_{ij} \rangle$ to the edge $j \rightarrow t$. MAP inference in original MRF corresponds to the s/t min cut on this augmented graph, with nodes on the s side of the cut getting a label of 0, and the nodes on the t side being assigned a label of 1.

4 Learning Feature Weights

Algorithm 1: MRF Learning algorithm

Data: Training set $\{X, \hat{q}\}$, MRF graph g, Slack penalty C, Iterations T, Step size α_t
Result: Weight vector w
$w \leftarrow 0$
$t \leftarrow 1$
$N_n \leftarrow$ number of nodes in g
$f_{opt} \leftarrow \infty$
$w_{opt} \leftarrow 0$
while $t \leq T$ **do**
    $g \leftarrow$ construct flow network from g
    $\tilde{q} \leftarrow$ s/t mincut of g
    $\nabla_w \xi(w) \leftarrow 2w + C(\hat{q} - \tilde{q})^T X$
    $w \leftarrow w - \alpha_t \nabla_w \xi(w)$
    Project w onto the positive orthant
    Compute function value f
    if $f < f_{opt}$ **then**
        $f_{opt} \leftarrow f$
        $w_{opt} \leftarrow w$
    end
    $t \leftarrow t + 1$
end
return w_{opt}

The submodularity restriction and binary labels, make efficient implementation of learning possible. We jointly learn both node and edge feature weights following the general max-margin framework described in (Taskar et al., 2004; Vernaza et al., 2008). Consider a graph with $\mathcal{N}$ nodes and $\mathcal{E}$ edges constructed as described above. Following Taskar *et al.*, the learning problem can be formulated in terms of the cut vector, such that, we minimize the norm of the weight vector subject to the constraint that the desired labeling scores better than an arbitrary labeling by an amount that scales with the Hamming distance between the desired and incorrect labelings.

$$\min_{\mathbf{w} \geq 0} \|\mathbf{w}\|^2 \tag{2}$$

subject to

$$\min_{\mathbf{q} \in Q} \sum_{i,j \in \mathcal{E}} \mathbf{w} \cdot \mathbf{x}_{ij}(q_{ij} - \hat{q}_{ij}) - (N_n - \hat{\mathbf{q}}_n^T \cdot \mathbf{q}_n) \geq 0$$

Here, Q is the set of all valid cuts and $q_{ij} \in \{0, 1\}$ indicates if edge $i \to j$ is cut ($q_{ij} = 1$). $\mathbf{q}_n$ is the cut vector for terminal edges with components q_{si} and q_{it}, where, $q_{si} = 1$ implies that i is labeled 1. $\hat{\mathbf{q}}$ is the cut vector corresponding to the desired labeling. The first component of the constraint captures the difference in cost of the min cut induced by the weights $\mathbf{w}$ and the desired labeling. The other component corresponds to the

number of labeling disagreements, N_n being the number of nodes in the graph (excluding s and t).

By rearranging terms, we obtain

$$\min_{\mathbf{w} \geq 0} \|\mathbf{w}\|^2 \tag{3}$$

subject to $\min_{\mathbf{q} \in Q} \sum_{i,j \in \mathcal{E}} (\mathbf{w}^T \cdot \mathbf{x}_{ij} + \hat{q}_{ij}(\delta_{is} + \delta_{jt})) q_{ij}$

$$\geq N_n + \sum_{i,j \in \mathcal{E}} (\mathbf{w}^T \cdot \mathbf{x}_{ij}) \hat{q}_{ij}$$

Here, δ_{ij} is the Kronecker delta. It can be shown that the left-hand-side and right-hand-side of the inequality in the constraint are equivalent (Vernaza et al., 2008). Moving the constraint to the objective, we get,

$$\min_{\mathbf{w} \geq 0} \|\mathbf{w}\|^2 + \mathcal{C}(N_n + \sum_{i,j \in \mathcal{E}} (\mathbf{w}^T \cdot \mathbf{x}_{ij}) \hat{q}_{ij} -$$

$$\min_{\mathbf{q} \in Q} \sum_{i,j \in \mathcal{E}} (\mathbf{w}^T \cdot \mathbf{x}_{ij} + \hat{q}_{ij}(\delta_{is} + \delta_{jt})) q_{ij})$$

Summing over all the documents in the training set, we get the final objective,

$$\min_{\mathbf{w} \geq 0} \|\mathbf{w}\|^2 + \sum_{d \in D} (\mathcal{C} (\mathcal{N}_d + \sum_{i,j \in \mathcal{E}_d} (\mathbf{w}^T \cdot \mathbf{x}_{ij}) \hat{q}_{ij} -$$

$$\min_{\mathbf{q} \in Q} \sum_{i,j \in \mathcal{E}_d} (\mathbf{w}^T \cdot \mathbf{x}_{ij} + \hat{q}_{ij}(\delta_{is} + \delta_{jt})) q_{ij}))$$

$$\tag{4}$$

Here, $\mathbf{w} = [\mathbf{w}_0^T \ \mathbf{w}_1^T \ \mathbf{w}_{00}^T \ \mathbf{w}_{11}^T]^T$, $\mathcal{N}_d$ is the number of nodes (excluding s and t) and $\mathcal{E}_d$ is the set of edges in the candidate entity MRF graph for a document $d \in D$, the set of all training documents, s and t are special source and sink nodes, respectively. The term $\mathcal{N}_d - \hat{q}_{ij}(\delta_{is} + \delta_{jt}) q_{ij}$ gives the number of misclassified nodes and $\sum_{i,j \in \mathcal{E}_d} \mathbf{w}^T \cdot \mathbf{x}_{ij} \hat{q}_{ij} - \mathbf{w}^T \cdot \mathbf{x}_{ij} q_{ij}$ is the total capacity of incorrectly cut edges in the flow graph. $\mathcal{C}$ is the penalty associated with the incorrect labeling. We solved the formulation (4) using the subgradient descent method as described in Algorithm 1.

4.1 Handling Unbalanced Training Data

The training data has many more entities labeled 0 as compared to those labeled 1. In our datasets, we observed a skew of about 3 : 1. This results in a bias towards the overrepresented class in the learning algorithm and the accuracy of the non-dominant class suffers. We addressed this problem by assigning separate misclassification penalties $\mathcal{C}_0$ and $\mathcal{C}_1$ for label 0 and 1 disagreements respectively in equation 4, where, disagreements are defined as below.

Definition 1. *Let $l_i \in \{0, 1\}$ and $\hat{l}_i \in \{0, 1\}$ be the predicted and actual labels of node i. We say that a node i has label 0 disagreement if $l_i \neq \hat{l}_i = 0$. Similarly it has label 1 disagreement if $l_i \neq \hat{l}_i = 1$.*

Proposition 1. *For an edge $i \rightarrow j$ with $q_{ij} \neq \hat{q}_{ij}$, exactly one of the nodes agrees on the label i.e. $l_i = \hat{l}_i$ (or $l_j = \hat{l}_j$) and the other node disagrees on the label i.e. $l_j \neq \hat{l}_j$ ($l_i \neq \hat{l}_i$).*

Proof. Case 1: Let $q_{ij} \neq \hat{q}_{ij} = 0$. This implies that the edge is not cut in the actual labeling and therefore $\hat{l}_i = \hat{l}_j$. However, $q_{ij} = 1$ implies that $l_i \neq l_j$. It follows that either $l_i = \hat{l}_i$ or $l_j = \hat{l}_j$. Case 2: Let $q_{ij} \neq \hat{q}_{ij} = 1$. Following a similar argument as that for case 1 above, we have that $\hat{l}_i \neq \hat{l}_j$ and $l_i = l_j$. Again, it follows that either $l_i = \hat{l}_i$ or $l_j = \hat{l}_j$. $\square$

Definition 2. *An edge $i \rightarrow j$ with $q_{ij} \neq \hat{q}_{ij}$, is said to have a label 0 disagreement if either $l_i \neq \hat{l}_i = 0$ or $l_j \neq \hat{l}_j = 0$. It is said to have a label 1 disagreement if either $l_i \neq \hat{l}_i = 1$ or $l_j \neq \hat{l}_j = 1$.*

4.2 Active Learning

Our online annotation system presents an opportunity to continuously update the model as more labeled data becomes available. The commonly used *passive learning* approach involves manual annotation of randomly and independently sampled data. Due to the time and cost associated with this process, often there is not enough training data to meet certain level of performance. *Active learning* (Lewis and Catlett, 1994) aims to minimize the labeling effort, by requesting labels for the most informative samples, so as to achieve a desired level of accuracy. While there are several approaches to querying examples for labeling (Li and Sethi, 2006), we follow a pragmatic approach, that can be characterized as *least certain querying* method. The method samples examples with the smallest difference between two highest probability classes. Our binary labeled MRF model labels a node, based on the collective effect of the node potential and the edge potentials on the edges connecting the node to its neighbors. We define cer-

tainty $C(i)$ at a node n_i as

$$C(i) = \left| \left(w_0 \cdot x_i + \sum_{(ij) \in \mathcal{E}: j \in N(i)} w_{00} \cdot x_{ij} \right) \right. \quad (5)$$
$$\left. - \left(w_1 \cdot x_i + \sum_{(ij) \in \mathcal{E}: j \in N(i)} w_{11} \cdot x_{ij} \right) \right|$$

where $N(i)$ is the set of all neighboring nodes of the node i. The certainty score $C(d)$ for a document d is then computed as the average certainty score across all nodes in that document.

$$C(d) = \frac{1}{|\mathcal{N}|} \sum_{i \in \mathcal{N}} C(i) \quad (6)$$

The active learning algorithm then queries for a document with the lowest $C(d)$ and presents the document for labeling. It might be possible to further reduce the labeling effort by requesting labels for only top k entities in the selected document, where the entities are ordered in increasing values of their $C(i)$.

5 Experiments and Results

5.1 Data Sets

We use $Wiki_{cur}$ (created by (Kulkarni et al., 2014)) for training our model and present cross-validation results. We also evaluate on several other datasets from the entity linking literature. (Kulkarni et al., 2009) had created a dataset ($IITB_{part}$) based on aggressive spotting but assuming single attachment. We, therefore, used our annotation system to manually complete annotations (to create $IITB_{cur}$) for the documents in this dataset.

5.2 Evaluation Measures

We follow the *fuzzy evaluation measure* (Cornolti et al., 2013) that accounts for slight syntactic and semantic variations in the match of a predicted and true annotation, where an annotation a is defined as the mention-entity pair $\langle m, e \rangle$. Using their notion of *weak annotation match* $M_w(a_1, a_2)$[4], we use as performance metrics, *Recall*, *Precision* and *F1* micro-averaged over all documents in a dataset. After factoring out spotter errors, we also separately report the accuracy of our disambiguation model alone (Referred to as "disambiguator only").

---

[4] which is true iff mentions m_1 and m_2 overlap in the input text and entities e_1 and e_2 are synonyms

Dataset	Disambiguator only			Weak annotation match		
	P	R	F	P	R	F
$Wiki_{cur}$	.82	.67	.74	.82	.56	.67
$IITB_{part}$	.82	.66	.73	.82	.50	.62

Table 1: Non-collective results (only node features) on $Wiki_{cur}$ set and $IITB_{part}$ datasets

5.3 Experiments with only Node Features

5.3.1 Is there merit in data curation?

The data curation process presents an opportunity for continuous training where our inference model periodically evolves, as more and more data gets curated. Optionally, in the absence of any curated data to start with (at time $t = t_0$ when our model is yet untrained), one could use a Logistic Regression model, trained on a large uncurated dataset, to warm-start the data curation process. As data gets curated and our model is trained, we switch to our trained model at time $t = t_k$.

We trained binary label LR models using 10000 randomly sampled Wikipedia documents, replacing an original Wikipedia document with its curated version from $Wiki_{cur}$, one at a time. Figure 2 plots the training accuracies of these models for an increasing number of curated documents. The improvement in accuracy could be explained by the reduction in false negatives achieved by virtue of aggressive tagging and multiple attachments in the curated dataset. Based on this observation, we claim (and verify it in section 5.4.3) that our MRF model too would benefit from data curation. At the same time, the use of an LR model for warm-starting an online annotation system as ours is strongly recommended.

5.3.2 How does our model perform?

Thereafter, we trained our candidate entity MRF model on $Wiki_{cur}$ dataset using the node features alone. We report two-fold cross-validation results on $Wiki_{cur}$ and test results on $IITB_{part}$ (Refer table 1). These serve as a baseline for our collective approach.

5.4 Collective Disambiguation

Next, we trained our model using node features and one or more edge features. Iterations T were fixed at 600, C was tuned as described below, and step size (at iteration t), $\alpha_t = K/\sqrt{t}$, where K was empirically set to 0.01.

5.4.1 Effect of C on accuracy

The C parameter in equation 4 acts as a regularizer and is indicative of the tolerance of disagreement between predicted and true labels. It was tuned on the training fold during two-fold cross-validation on $Wiki_{cur}$. Also, to account for the skew in label 0 and 1 instances in the dataset, we penalized label 0 and label 1 disagreements separately, using C_0 and C_1, respectively. A higher C_1 for instance, improves the label 1 recall while adversely impacting the precision. It is this recall-precision tradeoff for varying values of C_0, C_1, that we capture in Figure 3. We chose the best C_0 and C_1 from these for all our experiments.

5.4.2 Effect of Edge Features

Table 2 shows the effect of different edge features in a collective setting. The model seems to benefit the most from the inlink and outlink relatedness features, while context overlap-based features seem to be noisy. This is understandable as context overlap-based signals are useful only for topically coherent entities, which might not hold true for an aggressively tagged corpus like ours (Kulkarni et al., 2009).

Edge feature	Disambiguator only			Weak annotation match		
	P	R	F	P	R	F
Category	.72	.74	.73	.72	.63	**.67**
Outlink (O)	.84	.67	**.74**	.84	.57	**.68**
Inlink (I)	.80	.73	**.76**	.80	.62	**.70**
Frequent (F)	.84	.64	.73	.84	.54	.66
Synopsis	.69	.61	.65	.69	.52	.59
Syn. V/Adj.	.69	.67	.68	.69	.57	.62
Full text	.85	.63	.73	.85	.54	.66
All features	.44	.50	.47	.44	.42	.43
I+O	.85	.67	**.74**	.85	.56	**.68**
I+O+F	.79	.74	**.76**	.79	.63	**.70**

Table 2: Effect of edge features: two-fold cross validation on $Wiki_{cur}$. Edge features that showed improvement over node features are shown in bold.

5.4.3 Does training help?

We sampled 50 documents from the $Wiki_{cur}$ dataset, 5 at a time and used them for training, applying both passive (PL) and active learning (AL). The F_1 measure evaluated on an independent test set of 30 documents is shown in the plot (Refer to figure 4). The F_1 on training set seems to fluctuate, more so for *Train-AL* (Chen et al., 2006), but the F_1 on test set does show a steady improvement.

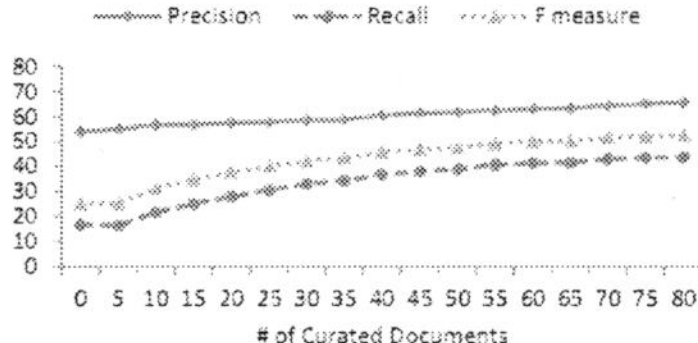
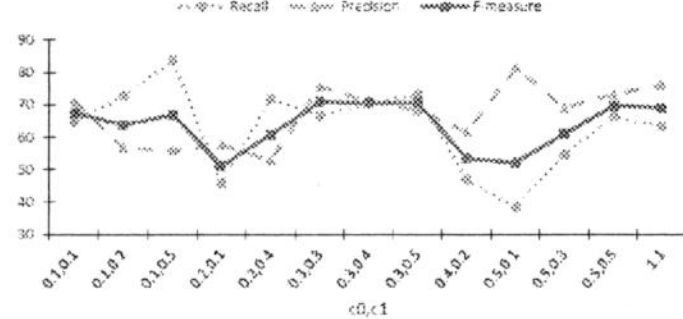
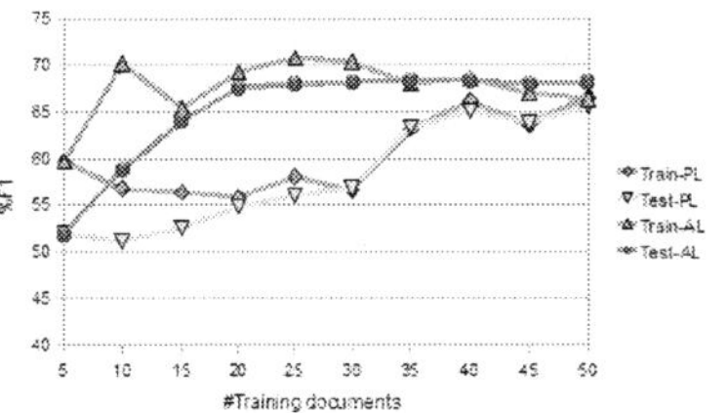

Figure 2: Effect of data curation

Figure 3: Effect of varying $\mathcal{C}$: $\mathcal{C}_0$ and $\mathcal{C}_1$

Figure 4: Effect of training

	$IITB_{part}$			AQUAINT			MSNBC		
Annotator	**F**	**P**	**R**	**F**	**P**	**R**	**F**	**P**	**R**
AIDA	.07	.66	.04	.21	.35	.15	.47	.75	.35
Wikify!	.37	.55	.28	.34	.29	.42	.41	.34	.51
TagMe	.44	.45	.42	.51	.46	.57	.52	.48	.55
Wikipedia Miner	.52	.57	.48	.47	.38	.63	.46	.55	.36
Illionis Wikifier	.44	.58	.36	.34	.29	.42	.41	.34	.51
Our Model (Node+I)	**.67**	.76	.60	.78	.81	.74	**.67**	.68	.66
Our Model (Node+I+O+F)	.65	.69	**.61**	**.79**	.82	**.75**	.66	.63	**.69**

Table 3: Comparison with publicly available systems (as reported by (Cornolti et al., 2013)) on three datasets

5.4.4 Comparison with collective approaches

We compared our system against several other collective annotation approaches: AIDA (Hoffart et al., 2011), Wikify! (Mihalcea and Csomai, 2007), TagMe (Ferragina and Scaiella, 2010), Wikipedia Miner (Milne and Witten, 2008) and Illionis Wikifier (Ratinov et al., 2011) on three datasets *viz.* $IITB_{part}$, AQUAINT (Wikipedia Miner) and MSNBC (Cucerzan, 2007). Our system consistently beats all these systems on all the three datasets (Table 3). Some of the other collective annotation systems like Cucerzan ($F_1 : .45$), CSAW (Kulkarni et al., 2009) ($F_1 : .69$), (Han et al., 2011) ($F_1 : .73$), and (Han and Sun, 2012) ($F_1 : .8$) have used CSAW's evaluation measure to evaluate on $IITB_{part}$. We achieved an F_1 of 0.6 using the same measure. The relatively lower F_1 on this dataset could be attributed to inconsistencies between the ground truth and our knowledge base. During our manual annotation of $IITB_{part}$, we came across over 8000 annotations that were either added or removed[5] to create the $IITB_{cur}$ dataset.

We evaluated our system on the ERD dataset and achieved R:.62, P:.66, $F_1 : .64$. We believe that our system benefits from model training, thereby performing better than that of (Kulkarni et al., 2014) ($F_1 : .61$). While some of the other systems (Cornolti et al., 2014) at ERD performed better, this could be attributed to their choice of features. Our system offers an end-end annotation framework that is interactive and jointly trains feature weights.

5.5 Results on $IITB_{cur}$

Section 6 shows some examples of incomplete annotations in the $IITB_{part}$ dataset. It is precisely such cases that we tried to correct during data preparation. Finally, we report the accuracy of our model on the $IITB_{cur}$ dataset - $P : 77.4\%$, $R : 54.3\%$, $F_1 : 63.8\%$.

5.6 Performance Evaluation

While our model allows for efficient inference and learning, graph construction itself is an expensive operation. For a document with $|E_d|$ candidate entities, the graph construction complexity is $O\left(|E_d|^2\right)$. For documents in the $Wiki_{cur}$ set with 190 candidate entities on an average, the average graph construction time was about 57 seconds. For the relatively larger documents in the $IITB_{cur}$ dataset, the average graph construction time was around 1.5 minutes. The performance could be improved by (a) pre-computing the entity-entity features for all entities in the knowledge base (b) dividing input document into chunks and performing graph construction and inference in parallel.

The running time for inference (Figure 5) shows a slightly quadratic behavior in the number of candidate entities $|E_d|$ of a document. Inference on most documents runs in under 0.5 seconds.On the relatively sparser *Inlink+Outlink* graphs (Refer to Figure 6), training is much faster than the more dense *Category* graphs. The faster training happens without trading off much on accuracy as can be seen in Table 2. For our experiments, the model was retrained at time t using all the available train-

---

[5]due to erroneous annotations or newer Wikipedia dump

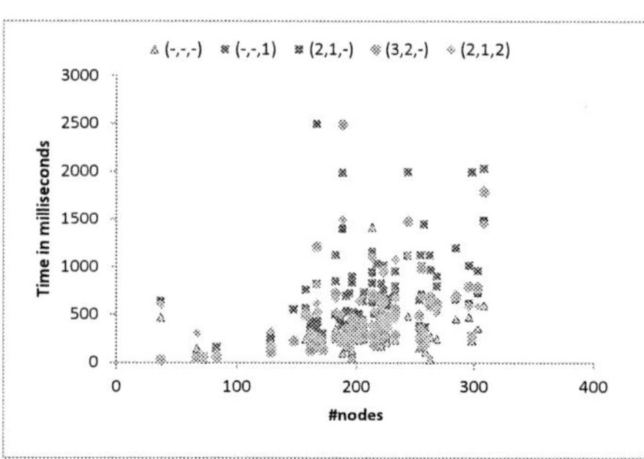

Figure 5: Running time for inference on $Wiki_{cur}$

ing data. While this might be acceptable for offline training, online systems might benefit from faster incremental training approaches.

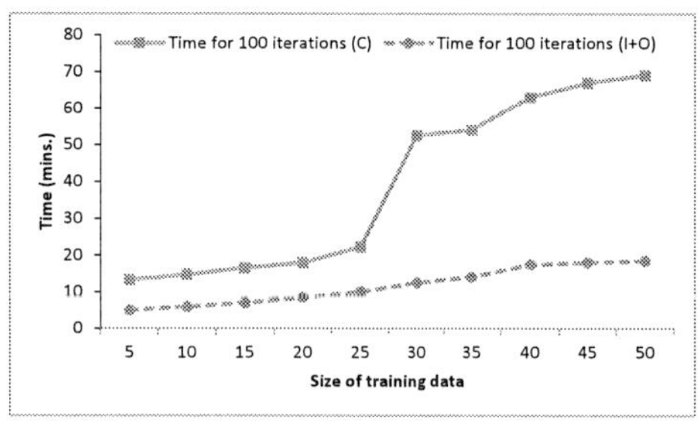

Figure 6: Scalability of training

6 Challenges with data curation

Data curation is a tedious and challenging task. Its inherent ambiguity often introduces annotator bias leading to either incomplete or ambiguous annotations in the curated data.

1. There might be cases when two or more entities are correct as attachments for a mention. *E.g.*, mention 'Barack Obama' can be tagged as *Barack Obama* or *President of United States*, and both might seem correct in the context that it appeared. A 'one entity per mention' assumption makes it impossible to honor such cases.

2. Human annotators often limit their attention to the candidate entities retrieved by the spotter and very rarely search the catalog for any missed candidates. This results in a lot of missed annotations and often many mentions getting no attachments (NA).

3. Annotators also seem biased towards entity names that match with the mention text. However, this is often not true. *E.g.* a mention of 'cone snail' disambiguates to *Conidae* and *Conus*.

4. Wikipedia contains many disambiguation pages that often show up in the candidate set for a mention. Tagging a mention with a disambiguation page seems to beat the very purpose of a disambiguation system. Ideally, the mention should be annotated with one of the entities on the disambiguation page or NA if none of them is semantically right.

Table 4 shows some of these cases from the $IITB_{part}$ dataset. It is cases like these that we attempted to correct in coming up with the curated $IITB_{cur}$ dataset.

7 Conclusion

We presented an approach to jointly train the node and edge features of a collective disambiguation model for the purpose of entity linking. Our system leverages active learning to bring down labeling effort. Experiments show that the model benefits from training and improves with the availability of more labeled data. We consistently performed better than many other systems on various datasets. It also scales reasonably well and with suggested tweaks can be used for large scale document annotation.

References

Indrajit Bhattacharya and Lise Getoor. 2006. A latent dirichlet model for unsupervised entity resolution. In *SIAM INTERNATIONAL CONFERENCE ON DATA MINING*.

Y. Boykov and V. Kolmogorov. 2004. An experimental comparison of min-cut/max-flow algorithms for energy minimization in vision. *Pattern Analysis and Machine Intelligence, IEEE Transactions on*, 26(9):1124–1137.

Razvan Bunescu and M Pasca. 2006. Using encyclopedic knowledge for named entity disambiguation. *Proceedings of EACL*, pages 9–16.

Soumen Chakrabarti, Kriti Puniyani, and Sujatha Das. 2006. Optimizing scoring functions and indexes for proximity search in type-annotated corpora. In

Ground Mention	Ground Entity	Predicted Entity	Remarks
lifestyle	Lifestyle	NA	Disambiguation page attachment
harsh reality	NA	Reality	Incomplete data
effort	NA	Energy	Incomplete data
self discipline	Discipline	self → Self, discipline → Discipline	Overlapping mentions
god	God (male deity)	God	Multiple correct entities
intellect	Intelligence	Intellect	Multiple correct entities

Table 4: Examples of predictions on the $IITB_{part}$ highlighting the challenges in data curation

Proceedings of the 15th international conference on World Wide Web, WWW '06, pages 717–726, New York, NY, USA. ACM.

Jinying Chen, Andrew Schein, Lyle Ungar, and Martha Palmer. 2006. An empirical study of the behavior of active learning for word sense disambiguation. In *Proceedings of the Main Conference on Human Language Technology Conference of the North American Chapter of the Association of Computational Linguistics*, HLT-NAACL '06, pages 120–127, Stroudsburg, PA, USA. Association for Computational Linguistics.

Tao Cheng, Xifeng Yan, and Kevin C. Chang. 2007. Entityrank: searching entities directly and holistically. In *VLDB '07: Proceedings of the 33rd international conference on Very large data bases*, pages 387–398. VLDB Endowment.

Marco Cornolti, Paolo Ferragina, and Massimiliano Ciaramita. 2013. A framework for benchmarking entity-annotation systems. In *Proceedings of the 22nd international conference on World Wide Web*, WWW '13, pages 249–260, Republic and Canton of Geneva, Switzerland. International World Wide Web Conferences Steering Committee.

Marco Cornolti, Paolo Ferragina, Massimiliano Ciaramita, Hinrich Schütze, and Stefan Rüd. 2014. The smaph system for query entity recognition and disambiguation. In *Proceedings of the First International Workshop on Entity Recognition & Disambiguation*, ERD '14, pages 25–30, New York, NY, USA. ACM.

Silviu Cucerzan. 2007. Large-scale named entity disambiguation based on wikipedia data. In *Proceedings of EMNLP-CoNLL*, volume 6, pages 708–716.

Stephen Dill, Nadav Eiron, David Gibson, Daniel Gruhl, R. Guha, Anant Jhingran, Tapas Kanungo, Sridhar Rajagopalan, Andrew Tomkins, John A. Tomlin, and Jason Y. Zien. 2003. Semtag and seeker: bootstrapping the semantic web via automated semantic annotation. In *Proceedings of the 12th international conference on World Wide Web*, WWW '03, pages 178–186, New York, NY, USA. ACM.

Angela Fahrni and Michael Strube. 2012. Jointly disambiguating and clustering concepts and entities with markov logic. In *COLING*, pages 815–832.

Paolo Ferragina and Ugo Scaiella. 2010. Tagme: on-the-fly annotation of short text fragments (by wikipedia entities). In *Proceedings of the 19th ACM international conference on Information and knowledge management*, CIKM '10, pages 1625–1628, New York, NY, USA. ACM.

William A. Gale, Kenneth W. Church, and David Yarowsky. 1992. One sense per discourse. In *Proceedings of the workshop on Speech and Natural Language*, HLT '91, pages 233–237, Stroudsburg, PA, USA. Association for Computational Linguistics.

Xianpei Han and Le Sun. 2012. An entity-topic model for entity linking. In *Proceedings of the 2012 Joint Conference on Empirical Methods in Natural Language Processing and Computational Natural Language Learning*, EMNLP-CoNLL '12, pages 105–115, Stroudsburg, PA, USA. Association for Computational Linguistics.

Xianpei Han and Jun Zhao. 2009. Named entity disambiguation by leveraging wikipedia semantic knowledge. In *Proceedings of the 18th ACM conference on Information and knowledge management*, CIKM '09, pages 215–224, New York, NY, USA. ACM.

Xianpei Han, Le Sun, and Jun Zhao. 2011. Collective entity linking in web text: a graph-based method. In *Proceedings of the 34th international ACM SIGIR conference on Research and development in Information Retrieval*, pages 765–774. ACM.

Johannes Hoffart, Mohamed Amir Yosef, Ilaria Bordino, Hagen Fürstenau, Manfred Pinkal, Marc Spaniol, Bilyana Taneva, Stefan Thater, and Gerhard Weikum. 2011. Robust disambiguation of named entities in text. In *Proceedings of the Conference on Empirical Methods in Natural Language Processing*, EMNLP '11, pages 782–792, Stroudsburg, PA, USA. Association for Computational Linguistics.

Gjergji Kasneci, Fabian M. Suchanek, Georgiana Ifrim, Shady Elbassuoni, Maya Ramanath, and Gerhard Weikum. 2008. Naga: harvesting, searching and ranking knowledge. In *Proceedings of the 2008 ACM SIGMOD international conference on Management of data*, SIGMOD '08, pages 1285–1288, New York, NY, USA. ACM.

Saurabh S. Kataria, Krishnan S. Kumar, Rajeev R. Rastogi, Prithviraj Sen, and Srinivasan H. Sengamedu. 2011. Entity disambiguation with hierarchical topic models. In *Proceedings of the 17th ACM SIGKDD international conference on Knowledge discovery and data mining*, KDD '11, pages 1037–1045, New York, NY, USA. ACM.

Sayali Kulkarni, Amit Singh, Ganesh Ramakrishnan, and Soumen Chakrabarti. 2009. Collective annotation of Wikipedia entities in web text. *Proceedings of the 15th ACM SIGKDD international conference on Knowledge discovery and data mining - KDD '09*, page 457.

Ashish Kulkarni, Kanika Agarwal, Pararth Shah, Sunny Raj Rathod, and Ganesh Ramakrishnan. 2014. System for collective entity disambiguation. In *Proceedings of the First International Workshop on Entity Recognition & Disambiguation*, ERD '14, pages 111–118, New York, NY, USA. ACM.

David D. Lewis and Jason Catlett. 1994. Heterogeneous uncertainty sampling for supervised learning. In *In Proceedings of the 11th International Conference on Machine Learning (ICML*, pages 148–156. Morgan Kaufmann.

Mingkun Li and Ishwar K. Sethi. 2006. Confidence-based active learning. *IEEE Trans. Pattern Anal. Mach. Intell.*, 28(8):1251–1261, August.

Xiaonan Li, Chengkai Li, and Cong Yu. 2010. Entityengine: answering entity-relationship queries using shallow semantics. In *Proceedings of the 19th ACM international conference on Information and knowledge management*, CIKM '10, pages 1925–1926, New York, NY, USA. ACM.

Thomas Lin, Mausam, and Oren Etzioni. 2012. Entity linking at web scale. In *Proceedings of the Joint Workshop on Automatic Knowledge Base Construction and Web-scale Knowledge Extraction*, AKBC-WEKEX '12, pages 84–88, Stroudsburg, PA, USA. Association for Computational Linguistics.

Paul McNamee. 2009. Overview of the tac 2009 knowledge base population track.

Rada Mihalcea and Andras Csomai. 2007. Wikify!: linking documents to encyclopedic knowledge. In *Proceedings of the sixteenth ACM conference on Conference on information and knowledge management*, pages 233–242. ACM.

David Milne and Ian H Witten. 2008. Learning to link with wikipedia. In *Proceedings of the 17th ACM conference on Information and knowledge management*, pages 509–518. ACM.

Lev Ratinov, Dan Roth, Doug Downey, and Mike Anderson. 2011. Local and global algorithms for disambiguation to wikipedia. In *Proceedings of the 49th Annual Meeting of the Association for Computational Linguistics: Human Language Technologies - Volume 1*, HLT '11, pages 1375–1384, Stroudsburg, PA, USA. Association for Computational Linguistics.

Ben Taskar and Daphne Koller. 2001. Learning Associative Markov Networks.

B. Taskar, V. Chatalbashev, and D. Koller. 2004. Learning associative markov networks. In *Proceedings of the twenty-first international conference on Machine learning*, page 102. ACM.

P. Vernaza, B. Taskar, and D.D. Lee. 2008. Online, self-supervised terrain classification via discriminatively trained submodular markov random fields. In *Robotics and Automation, 2008. ICRA 2008. IEEE International Conference on*, pages 2750–2757. IEEE.

Ben Wellner, Andrew McCallum, Fuchun Peng, and Michael Hay. 2004. An integrated, conditional model of information extraction and coreference with application to citation matching. In *Proceedings of the 20th Conference on Uncertainty in Artificial Intelligence*, UAI '04, pages 593–601, Arlington, Virginia, United States. AUAI Press.

Michael L. Wick, Aron Culotta, Khashayar Rohanimanesh, and Andrew McCallum. 2009. An entity based model for coreference resolution. In *SDM*, pages 365–376.

Yiping Zhou, Lan Nie, Omid Rouhani-Kalleh, Flavian Vasile, and Scott Gaffney. 2010. Resolving surface forms to wikipedia topics. In *Proceedings of the 23rd International Conference on Computational Linguistics*, COLING '10, pages 1335–1343, Stroudsburg, PA, USA. Association for Computational Linguistics.

Development of Speech corpora for different Speech Recognition tasks in Malayalam language

Cini kurian

Al-Ameen College, Edathala, Aluva

Abstract—**Speech corpus is the backbone of an Automatic speech Recognition system. This paper presents the development of speech corpora for different speech recognition tasks in Malayalam language. Pronunciation dictionary and Transcription file which are the other two essential resources for building a speech recognizer are also being created. Speech recognition performance of different speech recognition tasks are being presented. Speech corpus of about 18 hours have been collected for different speech recognition tasks.**

Keywords— Speech Recognition, corpus development, Malayalam

I. INTRODUCTION

One of the main challenges faced by speech scientist is the unavailability of the three important resources. The prime and most importantly, speech corpus (Speech Database), pronunciation dictionary and transcription file. Very fewer efforts have been made in Indian languages to make these resources available to public compared to English. Creation of these resources is time consuming, boredom and needs so much man power. Creating a well defined pronunciation dictionary needs through knowledge from phonetics, phonological rules, syntactic and semantic structure of the language.

It is necessary to have databases which comprises of appropriate sentences spoken by the typical users in realistic acoustic environment. Speech databases can be divided into two groups: (i) a database of speech normally spoken in a specific task domain. In this case, small amount of speech is sufficient to achieve acceptable recognition accuracy. (ii) a general purpose speech database that is not tuned to a particular task domain but consists of general text and hence can be used for recognition of any sentence in that language. The problem with most speech recognition systems is insufficient training data containing speech variations (spontaneous speech) caused by speaker variances (cover large number of speakers). To overcome these problems, a large vocabulary speech database is required to build a robust recognizer. The purpose of selection of phonetically-rich sentences is to provide a good coverage of pairs of phones in the sentence. The current work also aims at the development of databases for Malayalam speech recognition that will facilitate for acoustic phonetic studies, training and testing of automatic speech recognition systems. It is anticipated that the availability of this speech corpus would also stimulate the

basic research in Malayalam acoustic-phonetics and phonology.In this paper three sets of databases have been created (task specific databases , a general purpose database and a specially designed database for unique phoneme analysis) . The task specific database includes three domain based databases i.e isolated digit speech database, connected digit speech database and continuous speech database. The general purpose database includes a set of phoneme class wise speech database. Database designed for unique phoneme analysis includes, specially designed 32 minimal pair of words as well as a set of words which include unique phonemes in any word positions.

Section 2 discusses phonetic chart of Malayalam language and in section 3 the text corpus that has been prepared is detailed. In section 4 the method of speech data collection is being elaborated. The phoneme list prepared for the work is explained in section 5 followed by the creation of pronunciation dictionary in section 6. In section 7 the format and model of the transcription files being prepared is explained. Section 8 gives the results of various speech recognition tasks.

2. PHONETIC CHART

Malayalam has 52 consonant phonemes, encompassing 7 places of articulation and 6 manners of articulation, as shown in Table 1 below. In terms of manner of articulation, plosives are the most complicated, for they demonstrate a six-way distinction in labials, dentals, alveolar, retroflex, palatals, velars and glottal [1]. A labial plosive, for example, is either voiceless or voiced. Within voiceless labial plosives, a further distinction is made between aspirated and un-aspirated ones whereas for voiced labial plosives the distinction is between modal-voiced and breathy-voiced ones. In terms of place of articulation, retroflex are the most complex because they involve all manners of articulation except for semi vowels [2]. Phonetic chart as presented by Kumari, 1972 [3] for Malayalam language is given in table 1 and the same has been referred for this paper.

For all speech sounds, the basic source of power is the respiratory system pushing air out of the lungs. Sounds produced when the vocal cords are vibrating are said to be voiced, where the sound produced when the vocal cords are apart are said to be voiceless [4]. The shape and size of the vocal tract is a very important factor in the production of speech. The parts of the vocal tract such as the tongue and the

D S Sharma, R Sangal and E Sherly. Proc. of the 12th Intl. Conference on Natural Language Processing, pages 229–236,
Trivandrum, India. December 2015. ©2015 NLP Association of India (NLPAI)

lips that can be used to form sounds are called articulators (fig .1). The movements of the tongue and lips interacting with the roof of the mouth (palate) and the pharynx are part of the articulatory process [5]

Table 1 : Phonetic chart of Malayalam

		Labial		Dental		Alveolar		Retroflex		Palatal		Velar		Glottal
		voiced	unvoiced	voiced	unvoiced	Voiced	Unvoiced	voiced	unvoiced	voiced	unvoiced	voiced	unvoiced	
Stop / plosive — un aspirated		പ p	ബ b	ത t	ദ d	റ t	s ṭ	ഡ ḍ	ച c	ജ j	ക k	ഗ g	
Stop / plosive — aspirated		ഫph	ഭ bh	ഥ th	ധdh			O ṭh	ഢdh	ഛch	ഝjh	ഖkh	ഘgh	
Nasals		മ m		ന n		ന n̠		ണ ṇ		ഞ ñ		ങ ṅ		
Fricative		ഫ f		സ s				ഷ ṣ		ശ ś				ഹ h
Lateral						ല l		ള !		ഴ l				
rhotic						ര r		ഠ r						

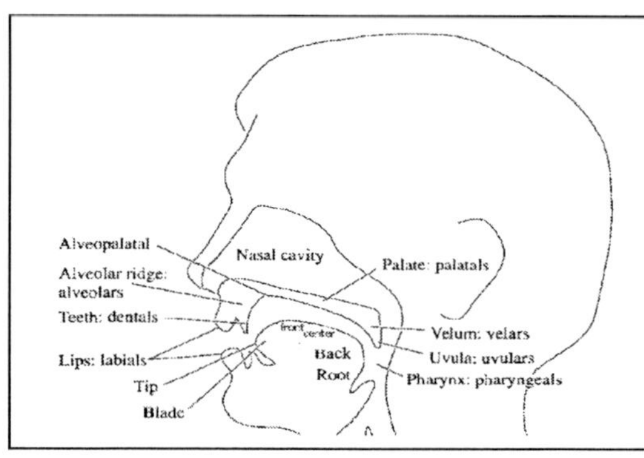

Figure 1: Place of articulation

3. Text Corpus

The first step followed in creating the speech database for automatic speech recognizers is the generation of optimal set of textual sentences to be recorded from the native speakers of the Malayalam language.

The following are the different set of text corpus collected for different tasks.

3.1 Isolated Digit Recognition Task

Digits from 0-9

3.2 Connected Digit Recognition Task

Text corpus consists of specially designed, twenty, 7 digit numbers so that maximum combinations of numbers as well as co-articulation of the numbers have been taken into account. It is assumed that speakers will be comfortable in reading 7-digit numbers. Accordingly, a sets of 7-digit numbers were generated, each set containing 20 numbers capturing all distinct word pairs. These sets were generated using different methods of generating word pairs. One such set of 20 numbers is shown in Table 2.

Table 2: An example of a list of twenty 7-digit numbers read by speakers

0098765	4159306	4725836	3567801
5432101	6927918	6828162	1345566
1975312	8908634	2612371	6778899
2964203	4074851	1460450	9011217
3952494	1733844	0570223	7913579

3.3 Continuous Speech Recognition task

For speaker independent speech recognition, speech data needs to be collected from a large number of speakers. It is not practical to ask speakers to speak/read a lot of sentences that contain all phonemes (in various phonetic contexts) of the language. Hence, it is desirable to construct sets of sentences that are phonetically rich. This construction is a laborious task. Phonetically rich sentences can be selected from a large set of text. Traditional sources of text data are books, magazines and periodicals. However a textual data is needed in electronic form so that it can be processed by a computer. Hence there are two choices: (a) Manually type in the printed data from articles, periodical, magazines etc., and store it in electronic form. (b) Use available online sources of text data. Example of such sources is articles on web and online news papers. There are several online newspapers that provide content in Malayalam language. Each online content uses its own grapheme encoding scheme to display Malayalam text. To collect the text data online Malayalam news papers being used. In order to compute the phonetic richness of sentences and select sentences, the Malayalam text (and the corresponding phoneme sequence) has to be represented using Roman symbols. However, such a grapheme to phoneme conversion programme for the different fonts was not available. Also, information about the coding scheme was not readily available. Hence a grapheme-to-phoneme (G2P) program was written to take care of most conventions of the font. A tools named Corpuscrt [6] from CMU (Carnie Melon University) is used to select the maximum phonetically rich sentences. Hence the selected text includes about 202 sentences, comprising of about 1600 words.

3.4 Analysis of Unique Phoneme Features for speech recognition

For the analysis of unique phoneme features of Malayalam language, the phonemes Alvelor plosive Q (t't'a) , Alvelor rhotic Ω (ra) , Retroflex lateral ള (l'a) ,Palatel lateral ഴ (zha) and Dental Nasal ന (n1a) have been selected. For this analysis, two set of words have been compiled.

i. The first set contains a word-list constituting each of these sounds in all permissible word-positions. In this category, a total of 340 words have been compiled. The following are (Table 3) the total number of section wise, categorization of words with these phonemes that have been collected for the study.

Table 3: List of Words with different categories of phonemes

Category	Total numbers
Alvelor plosive	27
Alvelor rhotic	48
Retroflex lateral	37
Palatel lateral	42
Dental Nasal	40
retroflex rhotic	49
alveolar lateral	44
alveolar nasal	53

ii. Since /la/ and /l'a/, /ra/ and /r'a/ are two pairs of contrastive phonemes and /zha/ contrasts in some instances with one or both of the laterals or in other instances with one or both of the rhotics, the data sets are designed to include minimal pairs. Accordingly 32 minimal pairs have been compiled (total of 64 words). In short a total of 404 words were designed for unique phoneme study.

3.5 Phoneme class wise speech recognition task

Five phoneme classes of words have been chosen for this task. The different phoneme classes are stop, lateral, fricative, nasals and rhotic. Maximum words have been included such that it should contain all phonemes in all word positions (start, middle and end).

Nasal class category contain 74 words which include labial, dental, alveolar and retroflex nasals. Category wise number of words is shown in table 4.

Table 4: List of words with Nasal class phonemes

Category	Total numbers
Labial nasals	20
Dental nasals	20
Alveolar nasals	14
Retroflex nasals	20

i. Lateral class words include a set of 54 words carefully designed which includes palatal, retroflex and alveolar lateral as detailed in table 5.

Table 5: List of words with lateral class phonemes

Category	Total numbers
Palatel lateral	15
Retroflex lateral	15
Alveolar lateral	24

ii. Fricative class words include a set of 70 words which includes dental, retroflex and palatal fricatives. Table 6 list the number of words of each type.

Table 6 : List of words with fricative class phonemes

Category	Total numbers
Dental fricative	23
Retroflex fricative	15
Palatel fricative	17
Glotal fricaitive	15

iii. Plosive/stop class words includes a total of 205 words in different categories such as labial voiced stop, labial unvoiced stop, dental voiced stop, dental unvoiced stop, velar voiced stop, velar unvoiced stop, retroflex unvoiced stop, palatal voice stop and palatal unvoiced stop. Table 7 lists the number of words in each category.

Table 7 : List of words with plosive/stop class phonemes

Category	Total numbers
Labial voiced stop	26
Labial unvoiced stop	20
Dental voiced stop	20
Dental unvoiced stop	20
Retroflex voiced stop	21

Retroflex unvoiced stop	15
Palatel voiced stop	20
Palatel unvoiced stop	22
Velar voiced stop	23
Velar unvoiced stop	19

iv. Rhotic class words includes 43 words which include both rhotics (alveolar rhotic and retroflex rhotics) as detailed in table 8.

Table 8: List of words with rhotic class phonemes

Category	Total numbers
Alvelor rhotic	23
Retroflex rhotic	20

4. Speech data collection

Speech data for all the recognition tasks is collected from the age group of 20 to 45 years keeping almost equal male and female ratio. Speakers were requested to read the word /sentences in a normal reading manner. Speech data is collected in normal office environment using a microphone with 1600 frequency. Mistakes made while recording have been corrected by re-recording or by making the corresponding changes in the transcription file. For all the tasks data have been collected from 25 speakers (13 female and 12 male speakers). The task wise list of speech corpus is detailed below.

- ➤ **Isolated Digit recognition task** - Digits zero to nine is uttered separately by speakers. Hence Size of the speech corpus for this task is 250 words.

- ➤ **Connected digit recognition task** - Text data as detailed in section 3.2 is read by the 25 speakers in normal reading manner. Size of the corpus is 500 words.

- ➤ **Continuous speech recognition task**- The 202 continuous sentences which are selected as described above were read by the speakers. Hence the size of the continuous speech corpus is 40000 words.

- ➤ **Unique, phoneme study** - The specially designed 404 words were read 25 speakers thereby enhancing the speech corpus by 10100 words.

- ➤ **Phoneme class wise recognition task** - For this category of speech corpus the 446 words as mentioned in section 3.5 were read by 25 speakers. Hence the size of speech corpus in this category is 11150 words.

These details are given in table 9 below.

Table 9: Speech corpus collection

Recognition task	Total text size in words	Number of speakers	Total size of speech corpus in words	Speech corpus in hrs
Isolated digit	10	male : 12 female :13	250	0.16
connected digit	20	male : 12 female :13	500	0.63
continuous speech recogntion task	1600	male : 12 female :13	40000	11.67
Analysis of Unique	404	male : 12 female :13	10100	3.9

5. Creation of Phoneme List

A phoneme is the basic unit of recognition. Therefore the preparation of a phoneme list is a vital step in creating a pronunciation dictionary. Each phone to be denoted by a set of phonetic notation rather than a single notation, which will be decided by the acoustic property of the phones. All unique phonemes of Malayalam language have been identified and phonetic notation has been assigned according to its phonetic properties. Table 10 lists all the phonemes used in this work along with its phonetic notation.

Table 10: Phoneme list

Malayalam	Phonetic Notation	Malayalam	Phonetic Notation	Malayalam	Phonetic Notation
അ	a	ച	clch ch	മ	m
ആ	aa	ഛ	clch chch	യ	y
ഇ	i	ജ	vbj j	ര	r
ഈ	ii	ഝ	clch chch	ല	l
ഉ	u	ഞ	nj'	വ	v
ഊ	uu	ട	clt' t'	ശ	sh
എ	e	ഠ	clt' t'h	ഷ	s'h
ഏ	e'	ഡ	vbd' d'	സ	s
ഐ	ai	ഢ	clt' t'h	സ	s1
ഒ	o	ണ	n'	ഹ	h
ഓ	o'	ത	clt t	ള	l'
ഔ	au	ഥ	clt th	റ	r'
ം	m	ദ	vbd d	ഴ	z
ഃ	-	ധ	clt th	റ	clr1 r1
ു	u'	ന	n (Dental nasal)	ഫ	ph1 (fan)
ക	clk k	ന	n1(alveolar nasal	ള	l'
ഖ	clk kh	പ	clp p	ണ	n'
ഗ	vbg g	ഫ	clp ph	ന	n1
ഘ	clk kh	ബ	vbb b	റ	r'
ങ	ng'	ഭ	clp ph	ല	l

6. Pronunciation Dictionary (PD)

In pronunciation dictionary all words in the training data to be mapped onto the acoustic units which are defined in the phone list. Theoretically, creation of phonetic dictionary is just a mapping of grapheme to phoneme. But this alone would not work especially for a language like Malayalam as many phonemes pronounced differently in different contexts. For example, ഫ (ph'a) pronounced differently in ഫലം (/ph'alam/-fruit) and ഫാന്‍ (/ph'aan'/ - fan) and ന (n1a and na - Nasal dental and Nasal alveolar) is pronounced differently even though the grapheme notation is same (eg. നനക്കുക/n1anaykkuka/- watering). Hence for creating pronunciation dictionary, initially mapping have been completed for all grapheme into the corresponding phoneme units. Then some phonological rules have been applied manually and edited the dictionary. Multiple pronunciations are also incorporated in the dictionary.

The format of pronunciation dictionary for isolated digit recognition is in table 11 and that of continuous speech recognition task is under table 12. The left segment represent orthographic transcription and right segment shows its actual pronunciation is taken from the training speech corpus. The dictionary creation to be done with utmost care and precision as the duplication of phone for different sounds will confuse the trainer and the model so created will give false information to the recognizer. The dictionary must have all alternate pronunciations marked with parenthesized serial numbers starting from (2) for the second pronunciation. The marker (1) is omitted for the first pronunciation. Thus pronunciation dictionary of 2480 words of Malayalam language have been prepared for different tasks.

The following are the size of pronunciation dictionary for different tasks/analysis

i. Digit recognition task - 10 words
ii. Connected word recognition tasks - 20 words
iii. Continuous speech recognition task - 1600 words
iv. Unique phoneme analysis - 404 words
v. Phoneme class wise recognition task - 446 words

Table 11: P.D for isolated digit recognition task

puujyam	clp p uu j y a m
onnu'	o n3 u'
raNtu'	r a n: vbd: d:
muunu'	m uu n3 u'
naalu'	n3 aa l u'
anchu'	a nj clc u'
aar'u'	aa r' u'
eezu'	ee zh u'
ettu'	e clt: t: u'
ompatu'	o m clp p a clt t u'
ompatu (2)	o n clp p a clt t u'

Table 12: Format of PD for continuous speech recognition task

aadyapaadattilum'	aa vbd d y a clpp aa vbd d a clt tt i l u m
aago'l'avipan'iyil_(2)	aa vbg g o' l' a v i clp p a n' i y i l
aago'l'avipan'iyil_	aa vbg g o' l' a v i clp p a n' i y i l
aakaashattu'ninnul'l'a	aa clk k aa sh a clt tt u' n i nn u l'l' a
aakar_s'hakamaayad'isainukal'il_	aa clk k a r' s'h a clk k a m aa y a vbd' d' i s ai n l u clk k a l' i l
aalappuza	aa l a clp pp u zh a
aam'bulan_su'	aa m vbb b u l a n s u'
aam'bulan_su'kit't'iyillenna	aa m vbb b u l a n s u' clk k i clt'l t'l i y i ll e n l n l a
aandhraprade'shu'	aa n clt th r' a clp p r' a vbd d e' sh u'
aapuro'gatiyum'	aa clp p u r o' vbg g a clt t i y u m
aaram'bhichchatu'	aa r a m clp ph i clch chch a clt t u'
aaram'bhikkum'	aa r a m clp ph i clk kk u m
aaram'bichchu	aa r a m vbb b i clch chch u

Transcription file

The transcription file contains the sequence of words transcribed orthographically, and non-speech sounds, written exactly as they occurred in the training speech, followed by a tag which can be used to associate this sequence with the corresponding training speech data. The acoustic speech file is transcribed into its corresponding orthographic representation. The transcription file is to be prepared for every training speech data after closely examining/hearing the wave file. Hence the transcription process is done manually considering even silence, noise or a breath. This is a herculean task and has to be done very carefully, since a minute error in the transcription file will mislead the recognizer and will lead into misclassification of training data. Hence transcription files prepared for a total of 62000 speaker utterances (wave file). Each task has a separate transcription file which consisting of transcriptions for each speaker utterance. Table 13 is a sample of transcription file created for continuous speech recognition task.

Table 13 : A sample of transcription file for continuous speech recognition task

```
<s> at'isthaanavilayil_ anj'chushatamaanam'maar_jin_
nalkan'amennaavashyappet't'ukon't'u' patimuunninu'
pet'ro'l'_panpukal'_ at'achchit't'upratis'he'dhikkuvaan_ vitaran'akkaar_
tiirumaanichchu </s>
<s> atinit'e vivaadamaayasid'i pibiyut'enir_de'shaprakaaram'
nir_michchataan'ennu nir_maataavum' sam'vidhaayakanum' po'liisino't'u
sammatichchit't'un't'u' </s>
<s> ate'samayam' prashnattil_ vaadam'ke'l'_kkunnatu'
teranj'nj'et'uppukammiis'han_ naal'atte'kkumaar'r'i </s>
<s> itu vivaadamaayappo'l'_ supriim'ko't'ati no't't'iisayachchu </s>
<s> intyan_ aayur_ve'davyavasaayam' naalaayirattiirunnuur'r'ianj'chu'
ko't'iyut'e'taan'u' </s>
<s> innale mukhar_jiye sit'iem'aar_aiskaanim'guka_l'_kku'
vidhe'yanaakki </s>
<s> iime'khalayil_ var_s'ham'to'r'um' e'zushatamaanam'
val'ar_chchayaan'ul'l'atu' </s>
```

8. Automatic Speech Recognition

Automatic Speech Recognition is the process of converting speech into text. Speech recognition systems perform two fundamental operations: Signal modeling and pattern matching [7]. Signal modeling represents process of converting speech signal into a set of parameters. Pattern matching is the task of finding parameter sets from memory which closely matches the parameter set obtained from the input speech signal [8]. Hence the two important methodologies used in this works are   MFCC Cepstral Coefficients [9] for signal modeling and Hidden Markov Model [10] for pattern matching. Mathematically stating computing the probability of a word given a pattern model is computed as the product of two components – acoustic model and language model.[11]

$$\hat{W} = \arg\max_W P\,(Y \mid W)\,P(W)) \,/\, P(Y) \qquad (1)$$

The right hand side of equation (1) has two components: i) the probability of the utterance of the word sequence given the acoustic model of the word sequence and ii), and the probability of sequence of words. The first component $P(Y/W)$, known as *the* observation likelihood, which is computed by the acoustic model. The Second component $P(Y)$ is estimated using the language model..

8.1 Acoustic model

The Carnegie Mellon University Sphinx-4[12] system is a frame-based, HMM-based, speech recognition system capable of handling large vocabularies. The word modeling is performed based on sub word units (phone set), in terms of which all the words in the dictionary are transcribed. Each phonetic unit considered in its immediate context (which we will refer to as tri-phone) is modeled by 3-state left-to-right HMM model [13] . To reduce the parameter estimation problem, data is shared across states of different tri-phones. These groups of HMM states sharing distributions between its member states are called senones [25]. The acoustic modeling component of the system has four important stages [14] . The first stage is to train the context independent model and then training context dependent models. Decision trees are built on the third stage and finally context independent tied models are created. Here, continuous Hidden Markov models are chosen to represent context dependent phones (tri-phones). The phone likelihood is computed using HMM. The likelihood of the word is computed from the combined likelihood of all the phonemes. The acoustic model thus built is a 3 state continuous HMM, with states clustered using decision tree [15] . The acoustic features used for recognition consist of 39-dimensional acoustic vectors derived every 10 ms spanning an analysis window of 20 ms. The feature vector consists of the first 13 cepstral coefficients (including, the frame energy) and two blocks of 13-dimensional coefficients, one composed of the "delta" cepstral features (velocity) and the other composed of "delta-delta" cepstral features (acceleration). Cepstral mean normalization is always applied at the utterance level to remove statistical biases of the mean which might have been introduced by linear channel distortion.

8.2 CREATION OF LANGUAGE MODEL

The language model employed in our recognition experiments is a tri gram-based language model developed using a training text corpus. These language models are smoothed using the Good-Turing discounting procedure [16].

Importance of a language model in a speech recognition system is vital as acoustic model alone cannot handle the problem of word ambiguity. Word ambiguity may occur in several forms such as similar sounding sounds and word boundaries. With similar sounding sounds, words are indistinguishable to the ear, but are different in spelling and meaning. The words "paat'am' (പാഠം and " paat'ham' (പാഠ്ഠ“are such examples. In continuous speech, word boundaries

are also challenging. For instance, the word " talasthaanam' (തലസ്ഥാനം) can be misconstrued as "tala sthaanam' (തല സ്ഥാനം). The use of language model resolves these issues by considering phrases and words that are more likely to be uttered. The trigram based language model with back-off is used for recognition in this work. The language model is created using the CMU statistical LM toolkit [17].

Training and testing is done by n –fold validation techniques. Word Error Rate (WER) is the standard evaluation metric used here for speech recognition. It is computed by SCLITE [18], a scoring and evaluating tool from National Institute of Standards and Technology (NIST)

8.3 Results of Different Speech Recognition Tasks

8.3.1 Isolated Digit Recognition Task

Table 14: Result of Digit Recognition Task

```
WORD RECOGNITION PERFORMANCE
Percent Total Error      =    7.1%   (    5)
Percent Correct          =   94.3%   (   66)
Percent Substitution     =    5.7%   (    4)
Percent Deletions        =    0.0%   (    0)
Percent Insertions       =    1.4%   (    1)
Percent Word Accuracy    =   92.9%
Ref. words               =            (   70)
Hyp. words               =            (   71)
Aligned words            =            (   71)
CONFUSION PAIRS                  Total          (4)
                                 With >=  1 occurances (4)
   1:     1  ->  എട്ട് ==> ഒന്ന്
   2:     1  ->  എഴ് ==> ആറ്
   3:     1  ->  എഴ് ==> ഒന്ന്
   4:     1  ->  ഒന്പത് ==> ഒന്ന്
   -------
   4
```

In isolated digit recognition task 92.9% accuracy being obatained as shown in table 14.

8.3.2 Connected Digit Recognition Tasks

Table 15: Result of Connected Digit Recognition Task

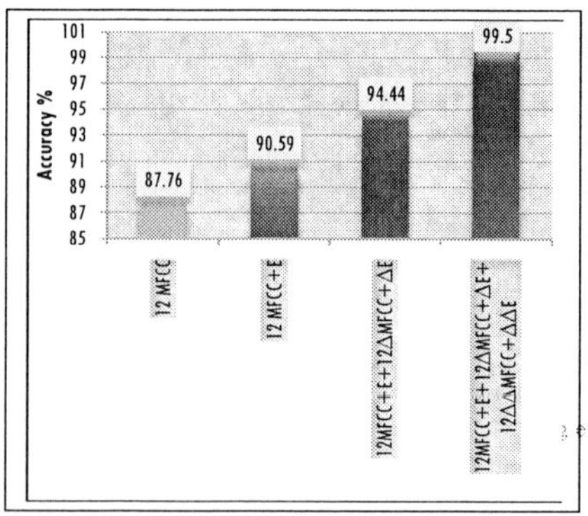

230

Speech recognition accuracy of the continuous speech recognition task using continuous and semi continuous model is detailed in table 16. For testing mode, a highest accuracy of 84% is obtained in continuous density hidden Markov model experiment.

9. Summary

Collection of essential resources for the development of speech recognizer for Malayalam language is discussed in this paper . A detailed description on the collection of text corpus and speech corpus for each tasks is being presented. The size of text and speech corpus used for each recognition tasks is detailed. Pronunciation dictionary, Transcription which are created based on these text and speech corpus are explained later with sufficient examples. A complete set of phone list which are prepared in connection with the recognition task is presented in table form. Thus we have created a total speech corpus of size 62000 words and a pronunciation dictionary of size 2480 words. It is anticipated that this work would bridge the start up issues such as collection of speech and text corpus, pronunciation dictionary creation etc, of Malayalam language speech research community to a greater extent.

References :

[1] Sadanandan, S. 1999. Malayalam Phonology: An Optimality   Theoretic Approach. Thesis (PhD). University of Southern California.

[2] Mohanan, K.P. and Mohanan, T. 1984. Lexical Phonology of the Consonant System in Malayalam. Linguistic Inquiry, 15, 575-602

[3]Kumari, S.B., 1972. Malayalam Phonetic Reader. Mysore: Central Institute of Indian Languages.

[4]Srikumar, K. and Reddy, N. 1988. An articulatory and acoustic study of trills in Malayalam. Osmania Papers in Linguistics, 14, 42-54.

[5]Radhakrishnan, S. 2009. Perception of Synthetic Vowels by Monolingual and Bilingual Malayalam Speakers . PhD thesis . Kent State University College

[6]Sesma Bailador , Alberto " CorpusCrt Politechnic University of   atalonia 1998

[7]   L.R.Bahl et.al, A method for the construction of Acoustic Markov Models for Words , IEEE Transactions on Audio, Speech and Language processing, Vol.1,No.4, Oct.1993

[8] B.H. Juang, C.H. Lee and Wu Chou, *Minimum classification error rate methods for speech recognition,* IEEE Trans. Speech & Audio Processing, T-SA, vo.5, No.3, pp.257-265, May 1997.

[9] Rabiner, L. Juang, B. H., Yegnanarayana, B., "Fundamentals of   Speech Recognition", Pearson   Publishers, 2010.

[10] L.R Rabiner and B.Gold , "Theory and Application of digital Signal processing , Prentice Hall,   Englewodd Cliffs , NJ,1975

[11] S. Young (1999). Acoustic Modelling for Large Vocabulary Continuous Speech Recognition.   Computational Models of Speech Pattern Processing: Proc NATO Advance Study Institute. K.   Ponting, Springer-Verlag: 18-3

[12] http://cmusphinx.sourceforge.net/wiki/tutorial

[13] C.H Lee, L.R Rabinar , R. Pieraccini, and J.G Wilpon , " Accoustic Modelling for Large Vocabulary speech Recognition ", Computer speech and Language , 4:127-165,1990 Vocabulary speech   Recognition ", Computer speech and Language , 4:127-165,1990

In connected digit recognition task, as per table 15, a very good accuracy is obtained i.e , 99.5 % (with 39   feature vectors) .Table 16 is the snapshot of the live decoder developed for connected digit recogntion task.

Table 16: Live decoder for Connected Digit Recognition Task

8.3.3 Continuous Speech Recognition Task

Table 16 Training and Testing results of Continuous Speech recognition - CDHMM vs. SCHMM Models

Sl.No	Continuous Model		Semi Continuous Model	
	Sentence Recognition Accuracy %			
	Train	Test	Train	Test
1	92.03	86.15	79.2	72
2	91.4	84.11	77.3	70.17
3	90.43	81.13	75	68.18
4	91	85.01	78	70.65
5	90.65	84.36	77.5	70.2
Average	91.102	84.152	77.4	70.24

[14]Levinson, S. E., Rabiner, L. R Sondhi, M. M., (1983). Speaker Independent Isolated Digit   Recognition Using Hidden Markov Model, In Proceedings of ICASSP,pp.1049-1052.

[15] S. Young, et. al., the HTKBook, http://htk.eng.

[16] K.F. Lee, Large-vocabulary speaker-independent continuous speech recognition: The Sphinx system, Ph.D. Thesis, Carnegie Mellon University, 1988.

[17]The   CMU-Cambridge   LM   toolkit   - http://www.speech.cs.cmu.edu/SLM/toolkit.html

[18] Fiscus, J. (1998) Sclite Scoring Package Version 1.5, US NationalInstitute   of   Standard   Technology(NIST),   URL   - http://www.itl.nist.gov/iaui/894.01/tools/.

POS Tagging of Hindi-English Code Mixed Text from Social Media: Some Machine Learning Experiments

Royal Sequiera, Monojit Choudhury, Kalika Bali
Microsoft Research Lab India
{a-rosequ,monojitc,kalikab}@microsoft.com

Abstract

We discuss Part-of-Speech(POS) tagging of Hindi-English Code-Mixed(CM) text from social media content. We propose extensions to the existing approaches, we also present a new feature set which addresses the transliteration problem inherent in social media. We achieve an 84% accuracy with the new feature set. We show that the context and joint modeling of language detection and POS tag layers do not help in POS tagging.

1 Introduction

Code Switching (CS) and Code Mixing (CM) are natural phenomena observed in all stable multilingual societies. Code Switching refers to the co-occurrence of speech extracts belonging to two different grammatical system (Gumperz, 1982) in a single utterance. Whereas, Code Mixing denotes the usage of linguistic units of one language into an utterance that belongs to another language(Myers-Scotton, 1993). In this paper, we will use CM to refer to both of these situations.

CM is predominately a speech-level phenomenon, though with the prevalence of social media and user-generated content that are more speech-like, we now observe CM quite commonly in text as well (Crystal, 2001; Herring, 2003; Danet and Herring, 2007; Cardenas-Claros and Isharyanti, 2009). Therefore, it is imperative that we develop NLP techniques for processing of CM text to analyze the user-generated content from and cater to the needs of multilingual societies.

In the recent past, there has been some work on CM data most of which has been focused on word level language identification (Solorio and Liu, 2008a; Saha Roy et al., 2013; Gella et al., 2013) and POS tagging of CM text which is one of the first steps towards processing of CM text. Parts-of-Speech tagging is another task which has been explored to a little extent for CM text (Solorio and Liu, 2008b; Vyas et al., 2014). POS tagging of CM data is an interesting problem to study both from a practical and a theoretical perspective because it requires modeling of the grammatical structures of both the languages as well as the syntactic constraints applicable on CM.

In this paper, we explore machine learning approaches for POS tagging of Hindi (**Hi**)-English (**En**) CM text from social media. We start with replication of the experiments presented in (Vyas et al., 2014) and (Solorio and Liu, 2008b), and reconfirm their results on our dataset. Then we extend the set of features used by (Solorio and Liu, 2008b) and do several feature selection experiments. Finally, we also propose and conduct a joint language labeling and POS-tagging task. Our experiments show that while there is marginal improvement due to use of certain additional features, joint modeling significantly hurts the results.

The rest of the paper is organized as follows: Sec 2 discusses the related work; in Sec 3, we introduce some basic concepts and definitions. Dataset is described in Sec 4 and the baseline experiments in Sec 5. Sec 6 discusses experiments with additional features and Sec 7 the joint modeling approach. Finally, we summarize our work and conclude in Sec 8.

2 Related Work

Parts-of-Speech tagging for monolingual text has been studied extensively with an accuracy as high as 97.3% for some languages (Toutanova et al., 2015). However, not much work has been done on POS tagging of CM text. Solorio and Liu (2008b) were the first to introduce this problem through their work on POS tagging of Spanish-English CM text collected by recording a conversation between three bilingual speakers and then manually transcribing the recording. They presented a set of rule-based methods which included tagging the

233

D S Sharma, R Sangal and E Sherly. Proc. of the 12th Intl. Conference on Natural Language Processing, pages 237–246,
Trivandrum, India. December 2015. ©2015 NLP Association of India (NLPAI)

Previous Work/Approaches	CM	Social Media	Machine Learning	Transliteration & Spelling Variation
(Solorio and Liu, 2008b)	✓	✗	✓	✗
(Gimpel et al., 2011)	✗	✓	✓	✓
(Vyas et al., 2014)	✓	✓	*	✓
(Jamatia and Das, 2014)	**	✓	✓	✗

Table 1: A comparison of the previous work
* Was not a primary focus but POS tagging of CM text was discussed.
** Did not use machine learning for developing a CM POS tagger but the individual POS taggers were trained using supervised machine learning.

Hi POS Tag	Universal POS Tag
NC	NOUN
NP	NOUN
NV	NOUN
NST	NOUN
VM	VERB
VAUX	VERB
PPR	PRON
PRF	PRON
PRC	PRON
PRL	PRON
PWH	PRON
JJ	ADJ
JQ	ADJ
DAB	PRON
DRL	PRON
DWH	PRON
AMN	ADV
ALC	ADV
PP	ADP
CSB	CONJ
CCL	CONJ
CX	PRT
CCD	CONJ
PU	.
RDX	NUM
RDF	X
RDS	.

Table 2: Mapping from **Hi** POS tag set to the Universal POS tagset

text through an English and a Spanish monolingual tagger and then choosing one of the two tags for a word based on some heuristics that used (a) the confidence scores of the taggers, (b) the lemma of the words, and (c) the language of the word as detected by several language detection techniques. They extend their framework by learning to predict the tag per word based on the output of the two monolingual taggers and several other features such as the confidence scores, language labels and the word itself. Naïve Bayes, SVM, Logic Boost and J48 were explored in their experimental setup. The machine learning based techniques achieved a word level tagging accuracy of around 93.5%, which is nearly a 4% improvment over the best of the rule-based systems. Note that since the speech conversations were manually transcribed, this dataset did not contain any spelling variations or transliteration, which are typical of social media text.

More recently, Vyas et al. (2014) presented an initial study on POS tagging of Hindi-English CM social media text. Apart from code-mixing, social media text poses other challenges as well, including transliteration (i.e., Romanization of Indic language words), intentional and unintentional spelling variations, short and ungrammatical text, etc. The authors created a corpora with multi-level annotations to represent the POS tag on the first level, language label on the second level and transliteration of the Hindi tokens in the final level. A simple language detection based heuristic was employed where first the text was divided into chunks of tokens belonging to a language, and then each chunk was tagged by the POS tagger for that language. Language detection and transliteration was carried out by a system described in Gella et al. (2013). Three different sets of experiments were conducted to study the effects of language detection and transliteration on the accuracy of POS tagging. With gold standard language labels and transliteration, a word level tagging accuracy of 79.02% has been reported, which is a good 15% improvement over the case where both language detection and transliteration were done automatically. This study not only highlights the importance of accurate language detection and transliteration for POS tagging of social media text, but also establishes the inherent hardness of the problem. Clearly, POS tagging of CM text cannot be solved by juxtaposition of two monolingual POS taggers.

Another recent study by Jamatia and Das (2015) briefly mentions POS tagging of Hindi-English CM tweets, though the primary focus of their work was tagging of monolingual Hindi tweets. They report 63.5% word level tagging accuracy for some Random Forest based pilot experiments on 400 CM utterances (all romanized) from Facebook and Twitter. On the other hand, the authors report around 87% accuracy on monolingual Hindi tweets written in Devanagari. Thus, this work also illustrates the hardness of POS tagging transliterated and CM social media text.

In this context, it is useful to note that there has been quite a few studies on POS tagging of monolingual social media content for English and a few other languages. Gimpel et al. (2011) proposed one of the first POS taggers for English tweets. A tag set for representing the POS tags in social media content was presented. They used a CRF tagger with arbitrary local features in a log-linear model adaptation. The feature set included context cues such as the the presence of digits or hyphens and capitalization in a word, and features representing suffixes upto length 3. The augmented feature set also amassed external linguistic resources, the domain specific properties of data and unlabeled in-domain data. An accuracy of 89.95% was reported.

Owoputi et al. (2013) proposed an improvement over this original Twitter POS tagger. In addition to the unsupervised word clustering features, the tagger exploits lexical features, which escalates the accuracy from aforementioned 90% to 93%. However, none of these studies consider code-mixing.

	#Matrices	
Type matrix	*Vyas et al. (2014)*	*Jamatia et al.(2014)*
#HiMono	126	9
#HiCM	61	213
#EnMono	189	0
#EnCM	30	0
Total Matrices	406	222
	#Tokens	
#Tokens	4,157	5,633
% of matrices with CM	22.4	95.94

Table 3: Data set statistics

Table 1 presents a comparative summary of the aforementioned approaches.

3 Basic Concepts and Annotation

With the advent of social media, we are now witnessing considerable amount of CM in text data, which is primarily due to the fact that social media data, and more generally other forms of CM such as e-mails,blogs are speech-like comments Bali et al. (2014). The following example for instance, demonstrates CS and CM in social media content:

Dude I think u should try again caz ye [this] tera [your] fault nahi [not] hai [is]. ye [this] CBSE walo [people] ki [of] fault hai [is].

The above utterance is an instance of both CM and CS. It is code-switched because the first part of the sentence "*Dude I think u should try again caz*" is in **En** matrix whereas the rest of the sentence is in **Hi** matrix. It is also code-mixed as there are **En** words such as fault is embedded within the **Hi** matrix.

More formally,

1. *Matrix Language:* The language governing the grammar of an utterance is called as the matrix language of the utterance. (plural: *matrices*)

2. *Embedded Language:* Refers to the language of the words that are not in the matrix language, but nevertheless, are *embedded* in the utterances.

3. *Switch Points:* Suppose that q :$<$ $w_1 w_2 w_3 \ldots w_n >$ is an utterance; i is a

switch point if and only if the language of the word w_i is different from w_{i+1}

Normalization is defined as the process of transforming an input text that might contain non-standard spellings and informal syntax to a standard or canonical representation of the spellings and grammar. If the language is not written in the script that is normally used, then the process of normalization would also involve back-transliteration from the non-native script to canonical word forms in the native script.

POS tagging of a CM text in social media is a challenging task due to the following reasons:

1. **Paucity of annotated CM data:** Annotating any data is a laborious task. However, there are further complications in CM data annotations. A bi-lingual speaker who is proficient at both the languages who also has matching linguistic background may be required for annotating POS tags of CM text. Although crowd-sourcing can be an alternative approach, it comes with the risk of inaccurate annotations. For this reason, crowd sourcing is not a very viable alternative for this kind of annotation (Jamatia and Das, 2014).

2. **Transliteration of tokens:** Traditionally, Indic languages are written in their native script. But, due to various socio-technical reasons, the computer mediated channels have been observing a lot of romanized content Sowmya et al. (2010). Bali et al. (2014) showed that less than 5% of the **Hi** content popular in social media are in native script. This can appear to be a challenging task for identifying the language of the words and thereby POS tagging of such words.

4 Data Set

For this study, we use data from two different sources. The first set was created by (Vyas et al., 2014). The corpora contains posts and comments belonging to Facebook pages of various celebrities and the BBC Hindi news page. The second source ocomes from Jamatia et al. (2015). The data is acquired from @BBCHindi and @aajtak using a Java based Twitter API. The statistics for each source is summarized by Table 3. There is a total of 628 utterances with 9,790 tokens and 48.4% of data features CM.

Vyas et al. (2014) mention the matrix language to be either **Hi** or **En**. But, for the sake of granular analysis we divide matrix language into four parts: Hindi-Monolingual (**HiMono**), Hindi-Code Mixed (**HiCM**), English-Monolingual (**EnMono**) and English-Code Mixed (**EnCM**). We also follow a multilevel annotation and the same illustrated by figure 1.

For our study, we use the tags generated by the individual POS taggers. But as the tag sets for **Hi** (Sankaran et al., 2008) (also known as **ILPOST** tagset) and **En** (Marcus et al., 1993) tagger are of different, we map both the tag sets to a universal POS tag set as proposed by(Petrov et al., 2011). The mapping from **En** tag set to the universal tag set has already been proposed by (Petrov et al., 2011); we present a mapping from **Hi** tag set to the universal POS tag set which is shown in Table 2.

5 Baseline Experiments

In this section we present baseline experiments for the VGSBC and SL model which is essentially the replication of the approaches proposes by Vyas et al. (2014) and Solorio and Liu (2008b) respectively. However, in the next section, we discuss additional features and extensions to the existing models.

5.1 VGSBC Baseline Experiments

Initially, we conduct the experiments proposed by (Vyas et al., 2014), and we refer to this model as VGSBC model following the names of the authors. The VGSBC model divides the text into chunks of tokens having same language. After which, the **Hi** chunks are tagged by the **Hi** POS tagger and **En** chunks are tagged by **En** POS tagger. The model presents three different experiments: The first experiment uses gold language labels(LL) and gold normalization (HN) of the token. On the other hand, the second experiment uses gold language labels but automated normalization of the tokens which helps one to individually study the effect of gold standard normalization. Finally, machine generated language labels and transliteration is used to establish the their combined role. We implement an n-gram based language identifier as proposed by (Gella et al., 2013; King and Abney, 2013a). For generating back-transliterations, we use a transliteration system inspired by (Gella et al., 2013). For **Hi**, a

```
<s>
  <matrix name="HiCM">
  Use_PRON=उसे realise_VERB krwao_VERB=करवाओ
  ki_CONJ=की tm_PRON=तुम uske_PRON=उसके liye_ADP=लिए
  kitna_PRON=कितना loyal_ADJ\E ho_VERB=हो use_PRON=उसे
  apni_PRON=अपनी sari_ADJ=सारी baten\NOUN=बाते share_VERB\E
  karo_VERB=करो
  </matrix>
</s>
```

Figure 1: An annotation example

	Matrix : Hindi			Matrix : English			Overall
	HiMono	HiCM	Overall	EnMono	EnCM	Overall	
Gold Std LL, Gold Std HN	0.794	0.764	0.769	0.827	0.817	0.825	0.782
Gold Std LL, Machine HN	0.775	0.759	0.762	0.754	0.722	0.749	0.759
Machine LL, Machine HN	0.759	0.741	0.744	0.544	0.556	0.546	0.698

Table 4: VGSBC results on the data set

CRF++ based Hindi POS Tagger is used which can be downloaded from `http://nltr.org/snltr-software/` and for **En**, we use the Twitter POS tagger (Owoputi et al., 2013) which is also freely available at `http://www.ark.cs.cmu.edu/TweetNLP/`. The tagger has an in-built tokenizer and normalizer specifically fabricated to handle social media content.

Result: Table 4 shows the results on our test data set using the VGSBC model. The accuracy is the highest (78.2%) when gold language labels and gold normalization is used. Also, VGSBC with gold language labels and gold normalization performs 6% better than VGSBC with machine generated language labels and automated normalization.

5.2 SL Baseline Experiments

The VGSBC model proposes a modest approach to POS tagging. As each chunk is tagged separately by either of the monolingual taggers, crucial information that can be captured by the other tagger is missed. Moreover, as the entire utterance is not tagged by the tagger, a right POS tag cannot be determined for every chunk. In other words, only completely monolingual utterances will be tagged appropriately by such an approach. Although the model uses language labels as well as the normalization of the tokens, it does not employ any machine learning algorithms to train a CM POS tagger. In contrast, SL model presents an approach which leverages the tags spawned by both the taggers. Furthermore, an entire utterance is passed to the individual taggers and either of the tags (from **Hi** POS tagger or **En** POS tagger) is chosen based on various heuristics:

5.2.1 Using Individual Taggers

We run the CM text through the individual taggers and measure the accuracy with respect to each tagger. As mentioned earlier, we pass the entire utterance to both taggers and then compute the accuracy for each tagger so as to determine how well monolingual the taggers work on CM text.

5.2.2 Using Language Labels

We also use the language labels to select the appropriate POS of the word in a CM text:

1. **Automatic Language Detection:** The language labels of words in the CM text was de-

	Matrix : Hindi			Matrix : English			Overall
	HiMono	HiCM	Overall	EnMono	EnCM	Overall	
ILPOST	0.800	0.722	0.735	0.192	0.252	0.207	0.610
Twitter	0.286	0.353	0.342	0.827	0.789	0.821	0.455
Automatic Language Detection	0.777	0.817	0.811	0.772	0.718	0.765	0.799
Human Language Detection	0.800	0.823	0.820	0.827	0.789	0.821	0.821
Oracle							0.864

Table 5: SL baseline accuracy

	Matrix : Hindi			Matrix : English			Overall
	HiMono	HiCM	Overall	EnMono	EnCM	Overall	
Naive Bayes	0.756	0.748	0.753	0.798	0.794	0.797	0.777
MaxEnt	0.795	0.795	0.795	0.862	0.849	0.861	0.831

Table 6: SL machine learning experiment

termined by using an n-gram based language identifier suggested by(Gella et al., 2013). The POS of the word is chosen based on its language label i.e. if the word is identified to be **En**, the output by **En** POS tagger will be considered as the POS of the word and similarly the POS of the **Hi** POS tagger is taken as the POS of the word if the language of the word is identified to be **Hi**.

2. **Gold Standard Language Detection:** The word level language labels of the CM text was done by a human annotator and the gold language labels of the words in CM text were used to choose the right POS of the word.

5.2.3 Oracle

Finally, to establish a baseline accuracy, we check if one of the POS tags generated by the individual POS taggers matches the gold POS tag and accordingly calculate the accuracy. In other words, Oracle gives the accuracy when the right tag is chosen from the available POS tags of monolingual POS taggers.

5.2.4 SL Baseline Results

As shown in Table 5, the monolingual taggers fail miserably as the CM text contains words that are foreign to the monolingual taggers. Therefore, an accuracy of 45.5% and 61.1% is obtained for **En** and **Hi** respectively. Unsurprisingly, the accuracy is high when the matrices are monolingual and when the appropriate POS tagger is used. When the gold language labels are used, the accuracy of the POS tags increases dramatically and an accuracy of 82.1% is obtained.

5.3 SL Machine Learning Experiments

We also conduct the machine learning experiments proposed by Solorio and Liu with the following features:**En** POS tag, **Hi** POS tag, POS confidence and the current token.

Due to the lack of information such as the confidence score and the tagger lemma, we could not conduct the experiments verbatim. However, the above mentioned features are closest to the features proposed by Solorio and Liu that we could replicate.

We use MALLET (MAchine Learning LanguagE Toolkit) which can be downloaded from `http://mallet.cs.umass.edu/` for training the CM POS tagger. As the data set is relatively smaller, a 10-fold cross validation was used for all the experiments. The experiment is conducted in three steps. We trained a Naïve Bayes and a MaxEnt based model aforementioned in the SL model.

5.3.1 Results

The accuracy obtained for each algorithm is as shown in Table 6. MaxEnt algorithm outperforms

Context	3	2	1	0
Accuracy	0.798	0.812	0.827	0.837

Table 7: Effect of context on learning

Scheme	Accuracy
Without Normalization (SL)	0.831
With Automated Normalization	0.834
With Gold Normalization	0.840

Table 8: Effect of Normalization on Accuracy

the Naive Bayes algorithm by 7%. Therefore, MaxEnt is chosen for further experiments.

5.4 Comparison of the Models

Let us now compare the numbers in table 4 and 5. When the gold standard language labels are used, the VGSBC model performs with 75.9% accuracy whereas the SL model has an accuracy of 82.1%. Similarly, when automated language labels are used, the VGSBC model works with an accuracy of 69.8% but the SL model performs with 82.1% accuracy. This clearly shows that tagging an utterance first and later choosing the POS tag based on the language label works better than dividing the utterance into chunks based on the language labels and then passing the chunks to the POS taggers.

The VGSBC and SL model show improvement in the accuracy (6% and 2% respectively) when gold language labels are used. The improvement in the accuracy can be owed to the fact that automatic language detection of a CM data plays a very important role and is far from a solved problem (Solorio et al., 2014). Further, the Oracle accuracy on our data set was found to be 86.4%.

The SL machine learning model works better than the SL baseline model with automatic language detection by 3% but is less than Oracle almost by the same margin. It is also seen that the machine learning model better than the SL baseline model (by 1%) with human language identification.

6 Additional Features and Joint Modeling

Although the SL models performs better than the VGSBC model, it does not use several features that the modern taggers use today. For instance,

the SL tagger does not utilize the contextual features, normalization features, sub-word features such as whether the first letter in a word is capitalized and so on. In this section, we propose additional features to the existing feature set used by the SL model and also propose extensions to the existing models.

6.1 The Feature Set

In addition to the feature set proposed by the SL model, we use the feature set proposed by Chittaranjan et al. (2014). The final augmented feature set is shown below:

Monolingual POS tagger Features: The output generated by the individual POS taggers mapped to the universal POS tag set is used as features. The confidence of the taggers is also used as a feature but as ILPOST does not generate a confidence score per tag, the confidence score generated by the Twitter tagger alone is used.

Normalization Feature: The words are normalized to their native script. That is, if the word is an **En** word, its standard form is used. Similarly, if the word is an **Hi** word, its gold transliteration is used. The rationale behind using this feature is that the text is written only in Roman script and is prone to non-standard spellings.

Contextual Features: These features include context cues such as the current token, an array of previous and next words, previous token and previous tag.

Capitalization Features: Indicates if the token is capitalized or not. These features signal an instance of Named Entity which could be a proper noun.

Special Character Features: Social media posts generally contain special characters like @, # etc.

Lexicon Features: They capture the existence of a token in lexicons. The lexicons include a **Hi** dictionary of most frequent words, **En** dictionary of most frequent words, a list of common NEs and a list of common acronyms.

Language Identifier Scores: We used character n-grams (King and Abney, 2013b) to train two language identifiers. We trained two separate language identifiers to identify words of **Hi** and **En**. We trained each such classifier with 5000 cases of positive instances and 5000 cases of negative instances. The classifiers were trained on $Maximum\ Entropy(MaxEnt)$ and the proba-

Features	*Accuracy*
Context	0.837
Hi and **En** LL	0.837
Lexicons	0.837
Hi Lexicon	0.838
NE and Acronym Lexicon	0.836
Hi, NE and Acronym Lexicon	**0.840**
Punctuation	0.838
Capitalization	0.836
Hi Normalization	0.830
Current Token	0.802
En Confidence	0.836
Hi, En POS and **En** Confidence	0.721
Capitalization, Punctuation and Lexicon	0.836

Table 9: The ablation experiment

bility scores for each label was used as a feature for CM POS tagger.

6.2 Experiments

In this section, we discuss various experiments with the new found features. We use *MaxEnt* algorithm for all the experiments discussed in this section with a 10-fold cross validation.

6.2.1 Context Based Experiments

Firstly, we choose the Monolingual POS tagger features (POS_{Hi}, POS_{En}, $Confidence_{En}$) along with Normalization Feature (NRM) and experiment for the best context. We run the experiment on different window size of words to determine the right context that produces the best accuracy. We begin with a context of three words (previous three words and next three words), i.e. window size = 3 and reduce the size by 1 for each experiment.

6.2.2 Normalization Experiments

We also propose extensions to SL model by using normalization of tokens as one of the features. Initially, we train a CM POS tagger with the aforementioned features without any normalization. This is exactly in line with what SL model proposes. In the next set of experiments, we use a machine transliteration of the token as the feature.

Finally, we use the gold transliteration as the feature to compare the gain with accuracy when the transliteration of the token is perfectly known.

6.3 Results

In the context based experiment, we observe that the accuracy increases consistently as the context decreases which is surprising as the context should have helped the learner. We also find that the word alone (no context) is the optimal context for the tagger. This is summarized by Table 7.

We see that the normalization slightly betters the performance. There is 1% increase in the accuracy when gold normalization is used. Table 8 exemplifies the gain in accuracy with the addition of normalization layer.

After choosing the right context size, we conduct a set of ablation experiments to study the effect of a set of features on the accuracy. We selectively turn off some of the features and observe the corresponding change in the accuracy for such a set of features. We conducted an elaborate feature selection step which is recapitulated by Table 9. From the table we observe that when the POS tags of the monolingual taggers are turned off, the accuracy drops steeply indicating that POS tags of the monolingual taggers contribute the most to the learning. The highest accuracy obtained is 84% when **Hi**, NE and Acronym lexicons are ablated and we call the corresponding model as SL++ model.

7 Joint Modeling

As the above proposed approaches use two separate layers viz. a language identification layer and a normalization layer, we propose a joint modeling of both the layer and investigate the resulting tagger. Our reasoning is that the the errors propagating through the layers can be avoided by designing a joint modeling system. To implement the above proposal, we come up with a new tag system which is a product of the POS tag set and language label set.

Let $\rho : POS_1, POS_2, ... POS_{12}$ be the POS tags.

Let $\Lambda : L_1, L_2, L_3$ be the language labels.
Then, the new tag set T obtained is defined as:

$$\mathcal{T} : \rho \times \Lambda$$

We choose the best model from Table 9 and run the joint modeling experiments. This approach yields an accuracy of 77.33%.

	Matrix : Hindi			Matrix : English			Overall
	HiMono	HiCM	Overall	EnMono	EnCM	Overall	
VGSBC	0.803	0.813	0.815	0.827	0.817	0.817	0.812
SL	0.849	0.861	0.851	0.926	0.930	0.911	0.913
SL++	0.852	0.861	0.859	0.930	0.908	0.915	0.926

Table 10: Matrix level accuracy of the systems

8 Discussion and Conclusion

In this study, we have seen that the VGSBC model performs poorly in comparison to the SL model baselines. This shows that passing the entire utterance to the monolingual POS tagger and then choosing the appropriate tags based on the language label works better than passing the monolingual fragments of the utterance to the respective monolingual tagger. We also see that the machine learning based technique described (Solorio and Liu, 2008) performs much better than all the baselines that only use some heuristics on top of the monolingual taggers. This essentially reestablishes the findings by Solorio and Liu (2008b).

Our extended feature experiments show that the context features do not help. In fact, the accuracy consistently increases as the context is narrowed down all the way until no context is used. Further, the SL model with the augmented features provides only marginal improvements. We believe that this is due to the paucity of training and test data. To verify this proposition, we trained and tested the VGSBC, SL and SL++ models on our entire dataset, the results of which are shown in 10. It is seen that the accuracy obtained for each model on the training data is consistently higher and that too by a large margin than when we did k-fold validation (all our previous experiments). Thus, it is clear that with context and other features, the models are over-fitting to the data and as a result we see no benefit. We do believe that some of the features, especially the context is useful and experiments on larger training set, will be able to bring this fact out. Similarly, the joint modeling approach also shows a degraded performance probably because of larger number of tags and insufficient data to learn from.

In order to understand the pain points of CM text processing, we also analyzed the correlation between the number of switch points in a sentence and the accuracy of POS tagging. Figure 2 shows the plot of number of switch points (so 0

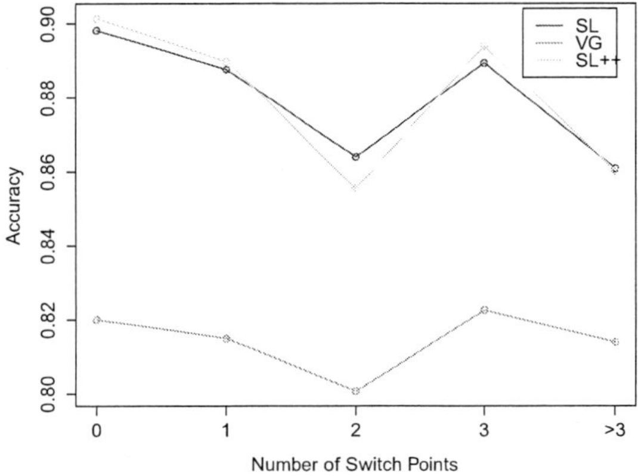

Figure 2: An annotation example

essentially refers to monolingual utterances) versus the word level accuracy of the tagger averaged on all test sentences with that many switch points. We see that with the increase of number of switch points, the accuracy falls dramatically for up to 2 switch points. However, the accuracy for three switch points is higher than one or two switch points. When we investigated into this, we found that there are very few examples in our test set with 3 or more switch points and as a result it is impossible to make any conclusions from there.

In future, we would like to address the data scarcity problem through a multi-pronged approach of (a) annotating more data, (b) using unsupervised machine learning techniques, and (c) better learning from monolingual utterances. Another promising direction of research could be to model this problem as a structured output prediction rather than a pointwise classification problem.

Acknowledgment

We would like to thank Amitava Das, IIIT-Sri City and Anupam Jamatia, NIT Agartala for sharing their annotated dataset. We are also grateful to Rafiya Begum, MSR India for her help with reviewing the annotations.

References

Kalika Bali, Yogarshi Vyas, Jatin Sharma, and Monojit Choudhury. 2014. ''i am borrowing ya mixing?'' an analysis of English-Hindi code mixing in Facebook. In *Proceedings of the First Workshop on Computational Approaches to Code Switching, EMNLP.*

Mónica Stella Cardenas-Claros and Neny Isharyanti. 2009. Code-switching and code-mixing in internet chatting: Between yes, ya, and si a case study. In *The JALT CALL Journal, 5.*

Gokul Chittaranjan, Yogrshi Vyas, Kalika Bali, and Monojit Choudhury. 2014. Word-level language identication using crf : Code-switching shared task report of msr india system. In *Proceedings of the First Workshop on Computational Approaches to Code Switching.*

David Crystal. 2001. *Language and the Internet.* Cambridge University Press.

Brenda Danet and Susan Herring. 2007. *The Multilingual Internet: Language, Culture, and Communication Online.* Oxford University Press., New York.

Spandana Gella, Jatin Sharma, and Kalika Bali. 2013. Query word labeling and back transliteration for indian languages: Shared task system description. In *FIRE Working Notes.*

Kevin Gimpel, N. Schneider, B. O'Connor, D. Das, D. Mills, J. Eisenstein, M. Heilman, D. Yogatama, J. Flanigan, and N. A. Smith. 2011. Part-of-speech tagging for twitter: Annotation, features, and experiments. In *Proceedings of ACL.*

John J. Gumperz. 1982. *Discourse Strategies.* Oxford University Press.

Susan Herring, editor. 2003. *Media and Language Change.* Special issue of Journal of Historical Pragmatics 4:1.

Anupam Jamatia and Amitava Das. 2014. Part-of-speech tagging system for Hindi social media text on twitter. In *Proceedings of the First Workshop on Language Technologies for Indian Social Media, ICON.*

Anupam Jamatia, Bjrn Gambck, and Amitava Das. 2015. Part-of-speech tagging for code-mixed english-hindi twitter and facebook chat messages. In *In the Proceeding of 10th Recent Advances of Natural Language Processing (RANLP).*

B King and S. Abney. 2013a. Labelling the languages of the world in mixed-language documents using weakly supervised methods. In *Proceedings of NACL-HLT, 2013.*

Ben King and Steven Abney. 2013b. Labeling the languages of words in mixed-language documents using weakly supervised methods. In *Proceedings of NAACL-HLT*, pages 1110–1119.

Mitchell P Marcus, Mary Ann Marcinkiewicz, and Beatrice Santorini. 1993. Building a large annotated corpus of english: The penn treebank. *Computational linguistics*, 19(2):313–330.

Carol Myers-Scotton. 1993. *Dueling Languages: Grammatical Structure in Code-Switching.* Claredon, Oxford.

Olutobi Owoputi, Brendan OConnor, Chris Dyer, Kevin Gimpel, Nathan Schneider, and Noah A. Smith. 2013. Improved part-of-speech tagging for online conversational text with word clusters. In *Proceedings of NAACL.*

Slav Petrov, Dipanjan Das, and Ryan McDonald. 2011. A universal part-of-speech tagset. *arXiv preprint arXiv:1104.2086.*

Rishiraj Saha Roy, Monojit Choudhury, Prasenjit Majumder, and Komal Agarwal. 2013. Overview and datasets of fire 2013 track on transliterated search. In *FIRE Working Notes.*

Bhaskaran Sankaran, Kalika Bali, Monojit Choudhury, Tanmoy Bhattacharya, Pushpak Bhattacharyya, Girish Nath Jha, S. Rajendran, K. Saravanan, L. Sobha, and K. V. Subbarao. 2008. A common parts-of-speech tagset framework for indian languages. In *Proceedings of LREC.*

Thamar Solorio and Yang Liu. 2008a. Learning to predict code-switching points. In *Proceedings of the Empirical Methods in natural Language Processing.*

Thamar Solorio and Yang Liu. 2008b. Parts-of-speech tagging for English-Spanish code-switched text. In *Proceedings of the Empirical Methods in natural Language Processing.*

Thamar Solorio, Elizabeth Blair, Suraj Maharajan, Steven Bethard, Mona Diab, Mahmoud Gohneim, Abdelati Hawwari, Fahad AlGhamdi, Julia Hirschberg, Alson Chang, and Pascale Fung. 2014. Overview for the first shared task on language identification in code-switched data. In *Proceedings of the First Workshop on Computational Approaches to Code Switching.*

V. B. Sowmya, Monojit Choudhury, Kalika Bali, Tirthankar Dasgupta, and Anupam Basu. 2010. Resource creation for training and testing of transliteration systems for indian languages. In *Proceedings of the Language Resource and Evaluation Conference (LREC).*

Kristina Toutanova, Dan Kleina, Christopher Manning, and Yoram Singer. 2015. Feature-rich part-of-speech tagging with a cyclic dependency network. In *In the Proceeding of 10th Recent Advances of Natural Language Processing (RANLP).*

Yogarshi Vyas, Spandana Gella, Jatin Sharma, Kalika Bali, and Monojit Choudhury. 2014. Pos tagging of English-Hindi code-mixed social media content. In *Proceedings of the First Workshop on Computational Approaches to Code Switching, EMNLP.*

Automated Analysis of Bangla Poetry for Classification and Poet Identification

Geetanjali Rakshit[1,2,3]   **Anupam Ghosh**[2]
Pushpak Bhattacharyya[2]   **Gholamreza Haffari**[3]
[1]IITB-Monash Research Academy, India, [2]IIT Bombay, India
[3]Monash University, Australia
{geet,pb}@cse.iitb.ac.in, anupam.ghsh@gmail.com
gholamreza.haffari@monash.edu

Abstract

Computational analysis of poetry is a challenging and interesting task in NLP. Human expertise on stylistics and aesthetics of poetry is generally expensive and scarce. In this work, we delve into the data to automatically extract stylistic and linguistic information which are useful for analysis and comparison of poems. We make use of semantic (word) features to perform subject-based classification of Bangla poems, and various stylistic as well as semantic features for poet identification. We have used a Multiclass SVM classifier to classify Tagore's collection of poetry into four categories: devotional, love, nature and nationalism. We identified the most useful word features for each category of poems. The overall accuracy of the classifier was 56.8%, and the analysis led us to conclude that for poetry classification, word features alone do not suffice, due to allusions often being used as a poetic device. We, next, used these features along with stylistic features (syntactic, orthographic and phonemic), for poet identification on a dataset of poems from four poets and achieved a performance of 92.3% using a Multiclass SVM classifier. While content-based and stylometric analysis of prose in Bangla has been done in the past, this is a first such attempt for poetry.

1 Introduction

Poetry is a creative expression of language that often makes use of one or more of the crafts of diction, sound, rhythm, imagery and symbolism. Processing creative writing such as poetry by computers is challenging, as opposed to ordinary everyday text, for computers are efficient in carrying out tasks of a more logical nature, as compared to those involving creativity. The volume of research in automated analysis of poetry has generally been low, and no work has been reported on Bangla poetry. Bangla is the seventh most spoken language in the world and has a rich literary tradition. While work on stylometry for prose (Chakraborty and Bandyopadhyay, 2011) and author identification (Das and Mitra, 2011) has been reported, our work is the first of its kind to analyse Bangla poetry.

The computational analysis of poetry is important, for not only can it lead to a better understanding of what makes rich literature, but it also has applications such as making recommendations to readers based on their literary tastes, as also in the psychological effects of poetry (Stirman and Pennebaker, 2001). Identifying the poet is also important for plagiarism detection.

We explore various kinds of features from Bangla poems to carry out specific analyses. Firstly, we perform a subject-based classification of poems into pre-determined categories from Tagore's poems using semantic features, the categories being *pooja* (devotional), *prem* (love), *prokriti* (nature), and *swadesh* (nationalism). With our experiments, we establish the fact that the words can help only so far, due to frequent use of poetic devices such as allusion and symbolism, which often leave poems open to multiple interpretations. Second, we observe that word features do fairly well for poet identification. The results improve when stylistic features (orthographic, syntactic and phonemic) are also introduced.

The paper is organized as follows. We dis-

D S Sharma, R Sangal and E Sherly. Proc. of the 12th Intl. Conference on Natural Language Processing, pages 247–253,
Trivandrum, India. December 2015. ©2015 NLP Association of India (NLPAI)

cuss the literature in Section 2, and describe our approach in Section 3. The system architecture and its details have been described in 4. The experimental setup and results are covered in sections 5 and 6, respectively. We delve into analysis of the results in Section 7. We conclude our work and discuss scope for future work in Section 8.

2 Related Work

Computational understanding of poetry has been previously studied for languages such as English (Kaplan and Blei, 2007), (Kao and Jurafsky, 2012), Chinese (Voigt and Jurafsky, 2013) and Malay (Jamal et al., 2012).

Kaplan and Blei (2007) analyse American poems in terms of style and visualise them as clusters. Kao and Jurafsky (2012) use various stylistic features to categorise poems into ones written by professional and amateur poets, and establish the importance of *Imagism* in poetry of high-quality. Lou et al. (2015) use of a SVM to classify poems in English into 3 main categories and 9 subcategories by combining tf-idf and Latent Dirichlet Allocation. All this work has been done for English. Voigt and Jurafsky (2013) observed through computational analysis the decline of the classical nature of Chinese poetry. Li et al. (2004) use a technique based on term connections for stylistic analysis of Chinese poetry. Jamal et al. (2012) have used a Support Vector Machine model to classify traditional Malay poetry, called pantun, into various themes.

No work in Bangla poetry has been so far reported in the literature. Chakraborty and Bandyopadhyay (2011) have used low-level, chunk-level and context-level features for semi-supervised detection of stylometry in Bangla prose on the writings of Rabindranath Tagore. Das and Mitra (2011) conducted experiments on author identification of Bangla prose on the works of three authors, namely Rabindranath Tagore, Bankim Chandra Chattopadhyay and Sukanta Bhattacharyay. They have used a Naive Bayes classifier using simple unigram and bigram features.

3 Our Approach

We use both word features and stylistic features that have reported in the literature. In the following section, we briefly describe them and go on to explain how they have been adapted to be used in our system for Bangla. One feature not previously reported for stylometry is *reduplication*, which is common, though not exclusive, to Indian languages. As compared to Indian languages, however, its literary merits in English might be arguable. Usage like *ha ha* doesn't generally act a poetic device.

3.1 Features

The stylometric features used for classification can be broadly classified into three kinds: orthographic, syntactic and phonemic. These are the same categories as reported in (Kaplan and Blei, 2007). Besides these, lexical features have been used.

Orthographic Features: Orthographic features deal with the measurements of various units of the poem. These features include word count, number of lines, number of stanzas, average line length, average word length, and average number of lines per stanza.

Syntactic Features: The syntactic features deal with the frequencies of the various parts of speech (POS) in the poem.

Phonemic Features: Sound plays an important role in poetry. Phonemic features deal with the sound devices used in a poem. Rhyme and metre are essential poetic devices. We make use of the following phonemic features: rhyme scheme, alliteration and reduplication.

Some common kinds of rhyme has been tabulated in Table 1.

Lexical Features: Each word type is a feature and its value is the tf-idf.

4 System Overview

The high-level view of the system is shown in Figure 1. The basic blocks of the system are: Alliteration and Reduplication, Rhyme Scheme Detector, Document Statistics, Shallow Parser and SVM classifier. Each one has been described in the subsequent subsections.

4.1 Alliteration and Reduplication

Alliteration is a poetic device which refers to the repetition of consonant sounds in the beginning of consecutive words. An example for this in Bangla would be অনাদরে অবহেলায়

Rhyme Type	Examples
Identical Rhyme: Identical phoneme sequence	cat-cat, বাঁকে-বাঁকে (*baanke-baanke*)
Perfect Rhyme: Same phoneme sequence from the ultimate stressed vowel onwards, but differing in the previous consonant	cat-rat, বাঁকে-থাকে (*baanke-thaake*)
Semi Rhyme: A perfect rhyme where one word has an additional syllable at the end	stick-picket জবা - অবাক (*joba-obaak*)
Slant Rhyme: Either identical ultimate stressed vowels or identical phoneme sequences following the ultimate stressed vowel, but not both	queen-afternoon কল্লোল - কোলাহল (*kallol-kolahol*)

Table 1: Types of Rhyme

(*anaadore abohelay*). To detect alliteration, we check the beginning sound of each word for every pair of consecutive words in a line.

Reduplication refers to the repetition of any linguistic unit such as a phoneme, morpheme, word, phrase, clause or the utterance as a whole (Chakraborty and Bandyopadhyay, 2010). It is mainly used for emphasis, generality, intensity or to show continuation of an act. It may be partial (খাওয়া দাওয়া *khaawa daawa*) or complete (আকাশে আকাশে *akaashe akaashe*). We check only for complete reduplication. We use a simple algorithm that basically checks if two consecutive words in the poem are identical.

4.2 Rhyme Scheme Detection

A rhyme scheme is the pattern of rhymes at the end of each line of a poem or song. The rhyme scheme of the poem can be determined by looking at the end word in each line of a poem. Various rhyme schemes are used. Ex: *abab*, *aabb*, *ababcc* and so on.

In the event of absence of Bangla Pronunciation Dictionary, we wrote the following algorithm. A character in Indian language scripts

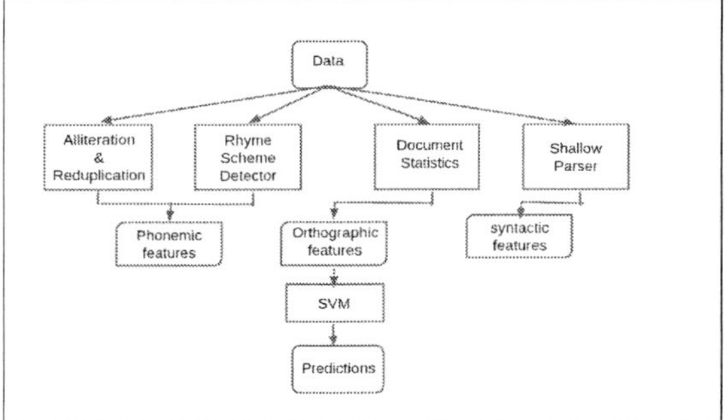

Figure 1: System Overview

is close to a syllable and there is one-to-one correspondence between what is spoken and what is written (Kishore and Black, 2003). In most cases, Bangla words are spoken as they are written. We also accomodate certain noncompliant cases, for instance for the case of হ-ending words, as explained in the subsequent algorithms.

In our system, we check for perfect rhyme and identical rhyme only. We grouped similar sounding vowels and consonants into groups, to allow for similar sounds to rhyme in case of perfect rhyme. This grouping was done as shown in Table 2. A detailed study of Bangla phonemics can be found in (Barman, 2011). The algorithm to detect the rhyme scheme is shown in Algorithm 1. The algorithm to check for rhyming words is described in Algorithm 2.

অ	আ	ই,ঈ	উ, ঊ	এ, ঐ
ও, ঔ	ক, খ	গ, ঘ	চ, ছ	জ, ঝ, য
ট, ঠ	ড, ঢ	ত, থ, ৎ	দ, ধ	ণ, ন
প, ফ	ব, ভ	ম	র, ড়	ল
শ, ষ, স	হ	য়		

Table 2: Sound Groupings

The *Find-rhyme-scheme* algorithm takes a poem and the length of a stanza in the poem as input, and returns the rhyme scheme for the poem. We first initialise a string variable *rhyme_scheme* to a sequence of consecutive English alphabets, which denotes the rhyme scheme. Next, we pick the end word for the first line and check if it rhymes with the end word of the next line (by calling *Check-rhyme()*). We keep checking until the last line, or until, a rhyming line is found. We then update the rhyme_scheme variable and check

---

Algorithm 1: Find-rhyme-scheme

Input: poem, len_of_stanza
Output: rhyme_scheme

Initialise: $rhyme\_scheme = "abcdefgh.."$
1. for i in range(0, $len\_of\_stanza - 1$)
2.   Read line and pick last word $word[i]$
3.   for j in range($i + 1$, len_of_stanza)
4.   Read line and pick last word $word[j]$
5.   Check-rhyme($word[i]$, $word[j]$)
6.   If true
7. $rhyme\_scheme[j] = rhyme\_scheme[i]$
8.   break
9. return rhyme_scheme height

---

from the next line onwards, and repeat the process until the last but one line is processed.

Algorithm 2: Check-rhyme

Input: $word_1$, $word_2$
Output: flag
V denotes vowel, C denotes consonant

Initialise: flag = 0
1. Pick last character z_1 and z_2 of $word_1$ and $word_2$, respectively
2.   if similar_sounding(z_1, z_2) or if either of z_1 or z_2 is C while the other is 'ো'
3.   pick the last but one character y_1 and y_2 of $word_1$ and $word_2$, respectively
4.   if both y_1 and y_2 are V or both y_1 and y_2 are C
5.   if similar_sounding(y_1, y_2)
6.   flag = 1
7.   if both z_1 and z_2 are C
8.   if y_1 and y_2 are C
9.   flag = 1
10.   if y_1 and y_2 are V
11.   if similar_sounding(y_1, y_2)
12.   flag = 1
13. return flag

The *Check-rhyme* algorithm takes as input two Bangla words, and returns whether or not they rhyme. It basically compares the last two characters of both words. The last two characters should either be identical to each other, or should be similar sounding, based on the groupings we made in Table 2. Thus words like মাঝে(*maajhe*) and লাজে (*laaje*) would rhyme.

Also, there is the special case of handling 'ো' (the vowel *o*). In most cases, when the last character in a Bangla word is a consonant, they have an implied *o* sound. This is kind of the reverse of the *inherent vowel suppression* in Hindi (Kishore and Black, 2003). Hence, words like দেহ (*deho*) and কেহ (*keho*) would rhyme. Thus, if one of the last character is a consonant, we need to check if the other word ends in 'ো'.

4.3 Document Statistics

The Document Statistics module basically takes as input a poem, and returns its orthographic features by counting the number of characters, words and stanzas. It also returns the tf-idf scores of the words.

4.4 Shallow Parser

The shallow parser gives the analysis of a sentence in terms of morphology, POS tagging, chunking, etc. We use the POS tags as features in our classification. The shallow parser for Bangla from IIIT Hyderabad has been used.

4.5 SVM

A Support Vector Machine (SVM) classifier was used for classification (Vapnik, 1998). based on the idea of learning a linear hyperplane from the training set that separates positive examples from negative examples. The hyperplane must be at the maximum distance possible from data instances of either class in order to obtain the best generalization. The SVM implementation of SVMLight was used for our experiments (Joachims, 1999).

5 Experimental Setup

For classification of poems into various categories, a bag of words model was trained using only lexical features. Five-fold cross-validation was done on 1341 poems, for training and testing. A linear kernel was used.

We crawled data from the website of *The Complete Works of Tagore* [1] to collect poems by Rabindranath Tagore in four categories: *pooja, prem, prokriti,* and *swadesh*. The data statistics are shown in Table 3.

For the poet identification task, we crawled data from the website of *Bangla Kobita* [2] by

---

[1] http://tagoreweb.in/
[2] http://www.bangla-kobita.com/

Category	Number of Poems
Pooja (Devotional)	617
Prem (Love)	395
Prokriti (Nature)	283
Swadesh (Nationalism)	46
Total	1341

Table 3: Data

four poets: *Rabindranath Tagore, Jibananada Das, Kazi Narul Islam,* and *Sukumar Roy.* The data statistics are shown in Table 4.

Poet	Number of Poems
Rabindranath Tagore	382
Jibanananda Das	348
Kazi Nazrul Islam	198
Sukumar Roy	130
Total	1058

Table 4: Data

We trained a Multiclass SVM classifier with a linear kernel for poet identification, using just lexical features (Model-lex) and using lexical as well as stylometric features (Model-lex+style). Five-fold cross-validation was done on the 1058 poems.

6 Results

The results for subject-based poem classification have been tabulated in Table 5 in terms of Precision, Recall and F-measure. The class *pooja* has the best score, and lowest score is for *swadesh.* The confusion matrix has been shown in Table 6. The precision for *swadesh* is high, but the recall is very low, which means instances of *swadesh* are often predicted to be of some other class. The overall performance is 56.8%.

The results for poet identification are shown in Table 7. We compare the results from the SVM classifier, with a Naive Bayes Classifier, in terms of lexical as well as stylistic features. The SVM trained on both lexical and stylis-

Class	P	R	F-measure
pooja	73.6	84.3	78.6
prem	58.9	55.4	57.1
prokriti	61.9	53.3	57.3
swadesh	83.3	21.7	34.4

Table 5: Results for Poem Classification

	pooja	prem	prokriti	swadesh
pooja	521	71	24	2
prem	110	219	66	0
prokriti	56	76	151	0
swadesh	27	6	3	10

Table 6: Confusion Matrix

tic features was found to have the best performance. When using a Multiclass SVM for classification, introducing stylistic features helped improve the overall performance by 2.2%.

Model	P	R	F-measure
Naive-Bayes-lex	90.3	89.2	89.5
Naive-Bayes lex+style	91.0	90.1	90.4
SVM-lex	92.0	87.9	89.9
SVM-lex+style	91.4	93.2	92.3

Table 7: Results for Poet Identification

In Table 8, we tabulate the effect of using various types of stylistic features on the prediction task. The syntactic features alone helped increase the performance by 1.2% over lexical features. Introducing orthographic and phonemic features further increased the performance slightly, by 0.5% and 0.7%, respectively.

7 Analysis and Discussion

From the confusion matrix in poem classification (Table 6), we observe that *swadesh* is often confused with *pooja.* A closer inspection of the poems from the category *swadesh* reveals that the presence of words like জপমালা (*japmala*), পবিত্র (*pobitro*), তীর্থ (*teertho*), etc., which mean *rosary, holy, pilgrimage,* respectively, might have caused the misclassification. One might note that in these poems, the words of worship such as pilgrimage, rosary, etc., have been used in the context of worship of one's motherland, and hence actually belong to the category *swadesh* or nationalism. On the other hand, in poems from *pooja* misclas-

Features	P	R	F-measure
lex+syn	91.2	92	91.1
lex+syn+orth	91.4	92.5	92
lex+syn+orth +phonemic	91.4	93.2	92.3

Table 8: Effect of various stylistic features

sified as *swadesh*, words like আঘাত (*aaghaat*), ভয় (*bhoy*), which mean *hit* and *fear*, respectively, might have caused the misclassification. Similarly, *prem* is most often confused with *pooja*, while *prokriti* is most often confused with *prem.*

Category	Most useful words
Pooja (Devotional)	*hridoy*(heart), *jibon*(life), *gobhir*(deep), *anando*(joy), *alo*(light), *alok*(light), *dhulo*(dust)
Prem (Love)	*sokhi*(friend), *hridoy*(heart), *pran*(life), *haashi*(smile), *madhur*(sweet), *nayan*(eyes), *aakulo*(eager), *aakhi*(eyes)
Prokriti (Nature)	*akash*(sky), *megh*(cloud), *hawa*(breeze), *phool*(flower), *baanshi*(flute), *gagan*(sky), *chhaaya*(shadow)
Swadesh (Nationalism)	*poth*(road), *bangla*(Bangla), *jaagrat*(awake), *bhai*(brother), *bharat*(India)

Table 9: Most distinguishing words from each category

Table 9 shows the most useful word features in identifying each category of poems.

It is observed that lexical features are very useful for poet identification, as poets often have a tendency to use the same set of or similar words. Stylistic features help only to a small extent, particularly, orthographic and phonemic features vary a lot across poems by the same poet, and hence are not much of a distinguishing feature in identifying the poet.

8   Conclusion and Future Work

We conducted what we presume to be the first reported computational analysis of Bangla poetry. With some preliminary investigation, we observed that words alone aren't always sufficient for classifying poems into categories, be-cause of poets often resorting to symbolism. It would be interesting to further investigate if this problem could be helped with Word Sense Disambiguation (WSD). We were able to determine the poet correctly 92.3% of the the time using the SVM classifier. The set of lexical and stylometric features could also be used to categorise poems into ones written by professional and amateur poets, which could throw some light on poetry appreciation, like (Kao and Jurafsky, 2012). The phonemic features could be further enhanced with checking of presence of rhyming words in the same line as also checking for style where each line in a poem begins with the same word. For example: অনেক কীর্তি, অনেক মূর্তি, অনেক দেবা-লয় (*onek keerti, onek smriti, onek debalaya*). The phonemic features may also be extended to detect metre and prosody (Dastidar, 2013), involving syllabification of the verse.

References

Binoy Barman. 2011. A contrastive analysis of English and Bangla phonemics. *Dhaka University Journal of Linguistics*, 2(4): 19–42.

Tanmoy Chakraborty and Sivaji Bandyopadhyay. 2011. Inference of Fine-grained Attributes of Bengali Corpus for Stylometry Detection. *Polibits*, Vol(44): 79–83. Instituto Politécnico Nacional, Centro de Innovación y Desarrollo Tecnológico en Cómputo.

Tanmoy Chakraborty and Sivaji Bandyopadhyay. 2010. Identification of reduplication in Bengali corpus and their semantic analysis: A rule-based approach. *NAACL Workshop on Computational Linguistics for Literature.*

Suprabhat Das and Pabitra Mitra. 2011. Author Identification in Bengali Literary Works. *Pattern Recognition and Machine Intelligence*, Vol(6744): 220–226. Springer Berlin Heidelberg.

Rimi Ghosh Dastidar. 2013. Symmetry in Prosodic Pattern of Rhyme and Daily Speech: Pragmatics of Perception. *Mining Intelligence and Knowledge Exploration*, 823–830. Springer.

Noraini Jamal, Masnizah Mohd and Shahrul Azman Noah. 2012. Poetry classification using support vector machines. *Journal of Computer Science*, Vol 8(9):1441.

T. Joachims. 1999. Making large-Scale SVM Learning Practical. *Advances in Kernel Methods - Support Vector Learning*, 169–184 MIT Press. Cambridge, MA.

David M. Kaplan and David M. Blei. 2007. A computational approach to style in american poetry. *In Data Mining, 2007. ICDM 2007. Seventh IEEE International Conference on.* 553–558. IEEE.

Justine Kao and Dan Jurafsky. 2012. A computational analysis of style, affect, and imagery in contemporary poetry. *In Proceedings of the NAACL-HLT 2012 Workshop on Computational Linguistics for Literature. Montreal, Canada,* 8–17.

S. Prahallad Kishore and Alan W. Black. 2003. Unit size in unit selection speech synthesis. *INTERSPEECH.*

Noraini Jamal, Masnizah Mohd and Shahrul Azman Noah. 2004. Poetry stylistic analysis technique based on term connections. *Machine Learning and Cybernetics, 2004. Proceedings of 2004 International Conference on,* Vol(5):2713–2718. IEEE.

Andres Lou, Diana Inkpen, and Chris Tanasescu. 2015. Multilabel Subject-Based Classification of Poetry. *The Twenty-Eighth International Flairs Conference.*

Shannon Wiltsey Stirman and James W. Pennebaker. 2001. Word use in the poetry of suicidal and nonsuicidal poets *Psychosomatic Medicine,* Vol 63(4):517–522. LWW.

Vladimir Naumovich Vapnik and Vlamimir Vapnik. 1998. *Statistical learning theory,* Vol 1. Wiley New York.

Rob Voigt and Dan Jurafsky. 2013. Tradition and Modernity in 20th Century Chinese Poetry. *23rd International Conference on Computational Linguistics.*

Bengali Shallow Parser http://ltrc.iiit.ac.in/analyzer/bengali/. *LTRC, IIIT Hyderabad.*

Sentence Boundary Detection for Social Media Text

Dwijen Rudrapal   **Anupam Jamatia**   **Kunal Chakma**
Dpt. of Computer Science and Engineering
National Institute of Technology
Agartala, Tripura, India
{dwijen.rudrapal, anupamjamatia, kchax4377}@gmail.com

Amitava Das
Indian Institute of Information Technology
Sri City
Andhra Pradesh, India
amitava.das@iiits.in

Björn Gambäck
Dpt. of Computer and Information Science
Norwegian University of Science and Technology
Trondheim, Norway
gamback@idi.ntnu.no

Abstract

The paper presents a study on automatic sentence boundary detection in social media texts such as Facebook messages and Twitter micro-blogs (tweets). We explore the limitations of using existing rule-based sentence boundary detection systems on social media text, and as an alternative investigate applying three machine learning algorithms (Conditional Random Fields, Naïve Bayes, and Sequential Minimal Optimization) to the task.

The systems were tested on three corpora annotated with sentence boundaries, one containing more formal English text, one consisting of tweets and Facebook posts in English, and one with tweets in code-mixed English-Hindi. The results show that Naïve Bayes and Sequential Minimal Optimization were clearly more successful than the other approaches.

1 Introduction

Sentences are basic units of the written language — just as words, phrases, and paragraphs — and detecting the beginning and end of sentences, or sentence boundary detection (SBD) is an essential prerequisite for many Natural Language Processing (NLP) applications, such as Information Retrieval, Machine Translation, Sentiment Analysis, and Document Summarization. For formal texts, sentence boundary detection has been considered a more or less solved problem since the 1990s, but the proliferation of social media has added new challenges to language processing and new difficulties for SBD, with state-of-the-art systems failing to perform well on social media, due to the coarse nature of the texts.

In spite of its important role for language processing, sentence boundary detection has so far not received enough attention. Previous research in the area has been confined to formal texts only, and either has not addressed the process of SBD directly (Brill, 1994; Collins, 1996), or not the performance related issues of sentence boundary detection (Cutting et al., 1992). In particular, no SBD research to date has addressed the problem in informal texts such as Twitter and Facebook posts.

The growth of social media is a global phenomenon where people are communicating both using single languages and using mixes of several languages. The social media texts are informal in nature, and posts on Twitter and Facebook tend to be full of misspelled words, show extensive use of home-made acronyms and abbreviations, and contain plenty of punctuation applied in creative and non-standard ways. The punctuation markers are also often ambiguous in these types of texts — in particular between actually being used as punctuation and being used for emphasis — creating great challenges for sentence boundary detection.

When analysing texts from Facebook and Twitter, we find a rich variety of practices to mark the end of a sentence, for example, with emoticons (such as ':)', ':(', ':D', '♡', etc.), with several consecutive punctuation markers (e.g., '!!!!' and '????') or several sequences of multiple periods (e.g., '... ...' or '...... .....'), and by mixing multiple punctuations in different combinations (e.g., '!?' or '...?'), as in the following three examples.

250

D S Sharma, R Sangal and E Sherly. Proc. of the 12th Intl. Conference on Natural Language Processing, pages 254–260,
Trivandrum, India. December 2015. ©2015 NLP Association of India (NLPAI)

(1) *Rick Ross b-day party at K.O.D $200 a head
... .. Im in the building ... ...*

(2) *after you can walk again?! whaaat, your
leg's broken???! LOL. makes no sense.*

(3) *@kirkfranklin happy birthday !!!! I'm so
glad you were born !*

In this work we concentrate on resolving the ambiguity of sentence end markers for social media text, and have carried out several experiments to detect sentence boundaries, using both rule-based and machine learning-based strategies.

The rest of the paper is organized as follows: In Section 2, we discuss some previous work on sentence boundary detection, which has mostly been on formal text. Corpora collection and annotation is discussed in Section 3, while Section 4 describes the rule-based and machine learning-based approaches used. Evaluation of the experimental results and error analysis are discussed in Sections 5 and 6, respectively. Finally, Section 7 concludes and points out some directions for future research.

2 Related Work

The approaches that have been taken to sentence boundary detection can on a general level be categorized as either machine learning-based or rule-based. State-of-the-art machine learning approaches perform well with an accuracy of around 99% on formal texts such as news-wire and financial newspaper texts, whereas rule-based approaches on the same type of texts typically report around 93% accuracy. Our approach investigates the use of different punctuations and patterns for marking the end of sentence in social media text and is based on comparing three machine learning algorithms — Conditional Random Fields, Naïve Bayes and Sequential Minimal Optimization — to a rule-based system, also with the rule-based strategy showing lower accuracy than the machine learning approaches, as described in the next sections. First, however, we will discuss some relevant previous work.

Riley (1989) proposed one of the earliest feature-based machine learning approaches, mainly for investigating the occurrences of periods as sentence end markers, and reported 99.8% accuracy on 25 million words of AP news-wire and the one million words tagged Brown corpus (Kučera and Francis, 1967).

Reynar and Ratnaparkhi (1997) presented a maximum entropy model trained on an annotated corpus. The model classifies each occurrences of '.', '?' and '!' as a valid or invalid sentence boundary. They proposed a domain-specific system which uses knowledge about the structure of English financial newspaper text, and a domain-independent system which uses the structure of English text genres. They report accuracy of 98.8% and 98.0%, for the domain-dependent and domain-independent system, respectively.

The *SATZ* system (Palmer and Hearst, 1997) uses a lexicon with part-of-speech probabilities and a feed-forward neural network. The system represents the context surrounding a punctuation mark as a series of vectors of probabilities. This probability of a word is used as input to the neural network to disambiguate sentence boundaries. *SATZ* reached an accuracy of 98.9% on Wall Street Journal (WSJ) text. Integrating the classifier with a heuristics-based approach increased the accuracy to 99.5%.

Gillick (2009) described a statistical system which focuses on full stops as candidate boundaries only. The system employs Support Vector Machines as a learning framework and reported accuracy rates of 99.75% on WSJ and 99.64% on the Brown corpus.

The *Punkt* system (Kiss and Strunk, 2006) introduced an unsupervised approach based on abbreviation identification. *Punkt* identifies abbreviations using three traits such as if an abbreviated word preceding a period and the period itself form a close bond. Abbreviations have the tendency to be rather short and often contain word-internal periods. *Punkt* achieved an accuracy of 98.35% on WSJ data and 98.98% on Brown texts.

Wong and Chao (2010) presented an incremental algorithm for sentence boundary detection using different features like if a word is capitalized, word length, potential punctuation, and the status of sign such as '$' and numbers, extracted from the trigram contexts of a training corpus. They report 99.98% accuracy on the Brown corpus, and slightly lower on the Tycho Brahe and Hoje Macau corpora with 96.51% and 98.73%, respectively.

The *iSentenizer-μ* system (Wong et al., 2014) presented an incremental tree learning architecture to detect sentence boundaries in a mixture of different text genres and languages. This model also utilized features derived from the trigram contexts of a training corpus. The system performance showed accuracy of 99.8%, 99.81% and 99.78% on the WSJ, Brown and Tycho Brahe corpora, respectively.

Rule-based to automatic sentence boundary detection have not been as succesful and hence also not as common as the various machine-learning based strategies. Grefenstette and Tapanainen (1994) describe one of the earliest rule-based systems, using a set of rules in the form of regular expressions to distinguish periods used in abbreviations, numbers, email and web addresses from those used as end of sentence markers. The system addressed periods only as sentence boundaries and showed an accuracy of 93.78%.

A more recent rule-based approach by Mikheev (2002) included a set of rules to detect capitalized words, abbreviations and other sentence termination punctuation such as periods, question marks, exclamation marks and semicolons. The system reached an accuracy of 99.55% on WSJ text and 99.72% on the Brown corpus, respectively.

3 Data Collection

In order to investigate the performance of sentence boundary detection on social media text and compare it to performance on more formal text, we have used three different text collections.

The first collection is a mixture of 3,000 tweets and Facebook posts in English, which we will call the"Social Media Corpus" (SMC). The tweets come from CMU's ARK Twitter data[1] (1,000 tweets) and Ritter[2] (1,000 tweets), while1,000 Facebook posts were randomly collected from campus-related billboard postings at different U.S. universities (CMU, Cornell, MIT, UCB, etc.).

The second collection is English-Hindi code-mixed twitter data (554 tweets) from the NITA corpus described by Jamatia et al. (2015), and the third collection consists of formal English text from the Brown corpus (1,125 messages), for comparison.

Utterance boundaries were manually inserted into the messages of the SMC by two human annotators. Due to the coarse nature of the corpus, also human annotators sometimes face difficulties in annotating sentence boundaries. Initially, the annotators agreed on only 61% of the utterance breaks. After discussions and corrections,

Corpus	Agreement
CMU ARK	92.3
Ritter	71.7
Facebook	76.2
NITA	92.5
Brown	99.8

Table 1: Inter annotator agreement (%) on the SMC, NITA and Brown corpora

the agreement between the annotators reached 80.06% on average over the entire corpus.

Details of the inter-annotator agreement values for annotation on SMC are given in Table 1, where an agreement on an utterance implies that both annotators had segmented it into the same number of sentences, all with the same word lengths. The resulting corpus has in total 6,444 sentences, of which 3,522 come from Twitter and 2,922 from Facebook posts.

The NITA and Brown corpora excerpts were also annotated by two humans, manually inserting sentence boundaries into the messages. The inter-annotator agreement ratios were 92.5% and 99.8% for the NITA corpus and the Brown corpus, respectively. The resulting segmented NITA corpus has 1,225 sentences and the Brown corpus part has 1,000 sentences.

4 System Description

To detect the sentence boundaries of social media texts, we first need to resolve the issues of ambiguous punctuation used for sentence boundaries. Punctuation markers such as period (.) , semicolon(;), comma(,), vertical-bar (|), tilde($\sim$), etc., are not only used as sentence separators. The period (.) is the most ambiguous separator: In our Twitter/Facebook social media corpus there are 5,664 periods and out of those, manual inspection showed that only 3,168 (i.e., 55.93%) were actually used as sentence end markers.

To mitigate the ambiguous nature of the period, the entire corpus was tokenized using the CMU tokenizer[3] originally developed by O'Connor et al. (2010) and specially designed for Twitter-related

---

[1]www.ark.cs.cmu.edu/TweetNLP
[2]www.github.com/aritter/twitter_nlp

[3]www.ark.cs.cmu.edu/TweetNLP

1. **IF** the current token matches one of the patterns shown in Table 2

   AND the current token is in the last token position of the string

   THEN the current token is a sentence end marker.

2. **IF** the current token **AND** the previous token match any of the patterns shown in Table 2,

   AND the next token is any punctuation other those in Table 2

   THEN the next token is a sentence end marker.

3. **IF** the current token **AND** both the two tokens before it match any of the patterns shown in Table 2

   AND the next token is a word-token (other than a symbol)

   THEN the current token is a sentence end marker.

Figure 1: Rule-based sentence boundary detection algorithm

English text. This tokenizer is a sub-module of CMU Twitter POS tagger developed by Gimpel et al. (2011). It was observed that tokenization resolved a large portion of the ambiguous punctuation, e.g., 'Mr.'; 'U.S.A'; `http://bit.ly/h1XIyQ`; '1019.0', etc.

After tokenization, we have developed two alternative approaches to automatically detect sentence boundaries, one rule-based approach and one approach based on applying machine learning. Three different machine learning algorithms were tested for automatic sentence boundary detection: Conditional Random Fields (CRF), Naïve Bayes (NB), and Sequential Minimal Optimization (SMO). The details of each approach will be discussed in following subsections.

4.1 Rule-Based Approach

A rule-based system was developed to automatically identify sentence boundaries in noisy social media text. The basic system splits Twitter and Facebook posts into sentences based on the punctuations that are normally used as sentence end markers, such as '.', '?', '!' and 'End-of-line'. 'End-of-line' will be used in this paper as a term refering to the cases where a social media post ends without any punctuation or any specific end marker; something which is quite common in informal texts, making the SBD task significantly more difficult.

The rule-based system correctly splits 2,468 posts of the in total 3,000 in SMC into 4,832 sentences with an F-measure of 72.34%, while the system was unable to split 532 of the posts. After observing the pattern of un-split posts in the corpus, we found that in addition to normal sentence end markers, a few other punctuation patterns have

been used as sentence end, as shown in Table 2.

Considering the above classes of sentence end markers, the rules shown in Figure 1 were incorporated into the basic system, in order to increase its performance.

After applying the above rules to the corpus, the rule-base system splits 2,604 posts into 5172 sentences withan F-measure of 78.72%. The remaining non-split 396 posts (13.2%) were analysed in detail, revealing that all those posts are exceptional. These exceptional cases are further discussed in Section 6.

Pattern	Total Count	Count as EoS
... (three consecutive periods with one or more instances)	548	538
.. (two consecutive periods with one or more instances)	139	139
!!!! (Two or more consecutive occurrences of !)	175	175
??? (Two or more consecutive occurrences of ?)	59	59
!!?? OR .... (combination of one or more different punctuations)	35	35

Table 2: Pattern of punctuations as End-of-Sentence (EoS)

4.2 Machine learning-based approach

The second approach to sentence boundary detection for social media text is based on machine learning. We experimented with applying three machine learning-based classification algorithms to the SBD task, Conditional Random Fields, Sequential Minimal Optimization and Naïve Bayes. The CRF implementation used comes from Miralium[4], while the other two classification were implemented using Weka[5].

Conditional Random Fields are widely used for text sequence labelling tasks. The CRF-based implementation here was trained on basic textual features such as Anchor Word (the current word) which is followed by Next Word, the Previous Word and the word before that (so two words before the Anchor Word). The CRF model provides simultaneously correlated word-level features, which gives greater freedom for incorporating a variety of knowledge sources.

Sequential minimal optimization (Platt, 1998) is an iterative optimization approach to training Support Vector Machines, SVM (Vapnik, 1995). SVM in turn is a binary classification algorithm that aims to separate two classes in a high-dimensional space by inserting hyper-planes between the instances.

5 Experimental Evaluation

To fully evaluate our proposed approaches, we experimented with using some state-of-art SBD systems. We tested the *OpenNLP Sentence Detector*,[6] which is a part of Apache OpenNLP library, and the *splitta* sentence boundary detection tool.[7]

The performance of all the proposed systems was tested on the social media corpus, on a portion of Brown corpus and on the NITA corpus. Details of experiments with results are shown in Table 3. The machine learning approaches were evaluated using 5-Fold cross validation.

The CRF implementation reached 99.81% average accuracy with a weighted average F1-score of 67.0%. The F-measures of Naïve Bayes (NB) and Sequential Minimal Optimization (SMO) are as given in Table 3. It is noticable that the SMO classifier gave the best result for the social media

---

[4]https://code.google.com/p/miralium/

[5]http://www.cs.waikato.ac.nz/ml/weka/downloading.html

[6]https://opennlp.apache.org/documentation/1.5.3/manual/opennlp.html

[7]https://code.google.com/p/splitta/

SBD Approach	Corpus based F Measure (in %)		
	SMC	Brown	NITA
Rule-based	78.7	70.6	64.3
SMO	**87.0**	93.3	84.3
NB	86.0	**99.6**	**84.5**
CRF	67.0	57.2	56.9
OpenNLP	68.4	97.5	44.1
splitta: NB	56.1	99.5	54.4
splitta: SVM	54.9	**99.6**	56.0

Table 3: SBD system performance on the corpora

corpus, whereas the Naïve Bayes classifier worked almost as well on SMC and was the best on the Brown corpus, with both those algorithms clearly out-performing CRF on all corpora.

Similarly, of the standard systems tested, the SVM and NB implementations in *splitta* were also succesful on the Brown corpus, but the state-of-the-art systems performed substantially worse on the social media data (SMC and NITA).

6 Error Discussion

The proposed approaches failed to recognize a few sentences in the SMC 3,000 Twitter and Facebook corpus. We analyzed those sentences and found usage of exceptional character sequences as sentence end markers. Patterns such as '|', '||' and '*' are used as sentence end markers, although they are not normally considered as any punctuation symbols. The presence of these patterns is perhaps due to the user's (the one who has posted) expression of the emphasis in the posts; to stress the meaning of the posts by splitting them into sentences.

For this reason, the tested and developed systems could not mark sentence boundaries in some of the exceptional cases. Some examples from the corpus are as follows.

(4) *@RockThatBieber We R Who We R - Keeeeshaa | Only Girl - Rihanna | Shake - Jesse McCartney .... :)*

(5) *@_shintarona_ Op corz gots eet , so now head is spinning with haaawt || Well the YT*

version I heard sounds exactly like that old one ...

(6) *Me * I love you DjHim * I love you too steph * AlwaysHim and forever :)*

In a few posts, periods have been either wrongly placed or intentionally inserted in between the texts, even though those periods are not actually marking the sentence end. For instance, in the following post

(7) *@syabillaedward honestly ? I have no idea . I just am ... all . the . time . :(*

there are periods (.) occurring at "all.the.time." In this example, the period (.) is inserted between texts to emphasize "all the time".

The tested machine learning algoriths performed well on the Brown corpus, with an F-measure of 93.3% with SMO and 99.6% for NB (Table 3). The reason for such a high score is that the nature of the Brown corpus is formal text where the significance of symbols such as '.', '?' and '!' are well defined. The machine learners are capable of identifying not only the regular meaning of these punctuation symbols, but also their occurrences in different situations. Therefore, it is most likely that our system would perform well on formal texts.

On the other hand, we observed that there is a slight drop in the F-measure of the SMO system from 87% to 84.3% when applied to the NITA English-Hindi code-mixed corpus as compared to the SMC social media corpus. SMC is purely based on English texts. Therefore, the boundaies of sentences within a post are easier to identify. In contrast, in the NITA code-mixed corpus, due to its complex nature, the difficulty of the SBD task increases in two differnt ways; one due to the code-switching at the sentence level and the other due to the code-mixing at the word level. In such a setting, identifying the beginning and end of a Hindi and an English sentence is comparatively difficult. For example:

(8) *Life Ok Dream Girl Ek Ladki Deewani Si Upcoming Tv show Story | Star Cast | Timing | Promo Wiki | Ne http://t.co/X9AhZRRPiD*

(9) *1 Ladke Ne ek Ladki Ko Call Ki Boy : I LOVE U Jaan Girl-Sacchi Boy-Mucchi Girl : ek 100ka Recharge Krwa Do Plz Boy-Sorry Didi Rong Number .*

The above examples are from the NITA English-Hindi code-mixed corpus, and show cases where the tested systems could not recognize the sentence boundaries. Example 8 is a sentence level code-mixed tweet; the following four sentences are there, but no sentence boundary markers were used.

(10) *Life Ok Dream Girl*

(11) *Ek Ladki Deewani Si*

(12) *Upcoming Tv show Story |*

(13) *Star Cast | Timing | Promo Wiki | Ne http://t.co/X9AhZRRPiD*

In Example 9, the English-Hindi code-mixing took place at the word level. This tweet can be split as follows into six sentences, even though there are no proper sentence end markers to define the sentence boundaries.

(14) *1 Ladke Ne ek Ladki Ko Call Ki*

(15) *Boy : I LOVE U Jaan*

(16) *Girl-Sacchi*

(17) *Boy-Mucchi*

(18) *Girl : ek 100ka Recharge Krwa Do Plz*

(19) *Boy-Sorry Didi Rong Number .*

7 Conclusion and Future Work

In this paper we have presented two different approaches to automatic sentence boundary detection in social media text. First, a rule-based system for the SBD task which achieved an F-measure of 78.7% in experiments on social media text. Second, a system based on machine learning approaches to detecting sentence boundaries. We adopted three different machine learning algorithms: Conditional Random Fields, Naïve Bayes, and Sequential Minimal Optimization, with SMO achieving the highest F-score on the social media corpus. For comparison, we also experimented with applying state-of-the art SBD systems to social media text, and with using the systems trained on social media on the more formal Brown corpus, as well as on an English-Hindi code-mixed corpus. This work is the first attempt towards SBD for social media text. Our next target is to make this SBD system more well-built and to make this system adequate for multilingual social media text.

Acknowledgements

Thanks to all the members of TweetNLP team (Carnegie Mellon University), Alan Ritter (Ohio State University), Dan Gillick (Google Research, Mountain View, CA), Robert Bley-Vroman (College of Languages, Linguistics, and Literature of the University of Hawai'i), and the Apache Software Foundation for making their datasets and tools available. Special thanks to the anonymous reviewers for their comments and suggestions that have helped to improve the paper.

References

Eric Brill. 1994. Some advances in transformation-based part of speech tagging. In *Proceedings of the Twelfth National Conference on Artificial Intelligence (Vol. 1)*, AAAI '94, pages 722–727, Menlo Park, CA, USA. American Association for Artificial Intelligence.

Michael John Collins. 1996. A new statistical parser based on bigram lexical dependencies. In *Proceedings of the 34th Annual Meeting on Association for Computational Linguistics*, ACL '96, pages 184–191, Stroudsburg, PA, USA. Association for Computational Linguistics.

Doug Cutting, Julian Kupiec, Jan Pedersen, and Penelope Sibun. 1992. A practical part-of-speech tagger. In *Proceedings of the Third Conference on Applied Natural Language Processing*, ANLC '92, pages 133–140, Stroudsburg, PA, USA. Association for Computational Linguistics.

Dan Gillick. 2009. Sentence boundary detection and the problem with the u.s. In *Proceedings of Human Language Technologies: The 2009 Annual Conference of the North American Chapter of the Association for Computational Linguistics, Companion Volume: Short Papers*, NAACL-Short '09, pages 241–244, Stroudsburg, PA, USA. Association for Computational Linguistics.

Kevin Gimpel, Nathan Schneider, Brendan O'Connor, Dipanjan Das, Daniel Mills, Jacob Eisenstein, Michael Heilman, Dani Yogatama, Jeffrey Flanigan, and Noah A. Smith. 2011. Part-of-speech tagging for Twitter: Annotation, features, and experiments. In *Proceedings of the 49th Annual Meeting of the Association for Computational Linguistics: Human Language Technologies*, volume 2: short papers, pages 42–47, Portland, Oregon, June. ACL.

Gregory Grefenstette and Pasi Tapanainen. 1994. What is a word, what is a sentence? problems of tokenization. In *Proceedings of the 3rd Conference on Computational Lexicography and Text Research*, Budapest, Hungary, July.

Anupam Jamatia, Björn Gambäck, and Amitava Das. 2015. Part-of-speech tagging for code-mixed English-Hindi Twitter and Facebook chat messages. In *Proceedings of 10th International Conference on Recent Advances in Natural Language Processing*, pages 239–248, in Hissar, Bulgaria, 7-9 September, September.

Tibor Kiss and Jan Strunk. 2006. Unsupervised multilingual sentence boundary detection. *Computational Linguistics*, 32(4):485–525, December.

Henry Kučera and W. Nelson Francis. 1967. *Computational Analysis of Present-Day American English*. Brown University Press, Providence, Rhode Island. http://www.sls.hawaii.edu/ bley-vroman/brown_corpus.html.

Andrei Mikheev. 2002. Periods, capitalized words, etc. *Computational Linguistics*, 28(3):289–318, September.

Brendan O'Connor, Michel Krieger, and David Ahn. 2010. Tweetmotif: Exploratory search and topic summarization for twitter. In *Proceedings of the Fourth International Conference on Weblogs and Social Media, ICWSM 2010, Washington, DC, USA, May 23-26, 2010*.

David D. Palmer and Marti A. Hearst. 1997. Adaptive multilingual sentence boundary disambiguation. *Computational Linguistics*, 23:241–267.

John C. Platt. 1998. Fast training of support vector machines using sequential minimal optimization. In *Advances in Kernel Methods — Support Vector Learning*. MIT Press, January.

Jeffrey C. Reynar and Adwait Ratnaparkhi. 1997. A maximum entropy approach to identifying sentence boundaries. In *Proceedings of the 5th Conference on Applied Natural Language Processing*, pages 803–806, Washington, DC, April. ACL.

Michael D. Riley. 1989. Some applications of tree-based modelling to speech and language. In *Proceedings of the Workshop on Speech and Natural Language*, HLT '89, pages 339–352, Stroudsburg, PA, USA. Association for Computational Linguistics.

Vladimir N. Vapnik. 1995. *The Nature of Statistical Learning Theory*. Springer-Verlag, New York, New York.

Fai Wong and Sam Chao. 2010. iSentenizer: An incremental sentence boundary classifier. In *Natural Language Processing and Knowledge Engineering (NLP-KE), 2010 International Conference on*, pages 1–7, Aug.

Derek F. Wong, Lidia S. Chao, and Xiaodong Zeng. 2014. iSentenizer-μ: Multilingual sentence boundary detection model. *The Scientific World Journal*.

Mood Classification of Hindi Songs based on Lyrics

Braja Gopal Patra, Dipankar Das, and Sivaji Bandyopadhyay
Department of Computer Science & Engineering, Jadavpur University, Kolkata, India
{brajagopal.cse, dipankar.dipnil2005}@gmail.com,
sivaji_cse_ju@yahoo.com

Abstract

Digitization of music has led to easier access to different forms music across the globe. Increasing work pressure denies the necessary time to listen and evaluate music for a creation of a personal music library. One solution might be developing a music search engine or recommendation system based on different moods. In fact mood label is considered as an emerging metadata in the digital music libraries and online music repositories. In this paper, we proposed mood taxonomy for Hindi songs and prepared a mood annotated lyrics corpus based on this taxonomy. We also annotated lyrics with positive and negative polarity. Instead of adopting a traditional approach to music mood classification based solely on audio features, the present study describes a mood classification system from lyrics as well by combining a wide range of semantic and stylistic features extracted from textual lyrics. We also developed a supervised system to identify the sentiment of the Hindi song lyrics based on the above features. We achieved the maximum average F-measure of 68.30% and 38.49% for classifying the polarities and moods of the Hindi lyrics, respectively.

1 Introduction

Studies on Music Information Retrieval (MIR) have shown moods as a desirable access point to music repositories and collections (Hu and Downie, 2010a). In the recent decade, much work on western music mood classification has been performed using audio signals and lyrics (Hu and Downie, 2010a; Mihalcea and Strapparava, 2012). Studies indicating contradictory emphasis of lyrics or audio in predicting music moods are prevalent in literature (Hu and Downie, 2010b). Indian music considered as one of the oldest musical traditions in the world. Indian music can be divided into two broad categories, "*classical*" and "*popular*" (Ujlambkar and Attar, 2012). Further, classical music tradition of India has two main variants; namely Hindustani and Carnatic. The prevalence of Hindustani classical music is found largely in north and central parts of India whereas Carnatic classical music dominates largely in the southern parts of India.

Indian popular music, also known as Hindi Bollywood music or Hindi music, is mostly present in Hindi cinemas or Bollywood movies. Hindi is one of the official languages of India and is the fourth most widely spoken language in the World[1]. Hindi or Bollywood songs make up 72% of the total music sales in India (Ujlambkar and Attar, 2012). Unfortunately, not much computational and analytical work has been done in this area.

Therefore, mood taxonomy especially for Hindi songs has been introduced here in order to closely investigate the role played by lyrics in music mood classification. The lyrics corpus is annotated in two steps. In the first step, mood is annotated based on the listener's perspective. In the second step, the same corpus is annotated with polarity based on the reader's perspective. Further, we developed a mood classification system by incorporating different semantic and textual stylistic features extracted from the lyrics. In addition, we also developed a polarity classification system based on the above features.

The paper is organized as follows: Section 2 reviews related work on music mood classification. Section 3 introduces the proposed mood classes. The detailed annotation process and the dataset used in the study have been described in Section 4. Section 5 describes the features of the

---

[1] www.redlinels.com/2014/01/10/most-widely-

D S Sharma, R Sangal and E Sherly. Proc. of the 12th Intl. Conference on Natural Language Processing, pages 261–267,
Trivandrum, India. December 2015. ©2015 NLP Association of India (NLPAI)

lyrics used in the experiments, which is followed by the results obtained so far and our findings and further prospect are discussed in Section 6. Finally Section 7 concludes and suggests the future work.

2 Related Work

Dataset and Taxonomy: Preparation of an annotated dataset requires the selection of proper mood classes to be used. With respect to Indian music, limited work on mood detection by considering audio features has been reported till today. Koduri and Indurkhya (2010) worked on the mood classification of South Indian Classical music, i.e. Carnatic music. The main goal of their experiment was to verify the *raagas* that really evoke a particular *rasa(s)* (emotion) specific to each user. They considered the taxonomy consisting of ten *rasas* e.g., *Srungaram (Romance, Love), Hasyam (Laughter, Comedy)* etc. Similarly, Velankar and Sahasrabuddhe (2012) prepared data for mood classification of Hindustani classical music consisting of 13 mood taxonomies (*Happy, Exciting, Satisfaction, Peaceful, Graceful, Gentle, Huge, Surrender, Love, Request, Emotional, Pure, Meditative*). Patra et al. (2013a) used the standard MIREX taxonomy for their experiments whereas Ujlambkar and Attar, (2012) experimented based on audio features for five mood classes, namely *Happy, Sad, Silent, Excited* and *Romantic* along with three or more subclasses based on two dimensional "*Energy and Stress*" model.

Mood Classification using Audio Features: Automatic music mood classification systems based on the audio features where spectral, rhythm and intensity are the most popular features, have been developed in the last few decades. The Music Information Retrieval eXchange[2] (MIREX) is an annual evaluation campaign of different Music Information Retrieval (MIR) related systems and algorithms. The "Audio Mood Classification (AMC)" task has been running each year since 2007 (Hu et al., 2008). Among the various audio-based approaches tested at MIREX, spectral features and Support Vector Machine (SVM) classifiers were widely used and found quite effective (Hu and Downie, 2010a). The "Emotion in Music" task was started in the year 2014 at MediaEval Benchmark Workshop. In the above task, the arousals and valence scores were estimated continuously in

time for every music piece using several regression models[3].

Notable work on music mood classification using audio features can be found on several music categories, such as Hindi music (Ujlambkar and Attar, 2012; Patra et al., 2014a, 2014b), Hindustani classical music (Velankar and Sahasrabuddhe, 2012) and Carnatic classical music (Koduri and Indurkhya, 2010).

Mood Classification from Lyric Features: Multiple experiments have been carried out on western music mood classification based on bag of words (BOW), emotion lexicons and other stylistic features (Zaanen and Kanters, 2010; Hu and Downie, 2010a, 2010b).

Multi-modal Music Mood Classification: Much literature on mood classification on western music has been published based on both audio and lyrics (Hu and Downie, 2010). The system developed by Yang and Lee, (2004) is often regarded as one of the earliest studies on combining lyrics and audio features to develop a multi-modal music mood classification.

To the best of our knowledge, Indian music mood classification based on lyrics has not been attempted yet. Moreover, in context to Indian music, multi-modal music mood classification also has not been explored either.

3 Taxonomy

In context to the western music, the Adjective list (Hevner, 1936), Russell's circumplex model (Russell, 1980) and MIREX taxonomy (Hu et al., 2008) are the most popular mood taxonomies used by several worldwide researchers in this arena. Though, several mood taxonomies have been proposed by different researchers, all such psychological models were proposed in laboratory settings and thus were criticized for the lack of social context of music listening (Hu, 2010; Laurier et al., 2009).

Russell (1980) proposed the *circumplex model* of affect (consisting of 28 affect words) based on the two dimensions denoted as "*pleasant-unpleasant*" and "*arousal-sleep*" (as shown in Figure 1). The most well-known example of such taxonomy is the *Valence-Arousal* (V-A) representation which has been used in several previous experiments (Soleymani et al., 2013). *Valence* indicates *positive* versus *negative* polarity whereas *arousal* indicates the *intensity* of moods.

---

[2] www.music-ir.org/mirex/wiki/MIREX_HOME

[3] http://www.multimediaeval.org/mediaeval2015/ emotion inmusic2015/

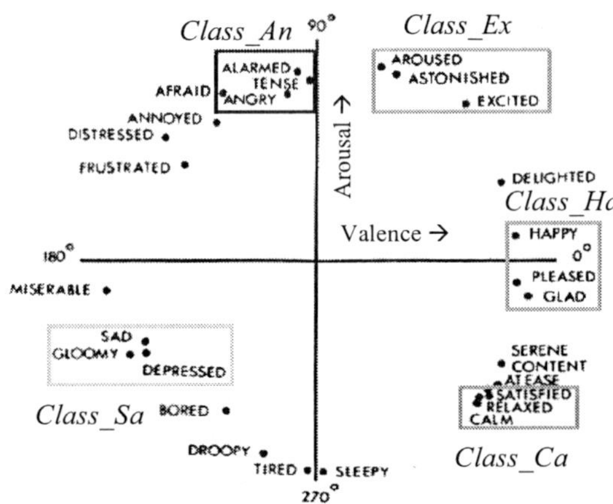

Figure 1. Russell's circumplex model of 28 affect words.

We opted to use Russel's circumplex model by clustering the similar affect words (as shown in Figure 1). For example, we have considered the affect words *calm, relaxed,* and *satisfied* together to form one mood class i.e., *Calm,* denoted as *Class_Ca.* The present mood taxonomy contains five mood classes with three subclasses in each.

One of the main reasons of developing such taxonomy was to collect similar songs and cluster them into a single mood class. Preliminary observations showed significant invariability in case of audio features of the subclasses over its corresponding main or coarse class. Basically the preliminary observations of annotation are related with the psychological factors that influence the annotation process while annotating a piece of music after listening to the song. For example, a *happy* and a *delighted* song have high valence, whereas an *aroused* and an *excited* songs have high arousal. The final mood taxonomy used in our experiment is shown in Table 1.

Class_Ex	Class_Ha	Class_Ca	Class_Sa	Class_An
Excited	Delighted	Calm	Sad	Angry
Astonished	Happy	Relaxed	Gloomy	Alarmed
Aroused	Pleased	Satisfied	Depressed	Tensed

Table 1. Proposed Mood Taxonomy

4 Dataset Annotation Perspective based on Listeners and Readers

Till date, there is no such mood annotated lyrics corpus available on the web. In the present work, we collected the lyrics data from different web archives corresponding to the audio data that was developed by Patra et al. (2013). Some more lyrics were added as per the increment of the audio data in Patra et al. (2013). The lyrics are basical-ly written in *Romanized English* characters. The pre-requisite resources like Hindi sentiment lexicons and stopwords are available in utf-8 character encoding. Thus, we transliterated the *Romanized English* lyric to utf-8 characters using the transliteration tool available in the EILMT project[4]. As we observed several errors in the transliteration process and hence corrected the mistakes manually.

It has to be mentioned that we have only used the coarse grain classes for all of our experiments. Also to be noted that, we started annotating the lyrics at the same time of annotating their corresponding audio files by listening to them. All of the annotators were undergraduate students worked voluntarily and belong to the age group of 18-24. Each of the songs was annotated by five annotators. We achieved the inter-annotator agreement of 88% for the lyrics data annotated with five coarse grain mood classes (as mentioned in bold face in Table 1). While annotating the songs, we observed that the confusions occur between the pair of mood classes like "*Class_An* and *Class_Ex*", "*Class_Ha* and *Class_Ex*" and "*Class_Sa* and *Class_Ca*" as these classes have similar acoustic features.

To validate the annotation in a consistent way, we tried to assign our proposed coarse mood classes (e.g., *Class_Ha*) to a lyric after reading its lexical contents. But, it was too difficult to annotate a lyric with such coarse mood classes as a lyric of a single song may contain multiple emotions within it. On the other hand, the annotators felt different emotions while listening to audio and reading its corresponding lyrics, separately. For example, *Bhaag D.K.Bose Aandhi Aayi*[5] is annotated as *Calss_An* while listening to it, whereas annotated as *Class_Sa* while reading the corresponding lyric. Therefore, in order to avoid such problem and confusion, we decided to annotate lyrics with one of the coarse grained sentiment classes, viz. *positive* or *negative*.

We calculated the inter-annotator agreement and obtained 95% agreement on the lyrics data annotated with two coarse grained sentiment classes. In order to emphasize the annotation schemes, we could argue that a song is generally considered as *positive* if it belongs to the *happy* mood class. But, in our case, we observed a different scenario. Initially, the annotators annotated

---

[4] http://tdil-dc.in/index.php?option=com_ vertical&parentid=72
[5] http://www.lyricsmint.com/2011/05/bhaag-dk-bose-aandhi-aayi-delhi-belly.html

a lyric with *Class_Ha* after listening to audio, but, later on, the same annotator annotated the same lyric with *negative* polarity while finished reading of its contents. Therefore, a few cases where the mood class does not always coincide with the conventional moods at lyrics level (e.g., *Class_Ha* and *positive*, *Class_An* and *negative*) are identified and we presented a confusion matrix in Table 2.

	Positive	Negative	No. of Songs
Class_An	1	49	50
Class_Ca	83	12	95
Class_Ex	85	6	91
Class_Ha	96	4	100
Class_Sa	7	117	125
Total Songs			**461**

Table 2. Confusion matrix of two annotation schemes and statistics of total songs.

5 Classification Framework

We adopted a wide range of textual features such as sentiment Lexicons, stylistic features and n-grams in order to develop the music mood classification framework. We have illustrated all the features below.

5.1 Features based on Sentiment Lexicons: We used three Hindi sentiment lexicons to classify the sentiment words present in the lyrics texts, which are Hindi Subjective Lexicon (HSL) (Bakliwal et al., 2012), Hindi SentiWordnet (HSW) (Joshi et al., 2010) and Hindi Wordnet Affect (HWA) (Das et al., 2012). HSL contains two lists, one is for adjectives (3909 *positive*, 2974 *negative* and 1225 *neutral*) and another is for adverbs (193 *positive*, 178 *negative* and 518 *neutral*). HSW consists of 2168 *positive*, 1391 *negative* and 6426 *neutral* words along with their parts-of-speech (POS) and synset id extracted from the Hindi WordNet. HWA contains 2986, 357, 500, 3185, 801 and 431 words with their parts-of-speech from *angry*, *disgust*, *fear*, *happy*, *sad* and *surprise* classes, respectively. The statistics of the sentiment words found in the whole corpus using three sentiment lexicons are shown in Table 3.

5.2 Text Stylistic Features: The text stylistic features such as the number of unique words, number of repeated words, number of lines, number of unique lines and number of lines ended with same words were considered in our experiments.

Classes	HWA	Classes	HSL	HSW
Angry	241			
Disgust	13	**Positive**	1172	857
Fear	13			
Happy	349			
Sad	107	**Negative**	951	628
Surprise	38			

Table 3. Sentiment words identified using HWA, HSL and HSW

5.3 Features based on N-grams: Many researches showed that the N-Gram feature works well for lyrics mood classification (Zaanen and Kanters, 2010) as compared to the stylistic or sentiment features. Thus, we considered Term Frequency-Inverse Document Frequency (TF-IDF) scores of up to trigrams as the results get worsen after including the higher order N-Grams. However, we removed the stopwords while considering the n-grams and considered the N-Grams having document frequency more than one.

We used the correlation based supervised feature selection technique available in the WEKA[6] toolkit. Finally, we performed our experiments with 10 sentiment features, 13 textual stylistic features and 1561 N-Gram features.

6 Results and Discussion

Support Vector Machines (SVM) is widely used for the for the western songs lyrics mood classification (Hu et al., 2009; Hu and Downie, 2010a). Even for the mood classification from audio data at MIREX showed that the LibSVM performed better than the SMO algorithm, K-Nearest Neighbors (KNN) implemented in the WEKA machine learning software (Hu et al., 2008).

To develop the automatic system for mood classification from lyrics, we have used several machine learning algorithms, but the LibSVM implemented in the WEKA tool performs better than the other classifiers available for the classification purpose in our case also. Initially, we tried LibSVM with the polynomial kernel, but the radial basic function kernel gave better results. In order to get reliable accuracy, we have performed 10-fold cross validation for both the systems.

We developed two systems for the data annotated with two different annotation schemes. In the first system, we tried to classify the lyrics into five coarse grained moods classes. In the

---

[6] http://www.cs.waikato.ac.nz/ml/weka/

second system, we classified the polarities (*positive* or *negative*) of the lyrics that were assigned to a song only after reading its corresponding lyrics. We have shown the system F-measure in Table 4.

In Table 4, we observed that the F-measure of the second system is high compared to the first system. In case of English, the maximum accuracy achieved in Hu and Downie (2010) is 61.72 over the dataset of 5,296 unique lyrics comprising of 18 mood categories. But, in case of Hindi, we achieved F-score of 38.49 only on a dataset of 461 lyrics and with five mood classes. The observations yield the facts that the lyrics patterns for English and Hindi are completely different. We have observed various dissimilarities (w.r.t. singer and instruments) of the Hindi Songs over the English music. There are multiple moods in a Hindi lyric and the mood changes while annotating a song at the time of listening to the audio and reading its corresponding lyric.

To the best of our knowledge, there is no existing system available for lyrics based mood classification in Hindi. As the lyrics data is developed on the audio dataset in Patra et al., (2013a), thus, we compared our lyrics based mood classification system with the audio based mod classification system developed in the Patra et al., (2013a; 2013b). Our lyrics based system performed poorly as compared to the audio based systems (accuracies of 51.56% and 48%), although lyrics dataset contain more instances than the audio based system. They divided a song into multiple audio clips of 60 seconds, whereas we considered the total lyrics of a song for our experiment. This may be one of the reasons for the poor performance of the lyrics based mood classification system as the mood varies over a full length song. But in the present task, we performed classification task on a whole lyric. It is also observed that, in context of Hindi songs, the mood aroused while listening to the audio is different from the mood aroused at the time of reading a lyric. The second system achieves the best F-measure of 68.30. We can observe that the polarity all over the music does not change, i.e. if a lyric is positive, then the positivity is observed through the lyric. We also observed that the N-Gram features yield F-measure of 35.05% and 64.2% alone for the mood and polarity classification systems respectively. The main reason may be that the Hindi is free word order language. The Hindi lyrics are also more free word order than the Hindi language itself as it matches the end of each line.

7 Conclusion and Future Work

In this paper, we proposed mood and polarity classification systems based on the lyrics of the songs. We achieved the best F-measure of 38.49 and 68.3 in case of the mood and polarity classification of Hindi songs, respectively. We also observed that the listener's perspective and reader's perspective of emotion are different in case of audio and its corresponding lyrics. The mood is transparent while adopting the audio only, where the polarity is transparent in case of lyrics.

In future, we plan to perform the same experiment on a wider set of textual features. Later on, we plan to develop a hybrid mood classification system based audio and lyrics features. We also plan to improve accuracy of the lyrics mood classification system using multi-level classification.

Acknowledgments

The first author is supported by Visvesvaraya Ph.D. Fellowship funded by Department of Electronics and Information Technology (DeitY), Government of India. The authors are also thankful to the anonymous reviewers for their helpful comments.

Systems	Features	Precision	Recall	F-Measure
System 1: Mood Classification	Sentiment Lexicon (SL)	29.82	29.8	29.81
	SL+Text Stylistic (TS)	33.60	33.56	33.58
	N-Gram (NG)	34.1	36.0	35.05
	SL+TS+ NG	**40.58**	**36.4**	**38.49**
System 2: Polarity Classification	SL	62.30	62.26	65.28
	SL+TS	65.54	65.54	65.54
	NG	65.4	63.0	64.2
	SL+TS+NG	**70.30**	**66.30**	**68.30**

Table 4. System performance

References

Aditya Joshi, A. R. Balamurali and Pushpak Bhattacharyya. 2010. A fall-back strategy for sentiment analysis in Hindi: a case study. In: *Proc. of the 8ht International Conference on Natural Language Processing (ICON -2010)*.

Akshat Bakliwal, Piyush Arora and Vasudeva Varma. 2012. Hindi subjective lexicon: A lexical resource for Hindi polarity classification. In: *Proc. of the 8th International Conference on Language Resources and Evaluation (LREC)*.

Aniruddha M. Ujlambkar and Vahida Z. Attar. 2012. Mood classification of Indian popular music. In: *Proc. of the CUBE International Information Technology Conference*, pp. 278-283. ACM.

Braja G. Patra, Dipankar Das and Sivaji Bandyopadhyay. 2013a. Automatic music mood classification of Hindi songs. In: *Proc. of 3rd Workshop on Sentiment Analysis where AI meets Psychology (IJCNLP 2013)*, Nagoya, Japan, pp. 24-28.

Braja G. Patra, Dipankar Das and Sivaji Bandyopadhyay. 2013b. Unsupervised approach to Hindi music mood classification. In: *Mining Intelligence and Knowledge Exploration*, pp. 62-69. Springer International Publishing.

Braja G. Patra, Promita Maitra, Dipankar Das and Sivaji Bandyopadhyay. 2015. MediaEval 2015: Feed-Forward Neural Network based Music Emotion Recognition. In *MediaEval 2015 Workshop*, September 14-15, 2015, Wurzen, Germany.

Braja G. Patra, Dipankar Das and Sivaji Bandyopadhyay. 2015. Music Emotion Recognition. In *International Symposium Frontiers of Research Speech and Music (FRSM - 2015)*.

Cyril Laurier, Mohamed Sordo, Joan Serra and Perfecto Herrera. 2009. Music mood representations from social tags. In: *Proc. of the ISMIR*, pp. 381-386.

Dan Yang and Won-Sook Lee. 2004. Disambiguating music emotion using software agents. In: *proc. of the ISMIR*, pp. 218-223.

Dipankar Das, Soujanya Poria and Sivaji Bandyopadhyay. 2012. A classifier based approach to emotion lexicon construction. In: *proc. of the 17th International conference on Applications of Natural Language Processing to Information Systems (NLDB - 2012)*, G. Bouma et al. (Eds.), Springer, LNCS vol. 7337, pp. 320–326.

Gopala K. Koduri and Bipin Indurkhya. 2010. A behavioral study of emotions in south Indian classical music and its implications in music recommendation systems. In: *Proc. of the ACM workshop on Social, adaptive and personalized multimedia interaction and access*, pp. 55-60. ACM.

James A. Russell. 1980. A Circumplx Model of Affect. *Journal of Personality and Social Psychology*, 39(6):1161-1178.

Kate Hevner. 1936. Experimental studies of the elements of expression in music. *The American Journal of Psychology*: 246-268.

Makarand R. Velankar and Hari V. Sahasrabuddhe. 2012. A pilot study of Hindustani music sentiments. In: *Proc. of 2nd Workshop on Sentiment Analysis where AI meets Psychology (COLING-2012)*. IIT Bombay, Mumbai, India, pages 91-98.

Menno V. Zaanen and Pieter Kanters. 2010. Automatic mood classification using TF*IDF based on lyrics. In: *proc. of the ISMIR*, pp. 75-80.

Mohammad Soleymani, Micheal N. Caro, Erik M. Schmidt, Cheng-Ya Sha and Yi-Hsuan Yang. 2013. 1000 songs for emotional analysis of music. In: *Proc. of the 2nd ACM international workshop on Crowdsourcing for multimedia*, pp. 1-6. ACM.

Philip J. Stone, Dexter C. Dunphy and Marshall S. Smith. 1966. *The General Inquirer: A Computer Approach to Content Analysis*. MIT Press, Cambridge, US.

Rada Mihalcea and Carlo Strapparava. 2012. Lyrics, music, and emotions. In: *Proc. of the 2012 Joint Conference on Empirical Methods in Natural Language Processing and Computational Natural Language Learning*, pp. 590-599. Association for Computational Linguistics.

Xiao Hu, J. Stephen Downie, Cyril Laurier, Mert Bay and Andreas F. Ehmann. 2008. The 2007 MIREX Audio Mood Classification Task: Lessons Learned. In proceedings of the 9th International Society for Music Information Retrieval Conference (ISMIR 2008), pages 462-467.

Xiao Hu, Stephen J. Downie and Andreas F. Ehmann. 2009. Lyric text mining in music mood classification. In proceedings of 10th International Society for Music Information Retrieval Conference (ISMIR 2009), pages 411-416.

Xiao Hu and J. Stephen Downie. 2010a. Improving mood classification in music digital libraries by combining lyrics and audio. In: *Proc. of the 10th annual joint conference on Digital libraries*, pp. 159-168. ACM.

Xiao Hu and J. Stephen Downie. 2010b. When lyrics outperform audio for music mood classification: A feature analysis. In: *proc. of the ISMIR*, pp. 619-624.

Xiao Hu. 2010. Music and mood: Where theory and reality meet. In: *proc. of the iConference*.

Xiao Hu, J. Stephen Downie, Cyril Laurier, Mert Bay and Andreas F. Ehmann. 2008. The 2007 MIREX audio mood classification task: lessons learned. In: *proc. of the ISMIR,* pp. 462-467.

Yi-Hsuan Yang, Yu-Ching Lin, Ya-Fan Su and Homer H. Chen. 2008. A regression approach to music emotion recognition. *IEEE Transactions on Audio, Speech, and Language Processing,* 16(2): 448-457.

Youngmoo E. Kim, Erik M. Schmidt, Raymond Migneco, Brandon G. Morton, Patrick Richardson, Jeffrey Scott, Jacquelin A. Speck and Douglas Turnbull. 2010. Music emotion recognition: A state of the art review. In: *proc. of the ISMIR,* pp. 255-266.

Using Skipgrams, Bigrams, and Part of Speech Features for Sentiment Classification of Twitter Messages

Badr Mohammed Badr
Dept. of Comp Sci & Engg
University College of Engineering
Osmania University, Hyderabad
`badr.md87@gmail.com`

S. Sameen Fatima
Dept. of Comp Sci & Engg
University College of Engineering
Osmania University, Hyderabad
`sameenf@osmania.ac.in`

Abstract

In this paper, we consider the problem of sentiment classification of English Twitter messages using machine learning techniques. We systematically evaluate the use of different feature types on the performance of two text classification methods: Naive Bayes (NB) and Support Vector Machines (SVM). Our goal is threefold: (1) to investigate whether or not part-of-speech (POS) features are useful for this task, (2) to study the effectiveness of sparse phrasal features (bigrams and skipgrams) to capture sentiment information, and (3) to investigate the impact of combining unigrams with phrasal features on the classification's performance. For this purpose we conducted a series of classification experiments. Our results show that POS features are useful for this task while phrasal features could improve the performance of the classification only when combined with unigrams.

1 Introduction

Due to the rapid growth of online opinion-rich resources with the advent of Web 2.0, a new area of text mining has emerged: sentiment analysis and opinion mining. The research of sentiment analysis is concerned with developing computational techniques that extract, categorize, and summarize subjective information (such as attitudes and sentiments) in textual resources. One fundamental task of sentiment analysis is to analyze a text fragment and detect the author's attitude with respect to a topic (e.g., determining whether a movie review is positive or negative towards the movie).

Twitter is an online, highly social microblogging service that enables subscribers to communicate with short text messages called "tweets".

Millions of people around the globe use Twitter on daily basis to publicly express their opinions regarding various aspects of their everyday lives. Thus, Twitter provides a massive data source which public and private organizations can harness to monitor the opinions of the crowd towards almost anything. Mining sentiments and opinions expressed in Twitter can provide indispensable information for various applications such as brand monitoring, customer management, and political forecasting.

Nevertheless, Twitter messages possess unique linguistic characteristics that make them distinguished from conventional user-generated content on the web (e.g., movie reviews). Tweets are short (maximum length is 140-character), cover a wide spectrum of topics, and written in an informal conversational style. The majority of tweets are poorly written and contain many non-standard lexical units such as emoticons (e.g., *_*), emojis (e.g., <3), neologisms (e.g., gr8), hashtags (e.g., #thingsilike), and acronyms (e.g., lol). In addition, most subscribers write their tweets using mobile devices, which increases the frequency of unintentional spelling mistakes. Petz et al. (2013) performed an empirical analysis on text samples collected from various social media, and they found misspellings ratio to be the highest in Twitter.

Because of the aforementioned reasons, sentiment analysis on Twitter text is considered much more challenging problem than other domains. The lexical variations of Twitter language affect the vector representation of the corpus. Saif et al. (2012) argued that data sparsity is the major challenge faced when dealing with Twitter text. They showed that Twitter text has much more low-frequency terms than movie reviews. This can be justified by the topic diversity and the large number of irregular words that occur in tweets. To get a closer look at this problem, we conducted a comparison between the Stanford Twitter Sen-

D S Sharma, R Sangal and E Sherly. Proc. of the 12th Intl. Conference on Natural Language Processing, pages 268–275,
Trivandrum, India. December 2015. ©2015 NLP Association of India (NLPAI)

timent (STS) dataset[1] and movie reviews dataset[2] in terms of vocabulary growth. Figure 1 shows the vocabulary growth rate of the two datasets. From Figure 1, it can be observed that the vocabulary of Twitter grows at a higher rate than movie reviews as the corpus size gets larger (measured by the total number of words). We manually inspected the low-frequency words in the Twitter vocbulary. Most of these words were informal abbreviations (e.g., 4eva), elongated words (e.g., beeeeer), and hashtag phrases (e.g., #mayblowyourmind).

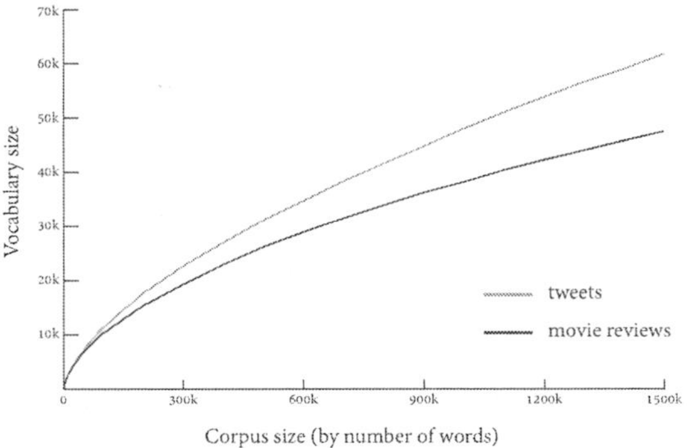

Figure 1: A comparison between the STS corpus and a movie reviews corpus in terms of vocabulary growth. Corpus size (x-axis) is plotted against the vocabulary size (y-axis).

In this paper, we address the problem of sentiment analysis of English tweets using machine learning-based classification techniques. We tackle this problem as a binary classification task where we have two classes: positive vs. negative.

2 Related Work

Using machine learning techniques to tackle the task of Twitter sentiment analysis has been the dominant technique in the literature (Go et al., 2009; Bifet and Frank, 2010; Pak and Paroubek, 2010; Kouloumpis et al., 2011; Asiaee T et al., 2012; Saif et al., 2012; Nakov et al., 2013). The pioneer work in this direction is Go et al. (2009) who used emoticons as noisy signals to obtain annotated training data. They experimented with SVM, Naive Bayes, and Maximum Entropy classifiers, and used unigrams, bigrams, and POS tags as features to build two-class sentiment classifiers. Their best classifier was Maximum Entropy

---

[1]http://www.sentiment140.com
[2]http://ai.stanford.edu/ amaas/data/sentiment

trained on a combination of unigrams and bigrams with an accuracy of 83.0%. Their results give an indication that combining different levels of n-gram features has a positive impact on the classifiers performance.

The impact of using POS features for Twitter sentiment classification was hotly debated in the literature. While Go et al. (2009) and Kouloumpis et al. (2011) concluded that POS features are not useful at all for Twitter sentiment classification, Pak and Paroubek (2010) showed that the distribution of POS tags is not uniform among different sentiment classes, which suggests that they can be used as discriminating features to train sentiment classifiers. In the latter approach, POS tags were used in conjunction with n-gram features to train a Naive Bayes classifier. However, they did not investigate how much improvement was gained when POS features were added to unigrams.

Fernández et al. (2014) experimented with different levels of skipgrams extracted from tweets to train an SVM sentiment classifier. Their results show that skipgram features outperform conventional n-gram features. Nevertheless, no other experiments were conducted to evaluate the effectiveness of skipgrams on other learning algorithms nor the imapct of combining skipgrams with unigrams on the classification performance.

3 Approach

Our approach is to extract different types of features from tweets and build sentiment classifiers using two supervised machine learning algorithms: Naive Bayes (NB) and Support Vector machines (SVM). We investigate the effectiveness of four different sets of features: unigrams, unigrams with part of speech tags, bigrams, and skipgrams. First, each set of features is used as a standalone feature set to train the two classifiers. Then, different feature sets are combined in order to study the impact of combining sprase feature sets on the classifiers' performance.

3.1 Twitter Sentiment Data

For the research conducted in this paper, we used the STS corpus which was created by Go et al. (2009). The STS training data was collected using the Twitter API and consists of a balanced set of 1.6 million tweets (800,000 tweets in each sentiment category). Tweets in the training set were automatically labeled using emoticons as noisy signals to detect the author's sentiment. For example, a tweet is considered positive if it contains any of the emoticons :), : -), :D, or =), and considered negative if it contains any of the emoticons : (or : - (. To filter out tweets of mixed sentiments, the authors removed tweets that contain both positive and negative emoticons. However, using emoticons as labels could produce noisy instances because the assumption of relating emoticons to the author's mood may not hold in all situations. Therefore, the work in this paper follows the Distant Supervision paradigm (Mintz et al., 2009).

A subset of the original STS training data was used to build the sentiment classifiers in this paper. We have randomly sampled a balanced set of 200,000 training instances from the original corpus. To evaluate the classifiers, the STS test dataset was used. The test data contains 182 positive and 177 negative tweets which were collected by querying the Twitter API with specific keywords including brands, products, and celebrities. Contrary to the training data, tweets in the test data were manually labeled by human annotators.

3.2 Linguistic Preprocessing

Twitter has its own conventions which makes tweets distinct from other online textual data. In addition, the raw text of tweets is noisy and usually contains non-standard lexical tokens (e.g., emoticons, acronyms, hashtags, etc.). Thus, tweets have to be processed using Twitter-specific tools followed by several steps of text normalization.

3.2.1 Tokenization and POS Tagging

In this step, we used CMU TweetNLP[3] to tokenize the tweets and produce the part-of-speech tags. TweetNLP is a Java-based microblogging-specific tool that was developed by Owoputi et al. (2013) to handle online conversational text such as Twitter messages. This POS tagger uses its own tag set which was crafted by Gimpel et al. (2011) for this kind of noisy and informal textual data. Figure 2 shows an example of a tweet that has been tagged with this tool.

3.2.2 Token Normalization

To reduce the number of word types, or the vocabulary size of the Twitter corpus, many preprocessing steps are necessary to normalize Twitter text. We use the same normalization steps as proposed

---

Figure 2: An example of a tweet that has been tagged by TweetNLP. The original tweet is *"ikr smh he asked fir yo last name so he can add u on fb lololol"*. This tweet can be formally writen as *"He asked for your last name so he can add you on Facebook"*. Figure taken from (Owoputi et al., 2013).

by Saif et al. (2012). These steps include the following:

- Case-folding: all tokens are first converted to lowercase letters.

- Username replacement: all user mentions are replaced by the token *MENTION*.

- Web links replacement: all URLs are replaced by the token *URL*.

- Punctuation replacement: all punctuation marks are replaced by the token *PUNCT*.

- Hashtags: the hash symbol (#) is removed from hashtags and they are treated as regular words afterwards.

- Digits: all digit characters are replaced by the token *DIGIT*.

- Word compression: any sequence of repeated letters is reduced to two letter. For example, *"coool"* and *"cooool"* are compressed as a single token *"cool"*.

Table 1 summarizes the effect of the normalization steps on the vocabulary size. It can be observed that the number of word types has been reduced by 58.5% due to token normalization.

3.3 Feature Extraction

For the purpose of this research, four different types of features were extracted from the preprocessed tweets. These features are: Unigrams (individual word tokens separated by a whitespace or a punctuation mark), Unigrams–POS (unigrams with their POS appended to the token), Bigrams (pairs of adjacent word tokens), and Skipgrams

---

[3]http://www.ark.cs.cmu.edu/TweetNLP

Normalization step	Vocab size	Reduction(%)
No normalization	196,630	0%
Case-folding	169,362	13.7%
Usernames	106,020	37.4%
URLs	97,088	5.5%
Punctuations	96,157	0.5%
Digits	85,961	10.5%
Hashtags	85,022	0.6%
Word compression	81,454	4.1%
Total Reduction		**58.5%**

Table 1: Effects of normalization steps on the vocabulary size.

(pairs of word tokens that are not necessarily adjacent). For example, consider the following preprocessed tweet:

" i love my new smartphone "

The extracted features are shown in Table 2. Each extracted feature in the table is enclosed within square brackets "[ ]".

It is worth mentioning that the skipgram features extracted in this step are actually k-skipbigrams, where k is the length of the tweet. In other words, we don't use a fixed window length to generate skipgram pairs, but the window length is allowed to expand for the entire text of the tweet. Using this approach to generate skipgram features will increase the size of the feature space by a considerable factor. In order to reduce the number of

Feature set	Extracted features
Unigrams	[i] [love] [my] [new] [smartphone]
Unigrams–POS	[i–O] [love–V] [my–D] [new–A] [smartphone–N]
Bigrams	[i–love] [love–my] [my–new] [new–smartphone]
Skipgrams	[i–love] [i–my] [i–new] [i–smartphone] [love–my] [love–new] [love–smartphone] [my–new] [my–smartphone] [new–smartphone]

Table 2: The extracted features from the sample tweet: *"i love my new smartphone"*.

the skipgram features, we used the following procedure: (1) Tokens tagged with parts of speech G (foreign words or abbreviations), \$ (digits and numbers), & (coordinating conjunction), U (URLs and emails), and P (pre- or post- postions) are removed from the set of candidate words for skipgrams generation. (2) We alphabetically arranged the words in each candidate pair. Thus, the features [i–love] and [love–i] are both represented as [i–love] regardless of the order in which each token appeared in the tweet. (3) Words that occur only once in the corpus (a.k.a. *hapaxes*) are excluded when generating features. Using this procedure allowed us to reduce the feature space substantially. Table 3 shows some summary statistics of the extracted features for each feature set.

Feature set	# Features	Hapaxes (%)
Unigrams	81,454	76.84%
Unigrams–POS	97,084	78.23%
Bigrams	656,440	87.57%
Skipgrams	3,084,656	92.04%

Table 3: Summary statistics for the extracted features.

3.4 Classification Methods

In this paper, we use machine learning techniques to build predictive models that can classify a tweet as positive or negative based on the sentiment expressed in the tweet. In other words, we tackle this problem as a binary text classification problem. We experimented with two learning algorithms that have been widely used for text classification tasks: Naive Bayes (NB) and Support Vector Machines (SVM).

In order to implement the aforementioned classification methods on our Twitter data sample, we adapted the same bag-of-features approach as in Pang et al. (2002) to convert extracted features from each tweet into a feature vector. We consider each tweet as a text document. Then, we extract a set of m features $\{f_1, \ldots, f_m\}$ from the entire Twitter corpus as shown in section 3.3. These features might include, for example, the unigram [*good*], the bigram [*really–good*], or the skipgram [*my–good*]. Finally, each tweet is represented as a feature vector $\mathbf{t} = (n_1(t), \ldots, n_i(t) \ldots, n_m(t))$, where $n_i(t)$ as the number of times a feature f_i occurs in a tweet $\mathbf{t}$.

3.4.1 Multinomial Naive Bayes

Naive Bayes classification is a probabilistic classification method which has been formulated based on Bayes theory. In this work, we used a multinomial Naive Bayes (MNB) model for text classification (Manning et al., 2008). To classify a tweet t, a MNB classifier assigns a class $c*$ as

$$c* = argmax_c P_{NB}(c|t)$$

$$P_{NB}(c|t) = \frac{P(c) \cdot P(t|c)}{P(t)}$$

The probability $P(t)$ is fixed for each class and has no role in estimating $c*$. Therefore, by applying the conditional independence of features assumption, $P_{NB}(c|t)$ can be estimated as

$$P_{NB}(c|t) = P(c)(\prod_{i=1}^{m} P(f_i|c)^{n_i(t)})$$

The probability $P(f_i|c)$ represents the relative frequency of the feature f_i in tweets belonging to class c and estimated through maximum likelihood. To deal with unknown features, the Laplace (add-one) smoothing technique is used to avoid zero-valued probabilities. Thus, $P(f_i|c)$ is estimated as

$$P(f_i|c) = \frac{count(f_i,c)+1}{\sum_{f \in V} count(f,c)+m}$$

where m represents the total number of features of a feature set.

3.4.2 Support Vector Machines

Joachims (1998) has shown that Support Vector Machines (SVM) is a highly effective classification technique for sparse text data. The motivation for using SVM for text classification problems originates from the capability of this algorithm to effectively handle sparse and highly dimensional data representations. Given a binary classification problem and a set of training examples, the aim of the training phase is to construct a hyperplane, denoted as a vector $\vec{w}$, that represents the largest possible separator between each class of the training examples. Thus, SVM classifiers are usually refereed to as maximum margin classifiers. When this largest margin separator is learned, deciding the class of unknown text documents is simply predicting which side of the hyperplane they might fall on.

The mathematical details of the SVM algorithm is beyond the scope of this paper. In our research, we used the LIBLINEAR package which includes a linear implementation of the SVM algorithm developed by Fan et al. (2008).

4 Evaluation

4.1 Experimental Set-up

We used a sample of the STS dataset described in section 3.1 as training data. We sampled 100,000 positive and 100,000 negative tweets from the original corpus. The STS testing dataset was used to evaluate the classifiers. Then, the same linguistic preprocessing and feature extraction steps were applied to both training and testing datasets. First, token normalization steps were applied to the output of TweetNLP tool using regular expressions. Second, we used a Python script to extract each of the feature sets described in section 3.3 from the preprocessed tweets. Features that occur only once were removed form the final feature sets. For classification, we used the multinomial Naive Bayes algorithm in-built in *WEKA*[4], the open source data mining software developed by Hall et al. (2009). The LIBLINEAR package was used for SVM with L2-regularized L2-loss and the cost parameter c was tuned to get the best performance of the SVM. We found that setting $c = 0.01$ works best for moderate number of features (Unigrams and Unigrams–POS), and $c - 0.005$ works best for large number of features (Bigrams, Skipgrams, and combinations of feature sets).

4.2 Experimental Results

In this section, we present the classification results, both from using each feature set in isolation and combining unigram features with phrasal features.

4.2.1 Individual Feature Sets

First, each set of features described in section 3.3 is used as a standalone feature set to train the classifiers. Table 4 shows the performance of each classifier as measured by accuracy.

From the results summarized in Table 4, it can be observed that SVM outperforms MNB when unigram features (both Unigrams and Unigrams–POS) are used to train the the classifiers. However, MNB outperforms SVM when phrasal features (both Bigrams and Skipgrams) are used. For Bigrams, and compared to the unigrams baseline, MNB accuracy has improved from 74.7% to 76.0% while SVM accuracy declined from 79.9% to 76.0%. The same can be observed for skipgram features, where MNB accuracy improved to 78.8%

[4]http://www.cs.waikato.ac.nz/ml/weka

Feature Set	MNB	SVM
Unigrams	74.7%	79.9%
Unigrams–POS	76.0%	**80.5%**
Bigrams	77.1%	76.0%
Skipgrams	**78.8%**	74.7%

Table 4: Classifications' accuracy for each set of features individually. Bold-faced accuracy scores denote the top-performing classifier for each learning algorithm.

Feature Set	MNB	SVM
Unigrams + Bigrams	78.3%	82.3%
Unigrams + Skipgrams	79.1%	83.0%
Unigrams–POS + Bigrams	78.6%	81.1%
Unigrams–POS + Skipgrams	**80.2%**	**83.6%**

Table 5: Classifications' accuracy for combined feature sets. Bold-faced accuracy scores denote the top-performing classifier for each learning algorithm.

while SVM declined to 74.7%. These results are comparable to those of Go et al. (2009) who observed similar behavior of their MNB and SVM classifier for unigram and bigram features. Therefore, one can conclude that the performance of SVM degrades as the sparsity degree of the feature representation increases, given that bigrams are sparser than unigrams, and skipgrams are sparser than bigrams. On the other hand, the sparsity degree does not negatively affect the performance of MNB.

Moreover, our results show that POS tags improve classification performance when they are attached to the unigrams. Compared to the unigrams baseline, accuracy of MNB improved from 74.7% to 76.0% while SVM accuracy slightly improved from 79.9% to 80.5%. These results contradict with the findings of Go et al. (2009) and Kouloumpis et al. (2011) who concluded that POS features are not useful for Twitter sentiment analysis. In both works, a general-purpose POS tagger was used to produce the POS tags. Therefore, our results provide evidence that using microblogging-specific POS tagger to produce POS features provide informative features for machine learning-based sentiment classifiers.

4.2.2 Combined Feature Sets

Next, we investigate the impact of combining unigram features with phrasal features on the classification's performance. To combine different feature sets, we merge two sets of features to generate a single feature set. For example, if the Unigrams feature set has n features is combined with the Bigrams feature set which has m features, the resulting feature space from the merge will have $n + m$ number of features. Table 5 shows the classification's accuracy for each combined features set.

From Table 5, one can observe the follow-ing: First, adding phrasal features to unigram features consistently enhance the classifiers' performance and yield an improvement over the classifiers trained on individual feature sets. Second, SVM classifiers consistently beat MNB when trained on combined features. Therefore, it can be concluded that using unigram features in combination with phrasal features improves the classification performance of learning algorithms. Moreover, skipgram features seem to be more capable of capturing informative sentiment terms than bigram features. Finally, combining Unigrams–POS and Skipgrams produced the optimal feature set of both learning algorithms as it achieved top performance (83.6% for SVM and 80.2% for MNB).

5 Discussion

Our classification results show that the two learning algorithms (MNB and SVM) behave differently in response to the sparsity degree of the text representation. Interestingly, the MNB classifier trained on skipgrams alone was optimal among the the other MNB classifiers even though the skipgram feature set is much more sparser than the other feature sets. Likewise, the MNB classifier trained on bigrams showed better performance than the unigram baseline. However, the increase in the sparsity degree hampers the performance of SVM as both classifiers trained on bigrams and skipgrams performed worse than the unigram baseline. Regarding POS features, and contrary to previous works in the literature, we found that adding POS features to unigrams improves the performance of the classification for both algorithms. We justify the difference in our result to the choice of the POS tagger, since the previous works used a general-purpose POS tagger that was trained on different domains other than social media text.

In addition, our results show evidence that combining unigram features with phrasal features always yields better performance than using feature sets in isolation. Sparse feature sets, which were less effective for SVM classifiers when used as standalone features, do not negatively impact the performance of SVM when combined with unigram features. Thus, we conclude that combining sparse phrasal feature sets with ungirams can be considered as a smoothing technique to alleviate the the sparsity problem and provide more informative features for sentiment classifiers.

In our experiments, we used a subset of the STS data as our training data (200,000 tweets). However, our optimal classifier in this research, the SVM trained Unigrams–POS and Skipgrams features combined, achieves 83.6% accuracy. This result outperforms all the classifiers of Go et al. (2009) which were trained on the entire original training dataset ($\sim$1.6M tweets) and evaluated on the same testing set. Their top performing classifier was the maximum entropy classifier trained on a combination of unigrams and bigrams (they reported 83.0% accuracy). This finding suggests that using skipgrams as features in combination with unigrams is a very good, yet simple solution to consider when the available training data is limited in size.

6 Future Work

In this paper, we showed that combining unigrams with skipgram features consistently improves the classification performance. Our skipgram features are actually k-skip-bigrams where k is the length of the tweet. For future work, one can investigate the impact of using fixed values for k on the classification performance as well as the sparsity degree.

Furthermore, we aim to expand the work conducted in this paper by considering the neutral class since not all tweets convey a polar sentiment. To tackle this task, the problem of Twitter sentiment classification would be reformulated as 3-class classification problem. The major challenge would be how to collect neutral tweets for training. One way to collect neutral tweets was suggested by Pak and Paroubek (2010) who used the Twitter feed of some newspapers and magazines as a source of objective tweets. Because newspapers headlines usually convey facts not opinions, they have considered Twitter news as neutral tweets.

7 Conclusions

The emergence of the social media, such as Twitter, has provided an open medium where people express their feelings and opinions at liberty. Twitter stream generates an enormous number of opinionated messages that cover all aspects of our daily lives. Effective sentiment analysis of Twitter messages can reveal high quality information regarding the concerns and preferences of the general public. However, the use of informal language and slang in Twitter, coupled with the high frequency of misspellings, makes this task more challenging than other domains where the text is well-edited. We showed that the vocabulary size of a Twitter text corpus grows in a higher rate than movie reviews corpus. By means of linguistic preprocessing, we were able to reduce the vocabulary size in our Twitter dataset by nearly 58%. Still, up to 76% of the words occur only once in the corpus. A manual inspection of the low-frequecnt terms has revealed that the vast majority of the words that occur only once are actually hashtag phrases, elongated words, and irregular acronyms.

In this paper, we systematically evaluated the effectiveness of four different feature sets: unigrams, unigrams with part of speech tags, bigrams, and skipgrams on the performance of MNB and SVM classifiers. First, each set of features is used as a standalone feature set to train the two classifiers. Our experimental results show that appending Twitter-specific POS tags to the unigrams consistently improves the performance of the classifiers compared to the unigrams baseline. We also find that MNB and SVM behaves differently in response to the sparsity degree of phrasal features (bigrams and skipgrams). While these features improve the performance of the MNB classifier compared to the unigram baseline, they hamper performance of SVM. To the best of our knowledge, this finding is unprecedented.

Furthermore, we investigated the impact of combining unigram features with phrasal features on the classification's performance. Interestingly, the results of combining different feature sets show improvements not only compared to the unigram baseline, but also over all individual feature sets. Therefore, we conclude that using a combination of unigrams and phrasal features is a very good, yet simple solution to improve the performance of Twitter sentiment classifiers, specially if the training data is limited.

References

Amir Asiaee T, Mariano Tepper, Arindam Banerjee, and Guillermo Sapiro. 2012. If you are happy and you know it... tweet. In *Proceedings of the 21st ACM international conference on Information and knowledge management*, pages 1602–1606. ACM.

Albert Bifet and Eibe Frank. 2010. Sentiment knowledge discovery in twitter streaming data. In *Discovery Science*, pages 1–15. Springer.

Rong-En Fan, Kai-Wei Chang, Cho-Jui Hsieh, Xiang-Rui Wang, and Chih-Jen Lin. 2008. Liblinear: A library for large linear classification. *The Journal of Machine Learning Research*, 9:1871–1874.

Javi Fernández, Yoan Gutiérrez, José M Gómez, and Patricio Martınez-Barco. 2014. Gplsi: Supervised sentiment analysis in twitter using skipgrams. In *Proceedings of the 8th International Workshop on Semantic Evaluation (SemEval 2014), number SemEval*, pages 294–299.

Kevin Gimpel, Nathan Schneider, Brendan O'Connor, Dipanjan Das, Daniel Mills, Jacob Eisenstein, Michael Heilman, Dani Yogatama, Jeffrey Flanigan, and Noah A Smith. 2011. Part-of-speech tagging for twitter: Annotation, features, and experiments. In *Proceedings of the 49th Annual Meeting of the Association for Computational Linguistics: Human Language Technologies: short papers-Volume 2*, pages 42–47. Association for Computational Linguistics.

Alec Go, Richa Bhayani, and Lei Huang. 2009. Twitter sentiment classification using distant supervision. *CS224N Project Report, Stanford*, 1:12.

Mark Hall, Eibe Frank, Geoffrey Holmes, Bernhard Pfahringer, Peter Reutemann, and Ian H Witten. 2009. The weka data mining software: an update. *ACM SIGKDD explorations newsletter*, 11(1):10–18.

Thorsten Joachims. 1998. *Text categorization with support vector machines: Learning with many relevant features*. Springer.

Efthymios Kouloumpis, Theresa Wilson, and Johanna Moore. 2011. Twitter sentiment analysis: The good the bad and the omg! *Icwsm*, 11:538–541.

Christopher D Manning, Prabhakar Raghavan, Hinrich Schütze, et al. 2008. *Introduction to information retrieval*, volume 1. Cambridge university press Cambridge.

Mike Mintz, Steven Bills, Rion Snow, and Dan Jurafsky. 2009. Distant supervision for relation extraction without labeled data. In *Proceedings of the Joint Conference of the 47th Annual Meeting of the ACL and the 4th International Joint Conference on Natural Language Processing of the AFNLP: Volume 2-Volume 2*, pages 1003–1011. Association for Computational Linguistics.

Preslav Nakov, Zornitsa Kozareva, Alan Ritter, Sara Rosenthal, Veselin Stoyanov, and Theresa Wilson. 2013. Semeval-2013 task 2: Sentiment analysis in twitter.

Olutobi Owoputi, Brendan O'Connor, Chris Dyer, Kevin Gimpel, Nathan Schneider, and Noah A Smith. 2013. Improved part-of-speech tagging for online conversational text with word clusters. Association for Computational Linguistics.

Alexander Pak and Patrick Paroubek. 2010. Twitter as a corpus for sentiment analysis and opinion mining. In *LREC*, volume 10, pages 1320–1326.

Bo Pang, Lillian Lee, and Shivakumar Vaithyanathan. 2002. Thumbs up?: sentiment classification using machine learning techniques. In *Proceedings of the ACL-02 conference on Empirical methods in natural language processing-Volume 10*, pages 79–86. Association for Computational Linguistics.

Gerald Petz, Michał Karpowicz, Harald Fürschuß, Andreas Auinger, Václav Stříteský, and Andreas Holzinger. 2013. Opinion mining on the web 2.0–characteristics of user generated content and their impacts. In *Human-Computer Interaction and Knowledge Discovery in Complex, Unstructured, Big Data*, pages 35–46. Springer.

Hassan Saif, Yulan He, and Harith Alani. 2012. Alleviating data sparsity for twitter sentiment analysis. CEUR Workshop Proceedings (CEUR-WS. org).

A Hybrid Approach for Bracketing Noun Sequence

Arpita Batra
LTRC, IIIT-Hyderabad
Hyderabad, India
arpita.batra@research.iiit.ac.in

Soma Paul
LTRC, IIIT-Hyderabad
Hyderabad, India
soma@iiit.ac.in

Abstract

For a resource poor language like Hindi, it becomes very difficult to bracket a noun sequence using approaches which are only based on corpus or lexical database. For semantic knowledge, power of both type of resources is needed to be combined. Therefore, affinity in between two nouns is preferred to be measured using backoff association which is the combination of lexical and conceptual association. Also, syntax is important for this task. But syntactic rules do not work for the compound nouns which is a special case of noun sequences and it may also occur as the sub-sequence. Using hybrid approach, accuracy of 86.33% has been obtained.

We have explored different variations like smoothing, frequency of synonyms and similar words for lexical association. And for conceptual association, different possible noun classes have been used for experiments. Authors have their own way of writing. Sometimes, two nouns can be written together as a single word or dash can be inserted in between the two. This helps in knowing that the two nouns have the tendency to be grouped together and hence this feature has been incorporated for the methods based on conceptual association.

1 Introduction

Complex noun sequence (NS) of Hindi was first discussed in Batra et al. (2014). We define

NS as a sequence of nouns in which the noun constituents may or may not be separated by the genitives - "kA", "kI" or "ke".[1] When nouns occur without any intervening postpositions, such special cases are called compound nouns (CN). Batra et al. (2014) have noticed that compound nouns have a tendency to be grouped first within a complex NS. They have called this concept, *local grouping*. This grouping takes place due to indeclinable nature of all the nouns except the last one in a CN. This can be formalized using following context-free grammar:[2]

$$G = \{V, \textstyle\sum, R, NS\}$$
$$V = \{NS, CN, genitive, noun\}$$
$$\textstyle\sum = \text{set of common nouns} \cup \text{set of genitives}$$

And rules R for this grammar are given by:
NS → NS genitive NS | CN | noun
CN → CN CN | noun CN | CN noun | noun noun
genitive → kA | kI | ke
noun → daravAja | kursI | kamarA | ...
      "door" "chair" "room"

Further, genitives and the head noun of the

---

[1] These allomorphic forms vary with gender, number and case values. Gender can have value - male(m) or female(f), number can have value - singular(s) or plural(p) and case can have - direct(d) or oblique(o) value. Morphological properties of genitives are:
kA - msd
kI - fsd or fso or fpd or fpo
ke - mso or mpd or mpo

[2] Context-free grammar has set of recursive rules which are used for generating strings from the non-terminals or the terminals (alphabets). It is represented using four tuples $\{V, \textstyle\sum, R, S\}$
V is the set of non-terminals
$\textstyle\sum$ is the set of terminals
R has the set of production rules from V to $(V \cup \textstyle\sum)*$
S is the start symbol

D S Sharma, R Sangal and E Sherly. Proc. of the 12th Intl. Conference on Natural Language Processing, pages 276–284,
Trivandrum, India. December 2015. ©2015 NLP Association of India (NLPAI)

sequence occurring just after the genitive should be in agreement.[3] Therefore, set V and rules can be expanded as shown below:

$$V = \{NS_{\text{msd}}, NS_{\text{mso}}, NS_{\text{mp}}, NS_{\text{f}}, CN_{\text{msd}},$$
$$CN_{\text{mso}}, CN_{\text{mp}}, CN_{\text{f}}, genitive_{\text{msd}},$$
$$genitive_{\text{mso}}, genitive_{\text{mp}}, genitive_{\text{f}},$$
$$noun_{\text{msd}}, noun_{\text{mso}}, noun_{\text{mp}}, noun_{\text{f}}\}$$

$NS \rightarrow NS_{\text{msd}} \mid NS_{\text{mso}} \mid NS_{\text{mp}} \mid NS_{\text{f}}$

$CN \rightarrow CN_{\text{msd}} \mid CN_{\text{mso}} \mid CN_{\text{mp}} \mid CN_{\text{f}}$

$genitive \rightarrow genitive_{\text{msd}} \mid genitive_{\text{mso}} \mid genitive_{\text{mp}} \mid$
$\quad\quad\quad genitive_{\text{f}}$

$noun \rightarrow noun_{\text{msd}} \mid noun_{\text{mso}} \mid noun_{\text{mp}} \mid noun_{\text{f}}$

$NS_{\text{f}} \rightarrow NS\ genitive_{\text{f}}\ NS_{\text{f}} \mid CN_{\text{f}} \mid noun_{\text{f}}$

$CN_{\text{f}} \rightarrow CN\ CN_{\text{f}} \mid noun\ CN_{\text{f}} \mid CN\ noun_{\text{f}} \mid$
$\quad\quad\quad noun\ noun_{\text{f}}$

$genitive_{\text{f}} \rightarrow kI$

$noun_{\text{f}} \rightarrow kursI \mid kursiyAZ \mid kursiyoM \mid ...$
$\quad\quad\quad$ "chair" "chairs"[4] "chairs"[5]

Similarly, rules can be expanded for NS_{msd}, NS_{mso} and NS_{mp}.

There exists an implicit relationship in between the noun constituents of a sequence. This semantic relation can not be captured using context-free grammar.

Parsing of complex NS is a very significant task for its correct interpretation. Parsing is the task of recognizing input string and assigning a structure to it (Jurafsky and Martin, 2000). Semantic parsing is important for understanding the meaning of a sequence. For this, nouns which have an implicit relationship in between them should be identified and then semantic role can be assigned to it. Bracketing helps in knowing the sub-sequence which are possible to be grouped together. It is difficult to add all the sequences in a dictionary because of the many possible combinations (Yosiyuki et al., 1994). And hence, to retrieve the meaning of a sequence, we cannot take dictionary as the reference. Some algorithm is needed for such type of work. Here, we have used approaches based on semantic and syntactic knowledge which are discussed later. Example

for some noun sequences with bracketing is shown below:

1. *((vidhAnasabhA chunAva)   prachAra)*
   "assembly"   "election" "propaganda"

2. *(sarakAra   kI (gaThana   nIti))*
   "government" *gen*[6]"formation" "policy"

3. *((gAoM   ke nAgarikoM) kI madada)*
   "village" *gen* "citizens"   *gen* "help"

The NS in example 3 can have two readings in two contexts as illustrated in the following examples:

(a) *gAoM   ke   nAgarikoM kI madada karo*
    "village" gen "citizens" gen "help" "do"
    "help the citizens of village"

(b) *gAoM   ke   nAgarikoM kI madada dvArA*
    "village" gen "citizens" gen "help" "by"
    ye   kAma   huA
    "this" "work" "happened"
    "This work happened by the help of village citizens"

The two interpretation can be represented using the following logical expressions:

(a) location(gAoM, nAgarikoM) && beneficiary(nAgarikOM, madada)

(b) location (gAoM, nAgarikoM) && agent (nAgarikOM, madada)

The meaning of the sequence can be ambiguous because of internal structure of the NS. Example:
gAon   ke kisAnoM ke   kheta
"village" *gen* "farmer" *gen* "farm"

It can be bracketed in two possible ways: (a) *((gAon ke kisAnoM) ke kheta)* and (b) *(gAon ke (kisAnoM ke kheta))*. Here, *gAon* refers to physical space which we can tag as village#1. The expression (a) conveys that farmers of the village#1 own farms and those farms are not necessarily located in the village#1, while in (b), farms are owned by some farmers which are located in village#1, but it is not necessary that farmers live in village#1. All the above cases of ambiguities can be resolved using contextual information. Legitimate bracketing will help in

---

[3] Agreement should be with gender, number and case

[4] plural(p) and direct(d)

[5] plural(p) and oblique(o)

[6] genitive

correct interpretation of NS.

In all the above examples, there are n-1 pairs of modifier and modified for a sequence containing n number of nouns. In example 3, "gAoM" and "nAgarikoM", "nAgarikoM" and "madada" are the two pairs. This can be represented using a tree in which parent nodes are modified and all the children nodes are modifiers. This type of structure is known as *modificational structure*. Knowing about modifiers and modifieds is the part of semantic parsing. And, every binary parse tree has an equivalent modificational structure (Lauer and Dras, 1994). Therefore, the task of bracketing becomes important for semantic parsing. And it also becomes important for information extraction and question answering. This task can also be used for inter-chunk and intra-chunk dependency parsing.

As we know, affinity of two nouns is judged semantically. Therefore, in Section 3, we have proposed algorithms which parse the sequence by judging the combination of nouns semantically. In Section 4, we have shown how agreement and grouping of compound noun can help in improving further accuracy, if applied first.

2   Related Work

We know that compound noun is a special case of noun sequences and we have included them in our study. In literature, many methods have been tested and proposed for parsing complex compound nouns in English. Some of the related works are discussed here in chronological order.

Grouping of two constituents in a compound noun depends on the affinity in between them. And this is determined semantically (Marcus, 1980; Lauer, 1994). Marcus (1980) has proposed a solution in which the better noun-noun pair (n_1n_2 or n_2n_3) in a compound noun $n_1n_2n_3$ is found. If either of the sub-constituent n_1n_2 or n_2n_3 is unacceptable, then the other parse is chosen. If both are acceptable, then the one with higher preference is chosen. The method of deciding preference order is not mentioned in the work. Liberman and Sproat (1992) have used mutual information for deciding the preference while Pustejovsky et al. (1993) have compared the

bigram frequency directly.

Marcus (1980) has proposed a method for parsing compound noun with more than three noun constituents. A buffer window of three constituents is taken. Initially, two components are grouped together from buffer. After this grouping, buffers are re-filled with the combined components, the component which has not been combined and the next component in a compound. The procedure of combining and filling the buffer is repeated till there exists the possibility of filling all the three buffers. This approach is a greedy approach and will fail for the compounds in which three leftmost nouns act only as the modifiers and not as the modified. Example of such parse structure are $(n_1(n_2(n_3n_4)))$, $((n_1(n_2(n_3n_4)))n_5)$ etc.

In previous methods, parsing is done using "lexical association". In such methods, grouping of nouns is resolved with the help of judging lexical preferences (Hindle and Rooth, 1993). Analysis which is based on lexical relationships faces the problem of data sparsity (Resnik, 1992; Resnik and Hearst, 1993). Word class information can also be used to measure the association. This type of association is termed as conceptual association (Resnik and Hearst, 1993). Lauer (1994) has used this concept for bracketing compound noun. This also helps in reducing the size of training data and is based on the assumption that all the nouns within a category behave in a similar manner (Lauer and Dras, 1994).

For training the data, Lauer (1994) has measured conceptual association using mutual information. A compound $n_1n_2n_3$ can be bracketed in two possible ways: $((n_1n_2)n_3)$ *and* $(n_1(n_2n_3))$. In first case, n_1 is modifying n_2 and n_2 is modifying n_3. And in second case, n_2 is modifying n_3 and n_1 is modifying n_3. This type of structure analysis is referred as *modificational structure* (Lauer and Dras, 1994). Models based on this concept were called dependency models and the models mentioned above were termed as adjacency models. Previous models were known as adjacency because the sub-sequences for which association is measured are adjacent to each other. For compound nouns with more than three nouns, they have proposed to multiply the conceptual associations. Lauer (1995) has shown that the dependency models perform better than the adjacency models. They have used similar algorithm with lexical association and have found that the method which uses conceptual association performs better. While, Lapata and Keller (2005) have shown that lexical association measure performs equivalent to the conceptual association measure when frequency for a sub-sequence is obtained from web.

Nakov and Hearst (2005) have also extracted lexical statistics from web search engine and have found that chi-square performs better than the measure which is similar to mutual information. For improving further accuracy, they have used some features like dash, possessive marker, capitalisation. They have searched the compound noun with these cues and have used this result to improve the score of both left and right bracketing. If the number of cues which support left bracketing are greater than the number of cues supporting right bracketing, then the result is left bracketed parse. Otherwise the result is right bracketed parse.

Girju et al. (2005) have used a C5.0 decision tree to determine the parse of noun compounds with three nouns. Three top semantic classes of all nouns were used as the feature.

Kulkarni and Kumar (2011) have used conditional probability to determine the constituency parse. In Sankrit, compounds are not separated by spaces and therefore, compatibity is decided after segments are obtained using a segmenter.

Kavuluru and Harris (2012) have used both non-greedy (global) and greedy based approach for bracketing compound nouns having four constituents ($n_1n_2n_3n_4$). For greedy approach, they have directly compared n-gram frequency as done by Pustejovsky et al. (1993). To determine the parse using non-greedy approach, cohesion value for all possible parse trees is calulated and the one with the highest value is chosen as the correct parse. Cohesion means togetherness and its value is obtained by calculating sum of jaccard index for each non-leaf node of a tree. Their approach uses adjacent sub-sequences for measuring association.

Not much work has been done in the area of parsing complex noun sequences. Sharma (2011) has used six syntactic and four semantic rules for parsing recursive genitive construction which is also the special case of noun sequences. Syntactic rules fail for the cases when the two genitive markers in the construction are same. For such cases, semantic rules are applied. List of words are classified using time, direction and measurement information which helps in applying semantic rules. And Batra et al. (2014) have used four approaches: adjacency greedy, adjacency global, dependency greedy and dependency global for constituency parsing. They have shown that dependency global performs the best. To the best of my knowledge, no other work has been done for noun sequences.

3 Parsing using Semantic Knowledge

Parsing the sequence requires world knowledge. It is not necessary that all information can be obtained from a corpus. Corpus can also be domain based and can be of limited size. Then for such cases, it becomes very difficult to find the parse using only lexical association. Generally, methods which use conceptual association performs better. For a resource poor language, conceptual association is also not sufficient because of the less coverage of words. Therefore, we propose a method which is the combination of lexical and conceptual association. First, we have covered the methods which depends on lexical association and then conceptual association based method has been explored.

Hindi is poor in resources. It is very difficult to find the sub-sequence formed by noun constituents with more than two nouns. Therefore, good accuracy can not be obtained when lexical association is measured between the whole constituents as proposed by Kavuluru and Harris (2012). Batra et al. (2014) calls this as adjacency global approach and had proven that dependency global approach performs better than this. This is based on modificational structure and can be obtained from binary parse tree by converting head noun of the left child into a modifier which modifies head noun of the right child. Cohesion value (CV) is measured by summing the association value (AV) for each node which have two children. For finding the best parse tree, cohesion value for all possible trees is calculated. The tree which has highest value is the result of bracketing.

$$CV(tree) = \sum_{\substack{n \in node \\ n \neq leaf\ node}} AV(H(lc(n)), H(rc(n)))$$

(1)

Association between head (H) of left and right child (*lc* and *rc*) of a non-leaf node 'n' can be found using lexical association or conceptual association. Lexical association uses frequency of noun constituents while conceptual association uses frequency of noun constituent's class. Association can be found using various measures. Some of the prevailing measures are pointwise mutual information, chi-square, jaccard index. Yang and Pedersen (1997) had shown that chi-square performs better than mutual information. This also has been shown by Nakov and Hearst (2005). Formula for jaccard index(ji), normalised pointwise mutual information(npmi) and chi-square(cs) are:

$$AV_{ji} = \frac{A}{A + B + C}$$

(2)

$$AV_{ji} = \frac{A}{freq(n_1) + freq(n_2) - A}$$

(3)

$$AV_{npmi} = \frac{\ln \frac{p(n_1,n_2)}{p(n_1)*p(n_2)}}{-\ln p(n_1, n_2)}$$

(4)

$$AV_{cs} = \frac{N(AD - BC)^2}{(A + C)(B + D)(A + B)(C + D)}$$

(5)

where,
A=freq($n_1 n_2$)
B=freq($n_1 \overline{n}_2$) = freq(n_1) - A
C=freq($\overline{n}_1 n_2$) = freq(n_2) - A
D=freq($\overline{n}_1 \overline{n}_2$)
N=A+B+C+D

p(n_1, n_2) = A/N
p(n_1) = freq(n_1)/N
p(n_2) = freq(n_2)/N

It is found that normalized pointwise mutual information is working better for lexical association and jaccard index is performing better for

conceptual association.

It is also not easy to find the bigrams in corpus. The count can be zero due to two reasons. First, two nouns can be combined but is unavailable. Another possibility is that the two nouns cannot be combined. If count of n_1 or n_2 is zero, then definitely, count of bigram is zero due to non-occurrence. Unseen bigrams and unigrams can be avoided using Kneser-Ney and Good Turing smoothing respectively. If smoothing is not applied, and default brackecting is chosen for the sequence, then it can add lot of noise. Therefore, for methods described below, smoothing and normalized pointwise mutual information has been used with lexical association and jaccard index for conceptual association. Below, we have discussed methods depending on various ways of calculating association value.

3.1 Lexical Association using Synonymns and Similar Words

It is not even too easy to find head of two subsequences together in a corpus. To increase the chances of finding the correct parse, we use the synonyms of the head of sub-sequences. Synonyms and similar words can be found using Hindi Wordnet. Synset can give set of synonyms. And similar words can be obtained using is-a specialization or hypernymy tree. Two words are similar to each other, if they share a hypernym. In English Wordnet, this is know as *co-ordinate term*. Example: "kuttA" (dog) and "nevalA" (mongoose) are co-ordinate terms as they both have a common hypernym "carnivore". Association using synset and coordinate terms can be found in various ways which are discussed below.

Sum of Frequency of Synonyms

For this method, we have used association similar to normalized pointwise mutual information. This depends on sum of frequency of all combinations formed using synonyms of both head nouns.

$$AV_{freq\_sum} = \frac{\ln \frac{sum(n_1,n_2)*N}{sum(n_1)*sum(n_2)}}{-\ln \frac{sum(n_1,n_2)}{N}}$$

(6)

$$CV = \sum_{\substack{n \in node \\ n \neq leaf\ node}} AV_{freq\_sum}(H(lc(n)), H(rc(n)))$$

(7)

$$sum(n_1, n_2) = \sum_{\substack{s_1 \in synonym(n_1) \\ s_2 \in synonym(n_2)}} freq(s_1, s_2),$$
$$sum(n_1) = \sum_{s_1 \in synonym(n_1)} freq(s_1),$$
$$sum(n_2) = \sum_{s_2 \in synonym(n_2)} freq(s_2)$$

Different authors can write a word with variations. Example, word "gehUZ" (wheat) can also be written as "geMhU". In synset, these variations are available in Hindi Wordnet. Using this approach for association, these variations can be captured. But problem with this method is that number of synonyms for the two head nouns may vary and hence, association value may be misleading.

Sum of Lexical Association of Synonyms

For this method, association in between two heads is calulated using summation of lexical associations between the pairs formed using synonyms of head constituents.

$$AV_{\text{LA\_sum}}(n_1, n_2) = \sum_{\substack{s_1 \in synonym(n_1) \\ s_2 \in synonym(n_2)}} AV_{\text{npmi}}(s_1, s_2) \tag{8}$$

$$CV = \sum_{\substack{n \in node \\ n \neq leaf\ node}} AV_{\text{LA\_sum}}(H(lc(n)), H(rc(n))) \tag{9}$$

This method suffers from the problem of collocation and different number of synonyms. Example for collocation: "vidhAna sabhA" (legislative assembly) is not referred as "kAnUna sabhA", despite the fact that "kAnUna" is the synonym of "vidhAna". Therefore, this method is not a good one.

Maximum of Lexical Association of Synonyms

For this method, association value is the maximum of all the values obtained using the combination of head noun synset.

$$AV_{\max}(n_1, n_2) = \max_{\substack{s_1 \in synonym(n_1) \\ s_2 \in synonym(n_2)}} AV_{\text{npmi}}(s_1, s_2) \tag{10}$$

$$CV = \sum_{\substack{n \in node \\ n \neq leaf\ node}} AV_{\max}(H(lc(n)), H(rc(n))) \tag{11}$$

This method does not have disadvantage of collocation, as we are trying to choose the best possible option from all the association values. Also, it does not even suffer from the problem of different number of synonyms. But disadvantage of this approach is the fact that different variations of writing a word is not taken into account.

3.2 Conceptual Association

Association between two constituents can also be measured using noun classes. We have used Hindi WordNet for finding the noun category and Jaccard Index as the association measure. Instead, of frequency of noun constituents, frequency of noun class is used which is obtained from training data. We have experimented using four types of classes: top node from hypernymy tree, second top node from hypernymy tree, second top node from ontology and third top node from ontology. First node from ontology is not considered as the class, because it tells that a word is noun and all the words in a sequence are noun except genitives. Therefore, it does not give any additional information.

$$CV = \sum_{\substack{n \in node \\ n \neq leaf\ node}} AV_{\text{ji}}(class_{\text{l}}(n), class_{\text{r}}(n)) \tag{12}$$

$$AV_{\text{ji}} = \frac{A}{A + B + C} \tag{13}$$

where,
$class_{\text{l}}(n)$ gives the class of head noun of left child
$class_{\text{r}}(n)$ gives the class of head noun of right child
$A = freq(c_1 c_2)$
$B = freq(c_1 \bar{c}_2)$
$C = freq(\bar{c}_1 c_2)$
and, c_i is the noun class of n_i

Author can write two noun compounds in various manners like dash can be used in between two nouns, two nouns can be combined together etc. Whenever, this feature is found for the two head nouns, then for that pair, one is added to the association value. Adding one, gives extra weightage to that pair and hence shows that these two should be grouped together. This feature is not used with lexical association because such cues were found to be very less frequent in the corpus.

3.3 Backoff Association

Due to less coverage of words in lexical database, conceptual association may not help in predicting the parse. If for any of the parse tree, any of the head noun is not found in lexical database, then normalized pointwise mutual information can be used as the lexical association measure. For lexical association, smoothed frequency is used. Synonyms and similar words based methods are not considered because of the non-significant difference in the result.

4 Bracketing using Hybrid Method

As it is evident from context-free grammar of noun sequences, compound nouns should be bracketed first and then these can be grouped with another compound noun or noun separated by genitives. Since, we use modificational structure for the task of parsing. Therefore, after the step of grouping compound nouns, whole sequence should be grouped using head nouns of these sub-sequences. If the compound noun has more than two nouns, then that sub-sequence is grouped internally using backoff association. Example:

hindU   samudAya ke logoM kI bhAvanAyeM
"Hindu" "community" "peoples"   "emotions"

In this sequence, hindU samudAya is the compound noun, therefore it should be grouped first as in "(hindU saumUdAya) ke logoM kI bhaAvanAyeM". Now, as the next step "samudAya ke logoM kI bhAvanAyeM" should be parsed.

Head nouns are grouped using agreement. If agreement is not satisfied, then the corresponding parse tree from all possible trees is discarded. In "samudAya ke logoM kI bhAvanAyeM", there are two possible bracketing options: "((samudAya ke logoM) kI bhAvanAyeM)" and "(samudAya ke (logoM kI bhAvanAyeM))". For the first case, "ke" and "logoM" should be in agreement and for second case, "ke" and "bhAvanAyeM" should be in agreement. "ke" and "logoM" are masuline while "bhAvanAyeM" is feminine. And, hence for the second case, "ke" and "bhAvanAyeM" are not in agreement. Therefore, this option should be discared. Now only one option is left: "((samudAya ke logoM) kI bhAvanAyeM)". Therefore, whole parse structure is: "(((hindU samudAya) ke logoM) kI bhAvanAyeM)". There can be the

cases, when more than one tree is left in option after the process of removal of trees. Then, for those trees, we find cohesion value using backoff association. If none of the parse tree is possible to be formed, then it has the ability to tell about grammatical error.

Syntactic rules are not used directly as done by Batra et al. (2014) and Sharma (2011), because they are valid for the presence of two genitives. We know that noun sequence can be of many possible length with different number of genitives. Therefore, it becomes difficult to increase the number of rules and hence we have used this procedure.

5 Experiments, Results and Observations

For experiments, 2365 noun sequences were extracted from Hindi Treebank. We have taken sequences with maximum five components because of less occurrence of larger sized sequences. Distribution of noun sequence on the basis of number of noun constituents is shown in Table 1. Since, conceptual association based approaches require training data, the data of noun sequences is divided into 2:1 ratio for training and testing respectively.

Noun Count	Distribution
3	78.30%
4	17.37%
5	3.55%
6	0.50%
7	0.25%

Table 1: Percentage distribution of noun sequences according to number of noun constituents

Batra et al. (2014) have shown that there exists more cases of left bracketing than right bracketing. Therefore, for all of the approaches, if two or more bracketing option has same cohesion value, then one with left bracketing is chosen out of the conflicts.

Further, a corpus of size 18200k, obtained using web crawling was used for finding frequency of noun constituents. Frquency is found for root form of the head nouns. And since, frequency for root form is used, therefore, root form of corpus is also used for finding the frequency. Also genitive construction as the paraphrase is used for increasing the bigram counts. For variations in lexical association, first we have experimented using different association measures with smoothed frequency. It has been observed that normalized pointwise mutual information performs the best. Also, three variations for lexical association depending on synonyms and similar words have been used. It has been observed that approaches using similar words is not performing as good as the one with only synonyms. A lot of noise is added for similar words due to the problem of collocation. For the same reason, summation of lexical association method is performing the worst. Even method based on summation of frequency is not performing too good. It is adding more noise due to difference in number of synonyms. The fact that it can be useful for capturing variation of spelling is overshadowed. Results for all these variations are shown in Table 2.

Type	Accuracy
jaccard index	58.49%
normalised pmi	59.00%
chi-square	58.23%
synset + frequency sum	58.49%
synset + association sum	45.08%
synset + association max	61.43%
similar + frequency sum	48.91%
similar + association sum	46.99%
similar + association max	49.04%

Table 2: Accuracy for methods using Lexical Association

For conceptual association, experiments have variation in terms of noun class. It has been observed that noun class obtained from hypernymy tree is performing better than the one obtained using onotology. Number of noun classes from hypernymy tree are greater than ontology. Therefore, it is able to capture variations of noun sequences as much as possible. Also, second top node of hypernymy is not performing better than the top node and third top node of ontology is performing worse than the second one. Inspite of the fact that number of noun classes are large, the accuracy is not good. Many times, no class is assigned because of small depth of hypernymy and ontology tree. For the association measure, normalised pointwise mutual information and jaccard index is used for all these methods. It has been seen that top hypernymy node is performing best with jaccard index.

Then, the feature of dash is taken into consideration for this approach. Results for all these variations are shown in Table 3.

Type	Accuracy
ji + 2nd top ontological node	50.70%
ji + 3rd top ontological node	48.02%
ji + top hypernymy node	59.64%
ji + 2nd top hypernymy node	54.91%
npmi + 2nd top ontological node	57.72%
npmi + 3rd top ontological node	55.93%
npmi + top hypernymy node	57.47%
npmi + 2nd top hypernymy node	57.47%
ji + top hypernymy + dash feature	60.66%

Table 3: Accuracy for methods using Conceptual Association

Hindi Treebank has the collection of news. Many english words can be found written in Hindi. It has been observed that these words have better chances to be found in corpus than lexical database. Therefore, for such cases, lexical association is working better than conceptual association.

For further experiments, cohesion value is obtained using backoff association. Then experiment is done with grouping compound nouns and bracketing head nouns using backoff association without considering agreement. As the part of the last experiment, agreement is also used. Results are shown in Table 4.

Type	Accuracy
backoff association (BA)	61.55%
BA + CN grouping	81.48%
BA + CN grouping + agreement	86.33%

Table 4: Accuracy for methods using Backoff Association

For baseline, left brcketing is applied. In Table 5, results for 3, 4 and 5 components are shown for left bracketing and the hybrid approach to show that these experiments are performing bettter than the baseline. Left bracketing is the parse tree of n-1 height and 'n' nodes. In this tree, every non-leaf node has the right child which is a leaf node. Example: (((((n1 n2) n3) n4), (((((n1 n2)n3)n4)n5) etc. As the number of constituents increases, number of possible bracketing options increases. Hence, the task becomes more and more difficult and this is also evident from the results shown in Table 5.

Noun Count	Left Bracketing	Hybrid
3	76.16%	92.16%
4	45.23%	68.25%
5	25.00%	43.75%

Table 5: Accuracy for left bracketing and hybrid approach

6   Conclusion

Each type of association has some advantages. Lexical association works good, if corpus size is big and unbiased. Similar words should be avoided as it adds lot of noise. Conceptual association has advantage of learning data. Increasing the learning data can help in improving the power of conceptual association. And when both associations are combined, then problem of less coverage of words in lexical database can be overcome for conceptual association. When problems of both association are removed, accuracy for methods using only semantic knowledge can be improved as shown for English compound nouns. Knowing about syntax of noun sequence and agreement feature also helps. Therfore, hybrid approach is generally good for the cases when small size of resources are available. For future work, spelling normalizer can be applied on noun sequences for improving methods using lexical association.

References

Amba Kulkarni and Anil Kumar. 2011. Statistical constituency parser for sanskrit compounds. *Proceedings of ICON*.

Arpita Batra, Soma Paul, and Amba Kulkarni. 2014. Constituency parsing of complex noun sequences in hindi. In *Computational Linguistics and Intelligent Text Processing*, pages 285–296. Springer.

Dan Jurafsky and James H Martin. 2000. *Speech & language processing*. Pearson Education India.

Donald Hindle and Mats Rooth. 1993. Structural ambiguity and lexical relations. *Computational linguistics*, 19(1):103–120.

James Pustejovsky, Peter Anick, and Sabine Bergler. 1993. Lexical semantic techniques for corpus analysis. *Comput. Linguist.*, 19(2):331–358, June.

Kobayasi Yosiyuki, Tokunaga Takenobu, and Tanaka Hozumi. 1994. Analysis of japanese compound nouns using collocational information. In *Proceedings of the 15th conference on Computational linguistics-Volume 2*, pages 865–869. Association for Computational Linguistics.

Mark Lauer. 1994. Conceptual association for compound noun analysis. In *Proceedings of the 32nd annual meeting on Association for Computational Linguistics*, pages 337–339. Association for Computational Linguistics.

Mark Lauer. 1995. Corpus statistics meet the noun compound: some empirical results. In *Proceedings of the 33rd annual meeting on Association for Computational Linguistics*, pages 47–54. Association for Computational Linguistics.

Mark Lauer and Mark Dras. 1994. A probabilistic model of compound nouns. *arXiv preprint cmp-lg/9409003*.

Mark Liberman and Richard Sproat. 1992. The stress and structure of modified noun phrases in english. *Lexical matters*, pages 131–181.

Mirella Lapata and Frank Keller. 2005. Web-based models for natural language processing. *ACM Transactions on Speech and Language Processing (TSLP)*, 2(1):3.

Mitchell P Marcus. 1980. *Theory of syntactic recognition for natural languages*. MIT press.

Philip Resnik. 1992. Wordnet and distributional analysis: A class-based approach to lexical discovery. In *AAAI workshop on statistically-based natural language processing techniques*, pages 56–64.

Philip Resnik and Marti Hearst. 1993. Structural ambiguity and conceptual relations. In *Proceedings of the Workshop on Very Large Corpora: Academic and Industrial Perspectives*, pages 58–64. Citeseer.

Preslav Nakov and Marti Hearst. 2005. Search engine statistics beyond the n-gram: Application to noun compound bracketing. In *Proceedings of the Ninth Conference on Computational Natural Language Learning*, pages 17–24. Association for Computational Linguistics.

Ramakanth Kavuluru and Daniel Harris. 2012. A knowledge-based approach to syntactic disambiguation of biomedical noun compounds. In *COLING (Posters)*, pages 559–568. Citeseer.

Roxana Girju, Dan Moldovan, Marta Tatu, and Daniel Antohe. 2005. On the semantics of noun compounds. *Computer speech & language*, 19(4):479–496.

Sapna Sharma. 2011. *Disambiguating the parsing of hindi recursive genitive constructions*. Ph.D. thesis, International Institute of Information Technology Hyderabad–500032 India.

Yiming Yang and Jan O Pedersen. 1997. A comparative study on feature selection in text categorization. In *ICML*, volume 97, pages 412–420.

Simultaneous Feature Selection and Parameter Optimization Using Multi-objective Optimization for Sentiment Analysis

Mohammed Arif Khan[1], Asif Ekbal[1] and Eneldo Loza Mencía[2]
[1]Dept. of Computer Science & Engineering, Indian Institute of Technology Patna, India
[2]KE Group, Dept. of Informatics, Technische Universitat Darmstadt, Germany
[1]{arif.mtmc13, asif}@iitp.ac.in
[2]eneldo@ke.tu-darmstadt.de

Abstract

In this paper, we propose a method of feature selection and parameter optimization for sentiment analysis in Twitter messages. Appropriate features and parameter combinations have significant effect to the performance of any classifier. As base learning algorithms we make use of Random Forest and Support Vector Machines. We perform sentiment analysis at the message level, and use the platform of SemEval-2014 shared task. We achieve substantial performance improvement with our proposed model over the systems that are developed with random feature subsets and default parameter combinations.

1 Introduction

Social media has grown enormously over the last decade. Huge amount of unstructured texts are generated through social media platforms such as Twitter, blogs etc. People's opinions on certain aspects or events are always important. Mining relevant information from such large amounts of text manually is almost impossible, and so there is an obvious need to develop automatic systems that can extract the most important information from these large data sets. Sentiment analysis or opinion mining, a multi-disciplinary area covering natural language processing, data mining and machine learning, aims at extracting emotions from texts. This is an active research area, which has been used in different applications such as financial prediction (Mittal and Goel, 2012), evaluating customer feedbacks (Maks and Vossen, 2013) and understanding users' opinions about products and/or services (Mukherjee and Bhattacharyya, 2012) etc. Literature shows that machine learning (Bo Pang and Vaithyanathan, 2002), (Boiy and

Moens, 2009) and lexicon-based (Maite Taboada and Stede, 2011), (Cataldo Musto and Polignano, 2014) approaches have more predominantly been used for sentiment analysis.

One of the earliest studies on sentiment analysis on microblogging websites was provided by (Alec Go and Huang, 2009). The work presents a distant supervised based approach for sentiment classification using hash tags in tweets. (Kevin Gimpel, 2011) propose an approach to sentiment analysis in twitter using Part-of-Speech (PoS) tagged n-gram features and some twitter specific hash tags. The scarcity of labelled data is often a bottleneck for any machine learning based system, and sentiment analysis is not an exception. A technique for automatically creating labelled datasets for sentiment analysis research has been proposed in (Pak and Paroubek, 2010). (Apoorv Agarwal and Passonneau, 2011) used tree kernel decision tree that made use of the features such as kernel decision, Part-of-Speech information, lexicon based features and several other features. Previous studies such as (Dmitry Davidov and Rappoport, 2010) observed that hash tags and smileys work good for sentiment analysis. (Nielsen, 2011) concluded that the AFINN word list performs slightly better than ANEW (Affective Norms for English Words) in twitter sentiment analysis. Most of the supervised approaches have used the features such as N-grams, PoS information, emoticons and opinion words. Among the supervised approaches, Support Vector Machine (SVM) (Vapnik, 1995) and Naive Bayes (Mitchell, 1997) have been popularly used.

The performance of any classification technique depends on the features used to represent training and test patterns. Feature selection (Liu and Yu, 2005; Liu and Motoda, 1998) is the technique of automatically selecting a subset of relevant features for a classifier. It helps to build a robust model and reduces the complexity of the learning

281

D S Sharma, R Sangal and E Sherly. Proc. of the 12th Intl. Conference on Natural Language Processing, pages 285–294,
Trivandrum, India. December 2015. ©2015 NLP Association of India (NLPAI)

algorithm. This is also termed as attribute selection/ subset selection etc. By removing most irrelevant and redundant features from the data, feature selection helps to improve the performance of a classifier. In a ML approach, appropriate feature selection can be thought of as an optimization problem. Some of the prior works where feature selection has been modelled within the frameworks of evolutionary optimization techniques include (Ekbal and Saha, 2012; Ekbal and Saha, 2013). These works primarily focussed on named entity recognition in multiple languages. In general a classifier has many parameters whose values heavily influence the performance of a classifier. Therefore, like feature selection, determining the appropriate values of parameters for a classifier is another important key issue.

In this paper we propose a method of feature selection and parameter optimization within the framework of multiobjective optimization (MOO) (Deb, 2001). We implement a diverse set of features, consider their various subsets, and optimise various functions such as recall and precision, F-measure and number of features etc. As the base learning algorithms we use Support Vector Machines (Vapnik, 1995) and Random Forest (Breiman, 2001). We have carried out experiments on the benchmark set up of SemEval-2014 shared task [1]. Evaluation shows that our proposed system achieves substantial performance improvement over the model developed with random feature subsets and default parameter settings. The key contributions of the paper are two-fold, *viz.* (i). proposing a joint model of feature selection and parameter optimization, especially for sentiment analysis and (ii) the use of MOO based evolutionary methods in the broad areas of opinion mining.

The rest of the paper is structured as follows. Section 2 describes the features that we implanted for sentiment analysis. In Section 3 we present our proposed method for feature selection and parameter optimization. In Section 4, we report the evaluation results with analysis and discussions. Finally, in Section 5 we conclude the paper.

2   Features for Sentiment Analysis

Feature plays an important role in sentiment classification. We implement 55 features, and we categorise these into the five groups.

1. *Emoticon Features:*

   Positive Smiley (pSmiley): It is a common practice that people represents emoticons through variety of smileys. A smiley present in a tweet directly represents its sentiment. A feature is defined that identifies whether the positive smiley(s) is/are present or not in a tweet. We used a set of positive smiles available at this web page [2].

   Negative Smiley (nSmiley): Similar to positive smiley, we also obtain a set of negative smileys from the same source. The value of this feature is set to "yes" or "no" depending upon whether the tweet contains the negative smiley or not.

   Last Token Smiley (LastTokenSmiley): This feature indicates whether the last token in a tweet is a smiley or not. The presence of this smiley clearly indicates that tweet can't be of neutral type.

2. *Lexicon Features:* We use three automatically built sentiment lexicons, namely NRC Hash tag Sentiment Lexicon (Saif Mohammad and Zhu, 2013) , Sentiment140 Lexicon (Saif Mohammad and Zhu, 2013) and Bing Liu Lexicon (Xiaowen Ding and Yu, 2008).

   NRC Hash tag Sentiment Lexicon: (Saif Mohammad and Zhu, 2013) showed that hashtagged emotion words are good indicators that the tweet as a whole (even without the hashtagged emotion word) is expressing the same emotion. We adapted that idea and obtain the following features from this Lexicon:

   (i) (LexNRC): Scores of all the words are summed up. A feature value is, thereafter, set to based on the overall score of the tweet. The feature values are set to +1 , 0 or -1 depending upon whether the overall score is above 1, varies within the range -1 and +1 or less than -1.

   (ii) (PositiveLexNrcToken): A feature is generated that takes the value equal to the number of words present in a tweet having their scores greater than zero.

---

[1] http://alt.qcri.org/semeval2014/task9/

[2] http://www.datagenetics.com/blog/october52012/index.html

(iii) (NegativeLexNrcToken): A feature is defined that takes the value equal to the number of words having the negative scores.

(iv) (MaxLexNrc): This feature indicates the maximum positive score among all the tokens in a tweet.

(v) (MinLexNrc): This feature indicates the minimum value (i.e. maximum negative score) of polarity among all the tokens of a tweet.

(v) (LastNonZeroScoreNrc): This feature corresponds to the polarity of the last token of the tweet. This feature has been defined based on the observation that the sentiment as expressed in the last word of the tweet has great influence on the overall sentiment of any tweet.

Sentiment140 Lexicon: In this lexicon, the individual scores of the tokens have been calculated based on the number of tweets in which these tokens co-occur with the positive or the negative emoticons. For every tweet in the data set, following features are defined using the sentiment score, i.e. *score(w)* of each token w in the tweet:

(i) (Lex140): Feature that corresponds to the total score = $\sum_{w \in tweet} score(w)$.

(ii) (PositiveLex140Token): Feature that indicates the number of tokens in the tweet with score(w) > 0

(iii) (NegativeLex140Token): Feature that indicates the number of tokens in the tweet with score(w) < 0

(iv) (MaxLex140): Feature that indicates the maximal score of any token in the tweet = $max_{w \in tweet} score(w)$

(v) (MinLex140): Feature that corresponds to the minimal score of any token in the tweet = $min_{w \in tweet} score(w)$

(vi) (LastNonZeroScore140): The score of the last positive token (score(w) > 0) in the tweet

Bing Liu's Lexicon: We define the following two features based on this lexicon.

(i) (BllPositiveWords): A feature is defined that has the value equal to the number of words of a tweet present in the BLL's (Bing Liu Lexicon) word list of positive lexicons.

(ii) (BllNegativeWords): This feature is defined based on the number of words of a tweet present in the BLL's (Bing Liu Lexicon) word list of negative lexicons.

3. *SentiWordNet Features:* Based on the SentiWordNet dictionary (Andrea Esuli and Sebastiani, 2010) we define the following features that depend on the number of words bearing positive, negative and neutral sentiments.

SWN Positive words (SwnPositiveTokenCount): This is an integer-valued feature that is set equal to the number of words having more positive sentiment.

SWN Negative words (SwnNegativeTokenCount): Similar to the feature defined above, this is also denoted by an integer-valued feature that takes the value equal to the number of words that bear more negative sentiments.

SWN Neutral words (SwnNeutralTokenCount): This feature determines the number of neutral words for a tweet. This is obtained by the following formula:
SWN Neutral words = (number of words in a tweet) - (number of SWN positive words + number of SWN negative words).

SWN Polarity (SwnPolarity): For every tweet a polarity score is assigned based upon the scores of the constituent tokens. Let x and y denote the sum of positive and negative sentiment scores, respectively, for all the words of a tweet. Now we assign the polarities of the words as follows. If (x-y) > 0.5 then polarity of the tweet is assigned to be positive; If (x-y) < -0.5 then polarity of the tweet is assigned to be negative; and if (x-y) lies between -0.5 to 0.5 then the polarity of the tweet is assigned to be neutral.

4. *Part-of-Speech (PoS) Features:* (CHRIS NICHOLLS, 2009) found that different PoS categories contribute to sentiment analysis in varying degrees. To extract the PoS of every word present in a tweet,

we use the CMU ARK tagger [3]. We define a feature vector that considers the number of PoS categories present in a tweet. These features are listed in Table 2 from feature number 30 to feature number 54.

5. *Miscellaneous Features:* Beside the above four categories of features, we also implemented the following features:

Hash Count (HashCount): This feature gives the difference of number of positive hashtags (ex, #excellent, #thankful) and negative hashtags (ex. #bad, #terror). A positive value (negative value) of this feature indicates positive (negative) sentiment.

Tweet Length (TweetLength): Generally, a long tweet have more number of stop words. This feature counts the number of words present in a particular tweet. More is the number of stop words present in a tweet higher is the chance of it not being of neutral polarity.

Capital Characters (InitCap): If majority of the words present in a tweet are capitalised then there is more chance that the overall sentiment of the tweet is non-neutral. We compute the ratio of captalised words with respect to the total number of words present in a tweet. If this ratio is above a certain threshold then we set the feature value to 1, otherwise 0.

All Cap Words (AllUpperWords): This is an integer-valued feature, the value of which is set to the number of words equal to the number of capitalised words. This feature is defined based on the assumption that the words written using only the capitalised letters express sentiments more strongly.

Negation (NotPresent): The presence of words such as "not", "couldn't", won't", "shouldn't" etc. reverts the polarity of the sentence. We manually create a list of all such words from the training data. A binary-valued feature is then defined that is set to "yes" or "no" depending upon the presence of such word in the tweet.

---

[3]http://www.ark.cs.cmu.edu/TweetNLP/

Stop Words (StopWords): In the previous study (Hassan Saif and Alani, 2012), it has been shown that the classifiers learned with stop words outperform those learned without stop words. Here we define a feature based on the number of stop words present in a tweet. If the number of stop words is greater than 20 % (in terms of the number of words) then the tweet has more possibility of being neutral.

Elongated Words (ElongatedWords): To represent strong emotions, people, in general, use to repeat the same character more than twice. Some of the examples are: "happpppy", "coooool" etc. We define this feature in such a way that checks whether there is at least one elongated words present in the tweet.

Last Token (LastToken): This feature checks whether "?" or "!" is present in the last position of the tweet or not. The presence of such token in the last position denotes that the overall sentiment expressed in the tweet may be neutral. For ex. "U remember her from the 90s?", "Hello Mumbai Gud morning!".

3 Proposed Approach

In this section, firstly we introduce the concept of multiobjective optimization (MOO), formulate the problem of simultaneous feature selection and parameter optimization and then describe the proposed approach.

3.1 Multi-objective Formulation for feature subset selection

Multiobjective optimization (MOO) deals with the concept of optimising more than one function at a time. Compared to single objective optimization (SOO) that concerns in optimising only one function at a time, it has the ability to produce more than one feasible solutions which are equally important from the algorithmic point of view. This concept has been widely used for solving many decision problems. Mathematically, MOO (Deb, 2001) can be described as follows:
Find the vectors

$$x^* = [x_1^*, x_2^*, ..., x_N^*]^T \qquad (1)$$

of decision variables that simultaneously optimize the M objective values

$$f_1(x), f_2(x), ..., f_M(x); N \geq M, N > 1, M > 1 \tag{2}$$

while satisfying the constraints, if any.

3.2 Formulation of the Problem

Performance of any classifier depends greatly on the parameters used. Generally we choose the best parameters of any classifier following a heuristics based method, where various combinations are tested on a held-out dataset and then finally the most promising one selected. This process is time-consuming and computation intensive, and therefore, some automatic techniques are most preferred.

Given a set of features F, appropriate parameters P and two classification quality measures, recall and precision, determine the feature subset F^* and parameter subset P^* such that maximize [recall, precision] where $F^* \subseteq$ F and $P^* \subseteq$ P.

In our case we use precision, recall, accuracy and the number of features as the objective functions. We build the following two frameworks as follows: (i). maximizing recall and precision, and (ii). minimising the number of features and maximising the accuracy. As precision and recall have trade-off (Buckland and Gey, 1994) so this combination will provide non-dominant pareto optimal solutions. In second framework we aim for high accuracy while using least computational cost (i.e. minimizing number of features). Along with these objective functions, we use the following parameters:
Random forest: Number of trees;
LibSVM: Cost and gamma parameters;
LibLinear: Cost parameter.
In Random Forest, more number of trees provides better accuracy but it uses more computational time. Cost parameter 'C' is a regularisation parameter, which controls the trade-off between achieving a low error on the training data and minimising the norm of the weights. It determines the influence of the misclassification on the objective function. As gamma increases, the algorithm tries harder to avoid misclassifying training data, which leads to overfitting.

3.3 Encoding of the Problem

If total number of features is N and the number of parameter to be optimized is M, then the length of the chromosome will be N+M. For an example, we encode a problem in Figure 1. The first 12 bits of the chromosome represent the features and the remaining bits encode the parameters. Each of the first 12 bits represents a feature, and this is randomly initialised to either 0 or 1. If the ith position of a chromosome is 1 then the ith feature participates in constructing the classifier else not. Here out of 12 features, 7 (first, fourth, fifth, sixth, eighth, tenth and eleventh) have been used to construct the classifier. If the population size is P then all the P number of chromosomes of this population are initialized in the same way.

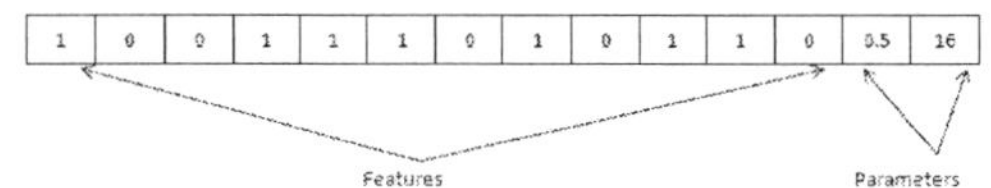

Figure 1: Encoding of the problem

3.4 Fitness Computation

For the fitness computation, the following procedure was executed.

(i) Let there are F number of features present in a particular chromosome (i.e. there are total F number of 1's present in the chromosome).

(ii) Construct a classifier with only these F features.

(iii). Perform 3-fold cross validation to compute the objective function values.

(iii) The aim is to optimize the values of the objective functions using the search capability of NSGA-II .

3.5 Other Operators

After fitness computation, we used binary tournament selection (Deb, 2001) as in NSGA-II, followed by crossover and mutation (Deb, 2001). The most characteristic part of NSGA-II is its elitism operation (Deb, 2001), where the non-dominated solutions among the parent and child populations are propagated to the next generation. The near pareto optimal strings of the last generation provide the different solutions to the feature selection problem. Each of these solutions is equally important from the algorithmic points of view.

3.6 Selection of Final Solution

MOO provides large number of non-dominated solutions (Deb, 2001) on the final Pareto optimal front. Although each of these solutions are equally important but sometimes the user may require a single solution. Hence, we develop a method for selecting a single solution from the set of solutions. For every solution of the final pareto optimal front, (i) classifier is trained using the features present in that particular solution (ii) evaluated for 3-fold cross validation on the training set (iii) selected the best feature combination that yileds the highest F-measure value and (iv). use this particular feature combination to report the final evaluation results.

3.7 Pre-processing and Experimental Setup

The data has to be pre-processed before being used for actual machine learning training. Each tweet is processed to extract only those relevant parts that are useful for sentiment classification. For example, we removed the tweets that don't have any label information in the training data; symbols and punctuation markers are filtered out; URLs are replaced by the word URL; words starting with digits are removed etc. Each tweet is then passed through the ARK tagger developed by CMU [4] for tokenization and Part-of-Speech (PoS) tagging.

From pre-processed tweets we build the final training set. For each tweet in the training set we extract the vectors based on all the features as defined above. As the base classifiers we make use of two different learning algorithms, namely Support Vector Machine (SVM) (Vapnik, 1995) and Random Forest (Breiman, 2001). For SVM we use two implementations as available in LibSVM (Chang and Lin, 2011) and LibLINEAR (Rong-En Fan and Hsieh, 2008).

4 Experiments and Result Discussion

In this section we describe the datasets we used for our experiments, report the evaluation results and provide necessary analysis.

4.1 Datasets

We use the data sets from SemEval-2014[5] shared task. The data sets contain 8,223 classified tweets in the training data and 8,987 tweets as part of the test data. Details of the data sets are shown in Table 1. Please note that we make use of our own evaluation script that also considers the accuracies of neutral classes when we perform evaluation. In contrast, the official evaluation of SemEval script simply ignores the neutral classes.

Table 1: Multi-class Data Sets

S.N.	Data Set	Class			Total
		Positive	Negative	Neutral	
1	Training	3071	1210	3942	8223
2	Test	3506	1541	3940	8987

4.2 Feature sets

We generate different models using the various feature combinations as shown in Table 2. Brief descriptions of these feature sets are described as below:

S55: is a set of 55 features as listed in Table 2. The intuition behind selection of the features in S55 is described in Section 2.

R20: is a subset of 20 features randomly selected from S55.

R30: is a subset of 30 features randomly selected from S55.

R40: is a subset of 40 features randomly selected from S55.

OS55 with FS & PO: This corresponds to the feature set on which joint feature selection and parameter optimization are performed.

OS55 with default parameters: This corresponds to the feature set where feature selection is performed but instead of using parameter optimization technique we make use of the default parameter settings.

4.3 Parameters for MOO

We use R20, R30 and R40 feature sets to construct the baseline models. Following parameter values are used for the NSGA-II. Population size = 32 ; Number of generations = 20; Number of objective functions = 2; Number of real variables = 2; Probability of crossover of real variable = 0.98; Probability of mutation of real variable = 0.50; Distribution index for crossover = 14; Distribution index for mutation = 38; Number of binary variables = 55

---

[4]http://www.ark.cs.cmu.edu/TweetNLP/

[5]http://alt.qcri.org/semeval2014/task9/

Table 2: Feature Sets of S55

Feature No	Features	R20	R30	R40	S55	OS55 for Exp-PR			OS55 for Exp-ANF		
						Random Forest	LibSVM	LibLINEAR	Random Forest	LibSVM	LibLINEAR
0	HashCount	1	0	1	1	0	0	0	0	0	0
1	TweetLength	1	0	1	1	0	1	0	0	0	0
2	InitCap	0	1	1	1	1	1	1	1	1	1
3	PercentCapital	0	1	0	1	0	1	0	1	1	1
4	AllUpperWword	0	0	1	1	1	0	1	0	0	0
5	NotPresent	0	1	0	1	1	0	0	0	0	0
6	pSmiley	1	0	1	1	0	0	0	1	0	1
7	nSmiley	0	1	1	1	1	1	1	1	1	1
8	LastTokenSmiely	0	1	1	1	1	0	0	1	0	0
9	StopWords	1	0	1	1	0	1	1	0	1	1
10	ElongatedWords	0	1	1	1	1	0	0	0	1	1
11	LastToken	0	0	1	1	1	0	0	0	1	0
12	SwnPositiveTokenCount	1	0	0	1	1	1	0	1	0	0
13	SwnNegativeTokenCount	0	1	1	1	1	1	1	0	1	1
14	SwnNeutralTokenCount	0	0	1	1	1	0	0	1	0	0
15	SwnPolarity	1	1	0	1	1	1	1	1	1	1
16	LexNRC	0	1	1	1	1	1	1	0	1	1
17	PositiveLexNrcToken	1	0	1	1	0	1	0	0	1	0
18	NegativeLexNrcToken	0	1	0	1	0	0	1	1	0	0
19	MaxLexNrc	0	0	1	1	1	1	1	1	1	1
20	MinLexNrc	1	0	1	1	1	1	1	1	1	1
21	LastNonZeroScoreNrc	0	1	1	1	0	0	1	0	0	0
22	Lex140	1	0	1	1	0	0	0	0	0	0
23	PositiveLex140Token	0	1	0	1	1	0	0	0	0	0
24	NegativeLex140Token	0	1	1	1	0	0	0	1	0	1
25	MaxLex140	1	0	1	1	0	0	1	0	0	0
26	MinLex140	0	0	1	1	1	0	0	1	0	0
27	LastNonZeroScore140	0	1	1	1	0	0	0	0	0	0
28	BllPositiveWords	1	0	1	1	1	1	1	1	1	1
29	BllNegativeWords	0	1	0	1	1	1	1	1	1	1
30	CommonNoun	0	1	1	1	1	0	1	1	1	0
31	Pronoun	1	1	0	1	0	1	0	0	1	0
32	NominalPossessive	0	0	1	1	1	0	0	0	1	1
33	ProperNnoun	0	1	1	1	0	0	0	0	0	0
34	ProperNounPossessive	1	1	0	1	1	1	1	1	0	1
35	NominalVerbal	0	0	1	1	1	0	1	1	0	0
36	ProperNounVerbal	0	1	0	1	0	0	1	1	0	1
37	VerbCoupla	1	0	1	1	1	0	0	1	0	0
38	Adjective	0	1	1	1	1	0	1	1	0	1
39	Adverb	0	1	0	1	0	1	0	1	1	0
40	Injection	0	0	1	1	0	1	0	0	1	0
41	Determiner	1	0	1	1	1	0	0	1	0	0
42	Preposition	0	1	1	1	1	0	1	0	0	1
43	ConditionalConjunction	0	0	1	1	0	1	1	0	1	1
44	VerbParticle	1	1	0	1	0	0	0	0	0	0
45	ExistentialPredeterminer	0	1	1	1	0	0	0	0	0	0
46	ExistentialPredeterminerVerbal	0	1	0	1	0	0	0	1	0	0
47	NumberOfHash	1	0	1	1	0	0	0	1	0	1
48	AtMention	1	0	1	1	1	1	1	1	0	1
49	DiscourseMarker	0	1	1	1	1	1	1	1	0	0
50	UrlEmail	1	0	1	1	1	0	0	1	0	0
51	Emoticon	0	1	0	1	1	1	1	1	1	1
52	Numeral	0	1	1	1	1	1	1	1	1	1
53	Punctuaion	0	1	0	1	1	1	0	0	0	1
54	OtherPOS	1	0	1	1	1	1	1	1	1	1
	Number of features	20	30	40	55	33	25	26	31	23	26

1 denotes the presence and 0 denotes the absence of a particular feature in the corresponding feature set

4.4 Experimental Results

At first we perform experiments using recall and precision as the two objective functions. Experimental results are shown in Table 3. Here we define the three models as follows: Model-1: Random Forest; Model-2: LibSVM and Model-3: LibLinear. The baseline model developed with random forest classifier shows the highest performance (i.e. 53.60%) for the system that makes use of 40 features. Random forest based baseline model developed with 20 features (i.e. R20) yields the F-measure values of 50.40% and the model developed with 30 features (i..e R30) shows the F-measure value of 52.30%. With LibLinear implementation of SVM we achieve the higher performance with 51.00% F-measure value. While considering both feature selection (FS) and parameter optimization (PO), we obtain the F-measure values of 59.30, 59.10 and 57.70 for the models optimal subset (OS55 with FS and PO) with respect to the first, second and third model, respectively. It is to be noted that when we perform only feature selection we observe the increments of 00.40, 14.80 and 04.90 percentage points for the respective models. However for the model which was developed both with feature selection and parameter optimization, we see the improvements of 04.20, 20.00 and 04.30 percentage points, respectively.

287

Table 3: Results for Exp-PR

S. N.	Feature Sets	Para-meters	Classifiers		
			Random Forest	LibSVM	Lib-LINEAR
1	R20	P	52.10	60.40	49.90
		R	52.70	56.30	53.20
		F1	52.30	50.60	50.10
2	R30	P	50.50	52.30	52.90
		R	50.80	44.60	52.10
		F1	50.40	31.00	50.40
3	R40	P	53.50	58.70	50.50
		R	54.10	53.50	52.20
		F1	53.60	46.20	51.00
4	S55	P	55.10	57.90	53.50
		R	55.60	49.20	55.10
		F1	55.10	39.10	53.40
5	OS55 with FS & PO	P	62.20	61.00	62.40
		R	61.00	60.60	60.30
		F1	59.30	59.10	57.70
6	OS55 default paameters	P	55.50	59.40	62.30
		R	56.10	57.30	60.60
		F1	55.50	53.90	58.30
% improvement due to FS			00.40	14.80	04.90
% improvement due to FS and PO			04.20	20.00	04.30

P=Precision, R=Recall, F1=F-measure (all in %) FS= Feature Selection, PO= Parameter Optimization

Table 4: Results for Exp-ANF

S. N.	Feature Sets	Para-meters	Classifiers		
			Random Forest	LibSVM	Lib-LINEAR
1	R20	A	52.65	56.33	53.32
		NF	20	20	20
		F1	52.30	50.60	53.10
2	R30	A	50.84	44.64	52.00
		NF	30	30	30
		F1	50.40	31.00	50.30
3	R40	A	54.11	53.49	55.20
		NF	40	40	40
		F1	53.60	46.20	54.10
4	S55	A	55.61	49.2	54.16
		NF	55	55	55
		F1	55.10	39.10	49.90
5	OS55 with FS & PO	A	61.32	60.58	59.06
		NF	31	23	26
		F1	59.70	59.20	55.50
6	OS55 default paameters	A	56.08	58.53	60.24
		NF	31	23	26
		F1	55.50	56.10	58.00
% improvement due to FS			00.40	17.00	08.10
% improvement due to FS and PO			04.60	20.10	05.60

A=Accuracy (in %), NF=Number of Features, F1=F-measure (in %), FS= Feature Selection, PO= Parameter Optimization

Hence it can be concluded that performing feature election and parameter optimisation together is better suited compared to the model that makes use of only the default parameters of the classifiers. However, third model achieves higher performance with the defaults parameters only. The parameters selected through MOO are shown in Table 5.

Results of the experiments when accuracy and number of features are optimised are shown in Table 4. Results show that both feature selection (FS) and parameter optimization (PO) yield better accuracies with F-measure values of 59.70, 59.20 and 55.50 for the respective models. When the selected feature set is used train the classifiers with default parameters, the models show the F-measure values of 55.50%, 56.10% and 58.00% for the three models, respectively. This again shows quite similar behaviours, i.e. first two classifiers perform superior with the joint model framework. However third model yields higher performance when the classifier is trained with the features selected through MOO based approach, but uses the default parameters.

Here we observe that in both the experiments, LibLinear implementation of SVM provides better result with default parameter configurations compared to their respective optimized parameter sets. This may be attributed to the fact that further attention is required to select the parameters of LibLinear model. Our approach is evolutionary in nature, and therefore, better accuracies can be achieved by either increasing the number of generations or size of the population or both.

Table 5: Optimized Parameters

S.N.	Classifier	Parameters	Experiment	
			Exp-PR	Exp-ANF
1.	Random Forest	Trees	862, 853	1990
2.	LibSVM	Cost	2^14	2^14
		Gamma	2^(-10)	2^(-9)
3.	LibLINEAR	Cost	4	2^(-2), 2^(-7), 2^(-8)

4.5 Comparisons

To compare our results with some of existing systems which were developed on the same data sets viz. NRC Canada-B (Xiaodan Zhu and Mohammad, 2014), Coooolll-B (Tang et al., 2014), TeamX-B (Miura et al., 2014), SAIL-B (Nikolaos Malandrakis and Narayanan, 2014), DAEDALUS-B(JulioVillena Roman, 2014) and SU-sentilab-B(Gizem Gezici and Saygin, 2013), we evaluate our best model (OS55 with FS & PO for Exp-ANF) using SemEval-14's scorer. This scorer considers only the F-measures for positive and negative classes. In Table 6 we present the results of comparisons. We observed that classification of neutral class was more challenging compared to the positive and negative classes. Hence in all our experiments we also considered neutral class along with positive and negative classes. It shows the F-measure values of 59.60, 37.30 and 67.50 for positive, negative and neutral class, respectively. When the official evaluation scorer was executed, the system yields the F-measure values of 64.16%, 74.75%, 68.39%, 60.62% and 35.48% for LiveJournal2014, SMS2013, Twitter2013, Twitter2014 and Twitter2014Sarcasm datasets, respectively which is named as 'Our System I'. Further we evaluate considering only positive and negative classes and named as 'Our System II'. Here 'Our System I' has much better F-measure than the average F-measure of our system which ignores the neutral class. This shows that our system provides better F-measure for neutral class.

Table 6: Comparisons with some existing systems

S. N.	System	F-measure					
		Live Journal 2014	SMS 2013	Twitter 2013	Twitter 2014	Twitter 2014 Sarcasm	Average
1.	NRC Canada-B	74.84	70.28	70.75	69.85	58.16	68.78
2.	Coooolll-B	72.90	67.68	70.40	70.14	46.66	65.55
3.	TeamX-B	69.44	57.36	72.12	70.96	56.50	65.27
4.	SAIL-B	69.34	56.98	66.80	67.77	57.26	63.63
5.	Our System I	64.16	74.75	68.39	60.62	35.48	60.68
6.	SU-sentilab-B	55.11	49.60	50.17	49.52	31.49	47.18
7.	Our System II	57.77	45.00	49.40	47.84	25.76	45.15
8.	DAEDALUS-B	40.83	40.86	36.57	33.03	28.96	36.05

5   Conclusion and Future Work

In this work, we have posed the problem of simultaneous feature selection and parameter optimization as a MOO problem, and evaluate this for sentiment analysis. We have implemented significantly diverse set of features for the task. Experiments show the effectiveness of the proposed approach with significant performance improvements over the various baselines developed with random feature subsets. It is also evident from the evaluation results that simultaneous feature selection and parameter optimization is better compared to the only feature selection.

In future, we would like to add more features to increase the baseline performance. More detailed parameter selection, for example, the kernel function of SVM need to be optimised to realise the effects of more systematic parameter optimization.

Acknowledgments

We thank the anonymous reviewers for their comments. This work is, in part, supported by German Academic Exchange Service (DAAD) through DAAD-IIT Master Sandwich Program.

References

[Alec Go and Huang2009] Richa Bhayani Alec Go and Lei Huang. 2009. Twitter sentiment classification using distant supervision. Technical report, Univ. stanford.

[Andrea Esuli and Sebastiani2010] Stefano Baccianella Andrea Esuli and Fabrizio Sebastiani. 2010. Sentiwordnet 3.0: An enhanced lexical resource for sentiment analysis and opinion mining. In *Seventh conference on International Language Resources and Evaluation LREC'10*, Valletta, Malta, May.

[Apoorv Agarwal and Passonneau2011] Ilia Vovsha Owen Rambow Apoorv Agarwal, Boyi Xie and Rebecca Passonneau. 2011. Sentiment analysis of twitter data. In *Proceedings of the Workshop on Languages in Social Media*, pages 30–38. Association for Computational Linguistics.

[Bo Pang and Vaithyanathan2002] Lillian Lee Bo Pang and Shivakumar Vaithyanathan. 2002. Thumbs up?: sentiment classification using machine learning techniques. In *Proceedings of the ACL-02 conference on Empirical methods in natural language processing-Volume 10*, pages 79–86. Association for Computational Linguistics.

[Boiy and Moens2009] Erik Boiy and Marie-Francine Moens. 2009. A machine learning approach to sentiment analysis in multilingual web texts. *Information retrieval*, 12(5):526–558.

[Breiman2001] Leo Breiman. 2001. Random forests. *Mach. Learn.*, 45(1):5–32, October.

[Buckland and Gey1994] Michael K. Buckland and Fredric C. Gey. 1994. The relationship between recall and precision. *JASIS*, 45(1):12–19.

[Cataldo Musto and Polignano2014] Giovanni Semeraro Cataldo Musto and Marco Polignano. 2014. A comparison of lexicon-based approaches for sentiment analysis of microblog posts. *Information Filtering and Retrieval*, page 59.

[Chang and Lin2011] Chih-Chung Chang and Chih-Jen Lin. 2011. Libsvm: A library for support vector machines. In *ACM Transactions on Intelligent Systems and Technology*.

[CHRIS NICHOLLS2009] FEI SONG CHRIS NICHOLLS. 2009. Improving sentiment analysis with part-of-speech weighting. In *Eighth International Conference on Machine Learning and Cybernetics*, Baoding, July.

[Deb2001] Kalyanmoy Deb. 2001. *Multi-objective Optimization Using Evolutionary Algorithms*. John Wiley and Sons, Ltd, England.

[Dmitry Davidov and Rappoport2010] Oren Tsur Dmitry Davidov and Ari Rappoport. 2010. Enhanced sentiment learning using twitter hashtags and smileys. In *Coling 2010: Poster Volume, pages 241–249*, Beijing, August.

[Ekbal and Saha2012] Asif Ekbal and Sriparna Saha. 2012. Multiobjective optimization for classifier ensemble and feature selection: an application to named entity recognition. *IJDAR*, 15(2):143–166.

[Ekbal and Saha2013] Asif Ekbal and Sriparna Saha. 2013. Full length article: Simulated annealing based classifier ensemble techniques: Application to part of speech tagging. *Inf. Fusion*, 14(3):288–300, July.

[Gizem Gezici and Saygin2013] Berrin Yanikoglu Dilek Tapucu Gizem Gezici, Rahim Dehkharghani and Yucel Saygin. 2013. Su-sentilab: A classification system for sentiment analysis in twitter. In *Proceedings of the International Workshop on Semantic Evaluation*, pages 471–477.

[Hassan Saif and Alani2012] Yulan He Hassan Saif and Harith Alani. 2012. Semantic sentiment analysis of twitter. In *11th international conference on The Semantic Web ISWC'12, Volume I*, Heidelberg.

[JulioVillena Roman2014] Gonzalez Cristobal Jose Carlos JulioVillena Roman, Janine Garcia Morera. 2014. Daedalus at semeval-2014 task 9: Comparing approaches for sentiment analysis in twitter.

[Kevin Gimpel2011] Nathan Schneider Kevin Gimpel. 2011. Part-of-speech tagging for twitter: Annotation, features, and experiments. In *Proceeding HLT '11 Proceedings of the 49th Annual Meeting of the Association for Computational Linguistics: Human Language Technologies: short papers - Volume 2 Pages 42-47*.

[Liu and Motoda1998] Huan Liu and Hiroshi Motoda. 1998. *Feature Selection for Knowledge Discovery and Data Mining*. Kluwer Academic Publishers, Norwell, MA, USA.

[Liu and Yu2005] Huan Liu and Lei Yu. 2005. Toward integrating feature selection algorithms for classification and clustering. *IEEE Trans. on Knowl. and Data Eng.*, 17(4):491–502.

[Maite Taboada and Stede2011] Milan Tofiloski Kimberly Voll Maite Taboada, Julian Brooke and Manfred Stede. 2011. Lexicon-based methods for sentiment analysis. *Computational linguistics*, 37(2):267–307.

[Maks and Vossen2013] Isa Maks and Piek Vossen. 2013. Sentiment analysis of reviews: Should we analyze writer intentions or reader perceptions? In *RANLP*, pages 415–419.

[Mitchell1997] Thomas M. Mitchell. 1997. *Machine Learning*. McGraw-Hill, Inc., New York, NY, USA, 1 edition.

[Mittal and Goel2012] Anshul Mittal and Arpit Goel. 2012. Stock prediction using twitter sentiment analysis. *Standford University*.

[Miura et al.2014] Yasuhide Miura, Shigeyuki Sakaki, Keigo Hattori, and Tomoko Ohkuma. 2014. Teamx: A sentiment analyzer with enhanced lexicon mapping and weighting scheme for unbalanced data. In *Proceedings of the 8th International Workshop on Semantic Evaluation (SemEval 2014)*, pages 628–632, Dublin, Ireland, August. Association for Computational Linguistics and Dublin City University.

[Mukherjee and Bhattacharyya2012] Subhabrata Mukherjee and Pushpak Bhattacharyya. 2012. Feature specific sentiment analysis for product reviews. In *Computational Linguistics and Intelligent Text Processing*, pages 475–487. Springer.

[Nielsen2011] F. Å. Nielsen. 2011. Afinn. Technical report, Richard Petersens Plads, Building 321, DK-2800 Kgs. Lyngby, March.

[Nikolaos Malandrakis and Narayanan2014] Colin Vaz Jesse Bisogni Alexandros Potamianos Nikolaos Malandrakis, Michael Falcone and Shrikanth Narayanan. 2014. Sail: Sentiment analysis using semantic similarity and contrast. *SemEval 2014*, page 512.

[Pak and Paroubek2010] Alexander Pak and Patrick Paroubek. 2010. Part-of-speech tagging for twitter: Annotation, features, and experiments. In *Seventh International Conference on Language Resources and Evaluation, LREC 2010*.

[Rong-En Fan and Hsieh2008] Kai-Wei Chang Rong-En Fan and Cho-Jui Hsieh. 2008. Liblinear: A library for large linear classification. In *Journal of Machine Learning Research*.

[Saif Mohammad and Zhu2013] Svetlana Kiritchenko Saif Mohammad and Xiaodan Zhu. 2013. Nrc-canada: Building the state-of-the-art in sentiment analysis of tweets. In *Proceedings of the seventh international workshop on Semantic Evaluation Exercises (SemEval-2013)*, Atlanta, Georgia, USA, June.

[Tang et al.2014] Duyu Tang, Furu Wei, Bing Qin, Ting Liu, and Ming Zhou. 2014. Coooolll: A deep learning system for twitter sentiment classification. In *Proceedings of the 8th International Workshop on Semantic Evaluation (SemEval 2014)*, pages 208–212, Dublin, Ireland, August. Association for Computational Linguistics and Dublin City University.

[Vapnik1995] Vladimir N. Vapnik. 1995. *The nature of statistical learning theory*. Springer-Verlag New York, Inc., New York, NY, USA.

[Xiaodan Zhu and Mohammad2014] Svetlana Kiritchenko Xiaodan Zhu and Saif M Mohammad. 2014. Nrc-canada-2014: Recent improvements in the sentiment analysis of tweets. *SemEval 2014*, 443.

[Xiaowen Ding and Yu2008] Bing Liu Xiaowen Ding and Philip S Yu. 2008. A holistic lexicon-based approach to opinion mining. In *Proceedings of the 2008 International Conference on Web Search and Data Mining*, pages 231–240. ACM.

Detection of Multiword Expressions for Hindi Language using Word Embeddings and WordNet-based Features

Dhirendra Singh Sudha Bhingardive Kevin Patel Pushpak Bhattacharyya

Department of Computer Science and Engineering,
Indian Institute of Technology Bombay.
{dhirendra,sudha,kevin.patel,pb}@cse.iitb.ac.in

Abstract

Detection of Multiword Expressions (MWEs) is a challenging problem faced by several natural language processing applications. The difficulty emanates from the task of detecting MWEs with respect to a given context. In this paper, we propose approaches that use Word Embeddings and WordNet-based features for the detection of MWEs for Hindi language. These approaches are restricted to two types of MWEs *viz., noun compounds and noun+verb compounds.* The results obtained indicate that using linguistic information from a rich lexical resource such as WordNet, help in improving the accuracy of MWEs detection. It also demonstrates that the linguistic information which word embeddings capture from a corpus can be comparable to that provided by Word-Net. Thus, we can say that, for the detection of above mentioned MWEs, word embeddings can be a reasonable alternative to WordNet, especially for those languages whose WordNets does not have a better coverage.

1 Introduction

Multiword Expressions or MWEs can be understood as idiosyncratic interpretations or *words with spaces* wherein concepts cross the word boundaries or spaces (Sag et al., 2002). Some examples of MWEs are *ad hoc, by and large, New York, kick the bucket, etc.* Typically, a multiword is a noun, a verb, an adjective or an adverb followed by a light verb (LV) or a noun that behaves as a single unit (Sinha, 2009). Proper detection and sense disambiguation of MWEs is necessary for many Natural Language Processing (NLP) tasks like machine translation, natural language generation, named entity recognition, sentiment analysis, etc. MWEs are abundantly used in Hindi and other languages of Indo Aryan family. Common part-of-speech (POS) templates of MWEs in Hindi language include the following: noun+noun, noun+LV, adjective+LV, adjective+noun, etc. Some examples of Hindi multiwords are पुण्य तिथि (*puNya tithi*, death anniversary), वादा करना (*vaadaa karanaa*, to promise), आग लगाना (*aaga lagaanaa*, to burn), धन दौलत (*dhana daulata*, wealth), etc.

WordNet (Miller, 1995) has emerged as crucial resource for NLP. It is a lexical structure composed of synsets, semantic and lexical relations. One can look up WordNet for information such as synonym, antonym, hypernym, etc. of a word. WordNet was initially built for the English language, which is then followed by almost all widely used languages all over the world. WordNets are developed for different language families *viz.* EuroWordNet[1] (Vossen, 2004) was developed for Indo-European family of languages and covers languages such as German, French, Ital-

---

[1] http://www.illc.uva.nl/EuroWordNet/

D S Sharma, R Sangal and E Sherly. Proc. of the 12th Intl. Conference on Natural Language Processing, pages 295–302,
Trivandrum, India. December 2015. ©2015 NLP Association of India (NLPAI)

ian, *etc.* Similarly, IndoWordNet[2] (Bhattacharyya, 2010) covers the major families of languages, *viz.*, Indo-Aryan, Dravidian and Sino-Tibetian which are used in the subcontinent. Building WordNets is a complex task. It takes lots of time and human expertise to build and maintain WordNets.

A recent development in computational linguistics is the concept of distributed representations, commonly referred to as *Word Vectors* or *Word Embeddings*. The first such model was proposed by Bengio et al. (2003), followed by similar models by other researchers *viz.,* Mnih et al. (2007), Collobert et al. (2008), Mikolov et al. (2013a), Pennington et al. (2014). These models are extremely fast to train, are automated, and rely only on raw corpus. Mikolov et al. (2013c; 2013b) have reported various linguistic regularities captured by such models. For instance, vectors of synonyms and antonyms will be highly similar when evaluated using cosine similarity measure. Thus, these models can be used to replace/supplement WordNets and other such resources in different NLP applications (Collobert et al., 2011).

The roadmap of the paper is as follows, Section 2 describes the background and related work. Our approaches are detailed in section 3. The description of the datasets used for the evaluation is given in section 4. Experiments and results are presented in Section 5. Section 6 concludes the paper and points to the future work.

2 Background and Related Work

Most of the proposed approaches for the detection of MWEs are statistical in nature. Some of these approaches use association measures (Church and Hanks, 1990), deep linguistics based methods (Bansal et

---

[2]IndoWordNet is available in following Indian languages: Assamese, Bodo, Bengali, English, Gujarati, Hindi, Kashmiri, Konkani, Kannada, Malayalam, Manipuri, Marathi, Nepali, Punjabi, Sanskrit, Tamil, Telugu and Urdu. These languages cover three different language families, Indo Aryan, Sino-Tibetan and Dravidian. http://www.cfilt.iitb.ac.in/indowordnet/

al., 2014), word embeddings based measures (Salehi et al., 2015), etc.

The work related to the detection of MWEs has been limited in the context of Indian languages. The reasons are, unavailability of gold data (Reddy, 2011), unstructured classification of MWEs, complicated theory of MWEs, lack of resources, etc. Most of the approaches of Hindi MWEs have used parallel corpus alignment and POS tag projection to extract MWEs (Sriram et al., 2007) (Mukerjee et al., 2006). Venkatapathy et al. (2007) used a classification based approach for extracting noun+verb collocations for Hindi. Gayen and Sarkar et al. (2013) used Random Forest approach wherein features such as *verb identity, semantic type, case marker, verb-object similarity, etc.* are used for the detection of compound nouns in Bengali using MaxEnt Classifier. However, our focus is on detecting MWEs of the type *compound noun* and *noun+verb compounds* while verb based features are not implemented in our case. We have used word embeddings and WordNet based features for the detection of above MWEs.

Characteristics of MWEs

MWE has different characteristics based on their usage, context and formation. They are as follows-

Compositionality: Compositionality refers to the degree to which the meaning of MWEs can be predicted by combining the meanings of their components. *E.g.* तरण ताल (*taraNa taala*, swimming pool), धन लक्ष्मी (*dhana laxmii*, wealth), चाय पानी (*chaaya paanii*, snacks), etc.

Non-Compositionality: In non-compositionality, the meaning of MWEs cannot be completely determined from the meaning of its constituent words. It might be completely different from its constituents. *E.g.* गुजर जाना, (*gujara jaanaa*, passed away), नजर डालना, (*najara Daalanaa*, flip through). There might be some added elements or inline meaning to MWEs that cannot be predicted from its parts. *E.g.* नौ दो ग्यारह होना (*nau do gyaaraha honaa*, run away).

Non-Substitutability: In non substitutability, the components of MWEs cannot be substituted by its synonyms without distorting the meaning of the expression even though they refer to the same concept (Schone and Jurafsky, 2001). *E.g.* in the expression चाय पानी (*chaaya paanii*, snacks), the word *paanii* (water) cannot be replaced by its synonym जल (*jala*, water) or नीर (*niira*, water) to form the meaning 'snacks'.

Collocation: Collocations are a sequence of words that occur more often than expected by chance. They do not show either statistical or semantical idiosyncrasy. They are fixed expressions and appear very frequently in running text. *E.g.* कड़क चाय (*kaDaka chaaya*, strong tea), काला धन (*kaalaa dhana*, black money), etc.

Non-Modifiability: In non-modifiablility, many collocations cannot be freely modified by grammatical transformations such as *change of tense, change in number, addition of adjective, etc.* These collocations are frozen expressions which cannot be modified at any condition. *E.g.*, the idiom घाव पर नमक छिड़कना (*ghaava para namaka ChiDakanaa*, rub salt in the wound) cannot be replace to *घाव पर ज्यादा नमक छिड़कना (*ghaava para jyaadaa namaka ChiDakanaa*, rub more salt in the wound) or something similar.

Classification of MWEs

According to Sag et.al (2002) MWEs are classified into two broad categories *viz.,* Lexicalized Phrases and Institutional Phrases. The meaning of lexicalized phrases cannot be construed from its individual units that make up the phrase, as they exhibit syntactic and/or semantic idiosyncrasy. On the other hand, the meaning of institutional phrases can be construed from its individual units that make up the phrase. However, they exhibit statistical idiosyncrasy. Institutional phrases are not in the scope of this paper. Lexicalized phrases are further classified into three sub-classes *viz.,* Fixed, Semi-fixed and Syntactically flexible expressions.

In this paper, we focus on *noun compounds* and *noun+verb compounds* which fall under the semi-fixed and syntactically fixed categories respectively.

Noun Compounds: Noun compounds are MWEs which are formed by two or more nouns which behave as a single semantic unit. In the case of compositionality, noun compounds usually put the stress on the first component while the remaining components expand the meaning of the first component. *E.g.* बाग बगीचा (*baaga bagiichaa*, garden) is a noun compound where *baaga* is giving the full meaning of the whole component against the second component *bagiichaa*. However, in the case of non-compositionality, noun compounds do not put stress on any of the components. *E.g.* अक्षय तृतीया (*axaya tRitiiyaa*, one of the festival), पुण्य तिथि (*puNya tithi*, death anniversary).

Noun+Verb Compounds: Noun+verb compounds are type of MWEs which are formed by sequence of words having noun followed by verb(s). These are type of conjunct verbs where noun+verb pattern behaves as a single semantic unit wherein *noun* gives the meaning for whole expression. *E.g.* वादा करना (*vaadaa karanaa*, to promise), मार डालना (*maar daalanaa*, to kill), etc.

3 Our Approach

The central idea behind our approach is that words belonging to a MWE co-occur frequently. Ideally, such co-occurrence can be computed from a corpus. However, no matter how large a corpus actually is, it cannot cover all possible usages of all words of a particular language. So, a possible workaround to address this issue can be as follows:

Given a word pair w_1 w_2 to be identified

as a MWE,

1. Find the co-occurrence estimate of w_1 w_2 using the corpus alone.

2. Further refine this estimate by using co-occurrence estimate of w_1' w_2', where w_1' and w_2' are synonyms or antonyms of w_1 and w_2 respectively.

In order to estimate co-occurrence of w_1 w_2, one can use *word embeddings or word vectors*. Such techniques try to predict (Baroni et al., 2014), rather than count the co-occurrence patterns of different tuples of words. The *distributional* aspect of these representations enables one to estimate the co-occurrence of, say, *cat* and *sleeps*, using the co-occurrence of *dogs* and *sleep*. Such *word embeddings* are typically trained on raw corpora, and the similarity between a pair of words is computed by calculating the cosine similarity between the embeddings corresponding to the pair of words. It has been proved that such methods indirectly capture co-occurrence only, and can thus be used for the task at hand.

While exact co-occurrence can be estimated using word embeddings, substitutional co-occurrence cannot be efficiently captured using the same. More precisely, if w_1 w_2 is a MWE, but the corpus contains w_1 $synonym(w_2)$ or $synonym(w_1)$ w_2 frequently, then one cannot hope to learn that w_1 w_2 is indeed a MWE. Such paradigmatic (substitutional) information cannot be captured efficiently by word vectors. This has been established by the different experiments performed by (Chen et al., 2013), (Baroni et al., 2014) and (Hill et al., 2014). So one needs to look at other resources to obtain this information. We decided to use WordNet for the same. Similarity between a pair of words appearing in the WordNet hierarchy can be acquired using multiple means. For instance, two words are said to be synonyms if they belong in the same *synset* in the WordNet.

Having these two resources at our disposal, we can realize the above mentioned approach more concretely as follows:

1. Use WordNet to detect synonyms, antonyms.

2. Use similarity measures either facilitated by WordNet or by the word embeddings.

These options lead to the following three concrete heuristics for the detection of *noun compounds* and *noun+verb* compounds for word pair $w_1 w_2$.

3.1 Approach 1: Using WordNet-based Features

1. Let WNBag $= \{w' \mid w' = IsSynOrAnto(w_1)\}$, where the function $IsSynOrAnto$ returns either a synonym or an antonym of w_1, by looking up the WordNet.

2. If $w_2 \in$ WNBag, then w_1 w_2 is a MWE.

3.2 Approach 2: Using Word Embeddings

1. Let WEBag $= \{w' \mid w' = IsaNeighbour(w_1)\}$, where the function $IsaNeighbour$ returns *neighbors* of w_1, i.e, returns the top 20 words that are close to w_1 (as measured by cosine similarity of the corresponding word embeddings).

2. If $w_2 \in$ WEBag, then w_1 w_2 is a MWE.

3.3 Approach 3: Using WordNet and Word Embeddings with Exact match

1. Let WNBag $= \{w' \mid w' = IsSynOrAnto(w_1)\}$, where the function $IsSynOrAnto$ returns either a synonym or an antonym of w_1, by looking up the WordNet.

2. Let WEBag $= \{w' \mid w' = IsaNeighbour(w_2)\}$, where the function $IsaNeighbour$ returns *neighbors* of w_2, i.e, returns the top 20 words that are close to w_2 (as measured by cosine similarity of the corresponding word embeddings).

3. If WNBag $\cap$ WEBag $\neq \phi$, then $w_1\ w_2$ is a MWE.

4 Datasets

MWE Gold Data

There is a dearth of datasets for Hindi MWEs. The ones that exists, have some shortcomings. For instance, (Kunchukuttan and Damani, 2008) have performed MWEs evaluation on their in-house dataset. However, we found this dataset to be extremely skewed, with only ~300 MWEs out of ~12500 phrases. Thus, we have created the in-house gold standard dataset for our experiments. While creating this dataset we extracted 2000 noun+noun and noun+verb word pairs each from the ILCI Health and Tourism domain corpus automatically. Further, three annotators were asked to manually check whether these extracted pairs are MWEs or not. They deemed 450 valid noun+noun and 500 noun+verb pairs to be MWEs. This process achieved an inter-annotator agreement of ~0.8.

Choice of Word Embeddings

Since Bengio et. al. (2003) came up with the first word embeddings, many models for learning such word embeddings have been developed. We chose the Skip-Gram model provided by word2vec tool developed by (Mikolov et al., 2013a) for training word embeddings. The parameters for the training are as follows: Dimension = 300, Window Size = 8, Negative Samples = 25, with the others being kept at their default settings.

Data for Training Word Embeddings

We used Bojar Hindi MonoCorp dataset (Bojar et al., 2014) for training word embeddings. This dataset contains 44 million sentences with approximately 365 million tokens. To the best of our knowledge, this is the largest Hindi corpus available publicly on the internet.

Data for Evaluating Word Embeddings

Before commenting on the applicability of word embeddings to this task, one needs to evaluate the quality of the word embeddings. For evaluating word embeddings of the English language, many word-pair similarity datasets have emerged over the years (Lev Finkelstein and Ruppin, 2002), (Hill et al., 2014). But no such datasets exists for Hindi language. Thus, once again, we have developed an in-house evaluation dataset. We manually translated the English word-pairs in (Lev Finkelstein and Ruppin, 2002) to Hindi, and then asked three annotators to score them in the range [0,10] based on their semantic similarity and relatedness[3]. The inter-annotator agreement on this dataset was 0.73. This is obtained by averaging first three columns of Table 1.

5 Experiments and Results

5.1 Evaluation of Quality of Word Embeddings

Entities	Agreement
human1/human2	0.74
human1/human3	0.68
human2/human3	0.77
word2vec/human1	0.65
word2vec/human2	0.54
word2vec/human3	0.63

Table 1: Agreement of different entities on the translated similarity dataset for Hindi

We have evaluated word embeddings that are trained on Bojar corpus on the word-pair similarity dataset (which is mentioned in the previous section). It is observed that, the average agreement between word embeddings (*word2vec* tool) and human annotators was ~0.61. This is obtained by averaging last three columns of Table 1.

---

[3]We are in the process of releasing this dataset publicly

Techniques	Resources used	P	R	F-score
Approach 1	WordNet	0.79	0.77	0.78
Approach 2	word2vec	0.75	0.64	0.69
Approach 3	word2vec+WordNet	0.76	0.68	0.72

Table 2: Results of noun compounds on Hindi Dataset

Techniques	Resources used	P	R	F-score
Approach 1	WordNet	0.75	0.82	0.78
Approach 2	word2vec	0.56	0.75	0.64
Approach 3	word2vec+WordNet	0.57	0.58	0.58

Table 3: Results of noun+verb compounds on Hindi Dataset

5.2 Evaluation of Our Approaches for MWEs detection

Table 2 shows the performance of the three different approaches at detecting noun compound MWEs. Table 3 shows the performance of the three different approaches at detecting noun+verb compound MWEs. As is evident from the Table 2 and Table 3, WordNet based approaches perform the best. However, it is also clear that results obtained by using word embeddings perform comparatively better. Thus, in general, these results can be favorable for word embeddings based approaches as they are trained on raw corpora. Also, they do not need much human help as compared to WordNets which require considerable human expertise in creating and maintaining them. In our experiments, we have used Hindi WordNet which is one of the well developed WordNet, and thus result obtained using this WordNet are found to be promising. However, for other languages with relatively underdeveloped WordNets, one can expect word embeddings based approaches to yield results comparable to those approaches which uses well developed Word-Net.

6 Conclusion

This paper provides a comparison of Word Embeddings and WordNet-based approaches that one can use for the detection of MWEs. We selected a sub-set of MWE candidates *viz., noun compounds and noun+verb compounds,* and then report the results of our approaches for these candidates. Our results show that the WordNet-based approaches performs better than Word Embedding based approaches for the MWEs detection for Hindi language. However, word embeddings based approaches has the potential to perform at par with approaches utilizing well formed WordNets. This suggests that one should further investigate such approaches, as they rely on raw corpora, thereby leading to enormous savings in both time and resources.

References

Mohit Bansal, Kevin Gimpel, and Karen Livescu. 2014. Tailoring continuous word representations for dependency parsing. Association for Computational Linguistics.

Marco Baroni, Georgiana Dinu, and German Kruszewski. 2014. Don't count, predict! a systematic comparison of context-counting vs. context-predicting semantic vectors. In *Proceedings of the 52nd Annual Meeting of the Association for Computational Linguistics (Volume 1: Long Papers)*, pages 238–247. Association for Computational Linguistics.

Yoshua Bengio, Réjean Ducharme, Pascal Vincent, and Christian Janvin. 2003. A neural probabilistic language model. *J. Mach. Learn. Res.*, 3:1137–1155, March.

Pushpak Bhattacharyya. 2010. Indowordnet. In *In Proc. of LREC-10*. Citeseer.

Ondřej Bojar, Vojtěch Diatka, Pavel Rychlý, Pavel Straňák, Vít Suchomel, Aleš Tamchyna, and Daniel Zeman. 2014. HindMonoCorp 0.5.

Yanqing Chen, Bryan Perozzi, Rami Al-Rfou, and Steven Skiena. 2013. The expressive power of word embeddings. In *ICML 2013 Workshop on Deep Learning for Audio, Speech, and Language Processing*, Atlanta, GA, USA, July.

Kenneth Ward Church and Patrick Hanks. 1990. Word association norms, mutual information, and lexicography. *Computational linguistics*, 16(1):22–29.

Ronan Collobert and Jason Weston. 2008. A unified architecture for natural language processing: deep neural networks with multitask learning. In William W. Cohen, Andrew McCallum, and Sam T. Roweis, editors, *ICML*, volume 307 of *ACM International Conference Proceeding Series*, pages 160–167. ACM.

Ronan Collobert, Jason Weston, Léon Bottou, Michael Karlen, Koray Kavukcuoglu, and Pavel Kuksa. 2011. Natural language processing (almost) from scratch. *J. Mach. Learn. Res.*, 12:2493–2537, November.

Vivekananda Gayen and Kamal Sarkar. 2013. Automatic identification of Bengali noun-noun compounds using random forest. In *Proceedings of the 9th Workshop on Multiword Expressions*, pages 64–72, Atlanta, Georgia, USA, June. Association for Computational Linguistics.

Felix Hill, Roi Reichart, and Anna Korhonen. 2014. Simlex-999: Evaluating semantic models with (genuine) similarity estimation. *arXiv preprint arXiv:1408.3456*.

Anoop Kunchukuttan and Om P Damani. 2008. A system for compound noun multiword expression extraction for hindi.

Yossi Matias Ehud Rivlin Zach Solan Gadi Wolfman Lev Finkelstein, Evgeniy Gabrilovich and Eytan Ruppin. 2002. Placing search in context: The concept revisited. *ACM Trans. Inf. Syst.*, 20(1):116–131, January.

Tomas Mikolov, Kai Chen, Greg Corrado, and Jeffrey Dean. 2013a. Efficient estimation of word representations in vector space. *CoRR*, abs/1301.3781.

Tomas Mikolov, Quoc V. Le, and Ilya Sutskever. 2013b. Exploiting similarities among languages for machine translation. *CoRR*, abs/1309.4168.

Tomas Mikolov, Wen-tau Yih, and Geoffrey Zweig. 2013c. Linguistic regularities in continuous space word representations. In *HLT-NAACL*, pages 746–751.

George A Miller. 1995. Wordnet: a lexical database for english. *Communications of the ACM*, 38(11):39–41.

Andriy Mnih and Geoffrey E. Hinton. 2007. Three new graphical models for statistical language modelling. In Zoubin Ghahramani, editor, *ICML*, volume 227 of *ACM International Conference Proceeding Series*, pages 641–648. ACM.

Amitabha Mukerjee, Ankit Soni, and Achla M Raina. 2006. Detecting complex predicates in hindi using pos projection across parallel corpora. In *Proceedings of the Workshop on Multiword Expressions: Identifying and Exploiting Underlying Properties*, pages 28–35. Association for Computational Linguistics.

Jeffrey Pennington, Richard Socher, and Christopher D Manning. 2014. Glove: Global vectors for word representation. *Proceedings of the Empirical Methods in Natural Language Processing (EMNLP 2014)*, 12.

Siva Reddy. 2011. An empirical study on compositionality in compound nouns. IJCNLP.

Ivan A. Sag, Timothy Baldwin, Francis Bond, Ann A. Copestake, and Dan Flickinger. 2002. Multiword expressions: A pain in the neck for nlp. In *Proceedings of the Third International Conference on Computational Linguistics and Intelligent Text Processing*, CICLing '02, pages 1–15, London, UK, UK. Springer-Verlag.

Bahar Salehi, Paul Cook, and Timothy Baldwin. 2015. A word embedding approach to predicting the compositionality of multiword expressions. In *Proceedings of the 2015 Conference of the North American Chapter of the Association of Computational Linguistics - Human Language Technologies (NAACL HLT)*.

Patrick Schone and Daniel Jurafsky. 2001. Is knowledge-free induction of multiword unit dictionary headwords a solved problem. Empirical Methods in Natural Language Processing.

R Mahesh K Sinha. 2009. Mining complex predicates in hindi using a parallel hindi-english corpus. In *Proceedings of the Workshop on Multiword Expressions: Identification, Interpretation, Disambiguation and Applications*, pages 40–46. Association for Computational Linguistics.

V Sriram, Preeti Agrawal, and Aravind K Joshi. 2007. Relative compositionality of noun verb multi-word expressions in hindi. In *published in Proceedings of International Conference on Natural Language Processing (ICON)-2005, Kanpur*.

Piek Vossen. 2004. Eurowordnet: a multilingual database of autonomous and language-specific wordnets connected via an interlingualindex. *International Journal of Lexicography*, 17(2):161–173.

Augmenting Pivot based SMT with word segmentation

Rohit More[†], Anoop Kunchukuttan[†],
Pushpak Bhattacharyya[†]
[†] Department of Computer Science
And Engineering
IIT Bombay, India
{rohit,anoop,pb}@cse.iitb.ac.in,

Raj Dabre[‡],

[‡] Graduate School of Informatics
Kyoto University
Japan
prajdabre@gmail.com

Abstract

This paper is an attempt to bridge two well known performance degraders in SMT, *viz.*, (i) difference in morphological characteristics of the two languages, and (ii) scarcity of parallel corpora. We address these two problems using "word segmentation" and through "pivots" on the morphologically complex language. Our case study is Malayalam to Hindi SMT. Malayalam belongs to the Dravidian family of languages and is heavily agglutinative. Hindi is a representative of the Indo-Aryan language family and is morphologically simpler. We use triangulation as pivoting strategy in combination with morphological pre-processing. We observe that (i) significant improvement in translation quality over direct SMT occurs when a pivot is used in combination with direct SMT, (ii) the more the number of pivots, the better the performance and (iii)word segmentation is a must. We achieved an *improvement* of 9.4 BLEU points which is over 58% compared to the baseline direct system. Our work paves way for SMT of languages that face resource scarcity and have widely divergent morphological characteristics.

1 Introduction

Hindi (hin) and Malayalam (mal) are two important languages from Indian sub-continent. Hindi is a language belonging to Indo-Aryan family with 300 million native speakers. Malayalam belongs to the Dravidian language family. It is spoken by over 38 million people.

The task of translation between Hindi and Malayalam proves to be a difficult one. This is due to scarcity of available parallel corpus and high agglutinative nature of Malayalam. Malayalam is a morphologically rich, agglutinative language in which complex words are formed by concatenating morphemes together. For example, "अगर बादल नहीं बरसे तो भी" (*if cloud not rain_verb then also*) in Hindi (5 words) would translate to "മഴാ പെയ്യുതിലെങ്ങിലും" (*rain_noun rain_verb+not+even_if+then_also*) in Malayalam (2 words).

In this paper, we present a case of translation from Malayalam to Hindi. Our approach is based on combined use of pivot strategies for Statistical Machine Translation (SMT) and word segmentation techniques. We show that word segmentation of source language as well as pivot language helps to improve the translation quality. Section 2 contains details about relevant work done in the field. Section 3 explains the design of our system in detail. Section 4 describes the experimental setup. Results of the experiments are discussed in Section 5. Section 6 includes concluding remarks on the mal-hin translation task.

2 Related Work

There is substantial amount on pivot-based SMT. De Gispert and Marino (2006) discuss translation tasks between Catalan and English with the use of Spanish as a pivot language. Pivoting is done using two techniques: pipelining of source-pivot and pivot-target SMT systems and direct translation using a synthesized Catalan-English. In Utiyama and Isahara (2007), the authors propose the use of pivot language through - phrase translation (phrase table creation) and sentence translation. Wu and Wang (2007) compare three pivot strategies *viz.* - phrase translation (*i.e.* triangulation), transfer method and synthetic method. Nakov and Ng (2012) try to exploit the similarity between resource-poor languages and resource-rich languages for the translation task. Dabre et al. (2014) used multiple decoding paths (MDP) to overcome

299

D S Sharma, R Sangal and E Sherly. Proc. of the 12th Intl. Conference on Natural Language Processing, pages 303–307,
Trivandrum, India. December 2015. ©2015 NLP Association of India (NLPAI)

the limitation of small sized corpora.Paul et al. (2013) discusses criteria to be considered for selection of good pivot language. Use of source-side segmentation as pre-processing technique has been demonstrated by (Kunchukuttan et al., 2014). Goldwater and McClosky (2005) investigates several methods for incorporating morphological information to achieve better translation from Czech to English.

Most of the pivot strategies mentioned above focus on the situation of resource-poor languages where direct translation is either very poor or not available. Our approach, like Dabre et al. (2014), tries to employ pivot strategy to help improve the performance of existing SMT systems. To the best of our knowledge, our work is the first attempt to integrate word segmentation with pivot-based SMT.

3 Our System

We propose a system which integrates word segmentation with triangulation and combines more than one SMT systems. The required concepts are explained as follows.

3.1 Pivoting by Triangulation

Wu and Wang (2007) discuss triangulation as a pivoting strategy. In this method, the source-pivot models and pivot-target models are trained using source(L_s)-pivot(L_p) and pivot(L_p)-target(L_t) corpora respectively. Using these two models, we induce a source-target model. The two important components to be calculated are - 1) phrase translation probability and 2) lexical weight.

The **Phrase translation probability** is estimated by marginalizing over all possible pivot phrase, along with the assumption that the target phrases are independent of the source phrase given the pivot phrase. The phrase translation probability can be calculated as shown below:

$$\phi\left(\vec{s}\|\vec{t}\right) = \sum_{\vec{p}} \phi\left(\vec{s}\|\vec{p}\right) \phi\left(\vec{p}\|\vec{t}\right) \qquad (1)$$

Where, $\vec{s}$, $\vec{p}$, $\vec{t}$ are phrases in languages L_s, L_p, L_t respectively.

The **Lexical Weight**, according to Koehn et al. (2003), depends on - 1) word alignment information a in a phrase pair (s, t) and 2) lexical translation probability $w(s|t)$.

Lexical weight can be modeled using following

equation,

$$p_w\left(\vec{f}\|\vec{e}, a\right) = \prod_{i=1}^{n} \frac{1}{\||j| (i, j) \in a\|} \sum_{\forall(i,j)\in a} w\left(f_i\|e_j\right) \qquad (2)$$

Wu and Wang (2009) discuss in detail about alignments information and lexical translation probability.

3.2 Word segmentation

We use unsupervised word segmentation as pre-processing technique. For this purpose, Morfessor (Virpioja et al., 2013) is used. It performs morphological segmentation of words of a natural language, based solely on raw text data. Morfessor uses probabilistic machine learning methods to do the task of segmentation. The trained models for word segmentation of Indian languages are available to use[1].

3.3 Integrating word segmentation with Triangulation

In our system, we use both phrase table triangulation and word-segmentation. The words in the source and pivot language training corpora are segmented before training the SMT systems. The target language is left unchanged. The phrase tables are then triangulated. This process is shown in Figure 1.

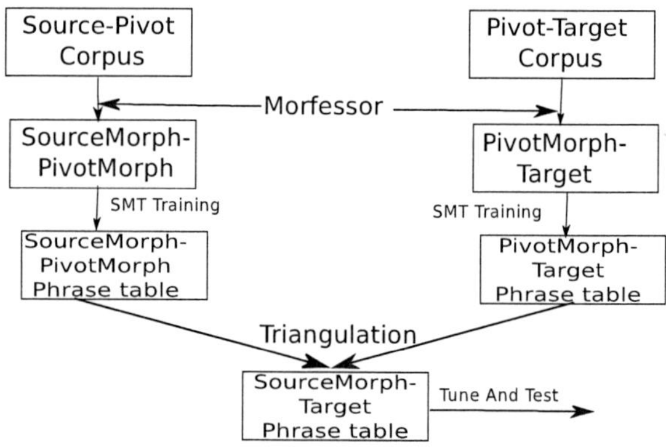

Figure 1: Integration of word segmentation with triangulation

3.4 Multiple Decoding Paths

We use the triangulated phrase table to supplement the direct phrase table. In order to integrate these two phrase tables, we use the multiple decoding paths (MDP) feature provided by the

---

[1] https://github.com/anoopkunchukuttan/indic_nlp_library

Moses decoder. Multiple decoding paths (Koehn and Hoang, 2007) allows us to lookup multiple translation models for hypothesis at decoding time, and the choice of best hypothesis at decoding time based on available evidence. We use MDP to combine one or more pivot-based MT systems with the direct MT system. This constitutes our **final decoding system**. We preferred this option over offline linear interpolation of phrase tables since the framework can dynamically consider phrases from multiple phrase tables and wouldn't need any hyperparameter tuning.

4 Experiments

The aim of experiments is to study impact of pivot strategies and word segmentation, separately and together.

4.1 Resource Details

We used the ILCI (Jha, 2010) multilingual corpora of around 50K sentences. The corpora belongs to Health and Tourism domain. Indian languages used in experiments are Bengali (ban), Gujarati (guj), Hindi (hin), Konkani (kok), Malayalam (mal), Marathi (mar), Panjabi (pan), Tamil (tam) and Telugu (tel).

Our data split was as follows: 46277 sentences are used for training, 500 sentences are used for tuning and 2000 sentences are used for testing.

For the experiments, we use phrase-based SMT training and 5-gram SRILM language model. Tuning is done using the MERT algorithm. The triangulated MT systems use default distance based reordering while direct systems use wbe-msd-bidirectional-fe-allff model

4.2 Experimental Setup

We trained various phrase based SMT systems by combining the basic systems mentioned in Section 3. We use a threshold of 0.001 for phrase translation probability to manage size of triangulated phrase table. The performance metric used is BLEU (Papineni et al., 2002). The following are the configurations we experimented with:

1. **DIR**: MT system trained on direct Source-Target corpus.

2. **DIR_Morph**: **DIR** system with source-text word-segmented.

3. **PIVOT**: MT system based on triangulated phrase table of Source-Target using a single Pivot language.

4. **PIVOT_Morph**: **PIVOT** system with both Source and Pivot texts segmented.

5. **PIVOT_SourceMorph**: **PIVOT** system with only Source text segmented.

6. **DIR+PIVOT**: MT system based on integration of **DIR** and **PIVOT** phrase tables using MDP.

7. **DIR_Morph+PIVOT_Morph**: MT system based on integration of **DIR_Morph** and **PIVOT_Morph** using MDP.

8. **DIR+All-PIVOT**: MT system based on integration of **DIR** and all 7 **PIVOT** systems using MDP.

9. **DIR_Morph+All-PIVOT_Morph**: MT system based on integration of **DIR_Morph** and all 7 **PIVOT_Morph** systems using MDP.

5 Results and Discussions

Table 1 shows BLEU scores for best performing MT systems for each experiment. Wherever a single pivot is used, it refers to the best supplementing pivot. In all the experiments, Punjabi was observed to be the best pivot.

Type of MT System	BLEU
DIR	16.11
DIR_Morph	23.35
PIVOT	15.72
PIVOT_Morph	23.02
PIVOT_SourceMorph	22.1
DIR+PIVOT	17.22
DIR_Morph+PIVOT_Morph	24.5
DIR+All-PIVOT	18.67
DIR_Morph+All-PIVOT_Morph	25.51

Table 1: BLEU Scores of MT systems

We can see that the pivot-only system gives translation accuracy comparable to the direct system for the best performing pivot language, Punjabi. Punjabi shares a large fraction of its vocabulary with Hindi. In addition, **pan** is morphologically simpler compared to other Indian languages. Hence, better word alignment can be achieved and during triangulation, more phrase pairs are obtained.

Though the **PIVOT** system does not better the performance of the **DIRECT** system, the combination of both the system *i.e.* **DIR+PIVOT** performs better than the **DIRECT** system.

DIR+PIVOT has relative improvement of 6.8% over **DIR** system. Addition of all **PIVOT** systems using multiple decoding paths shows that each pivot helps improve the BLEU score since each **PIVOT** system provides additional translation options. The all-pivot system *i.e.* **DIR+All-PIVOT** shows improvement of about 15% (2.56 BLEU points) over **DIR** system.

Pre-processing the corpus with word segmentation (**DIR_Morph** system) results in a substantial improvement of 44% over the **DIR** system. Use of word segmentation brings about a major improvement in the BLEU score. Since **mal** is morphologically rich, word segmentation reduces data sparsity, helps learn better alignment models and reduces the number of unknown words in test set.

We compared the use of word segmentation at source as well as pivot with word segmentation on the source language alone. Figure 2 compares these two system for various pivot languages.

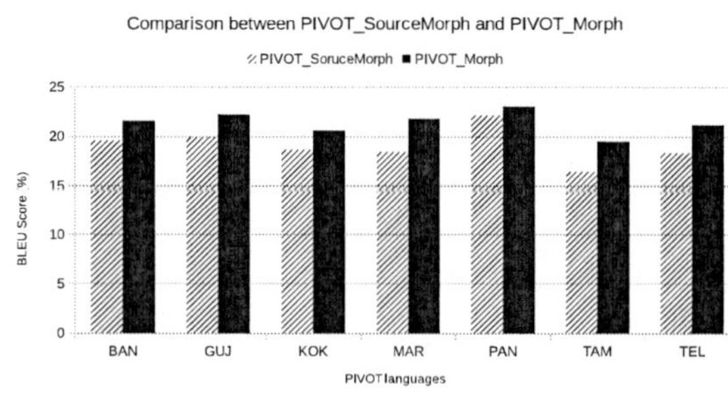

Figure 2: Comparison of PIVOT_Morph and PIVOT_SourceMorph MT systems

The additional use of word segmentation at pivot provides a 4% to 18% increase in the BLEU score.

The **DIR_Morph+All-PIVOT_Morph** system combines all pivot languages as well as source and pivot segmentation. This is the best performing system which achieves an improvement of 9.4 BLEU (58% improvement) over **DIR** system.

5.1 Examples

Below are few examples comparing baseline **DIR** and our final system *i.e.* **DIR_Morph+All-PIVOT_Morph**.

- **Example 1:**
  mal input: താമസിക്കുന്നതിനുള്ള സൗകര്യം സർക്കാർ വിശ്രമ ക്യാംപുകൾ കാർലാ ഹോട്ടൽ എന്നിവയിലുണ്ട്.
  tAmasikkunnatinuLLa saukarya.n sarkkAr vishrama kyA.npukaL kArlA hoTTal .ennivayiluNT)
  Baseline: के ठहरने की व्यवस्था सरकारी विश्राम कैंप कारला होटल एन्नीवयिलुण्ड के नाम से जाना जाता है ।
  (ke Thaharane kI vyavasthA sarakArI vishrAma kai.npa kAralA hoTala .ennivayiluNT ke nAma se jAnA jAtA hai)
  Final system: ठहरने की व्यवस्था सरकारी विश्राम कैंप कारला होटल भी उपलब्ध हैं ।
  (Thaharane kI vyavasthA sarakArI vishrAma kai.npa kAralA hoTala bhI upalabdha hai.n)
  Better translations for words are generated, and the number of unknown words is reduced.
- **Example 2:**
  mal input: ചെവിയിലെ കുരുക്കൾ ആരെയും ഉറങ്ങാൻ അനുവദിക്കില്ല.
  (c.eviyil.e kurukkaL Ar.eyu.n uRa N NAn anuvadikkilla)
  Baseline: कान की फुंसी को सोने के ।
  (kAna kI phu.nsI ko sone ke)
  Final system: कान की फुंसी किसी को भी नींद नहीं होने दिया ।
  (kAna kI phu.nsI kisI ko bhI nI.nda nahI.n hone diyA)
  The direct system is not able to translate some words, whereas out final system translates most words correctly.

6 Conclusions

We have shown that pre-processing using word segmentation and augmentation of direct systems with pivot-based systems provides significant advancement in translation quality. This is an attempt to integrate word segmentation with pivot-strategies. We achieved compelling results with our approach. The approach is applicable to any resource-scarce language pair with morphologically rich source side. In future, we will focus on applying our approach to other challenging language pairs. We will also work on MT tasks which involve morphologically rich target language.

Acknowledgements

We would like to thank the Technology Development for Indian Languages (TDIL) Programme and the Department of Electronics & Information Technology, Govt. of India for providing the ILCI corpus.

References

Raj Dabre, Fabien Cromieres, Sadao Kurohashi, and Pushpak Bhattacharyya. 2014. Leveraging small multilingual corpora for smt using many pivot languages.

Adrià De Gispert and Jose B Marino. 2006. Catalan-english statistical machine translation without parallel corpus: bridging through spanish. In *Proc. of 5th International Conference on Language Resources and Evaluation (LREC)*, pages 65–68. Citeseer.

Sharon Goldwater and David McClosky. 2005. Improving statistical mt through morphological analysis. In *Proceedings of the conference on Human Language Technology and Empirical Methods in Natural Language Processing*, pages 676–683. Association for Computational Linguistics.

Girish Nath Jha. 2010. The tdil program and the indian language corpora initiative (ilci). *Proceedings of the Seventh Conference on International Language Resources and Evaluation (LREC 2010). European Language Resources Association (ELRA).*

Philipp Koehn and Hieu Hoang. 2007. Factored translation models. In *EMNLP-CoNLL*, pages 868–876.

Philipp Koehn, Franz Josef Och, and Daniel Marcu. 2003. Statistical phrase-based translation. In *Proceedings of the 2003 Conference of the North American Chapter of the Association for Computational Linguistics on Human Language Technology-Volume 1*, pages 48–54. Association for Computational Linguistics.

Anoop Kunchukuttan, Ratish Pudupully, Rajen Chatterjee, Abhijit Mishra, and Pushpak Bhattacharyya. 2014. The iit bombay smt system for icon 2014 tools contest. In *NLP Tools Contest at ICON 2014.*

Preslav Nakov and Hwee Tou Ng. 2012. Improving statistical machine translation for a resource-poor language using related resource-rich languages. *Journal of Artificial Intelligence Research*, 44(1):179–222.

Kishore Papineni, Salim Roukos, Todd Ward, and Wei-Jing Zhu. 2002. Bleu: a method for automatic evaluation of machine translation. In *Proceedings of the 40th annual meeting on association for computational linguistics*, pages 311–318. Association for Computational Linguistics.

Michael Paul, Andrew Finch, and Eiichrio Sumita. 2013. How to choose the best pivot language for automatic translation of low-resource languages. *ACM Transactions on Asian Language Information Processing (TALIP)*, 12(4):14.

Masao Utiyama and Hitoshi Isahara. 2007. A comparison of pivot methods for phrase-based statistical machine translation. In *HLT-NAACL*, pages 484–491.

Sami Virpioja, Peter Smit, Stig-Arne Grönroos, Mikko Kurimo, et al. 2013. Morfessor 2.0: Python implementation and extensions for morfessor baseline.

Hua Wu and Haifeng Wang. 2007. Pivot language approach for phrase-based statistical machine translation. *Machine Translation*, 21(3):165–181.

Hua Wu and Haifeng Wang. 2009. Revisiting pivot language approach for machine translation. In *Proceedings of the Joint Conference of the 47th Annual Meeting of the ACL and the 4th International Joint Conference on Natural Language Processing of the AFNLP: Volume 1-Volume 1*, pages 154–162. Association for Computational Linguistics.

Using Multilingual Topic Models for Improved Alignment in English-Hindi MT

Diptesh Kanojia[1]   **Aditya Joshi**[1,2,3]

Pushpak Bhattacharyya[1] **Mark James Carman**[2]

[1]IIT Bombay, India, [2]Monash University, Australia

[3]IITB-Monash Research Academy, India

{diptesh,adityaj,pb}@cse.iitb.ac.in

mark.carman@monash.edu

Abstract

Parallel corpora are often injected with bilingual dictionaries for improved Indian language machine translation (MT). In absence of such dictionaries, a coarse dictionary may be required. This paper demonstrates the use of a multilingual topic model for creating coarse dictionaries for English-Hindi MT. We compare our approaches with: (a) a baseline with no additional dictionary injection, and (b) a corpus with a good quality dictionary. Our results show that the existing Cartesian product approach which is used to create the pseudo-parallel data results in a degradation on tourism and health datasets, for English-Hindi MT. Our paper points to the fact that existing Cartesian approach using multilingual topics (devised for European languages) may be detrimental for Indian language MT.

On the other hand, we present an alternate 'sentential' approach that leads to a slight improvement. However, our sentential approach (using a parallel corpus injected with a coarse dictionary) outperforms a system trained using parallel corpus and a good quality dictionary.

1 Introduction

Word Alignment is defined as the process of mapping synonymous words, using a parallel corpora. It is considered to be a valuable resource, and can be used for various applications such as word sense disambiguation, statistical machine translation (SMT), and automatic construction of bilingual text.

Statistical Machine Translation (SMT) is a technology for the automatic translation of text in one natural language into another. In a country like India where more than 22 official languages are spoken across 29 states, the task of translation becomes immensely important. A SMT system typically uses two modules: alignment and reordering. The quality of an SMT system is dependent on the alignments discovered. The initial quality of word alignment is known to impact the quality of SMT (Och and Ney, 2003; Ganchev et al., 2008). Many SMT based systems are evaluated in terms of the information gained from the word alignment results.

IBM models (Brown et al., 1993) are among the most widely used models for statistical word alignment. For these models, having a large parallel dataset can result in good alignment, and hence, facilitate a good quality SMT system. However, there is not a lot of parallel data available for English to Indian Languages, or for one Indian Language to another. Without sufficient amount of parallel corpus, it is very difficult to learn the correct correspondences between words that infrequently occur in the training data. Hence, a need for specialized techniques that improve alignment quality has been felt (Sanchis and Snchez, 2008; Lee et al., 2006; Koehn et al., 2007).

Mimno et al. (2009) present a multilingual topic model called PolyLDA, and apply it for Machine Translation for European and other languages such as Danish, German, Greek, English, Spanish, etc. Since multilingual topic models generate parallel topics: parallel clusters of words that are likely to be about the same theme, these topics provide coarse alignment that a Moses-like translation system can leverage on. The idea is to not rely on any external ontology such as WordNet and to rely purely on a parallel corpus to create such coarse alignments. The focus of our paper is to improve word alignments using multilingual Topic Models approach for English-Hindi MT. The key question that this paper attempts to answer is:

D S Sharma, R Sangal and E Sherly. Proc. of the 12th Intl. Conference on Natural Language Processing, pages 308–315,
Trivandrum, India. December 2015. ©2015 NLP Association of India (NLPAI)

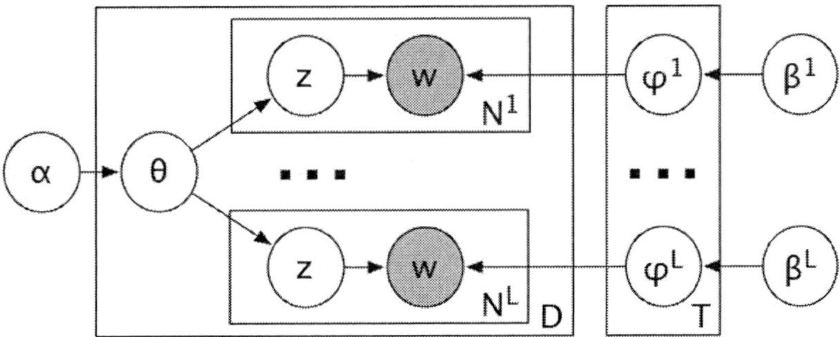

Figure 1: PolyLDA: Plate Diagram

'Can the information gained from multilingual topic models help in improving the quality of SMT for English - Hindi Machine Translation?'

The novelty of the paper lies in the following ways:

- Implementation of a multilingual topic model by Mimno et al. (2009) and applying it to English-Hindi MT using the Cartesian product approach.

- A novel approach to employ multilingual topics extracted by the multilingual topic model above. The approach called the sentential approach that performs better than the Cartesian product approach.

The paper is organized as follows. In section 2, we describe our related work. In section 3, we introduce multilingual Topic Models. In section 4 and 5, we describe the architecture of our work, and the experiment setup. We show the results obtained and our error analysis in section 6, and conclude in section 7.

2 Related Work

Our work covers two broad areas of research: Multilingual topic models and improvement of alignment in MT. We now describe the two in this section.

We implement the algorithm by Mimno et al. (2009) called PolyLDA. This model discovers topics for English - Hindi Parallel text, and use it to create pseudo-parallel data. They proposed Cartesian approach to inject the pseudo parallel data in the training corpora. They evaluate their topics for machine translation. Such multilingual topic models have been applied to a variety of tasks. Ni et al. (2009) extract topics from wikipedia, and use the top terms for a text classification task. They observe that parallel topics perform better than topic words that are translated into the target language. Approaches that do not rely on parallel corpus have also been reported. Jagarlamudi and Daumé III (2010) use a bilingual dictionary, and a comparable corpora to estimate a model called JointLDA. Boyd-Graber and Blei (2009) use unaligned corpus and extract multilingual topics using a multilingual topic model called MuTo.

The second area that our work is related to is improvement of alignment between words/phrases for machine translation. Och and Ney (2000) describe improved alignment models for statistical machine translation. They use both the phrase based and word based approaches to extend the baseline alignment models. Their results show that this method improved precision without loss of recall in English to German alignments. However, if the same unit is aligned to two different target units, this method is unlikely to make a selection. Cherry and Lin (2003) model the alignments directly given the sentence pairs whereas some researchers use similarity and association measures to build alignment links (Ahrenberg et al., 1998; Tufi and Barbu, 2002). In addition, Wu (1997) use a stochastic inversion transduction grammar to simultaneously parse the sentence pairs to get the word or phrase alignments. Some researchers use preprocessing steps to identity multi-word units for word alignment (Ahrenberg et al., 1998; Tiedemann, 1999; Melamed, 2000). These methods obtain multi-word candidates, but are unable to handle separated phrases and multiwords in low frequencies. Hua and Haifeng (2004) use a rule based translation system to improve the results of statistical machine translation. It can translate mul-

305

tiword alignments with higher accuracy, and can perform word sense disambiguation and select appropriate translations while a translation dictionary can only list all translations for each word or phrase. Some researchers use Part-of-speeches (POS), which represent morphological classes of words, tagging on bilingual training data (Sanchis and Snchez, 2008; Lee et al., 2006) give valuable information about words and their neighbors, thus identifying a class to which the word may belong. This helps in disambiguation and thus selecting word correspondences but can also give rise to increased vocabulary thus making the training data more sparse. Joshi et al. (2013) use in domain parallel data to inject additional alignment mappings for the news headline domain. Finally, Koehn et al. (2007) propose a factored translation model that can incorporate any linguistic factors including POS information in phrase-based SMT. It provides a generalized representation of a translation model, because it can map multiple source and target factors. It may help to effectively handle out-of-vocabulary (OOV) by incorporating many linguistic factors, but it still crucially relies on the initial quality of word alignment that will dominate the translation probabilities.

In this way, our paper attempts to verify the claim that multilingual topics can be used to address the problem of improved alignment generation. We use a baseline that contains no bilingual dictionary, and an approach that contains a good quality bilingual dictionary. This is similar to the approach in Och and Ney (2000).

3 Multilingual Topic Models: An Introduction

A topic model takes as input a set of documents, and generates clusters of words called 'topics'. These topics help to understand themes underlying a dataset. A popular topic model by Blei et al. (2003) called Latent Dirichlet Allocation (LDA) is an unsupervised model. This model takes as input the value of T as the number of topics, and a set of Dirichlet hyperparameters. LDA takes as input a dataset and models two kinds of distributions: (a) a document-topic distribution that determines the distribution of topics within a document, and (b) a word-topic distribution that determines the distribution of words across topics. The two distributions can be estimated using an Expectation-Maximization approach, or Gibbs sampling, among other approaches.

Multilingual LDA (PolyLDA) introduced by Mimno et al. (2009) is based on the idea of LDA, and extends it for extracting equivalent topics across languages. This topic model takes as input parallel documents (or sentences) across two or more languages, and discovers T topics in each of the languages. For example, a PolyLDA may discover an English topic '*book, books*' and the corresponding topic '*libre, libres*' in French, and '*libro, libri*' in Italian. Figure 1 shows the plate diagram for our implementation of PolyLDA. We use a simplified version of PolyLDA for two languages: *i.e.*, in our case $L = 2$.

Each document is modeled as a set of N^l words w where l ranges from 1 to L for L parallel languages. Each document has a distribution θ over all topics, over a total of D documents. Since L is 2 for us, There are two word-topic distributions ϕ_1 and ϕ_2 for English and Hindi, respectively. Thus, based on which language the word belongs to, it is picked from the appropriate distribution. α and β are the Dirichlet hyperparameters.

The output of PolyLDA is the estimation for ϕ for the two languages. The top n words for each topic are considered as candidates for generation of pseudo-parallel data.

4 Architecture

Indian languages are morphologically complex, and sometimes very agglutinative. English to Hindi poses a separate challenge of word ordering as well. We take help of multilingual topic models (MLTM) to obtain coarse alignments. In this section, we describe our architecture.

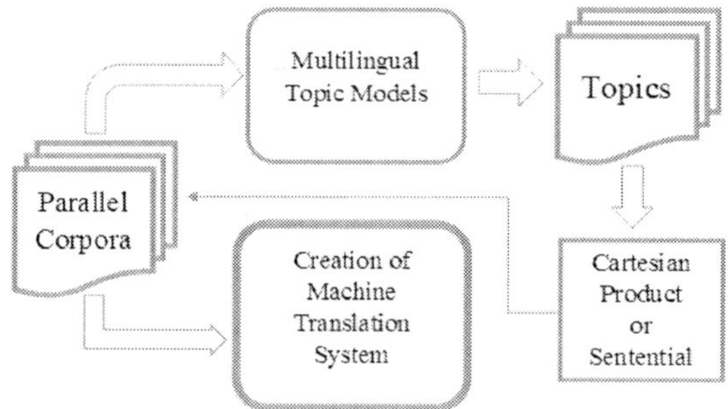

Figure 2: Our Architecture

The basic architecture is shown in Figure 2. We use multilingual topic models with the parameter of number of topics Z set. We thus obtain Z topics: each consisting of top k English and top k Hindi words. Using these topics, we generate *'pseudo-parallel'* data - parallel words or groups of words that may be translations of each other. Finally, this data is appended to the parallel corpus used for training a Moses-based MT system (Koehn et al., 2007).

The key step in the architecture is the approach used to create pseudo-parallel data. We consider two approaches to do so:

1. **Cartesian product Approach**: This approach was used by Mimno et al. (2009). In their work, they analyzed the characteristics of MLTM in comparison to monolingual LDA, and demonstrated that it is possible to discover aligned topics. They also demonstrated that relatively small numbers of topically comparable document tuples are sufficient to align topics between languages in non-comparable corpora. They then use MLTM to create bilingual lexicons for low resource language pairs, and provided candidate translations for more computationally intense alignment processes without the sentence-aligned translations. They conduct experiments for Spanish, English, German, French, and Italian. Figure 3 summarizes the approach. For parallel topic i with top 3 words, we add 9 pseudo-parallel sentences with one-to-one word alignment, as shown. Thus for T topics, and K top words, Cartesian product approach results in pseudo-parallel data of $T * K$ sentences of length 1 each. This is appended to the parallel corpus.

2. **Sentential Approach**: It is a novel approach which concatenates words belonging to the same topic as a pseudo-sentence. The approach is shown in Figure 4. We use the words aligned in topic models and put them in a sentence to create parallel sentences for the training corpora to be used in creating the MT system. Thus, the pseudo-parallel data generated in this case consists of 1 sentence per topic: $e_{i1}e_{i2}e_{i3}$ in parallel with $h_{i1}h_{i2}h_{i3}$. We use the sentential approach for the English - Hindi where the sentences constructed may not be word aligned but, unlike so many one to one Cartesian product alignments, our approach keeps them in the same sentence, thus reducing the chances of the system learning non synonymous candidate translations.

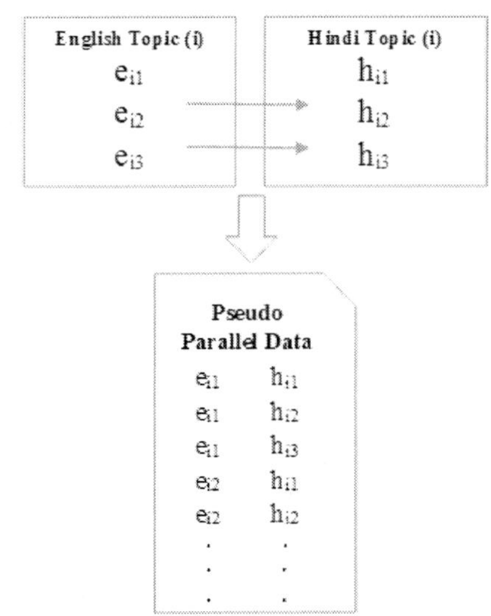

Figure 3: Existing Cartesian Product Approach to generate pseudo-parallel data

Thus for T topics, and K top words, sentential approach results in pseudo-parallel data of T sentences of length K each. This is appended to the parallel corpus.

The Cartesian product approach adds the word sets for every topic to a set of candidate translations. While it provides with a lot more pseudo parallel data to be injected, it also injects one to one aligned non synonymous words to the parallel data. On the other hand, sentential approach only provides fewer pairs. Thus, intuitively, sentential approach performs better in this regard, while injecting less noisy data to the parallel corpus.

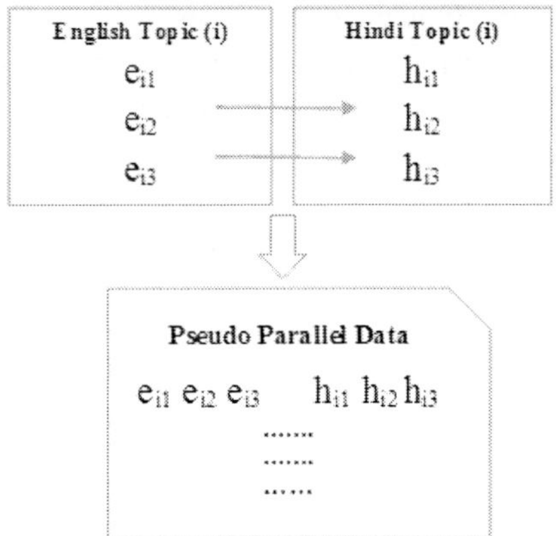

Figure 4: Our Sentential Approach to create pseudo-parallel data

TOPIC 1		TOPIC 2		TOPIC 3		TOPIC 4	
vitamin	मात्रा	clean	साफ	disease	रोग	cancer	कैंसर
quantity	विटामिन	acid	पथरी	blood	रक्त	nose	नाक
amount	महीने	ulcer	अल्सर	heart	हृदय	breast	शिकायत
large	बड़ी	stones	एसिड	diabetes	बीमारी	complaint	गर्भाशय
months	नाम	asthma	पड़ती	increases	बढ़	uterus	भूख

Figure 5: Parallel English-Hindi topics as generated by the topic model for the health dataset

TOPIC 1		TOPIC 2		TOPIC 3		TOPIC 4	
lake	झील	famous	प्रसिद्ध	worth	नाम	road	मार्ग
station	स्टेशन	country	देश	place	देखने	india	भारत
railway	रेलवे	state	प्रमुख	named	दर्शनीय	route	दिल्ली
nearest	धीरे	main	रूप	temples	नगर	path	सड़क
munnar	मुन्नार	centre	राज्य	city	मंदिरों	kms	रोड

Figure 6: Parallel English-Hindi topics as generated by the topic model for the tourism dataset

5 Experiment Setup

In this section, we describe the dataset, and setup for the experiments conducted.

5.1 Dataset

For our experiments, we use corpora from health and tourism domain by Khapra et al. (2010). These datasets contain approximately 25000 parallel sentences for English - Hindi language pair. We use these for both the creation of pseudo parallel data, and training Machine translation systems. We separate 500 sentences each for testing and tuning purposes. We ensure that they are not present in the training corpus.

5.2 Setup

We implemented the multilingual topic model in Java. Our implementation uses Gibbs sampling as described in the original paper. We used two configurations for our experiment. They vary in the pseudo parallel data which was included along with the training data used for MT system. We use MOSES Toolkit for all our experiments. We perform experiments and obtained results for 3 different data sets as indicated in Figure 7. We set K, the number of words in a topic model, to be 11 for our experiments. For the initial experiments, we use number of topics as 50.

1. **No dictionary (Baseline)**: A basic setup for creating an MT system requires training, testing and tuning corpora which we obtained for HEALTH and TOURISM domains.

2. **Cartesian product Approach**: In this approach the pseudo parallel data was created using MLTM approach described earlier, and added to the training data before training the MT systems. We added the pseudo parallel data to training data using the approach indicated in Figure 3. Thus, for 50 topics and 11 top words, we add 550 pseudo-parallel sentences, each of length 1.

3. **Sentential Approach**: We added the pseudo parallel data created using MLTM approach to the training data using the approach indicated in Figure 4. Thus, for 50 topics and 11 top words, we add 50 pseudo-parallel sentences, each of length 11.

4. **Full dictionary**: While the baseline uses no dictionary, this approach considered uses a good quality bilingual dictionary from `http://www.cfilt.iitb.ac.in/~hdict/webinterface_user/index.php`. The dictionary consists of more than 100,000 mappings between English and Hindi words.

6 Results

This section evaluates our implementation of the multilingual topic model for its impact on machine translation. We first present sample topics that are generated by the model. In the next subsection, we discuss the impact on machine translation.

6.1 Quantitative evaluation of Multilingual topics

Figures 5 and 6 show top 5 words for sample parallel English-Hindi topics for the health and tourism datasets respectively. The total number of topics, as stated before, is 50. Figure 5 shows four topics which correspond to four thematic components of the health dataset. Topic 1 is about administration of medicines, Topic 2 and 3 are about two kinds of diseases, while Topic 4 is about different types of cancer. We also see that translations of the English words appear in the corresponding Hindi side for each of the topics. They may not appear in the same order, since these are dependent on the frequency of the word in the specific language. Thus, our model is able to discover **coarse topics** underlying the datasets.

Similar trends are observed in case of 6. Consider topic 2. The word temples on English side aligns with two words on the Hindi side: one in the root form, and one in the inflected form. Thus, our model is able to discover **inflected forms** of words. Consider topic 4. The synonyms 'road', 'route' and 'path' occur on the English side. Three synonyms 'maarg', 'sadak' and 'road' also appear on the Hindi side. Thus, our model is able to discover **parallel synonyms** across the two languages.

Among 40 English words present in these figures, only 7 do not have a translation in the corresponding Hindi topic[1]. Similarly, for the 40 Hindi words, 6 do not have a translation in the corresponding English topic.

6.2 Benefit to MT

We now compare the baseline against the Cartesian product and sentential approaches that use multilingual topics. The total number of topics, as stated before, is 50. Table 1 shows the BLEU scores before and after injecting the multilingual topic modeling data, for the two datasets. We observe that BLEU score obtained on multilingual topic modeled data set using the Cartesian product approach for HEALTH domain is 25.98.

In the Cartesian product approach, we take parallel topics and map each topic word to every other parallel language topic word, and add them to training data. This may result in several incorrect translations being added to the parallel corpus.

---

[1]These are 'nearest, centre, asthma, diabetes, place, kms, breast'

	Health	Tourism
No dictionary (Baseline)	26.14	**28.68**
Cartesian product Approach (50 topics)	25.98	28.44
Sentential Approach (50 topics)	**26.25**	27.52
Full dictionary	**26.31**	**29.30**

Table 1: MT Results using no dictionary (baseline), good quality dictionary and coarse dictionary obtained through multilingual topic model (Cartesian product and Sentential approach)

This seems to be the likely cause for degradation from 26.14 to 25.98 in case of health dataset, and from 28.68 to 28.44 in case of tourism dataset. In case of health dataset, our sentential approach allows us to increase from baseline and move closer to using full dictionary.

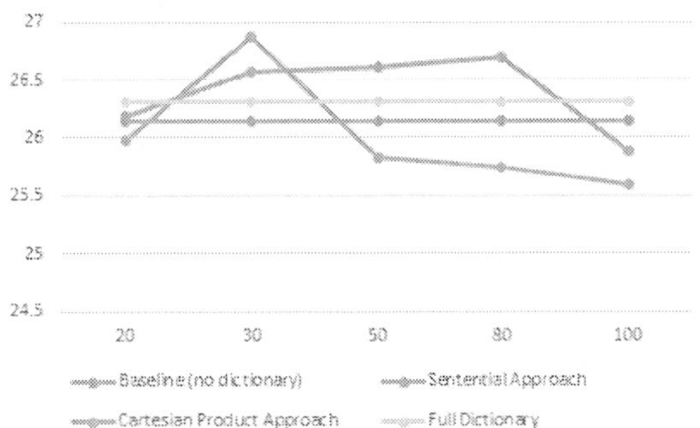

Figure 7: Change in BLEU scores for different value for Topics (T) for health domain

6.3 Impact of number of topics on MT

The degradation above is a parameter of number of topics; to ascertain that there is indeed degradation, we vary the number of topics. Hence, we conduct a separate run of our topic model for number of topics 20, 30, 50, 80 and 100. We then use different approaches as shown above, and show the results for health domain in the graph above (Figure 7). The x - axis represent the number of topics (T) varying from 20 to 100. The results of two topic modeled approaches namely Cartesian product approach and Sentence formation approach are shown above.

The baseline MT output is shown as a horizontal line as no topic model data is being added to it. The line representing the Cartesian product approach clearly shows the degradation of MT output for English - Hindi. On the other hand, the sentential approach shown minor improvements for a varied number of topic models. As more topics are added, sentential approach improves over the baseline. However, beyond 100, we observe a substantial degradation. This is because data sparsity along with too many topics introduces non-synonymous words in parallel topics.

For topics 30, 50 and 80, our approach of using a coarse dictionary obtained through multilingual topics surpasses using a full, good quality dictionary.

In summary, we see that existing Cartesian product approach using multilingual topics (devised for European languages) is detrimental for Indian language MT. A modified sentential approach results in marginal improvement.

7   Conclusion and Future Work

We implemented a multilingual topic model based on a past work to extract parallel English-Hindi topics. These parallel topics can be used by Moses to improve the alignment quality. We discussed two approaches to generate pseudo-parallel data. We used the Cartesian product approach that adds all combinations of top words in a topic. On the other hand, we introduced the sentential approach which adds all words together as a single sentence. We compared against a baseline with no bilingual dictionary, and an approach that uses a good quality dictionary in order to understand how beneficial it is to add coarse mappings obtained from the topic models. The strength of our model lies in that our approach using a coarse dictionary performs better than using a good quality dictionary.

On experimentation with tourism and health datasets, we observed that the existing Cartesian product approach leads to a degradation in the BLEU score from 26.14 to 25.98. On the other hand, our sentential approach is able to restrict this degradation, but **results in a improvement for a range of number of topics**.

Our paper points to the fact that existing approaches using multilingual topics (devised for European languages) may be detrimental for Indian language MT. In addition, using additional observed variables for inflections and morphological characteristics, and latent variables for semantic classes, new multilingual topic models can be designed.

References

Lars Ahrenberg, Mikael Andersson, and Magnus Merkel. 1998. A simple hybrid aligner for generating lexical correspondences in parallel texts. In *Proceedings of the 17th International Conference on Computational Linguistics - Volume 1*, COLING '98, pages 29–35, Stroudsburg, PA, USA. Association for Computational Linguistics.

David M Blei, Andrew Y Ng, and Michael I Jordan. 2003. Latent dirichlet allocation. *the Journal of machine Learning research*, 3:993–1022.

Jordan Boyd-Graber and David M Blei. 2009. Multilingual topic models for unaligned text. In *Proceedings of the Twenty-Fifth Conference on Uncertainty in Artificial Intelligence*, pages 75–82. AUAI Press.

Peter F. Brown, Vincent J. Della Pietra, Stephen A. Della Pietra, and Robert L. Mercer. 1993. The mathematics of statistical machine translation: Parameter estimation. *Comput. Linguist.*, 19(2):263–311, June.

Colin Cherry and Dekang Lin. 2003. A probability model to improve word alignment. In *Proceedings of the 41st Annual Meeting on Association for Computational Linguistics - Volume 1*, ACL '03, pages 88–95, Stroudsburg, PA, USA. Association for Computational Linguistics.

Kuzman Ganchev, Joo V. Graa, and Ben Taskar. 2008. Better alignments = better translations. In *in Proc. of the ACL.*

Wu Hua and Wang Haifeng. 2004. Improving statistical word alignment with a rule-based machine translation system. In *Proceedings of the 20th International Conference on Computational Linguistics*, COLING '04, Stroudsburg, PA, USA. Association for Computational Linguistics.

Jagadeesh Jagarlamudi and Hal Daumé III. 2010. Extracting multilingual topics from unaligned comparable corpora. In *Advances in Information Retrieval*, pages 444–456. Springer.

Aditya Joshi, Kashyap Popat, Shubham Gautam, and Pushpak Bhattacharyya. 2013. Making headlines in hindi: Automatic english to hindi news headline translation. *Sixth International Joint Conference on Natural Language Processing*, page 21.

Mitesh M Khapra, Anup Kulkarni, Saurabh Sohoney, and Pushpak Bhattacharyya. 2010. All words domain adapted wsd: Finding a middle ground between supervision and unsupervision. In *Proceedings of the 48th Annual Meeting of the Association for Computational Linguistics*, pages 1532–1541. Association for Computational Linguistics.

Philipp Koehn, Hieu Hoang, Alexandra Birch, Chris Callison-Burch, Marcello Federico, Nicola Bertoldi, Brooke Cowan, Wade Shen, Christine Moran, Richard Zens, Chris Dyer, Ondřej Bojar, Alexandra

Constantin, and Evan Herbst. 2007. Moses: Open source toolkit for statistical machine translation. In *Proceedings of the 45th Annual Meeting of the ACL on Interactive Poster and Demonstration Sessions*, ACL '07, pages 177–180, Stroudsburg, PA, USA. Association for Computational Linguistics.

Jonghoon Lee, Donghyeon Lee, and Gary Geunbae Lee. 2006. Interspeech 2006 improving phrase-based korean-english statistical machine translation.

I. Dan Melamed. 2000. Models of translational equivalence among words. *Comput. Linguist.*, 26(2):221–249, June.

David Mimno, Hanna M Wallach, Jason Naradowsky, David A Smith, and Andrew McCallum. 2009. Polylingual topic models. In *Proceedings of the 2009 Conference on Empirical Methods in Natural Language Processing: Volume 2-Volume 2*, pages 880–889. Association for Computational Linguistics.

Xiaochuan Ni, Jian-Tao Sun, Jian Hu, and Zheng Chen. 2009. Mining multilingual topics from wikipedia. In *Proceedings of the 18th international conference on World wide web*, pages 1155–1156. ACM.

Franz Josef Och and Hermann Ney. 2000. Improved statistical alignment models. In *Proceedings of the 38th Annual Meeting on Association for Computational Linguistics*, ACL '00, pages 440–447, Stroudsburg, PA, USA. Association for Computational Linguistics.

Franz Josef Och and Hermann Ney. 2003. A systematic comparison of various statistical alignment models. *Computational Linguistics*, 29(1):19–51.

Germn Sanchis and Joan Andreu Snchez. 2008. Vocabulary extension via pos information for smt.

Jorg Tiedemann. 1999. Word alignment step by step. In *Proceedings of the 12th Nordic Conf. on Computational Linguistics*, pages 216–227.

Dan Tufi and Anamaria Barbu. 2002. Lexical token alignment: Experiments, results and application. In *In Proc. of LREC-2002*, pages 458–465.

Dekai Wu. 1997. Stochastic inversion transduction grammars and bilingual parsing of parallel corpora. *Comput. Linguist.*, 23(3):377–403, September.

Triangulation of Reordering Tables: An Advancement Over Phrase Table Triangulation in Pivot-Based SMT

Deepak Patil, Harshad Chavan, Pushpak Bhattacharyya
Indian Institute of Technology Bombay, India
{deepakcp, harshadpc, pb}@cse.iitb.ac.in

Abstract

Triangulation in Pivot-Based Statistical Machine Translation(SMT) is a very effective method for building Machine Translation(MT) systems in case of scarcity of the parallel corpus. Phrase Table Triangulation helps in such a resource constrained setting by inducing new phrase pairs with the help of a pivot. However, it does not explore the possibility of extracting reordering information through the use of pivot. This paper presents a novel method for triangulation of reordering tables in Pivot Based SMT. We show that the use of a pivot can help in extracting better reordering information and can assist in improving the quality of the translation. With a detailed example, we show that triangulation of reordering tables also improves the lexical choices a system makes during translation. We observe a BLEU score improvement of 1.06 for Marathi to English MT system with Hindi as a pivot, and also significant improvements in 8 other translation systems by using this method.

1 Introduction

Pivot-Based Statistical Machine Translation(SMT) is a crucial and a well known methodology for building Machine Translation(MT) Systems for language pairs that are not so rich in terms of available resources. Low or no availability of parallel corpus for a language pair is one of the main reasons behind following a Pivot-Based approach. Pivot-Based approach makes use of a parallel corpus from source language to some language other than the target language, which is known as a "Pivot language" or simply a "Pivot", and a parallel corpus from the pivot language to the target language. Key idea behind using a pivot is, using one or more pivot languages to improve the quality of translation by making use of additional information that the pivot induces. This additional information is mainly in the form of a new set of phrase pairs that are extracted with the help of the pivot language. This method of extracting new phrase pairs in Pivot-Based SMT is known as the Triangulation method.

Current approaches and methods that discuss triangulation generally focus on the triangulation of the phrase tables from source language(source) to pivot language(pivot) and pivot language to target language(target). This improves the translation quality because of the newly added phrase pairs, but the reordering information for these newly added phrase pairs is not present in the reordering table. The focus of our work is to explore the possibility of extracting the reordering information for newly added phrase pairs by making use of the pivot language. To the best of our knowledge this is the first work that discusses the approaches for triangulation of reordering tables and shows significant improvements.

To begin with, Section 2 discusses the work related to Pivot-Based SMT and the Triangulation method. We then provide a background for our approaches for reordering table triangulation in Section 3. Section 4 discusses the mathematics involved in these approaches. We describe our approaches viz. Table Based approach and Count Based approach in detail, in Section 5. Section 6 explains the experimental setup. Results of our experiments are shown in Section 7 along with the discussion of those results. We conclude our work in Section 8 and also point out a few directions for future work.

2 Related Work

Use of a pivot in machine translation has been extensively studied by many researchers. Wang et al.

D S Sharma, R Sangal and E Sherly. Proc. of the 12th Intl. Conference on Natural Language Processing, pages 316–324,
Trivandrum, India. December 2015. ©2015 NLP Association of India (NLPAI)

(2006) demonstrated the use of pivot languages for extracting better word alignments when a source-target parallel corpus is either unavailable or is very small in size. Wu and Wang (2007) proposed the entire formulation for a pivot based approach and triangulation of phrase tables and showed that a pivot can be used for inducing new phrase pairs that were not extracted while building a phrase table from the training corpus. This forms a basis for a valid speculation that, pivot may also prove to be useful in extracting reordering information.

Several strategies have been proposed for the use of a pivot. Utiyama and Isahara (2007) proposed two strategies, a phrase translation strategy that is similar to the triangulation method and a sentence translation strategy that makes use of two different MT systems - one from source-pivot and other from pivot-target. They showed through their experiments that the phrase translation strategy performs significantly better than the sentence translation strategy. Wu and Wang (2009) additionally introduced a Synthetic Method for Pivot based SMT, that synthesizes the source-target corpus from source-pivot and pivot-target corpora. It was found through their experiments that the Triangulation Method outperforms the Sythetic method as well. This encouraged us to focus our work on the triangulation approach.

Nakov and Ng (2012) showed that merging the phrase tables by giving priority to the original table that is extracted from a direct parallel corpus(direct table) and using additional features is a good strategy. In case of an interpolation, it refers to giving higher weight values to the translation probabilities from a direct source-pivot phrase table. Dabre et al. (2015) studied the use of more than one pivots simultaneously. They also mentioned that the use of pivot for reordering would be an interesting problem.

The reordering model on which we focus in our work is a lexicalized reordering model discussed by Koehn et al. (2005). Lexicalized reordering was first proposed by Tillmann (2004). Similar approach was suggested by Ohashi et al. (2005). Mirkin (2014) proposed several ways for incrementally updating the lexicalized reordering model when new training data is introduced and described a way to combine new and existing reordering models. To the best of our knowledge, no work has been done on triangulation of reordering tables in specific.

3 Background for Our Approaches

Our aim is to generate a source language to target language reordering table given a source language to pivot language reordering table and a pivot language to target language reordering table. This is called as Triangulation of Reordering tables or Reordering Table Triangulation. In this paper, we propose two approaches for triangulation of reordering tables. Both of them make use of reordering tables, which have a peculiar format in Moses, a statistical machine translation system (Koehn et al., 2007). Before going forward with the description of our approaches, we explain the concepts of reordering orientations and give a short overview of the structure of a reordering table in Moses.

3.1 Reordering Orientations: Monotone, Swap and Discontinuous

Moses implements reordering using three kinds of orientations - Monotone, Swap and Discontinuous (Koehn et al., 2005; Koehn, 2009). For each phrase and its corresponding translation, there are three possible orientations.

Let S_1, S_2 be phrases in source sentence, T_1, T_2 be their corresponding translations in the target sentence and T_1 be a phrase that immediately precedes T_2 in the target sentence. Then for the phrase pair (S_2, T_2) the orientation is :

- **Monotone**, if S_1 is a phrase that immediately precedes S_2 in the source sentence.

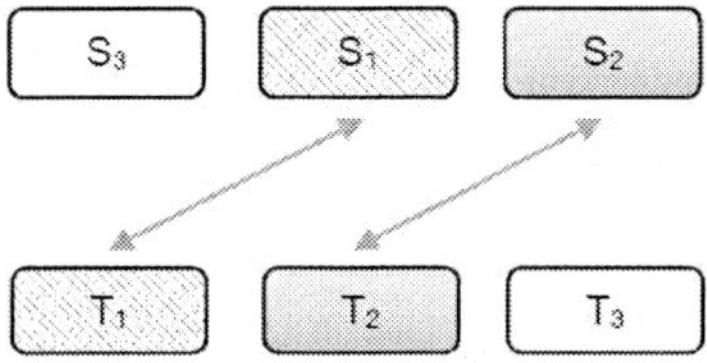

Figure 1: Monotone Orientation

- **Swap**, if S_1 is a phrase that immediately succeeds S_2 in the source sentence.

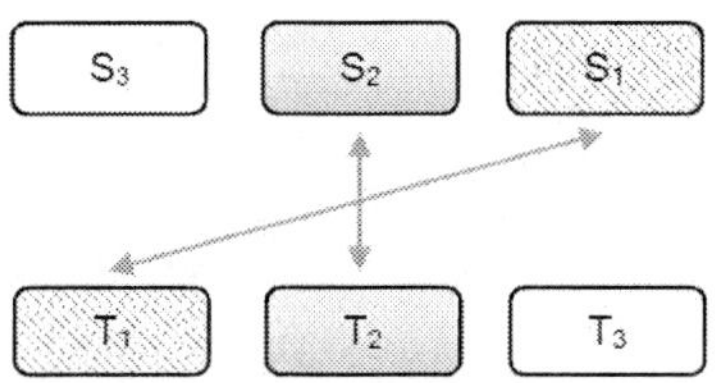

Figure 2: Swap Orientation

- **Discontinuous**, if S_1 and S_2 are not adjacent to each other in the source sentence.

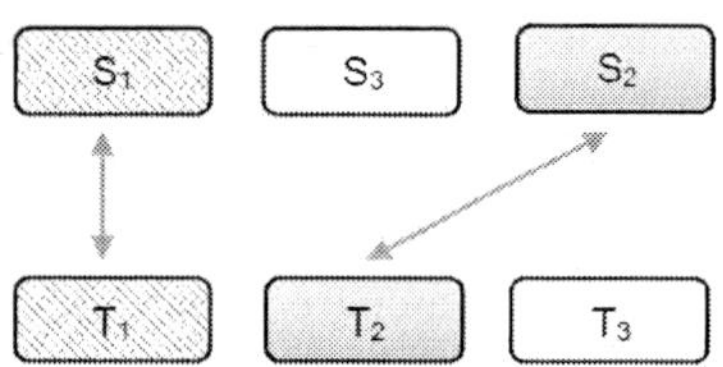

Figure 3: Discontinuous Orientation

Let us consider sentences from English-Marathi language pair shown in Figure 4.

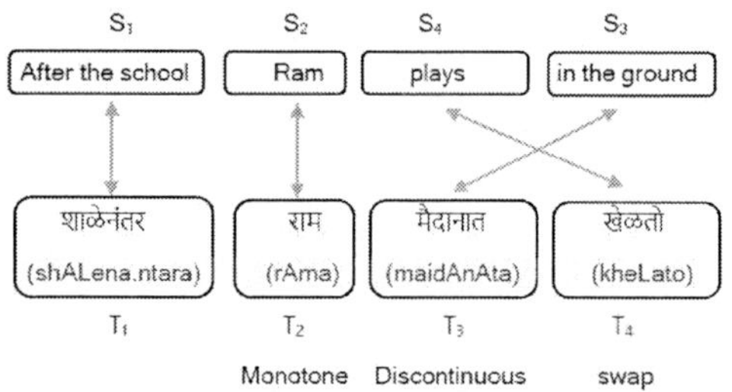

Figure 4: Example depicting all orientations

As per the definitions discussed above, the orientation exhibited by the phrase pair (Ram, राम) is a monotone since, the translation of the previous phrase of राम i.e. 'After the school' is also the previous phrase of 'Ram'. Similarly by definition, (plays, खेळतो) has a swap orientation and (in the ground, मैदानात) has a discontinuous orientation.

3.2 Structure of a Reordering Table in MOSES

As discussed in subsection 3.1, for each phrase pair, there are three reordering orientations possible. A typical reordering table in Moses consists of all such phrase pairs and their respective probability values for monotone, swap and discontinuous orientations.

Following is a sample entry from English-Marathi reordering table.

By looking ||| पाहिल्यावर |||0.2 0.2 0.6 0.2 0.2 0.6

The first three values are the probability values of a phrase pair (By looking, पाहिल्यावर) being a monotone, swap and discontinuous respectively, with respect to the previous phrase of पाहिल्यावर (pAhilyAvara) in the target sentence. The next three values are the probability values of a phrase pair (By looking, पाहिल्यावर) being a monotone, swap and discontinuous respectively,

with respect to the next phrase of पाहिल्यावर in the target sentence.

Reordering table is used during decoding to score the candidate translations. Scoring a particular candidate translation for reordering, involves scoring each phrase with respect to its previous and next phrase. This along with the Language Model, boosts up the scores assigned to better ordered candidate translations.

3.3 Objective of the Approach

Our objective is to determine the probability values discussed in Subsection 3.2, for phrase pairs that are newly extracted by phrase table triangulation, given the source-pivot and pivot-target reordering tables.

We propose two approaches for doing this. Our first approach only assumes the availability of two reordering tables mentioned above, whereas the second approach assumes the availability of a multilingual parallel corpus that is used for training, in addition to the two reordering tables.

4   Mathematical Formulation

For a language pair $L_1 - L_2$, (A, B) is a phrase pair if phrase A from L_1 translates to phrase B from L_2. We will use the notation $O(A \rightarrow B)$ to denote the orientation of a phrase pair (A, B). The possible values of O are $\{M,S,D\}$.
Where,
$M(A \rightarrow B)$: (A, B) has a Monotone orientation
$S(A \rightarrow B)$: (A, B) has a Swap orientation
$D(A \rightarrow B)$: (A, B) has a Discontinuous orientation

For the discussion in this section, let X,Y and Z be the phrases from source, pivot and target languages respectively which are all translations of each other. In other words, (X, Y) is phrase pair from source to pivot, (Y, Z) is a phrase pair from pivot to target and (X, Z) is a phrase pair from source to target.

Let us assume that (X, Z) is a phrase pair that was not originally present in the phrase table and was induced during the phrase table triangulation process. Then our task is to determine the probability values $P[M(X \rightarrow Z)]$, $P[S(X \rightarrow Z)]$ and $P[D(X \rightarrow Z)]$ in order to include an entry for phrase pair (X, Z) in the reordering table.

There can be more than one pivot phrases Y for a particular phrase pair (X, Z). There are also multiple combinations of source-pivot and pivot-target orientations possible for (X, Y) and

(Y, Z) respectively.
Marginalizing over these variables we get,

$$P[M(X \to Z)] =$$

$$\sum_{\substack{Y \\ O(X \to Y) \\ O(Y \to Z)}} P[M(X \to Z), O(X \to Y), O(Y \to Z)] \tag{1}$$

Applying the chain rule, we get,

$$P[M(X \to Z)] =$$

$$\sum_{\substack{Y \\ O(X \to Y) \\ O(Y \to Z)}} P[M(X \to Z)|O(X \to Y), O(Y \to Z)]. \\ P[O(X \to Y), O(Y \to Z)] \tag{2}$$

Since, $O(X \to Y)$ and $O(Y \to Z)$ are independent of each other, applying this independence assumption on second term, we get

$$P[M(X \to Z)] =$$

$$\sum_{\substack{Y \\ O(X \to Y) \\ O(Y \to Z)}} P[M(X \to Z)|O(X \to Y), O(Y \to Z)]. \\ P[O(X \to Y)].P[O(Y \to Z)] \tag{3}$$

$P[O(X \to Y)]$ and $P[O(Y \to Z)]$ are the reordering probability values from source-pivot and pivot-target and are directly available from the reordering tables that are used for triangulation. The first term i.e.

$$P[M(X \to Z)|O(X \to Y), O(Y \to Z)]$$

called a "**Multiplicative Factor**" henceforth, is a probability that for a particular orientation of $O(X \to Y)$ and $O(Y \to Z)$, source-target orientation for (X, Z) is a Monotone, in case of the calculation above. We worked out the mathematics for probability of (X, Z) being a Monotone. Similar calculations can be performed for determining the Swap and Discontinuous probability values. Therefore, similar kind of terms will exist for Swap and Discontinuous as well. The value for the Multiplicative Factor is not directly available to us. For calculating this value we propose two approaches in this paper.

5 Description of the Approaches

For calculating the Multiplicative Factor in Equation 3 we can follow one of the two paths, one is called a *Table Based Approach* and the other is called *Count Based Approach*.

5.1 Table Based Approach

This approach only assumes the availability of two reordering tables: a source language to pivot language reordering table and a pivot language to target language reordering table. Based on all possible source-pivot and pivot-target orientations, we designed an "**Orientation Table**" of all possible source-target orientations, which is shown in Table 1.

	M	S	D
Monotone (M)	M	S, D	S, D
Swap (S)	S	M, D	M, D
Discontinuous (D)	D	M ,S, D	M, S, D

Table 1: Orientation Table

The rows of the Orientation Table($O_i\,'s$) represent different orientations for a source-pivot phrase pair and the columns($O_j\,'s$) represent different orientation for a pivot-target phrase pair, where the pivot phrase is common. A cell which is in row O_i and column O_j lists all possible orientations from source-target when source-pivot orientation is O_i and pivot-target orientation is O_j. For example, assume that S, P, T are phrases from source, pivot and target languages respectively and are translations of each other. If the source-pivot orientation is a monotone for phrase pair (S, P) and the pivot-target orientation is swap for phrase pair (P, T), then for phrase pair (S, T) the orientation can either be a Swap or a Discontinuous. We studied numerous examples from the most general scenarios as well as from specific language pairs, in order to create this table.

We use this table for determining the Multiplicative Factor by looking up into the appropriate cell of the table while doing the computation. We also assume that if there are more than one orientations in a particular cell then all of them are equally likely. We have observed that there might be some wrong translations in the training data because of which the orientations which are not present in a particular cell may also be exhibited by some phrases in some situations, although, such occurrences are few in number. To factor in for such discrepancies, we assume that orientations present in the cells of the above table are the "most probable" ones and other orientations are also possible with a very small probability.

For example, for a phrase pair (S, P) the orientation is monotone and for (P, T) the orientation is

	En-Gu-Hi	En-Hi-Gu	En-Hi-Mr	Hi-Gu-En	Hi-Gu-Mr	Hi-Pa-En	Mr-Gu-Hi	Mr-Gu-En	Mr-Hi-En
DIR-DIR	25.97	16.03	10.12	29.87	33.69	29.78	41.66	16.72	16.77
INTER-DIR	25.83	17.37	13.11	30.01	36.09	29.86	42.58	17.97	19.04
INTER-TRI	25.08	16.94	12.57	28.54	36.13	28.38	42.47	17.70	19.09
INTER-INTER	26.30	17.71	13.19	30.52	36.28	30.39	42.67	18.55	20.10
IMPROVEMENT	**0.47**	**0.34**	**0.08**	**0.51**	**0.19**	**0.53**	**0.09**	**0.58**	**1.06**

Table 2: BLEU Scores for Count Based Approach

(IMPROVEMENT row shows improvement in INTER-INTER system over INTER-DIR system)

swap, then the multiplicative factor while calculating probability of (S, T) being a monotone i.e. $P[M(S \to T)|M(S \to P), S(P \to T)]$ can be assigned a small value, say 0.1, since monotone is not listed in the cell.

The other two orientations are assumed to be equally likely, so in this case

$$P[S(S \to T)|M(S \to P), S(P \to T)] = 0.45$$

and

$$P[D(S \to T)|M(S \to P), S(P \to T)] = 0.45$$

5.2 Count Based Approach

This approach assumes the availability of two reordering tables and the source-pivot-target multilingual parallel corpus that is used for training. By using the definition of probability, the Multiplicative Factor in equation (3) can be written as

$$P[M(S \to T)|O(S \to P), O(P \to T)]$$
$$= \frac{count[M(S \to T), O(S \to P), O(P \to T)]}{count[O(S \to P), O(P \to T)]}$$

Here the numerator is the count of the number of occurrences where phrase pair (S, T) has a monotone orientation when phrase pair (S, P) has a particular orientation O_1 and (P, T) has an orientation O_2. The denominator is the count of the number of occurrences where phrase pair (S, P) has a particular orientation O_1 and (P, T) has an orientation O_2.

Basic idea in the Count Based Approach is to extract these kind of counts from the corpus for each source-target phrase pair. For extracting these counts, say for a phrase pair (S, T), we need to look at the phrases which immediately precede or succeed phrase T in a target sentence and the position of their translations with respect to the position of phrase S in the source sentence. The

counts have to be extracted for each phrase pair and have to be stored separately in order to lookup while doing the computations for reordering table triangulation using this approach. This approach seems more intuitive since we use the parallel corpus for getting the count values and therefore we are likely to get more accurate values for the multiplicative factor.

6 Experimental Setup

We performed several experiments with both the approaches discussed in section 5. The parallel corpus used for the experiments was a Health and Tourism domain multilingual parallel corpus (Jha, 2010) which was divided into a training corpus of 46000 sentences, a tuning corpus of 500 sentences and a test corpus of 2000 sentences. The reason behind using a small sized corpus for our experiments is that, often in a realistic scenario, obtaining a large sized multilingual parallel corpus is difficult.

The tool used for translation was Moses 3.0 (Koehn et al., 2007). It was used for training, tuning(MERT based) and testing the translation systems. We experimented with four kinds of MT systems for 9 different source-pivot-target combinations from the language set {English(En), Hindi(Hi), Marathi(Mr), Gujarati(Gu), Punjabi(Pa)}, mentioned in Table 2. The differences in these systems were in the phrase table and reordering table which each system uses. A 'Direct Phrase table' and a 'Direct Reordering Table' are the tables that are obtained directly from source-target parallel corpus after training. A 'Triangulated Phrase Table' and a 'Triangulated Reordering Table' are the tables that are obtained through the process of triangulation. An 'Interpolated Phrase Table' is a phrase table ob-

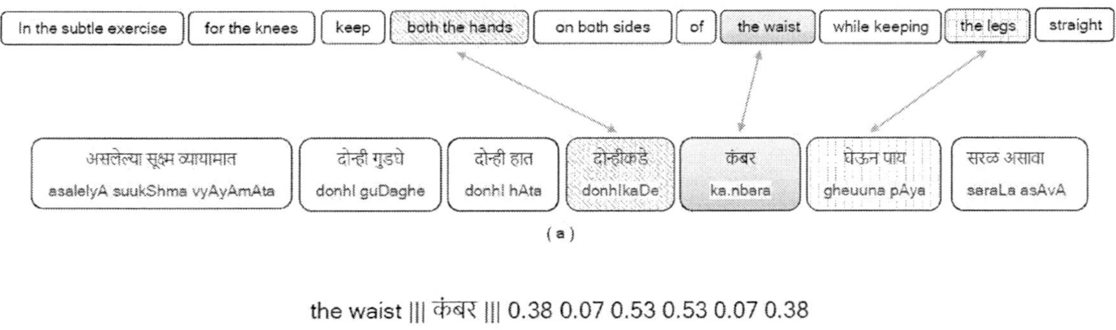

Figure 5: Sample Translation from English-Hindi-Marathi INTER-DIR MT System

tained by linear interpolation of values from Direct Phrase Table and Triangulated Phrase Table. Interpolation of reordering tables can be performed either by linear interpolation or by Fill-up interpolation (Dabre et al., 2015) of Direct and Triangulated Reordering Tables. With this terminology in place, below is a small description of each system.

- **DIR-DIR** : This system uses a Direct Phrase Table and a Direct Reordering Table.

- **INTER-DIR** : This system uses an Interpolated Phrase Table and a Direct Reordering table.

- **INTER-TRI** : This system uses an Interpolated Phrase Table and a Triangulated Reordering table.

- **INTER-INTER** : This system uses an Interpolated Phrase Table and an Interpolated Reordering table.

7 Results and Discussion

We performed experiments for both Table Based and Count Based approaches. The improvements were observed from the quantitative point of view - in the BLEU scores (Papineni et al., 2002) - as well as from the qualitative point of view - in the reordering of the translation that a system produces and better lexical choice in the translation.

7.1 Improvements in BLEU Scores

For the table based approach, we found an improvement of 0.48 in the BLEU score from 17.98 for INTER-DIR system to 18.46 for INTER-INTER system, for Marathi to English translation when Gujarati is used as a pivot. Small improvements were also observed for other systems,

like Hindi-Gujarati-English (0.4), Hindi-Punjabi-English (0.33) and Hindi-Gujarati-Marathi (0.16). The improvements in other five systems were not as significant as these. This was an expected pattern in the results since, the Table Based approach does not actually look at the training data while calculating the Multiplicative Factor. In this approach, Multiplicative Factor is calculated based on the Orientation Table which is training data independent. Therefore, the approach was expected to perform better in some situations than others.

On the other hand, the Count Based approach extracts the counts for orientations from the training corpus. Thus the calculated Multiplicative Factor is more accurate as compared to the Table Based approach. So we expected the Count Based approach to outperform the Table Based and produce an improvement in the BLEU score for most of the source-pivot-target language combinations. This is indeed the case and the results for Count Based approach are shown in Table 2. The improvements vary with language combinations because of the difference in the quality of the counts that are extracted for each combination.

The improvement from DIR-DIR system to INTER-DIR system is because of the phrase table triangulation and addition of newly extracted phrase pairs in the phrase table. Therefore, in order to quantify the improvement in BLEU score that is solely achieved by our approach, we consider INTER-DIR system as our baseline for all experiments. We can see from Table 2, that significant improvements are achieved by INTER-INTER systems over INTER-DIR systems in case of most language combinations. INTER-TRI system does not outperform INTER-DIR system since, it uses only the Triangulated Reordering ta-

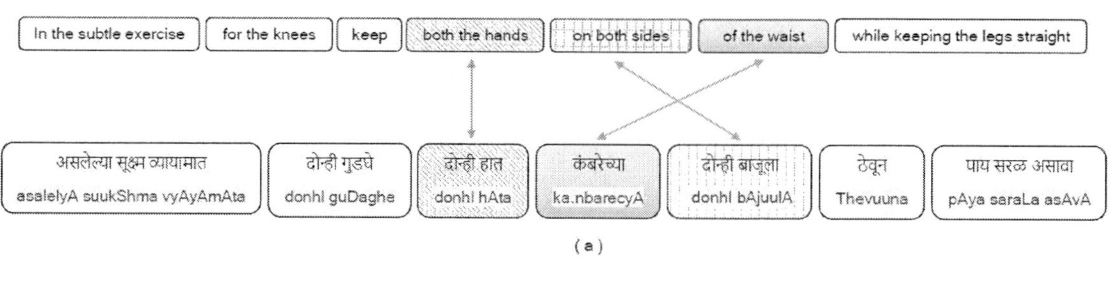

(a)

of the waist ||| कंबरेच्या ||| 0.27 0.27 0.45 0.27 0.45 0.27

(b)

Figure 6: Sample Translation from English-Hindi-Marathi INTER-INTER MT System

ble which mostly contains entries for only newly extracted phrase pairs. INTER-INTER systems perform better as expected, since knowledge from both, Direct and Triangulated Reordering tables is combined and used in these systems.

7.2 Qualitative Improvement in Reordering

Let us closely look at an actual translation example from the test corpus to clearly understand, how calculating reordering probability values for newly added phrase pairs helps in improving the quality of translation. It must be noted that, although the reordering information is not available for newly added phrase pairs in INTER-DIR system, they may still end up being a part of the best possible translation because of other factors involved such as Phrase Translation Probability and Language Model. For example, a newly induced phrase pair may have higher phrase translation probability than other phrase pairs, which results in that phrase being a part of the best candidate translation. This phenomenon is responsible for the improvement that is achieved by INTER-DIR system over DIR-DIR system.

Figure 5(a) shows the translation example from English-Hindi-Marathi INTER-DIR system and Figure 6(a) shows the translation example from English-Hindi-Marathi INTER-INTER system. From the phrase tables, we observed that the phrase pair (of the waist, कंबरेच्या) was added through triangulation of phrase tables. So, in INTER-DIR system, there are no reordering probability values available for this phrase pair, but in the INTER-INTER system, the reordering table has an entry for this phrase pair with reordering probability values. Figure 6(b) shows that reordering table entry for this phrase pair.

The translation produced by INTER-DIR system shown in Figure 5(a), will also be produced as a candidate translation by INTER-INTER system, but the INTER-INTER system discards it to choose the translation shown in Figure 6(a) as the best translation, since the reordering probability values for the new phrase pair play a vital role. If we look at figure 5(b), the reordering probability values for (the waist, कंबर) favour discontinuous orientation with respect to the previous phrase and monotone orientation with respect to the next phrase. But the translation that is generated has a discontinuous orientation for the phrase कंबर with respect to both previous and next phrases. Since the generated candidate is not in accordance with the values from reordering table, the candidate gets a relatively lesser score.

On the other hand, if we look at Figure 6(b), the reordering probability values for (of the waist, कंबरेच्या) favour discontinuous orientation with respect to the previous phrase and swap orientation with respect to the next phrase. The translation that is generated as a candidate, shown in Figure 6(a), also has discontinuous orientation with respect to the previous phrase and swap orientation with respect to the next phrase, for the phrase कंबरेच्या. Since the candidate is in accordance with the values from reordering table, the candidate gets a higher score as compared to the earlier candidate. There are also other factors like translation model and language model that contribute to the computation, but in this example the contribution by reordering probabilities is distinctly evident. We can see that the inclusion of reordering information for newly added phrase pair has also induced **better lexical choices** in the translation.

This leads to the translation shown in Figure

6(a) being selected as the best translation. It can be easily observed that the translation is a better one in terms of reordering. This shows that our approach works well to improve the quality of translation.

Following is another example from Marathi-Hindi-English system that shows qualitative improvement in the reordering of phrases in the output translation.

Input:
खूप अशक्त असूनही रुग्णाला आपले वजन जास्त वाटते.
(khuupa ashakta asuunahI rugNAlA Apale vajana jAsta vATate .)

English Equivalent (Reference):
Patient thinks his / her weight to be too much even on being very weak .

Output of INTER-DIR System:
Despite weight of the patient has to be extremely weak .

Output of INTER-INTER System:
despite being very weak patient feels more your weight .

It is evident from the example that the output of INTER-INTER system is better ordered than the output of INTER-DIR system. Except for the word "your", the meaning of the source sentence is better conveyed by the output of INTER-INTER system.

8 Conclusion and Future Work

The issue of data scarcity has been addressed effectively by Phrase Table triangulation. In this paper we went a step further and proposed two new approaches for the triangulation of reordering tables viz. Table Based approach and Count Based approach. We conducted experiments with both these approaches on 9 different translation systems, each using a different combination of source-pivot-target languages and found significant improvements in the BLEU scores for most of the systems. We also discussed actual translation examples that showed a qualitative improvement in the reordering of the output, thereby vindicating the fact that better reordering information can be extracted through a pivot. Examples also showed that the lexical choices made by the system improved when our approach was used. We also observed that Count Based approach performed better than Table Based approach for most of the language combinations.

The focus of our work was on finding the reordering probability values for phrase pairs that are newly added to the phrase table through the use of a pivot. The question that remains is, whether a pivot can help beyond extracting these reordering values. Another interesting question is whether this approach scales well to a scenario where more than one pivots are used simultaneously. We will try to focus on these points in the future.

Acknowledgement

We would like to thank Mr. Anoop Kunchukuttan and Mr. Rohit More from Centre For Indian Language Technology, IIT Bombay for their valuable inputs and suggestions and for the insightful discussions on the topic.

References

Raj Dabre, Fabien Cromieres, Sadao Kurohashi, and Pushpak Bhattacharyya. 2015. Leveraging small multilingual corpora for smt using many pivot languages. In *Proceedings of the 2015 Conference of the North American Chapter of the Association for Computational Linguistics: Human Language Technologies*, pages 1192–1202, Denver, Colorado, May–June. Association for Computational Linguistics.

Girish Nath Jha. 2010. The tdil program and the indian language corpora initiative (ilci). In *Proceedings of the Seventh Conference on International Language Resources and Evaluation (LREC 2010). European Language Resources Association (ELRA)*.

Philipp Koehn, Amittai Axelrod, Alexandra Birch, Chris Callison-Burch, Miles Osborne, David Talbot, and Michael White. 2005. Edinburgh system description for the 2005 iwslt speech translation evaluation. In *IWSLT*, pages 68–75.

Philipp Koehn, Hieu Hoang, Alexandra Birch, Chris Callison-Burch, Marcello Federico, Nicola Bertoldi, Brooke Cowan, Wade Shen, Christine Moran, Richard Zens, et al. 2007. Moses: Open source toolkit for statistical machine translation. In *Proceedings of the 45th annual meeting of the ACL on interactive poster and demonstration sessions*, pages 177–180. Association for Computational Linguistics.

Philipp Koehn. 2009. *Statistical machine translation*. Cambridge University Press.

Shachar Mirkin. 2014. Incrementally updating the smt reordering model. In *Proceedings of The 28th Pacific Asia Conference on Language, Information and Computing (PACLIC), Phuket, Thailand.*

Preslav Nakov and Hwee Tou Ng. 2012. Improving statistical machine translation for a resource-poor language using related resource-rich languages. *Journal of Artificial Intelligence Research*, pages 179–222.

Kazuteru Ohashi, Kazuhide Yamamoto, Kuniko Saito, and Masaaki Nagata. 2005. Nut-ntt statistical machine translation system for iwslt 2005. In *IWSLT*, pages 118–123.

Kishore Papineni, Salim Roukos, Todd Ward, and Wei-Jing Zhu. 2002. Bleu: a method for automatic evaluation of machine translation. In *Proceedings of the 40th annual meeting on association for computational linguistics*, pages 311–318. Association for Computational Linguistics.

Christoph Tillmann. 2004. A unigram orientation model for statistical machine translation. In *Proceedings of HLT-NAACL 2004: Short Papers*, pages 101–104. Association for Computational Linguistics.

Masao Utiyama and Hitoshi Isahara. 2007. A comparison of pivot methods for phrase-based statistical machine translation. In *HLT-NAACL*, pages 484–491. Citeseer.

Haifeng Wang, Hua Wu, and Zhanyi Liu. 2006. Word alignment for languages with scarce resources using bilingual corpora of other language pairs. In *Proceedings of the COLING/ACL on Main conference poster sessions*, pages 874–881. Association for Computational Linguistics.

Hua Wu and Haifeng Wang. 2007. Pivot language approach for phrase-based statistical machine translation. *Machine Translation*, 21(3):165–181.

Hua Wu and Haifeng Wang. 2009. Revisiting pivot language approach for machine translation. In *Proceedings of the Joint Conference of the 47th Annual Meeting of the ACL and the 4th International Joint Conference on Natural Language Processing of the AFNLP: Volume 1-Volume 1*, pages 154–162. Association for Computational Linguistics.

Post-editing a chapter of a specialized textbook into 7 languages: importance of terminological proximity with English for productivity

Ritesh Shah[1,2*], Christian Boitet[1†], Pushpak Bhattacharyya[2‡],
Mithun Padmakumar[1], Leonardo Zilio[1], Ruslan Kalitvianski[1],
Mohammad Nasiruddin[1], Mutsuko Tomokiyo[1], and Sandra Castellanos Páez[1]

[1]GETALP-LIG, Université Grenoble-Alpes, Grenoble, France
[2]CFILT, Indian Institute of Technology, Mumbai, India

Abstract

Access to textbooks in one's own language, in parallel with the original version in the instructional language, is known to be quite helpful for foreign students studying abroad. Cooperative post-editing (PE) of specialized textbook pretranslations by the foreign students themselves is a good way to produce the "target" versions, if the students find it rewarding, and not too time-consuming, that is, no longer than about 15-20 minutes per standard page (of 1400 characters or 250 words). In the experiment reported here, PE has been performed on a whole chapter of 4420 words (in English), or about 18 standard pages, into 7 languages (Portuguese, Japanese, Russian, Spanish, Bengali, Hindi, Marathi), native tongues of the participants. Average PE time has been measured, and when possible correlated with primary PE time (the time spent in editing a MT pre-translation in the PE text area). When terms are cognates of English terms (as in French, Spanish, Portuguese, and even Russian or Japanese), because neologisms are directly borrowed from English, or built using similar roots (often Latin or Greek) and similar word formation mechanisms (composition, affixation of special prefixes and suffixes), target terms can be "guessed" and PE time is in the order of 15 minutes per page, even if the target language is considered "distant" from English. On the other hand, PE times increase by a factor of 3 to 5 when the target language is terminologically distant from English. We found that is the case of Hindi, Bengali and Marathi, and probably of all Indic languages. Previous experiments seem to have missed that important point, because they were performed on too short texts (often, only a few paragraphs), and on "easy" pairs like English-French. A consequence is that, for terminologically distant language pairs, one should begin by separately collecting, or if necessary coining, the terms in the target languages.

1 Introduction

We are interested by using existing Machine Translation (MT) systems in the situations where their output does not (and often cannot, because, in its general form, MT is an "AI-complete" problem) provide "good enough" results. Post-editing MT results has been a professional activity in Japan since about 1985 (Nagao et al., 1985), and professional translators have begun to adopt that approach in other countries. Speaking of "translation accelerators", see for example the systems deployed at WIPO[1] and UN[2] (Pouliquen et al., 2013; Pouliquen and Mazenc, 2011a; Pouliquen and Mazenc, 2011b).

There are other situations in which MT outputs could be brought to a quality "good enough" for goals requiring a high level of precision and reliability. One of them is making pedagogical material accessible to foreign students in their own language. Cooperative post-editing (PE) of free MT pre-translations by the foreign students themselves is a good way to produce the "target" versions, if the students find it rewarding, and not too time-consuming., that is, if PE takes them no longer than about 15-20 minutes per standard page (of 1400 characters or 250 words).

---

*Ritesh.Shah@imag.fr
†Christian.Boitet@imag.fr
‡pb@cse.iitb.ac.in

[1]World Intellectual Property Organization
[2]The United Nations

D S Sharma, R Sangal and E Sherly. Proc. of the 12th Intl. Conference on Natural Language Processing, pages 325–332,
Trivandrum, India. December 2015. ©2015 NLP Association of India (NLPAI)

Having validated that idea since 2-3 years on the French-Chinese (fr-zh) language pair, with the participation of 6 Chinese students in an experiment concerning mainly informatics and mathematics, we wanted to investigate the feasibility of using that approach for other language pairs and other scientific domains. Note that, in that particular experiment, students had studied informatics at home before going abroad, knew most of the Chinese terminology, and had access to online French-English and English-Chinese lexicons. A natural question arises: is this approach usable for all situations < domain, instructional language, native tongue >? By 'native tongue', we understand not only the language spoken at home, but the language or languages of education, like Hindi and English in India.

In the fall of 2013, we had the opportunity to start an experiment involving a group of researchers, mostly PhD students, of 8 different native languages[3]: Portuguese (pt), Japanese (ja), Russian (ru), Spanish (es), Bengali (bn), Hindi (hi), Marathi (mr), and Malayalam (ml).

The Malayalam native speaker, PhD student of biological engineering, selected the text to be translated in his speciality, and organized the experiment, which lasted several months as we wanted it to be performed in realistic conditions, that is, with post-editors contributing occasionally. He could not do PE into Malayalam as there was no available en-ml MT system at the time, but he was initially expected to help with terminology in Hindi (his second language of education, English being his main one since college).

The text he selected was chapter 21 of the BEMbook (Malmivuo and Plonsey, 1995), a textbook in English on bioelectromagnetism, of about 700 pages, that is available freely online. This chapter contains 4420 words (in English) or about 18 standard pages.

The rest of this paper is organized as follows. We begin with more details on our motivations and discuss some related work on post-editing (PE). We then present the experimental setup and the use of the iMAG/SECTra tool along with the PE statistics. The next section gives quantitative and qualitative results, and analyzes why PE time, typically between 15 and 30 mn/page, was considerably longer for the 3 Indian languages (bn, hi, mr).

In short, the reason reported by the participants (post-editors) is that they ignored many existing technical terms *(latent terminology)*, or that, even worse, but a frequent case, there were no equivalent terms in their language *(absent terminology)*, in which case it was necessary to coin them after a long and fruitless search.

A deeper reason is probably that these languages are "terminologically distant" from English, that is, neologisms are not "cognates" of English neologisms: most of the time, they are not directly borrowed from English, and they are not built using similar roots (often Latin or Greek) and similar word formation mechanisms (composition, affixation of special prefixes and suffixes) as in English. Rather, they use roots coming from the Sanskrit or the Arabo-persian lexical store.

2 Motivations and objectives

2.1 Need for enabling access to pedagogical documents by foreign students

The needs for enabling access to pedagogical documents by foreign students in their native tongues has been long recognized. In Europe, the Bologna EU research project (2010-2013) attacked the task with the goal to make all syllabi of the European universities involved in the Erasmus project available in English and Chinese (Pietrzak et al., 2013; Depraetere et al., 2011; Depraetere and Van de Walle, 2012; Van de Walle et al., 2012b; Van de Walle et al., 2012a).

That was meant as a first step toward making course material also available, in those and more languages. The envisaged method was to build high-quality (HQ) specialized Statistical Machine Translation (SMT) systems to translate the corresponding web (*HTML*) pages and *PDF* files. Post-editing was seen only as a complement, to be added later if output quality did not meet expectations.

The choice of these 2 target languages was due to the large proportion of Chinese students in Europe, English being a natural "first step" as almost all European students studying within Erasmus must have quite good TOEIC[4], TOEFL[5] or IELTS[6] grades.

Like the proponents of the Bologna project, we think the real need is that foreign students get ac-

---

[3]Language code ISO639-2: https://www.loc.gov/standards/iso639-2/php/code_list.php

[4]Test of English for International Communication
[5]Test of English as a Foreign Language
[6]International English Language Testing System

cess not only to courses and tutorials, but also to notes from fellow students, in their respective languages, and possibly in parallel with the original (Kalitvianski et al., 2012).

Simultaneously, they should also be invited to participate and improve the translations as time progresses. A subgoal is also that they learn better the language of their host university.

2.2 Obstacles

The Bologna project started well, with clearly defined goals, and produced the beginning of a web service. However, very few syllabi were accessible, and the quality was not comparable with that of GT (Google Translate), Systran or Reverso. As no collaborative PE framework was included in the design, it could not be added afterwards and also could not produce a long-lasting service. This is no exception: less than 18 months after the end of the project, the Bologna web service was discontinued.

With our approach, immediate access in all languages for which MT is available is provided. But how to guarantee that a "good enough" quality level will be attained, and when?

A first answer is that students interested in accessing the content of these web pages and documents are usually only interested in some portion of them, and will "contribute" some corrections to improve segments they have not well understood. An important idea is that they will not do it only for themselves, to find "their" version when coming back later to the web page or document, but also for their fellows in the "virtual community" of the internauts sharing their language and wanting to access the same content.

A second answer is that "good enough" can be defined by some "self-scoring" mechanism. In SECtra/iMAG, each segment has a *reliability level*[7] and a *quality score* between 0 and 20[8].While the reliability level is fixed by the tool, the quality score can be modified by the post-editor (initially,

---

[7]* for dictionary-based translation, ** for MT output, *** for PE by a blingual contributor, *** for PE by a professional translatior, and ***** for PE by a translator "certified" by the producer of the content.

[8]10: pass, 12: good enough, 14: good, 16: very good, 18: exceptional, 20: perfect. 8-9: not satisfied with something in the PE. 6-7: sure to have produced a bad translation! 4-5: the PE corresponds to a text differing from that of the source segment. That happens when a senetnce has been erroneoulsy split into 2 segments and the order of words is different in the 2 languages. 2: the source segment was already in the target language.

it is that defined in his profile) or by any reader.

We can then say that the quality of the PE of a segment is deemed to be "good enough" if its quality score is higher or equal to 12/20.

2.3 Hypotheses and motivations behind the experiment

Our first hypothesis is that the objective is reachable only if PE is put at the center of the approach, and if foreign students that can benefit from it, do it themselves in a voluntary fashion.

Our second hypothesis is that we need to consider many more target languages than English and Chinese, including languages that are terminologically less equipped, for instance Arabic and South and South-East languages. Having the knowledge of an experiment (Wang and Boitet, 2013) in fr-zh for 1 year (in which the authors did not take part), we wanted to investigate the possiblity to do it for many languages, and to isolate the positive and negative factors, according to the target languages and to the profiles of the contributors.

3 Experiment

3.1 Setting

We considered the following constraints:

- to translate into as many target languages as possible, some of them being "distant" from English,

- to have as participants mostly PhD students, and all native speakers of the target languages,

- to tackle a text of significant length, in a representative document,

- to use available and free online MT systems.

3.1.1 Participants

The first thing was to assemble a team of volunteers, native speakers of several target languages. The candidate languages (native tongues of members of our lab) were Arabic, Bengali, Bulgarian, Chinese, French, German, Gujarati, Hindi, Japanese, Malayalam, Marathi, Portuguese, Russian, Somali, Spanish, Ukrainian, and Vietnamese. However, participants were available only for 8 languages (Portuguese, Japanese, Russian, Spanish, Bengali, Hindi, Marathi, Malayalam). Considering this set of target languages, and direct MT systems availability, English was the only choice for the source language. Unfortunately, at the time there was no MT system into Malayalam, so we had to skip the en-ml pair.

3.1.2   Choice of text

We had set up in 2011 an iMAG for the BEMbook(Malmivuo and Plonsey, 1995), for the benefit of a few French students in 2nd year of biology. Although they had bought the hard copy and knew English quite well (B2 level), they said it was quite helpful to access some difficult passages in French. In this case, MT outputs from GT were used, and the students post-edited 15% to 20% of the segments (sentences or titles) they accessed, but did not touch Chapter 21.

As said above, we selected chapter 21 because it was the most interesting for the PhD student in biology (native speaker of Malayalam).

This chapter has 374 segments, 4420 words and an average segment length of 22.22 words. It includes 10 diagrams, 13 equations, 11 section titles and sub-titles, 15 tables, 660 hapaxes (single-occurence words, and 6 scientific definitions spanning 62 segments.

Figure 1 below gives a screenshot of a typical passage from Chapter 21.

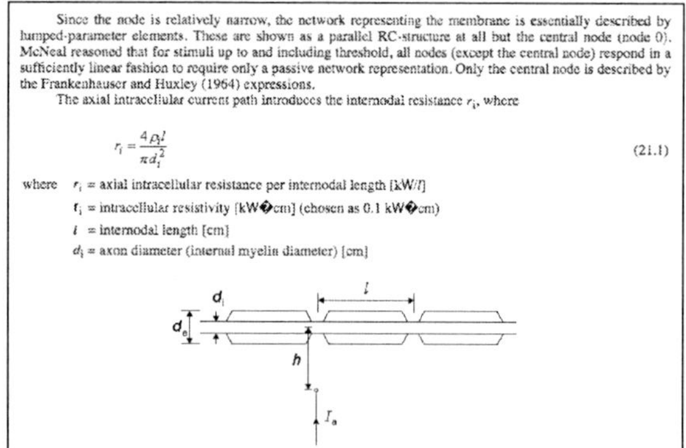

Figure 1: Passage of BEMbook Chapter 21, with 5 sentences. The 5th contains in-line mathematical symbols, not to be translated but kept as is, a numbered stand-alone mathematical equation. The last part is a diagram.

Segmentation is often a problem. For example, in Figure 2 we show 3 successive segments produced by Google's segmenter for the 5th sentence of that screenshot. Actually, the linguistic "segment", corresponding to a sentence, is much longer: the beginning of the sentence, then an in-line mathematical relation that can function as a verbal phrase or as a proper noun, and the end of the sentence, made of a "where" dominating 3 bullet items, each of them giving the definition of some symbol.

The axial intracellular current path introduces the internodal resistance r_i, where

$$r_i = \frac{4\rho_i l}{\pi d_i^2}$$

where ra = axial intracellular resistance per internodal length [kW/l]; ri = intracellular resistivity [kWcm] (chosen as 0.1 kWcm); 1 = internodal length [cm]; di = axone diameter(internal myelin diameter) [cm]

Figure 2. Segments produced by Google

3.1.3   Post-editing times

The time we want to measure is Tpe_{tot}, the *total PE time*, expressed in mn/p (minutes per page). That time can be split in two parts, Tpe_1 and Tpe_2, such that $Tpe_{tot} = Tpe_1 + Tpe_2$:

1. Tpe_1, the *primary PE time*, is the time taken to perform editing operations in SECTra PE text area, or in the iMAG palette text area.

2. Tpe_2, the *secondary PE time*, is the time taken to perform other activities, essentially looking for lexical equivalents.

For a segment seg, $Tpe_1(seg)$ is measured by SECTra when PE of seg is done in SECTra (advanced mode). It is not yet measured by the iMAG. An ongoing research shows however that $Tpe_1(seg)$ can be estimated from the "mixed PE distance" $\Delta_\alpha(pt, pe)$[9] between the pre-translation pt and its post-edition, pe.

---

[9]For two strings A and B, the distance in characters, $\Delta_c(A, B)$, is the usual Levenshtein distance, with all weights set to 1 (for inserting, deletion and exchange). If the words of A and B are $a_1 \ldots a_m$ and $b_1 \ldots b_n$, the distance in words, $\Delta_w(A, B)$, is again the edit distance, but this time considering the set of words in A and B to the a new "alphabet", and the weights of exchanges, insertions and deletions are the character distances: $EXC(u, v) = \Delta_c(u, v)$, $INS(u) = DEL(u) = \Delta_c(\varepsilon, u)$. Finally, $\Delta_\alpha(pt, pe) = \alpha\Delta_c(pt, pe) + (1 - \alpha)\Delta_w(pt, pe)$ with $\alpha \in [0, 1]$.

In this experiment, the post-editors have been asked to time their total times globally, that is, to record every time they did some PE, typically for less than 1 hour, the list of segments post-edited, and the total elapsed time. Using a proportional rule, we could then estimate $Tpe_{tot}(seg)$ for each segment seg.

3.2 Environment

We used the iMAG/SECTra tool as it was, without any special addition. PE is possible in both direct mode (on the web page) and advanced mode (on SECTra table-like PE interface). Figure 3 shows the direct interface (a palette on the web page, much like the Google Translate palette) and Figure 4 the advanced interface. Participants were asked to measure their overall time, and to use the interface to "self-score". As said above, PE time (only Tpe_1) is measured for each segment by the system, but only in the dedicated interface.

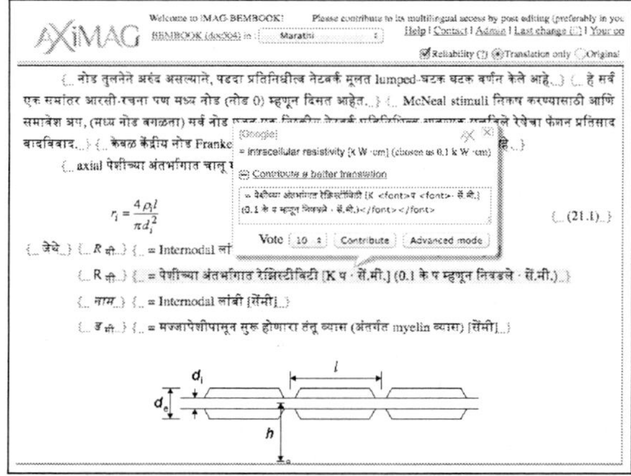

Figure 3. Post-editing on the web page. Reliability brackets appear around each segment: red for MT result, green for PE by a connected participant, orange for an anonymous contributor.

3.3 Unfolding

The experiment spanned about 9 months (1/10/2013-15/6/2014), because participants worked incrementally for short periods of time, which is what is expected in "real life".

3.3.1 Organization

A strong organization was not needed, but something of that kind emerged:

- There was a global "animation" by Par-

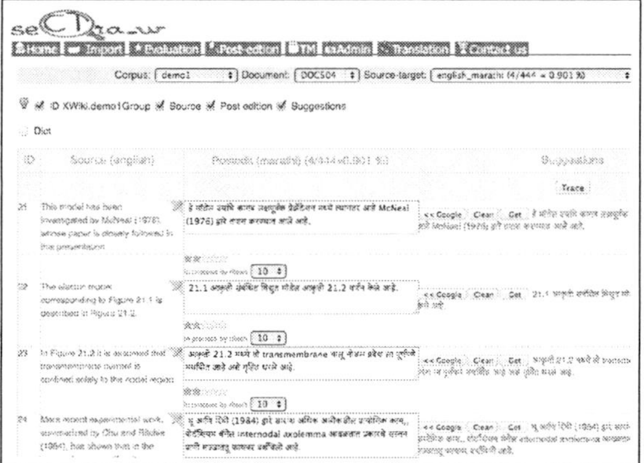

Figure 4. Table-like SECTra "advanced" PE interface. In this interface, the post-editor can choose from which MT result to start, in case more than one is available, and give himself or herself a score differing from the default score associated to his/her profile. The "reliability level" (between 3 stars and 5 stars) cannot be modified, but the "quality score" can. If a segment has been post-edited, the time taken in the PE window (Tpe_1) appears (in blue).

tic_ml[10], who could not PE himself due to the lack of MT into Malayalam.

- Joint work was done on Hindi and Marathi. It was coordinated and done 80% by Partic_hi_mr with the cooperation of Partic_ml.

- Partic_bn and other participants worked alone.

3.3.2 Particular points

Partic_sp had deadlines for exams and reports and could only post-edit about 60% into Spanish.

The terminological help initially expected from Partic_ml to find or create terms in Hindi did not materialize, because Partic_ml was educated in Malayalam and English, and learned Hindi only upto something like B2 level, with no introduction to technical terms, that are no more similar between Dravidian and Indo-Aryan languages than between English and Indo-Aryan languages.

By contrast, new terms can usually be coined quite easily from English (or French) terms that have a Latin or Greek etymology, into Romance languages as well as into Slavic languages. For Japanese (and French, for that matter), new terms

---

[10]Participant for Malayalam language.

are often initially directly borrowed from English, to be later (not always) superseded by terms coined using the lexical store and word formation methods of the language.

Some automatic term-coining from English into Bulgarian was already reported in (Nikolova and Nenova, 1982), and in this case it worked also into Russian.

4 Evaluation and discussion

4.1 Quantitative results

Language	Segments	Words	Words/segment (average)	Standard pages (250 words)	Time/std_page (seconds)	Time/std_page (minutes)
English (source)	*374*	*4420*	*11.82*	*17.7*	-	-
Portuguese	374	6232	16.66	24.9	926.2	15.5
Japanese	374	5000	13.37	20.0	937.2	15.6
Russian	374	4800	12.83	19.2	1037.4	17.2
Spanish	164	2583	15.75	10.3	1940.0	32.2
Bengali	365	4472	12.25	17.9	4666.5	**77.7**
Hindi	374	4547	12.16	18.2	6549.7	**109.2**
Marathi	374	4672	12.49	18.7	7087.6	**118.1**

Table 1. Time (Tpe_{tot}) taken for post-editing Chapter 21 of the BEMbook into 7 languages

From Table 1, we observe that PE was complete or nearly complete for all languages, save Spanish.

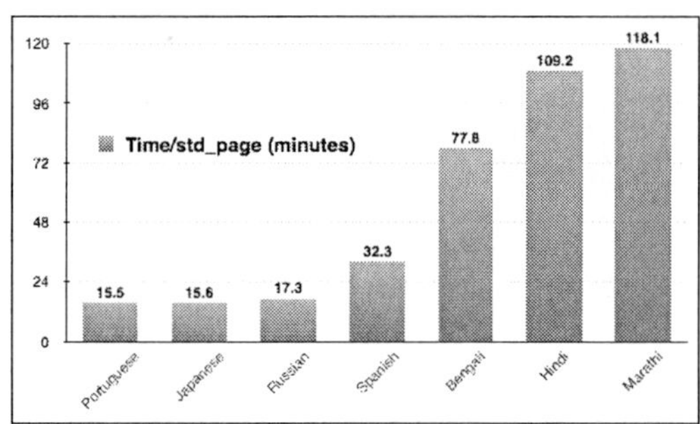

Figure 5: Plot of total post-editing times (in minutes per standard page)

4.2 Qualitative results

The final outputs obtained are all of the *expected quality level*. That means, as said above, that the quality score of each segment is higher or equal to 12/20. When the posteditors set that score, they do it by answering the question: "how good is this translation now for my usage, and presumably for the usage of future readers in my language?"

That means that, in this case, there is not much more one can do: producers are consumers of their own productions, hence they are in the bst position to judge them.

4.3 Impact of lack of terminology or terminological competence

As can be seen on Figure 5, the PE time per standard page is considerably higher for the Indic languages than for the others. Participants for the three Indic languages indicated that this increase was essentially due to lack of knowledge of specific terms, or to their absence in the language, meaning neologisms had to be created.

On the other hand, when terms are cognates of English terms (as in French, Spanish, Portuguese, and even Russian or Japanese), because neologisms are directly borrowed from English, or built using similar roots (often Latin or Greek) and similar word formation mechanisms (composition, affixation of special prefixes and suffixes), target terms can be "guessed" and PE time is in the order of 15 minutes per page, even if the target language is considered "distant" from English.

In fact, posteditors in the other languages (non Indic, here) had no problem to "deduce" terms in their languages from the English terms, by applying some simple spelling and transliteration changes.

4.3.1 Difficulty in finding an existing term in the 3 Indic languages considered

There were nearly 660 hapaxes in the post-edited chapter, about 300 of them being technical terms. Almost all these terms were understood by the Indian post-editors, but they did not know their equivalent in their languages. They of course began by looking for them in terminological sources, such as [http://cstt.nic.in] for instance, for English-Hindi pair. A successful search typically took 3 to 5 minutes, but an unsuccessful search (in several sources) took 4 times as much.

As a consequence, PE times increased by a factor of 3 to 5 when the target language was Hindi, Bengali and Marathi. The same thing would most probably happen with all other Indic languages.

4.3.2 How did we coin a non-existing term in Hindi or Marathi?

In case a term was not found, it had to be assembled (in case of a compound term in English), or transliterated. We give examples below. Assembling a term took typically 20 to 30 minutes, because there are usually several plausible choices, that had to be discussed between participants and sometimes with colleagues over the web.

Some examples of "assembled" terms are shown in Figure 6.

```
hyperpolarization अतिध्रुवण
stimulation उद् दीपन
electrode characteristics इलैक्ट्रोड अभिलक्षण (found together)
electrode current इलैक्ट्रोड धारा (found together)
electrode dissolution  इलैक्ट्रोड विलयन (found separately)
capacitance धारिता
nodal membrane निस्पंद/निस्पंदीय/नोड/नोडल झिल्ली (found separately with variations in dictionary itself)
threshold level देहली स्तर
```

Figure 6: Examples of "assembled" technical terms in Hindi

4.3.3 Why this factor is predominant but has not been considered in most previous studies?

Going from 15 mn/page to 1h15 mn/page makes of course a huge difference, and it is mainly attributable to the "terminological problem". However, previous studies such as (Green et al., 2013) did not mention it.

There may be several reasons for that. First, these experiments have usually been done on a few paragraphs only. Second, the material was selected in domains that were quite familiar to the participants, and not too specialized, so that post-editors always knew the lexical equivalents in their languages.

In fact, the *terminological problem* appears only (with that severity) when

- the 2 languages are terminologically distant (as defined above),

- the terminology in the target language is largely latent (hence, ignored by the post-editors), or worse absent.

5   Conclusion and perspectives

In this paper, we have presented an experiment in post-editing part of the online version of a textbook in English on bioelectromagnetism, the BEMbook, by a group 6 PhD students and a senior researcher, of 7 different native tongues (Portuguese, Japanese, Russian, Spanish, Bengali, Hindi, Marathi), using the iMAG/SECtra tool.

The goal was to investigate the feasibility of using that approach to make pedagogical material available to foreign students or to students studying abroad in their native tongues, with a PE time that was hoped to remain aound 15 mn/page.

The result is that it is quite possible, but that the post-editing time, typically between 15 and 30 mn/page, can considerably increase if many technical terms are ignored by the post-editors, or even worse when they are absent, which was the case for the 3 Indic languagues (bn, hi, mr). More precisely, about 1 hour per page can be added in case the lack (or ignorance) of terminology is significant.

A consequence is that, for terminologically distant language pairs, one should begin by collecting, or if necessary coining, the terms in the target languages, before asking foreign students to use our web service to access pedagogical material in their native languages, improving the quality of the text as a byproduct of their learning activity, spending a reasonable time in cooperative PE.

That is actually what is done in all professional or semi-professional translation and localization projects, for example in the localization projects integrated into large open source projects such as Mozilla.

In the context of "contributive PE", something more will be needed, so that the initially collected or coined bilingual terminology does not become obsolete with time, but "lives" with the PE activity using it.

What we plan, then, is to set up a contributive web service containing a multilingual lexical database with a simple "sharing-oriented" structure, like PIVAX (H.T. Nguyen 2008), and an instance of SepT[11], a kind of lexical network structure for collaboratively proposing terms as a kind of parallel "preterminological" activity.

Acknowledgements

We are grateful to UJF (Université Joseph Fourier), IRD (Institut de Recherche pour le Développement) and LIG (Laboratoire Informatique de Grenoble) for supporting this experiment.

References

Mohammad Daoud. 2010. *Usage of non-conventional resources and contributive methods to bridge the terminological gap between languages by developing multilingual "preterminologies"*. Ph.D. thesis, University of Grenoble, France.

Heidi Depraetere and Joeri Van de Walle. 2012. Bologna Translation Service: An enabler for international profiling and student mobility. In *"Proceedings of the 6th International Technology, Edu-*

---

[11]System for Eliciting pre-Terminology (Daoud, 2010).

cation and Development Conference", pages 5907–5912, Valencia, March. IATED.

Heidi Depraetere, Joachim Van den Bogaert, and Joeri Van de Walle. 2011. Bologna Translation Service: Online translation of course syllabi and study programmes in English. In *"Proceedings of the 15th Conference of the European Association for Machine Translation"*, pages 29–34, Leuven.

Spence Green, Jeffrey Heer, and Christopher D Manning. 2013. The efficacy of human post-editing for language translation. In *"Proceedings of the SIGCHI conference on Human factors in Computing systems"*, pages 439–448. ACM.

Ruslan Kalitvianski, Christian Boitet, and Valérie Bellynck. 2012. Collaborative computer-assisted translation applied to pedagogical documents and literary works. In *"Proceedings of the 24th International Conference on Computational Linguistics"*, pages 255–260, Mumbai. Citeseer.

Jaakko Malmivuo and Robert Plonsey. 1995. *Bioelectromagnetism: principles and applications of bioelectric and biomagnetic fields.* Oxford University Press.

Makoto Nagao, Jun-ichi Tsujii, and Jun-ichi Nakamura. 1985. The Japanese Government Project for Machine Translation. *Computational Linguistics*, 11(2-3):91–110.

Bonka Nikolova and Irina Nenova. 1982. An Automated System for Term Services. In J Horeckp, editor, *"Proceedings of the 9th Conference on Computational Linguistics"*, pages 265–270, Prague. North-Holland.

J Pietrzak, A Jauregi, Joeri Van de Walle, and A Eriksson. 2013. Improving access to educational courses via automatic machine translation - New developments in post-editing. In *"Proceedings of the INTED 2013 Conference"*, pages 5521–5529. IATED.

Bruno Pouliquen and Christophe Mazenc. 2011a. Automatic translation tools at WIPO. *Aslib, Translating and the Computer*, 33:17–18.

Bruno Pouliquen and Christophe Mazenc. 2011b. COPPA, CLIR and TAPTA: Three tools to assist in overcoming the patent language barrier at WIPO. In *"Proceedings of the 13th Machine Translation Summit"*, pages 24–30.

Bruno Pouliquen, Cecilia Elizalde, Marcin Junczys-Dowmunt, Christophe Mazenc, and José García-Verdugo. 2013. Large-scale multiple language translation accelerator at the United Nations. In *"Proceedings of the 14th Machine Translation Summit"*, pages 345–352.

Joeri Van de Walle, Heidi Depraetere, and J Pietrzak. 2012a. Bologna Translation Service: High-quality automated translation of study programmes into English. In *"Proceedings of the EDULEARN 2012 Conference"*, pages 5831–5835. IATED.

Joeri Van de Walle, Heidi Depraetere, and J Pietrzak. 2012b. Bologna Translation Service: Making study programmes accessible throughout Europe by means of high-quality automated translation. In *"Proceedings of ICERI 2012 Conference"*, pages 3910–3918. IATED.

Lingxiao Wang and Christian Boitet. 2013. Online production of HQ parallel corpora and permanent task-based evaluation of multiple MT systems: both can be obtained through iMAGs with no added cost. In *"Proceedings of the 2nd Workshop on Post-Editing Technologies and Practice at MT Summit 2013"*, pages 103–110, Nice, September.

Generating Translation Corpora in Indic Languages: Cultivating Bilingual Texts for Cross Lingual Fertilization

Niladri Sekhar Dash
Linguistic Research Unit
Indian Statistical Institute
Kolkata, India
Email: ns_dash@yahoo.com

Arulmozi Selvraj
Centre for ALTS
Central University of Hyderabad
Hyderabad, India
Email: arulmozi@gmail.com

Mazhar Hussain
Centre for Indian Languages
School of LL & CS
Jawaharlal Nehru University, Delhi
Email: mazharmehdi@gmail.com

Abstract

We address some theoretical and practical issues relating to generation, processing, and management of Translation Corpus (TC) in Indian languages, which is developed in a consortium-mode project (ILCI-II)[1] under the DeitY, Govt. of India. Issues are discussed here for the first time keeping in mind the ready application of TC in various domains of computational and applied linguistics. We first define what is a TC; describe the process of its construction; identify its features; exemplify the processes of text alignment in TC; discuss methods of text analysis; propose for restructuring of translational units; define the process of extraction of translational equivalents; propose for generating bilingual lexical database and TermBank from a structured TC; and finally identify areas where a TC and information extracted from it may be utilized. Since construction of TC in Indian languages is full of hurdles, we try to construct a roadmap with a focus on techniques and methodologies that may be applied for achieving the task. The issues are brought under focus to justify the work that generated TC for some Indian languages for future reference and application.

1. What is a Translation Corpus ?

Theoretically, a Translation Corpus (TC) suggests that it contains texts and their translation. It is entitled to include bilingual (and multilingual) texts as well as texts that may fit under *translation*. A TC, by virtue of its character and composition, is made of two parts: a text from a source language (SL) and its translation from a target language (TL) [15] [24], [39]. Although, a TC is normally bilingual and bidirectional [28], it can be multilingual and multi-directional as well [37], as it actually happens in case of the ILCI-I and ILCI-II projects for the Indian languages. In these two projects a new strategy is adopted where Hindi is treated as the only SL and several other Indian languages are treated as the TL (Fig. 1).

The issue of multi-directionality can be understood if all the target languages can establish linguistic links with each other as they are linked up with SL. Since the ILCI-I TC has not tried to venture into this direction, it makes sense to keep the present discussion confined within a scheme of bilingualism and bi-directionality, with, for example, Hindi

---

[1] Indian Languages Corpora Initiative-Phase II

as SL and Bangla as TL to understand the theoretical and practical issues involved in its text content, composition, structure, construction, processing, and utilization. Hence forth, our discussion will sail in this direction only.

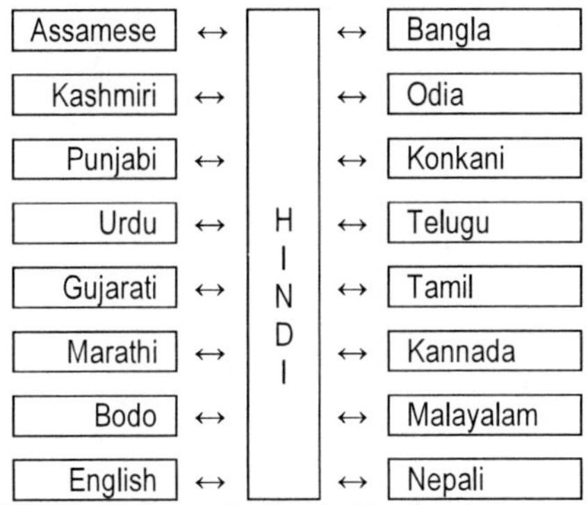

Fig. 1: Hindi as a SL and other Indian Languages as TL

Theoretically, a TC is supposed to keep meaning and function of words and phrases constant across languages [19], although alternation in structure (i.e., sequential order of words and phrases) is a permissible deviation. TC offers an ideal resource for comparing realisation of meanings (and structures) in two different languages under identical situations [3]. Also, it makes possible to discover the cross-linguistic variants, i.e., alternative renderings of meanings and concepts in the TL [4]. Thus a TC becomes useful for cross-language analysis and formulation of comparable lexical databases necessary for translation [1], [21], [26].

Since a TC contains texts from one language and its translations in another language, it is viewed as a sub-type of a parallel corpus, which, in principle, requires its texts to be maximally comparable to each other [28]. Therefore, it is better to consider a TC as a special corpus, which is identical in genre, similar in text type, uniform in format, parallel in composition, identical in content, comparable to each other and specific in utility [32], [37].

2. Construction of a Translation Corpus

The construction of a TC is a complicated task. It requires careful manipulation of SL and TL texts [18] [19]. A TC should be made in such a way that it is suitable to combine advantages of both comparable and parallel corpora [2].

Proceedings of ICON-2015: 12th International Conference on Natural Language Processing
Also accessible from http://ltrc.iiit.ac.in/proceedings/ICON-2015

D S Sharma, R Sangal and E Sherly. Proc. of the 12th Intl. Conference on Natural Language Processing, pages 333–342,
Trivandrum, India. December 2015. ©2015 NLP Association of India (NLPAI)

Text samples from the languages should be matched as far as possible in terms of text type, subject matter, purpose, and register [1]. The structure of a TC within two languages may be envisaged in the following manner keeping in mind the aim of the task and components to be integrated within a TC (Fig. 2).

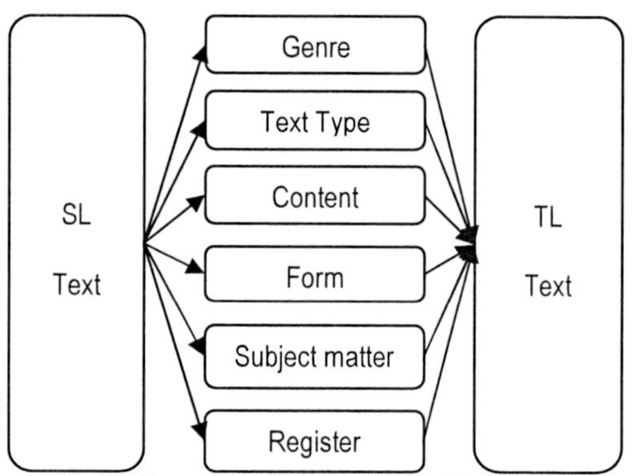

Fig. 2: Construction and composition of a TC

The diagram given above shows that a TC is designed in such a way that it can be used as a comparable as well as a parallel corpus. The reverse argument is not however true. That means a comparable or parallel corpus cannot be used as a TC unless it follows the conditions of its construction stated above. Therefore, selection of texts for constructing a TC needs to be guided by the following principles [34]:

- Written texts are included in a TC. Texts obtained from speech are ignored since the present state of TC targets written texts only.
- Texts should reflect on the contemporary language use although texts of earlier era may have relevance in case translating historical texts.
- Texts should be restricted to specific subject. It should include texts from specific domains of language use.
- Texts of the SL and the TL should be comparable as far as possible. They should match in **genre** (e.g. news), **type** (e.g. political), **content** (e.g. election), and **form** (e.g. report). They should also match in subject matter, register varieties, purpose, and type of user, etc.
- Texts must consist of fairly large and coherent extracts obtained from beginning to end of a breaking point (e.g. chapter, section, paragraph, etc.)
- Texts should faithfully represent regular as ell as special linguistic forms and elements of SL and TL. They may be large in size to encompass maximum varieties in content. Lexical varieties should be high in a TC.
- Texts should faithfully preserve domain-specific words, terms, idioms, phrases, and other lexical elements. Texts used in TC should be authentic and referential for future verification and validation.

- Texts should be available in machine-readable form for access and reference by users. Users may use language data in multiple tasks, such as, statistical sampling, text alignment, lexical database generation, text processing and translation, etc.
- Text samples should be preserved in annotated or non-annotated version. A POS tagged TC is a better resource than a non-tagged one.
- Linguistic and extralinguistic information should be captured in a systematic manner so that users can access information easily for future reference and validation.

Given below (Fig. 3) is a sample of Hind-Bangla translation corpus taken from the ILCI-I project.

Hindi Text
हृदय रोगी को नमक, मिर्च तथा तले-भुने भोजन का प्रयोग कम से कम करना चाहिए या हो सके तो नहीं करना चाहिए । हरी पत्तेदार सब्जियों तथा फल का सेवन अधिक मात्रा में करना चाहिए । यदि हृदय रोगी धूमपान, शराब या अन्य किसी नशीली वस्तु का सेवन करता है तो उसे शीघ्र ही इन पदार्थों का सेवन बंद कर देना चाहिए । हृदय रोगी को घी, मक्खन इत्यादि का सेवन कम से कम करना चाहिए । हृदय रोगी को आँवला तथा लहसुन का सेवन प्रतिदिन करना चाहिए । सेब के मुरब्बे का सेवन हृदय रोगियों को विशेषकर करना चाहिए ।

Bangla Translation
হৃদরোগীদের নুন, ঝাল ও আজেবাজে খাবার খাওয়া খুব কমিয়ে দেওয়া উচিত বা সম্ভব হলে বন্ধ করে দেওয়া উচিত । টাটকা সবজী ও ফল অধিক মাত্রায় ভোজন করা উচিত । যদি হৃদরোগী ধূমপান, মদ বা অন্য কোনো নেশা করেন তবে তাঁকে শীঘ্রই এই সব খাওয়া বন্ধ করে দিতে হবে । হৃদরোগীর ঘি, মাখন ইত্যাদি কম করে খাওয়া উচিত । হৃদরোগীকে প্রতিদিন আমলকী ও রসুন খাওয়ানো উচিত । আপেলের মোরোব্বা খাওয়া হৃদরোগীদের বিশেষ প্রয়োজন ।

Fig. 3: Hind-Bangla translation corpus

3. Features of a Translation Corpus

A TC has certain default features, which may vary for other types of corpus [32]. That means, a TC which does not possess these default features may be put outside its scope due to deviation from the norm. By all means, a TC should possess the following features:

3.1 Quantity of Data

A TC should be big with large collection of texts from SL and TL. Larger amount of text facilitates accessibility and reliability of translation. The number of sentences included in TC will determine its quantity. Since the primary goal of a TC is to include texts for translation, it should not be restricted with fixed number of sentences. The size of a TC is related to the amount of texts included in it. It is the total number of sentences that determines its size [31]. A TC that includes more number of sentences is more suitable, since size is an important issue in TC based linguistic works.

Proceedings of ICON-2015: 12th International Conference on Natural Language Processing
Also accessible from http://ltrc.iiit.ac.in/proceedings/ICON-2015

Making a TC large is linked with number of 'tokens' and 'types' included in it as well as with decisions of how many texts will be in it; how many sentences will be in each text; and how many words will be in each sentence [5]. A small TC, due to its limited number of texts, may fail to provide some advantages, which a large TC can provide. We find that a large TC has the following advantages:

- It presents better scope for variation of texts.
- It provides better spectrum of the patterns of lexical and syntactic usages in SL and TL.
- It confirms increment in number of textual citations that provide scopes for systematic classification of linguistic items in terms of their usage and meaning.
- It assures better opportunity for obtaining all kinds of statistical results far more faithfully for making various correct observations.
- It gives wider spectrum for studying patterns of use of individual words and sentences. This helps us to make generalization about syntactic structures of SL and TL.
- It helps to understand the patterns of use of multiword units like compounds, reduplicated forms, collocations, phrases, idioms and proverbs, etc. in SL and TL.
- It helps to identify coinage of new words and terms, locate their fields of usage, find variations of sense of terms, and track patterns of their usage in texts, etc.
- It gives scope for faithful analysis of usage of technical and scientific terms – a real challenge in translation.

A large TC is not only large in amount of data but also multidimensional in its composition, multidirectional in its form, and multifunctional in its utility. Thus quantity of data has an effect on validity and reliability of a TC. Also, it ensures diversity of SL/TL texts from which it is made. Since a TC is a minuscule form of SL and TL text varieties, in qualitative authentication of SL and TL properties, it is useless if it is not made large in amount of data [33].

3.2 Quality of Text

Quality relates to authenticity. That means texts should be collected from genuine communication of people from their normal discourse. The primary role of a TC generator is to acquire data for a TC generation in which he has no liberty to alter, modify or distort the actual image of the SL. He has no right to add information from personal observation on the ground that the data is not large and suitable enough to represent the language for which it is made. The basic point is that a TC developer will collect data faithfully following the predefined principles proposed for the task. If he tries to interpolate in any way within the body of the text, he will not only damage the actual picture of the text, but also damage heavily the subsequent analysis of data. This will affect the overall projection of the language, or worse, may yield wrong observations about the language in question. Therefore, at the time of constructing a TC, we had to observe the following conditions:

- Repetition of texts or sentences are avoided.
- Ungrammatical constructions are removed.
- Broken constructions are ignored.
- Incomplete constructions are separated.
- Mixed sentences are avoided.
- Texts from single field or domain are considered.
- Both synchronic and diachronic texts are considered.
- Standard forms of regular usage are considered.
- Text representation is maximally balanced, non-skewed, and wide.
- Texts are in homogeneous form without distortion of language data.

3.3 Text Representation

A TC should include samples from a wide range of texts to attain proper representation. It should be balanced to all disciplines and subjects to represent maximum number of linguistic features found in a language. Besides, it should be authentic in representation of a text wherefore it is made, since future analysis and investigation of TC may ask for verification and authentication of information from the TC representing a language. For example, when we develop a Hindi-Bangla TC, which is meant to be representative of a domain of the languages, it should to kept in mind that data are collected in equal proportion so that the TC is a true replica of the languages. This is the first condition of text representation.

Text samples should not be collected only from one or two texts. They should be maximally representative with regard to domains. A TC should contain samples not only from imaginative texts like fictions, novels, and stories but also from all informative texts like natural science, social science, earth science, medical science, engineering, technology, commerce, banking, advertisements, posters, newspapers, government notices and similar sources. To be truly representative, samples should be collected in equal proportion from all sources irrespective to text types, genres, and time variations. Although the appropriate size of sample of a TC is not finalised, we have collected 50,000 sentences from each domain where the number of sentences is divided equally among the sub-domains.

3.4 Simplicity

A TC should contain text samples in simple and plain form so that texts are easily used by translators without being trapped into additional linguistic information marked-up within texts. In fact, simplicity in texts puts the TC users in a better position to deal with the content of texts. However, it is not altogether a hurdle if TC texts are marked-up at word, phrase, and sentence level with grammatical, lexical, and syntactic information. The basic role of a mark-up process is to preserve some additional information, which will be useful for various linguistic works. Although these are helpful, these should be easily separable so that the original TC text is easily retrievable. There are some advantages in using mark-ups on a TC. In information

Proceedings of ICON-2015: 12th International Conference on Natural Language Processing
Also accessible from http://ltrc.iiit.ac.in/proceedings/ICON-2015

retrieval, machine learning, lexical database generation, termbank compilation, and machine translation, a TC built with marked-up texts is more useful for searching and data extraction from the texts, which results in development of systems and tools. Marked-up TCs are also quite useful for sociolinguistic researches, dictionary compilation, grammar writing, and language teaching.

3.5 Equality

Each text sample should have equal number of sentences in TC. For instance, if a SL text contains 1000 sentences, each TL text should also contain the same number of sentences. We propose this norm because we argue that sentences used in TC should be of equal number so that translation mechanism can work elegantly. However, there may be some constraints, which may not be avoided at the time of TC generation:

- Number of texts available in SL may be more than that of TL.
- Collection of equal number of sentences from SL and TL may not be an easy task.
- Parity in number of sentences is deceptive, because sentences never occur in equal number in SL and TL.
- A sentence in SL may be broken into two or more sentences in TL. Reversely, several sentences in SL may be merged into one sentence in TL.
- Equal number of sentences cannot be collected from SL and TL in a uniform manner, since size varies.

3.6 Retrievability

The work of TC generation does not end with compilation of texts. It also involves formatting the text in a suitable form so that the data becomes easily retrievable by end users. That means data stored in a TC should be made easily retrievable for users. Anybody interested in TC should be able to extract relevant information from it. This directs our attention towards the techniques and tools used for preserving TC in digital format. The present technology has made it possible for us to generate a TC in PCs and preserve it in such a way that we are capable to retrieve and access the texts. The advantage, however, goes directly to those people who are trained to handle language databases in computer.

This, however, does not serve the goals of all TC users, since utility of TC is not confined to computer people only. A TC is made for all (computer experts, linguists, social scientists, language experts, teachers, students, researchers, historians, advertisers, technologists, and general people). Its goal is accomplished when people coming from all walks of life can access it according to their needs. In reality, there are many people who are not trained for handling computer or digital TC, but need TC to address their needs. Therefore, TC must be stored in an easy and simple format so that common people can use it.

3.7 Verifiability

Texts collected in a TC should be open for all empirical verifications. It should be reliable and verifiable in the context of representing a language under study. Until and unless a TC is fit for all kinds of empirical analysis and verification, its importance is reduced to nothing. Text samples, which are collected and compiled in a TC to represent SL and TL should honestly register and reflect on the actual patterns of language use. To address this need, a TC should be made in such a way that it easily qualifies to win the trust of users who after verifying texts, agree that what is stored in TC is actually a faithful reflection of SL and TL. For instance, when we develop a TC for Hindi and Bangla we are careful that texts stored in the TC qualify to reflect properly on the respective languages. A TC thus attests its authenticity and validity.

3.8 Augmentation

A TC should grow with time with new texts to capture the changes in content and form. Also it should grow to register variations in texts. Although most of the present TCs are synchronic, we should take effort to make diachronic TCs so that we find a better picture of the languages involved in the game. A synchronic TC, by addition of texts, may become diachronic. This can have direct effects on size, quantity, coverage, and diversity of a TC. *Augmentation* thus becomes an important feature of a TC.

3.9 Documentation

It is necessary to preserve detail information of the sources wherefrom texts are collected in TC. It is a practical requirement on the part of TC designer to deal with problems related to verification and validation of SL and TL texts and dissolving copyright issues. It is also needed to dissolve linguistic and extralinguistic issues relating to sociolinguistic investigations, stylistic analyses, and legal enquiries, etc. which ask for verification of information of SL and TL texts. As TC maker we document meticulously all extralinguistic information relating to types of text, source of text, etc. There are directly linked with referential information of physical texts (e.g., name of book, name of topics, newspaper, year of first publication, year of second edition, numbers of pages, type of text, sex, profession, age, social status of author(s), etc.).

Documentation information of a TC should be separated from the texts itself in the form of Metadata. We keep all information in a Header File that contains all references relating to texts. For easy future access, management, and processing of TC this allows us to separate texts from the tagset quickly. We follow the TEI format (*Text Encoding Initiative*), which has a simple minimal header containing reference to texts. For management of a TC, this allows effective separation of plain texts from annotation with easy application of Header File separation.

Proceedings of ICON-2015: 12th International Conference on Natural Language Processing
Also accessible from http://ltrc.iiit.ac.in/proceedings/ICON-2015

4. Alignment of Texts in Translation Corpus

Aligning texts in TC means making each Translation Unit (TU) of SL correspond to an equivalent unit in TL [27]. TU covers small units like words, phrases, and sentences [12] as well as larger units like paragraphs and chapters [30] (Fig. 4). Selection of TU depends largely on the point of view selected for linguistic analysis and the type of corpus used. If a TC asks for a high level faithfulness to original, as it happens in legal and technical texts, close alignment between sentences, phrases or even words is mandatory. In case of non-technical texts (e.g. fiction), alignment at larger units at paragraph or chapter level will suffice [38]. Thus, operation of alignment may be refined based on the type of corpus used in the work. The faithfulness and linearity of human translations may guide to align a TC, although this is predominantly true for technical corpora. Literary TC, on the other hand, lends itself to reliable alignment of units beyond sentence level if translational equivalency observed in TC is previously formalised [11].

<table>
<tr><td></td><td>SL Text</td><td>↔</td><td>TL Text</td></tr>
<tr><td></td><td colspan="3" align="center">↓   ↓</td></tr>
<tr><td rowspan="4">Small TUs</td><td>Character</td><td>↔</td><td>Character</td></tr>
<tr><td>Word</td><td>↔</td><td>Word</td></tr>
<tr><td>Phrase</td><td>↔</td><td>Phrase</td></tr>
<tr><td>Sentence</td><td>↔</td><td>Sentence</td></tr>
</table>

Large TUs	Paragraph	↔	Paragraph
	Chapter	↔	Chapter

Fig. 4: Layers of translation unit alignment in TC

Since so-called 'free translations' present a problems in processing due to missing sequence, change in word order, modification of content, etc. it is sensible to generate sets of 'corresponding texts' having mutual conceptual parallelism. The main goal is not to show structural equivalences found between the two languages, but pragmatically, to search TL text units, which appear to be closest to SL text units. Such rough alignment yields satisfactory results at sentence level [17] especially when supported by some statistical methods [6] with minimal formalisation of syntactic phenomena of texts [7].

Sentence level alignment is an important part of TC alignment. It shows correspondences down to the level of sentence, and not beyond that [8]. For this work, a weak translation model serves the purpose, since this is one of the primary tools required at the initial stage of TC analysis [29]. Given below is a sample of Hind-Bangla TC where sentences are largely aligned (Fig. 5).

Alignment of TC helps to optimize mapping between two equivalent units in order to obtain better translation output. It involves associating equivalent units (e.g. words, multiword units, idioms, phrases, clauses, and sentences, etc.) endowed with typical formal structures. However, the basic purpose of this process alignment is to allow pairing

mechanism to be broken into following three parts in a systematic way:

- Identification of potential linguistic units, which may be grammatically associated in TC.
- Formalisation of structures of associable units by way of using sets of morphosyntactic tags.
- Determination of probability of proposed structures comparing the forms with effective texts collected from manually translated corpora.

Sentence ID	Hindi-Bangla Aligned Sentences
HNHL_296	हृदय रोगी को घी, मक्खन इत्यादि का सेवन कम से कम करना चाहिए ।
BNHL_296	হৃদরোগীর ঘি, মাখন ইত্যাদি কম করে খাওয়া উচিত ।
HNHL_297	हृदय रोगी को आँवला तथा लहसुन का सेवन प्रतिदिन करना चाहिए ।
BNHL_297	হৃদরোগীকে প্রতিদিন আমলকী ও রসুন খাওয়ানো উচিত ।
HNHL_298	सेब के मुरब्बे का सेवन हृदय रोगियों को विशेषकर करना चाहिए ।
BNHL_298	আপেলের মোরোব্বা খাওয়া হৃদরোগীদের বিশেষ প্রয়োজন।

Fig. 5: Sentences aligned in Hind-Bangla TC

By subdividing the process into three parts a relatively simple system module may be developed to identify the units likely to correlate with analysis of TC [24]. It is not, however, necessary to analyse all sentences used in TC to find out all matches. Analysis of type constructions, rather than full set of tokens, serves the initial purpose, because:

(a) In a language there are units, which are identical in form and sense. That means a NP in SL may correspond structurally to other NPs within a text. This is true to both SL and TL.
(b) Sequence and interrelation between the units in TL text may be same with those in SL text if TC is developed from two sister languages.
(c) There are certain fixed reference points in texts (e.g., numbers, dates, proper names, titles, paragraphs, sections, etc.), which mark out texts and allow rapid identification of translation units.

It is always necessary to fine-tune alignment process of TC to enhance text processing and information retrieval. However, it requires identification and formalisation of 'translation units' and utilisation of bilingual dictionaries. So, there is no need for exhaustive morphosyntactic tagging of each text, since machine can do it with a statistical support to find out equivalent forms by comparing TC that exhibit translational relations. However, to ensure quality

Proceedings of ICON-2015: 12th International Conference on Natural Language Processing
Also accessible from http://ltrc.iiit.ac.in/proceedings/ICON-2015

performance of a system the following things should be taken care of:

(a) Standard of TC should be high. Aligned bilingual texts may pose problem if the quality of TC is poor or if texts are not put under strict vigilance of linguists.
(b) Quality and size of bilingual dictionary should be high. Dictionary is a basic resource in terms of providing adequate lexical information. Moreover, it should have provision to integrate unknown words found in TC.
(c) Robustness of the system and the quality of translation will depend on the volume of training data available.
(d) Level of accuracy in TC will rely heavily on the levels of synchronisation between the texts of TC.

Alignment of TC is a highly complicated task. Impetus for progress must come from linguistic and extralinguistic sources. It is a highly specialised work, which unlike most others, is a worthy test bed for various theories and applications of linguistics and language technology. It verifies if theories of syntax, semantics, and discourse are at all compatible to it; if lexicon and grammar of SL and TL are fruitfully utilised; if algorithms for parsing, word sense analysis and pragmatic interpretations are applicable; and if knowledge representation and linguistic cognition have any relevance in it. Alignment of text is greatly successful in domain-specific TC with supervised training where all syntactic, lexical and idiomatic differences are adequately addressed [35]. This usually narrows down the gulf of mutual intelligibility to enhance translatability between the two languages.

5. Translation Corpus Analysis

TC analysis has three goals. First, to structure translations in such a way that these are usable in production of new translations. Using *TransSearch System* [16] we can mark out bilingual correspondences between SL and TL texts. Second, to draft translations to detect translation error, if any, in TC. It is possible to certify that a translation is complete, in the sense that larger units (pages, paragraphs, sections, etc.) of SL texts are properly translated in TL text. Last, to verify if any translation is free from interference errors resulted from 'deceptive cognates'. For instance, the Hindi word *sandes* 'news' and Bangla word *sandes* 'sweet' cannot be accepted as good cognates for mutual translation, although they appear similar in form in the two languages. Similarly, Hindi word *khun* and Bangla word *khun* should not be treated as identical, because while the Hindi word means 'blood', Bangla word means 'murder'.

A TC, once aligned, is available for linguistic analysis. In general, it involves the following tasks:

(a) **Morphological Analysis:** Identify form and function of constituting morphemes.
(b) **Syntactic Analysis:** Identify form and function of syntagms in respective corpus.

(c) **Morphosyntactic Analysis:** Identify interface involved within surface forms of lexical items used in TC.
(d) **Semantic Analysis:** Identify meaning of linguistic units (i.e., words, idioms, phrases, etc.) as well as ambiguities involved therein.

For effective linguistic analysis, we may use descriptive morphosyntactic approach along with some statistical approaches for probability measurement. We take support from standard descriptive grammars and morphosyntactic rules of SL and TL. At this stage, part-of-speech tagging is done by comparing texts of SL and TL manually. Our traditional grammatical categories have good referential value on quality of part-of-speech tagging, since a MT system with few POS tags shows greater success than a system with exhaustive POS tags [10]. Based on analysis of equivalent forms obtained from TC, we find three types of matching:

- **Strong match:** Here number of words, their order, and their meaning are same.
- **Approximate match:** Here number of words and their meanings are same, but not the order in which they appear in texts.
- **Weak match:** Here order and number of words are different, but their dictionary meanings are same.

In case of translating texts from Hindi to Bangla, most of the grammatical mappings are 'strong matches', as the languages belong to same typology. In such a situation, alignment of texts in TC can rely on syntactic structure of respective texts although greater emphasis should be on semantic match. We argue that if 70% words in a sentence of Hindi text semantically correspond to 70% words in a sentence in Bangla text, we can claim that sentences have semantic equivalency to have a translational relationship.

Research is going on to develop TC analyser, which can account for translation equivalence between words, idioms, and phrases in TC. Statistical algorithms are also used to find keywords to retrieve equivalent units from TC. Once these are found, these are verified and formalised by human translators as model inputs and stored in bilingual lexical database [13], [28].

6. Restructuring Translation Units

Restructuring a Hindi sentence into Bangla is an attempt to maximize all linguistic resources, strategies and methods deployed in manual translation, as Hindi and Bangla exhibit close typological, grammatical, and semantic similarities due to their genealogical linkage. Since both the languages belong to the same family, it has been, to a large extent, an easy task for us to restructure Hindi phrases in Bangla with utilization of lexico-grammatical stock of both languages. The linguistic knowledgebase and information obtained from this kind of experiment can help to design system for Machine Aided Translation between the two languages.

Proceedings of ICON-2015: 12th International Conference on Natural Language Processing
Also accessible from http://ltrc.iiit.ac.in/proceedings/ICON-2015

(a) Hindi : Hindu dharm mein tIrtha kA baRA mahattva hyay.
(b) Bangla : Hindu dharme tirther bishes guruttva ache.

The type of restructuring referred to in the following table (Table 1) is called 'grammatical mapping' in TC. Here, words of the SL text are 'mapped' with words of the TL text to obtain meaningful translation. Although there are various schemes for mapping (e.g., lexical, morphological, grammatical, phrasal, clausal, etc.), the most common form of grammatical mapping is phrase mapping within the two languages considered in TC.

Input	Hindu (a) dharm (b) mein (c) tIrtha (d) kA (e) baRA (f) mahattva (g) hyay (h)
Literal Output	Hindu (1) dharma (2) -e (3) tirtha (4) -er (5) bishes (6) guruttva (7) ache (8)
Restructuring	Hindu (1) dharme (2+3) tirther (4+5) bishes (6) guruttva (7) ache (8)
Actual Output	(1) (2+3) (4+5) (6) (7) (8)

Table 1: Restructuring Hindi and Bengali sentences

In above examples (a & b) we see how we need to map the case markers with nouns to get appropriate outputs in Bangla translation. In Bangla, case markers are tagged with nouns and pronouns, while in Hindi, they remain separate from nouns and pronouns and appear as independent lexical items in sentence. That means at the time of translation from Hindi to Bangla, the multi-word units (particularly of verb class) have to be represented as a single-word unit in Bengali.

Grammatical mapping is highly relevant in the context of MT between the two languages, which are different in word order in sentence formation. In the present context, while we talk about MT system from Hindi to Bangla, this becomes relevant, as Hindi phrases need to be restructured in the framework. Therefore, grammatical mapping and reordering of words is needed for producing acceptable outputs in Bangla.

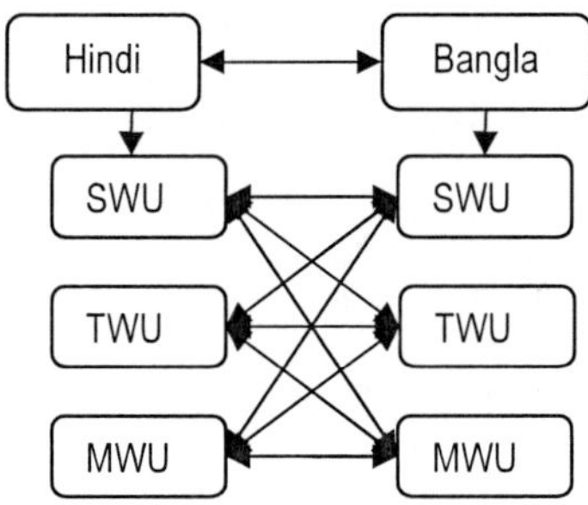

Fig. 6: Lexical Mapping between Hindi and Bangla

At the lexical level, on the other hand, to achieve good output in Bangla, words used in Hindi sentence need to be mapped with words used in Bangla in the following manner (Fig. 6). However, it is found that mere lexical mapping is not enough for proper translation. A Hindi sentence may contains an idiomatic expression, which requires pragmatic knowledge to find a similar idiomatic expression in Bangla to achieve accuracy in translation. Therefore, we need to employ pragmatic knowledgebase to select the appropriate equivalent idiomatic expression from the TL.

7. Extraction of Translational Equivalent Units

Search for translation equivalent units (TEU) in TC begins with particular forms that express similar sense in both the languages. Once these are identified in TC, these are stored in a separate lexical database. Normally, a TC yields large amount of TEU, which are good to be used as alternative forms. The issues that determine the choice of appropriate equivalent form are measured on the basis of recurrent patterns of use of the forms. The TEUs are verified with monolingual text corpora of the two languages from which TC is made. It follows a scheme (Fig. 7) through which we generate a list of possible TEUs from the TC.

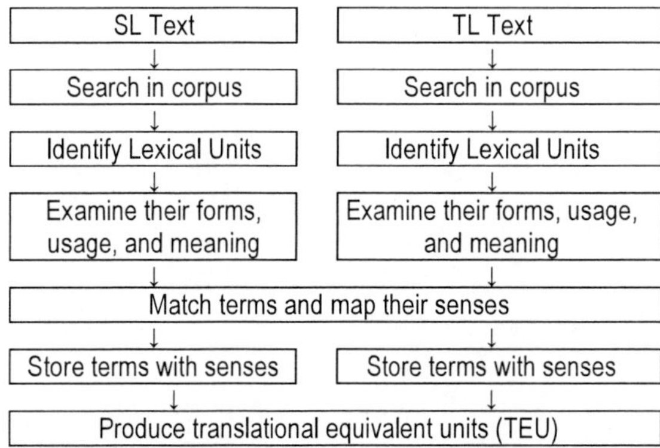

Fig. 7: Extraction of TU from a Translation Corpus

We find that even within two closely related languages, TEUs seldom mean the same thing in all contexts, since these are seldom used in the same types of syntactic and grammatical construction [12]. Moreover, their semantic connotations and degree of formality differ depending on language-specific contexts. Sometimes a lemma in TL is hardly found as a true TEU to a lemma of SL, even though they appear conceptually equivalent. Two-way translation is possible with proper names and scientific terms, but hardly with ordinary lexical units [25]. This signifies that ordinary texts will create more problems due to differences in sense of words. It requires a high degree of linguistic sophistication to yield better outputs. In general, we extract the following types of TEUs from a TC to build up useful resource for multiple applications:

- Extract good TEU including words, idioms, compounds, collocations, and phrases.
- Learn how TC help in producing translated texts that display 'naturalness' of the TL.

- Create new translation databases that will enable us to translate correctly into the languages on which we have only limited command.
- Generate Bilingual Lexical Database (BLD) for man and machine translation.
- Generate Bilingual Terminology Database (BTB) as it is neither standardised nor developed for Indic languages.

Process of extracting TEUs from TC and their subsequent verification for authentication with monolingual corpora is schematized below (Fig. 8). To find out TEU from a TC we use various searching methods to trace comparable units (i.e., words and larger units than words) which are similar in meaning. Findings are further schematized with bilingual lexical dictionary and term databases to enrich the MT knowledgebase for the battles ahead.

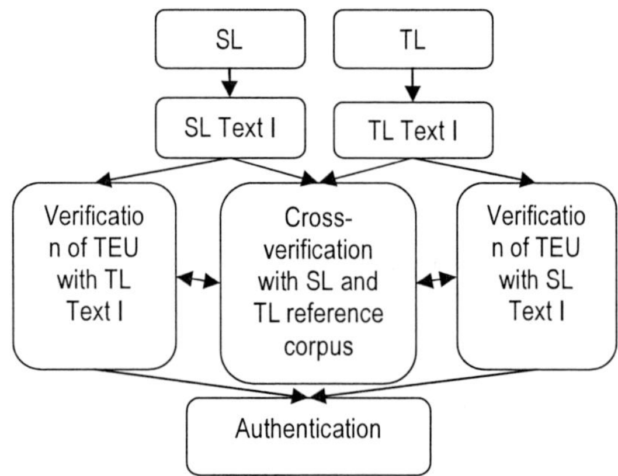

Fig. 8: Verification of TEUs with monolingual corpus

8. Bilingual Lexical Database

Development of a Bilingual Lexical Database (BLD) from a TC is an essential task the lack of which is one of the bottlenecks of present MT works in Indian languages. Traditional dictionaries cannot compensate this deficiency, as they do not contain information about lexical sub-categorisation, lexical selection restriction, and domains of application of lexical items [14]. Using POS-tagged TC we can extract semantically equivalent words for the BLD [9]. A BLD may be developed from untagged corpora when POS-tagged TC is not available for the purpose.

Formation of BLD is best possible within those cognate languages, that are typologically or genealogically related (e.g. Bangla-Odia, Hindi-Urdu, Tamil-Malayalam, etc.) because cognate languages usually share many common properties (both linguistic and non-linguistic) hardly found in non-related languages [22]. Also, there is a large chunk of regular vocabulary similar to each other not only in phonetic/orthographic and representations but also in sense, content (meaning), and connotation.

Lexical Items	Bangla: Odia
Relational terms	bAbA: bapA, mA:mA, mAsi:mAusi, didi:apA, dAdA:bhAinA, boudi:bhAuja, bhAi:bhAi, chele:pilA, meye:jhia,
Pronouns	Ami:mu, tumi:tume, Apni:Apana, tui:tu, se: se
Nouns	lok:loka, ghar:ghara, hAt:hAta, mAthA:munda, pukur: pukhuri, kalA: kadali, am:ama,
Adjectives	bhAla:bhala, bhejA:adA, satya:satya, mithyA:michA
Verbs	yAchhi:yAuchi, khAba:khAiba, balechila:kauthilA, balbe:kAhibe, Asun:Asantu, basun: basantu, bhAlabAse: bhalapAy
Postpositions	kAche:pAkhare, mAjhe:majhire, nice:talare
Indeclinable	ebang:madhya, kintu:kintu

Table 2: Similar vocabulary of Bengali and Oriya

For instance, the list above (Table 2) shows examples where regular vocabulary are similar in sense in Bangla and Odia – two sister languages. To generate a BLD, we use the following strategies on POS tagged TC:

- Retrieve comparable syntactic blocks (e.g. clauses and phrases, etc.) from a TC.
- Extract content words from syntactic blocks (e.g. nouns, adjectives, and verbs).
- Extract function words from syntactic blocks (e.g. pronouns, postpositions, adverbs, etc.).
- Select those lexical items that show similarity in form, meaning, and usage.
- Store those lexical items as translation equivalent units (TEU) in BDL.

Since we do not expect total similarities at morphological, lexical, syntactic, semantic and conceptual level within the two languages (even though languages are closely related), similarities in form, meaning, and usage are enough for selection of TEU.

9. Bilingual Terminology Databank

Collection of Scientific and Technical Terms (STTs) from a TC asks for introspective analysis of a TC. The work is to search through TC to find out STTs which are equivalent or semi-equivalent in TL and TL. While doing this, we need to keep various factors in mind regarding the appropriateness, grammaticality, acceptance and usability of STTs in TL. But the most crucial factor is 'lexical generativity' of the STTs so that many new forms are possible to generate by using various linguistic repertoires available in TL.

TC has another role in choice of appropriate STTs from a list of multiple synonymous STTs that try to represent a particular idea, event, item, and concept. It is observed that the recurrent practice of forming new STTs often goes to such an extreme level that we are at loss to decide which

Proceedings of ICON-2015: 12th International Conference on Natural Language Processing
Also accessible from http://ltrc.iiit.ac.in/proceedings/ICON-2015

STT is to select over other suitable candidates. Debate may also arise whether we should generate new STTs or accept STTs of SL already absorbed in TL by regular use and reference. Some STTs are so naturalised that it becomes almost impossible to trace their actual origin. In this case, we have no problem, because these terms are 'universally accepted' in TL. For instance, the Bengali people face no problem in understanding terms like *computer, mobile, calculator, telephone, tram, bus, cycle, taxi, rickshaw, train, machine, pen, pencil, pant, road, station, platform,* etc. because these are accepted in Bangla along with respective items. Their high frequency of use in various text types makes them a part of Bangla vocabulary. There is no need for replacement of these STTs in the TL texts.

A TC is a good resource for selection of appropriate STTs presenting new ideas and concepts. As a TC is made with varieties of texts full of new terms and expressions, it provides valuable resource of context-based example to draw sensible conclusions. Here a TC contributes in two important ways:

(a) It helps to assemble STTs for SL and TL along with information of dates and domains of their entry and usage, and
(b) It supplies all possible native coinage of STTs along with information of domains and frequency of use in SL and TL.

These factors help to determine on relative acceptance or rejection of STTs. Examination of some instances derived from the Hindi-Bangla ILCI-I corpus shows that a TC is highly useful in collection of appropriate STTs – an essential element in translation.

The entire scheme of TC generation and processing may be visualised from the following block diagram (Fig. 9)

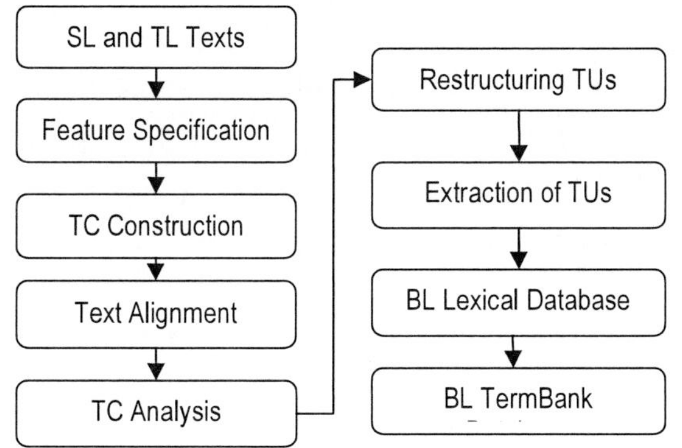

Fig. 89: Scheme of TC generation and processing

10. Conclusion: Value of a Translation Corpus

The question that arises at the time of TC building is: who is going to use it and for what purposes? That means the issue of determining target users is to be dissolved before the work of TC development [36]. But why it is necessary to identify target users? There are some reasons:

- The event of TC generation entails the question of its possible application in various research activities.
- Utility of a TC is not confined within MT. It has equal relevance in general and applied linguistics,
- Each research and application in MT requires specific empirical databases of SL and TL,
- People working in different fields of LT require TC for research and application.
- Form and content of a TC are bound to vary based on users both in linguistics and language technology,
- In language teaching, teachers and instructors require TC for teaching translation courses,
- People studying language variation in SL and TL need TC to initiate their research and investigation,
- Lexicographers and terminologists need TC to extract linguistic and extralinguistic data and information necessary for their works.

These application-specific needs can be easily fulfilled by a TC. Hence, question of selecting target users becomes pertinent in TC construction. However, although prior identification of target users is a prerequisite in TC generation, it does not imply that there is no overlap among target users with regard to utilisation of a TC. In fact, our past experience shows that multifunctionality is an inherent feature of a TC due to which a TC attracts multitudes of users from various fields [15].

This signifies that a TC designed and developed for specific use may be useful for other works. For example, although TC is suitable for lexicographers, it is useful for lexicologists, semanticists, grammarians, texts experts and social scientists. Also it is useful for media persons to cater their needs related to language and society. A TC can be used as a resource for works of language technology as well as an empirical database for mainstream linguistics [36]. In essence, it has application relevance to people interested in SL and TL texts full of exciting features both in content and texture. For Indian languages, a TC is a primary resource, which we need for linguistics and language technology.

References

[1] Altenberg, B. & K. Aijmer. 2000. The English-Swedish parallel corpus: a resource for contrastive research and translation studies. In: C. Mair & M. Hundt (Eds.) *Corpus Linguistics and Linguistics Theory.* Amsterdam-Atlanta, GA: Rodopi. Pp. 15- 33.

[2] Atkins, S., J. Clear, & N. Ostler. 1992. Corpus design criteria. *Literary and Linguistic Computing.* 7(1): 1-16.

[3] Baker, M. 1993. Corpus linguistics and translation studies: implications and applications. In: M. Baker, G. Francis & E. Tognini-Bonelli (E.ds) Text and Technology: In Honour of John Sinclair, Amsterdam: John Benjamins, pp. 233-250.

[4]   Baker, M. 1995. Corpora in translation studies: an overview and suggestions for future research. *Target.* 7(2): 223-43.

[5]   Baker, M. 1996. Corpus-based translation studies: the challenges that lie ahead. In: H. Somers (Ed) *Terminology, LSP and Translation.* Amsterdam: John Benjamins. Pp. 175-186.

[6]   Brown, P. & M. Alii. 1990. A statistical approach to machine translation. *Computational Linguistics.* 16(2): 79-85.

[7]   Brown, P. & M. Alii. 1993. The mathematics of statistical machine translation: parameter estimation. *Computational Linguistics.* 19(2): 145-152.

[8]   Brown, P., J. Lai, & R. Mercer. 1991. Aligning sentences in parallel corpora. *Proceedings of the 29th Meeting of ACL.* Montreal, Canada.

[9]   Brown, R.D. 1999. Adding linguistic knowledge to a lexical example-based translation system. *Proceedings of the MTI-99,* Montreal. Pp. 22-32.

[10] Chanod, J.P. & P. Tapanainen. 1995. Creating a tagset, lexicon and guesser for a French tagger. *Proceedings of the EACL SGDAT Workshop on Form Texts to Tags Issues in Multilingual Languages Analysis,* Dublin. Pp. 58-64.

[11] Chen, K.H & H.H. Chen. 1995. Aligning bilingual corpora especially for language pairs from different families. *Information Sciences Applications.* 4(2): 57-81.

[12] Dagan, I., K.W. Church, and W.A. Gale. 1993. Robust bilingual word alignment for machine-aided translation. *Proceedings of the Workshop on Very Large Corpora: Academic and Industrial Perspectives,* Columbus, Ohio.

[13] Gale, W. & K.W. Church. 1993. A program for aligning sentences in bilingual corpora. *Computational Linguistics.* 19(1): 75-102.

[14] Geyken, A. 1997. Matching corpus translations with dictionary senses: two case studies. *International Journal of Corpus Linguistics.* 2(1): 1-21.

[15] Hunston, S. 2002. *Corpora in Applied Linguistics.* Cambridge: Cambridge University Press.

[16] Isabelle, P., M. Dymetman, G. Foster, J.M. Jutras, E. Macklovitch, F. Perrault, X. Ren & M. Simard. 1993. Translation analysis & translation automation. *Proceedings of the TMI-93,* Kyoto, Japan.

[17] Kay, M. & M. Röscheisen. 1993. Text-translation alignment. *Computational Linguistics.* 19(1): 13-27.

[18] Kenny, D. 1997. (Ab)normal translations: a German-English parallel corpus for investigating normalization in translation. In: B. Lewandowsk-Tomaszczyk & P. Janes Melia (eds) *Practical Applications in Language Corpora. PALC '97 Proceedings,* Lódz: Lódz University Press, pp. 387-392.

[19] Kenny, D. 1998. Corpora in translation studies. In: M. Baker (Ed) *Routledge Encyclopaedia of Translation Studies,* London: Routledge, Pp. 50-53.

[20] Kenny, D. 1999. The German-English parallel corpus of literary texts: a resource for translation scholars. *Teanga.* 18: 25-42.

[21] Kenny, D. 2000. Lexical hide-and-seek: looking for creativity in a parallel corpus. In: M. Olohan (Ed) *Intercultural Faultlines. Research Models in Translation Studies I:* Manchester: St. Jerome, pp. 93-104.

[22] Kenny, D. 2000. Translators at play: exploitations of collocational norms in German-English translation. In: B. Dodd (Ed) *Working with German Corpora,* Birmingham: University of Birmingham Press, 143-160.

[23] Klaudy, K. & K. Karoly. 2000. The text-organizing function of lexical repetition in translation. In: M. Olohan (ed.) Intercultural Faultlines. Research Models in Translation Studies I: Textual and Cognitive Aspects, Manchester: St. Jerome, pp. 143-159.

[24] Kohn, J. 1996. What can (corpus) linguistics do for translation?. In: K. Klaudy, J. Lambert & A. Sohar (eds.) Translation Studies in Hungary, Budapest: Scholastica, Pp. 39-52.

[25] Landau, S.I. 2001. *Dictionaries: The Art and Craft of Lexicography.* Cambridge: Cambridge University Press.

[26] Mauranen, A. 2000. Strange strings in translated language: a study on corpora. In: M. Olohan (Ed) Intercultural Faultlines. Research Models in Translation Studies I: Textual and Cognitive Aspects, Manchester: St. Jerome, Pp. 119-141.

[27] McEnery, T. and M. Oakes. 1996. Sentence and word alignment in the CARTER Project. In: J. Thomas & M. Short (Ed) *Using Corpora for Language Research.* London: Longman. Pp. 211-233.

[28] Oakes, M. & T. McEnery. 2000. Bilingual text alignment — an overview. In: Botley, S.P., A.M. McEnery, & A. Wilson (Eds.) *Multilingual Corpora in Teaching and Research.* Amsterdam-Atlanta, GA.: Rodopi. Pp. 1-37.

[29] Simard, M., G. Foster, & P. Isabelle. 1992. Using cognates to align sentences in parallel corpora. *Proceedings of TMI-92.* Canadian Workplace Automation Research Center. Montreal.

[30] Simard, M., G. Foster, M-L. Hannan, E. Macklovitch, and P. Plamondon. 2000. Bilingual text alignment: where do we draw the line?. In: Botley, S.P., Tony McEnery & A. Wilson (ed.) *Multilingual Corpora in Teaching and Research.* Amsterdam-Atlanta, GA.: Rodopi. Pp. 38-64.

[31] Sinclair, J. 1991. *Corpus, Concordance, Collocation.* Oxford: Oxford University Press. Pp. 20.

[32] Stewart, D. 2000. Conventionality, creativity and translated text: implications of electronic corpora in translation. In: M. Olohan (ed) Intercultural Faultlines. Research Models in Translation Studies I: Textual and Cognitive Aspects, Manchester: St. Jerome, pp. 73-91.

[33] Stewart, D. 2000. Poor relations and black sheep in translation studies. *Target* 12(2): 205-228.

[34] Summers, D. 1991. *Longman/Lancaster English Language Corpus: Criteria and Design.* Harlow: Longman.

[35] Teubert, W. 2000. Corpus linguistics — a partisan view. *International Journal of Corpus Linguistics.* 4(1): 1-16.

[36] Tymoczko, M. 1998. Computerized corpora and the future of translation studies. *Meta* 43(4): 652-659.

[37] Ulrych, M. 1997. The impact of multilingual parallel concordancing on translation. In: B. Lewandowska-Tomaszczyk and P.J. Melia (eds.) Practical Applications in Language Corpora, Lodz: Lodz University Press, pp. 421-436.

[38] Véronis, J. (ed.). 2000. *Parallel Text Processing: Alignment and Use of Translation Corpora.* Dordrecht: Kluwer Academic Publishers.

[39] Zanettin, F. 2000. Parallel corpora in translation studies: issues in corpus design and analysis. In: M. Olohan (ed.) Intercultural Faultlines. Research Models in Translation Studies I: Textual and Cognitive Aspects, Manchester: St. Jerome. Pp., 105-118.

Translation Quality and Effort: Options versus Post-editing

Donald Sturgeon[*]
Fairbank Center for Chinese Studies
Harvard University
djs@dsturgeon.net

John S. Y. Lee
Department of Linguistics and Translation
City University of Hong Kong
jsylee@cityu.edu.hk

Abstract

Past research has shown that various types of computer assistance can reduce translation effort and improve translation quality over manual translation. This paper directly compares two common assistance types – selection from lists of translation options, and post-editing of machine translation (MT) output produced by Google Translate – across two significantly different subject domains for Chinese-to-English translation. In terms of translation effort, we found that the use of options can require less technical effort than MT post-editing for a domain that yields lower-quality MT output. In terms of translation quality, our analysis suggests that individual preferences play a more decisive role than assistance type: a translator tends to consistently work better either with options or with MT post-editing, regardless of domain and of their translation ability.

1 Introduction

State-of-the-art computer-assisted translation (CAT) systems offer many types of assistance to the human translator. Most studies have focused on investigating whether such assistance — including translation memory, Machine Translation (MT) output, and word and phrase translation options — results in higher productivity and better quality when compared with unassisted translation (Plitt & Masselot, 2010; Zhechev, 2012; Green et al., 2013; Aranberri et al., 2014; Gaspari et al., 2014). Less attention, however, has been devoted to comparing the relative merits of these assistance types. This paper presents a direct comparison between two common types, namely, selection from translation options, and post-editing of MT output, with Goo-gle Translate as the MT system. We analyze these two assistance types along two dimensions:

Translation effort. Translation effort can be measured in terms of time or the amount of editing. Previous research has found between-translator variance of the number of post-editing operations to be lower than that of post-editing time (Tatsumi and Roturier, 2010; Koponen, 2012; Koponen et al., 2012). Therefore, we will hold temporal effort as constant, and instead measure technical effort (Krings, 2001), by explicitly measuring the amount of editing and the number of clicks needed for selecting options. We investigate which assistance type requires less effort, across two domains that differ in terms of MT output quality.

Translation quality. We measure whether either of these assistance types results in better human translations. Past studies have suggested that individual work style is an important factor (e.g., Koehn and Germann, 2014); this study provides further evidence by analyzing a number of other possible factors, including the effect of different domains and translator abilities.

2 Previous work

As publicly available MT systems continue to improve, human translators increasingly adopt post-editing of MT output to boost their productivity. Naturally, the quality of the output is a major factor that determines its benefits. It has been shown that better MT systems generally yield greater productivity gains (Koehn and Germann, 2014). Even state-of-the-art MT systems, however, tend to produce lower-quality output for source sentences from more specialized domains, because of mismatched data. For these domains, the available bilingual data is often insufficient to train a statistical MT system. An alternative is to infer word and phrase alignments from the limited data available,

---

[*] The first author conducted this research at the Department of Linguistics and Translation at City University of Hong Kong.

339

D S Sharma, R Sangal and E Sherly. Proc. of the 12th Intl. Conference on Natural Language Processing, pages 343–350,
Trivandrum, India. December 2015. ©2015 NLP Association of India (NLPAI)

to be offered as translation options to the human translators. A research question that remains under-investigated is whether the use of options or MT output post-editing is more suitable for domains with varying levels of MT output quality.

Two previous studies have evaluated both the use of options and MT post-editing,[1] but on only a single domain. One involved monolingual translators with no knowledge of the source language (Koehn, 2010). They were asked to translate news stories from Arabic and Chinese to English, aided by post-editing and translation options. The study found no significant difference between the two assistance types for Arabic but better performance with options for Chinese. The other study was concerned with French-to-English translation on the news domain (Koehn, 2009b). Each of three kinds of assistance – prediction of the next word/phrase, options, and MT post-editing – improved translation productivity and quality overall. Most relevant for our study, MT post-editing outperformed options, saving 1 second per word and achieving a 4% higher correctness rate (Koehn, 2009b:p.250, Table 2).

This paper further compares these two assistance types in terms of a number of other factors. One factor is the subject domain. We consider whether two domains, one resource-rich and the other resource-poor, may favor different assistance types. Another factor is individual preference for specific assistance types. In the aforementioned study, half of the subjects achieved higher rates of correct translations with options, and the other half the opposite (Koehn, 2009b:p.250, Table 2). Using a larger pool of subjects, we investigate correlations between translation quality and other variables, namely, different domains and translator abilities.

3 Experimental setup

3.1 Domains

We chose two contrasting domains on which to conduct our experiments. The first is a resource-rich domain with many commercial MT systems trained with similar bilingual data; the second is resource-poor with limited samples of bilingual sentences, and would be considered out-of-domain for most commercial MT systems.

- ***"Multi UN" domain***. This domain consists of a corpus of United Nations documents published between January 2000 and March 2010 (Eisele and Chen, 2010). Among the largest parallel corpora available for Chinese and English (Tian et. al, 2014), the corpus has a total of 9.6 million aligned sentences.
- ***"Literary" domain***. This domain is derived from the first 51 chapters of the Chinese classic novel, *Romance of the Three Kingdoms*, and an English translation by C.H. Brewitt-Taylor.[2] These chapters contained 1563 paragraph alignments and 249390 characters.

3.2 Translation assistance types

For each domain, we compared two translation assistance types:

- ***Translation options***. The user first selects translation options for phrases in the source sentence, and then further edits the resulting target sentence (see next section for a description of the interface). For each of the two domains we compiled a phrase table to store these options. Both tables contain bilingual dictionary data from CEDICT (cc-cedict.org) and from the Chinese Text Project (ctext.org). The table for the Multi UN domain is further enriched with word and phrase correspondences extracted from the corpus of UN documents (Eisele and Chen, 2010); the table for the Literary domain, with those from the aforementioned bilingual data from the *Romance of the Three Kingdoms*. While the UN corpus provides sentence alignments,[3] we aligned the Chinese and English texts in the Literary domain using Microsoft's "Bilingual Sentence Aligner" tool,[4] followed by manual review to exclude false matches. We then used Giza++

---

[2] http://ctext.org/sanguo-yanyi
[3] Sentences with over 40 Chinese characters were excluded.
[4] The aligner implements the algorithm described by Moore (2002). See http://research.microsoft.com/en-us/downloads/aafd5dcf-4dcc-49b2-8a22-f7055113e656/

340

(Och and Ney, 2003) to extract alignments between Chinese and English and used these to construct our phrase table.

- ***MT output post-editing***. The user post-edits the translation produced by a fully automatic MT system; in our case, the Google Translate system (translate.google.com). An alternative approach would have been to train statistical machine translation models using the respective bilingual datasets described in the previous section. We trained such a model for the Multi UN domain using Moses MT (Koehn et al., 2007); the resultant model achieved a TER of 56.9 on the test set (see Section 3.4) when measured against the reference translation, which was on a par with the TER of 58.3 achieved by Google Translate. For the Literary domain, however, it would be impractical to train such a model, given the limited amount of data available. A possible mitigation is to attempt domain adaptation (e.g., Song et al., 2012), but this method would introduce a possibly confounding variable. Instead, for more straightforward comparison, we made use of Google Translate, a general-purpose and widely used MT system, on both domains.

3.3 Interface

Figure 1 shows the interface used in our experiments for displaying translation options. The user is presented with a list of translation options for phrases in the source sentence, in decreasing order of the frequency with which they occur in the training data.[5] Such matches may be strings of any length, and are chosen using forward maximal matching against the phrase table. For each matched phrase, the translation with the highest frequency is pre-selected by default; for example, "China is a" is pre-selected on the first row in Figure 1. The user may substitute one of the proposed alternatives in place of the pre-selected option. Selections are made as an on-off toggle with a maximum of one selection per row, and a null selection can be made by clicking any selected translation to deselect it. Clicking on an item immediately substi-

tutes it into the appropriate location in the proposed translation string. For example, in Figure 2, the English translation "contraction" has been selected over the default "austerity" on the fifth row; and the null selection has been made on the second and seventh rows. Once all such choices have been made, the user edits the string composed of the choices made for each phrase.

Additional features commonly included in production CAT systems, such as the ability to add new entries to the phrase table and to dynamically update frequencies of phrase table items were disabled during our experiment to avoid complicating our results with factors that would likely vary depending upon the amount of text reuse within each passage in the test set.

To make the translation procedure as similar as possible in both MT post-editing and options cases, the text for the MT post-editing evaluations was fetched beforehand from Google Translate and imported into the same environment used for the options experiments, where it was presented for post-editing in the same manner as for the options case, but without displaying any matches from a phrase table.

In what follows, we use "default selections" to refer to the initial selections as presented to the user (and their concatenation), "user selections" for the actual combination of selections ultimately chosen by the user (and the corresponding string), and "final translation" for the finished translation created by post-editing of the user selections.

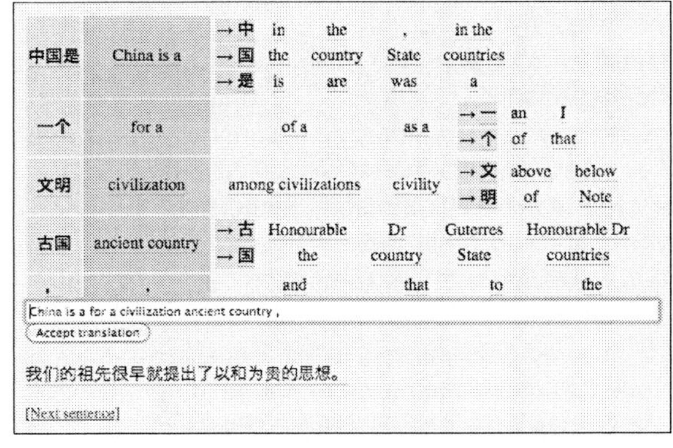

Figure 1. The interface for displaying translation options, shown with default selections highlighted, on a Chinese-to-English translation task.

---

[5] We use the word "phrase" to refer to an arbitrary string of terms rather than any particular linguistic construction.

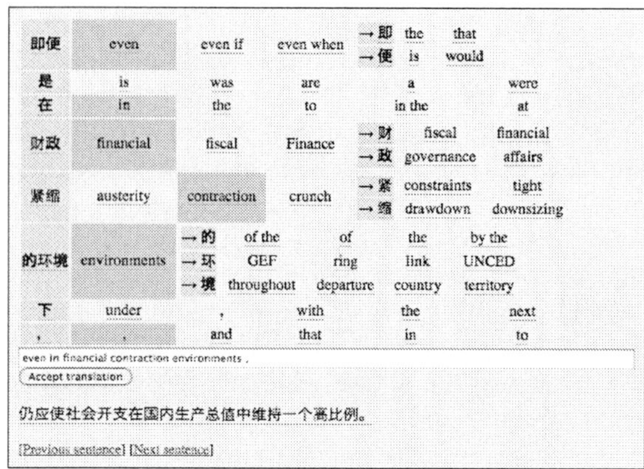

Figure 2. The interface for displaying translation options, with two null selections (rows 2 and 7) and one alternative selection (row 5). This set of selections corresponds to a total of three clicks, the minimum number required to produce this set of selections.

3.4 Procedure

Twenty-four Masters-level students in the Translation Department, at a university in which English is the primary language of teaching, participated in this study.[6] They were all native speakers of Mandarin and highly competent in English.

The students performed translations in four 45-minute sessions: Multi UN post-editing, Multi UN options, Literary post-editing, and Literary options. In each session, they translated continuous passages of Chinese text from the appropriate domain into English using the interface describe above. For the post-editing sessions, the output of Google Translate was provided in the same interface, with the options table hidden. The students were not allowed to use any additional translation aids, with the exception of a single specified online dictionary (cdict.net). The translation had to be completed in the allotted time; thus, we held translation time as a constant, and measured differences in translation effort and quality in the four sessions.

Our test sets contained data similar to but excluded from the data used to create the phrase table. For the Literary domain, this consisted of sections of text from chapters 52 onwards; for the Multi UN

domain, we selected document fragments immediately post-dating the latest documents in the corpus.[7] For each domain, we used the same test set for both assistance types, while ensuring that each student translated a different source text using options to the text they post-edited from MT. We asked two different students to translate the same passage under each condition.

After the translations had been completed, each student was asked to evaluate the quality of the translations of four other students, two of whom had translated the same passage using options and two of whom had translated this same passage by post-editing MT output. These four translations were presented in a differing random order each time so that the evaluators had no way of knowing which translator or which assistance type corresponded to any given part of the translation. Students were asked to give a holistic rating from 1 to 5 of the quality of each translation. There was substantial agreement among the annotators. 43% of quality annotations differed by 1 or less between the two annotators who evaluated the same translation, and 87% differed by 2 or less.

4 Experimental results

We first discuss our results on the amount of translation effort required (Section 4.1), and then the factors impacting translation quality (Section 4.2).

4.1 Translation effort

Table 1 reports the average technical translation effort for each of the four sessions. For MT post-editing ("PE$_{MT}$"), we measure the effort using Translation Edit Rate (TER) (Snover et. al, 2006). This metric, used also in a number of previous studies (e.g., Koponen 2012; Koponen 2013; Koehn and Germann 2014), reflects the number of edit operations performed per 100 words of the final translation.

For the use of options, we measure two kinds of effort ("Options+PE$_{user}$"). The first kind is the effort for selecting options ("Options"). Rather than the raw number of clicks, we report instead the number of clicks (i.e. options chosen) per 100 words of the final translation, to facilitate a more

---

[6] Although a total of 25 students participated, one student failed to fully observe the rules of the experiment, and so this student's data is excluded from the data presented in this paper.

[7] Document fragments from April 2010 available through http://documents.un.org/, the UN documents site from which the Multi UN corpus was extracted.

natural comparison with the TER figures. We considered only the final user selection – i.e. for a given word, clicking the second suggested translation, and then clicking the third suggestion thereby replacing it, would count as one click not two. The second kind is the effort for post-editing the user selections into the final translation ("PE_{user}"), again reported as TER. As a baseline, we also include the hypothetical TER for post-editing the default selections into the final translation without using options ("$PE_{default}$").

As shown in Table 1, for every 100 words in the Literary domain, the use of options reduced the number of edits (TER) from 65.1 to 48.8, at the cost of 25.7 clicks. The editing effort compares favorably to MT post-editing, whose relatively high TER of 61.0 reflects the poor quality of MT output in the face of out-of-domain sentences. Assuming that less effort is needed to click than to edit a word, it can be argued that the use of options requires less technical effort for this domain.

In the Multi UN domain, the use of options again reduced the TER, from 47.4 to 36.1, at the cost of 12.0 clicks. The TER for MT post-editing, however, was even lower, at 27.3. This result suggests that for a resource-rich domain with MT systems trained with matching data, the higher quality of the MT output outweighs the reduction in effort brought by the options.

The number of clicks per 100 words is notably higher for the Literary domain than the Multi UN. This can be explained by modern Chinese having longer average word length than literary Chinese. Furthermore, UN documents tend to contain repeated technical terms and phrases that are identified and matched as single phrases when they reoccur.

One factor that could potentially influence our results is the degree to which the translator selects the option in the "optimal" manner. As observed by Koehn (2009b), when the translator saw an option that was suitable, he or she might have simply typed it in, rather than using the clicking mechanism to insert. To investigate whether this was a common phenomenon, we needed to compare actual user selection of options to the hypothetically "ideal" selections, given the final translation. To do this, we calculated the optimal set of selections that would have resulted in the closest string to that user's final translation, as measured by TER. On the Literary domain, the selections chosen by sev-

eral translators had the same TER as the optimal selections, and average user selection performance was within 10% of ideal performance.[8] On the Multi UN domain, only one translator's selections scored the same as the ideal selections, and average user performance was within 20% of ideal. These figures confirm that while translators may have been influenced by options that they did not select, they only rarely failed to select options that would have reduced the technical effort required for their final translation.

Domain	Assistance Type	Clicks	TER
Multi UN	$PE_{default}$	0	47.4
	Options+PE_{user}	12.0	36.1
	PE_{MT}	0	27.3
Literary	$PE_{default}$	0	65.1
	Options+PE_{user}	25.7	48.8
	PE_{MT}	0	61.0

Table 1. Technical translation effort for using MT post-editing ("PE_{MT}") and options ("Options+PE_{user}"), and the baseline of post-editing directly from default selections without using options ("$PE_{default}$"). The effort is expressed by the number of clicks per 100 words for selecting options, and by the TER for post-editing from Google Translate output ("PE_{MT}") or from the user selections ("PE_{user}").

4.2 Translation quality

Table 2 shows the average translation quality for different combinations of domains and assistance types. Despite their different levels of translation effort, all four yielded similar average quality scores, with MT post-editing on the Multi UN domain scoring slightly higher. This is likely explained in part by the fact that Google Translate uses UN documents as training data, and thus performs particularly well on material from this domain.[9] These averages, however, mask some

____

[8] That is, on average the amount of post-editing work that a user could have avoided if he or she had chosen precisely those options that would minimize such work was less than 10% of his or her total post-editing work, as measured by the TER metric.

[9] http://www.reuters.com/article/2007/03/28/us-google-translate-idUSN1921881520070328

significant variations, to which we now turn our attention.

Domain	Assistance Type	Quality score
Multi UN	PE_{MT}	4.25
	Options+PE_{user}	4.06
Literary	PE_{MT}	4.06
	Options+PE_{user}	4.09

Table 2. Average translation quality by assistance type and domain as measured by manual evaluation.

Options vs. post-editing. Of the 24 students, 10 scored higher in both domains when using options, 11 scored higher in both domains using post-editing; only three scored higher on the Literary domain using options but scored lower with it on the UN domain. There was thus a strong correlation between difference in options-based quality and post-edit-based quality in the two domains (Pearson correlation coefficient: r=0.84, p<0.01). Figure 3 illustrates this correlation as a graph; with the exception of the three data points in the lower-right quadrant, x-y pairs are always either both positive or both negative. In other words, the options consistently helped some students to create higher quality translations, while other students consistently produced higher quality translations by post-editing, even for two domains with significant differences in MT output quality.

We can thus divide our translators into two main groups: those who on both domains improved their translation quality with options (which we term the "Options+" group), and those who showed improved quality with MT post-editing ("Options-"). Table 3 shows the consistent gap in average quality score between options and MT post-editing for these two groups.

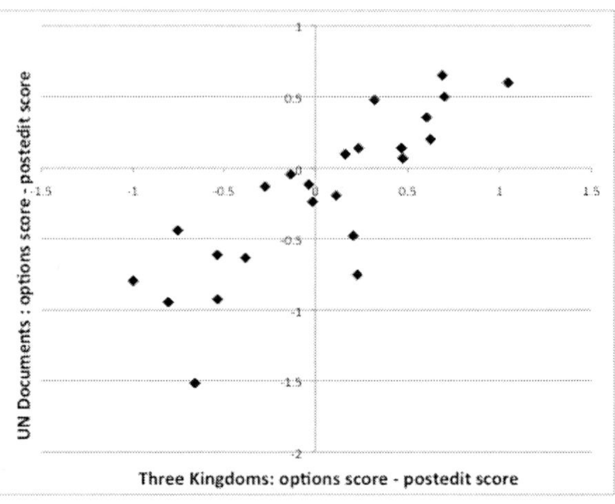

Figure 3. Improvement in manual quality assessment score using options on the Multi UN domain vs. improvement using options on the Literary domain.

Group	Domain	Assistance Type	Quality Score
Options+	Multi UN	PE_{MT}	3.93
		Options+PE_{user}	*4.25*
	Literary	PE_{MT}	3.83
		Options+PE_{user}	*4.36*
Options-	Multi UN	PE_{MT}	*4.45*
		Options+PE_{user}	3.87
	Literary	PE_{MT}	*4.22*
		Options+PE_{user}	3.76

Table 3. Translation quality as measured by manual evaluation, grouped by those whose translation quality increased with options (+) and those whose quality decreased (-).

Assistance uptake. We next investigated whether members of the Options- group were unable or unwilling to make use of the options, similar to the "refuseniks" identified by Koehn (2009b). As shown in Table 4, the average number of clicks per 100 words among members of the Options- group was somewhat below those of Options+ for both domains (22.6 vs 26.2 for Literary, and 11.1 vs 12.2 for Multi UN); but these figures are still broadly comparable, indicating that both groups did make use of options. Additionally, both the highest and lowest numbers of clicks per 100 words (2.0 and 47.2 respectively) for a document in the Literary domain occurred in the Options-group, strongly suggesting that other factors beyond whether or not users made use of options affected the degree to which they benefited from their presence. There was however a clear correlation (r=0.69, p<0.01) between how often an individual user clicked on one domain and on the other, indicating that user preference is a more important factor than domain in determining assistance uptake.

Domain	Group	Clicks per 100 words
Multi UN	Options+	12.2
	Options-	11.1
Literary	Options+	26.2
	Options-	22.6

Table 4. The average number of clicks (i.e., option selections) per 100 words, compared between the Options+ and Options- groups and across domains.

Translator ability. Finally, we considered the possibility that only more advanced translators benefited from the options, or vice versa. The average per-translator per-domain quality scores ranged from 3.3 to 4.9, confirming the existence of variation in individual translator ability. Looking at the absolute quality scores for the Options+ and Options- groups, we found the same average score of 4.1 for both groups when averaged over all four of each individual's translations. The strongest and weakest performing individuals were both in the Options+ group, demonstrating that both strong and weak translators can and do benefit from options, though not all do. These results suggest that translator ability does not determine whether or not options are beneficial.

In summary, regardless of the differences in domain and the quality of MT output, and regardless of their translation competence, some translators consistently produced better translations with MT post-editing than with options, even though they made full use of options; others showed the opposite tendency, again consistently so.

5   Conclusions

This paper has presented a study on the use of word and phrase translation options and MT post-editing. We compared a resource-rich domain that benefits from an MT system with matching training data, and a resource-poor one that yields lower-quality MT output. We found that the use of options required less technical effort than MT post-editing for the latter domain, but not for the former. In terms of translation quality, however, we found that individual translators exhibited consistent preferences for either options or MT post-editing across two domains: those whose translations improved when using options as compared with MT post-editing benefitted more from this type of assistance regardless of domain, and likewise those who did better without it again did so without respect to domain. Furthermore, we found that improvement in translation quality was not simply a function of translation ability, nor was it merely a matter of whether or not translators engaged with options selecting functionality of the CAT system. We therefore echo Koehn (2009b)'s suggestion that more study is needed into the cognitive processes of translation and how these may explain these different outcomes.

Acknowledgements

The work described in this paper was supported by a Teaching Development Grant from City University of Hong Kong (Project No. 6000489).

References

Nora Aranberri, Gorka Labaka, Arantza Diaz de Ilharraza, and Kepa Sarasola. 2014. Comparison of post-editing productivity between professional translators and lay users. *Proc. AMTA Workshop on Post-Editing Technology and Practice.*

Andreas Eisele, Yu Chen. 2010. MultiUN: A Multilingual Corpus from United Nation Documents. *Proc. Seventh conference on International Language Resources and Evaluation*, p. 2868-2872.

Federico Gaspari, Antonio Toral, Sudip Kumar Naskar, Declan Groves, and Andy Way. 2014. Perception vs. Reality: Measuring Machine Translation Post-editing Productivity. *Proc. Third Workshop on Post-Editing Technology and Practice.*

Spence Green, Jeffrey Heer, and Christopher D. Manning. 2013. The Efficacy of Human Post-Editing for Language Translation. *Proc. ACM Human Factors in Computing Systems (CHI).*

A. Guerberof. 2009. Productivity and quality in MT post-editing. 2009. *Proc. MT Summit Workshop on New Tools for Translators.*

Chung-chi Huang, Mei-hua Chen, Ping-che Yang and Jason S. Chang. 2013. A Computer-Assisted Translation and Writing System. *ACM Transactions on*

Asian Language Information Processing 12(4): Article 15.

Philipp Koehn, Hieu Hoang, Alexandra Birch, Chris Callison-Burch, Marcello Federico, Nicola Bertoldi, Brooke Cowan, Wade Shen, Christine Moran, Richard Zens, Chris Dyer, Ondrej Bojar, Alexandra Constantin and Evan Herbst. 2007. Moses: Open Source Toolkit for Statistical Machine Translation, *Annual Meeting of the Association for Computational Linguistics (ACL)*, demonstration session, Prague, Czech Republic.

Philipp Koehn. 2009a. A web-based interactive computer aided translation tool. *Proc. ACL-IJCNLP 2009 Software Demonstrations*, p. 17-20.

Philipp Koehn. 2009b. A process study of computer-aided translation. *Machine Translation* 23(4):241-263.

Philipp Koehn. 2010. Enabling Monolingual Translators: Post-Editing vs. Options. *Proc. Human Language Technologies: The 2010 Annual Conference of the North American Chapter of the ACL.*

Philipp Koehn and Ulrich Germann. 2014. The Impact of Machine Translation Quality on Human Post-editing. *Proc. Workshop on Humans and Computer-assisted Translation.*

Maarit Koponen. 2012. Comparing human perceptions of post-editing effort with post-editing operations. *Proc. 7th Workshop on Statistical Machine Translation*, p.181-190.

Maarit Koponen, Wilker Aziz, Luciana Ramos, and Lucia Specia. 2012. Post-editing time as a measure of cognitive effort. *AMTA 2012 Workshop on Post-Editing Technology and Practice*, p.11-20.

Maarit Koponen. 2013. This translation is not too bad: An analysis of post-editor choices in a machine translation post-editing task. *Proc. MT Summit XIV Workshop on Post-editing Technology and Practice.*

Hans P. Krings. 2001. *Repairing texts: Empirical investigations of machine translation post-editing process.* Kent State University Press.

Philippe Langlais, Sébastien Sauvé, George Foster, Elliott Macklovitch, Guy Lapalme. 2000. Evaluation of TRANSTYPE, a Computer-aided Translation Typing System: A comparison of a theoretical- and a user- oriented evaluation procedures. *Proc. LREC.*

Samuel Laubli, Mark Fishel, Gary Massey, Maureen Ehrensberger-Dow, and Martin Volk. 2013. Assessing post-editing efficiency in a realistic translation environment. *Proc. MT Summit XIV Workshop on Post-editing Technology and Practice.*

Robert C. Moore. 2002. Fast and Accurate Sentence Alignment of Bilingual Corpora. *Proceedings of the 5th Conference of the Association for Machine Translation in the Americas on Machine Translation*, p. 135-144.

Sharon O'Brien. 2011. Towards predicting post-editing productivity. *Machine Translation* 25:197-215.

Franz Josef Och and Hermann Ney. 2003. A Systematic Comparison of Various Statistical Alignment Models. *Computational Linguistics* 29(1):19-51.

M. Plitt and F. Masselot. 2010. A productivity test of statistical machine translation post-editing in a typical localization context. *Prague Bulletin of Mathematical Linguistics* 93:7-16.

Matthew Snover, Bonnie Dorr, Richard Schwartz, Linnea Micciulla, and John Makhoul. 2006. A Study of Translation Edit Rate with Targeted Human Annotation. *Proc. 7th Conference of the Association for Machine Translation in the Americas*, p. 223-231.

Yan Song, Prescott Klassen, Fei Xia and Chunyu Kit. 2012. Entropy-based Training Data Selection for Domain Adaptation. *Proc. COLING 2012*, p.1191-1200.

Lucia Specia, Nicola Cancedda, Marc Dymetman, Marco Turchi and Nello Cristianini. 2009. Estimating the Sentence-Level Quality of Machine Translation Systems. *Proc. 13th Annual Conference of the EAMT*, p. 28-35.

Midori Tatsumi and Johann Roturier. 2010. Source Text Characteristics and Technical and Temporal Post-Editing Effort: What is Their Relationship? *Proc. 2nd Joint EM+/CNGL Workshop "Bringing MT to the User: Research on Integrating MT in the Translation Industry" (JEC).*

Irina Temnikova. 2010. Cognitive Evaluation Approach for a Controlled Language Post-Editing Experiment. *Proc. LREC.*

Liang Tian, Derek F. Wong, Lidia S. Chao, Paulo Quaresma, Francisco Oliveira, Shuo Li, Yiming Wang, Yi Lu. 2014. UM-Corpus: A Large English-Chinese Parallel Corpus for Statistical Machine Translation. *Proceedings of the 9th International Conference on Language Resources and Evaluation (LREC'14).*

Joseph P. Turian, Luke Shen, and I. Dan Melamed. 2013. Evaluation of machine translation and its evaluation. *Proc. MT Summit IX.*

Lucia Morado Vazquez, Silvia Rodriguez Vazquez, and Pierrette Bouillon. 2013. Comparing forum data post-editing performance using phrase table and machine translation output: a pilot study. *Proc. XIV Machine Translation Summit.*

V. Zhechev. 2012. Machine translation infrastructure and post-editing performance at Autodesk. *Proc. AMTA Workshop on Post-editing Technology and Practice.*

Investigating the potential of post-ordering SMT output to improve translation quality

Pratik Mehta, Anoop Kunchukuttan, Pushpak Bhattacharyya
Center for Indian Language Technology
Department of Computer Science and Engineering
Indian Institute of Technology Bombay
`{pratikm,anoopk,pb}@cse.iitb.ac.in`

Abstract

Post-ordering of Statistical Machine Translation (SMT) output to correct word order errors could be a promising area of research to overcome structural divergence between language pairs. This is especially true when it is difficult to incorporate rich linguistic features into the baseline decoder. In this paper, we propose an algorithm for generating oracle reorderings of MT output. We use the oracle reorderings to empirically quantify an upper bound on improvement in translation quality through post-ordering techniques. In our study encompassing multiple language pairs, we show that significant improvement in translation quality can be obtained by applying reordering transformations on the output of the SMT system. This presents a strong case for investing effort in exploring the post-ordering problem.

1 Introduction

Word order divergence is a central problem in Statistical Machine Translation (SMT) and major stumbling block to generating comprehensible translations. Many solutions for reordering have been proposed to bridge this divergence. Word order divergence is generally handled within the core SMT model or using source-side reordering as a pre-processing step. In the core SMT system, word order can be tackled using a variety of models of varying complexity: word-level alignment models (Brown et al., 1993), lexicalized reordering models (Tillmann, 2004; Galley and Manning, 2008), hierarchical SMT (Chiang, 2005), syntax based SMT (Yamada and Knight, 2002), *etc*. SMT models like phrase-based SMT are not good at bridging word order divergence (Marie et al., 2014). In these cases, source-side reordering is used as a pre-processing step to convert the source sentence to target language word order (Collins et al., 2005; Ramanathan et al., 2008). The best performing approaches generally rely on parse information on the source side to generate the correct word order. However, it has proved to be a very difficult problem which is far from being solved, especially when parse information is not forthcoming. The computational complexity of searching through a large space of potential reorderings and the need for incorporating higher level linguistic information are the primary challenges in tackling the reordering problem.

While there is active research in preordering and in-decoder approaches, there has been little work on the problem of post-ordering of SMT output. We define the word-order post-ordering as follows:

Given the output of an MT system, permute the words of the output to generate a better word order.

The following example shows how simply reordering the words in the SMT output can improve translation quality:

Source:

य बीत पांच सालों म ग्रीस को मिलन वाला तीसरा राहत पकज ह

Translation (Google Translate[1]):

```
They meet Greece in the last five years is the
third bailout package
```

Post-ordered Translation:

```
They is the third bailout package in the last
five years meet Greece
```

The following are a few reasons why post-ordering may be an interesting direction to explore:

- SMT decoders have to search through a very large search space to find the best translations. Hence, the translation models are generally simple and use a limited number of fea-

---

[1] `https://translate.google.com/`

D S Sharma, R Sangal and E Sherly. Proc. of the 12th Intl. Conference on Natural Language Processing, pages 351–356,
Trivandrum, India. December 2015. ©2015 NLP Association of India (NLPAI)

tures so as to make decoding computationally tractable. Generating correct word order generally requires richer models which can look at long distance dependencies. The post-ordering stage is a good stage in the SMT pipeline where richer models can be applied to the best translation candidates to correct word order errors.

- If the target language is resource rich, we can use resources of the target language. For instance, chunkers, constituency/dependency parsers, *etc.* may be available for the target language. This is the case for translation from many Indian language to English. Hence, our experiments in the paper have focussed on Indian language to English translation. However, an important limitation of this approach could be the inability of these tools to perform with high accuracy in the face of errors in the baseline translation output.

- Post-ordering can take advantage of human-postediting of MT output. The post-edited output can be useful to learn post-ordering models that are customized to the baseline SMT system.

- Even if human post-edited output is not available, aligning the baseline output with the reference translation can help construct oracle reorderings. The parallel corpus comprising the baseline output and their oracle reorderings could be used to learn post-ordering models customized to the baseline SMT system.

Before embarking of designing post-ordering methods, it would be prudent to estimate if post-ordering methods can actually improve translation quality. In this paper, we study the viability of post-ordering *i.e. can significant improvements in translation quality be obtained by simply permuting the underlying MT system output's word order?*. We try to answer this question by estimating an upper bound on the translation accuracy after post-ordering. For this, we propose to compute oracle reorderings of the translation output by comparing it with the reference translation. Our experiments using this approach show significant improvement in translation quality over baselines, as measured by both automatic and manual evaluation metrics. This puts forward a good case for exploring post-ordering methods for machine translation.

The following is an outline of the paper. In Section 2, we describe related work. In the remainder of the paper, we estimate an upper bound on the potential gains in translation accuracy by post-ordering. Section 3 describes our method for computing oracle reorderings from the translation output, which is used to estimate the upper bound. Section 4 describes our experimental setup and 5 presents the results and discusses the observations. Section 6 concludes the paper and points out future work.

2 Related Work

Oracle translations have been used by many researchers for diagnosing translation output. Auli et al. (2009) and Wisniewski and Yvon (2013) have used oracle translations to do reference reachability analysis and identify model and search errors. Wisniewski and Yvon (2013) have used the oracle translations to conduct various kinds of failure analysis and study effect of various search parameters. Dreyer et al. (2007), Li and Khudanpur (2009) and Wisniewski and Yvon (2013) use oracle translations to understand the limitations of various reordering constraints imposed on translation decoders. In the same spirit, we try to estimate an upper bound on the benefits of post-ordering the baseline SMT output.

Though we do not tackle the problem of post-ordering in this work, we summarize the existing work on post-ordering for SMT. There has been work on post-editing of machine translation output. The method described in (Simard et al., 2007) is most commonly used. It involves automatically post-editing the output of an MT system using another phrase-based MT system trained on parallel data constructed from previously decoded output (e) and corresponding references (e'). Béchara et al. (2011) improvizes on this approach by appending source words (f) to the output part of the parallel data (e), creating a new language (e'#f) and retaining source context. Marie et al. (2014) use a second-pass decoder to improve translation quality. However, none of these works have focussed on word order and the effect on the word order has not been explicitly evaluated.

Post-ordering as a problem has been introduced by Sudoh et al. (2011). However, it is not a

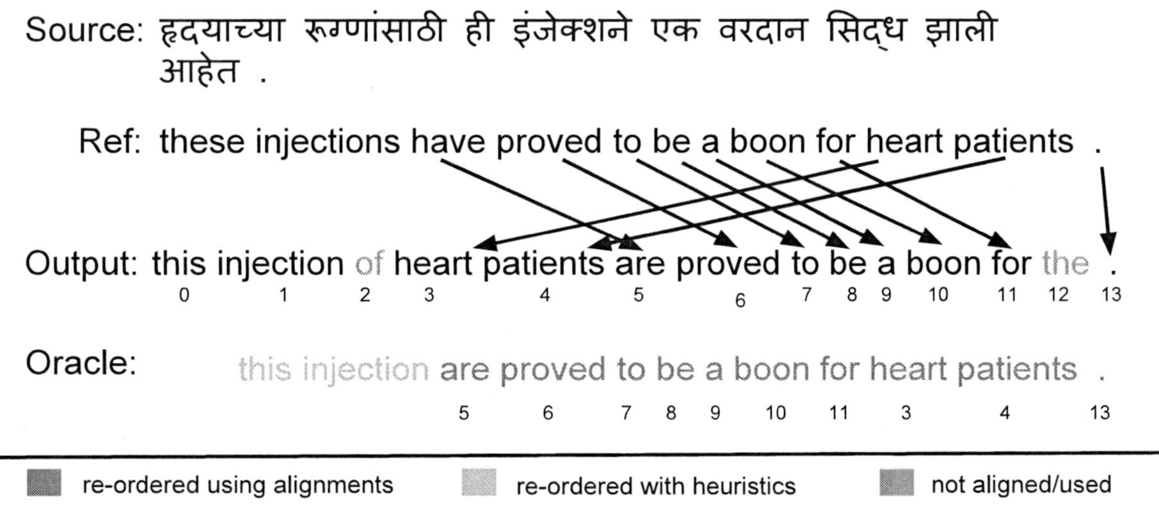

Figure 1: Construction of Oracle reordering

post-ordering system in the sense in which we have defined it. Theirs is actually a two stage translation system that decomposes the translation problem into lexical transfer and reordering sub-problems. Goto et al. (2012) and Goto et al. (2013) also propose post-ordering systems with the same architecture, but different reordering methods in the second stage. The motivation in these post-ordering methods is not to improve upon the word order. Rather, lexical mappings are learnt in the first stage after reordering the target text to match the source order, thus necessitating the second re-ordering stage.

3 Generating Oracle Translations

To estimate an upper bound on the improvement in translation accuracy possible with post-ordering, we generate *oracle* reorderings of the baseline SMT output hypothesis. An *oracle* reordering is the best possible word order of the hypothesis, in terms of fluency and syntactic correctness. We propose the following algorithm for computing the oracle reordering.

1. Obtain word alignments between the hypothesis and reference using the monolingual aligner algorithm in METEOR (Denkowski and Lavie, 2014).

2. Construct a new sentence by rearranging aligned words from the hypothesis using the word-order from the reference.

3. Use additional heuristics to include as many unaligned words from the hypothesis into the *oracle* reordering as possible. In our experiments, the words in the hypothesis that were not aligned by METEOR but found a stem-match in the reference were inserted in the oracle sentence.

The resulting oracle hypothesis is a permutation of a subset of words in the original MT decoding step, such that they reflect the word order in the reference.

4 Experimental Setup

We studied different SMT systems from 10 Indian languages to English for quantifying the potential improvement in translation accuracy. The experiments were carried across 10 Indian languages included in the multilingual ILCI corpus (Jha, 2010), which contains nearly 50,000 parallel sentences . For each language pair, the corpus was split into 46,277 sentences for training, 500 sentences for tuning and 2000 sentences for testing. We trained phrase-based and hierarchical phrase-based systems on this data.

The phrase-based systems were trained using the Moses SMT toolkit (Koehn et al., 2007) with the *grow-diag-final-and heuristic* for phrase extraction and the *msd-bidirectional-fe* model for lexicalized reordering. The trained models were tuned with Minimum Error Rate Training (MERT) (Och, 2003) with default parameters. We trained

349

Score	Adequacy	Fluency
1	No meaning	Incomprehensible
2	Little meaning	Disfluent
3	Much meaning	Non-native fluency
4	Most meaning	Good fluency
5	All meaning	Flawless fluency

Table 1: Description of scores for manual evaluation

5-gram language models on the training-set using Kneser-Ney smoothing with SRILM (Stolcke and others, 2002). The hierarchical systems were also trained with Moses using default parameters.

For three phrase-based SMT systems with Hindi, Marathi and Malayalam respectively as source and English as target language, qualitative analysis was performed through manual evaluation of output sentences by native speakers of each of the source languages. Given the source and gold reference, the evaluators were asked to rate the adequacy and fluency of a system's output and oracle sentences on a scale of 1 to 5, as described in (Koehn and Monz, 2006) (see Table 1). The weighted average of the scores over all sentences was then calculated as:

$$average\_score = \sum_{s=1}^{5} s.f(s) \qquad (1)$$

where, s: the score ranging from 1 to 5
$f(s)$: frequency of occurrence of score s

5   Results & Discussion

Table 2 shows the results in case-insensitive BLEU (Papineni et al., 2002). There was significant improvement in oracle reordering over the baseline SMT systems. This trend was consistent across all studied language-pairs and in both phrase-based and hierarchical SMT systems. We see that the oracle sentences were often shorter than the translation hypotheses because words that were not aligned with the reference translations nor accounted for by the heuristics were left out. For fair evaluation, we removed these *outlier* words from the original translations to create *pruned* hypotheses containing the same bag of words as their corresponding oracle sentences and compute BLEU scores. The average improvement in oracle BLEU scores over all language pairs was 59.5% for phrase-based systems, and 60.45% for hierarchical systems. Table 4 shows examples illustrat-

Lang-pair	Model	Original	Pruned	Oracle
hin-eng	PBSMT	22.77	23.12	36.74
	HPBMT	23.87	24.5	37.36
mar-eng	PBSMT	12.6	11.23	18.07
	HPBMT	14.65	13.95	21.97
ben-eng	PBSMT	16.24	15.67	24.38
	HPBMT	14.69	14.01	24.59
guj-eng	PBSMT	17.66	17.03	26.32
	HPBMT	15.96	15.17	24.59
kon-eng	PBSMT	15.56	14.74	22.7
	HPBMT	13.67	12.77	20.85
pan-eng	PBSMT	19.98	19.87	32.72
	HPBMT	20.12	20.00	30.64
urd-eng	PBSMT	17.31	17.17	29.89
	HPBMT	19.05	18.58	29.52
tam-eng	PBSMT	10.54	8.9	14.77
	HPBMT	10.3	9.0	15.4
tel-eng	PBSMT	12.63	11.42	17.96
	HPBMT	11.9	10.66	17.42
mal-eng	PBSMT	8.3	6.03	10.32
	HPBMT	8.46	6.48	11.24

Table 2: Experimental results (BLEU) ISO-639-2 language codes are shown

ing the oracle reorderings from the Hindi-English phrase-based SMT experiment.

In the manual evaluation task, the evaluators frequently rated oracle sentences as being more fluent than the decoded sentences. Average fluency scores across all evaluated sentences improved by a margin of 0.45 in Hindi (16.4%), 0.15 in Malayalam (6.8%) and 0.11 in Marathi (3.9%), as seen in Table 3. The small drop in adequacy of oracle was expected because of imperfect alignments between the disfluent output and their references, which affected the construction of complete oracle sentences. We suspect that this loss in adequacy must also have affected the perception of fluency in cases where the oracle sentence was significantly shorter than the original output. With better alignment aided by transliteration and more sophisticated heuristics, construction of more adequate oracle sentences would be possible. However, this will only serve to reinforce belief in post-ordering as a beneficial exercise - something our results already show.

Lang-pair	Test	Adequacy	Fluency
hin-eng	Original	3.29	2.74
	Oracle	3.19	3.19
mar-eng	Original	3.12	2.83
	Oracle	2.96	2.94
mal-eng	Original	1.92	2.19
	Oracle	1.40	2.34

Table 3: Manual evaluation scores

6 Conclusion

We see that the BLEU score of oracle reorderings show substantial improvements of upto 60.45% over the baseline output. Manual evaluation of MT output also shows 20% improvement in fluency of translations. These improvements were obtained by simply reordering the output of the baseline SMT systems. Our study thus establishes the potential for further research in post-ordering of machine translation output to provide significant gains in translation quality. The post-ordered parallel translation corpus obtained by oracle alignment may be used for learning post-ordering models.

Acknowledgements

We thank the Technology Development for Indian Languages (TDIL) Programme and the Department of Electronics & Information Technology, Govt. of India for providing the ILCI corpus. We thank the National Knowledge Network for making available computational facilities on the Garuda Cloud for performing computationally intensive tasks. Thanks to Aditya Joshi, Joe Cheri Ross and Anupam Ghosh for helping us in evaluation of the MT outputs and for their feedback on translation quality.

References

Michael Auli, Adam Lopez, Hieu Hoang, and Philipp Koehn. 2009. A systematic analysis of translation model search spaces. In *Proceedings of the Fourth Workshop on Statistical Machine Translation*, StatMT '09, pages 224--232, Stroudsburg, PA, USA. Association for Computational Linguistics.

Hanna Béchara, Yanjun Ma, and Josef van Genabith. 2011. Statistical post-editing for a statistical mt system.

Peter F Brown, Vincent J Della Pietra, Stephen A Della Pietra, and Robert L Mercer. 1993. The mathematics of statistical machine translation: Parameter estimation. *Computational linguistics.*

David Chiang. 2005. A hierarchical phrase-based model for statistical machine translation. In *Proceedings of the 43rd Annual Meeting on Association for Computational Linguistics*, pages 263--270. Association for Computational Linguistics.

Michael Collins, Philipp Koehn, and Ivona Kučerová. 2005. Clause restructuring for statistical machine translation. In *Proceedings of the 43rd annual meeting on association for computational linguistics*, pages 531--540. Association for Computational Linguistics.

Michael Denkowski and Alon Lavie. 2014. Meteor universal: Language specific translation evaluation for any target language. In *Proceedings of the EACL 2014 Workshop on Statistical Machine Translation.*

Markus Dreyer, Keith Hall, and Sanjeev Khudanpur. 2007. Comparing reordering constraints for smt using efficient bleu oracle computation. In *Proceedings of the NAACL-HLT 2007/AMTA Workshop on Syntax and Structure in Statistical Translation*, pages 103--110. Association for Computational Linguistics.

Michel Galley and Christopher D Manning. 2008. A simple and effective hierarchical phrase reordering model. In *Proceedings of the Conference on Empirical Methods in Natural Language Processing*, pages 848--856. Association for Computational Linguistics.

Isao Goto, Masao Utiyama, and Eiichiro Sumita. 2012. Post-ordering by parsing for japanese-english statistical machine translation. In *Proceedings of the 50th Annual Meeting of the Association for Computational Linguistics: Short Papers - Volume 2*, ACL '12, pages 311--316, Stroudsburg, PA, USA. Association for Computational Linguistics.

Isao Goto, Masao Utiyama, and Eiichiro Sumita. 2013. Post-ordering by parsing with itg for japanese-english statistical machine translation. 12(4):17:1--17:22, oct.

Girish Nath Jha. 2010. The tdil program and the indian language corpora initiative (ilci).

Philipp Koehn and Christof Monz. 2006. Manual and automatic evaluation of machine translation between european languages. In *Proceedings of the Workshop on Statistical Machine Translation*, pages 102--121. Association for Computational Linguistics.

Philipp Koehn, Hieu Hoang, Alexandra Birch, Chris Callison-Burch, Marcello Federico, Nicola Bertoldi, Brooke Cowan, Wade Shen, Christine Moran, Richard Zens, et al. 2007. Moses: Open source toolkit for statistical machine translation. In *Proceedings of the 45th annual meeting of the ACL on interactive poster and demonstration sessions*, pages 177--180. Association for Computational Linguistics.

Source	मैंने अमेजन नदी के बियाबान एवं नदी तटों की सुंदरता के बारे में पढ़ा व सुना है ।
Reference	I have read and heard about the beauty of the wilderness and river banks of the Amazon river .
Original hypothesis	I Amazon and river banks of the river wilderness about the beauty of read and have heard.
Pruned hypothesis	I Amazon and river banks of the river wilderness about the beauty of read and have heard .
Oracle	I have read and heard about the beauty of wilderness and river banks of the Amazon river .

Source	इस अध्ययन में 5800 परिवारों के 14 हजार बच्चों को शामिल किया गया था ।
Reference	In this study 14 thousand children of 5800 families were included .
Original hypothesis	In this study 5800 families of 14 thousand children had been included.
Pruned hypothesis	In this study 5800 families of 14 thousand children had included .
Oracle	In this study 14 thousand children of 5800 families had included .

Table 4: Oracle post-ordering examples for Hindi-English

Zhifei Li and Sanjeev Khudanpur. 2009. Efficient extraction of oracle-best translations from hypergraphs. In *Proceedings of Human Language Technologies: The 2009 Annual Conference of the North American Chapter of the Association for Computational Linguistics, Companion Volume: Short Papers*, pages 9--12. Association for Computational Linguistics.

Benjamin Marie, Lingua et Machina, and Aurélien Max. 2014. Confidence-based rewriting of machine translation output. In *Conference on Empirical Methods in Natural Language Processing*, pages 1261--1272.

Franz Josef Och. 2003. Minimum error rate training in statistical machine translation. In *Proceedings of the 41st Annual Meeting on Association for Computational Linguistics-Volume 1*, pages 160--167. Association for Computational Linguistics.

Kishore Papineni, Salim Roukos, Todd Ward, and Wei-Jing Zhu. 2002. Bleu: a method for automatic evaluation of machine translation. In *Proceedings of the 40th annual meeting on association for computational linguistics*, pages 311--318. Association for Computational Linguistics.

Ananthakrishnan Ramanathan, Jayprasad Hegde, Ritesh M Shah, Pushpak Bhattacharyya, and M Sasikumar. 2008. Simple syntactic and morphological processing can help english-hindi statistical machine translation. In *IJCNLP*, pages 513--520.

Michel Simard, Nicola Ueffing, Pierre Isabelle, and Roland Kuhn. 2007. Rule-based translation with statistical phrase-based post-editing.

Andreas Stolcke et al. 2002. Srilm-an extensible language modeling toolkit.

Katsuhito Sudoh, Xianchao Wu, Kevin Duh, Hajime Tsukada, and Masaaki Nagata. 2011. Post-ordering in statistical machine translation. In *Proc. MT Summit*.

Christoph Tillmann. 2004. A unigram orientation model for statistical machine translation. In *Proceedings of HLT-NAACL 2004: Short Papers*, pages 101--104. Association for Computational Linguistics.

Guillaume Wisniewski and François Yvon. 2013. Oracle decoding as a new way to analyze phrase-based machine translation. *Machine translation*, 27(2):115--138.

Kenji Yamada and Kevin Knight. 2002. A decoder for syntax-based statistical mt. In *Proceedings of the 40th Annual Meeting on Association for Computational Linguistics*, pages 303--310. Association for Computational Linguistics.

Applying Sanskrit Concepts for Reordering in MT

Akshar Bharati, Sukhada, Prajna Jha, Soma Paul and Dipti M Sharma
Language Technology Research Center
International Institute of Information Technology
Hyderabad, India
sukhada@research.iiit.ac.in, pragya.jha.jk@gmail.com
soma@iiit.ac.in, dipti@iiit.ac.in

Abstract

This paper presents a rule-based reordering approach for English-Hindi machine translation. We have used the concept of *pada,* from Pāṇinian Grammar to frame the reordering rules. A *pada* is a word form which is ready to participate in a sentence. The rules are generic enough to apply on any English-Indian language pair. We tested the rules on English-Hindi language pair and obtained better comprehensibility score as compared to Google Translate on the same test set. In assessing the effectiveness of the rules on padas which are analogous to minimal phrases in English, we achieved upto 93% accuracy on the test data.

1 Introduction

Like many other languages, Hindi word order differs from English. That is why in machine translation (MT), in addition to finding appropriate word senses, reordering of words plays a crucial role. Reordering in rule-based MT is a stage where the positions of the words of the source language (SL) sentence are reordered according to the target language (TL) syntax.

Hindi is a relatively free word-order language. The relations between constituents are marked explicitly with the help of postpositions. The morphological richness of the language allows the constituents to change their positions freely within a clause (Kachru, 2006; Chatterjee et al., 2007). In spite of that, not all the words can occur freely at any position (Kachru, 2006). For example,

- Postpositions follow their objects

- Verbs always precede their auxiliaries

- Modifiers such as prepositional modifiers, adjectival modifiers or determiners precede their head

For such reasons and many more described in Section 4, one needs to reorder the sentences to arrive at a natural translation.

Statistically trained systems give good results in less amount of time and manual effort. But any statistically trained system requires huge parallel corpus. Indian languages (ILs) lack a reasonable parallel corpus size for English and IL pairs. Hence, we explore a rule based approach for reordering taking insights from Pāṇinian Grammar (PG).

The available reordering approaches are discussed in Section 2. Our reordering approach is described in Section 3. Section 4 talks about major divergences between English and Hindi. Reordering rule formation is described in Section 5 and Section 6 presents experiments and results. Section 7 does error analysis and Section 8 concludes the paper.

2 Related Work

There are many approaches to handle TL word ordering. Some of them are described below:

1. Koehn et al (2003) perform reordering by using relative distortion probability distribution model trained from joint probability distribution model $\phi(\bar{e}, \bar{f})$. Their model relies on the language model to produce words in right order (Koehn, 2009).

2. Kunchukuttan et al (2014) developed a phrase based system for English-Indian Language (henceforth En-IL) pairs that uses two extensions- (i) source reordering for En-IL translation using source side reordering rules developed by (Patel et al., 2013) and (ii) describing untranslated words for Indian-IL translation by using transliteration procedure.

D S Sharma, R Sangal and E Sherly. Proc. of the 12th Intl. Conference on Natural Language Processing, pages 357–366,
Trivandrum, India. December 2015. ©2015 NLP Association of India (NLPAI)

3. A statistical translation model introduced by Yamada and Knight (2001) incorporates features based on syntax and converts SL parse tree according to TL with the help of probabilistic operations at required nodes using expectation-maximization algorithm. This model accepts parse trees as an input on which it performs child node reordering according to the TL.

4. Costa-Jussà and Fonollosa (2009) used an Ngram-based Reordering (NbR) method that uses SMT techniques to generate reordering graph, which utilizes word classes and NbR model for reordering. It produces an intermediate representation of source corpora where word-order of SL is represented more closely to the order of TL.

5. Universal Networking Language (UNL) is an interlingual representation of MT systems through semantic graphs, which comprise of semantic relations, attributes and universal words. The UNL approach transforms the lexicon into semantic hyper-graph which decides the word-order of the TL through parent-child positioning and relationship priority (Singh et al., 2007).

3 Our Approach

We present a rule based approach which is based on PG, particularly on the concept of *pada*. Though this paper presents an English-Hindi (En-Hi) reordering approach, we claim that the same system is generic enough to be used for any English-IL pair with some modifications.

PG analyses a word as a combination of a root/stem (*prakṛti*) and an affix (*pratyaya*) (Bharati et al., 2015). It is both the root and the affix that jointly denote the meaning – *prakṛtipratyayau sahārtham brūtaḥ* (Lit. root and affix together convey the meaning) (Rathore, 1998). PG deals with morphology which is not separated but is interlinked with syntax and semantics (Subrahmanyam, 1999). This in a way helps capture "how languages encode information" and "how the information flows in language". Let us explore it through example 1, taken from Bharati et al. (2015).

(1) a. mārjārāḥ   mūṣakān
         cat.PL,NOM rat.PL,ACC

mārayanti
kill.3,PL,PR
'Cats kill rats.'

   b. mūṣakān mārjārāḥ mārayanti

   c. mārjārāḥ mārayanti mūṣakān

   d. mārayanti mārjārāḥ mūṣakān

   e. mūṣakān mārayanti mārjārāḥ

   f. mārayanti mūṣakān mārjārāḥ

The words in Sanskrit, in example 1a, can be ordered in any possible combination as shown through 1b to 1f. Still, they convey more or less the same meaning, but in English, changing the order of the subject and object as in "Rats kill cats" changes the meaning of the sentence all together.

The words in 1a have explicit morphemes called *vibhaktis* attached to them which mark the desired information explicitly. In other words, all the words have formed *padas* (described in Section 3.1), hence, they can occur freely at any position in the sentence. This gives us the clue to identity the relational morphemes and attach them with their relata.

3.1 *Pada* Formation

In PG, a *śabda* denotes a linguistic expression ranging from individual speech sound to an utterance (Singh, 1991) whereas a *pada* is a primary structural unit that occurs in actual sentences. Sanskrit has a grammatical rule *apadaṁ na prayuñjīta* (Dvivedi, 1953) which says: "a word which is not a *pada* should not be used in a sentence". Pāṇini defines a *pada* as follows: "A finished word form which is ready to participate in a sentence" (Mahavir, 1984; Bharati et al., 2015).

The sūtra *suptiṅantaṁ padam* (A 1.4.14i) states: "a word ending in *sup* (nominal suffix) or *tiṅ* (verbal suffix) is called a *pada*". The *sup* and *tiṅ* are the nominal and verbal grammatical inflections. The *sup* is the nominal case and the *tiṅ* is finite verb inflection. *Vibhakti* is a general term in Sanskrit used for both the nominal as well as verbal suffixes.

According to the sūtra (A. 1.4.14),

1. *Prātipadika + sup = subanta pada*
   (nominal stem + nominal suffix = nominal *pada*)

2. *Dhātu + tiṅ = tiṅanta pada*
   (verbal stem + finite verbal suffix = verbal *pada*)

Hence *pada* is a grammatically inflected word form which is ready to participate in a sentence expressing its role and relations with other words in the sentence.

3.2 The *subanta* and *tiṅanta padas* in English

Let us take some English sentences and use Pāṇinian primitives such as *sup*, *tiṅ* and *pada* etc. to analyse them.

(2) Rama laughed.

The constituency tree diagram for sentence 2 is shown in Figure 1. The word *Rama* is the subject and thus does not carry any case marker. We are now looking for the criteria equivalent to the notion of *sup* Bharati et al (1996) show that English has the notion of generalized vibhakti. which corresponds to the *sup* suffixes in Sanskrit. The generalized vibhakti is realized either through subject[1] or object positions or through prepositions. Thus in sentence 2, *Rama* occurring at subject position seems to carry no *sup*, but according to Bharati et al., (1996), since it occurs at the subject position it carries a generalized vibhakti in terms of subject position, hence, it is a *subanta pada*.

The verb *laughed* has *-ed* suffix as a *tiṅ*, hence it can be called as a *tiṅanta* pada. See Figure 1 where each box represents an independent *pada*.

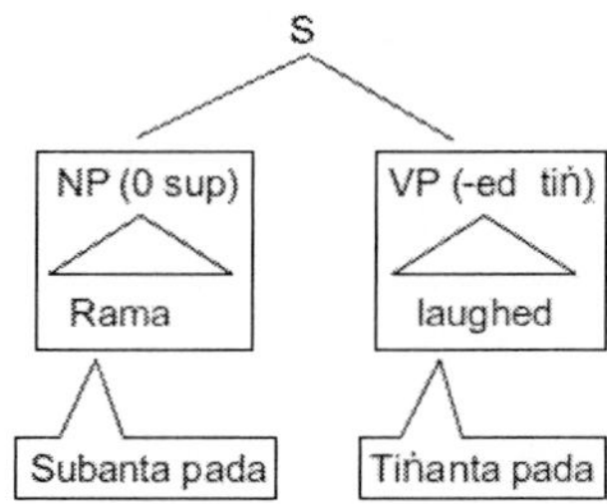

Figure 1: *Pada* information in tree diagram for 2

Example 2 contains only minimal phrases where each phrase consists of a single word, hence just by applying the sūtra *suptiṅantaṁ padam* (A 1.4.14) we can conclude that minimal phrase is a *pada* from Pāṇinian viewpoint. But what about the phrases which consist of more than one word? For example,

(3) The new students have been working on this problem.

In sentence 3, the word group *the new students* is an NP and *have been working on this problem* is a VP which consists of a verb group and a prepositional phrase. The verb group *have been working* contains *work* as a verb and *have been -ing* as a *tiṅ*/auxiliaries, hence, it can be taken as a *tiṅanta* pada. But, how many padas should we consider in the constituents *the new students* and *on this problem*?

The constituent *the new students* in sentence 3 occurs at subject position, hence, as stated by Bharati et al., (1996) it carries a generalized vibhakti in terms of subject position. Also, if the constituent *the new students* occurs in a prepositional phrase all three words take only a single preposition as in *I gave a book **to the new students***. The head noun *students* along with its modifiers *new* and *the* takes only one-vibhakti/*ekasup* 'to', Therefore, in example 3, the whole group, *the new students* can be taken as a single *subanta* pada. Similarly, *on this problem* can also be taken as a *subanta* pada which carries the preposition *on* as a *sup*.

As said before, a *tiṅanta pada* is formed by adding *tiṅ* suffixes to the verbal stems.

The finite verb phrases (VPs) are exceptional cases in English where an adverbial phrase can occur between a finite verb group. For example, take sentence 4:

(4) The child   is   impatiently
         baccā *AUX* besabrī se
    waiting   for
    pratīkṣā kara.3.SG.PR.CONT kī
    her   mother.
    vaha.GEN.SG māṃ
    'baccā besabrī se apanī māṃ kī pratīkṣā
    kara rahā hai'

In 4, the adverb 'impatiently' is embedded in the *tiṅanta pada*, *is waiting*. This is a frequent phenomenon in English. Hence, identification of *tiṅanta padas* helps in forming a verb group whereby translation of verb and its suffixes can be handled properly by grouping the verb root and verbal affixes the *tiṅ*.

In literature, a quite similar concept is mentioned by the name of Local Word Grouping (LWG), whereby word groups are formed based on the local (adjacent) word information (Bharati et al., 1995). In our attempts, we form word groups on the basis of nearby verbal and nominal suffixes called *sup* and *tiṅ* inspired by Pāṇinian

---

[1]In linguistics, the notion of subject in ILs is much debatable (Bharati and Kulkarni, 2011).

grammar which is linguistically more precise and satisfactory. This also facilitates the study of relational information that binds the words into a meaningful sentence.

In Hindi and Hindi like languages where the grammatical information is lexicalized, we group the postpositions with the nouns for *subanta* and auxiliaries with the verb for *tinanta*. Since auxiliaries and postpositions are grouped with the verbs and nouns, we get the padas and we can directly substitute them. In English also the auxiliaries carry the *tin* information for the verbs. We are treating prepositions as the *sup* for nouns. In this way, the prepositions and postpositions for nouns and auxiliaries for verbs with respect to word order are taken care of by this step.

This approach handles grouping of noun with *sup* inflection and verb with *tin* inflection. Hence, we do not need to have separate reordering rules for this. However, reordering between En-Hi pair is a more complex task, because, in English, a lot of relational information is encoded in position, which makes syntax of English very diverse from Hindi.

4 Major Divergences between English and Hindi

Language divergence includes lexical, structural and conflational divergences (Dorr, 1993). Dave et al (2001) discuss the major structural divergences with respect to English and Hindi. Table 1 summarizes the major structural divergences between English and Hindi.

English	Hindi
SVO	SOV
head first	head last
prepositional	postpositional
subject is sacrosanct	subject may be dropped

Table 1: Major structural divergences between English and Hindi

5 Formation of Reordering Rules

Hindi and English follow 'mirror structure' in terms of structural word order. Hence the daughters of English verb phrase (VP) and prepositional phrase (PP) come in mirror image when translated into Hindi. In other words, the SL VP looks like a mirror image of the TL VP and vice versa.

The concept of 'mirror structure' is illustrated with example 5. The constituency tree for sentence 5 is shown in Figure 2. The mirror image of its VP as shown in Figure 3 gives a perfectly ordered Hindi sentence.

(5) Queen Victoria opened Blackfriars Bridge in November 1869.

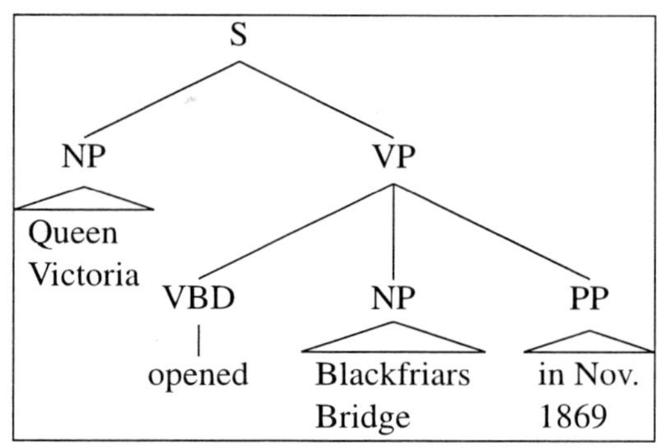

Figure 2: Showing constituency parse for 5

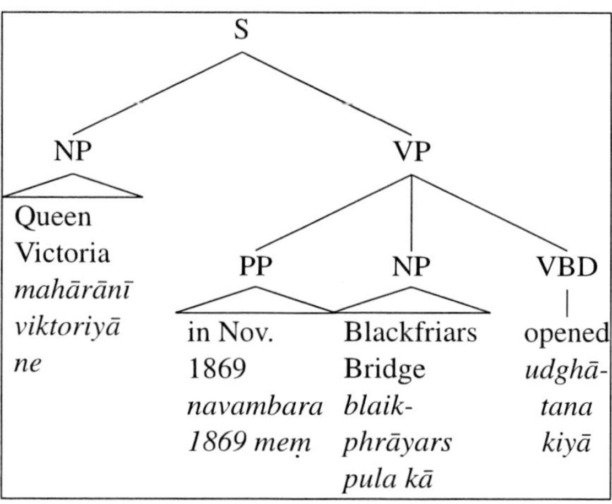

Figure 3: Showing mirror image of the constituency parse for 5

When mere 'mirror structure' does not suffice to arrive at a fluent Hindi sentence, we take advantage of dependency parse to handle such peculiarities in order to put the phrase at the desired place in TL. For example, indirect object tends to precede the direct object in Hindi. In 6a, the indirect and direct object reversal is restricted using dependency relations, since 6a sounds more natural than 6b to the native speakers of Hindi.

(6) a. Hari ne   use   eka
        Hari.PROPN,NOM he.DAT a

356

billī   dī
cat.ACC,SG give.PT,SG,FEM

'Hari gave her a cat.'

  b. Hari ne   eka billī
Hari.PROPN,NOM a   cat.ACC,SG
use   dī
he.DAT give.PT,SG,FEM

'Hari gave her a cat.'

5.1   Special Cases in Hindi

Apart from the cases described in Section 1, there are constructions which are not so flexible in terms of word order. This section describes some of them.

- Starting point and end point: While talking about a range or a span, the phrase describing an initial point precedes the phrase that describes the end point. This phenomenon seems to be common in all languages. Some such examples are shown from English in 7.

  (7)   a. In Kashmir, fishing is a good business and the ideal season is **from April to October**.

        b. I shall continue to work **from 6 a.m. till midnight**, even if it kills me.

        c. **October to March** is the best time to visit the Jaipur city.

        d. In the south, Jammu is a transition zone **from the Indian plains to the Himalayas**.

  In 7, all the phrases shown in bold letters do not change their positions. Only forming the padas by identification of *sup* and *tiṅ* gives perfect word order in Hindi, hence, no movement is required.

- Relative order of arguments of a verb: The internal order of theme and recipient roles in English can be expressed in two ways: (i) through position as shown in 8 and (ii) through preposition as shown in 9.

  (8)   John gave **Harry** a book.

  (9)   John gave a book **to Harry**.

  In Hindi, 8 and 9 both the sentences can be translated as in 10 and 11 respectively. Since Hindi is morphologically rich, it marks relations through morphemes. Therefore, as mentioned above, the order can be relatively free.

  (10)   John ne **Harry ko** eka kitāba dī.

  (11)   John ne eka kitāba **Harry ko** dī.

  However, more natural one is 10. This is the default order in Hindi. This is consistent with the SOV order of Hindi.

- Source and destination phrases: Source and destination phrases tend to occur immediately before their verbal head as shown in 12 and 13. For instance, *vaha use skūla le gayā.* sounds more natural than *vaha skūla use le gayā.* in Hindi.

  (12)   He   **took**   her **to the school**.
  vaha **le gayā** use   **skūla**
  'vaha use **skūla le gayā**.'

  (13)   He   **picked** her **from the party**
  vaha **le āyā** use **se**   **pārtī**
  'vaha use **pārtī se le āyā**.'

  Whereas if source and destination both occur as arguments of a same verb then destination phrase tends to occur immediately before the verb as shown in 14.

  (14)   He   **took**   her **home** from the
  vaha **le gayā** use **ghara** se
  party.
  pārtī
  'vaha use pārtī se **ghara le gayā**.'

- Marking negation: In English negation markers 'no' and 'not' occur with nouns and verbs respectively. Whereas in Hindi, if the head of the negation marker 'no' is a verb modifier then the negation marker comes before the verb. There also, if the verb is a conjunct verb (Begum et al., 2011) then it come before the helping verb as shown in 17.

  (15)   **No**   politician is
  koi nahīṃ rājanetā   hai
  completely   honest.
  pūrī taraha se īmānadāra

  '**koi** rājanetā pūrī taraha se īmānadāra **nahīṃ** hai'

(16) We   seek   **no**
hama cāhate haiṃ **koi nahīṃ**
reward.
ināma
'hama **koi** ināma **nahīṃ** cāhate haiṃ'

(17) He   did   **not**   **wait**
vaha *PAST* **nahīṃ pratīkṣā kara**
for me.
liye mere
'usane mere liye **pratīkṣā nahīṃ kī**'

- Yes/no interrogative question: The yes/no interrogative morpheme is missing in English (Anantpur, 2009). Therefore, it inverts the positions of subject and verb/auxiliary to mark a yes/no interrogative. Whereas in Hindi, yes/no interrogative question marker *kyā* is lexicalized and normally occurs at sentence initial position. As a consequence, in addition to word order, one needs to insert the morpheme *kyā* in Hindi, as shown in 18.

(18) Did   you   eat?
PAST,yes/no āpane khā
'**kyā** āpane khaya?'

Section 5.2 and 5.3 describe some important reordering rules which are sufficient to give an overview of our approach.

5.2   Rules Based on 'Mirror Structure'

The rules based on 'mirror structure' are very productive. These rules give around 70% constituent reordering accuracy.

We followed Penn tagset to represent constituents. The rules are written using the following convention: *[.mother child1 child2 child3]* → *[.mother child3 child2 child1]*, where the part before '→' denotes SL parse tree and the later part denotes TL parse tree. The item marked with dot (.) represents the mother node followed by its child nodes. The rules are written in following format: first, we give the rule and then the rules are described with an example/s.

RBMS1[2]: VP is reversed to allow 'mirror structure' as discussed in Section 3. See example 5.

RBMS2: [.ADVP RB NP] → [.ADVP NP RB]
RB should be the last child of an ADVP.

---

[2]The rules based on 'mirror structure are named as *RBMS + a number* and the rules for restricting 'mirror structure' are named as *RRMS + a number.*

(19) It   was **down about**   **35 points**.
yaha thā **nīce   lagabhaga 35 aṃka**
'yaha **lagabhaga 35 aṃka nīce** thā.'

RBMS3: [.SBAR IN S] → [.SBAR S IN] iff *IN* != sentential conjunction
SBAR introduced by preposition is reversed as in 20, except when it is not a sentential conjunction as in 21.

(20) I   expect   a rough   market **before**
maiṃ āśā kara   asthira bājāra **pahale**
prices stabilize.
mūlya sthira ho
'maiṃ **mūlya sthira hone se pahale**
asthira bājāra ki āśā karatā hūṃ'

(21) It was so   dark   **that** I   could
thaā itanā andherā **ki**   maiṃ saka
not   see   anything.
nahīṃ dekha.PT kucha
'itanā andherā thā ki maiṃ kucha nahīṃ
dekha sakā'

RBMS4: [.NP [.NP *] [.PP *] [.* *]] → [.NP [.* *] [.PP *] [.NP *]]

(22) The boy   **in   blue shirt**   is   here.
ladakā **vālā nīlī   kamīja** hai yahāṃ
'**nīlī kamīja vālā** ladakā yahāṃ hai

5.3   Rules for Handling Exceptional Cases

Even after applying 'mirror structure' on VP, some cases remain non-fluent and/or incomprehensible because of the inflexibility of some of the constituents to precede/follow the other constituents as pointed out in Section 1. This section describes some rules which are exceptions of 'mirror structure'.

RRMS1: [.VP * V] → [.VP * V]
Since Hindi is a verb final language, we restrict VP inversion iff verb is its last child, as in 23.

(23) The prices   of winter wheat   **now**
mūlya.PL kā śarada geṃhūm **aba**
being   planted will not   fall soon.
-jā rahe bo.PSSV *FUT* nahiṃ gira jaldī
'**aba boye jā rahe** śarada geṃhūm ke
mūlya jaldī nahiṃ gireṃge'

RRMS2: [.ADJP RB JJ PP] → [.ADJP PP RB JJ]
ADJP having a PP clause, is reversed in order to emphasize PP or sentential clause. See 24.

(24) She is **very good at her**
vaha hai **bahuta acchī meṃ apane**
work.
kārya
vaha **apne kārya meṃ bahuta acchī** hai

RRMS3: [.SQ WHNP VBD NP VP] → [.SQ
VBD NP WHNP VP]

Wh-element of a sentence should be placed before the verb of the sentence/clause.

(25) **How many people** did you see?
kitane loga *PT* āpa mila
'āpa **kitane logoṃ** se mile?'

5.4 Illustration of Reordering Rules

The rules are written using CLIPS (Giarratano
and Riley, 1998) where higher precedence rules
are given higher salience. In general, specific
rules have higher salience than a general rule. An
overview of the reordering rules is given in Table
2 where first column shows the reordering rules or
procedure and second column shows the effect of
that particular step.

6 Experiments and Results

We picked 500 Full-text sentences from COCA
(Davies, 2010) as SL input. These sentences were
divided into 20 sets of 25 sentences each. All these
input sets were translated in TL Hindi, using our
system and Google Translate. One human evaluator evaluated two different sets and each set was
evaluated by three evaluators. In total 30 evaluators rated the translation quality of both the systems on a scale of 0-4 (Bharati et al., 2004). As
per Bharati et al (2004) , this scale assesses translation quality in terms of comprehensibility. Note
that the identity of any system was not disclosed
to the human evaluators for unbiased ratings. We
found that on this scale Google Translate obtained
44.2% comprehensibility score while our system
obtained 51.8% comprehensibility score.

Out of these 20 sets, we selected 4 sets for En-
Hi word ordering quality assessment. The evaluators were asked to rank these sets on the basis of
word order quality without giving much emphasis on translation quality. The evaluators rated the
sentences '0' if the word order was unacceptable
(but still the sentence might be comprehensible in
some cases) and '1' if the order was acceptable.

The reordering rules for our system were tested
for both gold and automatic constituency parse

Input	(S (PP (IN In) (NP (CD 2006))) (, ,) (NP (DT the) (JJ Lebanese) (NNP Hezbollah) (NN militia)) (VP (VBD seemed) (ADJP (JJ able) (S (VP (TO to) (VP (VB rain) (NP (NNS rock- ets)) (PP (IN at) (NP (NN will)))) (PP (IN during) (NP (NP (DT a) (JJ monthlong) (NN conflict)) (PP (IN with) (NP (DT the) (JJ Jewish) (NN state)))))))))))
Pada forma- tion	(S 2006 In , the Lebanese Hezbollah militia (VP (VBD seemed) (ADJP (JJ able) (S (VP (VP (VB rain) to (NP (NNS rockets)) (PP will at)) (PP (NP (NP a monthlong conflict during) (PP (NP the Jewish state with))))))))
RBMS1	(S 2006 In , the Lebanese Hezbollah militia (VP (VBD seemed) (ADJP (JJ able) (S (VP will at rockets rain to (PP (NP (NP a monthlong con- flict during) (PP (NP the Jewish state with))))))))
RBMS1	(S 2006 In , the Lebanese Hezbollah militia (VP (VBD seemed) (ADJP (JJ able) (S (NP (NP a monthlong conflict during) (PP the Jewish state with)) will at rockets rain to))))
RRMS2	(S 2006 In , the Lebanese Hezbollah militia (VP (VBD seemed) (ADJP (S (NP (NP a monthlong conflict dur- ing) (PP the Jewish state with)) will at rockets rain to able))))
RBMS1	(S 2006 In , the Lebanese Hezbollah militia (NP (NP a monthlong conflict during) (PP the Jewish state with)) will at rockets rain to able seemed)
RBMS4	2006 In , the Lebanese Hezbollah militia the Jewish state with a month- long conflict during will at rockets rain to able seemed
lexical substi- tution	2006 meṃ, lebānī hijabullāha laḍāke yahūdī rājyoṃ ke sātha mahīnā bhara lambe saṃgharṣa ke daurana icchānusāra rauketa barasāne meṃ sakṣama dikhe

Table 2: Illustration of reordering rules

based reordering accuracy. Table 3 shows the reordering results.

The reordering rules were also tested on gold

Anusāraka with gold parse	67%
Anusāraka with automatic parse	65.5%
Google Translate	42%

Table 3: Reordering accuracy results evaluated by common people

and automatic constituency parse based input by the developers but the reordering scale for developers was between 0-2 as shown in Table 4. See the results in Figure 4.

0	unacceptable
1	non-fluent but acceptable
2	fluent/acceptable

Table 4: Reordering evaluation criteria for developers

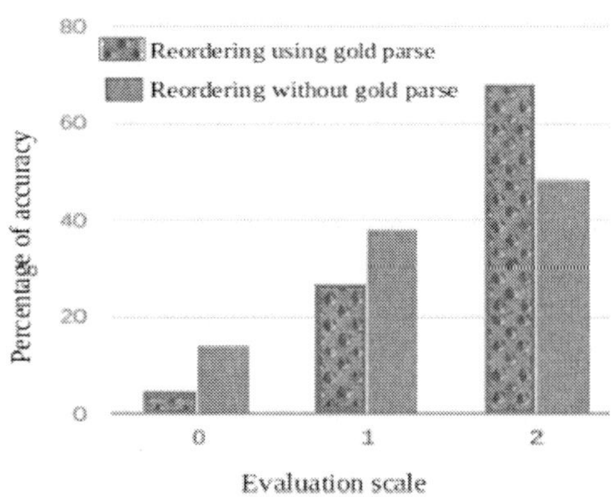

Figure 4: Percentage of reordering accuracy for En-Hi with and without gold parse

As expected, the results of the gold parse based word order are slightly better than the automatic parse based word ordering in case of developers' as well as common peoples' evaluation. The results confirm that a rule based reordering system performs better than a SMT based system.

#Sentences	#Words	#Phrases
100	2151	1637

Table 5: Test Corpus

We also report phrase reordering accuracy rather than sentence reordering accuracy, since our rules basically reorder phrases/padas and just because of incorrect reordering of one phrase, penalizing sentences of around 50 word length does not sound justified.

	#Phrases ordered correctly	#Phrases ordered incorrectly
Gold parse	97.5%	2.5%
Automatic parse	93%	7%

Table 6: Reordering results based on gold and automatic parse

Using our tool, Karan et al., (2014) have reported 21.84 BLEU score improvement over the baseline 20.04. After that the system has been improved. It should also be noted that their paper was not on reordering.

7 Error analysis

This section analyses various types of errors in TL reordering output.

Some cases rated as '0' were actually ordered correctly but the evaluators rated them low due to incorrect TL word substitutions. For instance, in 26, *reported* is translated as *sūcanā dī*, but in system generated output it was translated as *pāyā*.

(26) Hubbard   reported   from
      Hubbard.NOM sūcanā de.PT se
      Cairo.
      Cairo
      'Hubbard ne Cairo se sūcanā dī.'

In most of the cases, the adverbs like *now, mainly, likely*, etc. were misplaced as shown in 27. Or incorrect insertions of the words like *ki* (that), *isaliye* (hence), etc. were made in TL as shown in 28. For example,

(27) Saleh is **now** in the U.S. for further medical treatment.

      'Saleh **aba** āge kī cikitsā ke liye U.S. meṃ hai'

      'Saleh āge kī cikitsā ke liye **aba** U.S. meṃ hai'

      '*Saleh āge kī cikitsā ke liye U.S. meṃ **aba** hai'

(28) Since chalk first touched slate, schoolchildren have wanted to know: What is on the test?

In 28, insertion of *taba se* (thenceforth) is required for a fluent and comprehensible sentence in Hindi.

We noticed an interesting case where the shared verb should be repeated while translation in Hindi. For instance, in 29, the shared verb *swim* makes two *tiṅanta* padas with each auxiliary/*tiṅ*, *can* and *help*. There also, if the shared verb is a conjunct verb, then the verbalizer/helping verb (Begum et al., 2011) behaves as a *dhātu* and makes an independent *pada* with the auxiliary as shown in bold in 30.

(29)   She can   and will **swim**.
       vaha *BE ABLE TO* aura *FT* **taira**

       'vaha **taira sakatī hai** aura **tairegī**'

(30)   ... he **can**   and **will**
       ... vaha *BE ABLE TO* aura *FT*

       help   fight   the country's active
       madada kara ladanā   deśa kī   sakriya
       Al-Qaida branch.
       Al-Qaida śākhā

       '... vaha deśa meṃ sakriya Al-Qaida śākhā' se ladane meṃ **madada kara sakatā hai** aura **karegā**'

8   Conclusion and Future Work

This paper presented reordering rules for English-Hindi language pair using the concept of *pada* from Pāṇinian Grammar. We developed rules for generating fluent English-Hindi word order. We obtained better results than the SMT system Google Translate which show that the rules are accurate enough to enhance the translation quality. We elaborated on the concept of *pada* and presented a method for identification of *pada* and generation of reordering rules. We have also claimed that the approach presented in this paper is generic enough to be applied on English-Indian language MT systems.

Acknowledgments

We would like to express our special thanks to Prof. Vineet Chaitanya for his expert guidance and support. We would like to extend our thanks to Mrs. Sirisha Manju, Mrs. P Roja Laxmi, Mrs. Mahalaxmi, Mr. KRS Harsha, Ms. Pratibha Rani, Mr. Ganesh Katrapati and the evaluators for their help in implementing the rules, preparing the data, conducting the experiments and evaluation.

References

Amba Padmanathrao Anantpur. 2009. *Anusaaraka: An approach for MT taking insights from the Indian Grammatical Tradition.* Ph.D. thesis, University of Hyderabad.

Rafiya Begum, Karan Jindal, Ashish Jain, Samar Husain, and Dipti Misra Sharma. 2011. Identification of Conjunct verbs in Hindi and its effect on Parsing Accuracy. In *Computational Linguistics and Intelligent Text Processing*, pages 29–40. Springer.

Akshar Bharati and Amba Kulkarni. 2011. 'subject' in english is *abhihita*.

Akshar Bharati, Vineet Chaitanya, and Rajeev Sangal. 1995. *Natural language processing: a Paninian perspective.* Prentice-Hall of India New Delhi.

Akshar Bharati, Medhavi Bhatia, Vineet Chaitanya, and Rajeev Sangal. 1996. Paninian grammar framework applied to English. *Department of Computer Science and Engineering, Indian Institute of Technology, Kanpur.*

Akshar Bharati, Rajni Moona, Smriti Singh, Rajeev Sangal, and Dipti Mishra Sharma. 2004. Mteval: an evaluation methodology for machine translation systems. In *Proc. SIMPLE Symp on Indian Morphology, Phonology and Lang Engineering.*

Akshar Bharati, Sukhada, Dipti M Sharma, and Soma Paul, 2015. *Sanskrit and Computational Linguistics*, chapter Anusāraka Dependency Schema from Pāṇinian Perspective. D. K. Publishers.

Niladri Chatterjee, Anish Johnson, and Madhav Krishna. 2007. Some improvements over the BLEU metric for measuring translation quality for Hindi. In *Computing: Theory and Applications, 2007. ICCTA'07. International Conference on Computing: Theory and Applications*, pages 485–490. IEEE.

Marta R Costa-Jussà and José AR Fonollosa. 2009. An Ngram-based reordering model. *Computer Speech & Language*, 23(3):362–375.

Shachi Dave, Jignashu Parikh, and Pushpak Bhattacharyya. 2001. Interlingua-based English–Hindi machine translation and language divergence. *Machine Translation*, 16(4):251–304.

Mark Davies. 2010. The corpus of contemporary american english as the first reliable monitor corpus of english. *Literary and linguistic computing*, pages 447–464.

Bonnie Jean Dorr. 1993. *Machine translation: a view from the Lexicon.* MIT press.

Kapildev Dvivedi. 1953. *Rachanānuvādakaumudī.* Vishwavidyalaya Prakashan.

Joseph C Giarratano and Gary Riley. 1998. *Expert systems.* PWS Publishing Co.

Yamuna Kachru. 2006. *Hindi.* London Oriental and African Language Library, John Benjamins.

Philipp Koehn, Franz Josef Och, and Daniel Marcu. 2003. Statistical phrase-based translation. In *Proceedings of the 2003 Conference of the North American Chapter of the Association for Computational Linguistics on Human Language Technology-Volume 1*, pages 48–54. Association for Computational Linguistics.

Philipp Koehn. 2009. *Statistical machine translation.* Cambridge University Press.

Anoop Kunchukuttan, Abhijit Mishra, Rajen Chatterjee, Ritesh Shah, and Pushpak Bhattacharyya. 2014. Sata-Anuvadak: Tackling Multiway Translation of Indian Languages. *pan*, 841(54,570):4–135.

Mahavir. 1984. *Samartha Theory of Pāṇini and Sentence Derivation.* Munshiram Manoharlal Publishers.

Raj Nath Patel, Rohit Gupta, Prakash B Pimpale, and Sasikumar M. 2013. Reordering rules for English-Hindi SMT.

Sandhya Rathore. 1998. Kaunda bhatta's vaiyakaranabhusanasara: an analytical study. *Indian Council of Philosophical Research (distributed by Munshiram Manoharlal, Delhi).*

Smriti Singh, Mrugank Dalal, Vishal Vachani, Pushpak Bhattacharyya, and Om P Damani. 2007. Hindi generation from interlingua. *Machine Translation Summit (MTS 07), Copenhagen.*

Jag Deva Singh. 1991. *Pāṇini, his description of Sanskrit: An analytical study of Aṣṭādhyāyī.* Munshiram Manoharlal Publishers.

Karan Singla, Kunal Sachdeva, Diksha Yadav, Srinivas Bangalore, and Dipti Misra Sharma. 2014. Reducing the impact of data sparsity in statistical machine translation. *Syntax, Semantics and Structure in Statistical Translation.*

Prakya Sreesaila Subrahmanyam. 1999. *Pa:ṇinian Linguistics.* Institute for the Study of Languages and Cultures of Asia and Africa, Tokyo University of Foreign Studies.

Kenji Yamada and Kevin Knight. 2001. A syntax-based statistical translation model. In *Proceedings of the 39th Annual Meeting on Association for Computational Linguistics*, pages 523–530. Association for Computational Linguistics.

Dialogue Act Recognition for Text-based Sinhala

Sudheera Palihakkara, Dammina Sahabandu, Ahsan Shamsudeen, Chamika Banda-ra, and Surangika Ranathunga

Department of Computer Science and Engineering

University of Moratuwa

Katubedda 10400, Sri Lanka

{sudheera.10,dammina.10,ahsan.10,chamika.10,surangika}@cse.mrt.ac.lk

1   Abstract

This paper discusses the application of classical machine learning approaches to the task of Dialogue Act Recognition for text-based Sinhala. A study was carried out to identify a dialogue act tag set for Sinhala. A new corpus using Sinhala subtitles for English movies was created and was annotated with the selected dialogue acts. Evaluation of the dialogue act recognition system was performed using features that were used for English language, plus the newly identified features for Sinhala. Although Sinhala is an under-resourced language without even the basic tools such as a PoS tagger, we managed to achieve good classification accuracy by exploiting Sinhala specific features. As far as we are aware, this is the first research on dialogue act recognition on the family of Indo-Iranian languages.

1   Introduction

Sinhala is the native language of the Sinhalese people, the largest ethnic group in Sri Lanka numbering about 16 million. Considering the other ethnic groups using Sinhala as the second language, Sinhala can be said to be actively used by 19 million people.

Sinhala is the only language that most of the Sinhalese are fluent in. According to the Department of Census and Statistics Sri Lanka, as of 2007, roughly about 50% of the urban youth can read an English newspaper, while in rural areas, this value is well below 40%[1]. In contrast, the overall literacy rate of the country is 98.1%. Therefore there is a dire need for Sinhala language computing. With the implementation of Sinhala Unicode, the platform for this has been set. However the amount of research carried out in the area of Natural Language Processing (NLP) for Sinhala is not adequate. Unlike languages such as English, Spanish or French that are being used by larger populations in the world, Sinhala is restricted to Sri Lanka. This has an adverse impact on the progress made in Sinhala NLP research. Although there exists some preliminary-level research in areas such as Sinhala-English translation (Silva and Weerasinghe, 2008), Sinhala-Tamil (the other official language in Sri Lanka) translation (Sripirakas et al., 2010), and Sinhala spell checking (Jayalatharachchi et al., 2012), the attention paid for processing of spoken and written Sinhala conversations is very low.

The aim of this paper is to lay the first stone to fill this void in processing spoken and written Sinhala conversations. It makes use of the already existing research for Dialogue Act (DA) Recognition for English and explores how it can be used in the context of Sinhala. Given the fact that dialogue act recognition is an important step in understanding spontaneous dialogue, we envisage that this research would pave the path to research in areas of Sinhala NLP such as meeting summarization, question-answering systems, and automated assistance.

As the first step in the process, a corpus was created from Sinhala subtitles for English movies. A set of dialogue acts was identified based

---

[1]http://www.statistics.gov.lk/MDG/Mid-term.pdf

D S Sharma, R Sangal and E Sherly. Proc. of the 12th Intl. Conference on Natural Language Processing, pages 367–375,
Trivandrum, India. December 2015. ©2015 NLP Association of India (NLPAI)

on the commonly used dialogue acts for English. Part of the corpus was annotated with these dialog acts. Similarly, feature selection was started with the common features used for English, and later on the study Sinhala-specific features were identified and introduced to improve the classification accuracy. We also experimented with multiple classifiers to select the best performing classifier for Sinhala.

When carrying out Dialogue Act recognition for Sinhala, unavailability of foundational NLP research for Sinhala was a major limitation. For example, Part of Speech (PoS) tags are considered as a successful candidate in the feature set for dialogue act recognition (Verbree et al., 2006). The set of PoS tags has been identified for English and there are many English PoS taggers giving very good accuracy. In contrast, Sinhala PoS tagging is at its inception stage (Herath and Weerasinghe, 2004). Despite these limitations, we managed to achieve a good level of accuracy for Sinhala Dialogue act recognition, by exploiting the Sinhala language-specific features. As far as we are aware, this is the first research on dialogue act recognition on the family of Indo-Iranian languages.

The rest of the paper is organized as follows. Section 2 discusses some important characteristics of Sinhala language and related research in Sinhala language computing. Section 3 gives a brief introduction to the area of dialogue act recognition. Sections 4, 5 and 6 discuss the corpus we created, the dialogue act tag set used in the study, and a discussion on feature selection, respectively. Section 7 presents the results of the study, and finally Section 8 concludes the paper.

2 Sinhala Language and Computing in Sinhala

Sinhala language is more than two thousand years old. It is a language akin to Hindi, Bengali and other north Indian languages. Its closest relative is the language spoken in Maldives islands, Divehi (Pannasara and Arachchi, 2011). Contemporary Sinhala has been influenced by a wide variety of languages including Pali, Sanskrit, Tamil, Portuguese, Dutch and English. Sinhala alphabet is an abugida used in Sinhala writing system, which is a member of Brahmic family script. It is one of the longest alphabets in use today.

As shown in Figure 1, Sinhala belongs to the Indo-Aryan branch of Indo-Iranian language family, which along with Germanic belongs to the larger Indo-European language family. English and German languages are descendants of the Germanic branch.

European family, the Uralic family, the Altaic family, the Sino-Tibetan family, the Afro-Asiatic family and the Niger-Congo family can be considered as the origins of some of the major modern languages (Holman et al., 2011). As depicted in Figure 1, both Sinhala and English languages are descendants of the Indo-European language family.

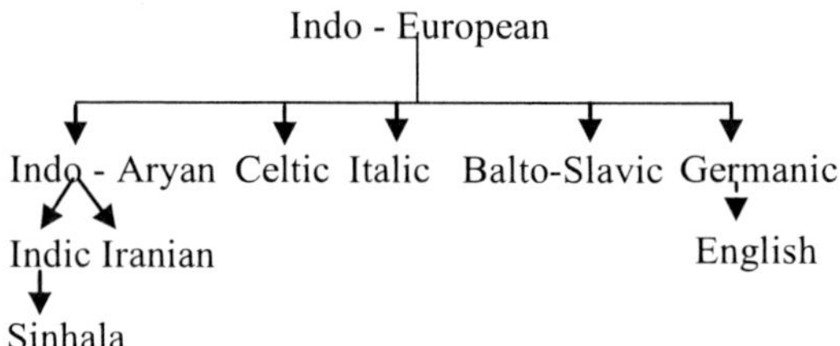

Figure 1. Language Families

Following are some examples on how spoken Sinhala differentiates from spoken English.

In English, the tag question, "isn't it.", "aren't you" or "don't they" agrees with the subject of the sentence that precedes. Its Sinhala equivalent is simply " නේ (ne)?" tagged to the end of the sentence, irrespective of its subject. Some examples are provided in Table 1.

Sentence in Sinhala	Phonetic Pronunciation	English Meaning
ඔයා වතුර බොනවනේ?	oya wathura bonava, ne?	You drink water, don't you?
අපි වතුර බොමුනේ?	api wathura bomu, ne?	Let's drink water, shall we?
ඔයා ඇමෙරිකන් නේ?	oya aemeri-kan, ne?	You're American, aren't you?

Table 1. Tag Questions in Sinhala and English

To intensify the meaning of an adjective (such as 'large'), English speakers add 'very' before it: very large. Sinhala speakers have another way of intensifying the meaning of adjectives by lengthening a vowel of the adjective itself. Thus the term 'ලොකු (loku)' (large) can be made into 'ලෝකූ (lokuuu)' (very large).

Although there exists much dissimilarity between Sinhala and English, it is not difficult to identify some similarities between the two languages through a much closer inspection.

If we consider the phonetic pronunciation of different words, we can observe similarities in languages of the Indo-European family. For an example the English word month pronounced in German as *Monat*, in Welsh as *mis*, in Italian as *mese* and in Sinhala as *masaya*[2].

Moreover, the set of punctuation marks used in both Sinhala and English are identical, although the ancient Buddhist scriptures did not use such punctuations. This could be due to the influence that Colonial English had over Sinhala.

As mentioned earlier, there exists some preliminary NLP research for Sinhala such as a Sinhala PoS tagger (Herath and Weerasinghe, 2004), a Sinhala WordNet (Wijesiri et al., 2014), English-Sinhala translation (Silva and Weerasinghe, 2008), and Sinhala-Tamil translation (Sripirakas et al., 2010). However, none of this work can be said to be comprehensive or completed. Still there is a considerable amount of work to be done in implementing the basic NLP tools for Sinhala.

3 Dialogue Act Recognition

To understand a spontaneous dialogue, it is important to model and automatically identify the structure of that dialogue, because it will make it easier to get a better interpretation of that spontaneous dialogue. How to model a spontaneous dialogue precisely is still an open issue, though some of the specific characteristics for modelling a spontaneous dialogue have already been identified. Among these clearly identified characteristics, "Dialogue Acts" hold an important place.

3.1 Speech Acts and Illocutionary Forces

A speech act in linguistics is an utterance that has performative function in language and communication (Searle, 1985). In general, speech acts are acts of communication such as statements, requests, questions, apologies and thanking. These acts of communication are for expressing a certain attitude, and the type of speech act being performed corresponds to the type of attitude or intention being expressed. For example, a statement expresses a belief, a request expresses a desire, and an apology expresses regret.

As an act of communication, a speech act succeeds if the audience identifies, in accordance with the speaker's intention, the attitude being expressed.

Dialogue acts are a specialized version of these speech acts. For example, "Question" is a speech act, but "Yes-No-Question" is a dialogue act. Therefore although the number of speech acts is somewhat stable, usually ten, the number of dialogue acts depends. For example, if the requirement is to process a questionnaire system, it is required to have different kinds of questions such as yes-no-questions, and open questions. However having different kinds of greetings is useless for that application. That explains how the set of dialogue acts and the size of the set depend on the application.

Austin (1975) defines a dialogue act as the "meaning of an utterance at the level of illocutionary force". The illocutionary force of an utterance is the speaker's intention in producing that utterance. Instance of a culturally defined speech act type is known as an illocutionary act, it is characterised by a particular illocutionary force. It has several types of acts, such as Asserting, Promising, Excommunicating, Exclaiming in pain, Inquiring and Ordering. For example, if we consider a speaker who asks "How is that work going on?, isn't it finished yet?" as a way of enquiring about the work, his or her *intent* may be in fact to make the person to finish the work. Thus the illocutionary force of the utterance is not an inquiry about the progress of the work going on, but a force for the work to be finished.

3.2 Process of Identifying Dialogue Acts

The process of identifying the Dialogue Act of an utterance in a particular language consists of a fixed set of steps (Král and Cerisara, 2012). This process is independent of the natural language used for the Dialogue Act Recognition. First and foremost step of the dialogue act recognition procedure is to identify the set of DA tags that is relevant for the task. After that, relevant informative features have to be computed from the speech signal. This is a very critical step since the accuracy of identifying the Dialogue Acts heavily depends on the identified feature set. Then DA models will be trained on these identified features set. The trained DA model can be used to determine the dialogue act of a given utterance. To make the process of dialogue act recognition easier, segmentation of the dialogues

---

[2]Used Google translator.

into utterances needs to be carried out independently, or alternatively realized during the recognition step with joint DA recognition and segmentation models.

4 Corpus

Since no corpus was available for dialogue act recognition for Sinhala, it was required to build a standard corpus from the scratch. We identified several approaches for this task:

1. Translate an existing standard English corpus
2. Collect written (typed) conversations from a Sinhala chat tool
3. Collect Sinhala subtitles in English movies
4. Collect conversations from Sinhala novels.
5. Collect telephone conversations carried out in Sinhala.

Among above approaches, the last one is a very difficult task to perform, because there is no solid research for speech-to-text conversion of Sinhala. Collecting conversations from Sinhala novels was found to be not possible due to the public unavailability of novels in digital format. Finding translators was not possible so we abandoned the first option.

Then we deployed a Sinhala chat tool for public use and collected conversations. At the beginning, this approach seemed promising but the process was slow because it was difficult to get volunteers. Moreover, volunteers tend to use English words in the middle of Sinhala utterances. Also they used slangs and urban words more often, which makes the classification more complex. Although we understand that a dialogue act recognition system should accept the existence of such non-standard words, this was considered out of scope for the current research.

Then we extracted utterances from Sinhala subtitles of English movies. The translation of English movies is a result of a community-based crowd sourcing effort. About 10 full-time translators are contributing to this under the trade name of "baiscope.lk"[3]. In Sri Lanka, there is a large population that enjoys Hollywood movies and TV series. However, their low English literacy is a problem when understanding these movies and TV series. The aim of baiscope.lk is to provide Sinhala subtitles for English movies

and TV series. The subtitle creation process is governed by a set of rules and regulations. The subtitles are almost in grammatically correct Sinhala.

One issue with this method is that some movies have frequent scene changes. This is problematic for extracting consistent conversations. To overcome this we had to manually select the movies that contained long consistent scenes. We collected about 1.8 million utterances using this method for 2306 movies. A common characteristic of these selected movies was that they involved realistic characters and real life situations. Therefore the conversations taking place in these movies are general human conversations that do not refer to any specific domain (e.g. war). This is exactly what we required, in order to carry out dialog act recognition in general human conversations.

Extraction and segmentation of utterances were done in a semi-automatic manner to build a more conversation-oriented corpus. Extracting the utterances from a subtitle file consists of several steps. First step is to omit the time-related information mentioned alongside utterances. Then the filtering out of advertisements and symbolic characters takes place. Finally improperly used punctuation marks are removed. These include the use of multiple exclamation/question marks in order to emphasize the emotion conveyed in the movie scene instead of using just one right after an utterance. Segmentation is done manually by checking each line, because one statement is sometimes broken into few lines in the subtitles due to a scene change in the middle of an utterance in the movie. If any such lines are found, they can be combined into a single line.

The final "Sanwada" corpus contains 1.8 million utterances including tagged 12,000 utterances. In Sinhala, the term "Sanwada" means conversation.

5 Tag Set

There exists many research related to dialog act tag sets, and dialog act annotation (Bunt et al., 2010, Bunt et al., 2012). To select a suitable tag set for Sanwada corpus, we adapted a generic tag set by referring to the DAMSL (Allen and Mark, 2013) tag set and the study by Stolcke et al., (2000). To measure the necessity and sufficiency of this tag set for tagging Sanwada corpus, we performed several iterations of manual tagging

---

[3] http://www.baiscopelk.com/

for a separate a set of samples. These samples were chosen from a set of tagged utterances that were not included in the "Sanwada" corpus. In each iteration, we added necessary new tags and removed unnecessary tags from the set. Table 2 lists the final tag set along with the percentage of occurrence in the manually tagged Sanwada corpus.

Dialogue Act Tag	Percentage
Statement	48.51%
Yes-No Question	12.87%
Request/Command/Order	10.23%
Open Question	9.78%
Back-channel/Acknowledge	7.39%
Conventional Opening	2.58%
Backchannel Question	2.31%
No Answer	1.42%
Yes Answers	1.36%
Apology	1.33%
Thanking	0.75%
Opinion	0.44%
Aadoned/Uninterpretable/Other	0.44%
Conventional Closing	0.31%
Expressive	0.17%
Reject	0.11%

Table 2. Selected Dialogue Act Tag Set

Wh-Question is one of the major tags used in related work (Stolcke et al., 2000). The presence of 'WH' letters as in 'what', 'when', 'why', 'which' etc. in an utterance is used as a feature in order to identify Wh-Questions. But considering the lexical characteristics of Sinhala this tag is not applicable. For example, in Sinhala, 'මොකක්ද' means 'what', 'කියටද' means 'when', and 'ඇයි' mans 'why'. As can be seen, the first character of these Sinhala words is different in each word, as opposed to the English words. Therefore we used more generic tag Open-Question for questions in general unless it is a Yes-No Question or a Backchannel Question.

In the initial tag set we had two separate tags for Request and Command/Order. For English there is a clear separation in utterances between these two tags. Most of the Requests include the word "please" or a similar phrase in contrast to Command/Orders where it does not. In Sinhala, different forms of the same word are used to indicate whether it is a request or a command. For example, වහන්න (wahanna) is used in requests in a polite manner to say close something (e.g. a door) where වහපං (wahapan) is used in orders.

It should also be noted here that English-Sinhala translation in baiscope.lk is not just a mere one-to-one mapping from English to Sinhala. This is because the translation process is subjective. The translators generate subtitles while watching the movie. Therefore they capture the prosodic and other contextual information in the Sinhala subtitles to a great extent. For example, consider a movie scene where an actor asks another actor to "close that door" in a very harsh tone. The corresponding Sinhala subtitle uses command-type words "දොර වහපං" (dora wahapan) instead of request-type words "දොර වහන්න" (dora wahanna).

The rate of occurrence of Backchannel Questions is comparatively high in Sinhala. Therefore we introduced it as a separate tag. Backchannel questions are Back-Channels or Acknowledges in question form. For example, in Sinhala conversations we often come across the phrase "එහෙමද?" (ehemada?) in response, roughly it means "is it?". It should also be noted that there is no relevant Sinhala phrase for the commonly used English term "isn't it".

To tag the Sanwada corpus using the tags listed in Table 2, we have selected four independent contributors. After tagging the complete corpus manually, we have calculated the inter-annotator agreement among them using Fleiss kappa (Fleiss, 1981) value and the agreement was 0.8161. To calculate the kappa value we implemented a tool based on the equations introduced by Fleiss (1981).

6   Feature Selection

Our target was to test the performance of features already identified in related work for English and distinguish the relevant features for Sinhala. Also we have identified several new features exclusive for Sinhala.

6.1   Identified features from related work

We have identified 14 features that can be used in textual dialogue act recognition from previous studies (Verbree et al., 2006; Rosset and Lamel, 2004). Among those 14 features we selected only 7 features for our study considering the applicability to Sinhala and other few concerns that are discussed below. Table 3 lists these 14 features along with their selection status.

Since we are using Bigrams as a feature, feature 8 and 9 were omitted. Feature 10 is omitted due to the unavailability of a Sinhala PoS tagger. Taking previous Dialogue Acts as a feature can introduce a cumulative error as described by Lendvai et al., (2003). Unigrams are ineffective for long utterances, although their effectiveness has been shown for chat messages (Ivanovic, 2008).

Feature	Status
1. Number of words in the segment	Selected
2. Bigrams/Trigrams of words	Selected
3. Previous Dialogue Act	Selected
4. Verb of the Sentence	Selected
5. Punctuation marks	Selected
6. Grammar pattern	Selected
7. Frequent words for each tag	Selected
8. First two words	Not-selected
9. Last two words	Not-selected
10. First verb type/ Second verb type	Not-selected
11. Words in last 10 Dialogue Acts	Not-selected
12. N-grams of previous Dialogue Acts	Not-selected
13. Bag-of –words	Not-selected
14. Unigrams	Not-selected

Table 3. Selected Features

6.2 Exclusive features for Sinhala

Last letter of the last word of the utterance is one feature that we have identified. Unlike in English, the last letter of the utterance makes a big impact on the dialogue act of the utterance. For instance, most of the Yes/No questions end with the letter 'ද'(da), most of Request/Command/Order ends with one of the letters 'න්'(n), 'න'(na), or ' නු'(nu), and most of the open questions end with 'නේ'(ne). Not only the last letter but also the last word of an utterance is an exclusive feature for Sinhala.

The presence of specific Sinhala cue phrases is another identified feature. Table 4 lists some identified cue phrase sets.

6.3 Identified Features

Next follows all the major features that could be used for dialogue act recognition.

1. *Cue Phrases*: presence of connective expressions.
2. *Number of words in the segment*: self-explanatory.
3. *Bigrams/Trigrams of words*: Adjacent two words in an utterance is considered as a bigram, likewise trigram is adjacent three words.
4. *Previous Dialogue Act*: The dialogue act of the previous utterance.
5. *Verb of the Sentence*: self-explanatory
6. *Punctuation marks*: The appearance of the question mark, exclamation mark, Full stop, etc. in the utterance. In Sinhala same punctuation marks are used as in English.
7. *Grammar pattern*: The Sinhala grammar pattern(s) of the sentences in the utterance.
8. *Last word of the utterance*: self-explanatory.
9. *Frequent words for each tag*: For each tag the most frequent words appear in the training set of utterance.
10. *End letter of the last word of the sentence*: self-explanatory.

Sinhala cue phrase(s)	Phonetic Pronunciation	English cue phrase
ඇත්තෙන්ම	aeththenma	actually
සහ, හා	saha, haa	and
නිසා, හින්ද	nisa, hinda	because
එසේම	esema	also
එහෙත්, නමුත්	eheth, namuth	but
වගේ, වැනි, වාගේ	wage, waeni, waage	like
ඉතින්, එවිට	ithin, ewita	then
හෝ	ho	or
හරි	hari	well
එනිසා, එබැවින්	enisaa, ebawin	so

Table 4. Cue Phrases

6.4 Feature Selection Experiments

The idea of the experiments is to identify the most contributing features for classifying and the most effective combinations of the features. From the aforementioned 10 features, 8 were selected based on the performance evaluation (with 10 features, it is computationally expensive than for 8 features to go through all possible combinations)[4].

---

[4] For 10 features have to go through 2^{10} i.e. 1024 combinations where for 8 features it's only 2^8 i.e. 256.

We used WEKA (Hall et al., 2009) toolkit for classification. To achieve above described task we used the InfoGain Attribute Evaluator of WEKA and obtained the InfoGain values. Table 5 displays the results. The InfoGain value evaluates the worthiness of a feature by measuring the information gain resulted only by that particular feature. For example, a feature with an InfoGain value of 1 means that all of the information available in that feature contributes to classification. However this does not mean that the use of that feature alone is able to conduct the entire classification.

Rank	Feature	InfoGain
1	Punctuation marks	0.71
2	Last word of the utterance	0.60
3	Frequent words for each tag	0.42
4	Trigrams/Bigrams	0.31
5	Last letter of the last word of the sentence	0.30
6	Verb of the Sentence	0.24
7	Number of words in the segment	0.18
8	Cue Phrases	0.17

Table 5. Individual Feature Performance

From this result set we can observe that the most contributing feature for the task is punctuation marks. The processed subtitles that we used have been properly written with the use of punctuation marks. This particular feature has been effective in distinguishing questions (Open Question, Yes/No Questions and Back-channel Questions) from other tags. Some of the features that we identified as exclusive features for Sinhala (last word of the utterance and last letter of the utterance) also contribute a considerable amount.

Feature 3 in the table (Frequent words for each tag) keeps track of the most frequent words used in the entire corpus and uses the presence of those words in a particular utterance as a feature for the classifier. For this task we used WEKA's StringToWordVector option with the word count of 100. This feature has not been widely used in related work but we could observe that this feature works well.

There were limitations on finding the verb of the sentence precisely due to the lack of resources for PoS tagging for Sinhala. Therefore we used a set of commonly used Sinhala verbs and checked the presence of those verbs in a given utterance as feature.

From the above mentioned features we have selected the best performing six features listed in the Table 6 by testing all the combinations of features on the J48 WEKA classifier.

Feature
Punctuation marks
Last word of the utterance
Trigrams/Bigrams
Last letter of the last word of the sentence
Frequent words for each tag
Cue Phrases

Table 6. Best Performing Features

For the 8 different features there are 256 different combinations of feature sets. We went through all these different combinations and classified them using a trained J48 classifier. The features mentioned in Table 6 yielded the maximum accuracy on the testing set. This feature set achieved F-measure value of 0.755 with a precision 0.788 and recall 0.755.

7 Results

For classification task we have used 8000 utterances as training set and 4000 utterances as testing set. Each entry was labeled with exactly one dialog act. As the first step we have tested the classification accuracy by just using the features used for dialogue act recognition in English. From the best performing features stated in Table 6, Punctuation marks, Trigrams/Bigrams and Frequent words for each tag are the three features used in the related work. The other three features are specific for Sinhala. Using those three features used for English we were able to gain an accuracy of 71.14% in classification using the J48 classifier. Then we have used all six features and classified using the same classifier and we were able to improve the accuracy to 78.68%.

As the next step we have used the same feature set and classified the same data set using different classifiers to model the performance of different classifiers on Sinhala. Table 7 lists the classifiers in the descending order of F-measure value. F-measure represents a value of accuracy of the tests performed, which is calculated using recall and precision values. We can observe that RandomForest, SimpleLogistic and LMT classifiers give the highest F-measure.

Classifier	Recall	Precision	F-measure
RandomForest	0.792	0.780	0.776
SimpleLogistic	0.794	0.772	0.765
LMT	0.794	0.760	0.762
PART	0.786	0.757	0.756
J48	0.789	0.773	0.755
NaiveBayes	0.756	0.728	0.732
REPTree	0.782	0.761	0.731
DecisionTable	0.761	0.757	0.727
SMO	0.769	0.728	0.708
DecisionStump	0.639	0.413	0.501
HoeffdingTree	0.677	0.522	0.577

Table 7. Classifier Performance

8 Conclusion

This paper explored how Dialog Act recognition can be carried out for Sinhala, which is an under-resourced language. We built a corpus using Sinhala movie subtitles, and defined a suitable dialogue act tag set for this corpus based on the results of a few tests performed on the corpus. The experiments done on the corpus for recognizing dialogue acts obtained reasonable results and showed that Sinhala-specific features can be used to improve Sinhala dialogue act recognition.

The feature selection test explored new ways of extracting information from the utterances and we identified a best performing feature set for the Sinhala Language. Despite the small size of the feature set, we managed to achieve a reasonable accuracy in different classifiers. The classifier tests revealed that most of the classifiers perform well with the Sinhala corpus without any classifier parameter tuning. We reached to 78.68% accuracy of dialogue act tagging with Random-Forest classifier.

As future work, we suggest taking lower level information such as prosody into the picture and defining features related to it. Since we have a very large unlabelled data set, it is possible to explore the use of unsupervised learning techniques for dialog act recognition for Sinhala. We also envisage that this research would pave the path for more Sinhala related research such as meeting summarization in Sinhala and Sinhala question answering systems.

Reference

JM Allen and Mark Core. 1997. draft of DAMSL: Dialog act markup in several layers.

John Langshaw Austin. 1975. How to do things with words, volume 367. Oxford university press.

Harry Bunt, Jan Alexandersson, Jean Carletta, Jae-Woong Choe, Alex Chengyu Fang, Koiti Hasida, Kiyong Lee et al. 2010 Towards an ISO standard for dialogue act annotation. In Seventh conference on International Language Resources and Evaluation.

Harry Bunt, Michael Kipp and Volha Petukhova. 2012. Using DiAML and ANVIL for multimodal dialogue annotations. In proceedings of the Language Resources and Evaluation Conference.

Joseph L Fleiss. 1981. The measurement of interrater agreement. Statistical methods for rates and proportions, 2:212–236.

Mark Hall, Eibe Frank, Geoffrey Holmes, Bernhard Pfahringer, Peter Reutemann, and Ian H Witten. 2009. The WEKA data mining software: an update. ACM SIGKDD explorations newsletter, 11(1):10–18.

Dulip Lakmal Herath and Ruvan Weerasinghe. 2004. A stochastic part of speech tagger for Sinhala. In Proceedings of the 06th International Information Technology Conference, pages 27–28.

Eric W Holman, Cecil H Brown, Søren Wichmann, André Müller, Viveka Velupillai, Harald Hammarström, Sebastian Sauppe, Hagen Jung, Dik Bakker, Pamela Brown, et al. 2011. Automated dating of the worlds language families based on lexical similarity. Current Anthropology, 52(6):841–875.

Edward Ivanovic. 2008. Automatic instant messaging dialogue using statistical models and dialogue acts. Master's thesis, University of Melbourne.

Eranga Jayalatharachchi, Asanka Wasala, and Ruvan Weerasinghe. 2012. Data-driven spell checking: The synergy of two algorithms for spelling error detection and correction. In International Conference on Advances in ICT for Emerging Regions, pages 7– 13. IEEE.

Pavel Král and Christophe Cerisara. 2012. Dialogue act recognition approaches. Computing and Informatics, 29(2):227–250.

Piroska Lendvai, Antal van den Bosch, and Emiel Krahmer. 2003. Machine learning for shallow interpretation of user utterances in spoken dialogue systems. In Proceedings of the EACL-03 Workshop on Dialogue Systems: Interaction, Adaptation and Styles of Management, pages 69–78.

Okampitiyc Pannasara and V. Arachchi. 2011. Sinhala bhasha vikashaya saha shilalekhana wimarshana. Colombo.

Sophie Rosset and Lori Lamel. 2004. Automatic detection of dialog acts based on multi-level information. pages 540–543.

John R Searle. 1985. Expression and meaning: Studies in the theory of speech acts. Cambridge University Press.

Anne Mindika Silva and Ruvan Weerasinghe. 2008. Example based machine translation for English-Sinhala translations. In Proceedings of the 09th International IT Conference, pages 27–28.

Sakthithasan Sripirakas, Ruvan Weerasinghe, and Dulip L Herath. 2010. Statistical machine translation of systems for Sinhala-Tamil. In International Conference on Advances in ICT for Emerging Regions, pages 62–68. IEEE.

Andreas Stolcke, Klaus Ries, Noah Coccaro, Elizabeth Shriberg, Rebecca Bates, Daniel Jurafsky, Paul Taylor, Rachel Martin, Carol Van Ess-Dykema, and Marie Meteer. 2000. Dialogue act modeling for automatic tagging and recognition of conversational speech. Computational linguistics, 26(3):339–373.

Daan Verbree, Rutger Rienks, and Dirk Heylen. 2006. Dialogue-act tagging using smart feature selection; results on multiple corpora. In Spoken Language Technology Workshop, pages 70–73. IEEE.

Indeewari Wijesiri, Malaka Gallage, Buddhika Gunathilaka, Madhuranga Lakjeewa, Daya C Wimalasuriya, Gihan Dias, Rohini Paranavithana, and Nisansa de Silva. 2014. Building a WordNet for Sinhala. In Seventh Global Wordnet Conference, pages 100–108.

A Semi Supervised Dialog Act Tagging for Telugu

Suman Dowlagar
suman.d@research.iiit.ac.in

Radhika Mamidi
radhika.mamidi@iiit.ac.in

Abstract

In a task oriented domain, recognizing the intention of a speaker is important so that the conversation can proceed in the correct direction. This is possible only if there is a way of labeling the utterance with its proper intent. One such labeling techniques is Dialog Act (DA) tagging. This work focuses on discussing various n-gram DA tagging techniques. In this paper, a new method is proposed for DA tagging in Telugu using n-gram karakas with back-off as n-gram language modeling technique at n-gram level and Memory Based Learning at utterance level. The results show that the proposed method is on par with manual DA tagging.

Keywords: Dialog Acts, Intention Recognition, Dialog System, n-grams, Karaka Dependencies, Back-off, Memory Based Learning.

1 Introduction

The term 'dialog' origins from the Greek word *dialogos* which means conversation. A Dialog system which is a conversational agent which converses with human.

విద్యార్థి	:	నమస్కారం సర్.
student	:	Hello sir.
లైబ్రేరియన్	:	నమస్కారం.
librarian	:	Hello.
విద్యార్థి	:	నాకు ఈ పుస్తకము జారీ చేయండి.
student	:	I want to issue this book.

Table 1: Conversation between a student and a librarain from ASKLIB corpus in Telugu with English translation

The crucial use of a dialog system is to convert simple yet complicated tasks from manual to automated. The process of understanding and generating the dialogs is known as dialog modeling. In dialog modeling, to understand the dialogs, speaker's intent must be recognized. The recognition of the speaker's intent is done with the help of Dialog Acts. Dialog Acts is a tagset that classifies utterances based on pragmatic, semantic and syntactic features. Dialog Acts are similar to Austin's speech acts. According to Austin (1975), a speech act represents the meaning of an utterance at the level of illocutionary force. DA tagging is assigning a Dialog Act to an utterance from the given DA tagset.

Earlier, research in DA tagging was limited to linguistic domain, but now with the help of statistics, machine learning and pattern matching, automated DA tagging with various DA recognition approaches (Král and Cerisara, 2012) have come into existence. Some of the DA tagging methods include word based DA tagging (Garner et al., 1996), which shows that individual words are the potential source for tagging utterances in dialogs. On the other hand, (Webb et al., 2005) used n-grams with *predictivity criterion* for DA tagging which shows that instead of considering all n-grams, take only those which surpass the threshold. (Klüwer et al., 2010), proved that n-grams obtained from dependency parsing are powerfull enough for DA tagging. (Liu et al., 2013) and (Rotaru, 2002), proved that memory based learning techniques can be used for DA tagging. Other methods for DA tagging include Naive Bayesian interpretation (Reithinger and Klesen, 1997), Hidden Markov Models (Stolcke et al., 2000).

Telugu is a free word order language. Existing n-gram cue based methods are mainly

D S Sharma, R Sangal and E Sherly. Proc. of the 12th Intl. Conference on Natural Language Processing, pages 376–383,
Trivandrum, India. December 2015. ©2015 NLP Association of India (NLPAI)

Tag list	%	Description of Tags	Example of utterances translated to English
RETURN	2.93	Utterance intent is to return the book	*I am returning this book.*
TIME_ASSERT	0.55	Speaker makes a claim with respect to library timings	*Now the time is 6.30pm.*
ISSUE_INFO_REQUEST	1.92	Utterance is bound to provide answer related to issue of book	*Do you want to issue this book?*
ISSUE	3.88	Utterance intent is to issue the book	*Issue this book to me*
REISSUE_INFO_REQUEST	1.92	Utterance is bound to provide answer related to reissue of book	*Are you willing to reissue this book?*
ISSUE_ASSERT	3.68	Speaker makes a claim while issuing the book	*You have to return this book in a month, or else you will be charged.*
ACCEPT_ACKNOWLEDGE	6.46	Utterance indicates speaker has understood and accepted the stated fact.	*Ok sir, I will return this book in a month.*
ASSERT	0.25	Speaker states a general fact with out any relation to issue, reissue, return etc	*Days have passed since I saw you.*
COMMIT	9.99	Utterance states that speaker is committing to perform the action in future.	*Ok sir, I will come tomorrow.*
GREETINGS_REPLY	12.26	Utterance is replying to a greet so as to maintain the conversation	*I am fine.*
ANSWER	2.37	Utterance is answering to the question	*The author of this book is Dan Jurafsky.*
GREETINGS	7.67	Utterance states that the conversation is started	*Good Morning sir.*
ACCEPT	6.16	Utterance shows speakers agreement to the proposal or claim	*Ok sir.*
INFO_REQUEST	6.76	Utterance that is a generic question without relation to any domain specific task	*How are you sir?*
RETURN_ASSERT	3.08	Speaker makes a claim while issuing the book	*I am deleting this book from your account.*
GREETINGS_EOC	12.26	Utterance states that the conversation is completed	*Thank you.*
RETURN_INFO_REQUEST	2.32	Utterance is bound to provide answer related to return of book	*Do you want to return this book?*
REISSUE_ASSERT	2.77	Speaker makes a claim while returning the book	*I am extending the book's due date.*
REISSUE	3.13	Utterance intent is to reissue the book	*Please, reissue this book to me.*
ACTION_DIR	9.64	Utterance intent is to make hearer, perform an action	*Give me the id card and the book.*

Table 2: Showing the tagset, its percentage in corpus, description of each tag with an example (written originally in Telugu) translated to English.

Speaker		Dialog in Telugu with English Translation	DA tag
విద్యార్థి	:	నమస్కారం సర్.	GREETINGS
student	:	Hello sir	
లైబ్రేరియన్	:	నమస్కారం.	GREETINGS_REPLY
librarian	:	Hello	
విద్యార్థి	:	నాకు ఈ పుస్తకము జారీ చేయండి.	ISSUE
student	:	I want to issue this book	

Table 3: Conversation between a student and a librarian with its respective DA tags

developed for English, When these are applied to DA tag Telugu dialogs, the baseline accuracy is not reached, because n-gram methods are position dependent. In this paper, a new method is proposed for DA tagging in Telugu using n-gram karakas with back-off and Memory Based Learning such as kNN. The novel method is compared with n-gram and a combination of unigram methods. The results show that the proposed method does better DA tagging for Telugu.

This paper is organized as follows. Section 2 gives an overview of the corpus and tagset used. In section 3 we present our work, section 4, results are tabulated, section 5 draws some important conclusions and finally section 6 gives the scope for future work.

2 Corpus

At present, there is no available corpus related to task oriented Telugu dialogs. Our work started with the construction and acquisition of the dialogs in Telugu.

The focus was on task oriented, domain dependent dialogs with *'Library'* as the domain. We named the corpus as ASKLIB. ASKLIB consists of nearly 225 dialogs that took place between students and the librarian. This corpus is also collected by frequently visiting different libraries and observing how people interact with the librarian. The data acquisition was also done through the *Wizard of Oz* technique. 27 active participants were told to assume the scenario of a library and were asked to write a few generic 2 party conversations. After the corpus acquisition, we observed that the dialogs pertaining to the library domain could be broadly classified into 4 types, viz. ISSUE, REISSUE, RETURN,

ENQUIRY. In other words, a person's interaction with a librarian can result in either issue, reissue or return of a book or any enquiry related to a book/the library. The data that was collected has undergone various layers of automated spell checking using CALTSLAB Spell Checker (`http://caltslab.uohyd.ernet.in/spell_checker.php`) and manual spell checking to make the corpus reliable and correct.

Words	Dialogs	Utterances per Dialog
12826	225	7-9

Table 4: Corpus Statistics

Table 4 gives the information about the number of words, dialogs and utterances per dialog present in ASKLIB corpus.

The DA tagset is based on DAMSL (Core and Allen, 1997) and some domain dependent tags. DAMSL is one of the domain independent tagsets used for DA Tagging. The reason for choosing domain dependent tags is that, as the ASKLIB data is categorized to 4 types, the questions raised and assertions clamied in each category will be different. Hence, a modified DAMSL tagset is created to suit the library domain by adding a set of domain dependent tags along with some of the DAMSL tags. At present, our tagset consists of a total of 21 tags. The tagset and its related information is given in table 2. Table 3 gives a sample conversation taken from ASKLIB corpus with DA tags; the utterances are given in Telugu with their English translation.

3 Classification Algorithms

Of all the methods developed for DA tagging, the easiest way to automatically tag the test utterance is by matching the test utterance to any of the utterances present in the training data. The problem with this method is the unlikely occurence of the same utterance in both the training data and the test data. It will also occupy a lot of memory (for huge corpus) as each and every unique utterance with its corresponding tag is stored in the training data. As the huge corpus was difficult to handle, the focus was made on words. The problem of considering only words is that words do not contain any local contextual information. Later, the methods were extended to n-grams. The n-gram methods consist of splitting the utterances into a sequence of n words. These n-grams are called cues. In cue based n-gram DA tagging techniques, the n-grams obtained from the training data act as cues. By matching n-grams of the training data with n-grams of test data, an appropriate tag to the test data was given. Also, the size of unique n-grams obtained from training data is very less when compared to the size of unique utterances in training data.

In this paper, we talk about three methods. They are:

1. DA tagging using n-grams,

2. Combinations of unigrams with Naive Bayesian plus k Nearest Neighbors(kNN) and

3. Our method, n-grams with karaka dependency relations between them using back-off plus Memory Based Learning such as kNN.

3.1 N-gram Method

Of all the approaches in DA tagging, cue based n-gram tagging methods are proven to be the easiest and the most powerful DA tagging scheme. In n-gram methods, the tag of the test utterance is obtained by converting the test utterance into a set of contiguous sequence of n words. Thus, allowing the obtained sequence to be compared with other n-gram training sequences using efficient algorithms. These DA tagging schemes are mostly developed for corpus related to English language because English has a fixed syntactic structure. For English, in both training and test data, the position of the words in an utterance will remain mostly the same. By comparing the n-grams obtained from training data with the n-grams obtained from test data, the best tag for the test utterance is obtained. As this method gives high accuracy for English, the same method is applied to the Telugu ASKLIB corpus.

For choosing the best tag, Naive Bayesian interpretation is used,

$$\hat{T} = \underset{T}{\operatorname{argmax}} \ \frac{P(U, T)}{P(U)} \tag{1}$$

where $\hat{T}$ is the correct tag, from the tagset T for the utterance U.

For n-grams, the above equation is modified to

$$\hat{T} = \underset{T}{\operatorname{argmax}} \ \prod_{i=1}^{N} \frac{P(w_i, T)}{P(w_i)} \tag{2}$$

where w_i represents the n-gram sequence and N is equal to the list of n-grams obtained for the utterance U.

3.2 Combinations of Unigrams and kNN

The n-gram method will have a low accuracy for free word order languages like Telugu. In free word order languages like Telugu, even though the speaker's intent might be the same, the position of the words (the syntactic structure) might change. Hence the n-grams method will not work. So word position independent methods must be considered, One such method is to extract n-grams by considering combinations of unigrams. For example: In the combinations of unigrams for n=2 we get bigrams. Here, each word will appear with all the other words in the given utterance and with itself. The problem with this approach is that the time complexity increases when n value increases. As low order n-grams will capture less context, for further processing Memory Based Learning(MBL) method such as k Nearest Neighbors(kNN) (Cover and Hart, 1967) is applied. In MBL the pattern of the training data will be tested against the pattern of the test data with the word sequence independence as one of the criteria. This method gives the tag of the nearest training utterance to the test utterance without considering the position of words in an utterance in both the training data and the test data.

In combinations of unigrams and kNN method, for choosing the best tag, Naive Bayesian interpretaion in combination with kNN is used.

The above equation 2 will undergo a small modification by considering combinations of unigrams.

$$\hat{T} = \operatorname*{argmax}_{T} \prod_{i=1}^{N_{all}} \frac{P(w_i, T)}{P(w_i)} \qquad (3)$$

where N_{all} is equal to the list of combinations of unigrams

The kNN method is

$$DA(U_{test}) = DA(U_{train})$$
$$if : |U_{test} - U_{train_i}| = min \ |U_{test} - U_{train_N}|$$
$$\text{for N = 1,2,...(no of unique train utterances)} \qquad (4)$$

where U_{test}, U_{train} represents train and test utterances respectively

3.3 N-grams related with Karaka Dependency relations with Language Modeling and kNN

In Paninian framework (Bharati et al., 1995), for free word order Indian languages like Telugu, it is proven that the karaka based dependency relations will remain the same even though the syntactic structure of the sentence changes. By using these karaka dependencies, the syntactico-semantic relationships between the words is captured in the *modifier-karaka-modified* format. On careful inspection, this format seems similar to the n-grams with karaka relationships between them. After extracting all the n-grams with karaka dependencies, language modeling technique i.e. Katz's back-off model (at n-gram level) and memory based learning technique i.e. kNN (at utterance level) will be applied. The combination of the above two will give the best tag to test utterances when compared to the above models.

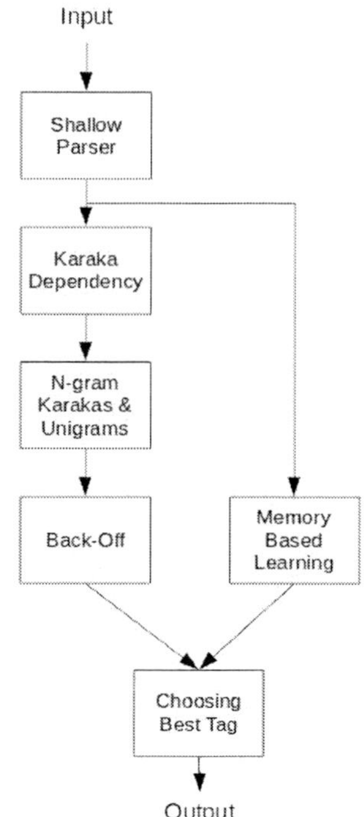

Figure 1: Figure showing the Karaka Dependency method with Back-off and Memory Based Learning for DA tagging.

Why Katz's back-off model? why not just check for karaka dependencies with smoothing algorithms and tag it?

Linguistically speaking, for an utterance to be given a specific tag, each and every word in the utterance must contribute to the tag. So in the test utterance, after extracting all the words with karaka relations between them, there will be certain words whose dependencies are missed. It might be due to any of the following reasons given below.

1. Some karaka dependencies are currently not annotated in the Telugu tree bank.

2. The n-grams have a different karaka dependency between them.

3. Telugu is a morphologically rich language. In n-gram karakas, the root word and the karaka dependency might be the same but the suffix might change.

4. The words themselves are not present in the training data.

Telugu utterance WX-format	VixyArWi : nenu I puswakaM wIsukuMtAnu
Gloss	Student : I this book take+future
Translation	Student : I will take this book
Karaka Dependencies extracted in modifier-karaka-modified format	[WisukuMtAnu]-k1-[nenu],[WisukuMtAnu]-k2-[I puswakaM]

Table 5: Example of n-gram karaka format extraction for an utterance

Hence, for those n-gram with karaka relationships the karaka dependencies form the test data are dropped. It is verified that they are mostly unigrams. Hence back-off to unigrams is considered. One of the basic back-off techniques is Katz's back-off model, which is presently proven as an effective LM algorithm for the given training and test data.

The algorithm is:

1. Extracting n-grams with karaka dependencies:

    (a) The training data is run through the shallow parser tool (`http://ltrc.iiit.ac.in/analyzer/telugu/`) for clustering the words and morph related information (PVS and Karthik, 2007).

    (b) Telugu tree bank (which consists of huge data containing karaka dependencies) is used as annotated data for karaka dependencies.

    (c) The karaka dependencies are extracted for the words present in each utterance (for both training and test data). An example of karaka dependencies is shown in Figure 2

    (d) The karaka dependencies between the words or word clusters will be converted to *modifier-karaka-modified* format as shown in table 5.

    (e) By observation, the format will be similar to n-grams with just karakas present between them. They are abbreviated as n-gram karakas.

2. Language Modeling technique:

    (a) After extracting n-grams with karaka dependencies for all the training and test utterances, Katz's back-off model (Katz's back-off model, 2015) is applied.

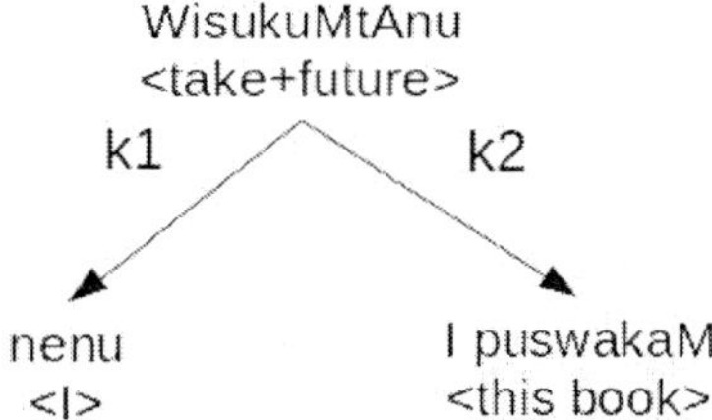

Figure 2: Showing karaka dependencies for an example utterance given in table 5

    (b) In Katz's back-off model, it is verified whether n-gram karakas are present or not in the training data, if present then tag probabilities are updated

    (c) If not, as Telugu is a morphologically rich language, we back-off to morphed n-gram karakas.

    (d) If the morphed n-gram karakas are not present in the training data then, it is known that particular dependencies are not annotated in the training data

    (e) Then the n-gram karakas will be decomposed to non karaka dependency words i.e. we back-off to unigrams and further to unigram morphs.

    (f) When all the above steps fail, smoothing method is considered.

3. k Nearest Neighbor:

    (a) To capture the utterance level information and to provide a strong ground for the respective tag, kNN is used.

    (b) kNN technique applied is same as given in equation 4

Katz's back-off model for n-gram karakas with back-off to morphed n-gram karakas is given in equation 5.

Katz's back-off model for non dependencies i.e. unigrams with back-off to morphed unigrams is given in equation 6.

$$p_{bo}(n\_gram\_karaka_i, T) =$$

$$\begin{cases} discount_1 \frac{C(n\_gram\_karaka_i, T)}{C(n\_gram\_karaka_i)} \\ if\ C(n\_gram\_karaka_i, T) > 0 \\[2ex] \alpha_1 \frac{C(morph\_n\_gram\_karaka_i, T)}{C(morph\_n\_gram\_karaka_i)} \\ if\ C(morph\_n\_gram\_karaka_i, T) > 0 \\[1ex] (otherwise) \end{cases}$$

$$(5)$$

$$p_{bo}(unigram_i, T) =$$

$$\begin{cases} discount_2 \frac{C(unigram_i, T)}{C(unigram_i)} \\ if\ C(unigram_i, T) > 0 \\[2ex] \alpha_2 \frac{C(morph\_unigram_i, T)}{C(morph\_unigram_i)} \\ if\ C(morph\_unigram_i, T) > 0 \\[1ex] (otherwise) \end{cases}$$

$$(6)$$

where $discount_1, discount_2$ are discounts obtained by Good Turing estimation as C^*/C and α_1, α_2 are back-off weights

4 Experiments and Results

The testing is done on our ASKLIB corpus using all the three algorithms. The corpus consisting of 225 dialogs is divided into four parts, each time one part is used for the testing and the remaining are combined for the training.

Firstly, the experiment is run on an n-gram method with Bayesian interpretation where n-grams of length 1-3 are considered. The results are shown in table 6

n-grams	Accuracy
n = 1	58.17%
n = 2	54.71%
n = 3	47.79%

Table 6: Accuracy obtained for n-grams.

From the results in table 6, it is clear that the n-grams are not sufficient for DA tagging for free word order languages like Telugu. When the n-gram length increases, there is a decrease in accuracy. The explanation is that, as Telugu is a free word order language, even though the intent is the same, the position of

words will not be the same in both the training data and the test data. Hence this method will not work for free word order languages like Telugu.

Next, n-grams with position independence are considered by taking combinations of unigrams from the training data and the test data combined with the kNN algorithm. The results are shown in table 7

Combinations of unigrams with kNN	Accuracy
n = 1 + kNN	66.67%
n = 2 + kNN	71.80%

Table 7: Accuracy obtained for combinations of unigrams.

From the results in table 7, it can be seen that, combinations of unigrams combined with kNN does show a good response in accuracy. The problem with this method is that, for an utterance of n words, each word is repeated n times which results in an increase in time complexity.

Now consider n-grams with karaka dependencies using back-off and kNN. This method is applied on ASKLIB corpus. The results are as shown in table 8

n-gram karakas using back-off and kNN	Accuracy
n-gram karakas + back-off + kNN	73.34%

Table 8: Accuracy obtained for n-gram karakas using back-off and kNN.

For free word order languages like Telugu, it is known that the karaka dependencies remain the same even though the word order changes. Hence there is no need to consider the methods such as combinations of unigrams. From this, there will be no problem of time complexity. There will be an advantage of morphs during back-off. Also, utterance level contextual information is captured using kNN. Due to the above reasons, from the results in table 8 we can see that the accuracy has risen to 73.34%.

When karaka based dependency method is

compared with the position specific n-grams methods and also combinations of unigrams, we can surely see the increase in accuracy, which proves that our method performs better.

5 Conclusion

Various classification algorithms are considered to tag the utterance using DA tagging scheme for ASKLIB corpus. Out of them, the proposed novel method obtained by considering the n-grams karaks with the Language Modeling technique (back-off) at intra utterance level in combination with Memory Based Learning such as k Nearest Neighbor method at the utterance level is applied. This method for DA tagging provided an accuracy of 73.34% when compared to the other methods. The results given in table 8 prove that this method performs better when compared to the other methodologies and is best suited for the DA tagging in Telugu task oriented dialogs.

6 Future Work

The given method will be tested on several Dravidian Languages like Kannada, Malayalam and Tamil etc. ASKLIB corpus is currently being developed in Kannada, Malayalam and Tamil. Further, new algorithms will also be applied taking the concept of karaka dependencies with contextual handling of previous utterances in dialogs as well.

References

Austin, J. L. 1975. *How to do things with words* volume 367. Oxford university press.

Bharati, A., Chaitanya, V., Sangal, R., & Ramakrishnamacharyulu, K. V. 1995. *Natural language processing: a Paninian perspective*, 67–71. New Delhi: Prentice-Hall of India.

Core, M. G., & Allen, J. 1997. Coding Dialogs with the DAMSL Annotation Scheme. *AAAI Fall Symposium on Communicative Action in Humans and Machines* 28–35

Cover, T. M., & Hart, P. E. 1967. Nearest neighbor pattern classification. *Information Theory, IEEE Transactions on*, 13(1):21–27.

Garner, P. N., Browning, S. R., Moore, R. K., & Russell, M. J. 1996. A theory of word frequencies and its application to dialogue move recognition. *In Spoken Language, 1996. ICSLP 96. Proceedings., Fourth International Conference on*, volume 3, 1880–1883. IEEE.

Katz's back-off model. 2015. *In Wikipedia, The Free Encyclopedia.* https://en.wikipedia.org/w/index.php?title=Katz\%27s_back-off_model&oldid=647273356

Klüwer, T., Uszkoreit, H., & Xu, F 2010. Using syntactic and semantic based relations for dialogue act recognition. *In Proceedings of the 23rd International Conference on Computational Linguistics : Posters*, pp. 570-578 Association for Computational Linguistics.

Král, P., & Cerisara, C. 2012. Dialogue act recognition approaches. *Computing and Informatics*, 29(2):227–250.

Liu, P., Hu, Q., Dang, J., Jin, D., & Cao, J. 2013. Dialog Act classification in Chinese spoken language. *In Machine Learning and Cybernetics (ICMLC), 2013 International Conference on*, volume 2, 516–521 IEEE.

PVS, A., & Karthik, G. 2007. Part-of-speech tagging and chunking using conditional random fields and transformation based learning. *Shallow Parsing for South Asian Languages, 21.*

Reithinger, N. & Klesen, M. 1997. Dialogue act classification using language models. G. Kokkinakis, N. Fakotakis & E. Dermatas (eds.), *EUROSPEECH,*:ISCA

Rotaru, M. 2002. Dialog act tagging using memory-based learning. *Term project, University of Pittsburgh*, 255–276

Stolcke, A., Ries, K., Coccaro, N., Shriberg, E., Bates, R. A., Jurafsky, D., Taylor, P., Martin, R., Ess-Dykema, C. V. & Meteer, M. 2000.perform Dialog Act Modeling for Automatic Tagging and Recognition of Conversational Speech. *Computational Linguistics*, 26, 339–373

Webb, N., Hepple, M., & Wilks, Y. 2005. Dialogue act classification based on intra-utterance features. In *Proceedings of the AAAI Workshop on Spoken Language Understanding*

Ranking Model with a Reduced Feature Set for an Automated Question Generation System

Manisha Satish Divate
Department of Computer science
University of Mumbai
India
divate.manisha.79@gmail.com

Ambuja Salgaonkar
Department of Computer science
University of Mumbai
India
ambujas@gmail.com

Abstract

A metric has been proposed to automatically generate well-formed-ness rank for machine generated questions. The grammatical correctness of a question, challenge due to the negation in the source text and number of transformations required to convert an ill-formed (not appealing to humans) question to a well-formed (meaningful and human appealing) question seem the prominent features.

We used 135 questions generated by Heilman and Smith's system (Heilman and Smith, 2011), developed a regression model using our feature set and tested it. The R-squared value is 93.5% which is quiet acceptable. Relevance of the model has been corroborated by means of the residual plot. (Heilman and Smith, 2011) Metric is of 187 features and that of (Liu, 2012) is of 11. We suggested 16 features for a general automatic question quality enhancer to look into. However, the present model has been built by considering only 10 out of them. (Heilman and Smith , 2011)generated questions do not possess any infirmities indicated by the remaining ones. 75 questions were used in training and 60 were tested. Recognition accuracy is 94.4%.

1. Introduction

Automatic question generation systems (AQG) have been attempted since the mid-1970s (Wolfe J.H., 1976). A significant amount of work has been reported during the last decade, see details in Sec-
tion 2 below. To a certain extent AQGs have assisted human question-paper setters, but the quality of the automatically generated questions is often found to be inadequate. The strength and weaknesses of AQGs and a few remedies to enhance the quality of the questions have been discussed by us in (Salgaonkar and Divate, 2013).

It is necessary to formally compute the worth of an AQG by employing a quality metric. Developing such a metric for a given set of questions and therefore for an AQG is a research problem. The quality metric would serve the purpose of evaluating any automatic system that claims to provide quality enhancement of a set of questions. Call such a system an "automatic question quality enhancer" (AQQE). In the present paper we propose a new quality metric for questions generated by an AQG, suggest a framework for an AQQE, and demonstrate the improvement in quality due to this framework.

It goes without saying that the attributes of a question are the arguments of the quality function, and that, to improve the quality of a question, the attribute values have to be changed appropriately. Therefore the task of the AQQE is to rearticulate a given question in such a way that the changed attribute values yield a higher quality according to the metric. To improve the productivity of an AQG, our aim has to be optimization of the "objective function" of the metric, since we aspire to make a system to generate more and more questions that are acceptable to humans.

2. Previous Research

D S Sharma, R Sangal and E Sherly. Proc. of the 12th Intl. Conference on Natural Language Processing, pages 384–393,
Trivandrum, India. December 2015. ©2015 NLP Association of India (NLPAI)

AQGs that attempt to measure *factual* as well as *deep learning*, including reading comprehension, writing ability and vocabulary, have been proposed in (Kunichika *et al.,* 2004; Brown *et al.,* 2005; Liu *et al.,* 2005; Chen *et al.,* 2006; Liu *et al.,* 2012). Systems generating MCQ type, fill-in-the-blank type or wh-type questions are another thrust area (Aist, 2001; Hashino and Hiroshi, 2005; Aldabe *et al.,* 2006; Mitkov, 2006; Prasad et al.,2008; W. Chen *et al.,* 2009; Chen *et al.,* 2009; Heilman and Smith, 2009; Ali *et al.,* 2010; Liske, 2011; Agarwal and Mannem, 2011a; Agarwal and Mannem, 2011b).

Incorrect articulation of linguistic structures and an undue focus on relatively less important points are two commonly observed flaws in automatically generated questions. The statistics of the other types of errors observed in our experiments is given in the Table 1 below

Error Type	%
No error	43.10
Wrong WH	30.17
Vague	11.21
Formatting error	6.90
Ungrammatical	5.17
Does not make sense	4.31
Co reference not resolve	3.45

Table 1: Flaws observed in system generated questions

According to (Heilman and Smith, 2009), only 27.3% of the questions among the ones generated through their system are acceptable [Henceforth, the two authors are abbreviated as H&S]. The rank of a question has been computed by employing the linear regression model with 187 features (H&S, 2010). Among them, 53 features are as follows: length-based (3), language model (6), grammatical aspects (23), transformations (8), vagueness (3), negation (1), and wh-words (9). The remaining 134 are values computed from binary histograms of length and count features that serve as thresholds for controlling non-linearity among the numerical parameters used for describing syntax, length and linguistic features.

Empirical testing of the automatically generated questions revealed that out of the top ranked 20% (86 out of 428 questions), 52.3% were acceptable, where top rank is defined to be rank 3.5 and above on a 5-point scale, as selected by a team of human raters.

(Liu, 2012) is another notable work in the area of AQGs. This system helps in review writing and extracting citations from a given text. Further, the system categorizes the text and identifies the keywords that are used to fill in suitable question templates from the authors' question template library.

Among the approaches used in (Liu, 2012) to rank a question, two give the best results: point-wise logistic regression and pair wise support vector machines (the later technique is named RankSVM). With 11 features, when considering the top 25% ranked questions the acceptability of RankSVM was found to be 75.8%, while that of logistic regression was 74.2%, whereas 71.3 % of the top 50% are found acceptable. This figure is comparable to the result of (H&S, 2009). Also, it confirms the later result (H&S, 2011) that the increase in the percentage of acceptable questions is statistically significant when considering only the top ranked ones.

The 187 features of (H&S, 2010 and 2011) is arguably a large number, because a dozen features of (Liu, 2012) has led to a comparable result. Therefore the hypothesis arises whether it is possible to independently develop yet another reliable quality metric for questions using a model with a small number of features.

The findings about our 10 features regression model are reported in this paper. Section 3 is on nomenclature that is to set up a background for a novice reader. Details of our experiment are listed in Section 4. Observations and interpretations are presented in Section 5. Findings are summarized in the end of the paper.

3. Nomenclature

A question is *ill-formed*, i.e., unacceptable, if one or more flaws of the following types are observed in its articulation: incorrect grammar, semantic inadequacy, vagueness with respect to the answer, inadequate data, a wrong choice of WH form while presenting a question, or some editing is needed (H&S, 2009; Mannem et. al, 2010).

A question is *well-formed*, hence acceptable, if it is not ill-formed, i.e., it does not have any of the 6 flaws mentioned above.

A Base sentence is the source text for generating the questions.

An *answer phrase* is a machine-selected portion of the base sentence that is expected to be an answer to one or many potential questions that would be generated by an AQG.

Example (base sentence): *As is the case in a Parliamentary system, the government is formed by the party, alliance or group of assembly members who command the majority.*

(Answer phrase) by the party, alliance or group of assembly members who command the majority

IFQ (generated by HSAQG): *What is the government formed by?*

WFQ (manually generated): *Who forms the government in a Parliamentary system?*

Flaw: Wrong choice of wh-form.

4. Methodology

Base text database consisted of five randomly selected paragraphs, of length 1 to 6 sentences, from wiki articles on a variety of topics: University of Mumbai, Lokmanya Tilak as a journalist, Government of Maharashtra, renewable energy, solar technology [Appendix 1].

135 questions were generated with HSAQG, out of which we randomly selected 75 as a training set. 13 questions (17.33% or a little over 1/6) were found to be redundant. Of the remaining 62, we found that 26 questions (42%) were acceptable to humans or WFQ, and 36 questions (58%) needed reframing in order to make them WFQs.

It appears that there is enough scope for further improvement in systems like HSAQG, hence this is a substantive research problem. Inspection of the data reveals that the changes required to improve the acceptability of the AQG-generated questions include removal of formatting errors, extra precision of questions to enhance clarity, more complete selection of answer phrases.

In the first step we analyzed the system generated IFQs with respect to the corresponding WFQs that were provided by a human expert. This exercise laid the foundation for generating the 16 dimensional vector representation of a question which is the core of our quality metric.

In the Table 2 below we list a few sample IFQs from our experiment, the corresponding WFQs and the flaws observed in each case.

Sentence simplification is another challenge in AQG systems. AQG system frames all possible questions from the modifier phrase, subordinate clause, appositives phrases, and from leading prepositional phrases. Those questions are unacceptable because they are *vague* or *grammatically incorrect*, or *do not make sense*. Our analysis reveals that AQGs fail to produce WFQs from the negative sentences.

In the next step we had a team of 5 human raters rank each of the questions on a 5-point scale. The protocol for generating the rank of a question was that the majority carries the vote. In case of much divergence in perceived rank, we took cognizance of others' views before choosing a rank. The sentiments of the raters were shared, which gave us an idea about what is not appealing to them. We formalized this feedback using the grammatical framework of English sentence structure. This exercise led to 16 rules for computing the rank of a question. These rules have been listed as R1 to R16. Only 10 rules (*-marked) were applicable for the H&S AQG that we used. Examples for remaining 6 rules (which are not *- marked) are taken from various internet sources. Ill-articulations are underlined and corrections are in bold.

R1(verbTenseInQuestion): Verb exists AND Verb Tense is correct => 1 else 0

Base sentence: *The Martians landed **near the aqueduct.***

IFQ: *Where did the Martians landed?*

WFQ: *Where did the Martians **land**?*

* R2(AuxVerb): AuxiliaryVerb is present in the base sentence AND (incorrect or no use of AuxiliaryVerb in the question) => 0 else 1

The University of Mumbai was established 1857 by Dr John Wilson (after whom Wilson College in Mumbai is named), according to

Sr No	Base Sentence	Answer phrase	IFQ	WFQ	Flaw	Flaw type
1	Maharashtra has bicameral legislature, i.e., it consists of two houses, Vidhan Sabha and Vidhan Parishad.	a bicameral legislature i. e.	What does Maharashtra consist of two houses-- Vidhan Sabha and Vidhan Parishad Maharashtra has?	Which type of legislature does Maharashtra have? Which legislature has two houses?	it refers to Maharashtra but, actually it should refer to the word bicameral	Inappropriate resolution of co-reference
2	Following this, on 22 June 1897, Commissioner Rand and another British officer, Lt. Ayerst, were shot and killed by the Chapekar brothers and their other associates	Commissioner Rand and another British officer	Who were shot? Who were killed?	Who were shot and killed A clearer question could be: Who were shot and killed on 22 June 1897 by the Chapekar brothers and their other associates?	Shoot and kill refers to an instance; Shoot and kill are not to be treated as two different instances.	Verbs come with a conjunction; question is too short
3	Tilak was born in a Chitpavan Brahmin family in Ratnagiri Maharashtra on 23July 1856	23rd july 1856	When was Tilak born in a Chitpavan Brahmin family on 23 July 1856?	When was Tilak born ?	Date, family and place need to be treated as three different things	Additional context is to be removed
4	Tilak was born in a Chitpavan Brahmin family in Ratnagiri Maharashtra on 23July 1856	on 23	What was Tilak born in a Chitpavan Brahmin family in Ratnagiri Maharashtra on July 1856?	When was Tilak born?	23 July 1856 is a phrase	Answer phrase is partially selected
5	Based on REN21's 2014 report, renewables contributed 19 percent to our energy consumption and 22 percent to our electricity generation in 2012 and 2013, respectively	to our energy consumption and 22 percent-	What did renewables contribute 19 percent to to our electricity generation in 2012 and 2013, respectively?	what [according to REN21's report] in 2012 renewables contributed 19 percent to?	Words order is incorrect. Question becomes ungrammatical.	Grammatically incorrect

Table Continued…..

Sr No	Base Sentence	Answer phrase	IFQ	WFQ	Flaw	Flaw type
6	Following this, on 22 June 1897, Commissioner Rand and another British officer, Lt. Ayerst were shot and killed by the Chapekar brothers and their other associates	yes/no	Did Commissioner Rand and another British officer follow this?	Did Chapekar brothers and their other associates kill and shoot Commissioner Rand and another British officer, Lt. Ayerst on 22 June 1897?	"Following this" indicates an event.	Does not make sense
7	Maharashtra has a bicameral legislature i. e. it consists of two houses-- Vidhan Sabha (legislative assembly) and Vidhan Parishad (legislative council).	yes/no	Does Maharashtra consist of two houses-- Vidhan Sabha and Vidhan Parishad Maharashtra has a bicameral legislature i. e.?	does maharashtra consist of two houses Vidhan sabha and Vidhan parishad?	Removal of "-" and "i.e" from question.	Formatting error
8	In 1792, Carey, a Baptist, who was not only a cobbler, but a linguist of the highest order.	Carey	Who was not only a cobbler, but a linguist of the highest order in 1792?	Who was Baptists, cobbler and linguist of highest order in 1972?	Frame affirmative question.	Negative sentence

Table 2: Sample IFQs with flaw types and suggested WFQ

``Wood's dispatch'', drafted by Sir Charles
IFQ : *Who <u>was</u> ``Wood's dispatch'' drafted by in 1854?*
WFQ: *Who **drafted** "Woods dispatch" ?*
*R3(AnsPronoun): Correct Wh-phrase with respect to the Pronoun phrase in Answer => 1 else 0
Base Sentence: *<u>It</u> has 711 affiliated colleges*
IFQ: *What has 711 affiliated colleges?*
WFQ: *What has 711 affiliated colleges?*
*R4(PronounAsSubjectInQuestion): Subject of the question phrase is pronoun => 0 else 1
Base Sentence: ***It** has 711 affiliated colleges*
IFQ: *What does <u>it</u> have?*

WFQ: *How many affiliated colleges does **University of Mumbai** have?*
*R5(AnsPhraseAsPP): Answer phrase is a propositional phrase => 0 else 1
Base Sentence: *The Government of Maharashtra is the government for the state of Maharashtra <u>in Western India</u>.*
IFQ: *What is the Government of Maharashtra the government for the state of Maharashtra in?*
WFQ: *Where in India is the Government of Maharashtra the government for the state of Maharashtra?*

*R6(SubordinateClause): Subordinate clause in question => 0 else 1

> Base Sentence: *Solar technologies are broadly characterized as either passive solar or active solar depending on the way they capture, convert and distribute solar energy.*
>
> IFQ: *What are Solar technologies broadly characterized as they capture, convert and distribute solar energy?*
>
> WFQ: *What are the ways to characterize Solor Technologies?*

*R7(NounPhraseInsidePP): Noun phrase that is the answer phrase is a part of a propositional phrase => 0 else 1

> Base Sentence: *The Government of Maharashtra is the government for the state of Maharashtra in Western India.*
>
> IFQ: *What is the Government of Maharashtra the government for in Western India?*
>
> WFQ: *Which state in Western India the Government of Maharashtra is the government for?*

R8(SubjectMovement): Answer phrase is not a subject AND correct Subject-Auxiliary Verb movement => 1 else 0

> Base Sentence: *Sam is reading the paper.*
>
> IFQ: *what Sam is reading?*
>
> WFQ: *What is Sam reading?*

R9(RemovedAppositives): Appositive phrase => 0 else 1

> Base Sentence: *In June of 1987, The Bridge of Trinquetaille, Vincent van Gogh's view of an iron bridge over the Rhone, sold for $20.2 million.*
>
> IFQ: *what was Vincent van Gogh's view of an iron bridge over the Rhone sold for $20.2 million?*
>
> WFQ: What was sold for $20.2 million?*

R10(LeadConjunction): Leading conjunction phrase => 0 else

> Base Sentence: *Since they had misbehaved, the boys were given one week suspensions from school.*
>
> IFQ: *who had misbehaved since?*
>
> WFQ: *who had misbehaved?*

R11(NounParticiple): Noun participle without the noun => 0 else 1

> Base sentence: *Having been on the road for four days, the Todds were exhausted.*
>
> IFQ: *Who were exhausted having been on the road for four days?*

WFQ: *Who were exhausted?*

*R12(LeadingPP): Leading proposition phrase of a base sentence appearing in the question AND not moved to the end of the question => 0 else 1

> Base sentence: *Based on REN21's 2014 report, renewables contributed 19 percent to our energy consumption and 22 percent to our electricity generation in 2012 and 2013, respectively*
>
> IFQ: *Who were based on REN21's 2014 report?*
>
> WFQ: *What [according to REN21's 2014 report] contributed 19 percent to our energy consumption in 2012?*
>
> Base sentence: *For convocation, I will go to the University.*
>
> IFQ: *For what will you go to the University?*
>
> WFQ: *What will you go to the University for?*
>
> WFQ: *Why will you go to the University?*
>
> WFQ with a lesser rank: *When will go to the University? (The correct answer of this question will be "convocation day" or "on convocation day").*

*R13(Wh-PhraseAsPerANS): Correct Wh-phrase with respect to the Answer in the Answer phrase => 1 else 0

> Base Sentence: *Tilak was born in a Chitpavan Brahmin family in Ratnagiri, headquarters of the eponymous district of present day Maharashtra (then British India) on 23 July 1856.*
>
> IFQ: *Who was headquarters of the eponymous district of present day?*
>
> WFQ: *what was the headquarters of the eponymous district of present day Maharashtra?*

*R14(LengthAnsPhrase): NOT (Answer phrase longer than 4 words OR Answer phrase lesser than 4) OR Answer phrase is a named entity => 1 else 0

> Base Sentence: The University of Mumbai offers Bachelors, Masters and Doctoral degrees apart from **diplomas and certificates in many disciplines.**
>
> IFQ: *What does the University of Mumbai offer Bachelors, Masters and Doctoral degrees apart from?*
>
> WFQ: *Which courses does University of Mumbai offer along with Bachelors, Masters and Doctoral degrees?*

R15(ChkNegation): Base sentence is a negation AND Question form is negative => 0 else 1
If question is not affirmative then rank 0 else 1

Base sentence: *In 1792, Carey, a Baptist, who was not only a cobbler, but a linguist of the highest order.*

IFQ: *Who was not only a cobbler, but a linguist of the highest order in 1792?*

WFQ: *Who **was cobbler and linguist** of higher order in 1792?*

*R16(Wh-PhraseChange): WFQ => 0 else number of modifications required to make it a WFQ

Base Sentence: *Maharashtra has a bicameral legislature i. e. it consists of two houses-- Vidhan Sabha (legislative assembly) and Vidhan Parishad (legislative council).*

IFQ: *Does Maharashtra consist of two houses--Vidhan Sabha and Vidhan Parishad Maharashtra has a bicameral legislature i. e.?*

WFQ: *does Maharashtra consist of two houses Vidhan sabha and Vidhan parishad?*

A question is represented as a 16 dimensional vector, of which all values but the last are either 0 or 1. Together with the human rated rank of each question as the dependent variable in the 17th place, we got a system of 62 equations in 16 independent variables (equivalently, 62 observations with 16 parameters). We attempted a solution of this system by employing a multiple linear regression.

5. Result and Discussion:

At 93.5%, the R-squared value, or the coefficient of determination, is satisfactory. We tested the model by using 61 observations that were independent of the training sample. Of which 6 questions were found redundant. The precision of the model from a sample of size 54 is 0.934.

As shown in the Figure 3 (a) and (b), the points in the residual plot when employed our model, are randomly dispersed. It confirms that the linear regression model is appropriate for this data.

We derived a quality metric for computing "how well-formed a question is":

$Y= 0.097*AuxVerb + 0.194*LeadingPP + 0.246*LengthAnsPhrase + 0.017*Wh-PhraseAsPerANS + 0.714*AnsPronoun - 0.010*PronounAsSubjectInQuestion - 0.215*SubordinateClause + 0.208*NounPhraseInsidePP - 0.037*AnsPhraseAsPP - 0.588*Wh-PhraseChange + 3.746$

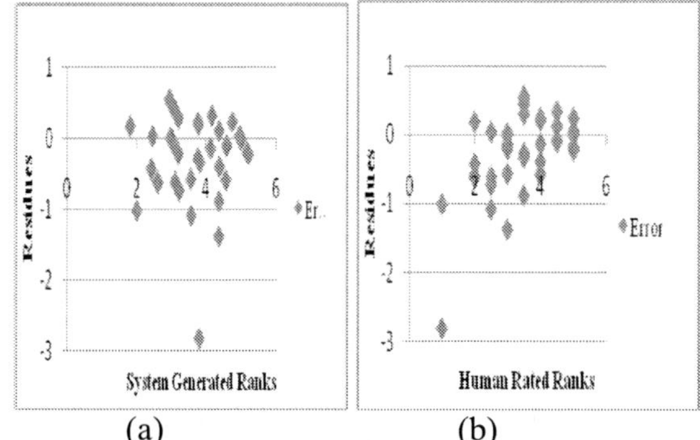

(a)   (b)

Figure 3 (a): Residual plot for ranks generated by LR model

Figure 3 (b): Residual plot for Human rated ranks

We observed a few interesting facts a majority of errors (30.17%) are because of wrong choice of Wh-phrase. It may be due to the fact that formulating a question using *what* is relatively easier and not incorrect per se. Therefore, AQGs employ this technique most of the time while generating a Wh-question. However, such questions are vague, imprecise so we classify them as IFQ. Articulating a question with a right Wh-phrase involves analysis of the answer term. Recall the example from [Section 4], namely, *Why will you go to the University?* The articulation of this *WFQ* requires the understanding that convocation is an event at the University and that has a purpose for its visitors. Interpretation of the event as a temporal entity gives rise to a less pertinent question: *When will you go to the University?*

In the case of an IFQ with a flaw, a wrong choice of Wh-phrase requires up to 5 modifications while transforming it into a WFQ. A list of sample templates for a variety of Wh-questions and the corresponding transformations is given below.

Sample question prototypes

Example1: <What Verb Object?>: *What drink chocolate of us?*

Example2: <What do-support Subject Verb?>: *What did you eat (today)?*

Example3: <How many Helping noun Verb Object?>: *How many of us drink chocolate?*

Example3: <How many Helping noun do-support Subject Verb?>: How many modifications do we need?

To change the Wh-phrase from a *what* [Example1] type question to *How many* [Example3] type we need to change the Wh-phrase and

386

the addition of a helping noun. We modify the question in 2 steps.

Ex: Base Sentence : *Tilak obtained his Bachelor of Arts **in first class** in Mathematics from Deccan College of Pune in 1877.*

Answer phrase: *in first class*

IFQ : *What did Tilak obtain his Bachelor of Arts in from Deccan College of Pune in 1877?*

WFQ: *which class did Tilak obtain in his Bachelor of Arts in Mathematics from Deccan College of Pune in 1877.*

To change IFQ to WFQ we need to perform changes like *What→Which* ; insert *→class* ; Add preposition → *in* before possessive noun. We assign value 3 for 16th feature which indicates the number of modification required to make WFQ from given IFQ.

A too-long answer phrase leads to the formation of a wrong Wh-question, as it may contain sub-phrases or may lead to the formation of vague questions, since very little information remains in hand for formulating the questions. For example, with *"It is an elected government with 288 MLAs elected to the legislative assembly for a 5-year term"* as a base sentence and *"with 288 MLAs elected to the legislative assembly for a 5-year term"* as an answer phrase the choice of a question is *"Who is it an elected government with?"* lead to the formation of Wrong Wh-question.

The system generated ranks (R) labeled A to E (where A is the best, and E is not acceptable) as follows: A is 4 to 5, B is 3 to 4, C is 2 to 3, D is 1 to 2, E is 0 to 1 (upper bound is included, lower bound excluded). For classification we used J48 classifier, to classify the test data of 54 questions into defined five classes (A-E).

Systems performance is evaluated by calculating Precision and F1 measure using formula mentioned below.

Precision (PPV) = TP /(TP + FP)

F1= 2TP/(2TP+FP+FN)

Study results shows average precision value for all classes is 0.934 and F1-score as 0.944.

Towards the conclusion of our experiment, we manually modified each IFQ such that its vector representation will yield an optimum value and computed its rank by applying H&S metric as well as our metric. There were 4, 13, 18 and 20 questions were of the ranks up to 2, 3, 4 and 5 respectively. It revealed that the ranks of all but the

question numbers 5 and 41 have been upgraded to 5. Rank of question number 5 and 41 were upgraded to 4. Answer phrase in these cases has been a pronoun phrase, *following this.* In the absence of background knowledge resolution of the pronoun reference is a challenge while framing a WFQ of rating 5.

6. Conclusion

This study reveals that researching AQGs is worth for their enhancement. HSAQG generated questions are free from the 6 types of infirmities, namely, correct verb tense, Subject-Auxiliary Verb movement, leading conjunction phrase, Appositive phrase, question form is negative. Our linear regression model with 16 features is simple and effective for ranking a question for its well-formedness. The inputs generated by it are worth looking while designing an AQQE. AQQE is a challenge that has immediate applications.

References

Agarwal, M., & Mannem, P. (2011a, June). *Automatic gap-fill question generation from text books*. In Proceedings of the 6th Workshop on Innovative Use of NLP for Building Educational Applications (pp. 56-64). Association for Computational Linguistics.

Agarwal, M., Shah, R., & Mannem, P. (2011b, June). *Automatic question generation using discourse cues.* In Proceedings of the 6th Workshop on Innovative Use of NLP for Building Educational Applications (pp. 1-9). Association for Computational Linguistics.

Aist G.(2001) *Towards automatic glossarization: automatically constructing and administering vocabulary assistance factoids and multiple-choice assessment.* International Journal of Artificial Intelligence in Education, 12, 212-231

Aldabe, I., de Lacalle, M. L., Maritxalar, M., Martinez, E., & Uria, L. (2006, January*). Arikiturri: an automatic question generator based on corpora and nlp techniques.* In Intelligent Tutoring Systems (pp. 584-594). Springer Berlin Heidelberg.

Ali, H., Chali, Y., & Hasan, S. A. (2010, June). *Automation of question generation from sentences.* In Proceedings of QG2010: The Third Workshop on Question Generation (pp. 58-67).

Brown, J. C., Frishkoff, G. A., & Eskenazi, M. (2005, October). *Automatic question generation for vocabulary assessment.* In Proceedings of the conference on Human Language Technology and Empirical Methods in Natural Language Processing (pp. 819-826). Association for Computational Linguistics.

Chali, Y., & Hasan, S. A. (2012). *Towards Automatic Topical Question Generation.* In *COLING* (pp. 475-492).

Chen, W. (2009). Aist, G., Mostow, J.: *Generating questions automatically from informational text.* In Proceedings of the 2nd Workshop on Question Generation (AIED 2009) (pp. 17-24).

Chen, C. Y., Liou, H. C., & Chang, J. S. (2006, July). *Fast: an automatic generation system for grammar tests.* In Proceedings of the COLING/ACL on Interactive presentation sessions (pp. 1-4). Association for Computational Linguistics.

Heilman, M., & Smith, N. A. (2009). *Question generation via overgenerating transformations and ranking.* (No. CMU-LTI-09-013). CARNEGIE-MELLON UNIV PITTSBURGH PA LANGUAGE TECHNOLOGIES INST.

Heilman, M., & Smith, N. A. (2010b, June). *Good question! statistical ranking for question generation.* In Human Language Technologies: The 2010 Annual Conference of the North American Chapter of the Association for Computational Linguistics (pp. 609-617). Association for Computational Linguistics.

Heilman, M., & Smith, N. A. (2010c, June). *Rating computer-generated questions with Mechanical Turk.* In Proceedings of the NAACL HLT 2010 Workshop on Creating Speech and Language Data with Amazon's Mechanical Turk (pp. 35-40). Association for Computational Linguistics.

Heilman, M., & Smith, N. A. (2009, July). *Ranking automatically generated questions as a shared task.* In The 2nd Workshop on Question Generation (Vol. 1, pp. 30-37).

Heilman, M. (2011). *Automatic factual question generation from text* (Doctoral dissertation, Carnegie Mellon University).

Hoshino, A., & Nakagawa, H. (2005, June). *A real-time multiple-choice question generation for language testing: a preliminary study.* In Proceedings of the second workshop on Building Educational Applications Using NLP (pp. 17-20). Association for Computational Linguistics.

Kunichika, H., Katayama, T., Hirashima, T., & Takeuchi, A. (2004). *Automated question generation methods for intelligent English learning systems and its evaluation.* In Proc. of ICCE.

Liske, H. (2011, June). *A framework for automated generation of examination questions from web based semantically treated search results.* In Proceedings of the 12th International Conference on Computer Systems and Technologies(pp. 510-515). ACM.

Liu, M., Calvo, R. A., & Rus, V. (2010, January). *Automatic question generation for literature review writing support.* In Intelligent Tutoring Systems(pp. 45-54). Springer Berlin Heidelberg.

Liu, M., & Calvo, R. A. (2011, January). *Question taxonomy and implications for automatic question generation.* In Artificial Intelligence in Education (pp. 504-506). Springer Berlin Heidelberg.

Liu, M., Calvo, R., Aditomo, A., & Pizzato, L. A. (2012). *Using wikipedia and conceptual graph structures to generate questions for academic writing support.* Learning Technologies, IEEE Transactions on, 5(3), 251-263.

Liu, M., Calvo, R. A., & Rus, V. (2012). G-Asks: *An intelligent automatic question generation system for academic writing support.* Dialogue and Discourse: Special Issue on Question Generation, 3(2), 101-124.

Mannem, P., Prasad, R., & Joshi, A. (2010, June). *Question generation from paragraphs at UPenn: QGSTEC system description.* In Proceedings of QG2010: The Third Workshop on Question Generation (pp. 84-91).

Mitkov, R., An Ha, L., & Karamanis, N. (2006). *A computer-aided environment for generating multiple-choice test items.* Natural Language Engineering, 12(02), 177-194.

Pal, S., Mondal, T., Pakray, P., Das, D., & Bandyopadhyay, S. (2010). *Qgstec system description–juqgg: A rule based approach.* In Proceedings of the Third Workshop on Question Generation, pp.76-79

Prasad, R., & Joshi, A. (2008, September). *A discourse-based approach to generating why-questions from texts.* In Proceedings of the Workshop on the Question Generation Shared Task and Evaluation Challenge (pp. 1-3).

Rus, V., & Lester, J. (2009, July). *The 2nd Workshop on Question Generation.* In AIED (p. 808).

Salgaonkar A. and Divate M.(2014c*) Ill-Formed to Well Formed Question Generator.* In ICCI'14, Mumbai.

Wolfe, J. H. (1976, February). *Automatic question generation from text-an aid to independent study.* In ACM SIGCUE Outlook (Vol. 10, No. SI, pp. 104-112). ACM.

Appendix (source Wikipedia)

Paragraph1:

The University of Mumbai offers Bachelors, Masters and Doctoral degrees apart from diplomas and certificates in many disciplines. The University of Mumbai is one of the largest universities in the world in terms of the number of students. In 2011 the total number of enrolled students was 5,49,432. It has 711 affiliated colleges. The University of Mumbai was established in 1857 by Dr John Wilson (after whom Wilson College in Mumbai is named), according to ``Wood's dispatch", drafted by Sir Charles Wood in 1854.The name of the University has been changed from ``University of Bombay" to ``University of Mumbai" as per a gazette of the Government of Maharashtra dated September 4,1996.

Paragraph 2:

The Government of Maharashtra is the government for the state of Maharashtra in Western India. Maharashtra has a bicameral legislature i. e. it consists of two houses-- Vidhan Sabha (legislative assembly) and VidhanParishad (legislative council).It is an elected government with 288 MLAs elected to the legislative assembly for a 5-year term. The leader of the majority in assembly becomes the Chief Minister and selects the cabinet members. As is the case in a Parliamentary system, the government is formed by the party, alliance or group of assembly members who command the majority.

Paragraph 3 :

Based on REN21's 2014 report, renewables contributed 19 percent to our global energy consumption and 22 percent to our electricity generation in 2012 and 2013, respectively. n 2011, the International Energy Agency said that "the development of affordable, inexhaustible and clean solar energy technologies will have huge longer-term benefits. Renewable energy replaces conventional fuels in four distinct areas: electricity generation, hot water\/space heating, motor fuels, and rural energy services. Wind power is growing at the rate of 30% annually, with a worldwide installed capacity of 282,482 megawatts (MW) at the end of 2012, and is widely used in Europe, Asia, and the United States. Renewable energy is generally defined as energy that comes from resources which are naturally replenished on a human timescale such as sunlight, wind, rain, tides, waves.

Paragraph4

Tilak was one of the first and strongest advocates of "Swaraj" (self-rule) and a strong radical in Indian consciousness. Tilak was born in a Chitpavan Brahmin family in Ratnagiri headquarters of the eponymous district of present-day Maharashtra (then British India) on 23 July 1856. He obtained his Bachelor of Arts in first class in Mathematics from Deccan College of Pune in 1877. In 1879 he obtained his LL.B degree from Government Law College. Following this, on 22 June 1897, Commissioner Rand and another British officer, Lt. Ayerst were shot and killed by the Chapekar brothers and their other associates.

Paragraph 5:

Venus Express is outfitted with a camera that can take images in infrared and visual spectrums as well as a device called the Flux Gate Magnetometer, which searches for lightning signal

Paragraph 6:

Solar technologies are broadly characterized as either passive solar or active solar depending on the way they capture, convert and distribute solar energy.

Natural Language Processing for Solving Simple Word Problems

Sowmya S Sundaram
Indian Institute of Technology, Madras
Chennai 600036
sowmya@cse.iitm.ac.in

Deepak Khemani
Indian Institute of Technology, Madras
Chennai 600036
khemani@iitm.ac.in

Abstract

This paper describes our system which solves simple arithmetic word problems. The system takes a word problem described in natural language, extracts information required for representation, orders the facts presented, applies procedures and derives the answer. It then displays this answer in natural language. The emphasis of this paper is on the natural language processing(NLP) techniques used to retrieve the relevant information from the English word problem. The system shows improvements over existing systems.

1 Introduction

The aim of this work is to solve a mathematical problem involving addition/subtraction which is given in English. It uses the principles of NLP to extract information from the text. Then, it uses some pre-stored routines to calculate the answer. To illustrate, a sample input and the corresponding output is shown below.

Input: John has 3 apples. He gave 1 apple to Mary. How many apples does John have now?

Output: John has 2 apples.

The system extracts the information that, to use the parlance of (Bakman, 2007), an owner "John" has 3 apples. The natural language processor maps the word "give" to the knowledge that it must happen between two owners, where the first owner loses something and the second owner gains it. This information is coded in the form of schemas which are templates describing different scenarios. For example, the above scenario is known as a "Transfer-In-Ownership" or "Change-Out" which says John loses one apple and Mary gains it.

The issues in this simple example are many. The pronoun, "He" must be mapped to "John". The

order of the sentences matter. If the problem was "John gave 1 apple to Mary. He has 3 apples now. How many apples did John have?", then the answer is completely different.

To elaborate, the problem solving process begins by processing the question that is expressed in natural language. After processing the question, the information required by the knowledge representation is extracted. This is a knowledge-based natural language processing system. Hence, the domain knowledge provided by the underlying representation can also help clear ambiguities faced by the natural language processor.

For example, one of the heuristics used is described as follows. If the problem is, "There are 2 pencils in the drawer. Tim placed 3 pencils in the drawer. How many pencils are now there in total?", the natural language processor does not understand whether the question is about the pencils with Tim or the ones in the drawer. However, after representing the knowledge, it is clear that the "drawer" has a change in state and more probably, the question is about the ones in the drawer.

The given word problem is split into constituent sentences. Every sentence is analysed and the information required by the representation is extracted using Stanford Core NLP Suite (Manning et al., 2014) in a manner that is described in detail in the following sections. The answer is again displayed in natural language.

For evaluation, the datasets provided by (Hosseini et al., 2014) are used. The proposed system shows an improvement because of the exploitation of knowledge representation and using keywords other than verbs.

2 Related Work

Such a problem was first attempted by Bobrow as part of his PhD dissertation in 1964. The

D S Sharma, R Sangal and E Sherly. Proc. of the 12th Intl. Conference on Natural Language Processing, pages 394–402,
Trivandrum, India. December 2015. ©2015 NLP Association of India (NLPAI)

system described in (Bobrow, 1964) could solve an algebra problem given in a subset of natural language. A common trait of most systems that use this approach is to work with a subset of the natural language, most commonly via a Controlled Natural Language. This work attempts to extract information from the ambiguous English sentences themselves. The latest in this line of work for mathematical algebraic word problems, without using empirical methods, is in (Bakman, 2007) which proposed a method that improved upon (Dellarosa, 1986). Dellarosa used "schemas" to solve addition/subtraction problems in 1986 with some improvements over (Fletcher, 1985) for classifying entities like "dolls" are "toys". Schemas are templates for problem solving. (Bakman, 2007) extends schemas to handle extraneous information and can solve multi-step problems unlike its predecessors. In a review of such knowledge-based systems by (Mukherjee and Garain, 2009), it was remarked that there are no datasets to compare performances. The recent empirical methods that are cited below provided datasets that can now be used for evaluation. For example, (Kushman et al., 2014) proposed a word problem solver which uses statistical analysis to solve word problems. They handled a more complex class of word problems which involve solving a set of simultaneous linear equations. More recently, (Hosseini et al., 2014) attempted the same addition/subtraction word problem framework where they concentrated on classifying the verbs in a given problem into semantic classes. They were able to show remarkable improvement over (Kushman et al., 2014). They used a state representation to depict temporal ordering. However, the system could not reason about existing scenarios like questions that involved comparisons. There is some development in this direction by the mathematical modelling conglomerate WolframAlpha (2015).

3 Architecture

The architecture of the system is described in Figure 1. The given problem is first simplified such that every sentence in the new problem has exactly one verb. Then, linguistic information is extracted from each sentence and passed on for the Knowledge representation. For example, "Ruth has 3 apples" will be translated as "owner = Ruth; entity.name = apples, entity.value = 3; verb = has".

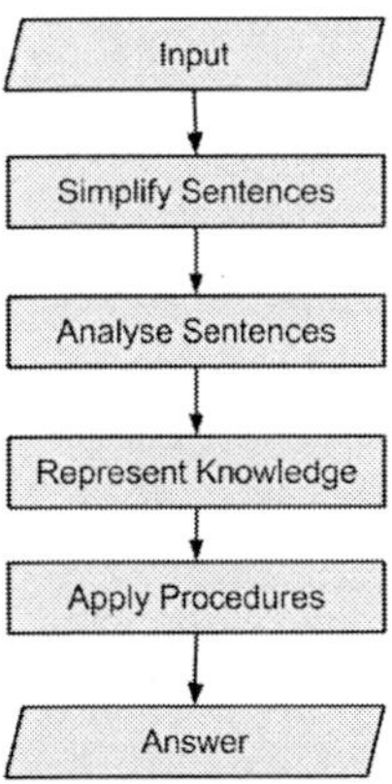

Figure 1: Architecture of Word Problem Solver

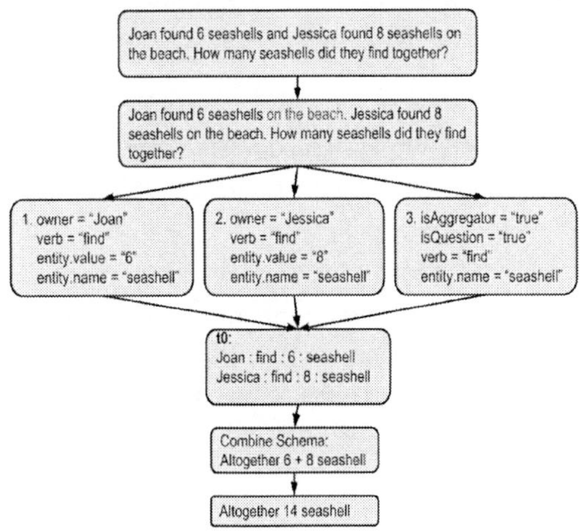

Figure 2: Example of the Problem Solving Process

During the knowledge representation phase, all the sentences are taken into consideration the events are ordered according to time. Then, the problem is solved using the procedures stored in it. These units are explained in more detail in the following sections. An example that depicts how a problem is solved is shown in Figure 2.

4 Knowledge Representation

4.1 Schemas

A popular representation idea is to use schemas. Schemas are templates that describe how entities interact. In this discussion, the schemas described by (Bakman, 2007) are explained. For instance, "John had 3 apples. He forfeited 1 apple. How many apples does he have now?" will trigger the "Transfer in Ownership" schema because of the keyword "forfeit". This situation is described below.

(owner) had (X) (object)
(owner) (transfer-in-ownership) (Y) (object)
(owner) has (Z) (object)

To elaborate, each sentence is examined sequentially until a keyword is encountered. In the second sentence, the word "forfeit" is such a word that maps to the "transfer-in-ownership" schema. This is matched against the second statement in the schema description and the owner is identified as "John" and Y = 1 and object as "apple". Now the problem is re-examined searching for sentences with "John" and "apple" to match.
(owner) = John, (X) = 3, (Y) = 1, (object) = apple, (transfer-in-ownership) = forfeit
Y + Z = X.
The equation is attached to every schema.

ROBUST, the system developed by (Bakman, 2007), was able to solve multi-step problems with extraneous information.

Disadvantages of ROBUST:

- Sometimes, due to the lack of some implicit common sense knowledge, the problem cannot be solved. To illustrate, "A farmer bought 3 apples and lost 2 of them. How many fruits does he have now?". This problem cannot be solved by schemas as there is no explicit statement saying the farmer had no apples initially.

- There is a search overhead to match sentences against all possible schemas because all the sentences are examined whenever a keyword is encountered.

4.2 Temporal Schemas

In this paper, by using time, default assumptions and heuristics, a large number of problems are solved. To illustrate, the following problem is taken.
"John buys 11 peaches. He eats 9 peaches. How many does John have now?"
The first sentence is represented as:

t_0
$John : has : peaches : x_1$
$unknown_0 : has : peaches : x_2$
t_1
$John : buy : peaches : 11$

t_2
$John : has : peaches : x_1 + 11$
$unknown_0 : has : peaches : x_2 - 11$

This represents the knowledge that the keyword "buy" signifies a "Change Out" in ownership for "John", the buyer and "$unknown_0$", the unnamed seller. As we don't know some values, they are kept as variables. The time stamp t_0 is the initial default one.

When the next sentence is read, "John eats 9 peaches", it is updated as:

t_0
$John : has : peaches : x_1$
$unknown_0 : has : peaches : x_2$
t_1
$John : buy : peaches : 11$
t_2
$John : has : peaches : x_1 + 11$
$unknown_0 : has : peaches : x_2 - 11$
t_3
$John : eat : peaches : 9$
t_4
$John : has : peaches : x_1 + 11 - 9$
$unknown_0 : has : peaches : x_2 - 11$

Now, once the system encounters the question, it retrieves the most recent value of John's peaches. Hence, it retrieves "x_1 + 11 - 9". By making an assumption that John had no peaches in the beginning, we compute "11-9", that is "2" and display the answer.

There are situations when an expression has to be substituted by a value. For example, John may have 6 apples. Then, we come to know that John has 3 more apples than Mary and we do not know how many apples Mary has (say x apples). After applying the schema, we know that John has (x+3) apples. When John has two consistent values at the same time, an equation 6 = 3 + x is created and solved. The fact that Mary has 3 apples is stored.

Sometimes, we may require a value that occurs in the first time step. By analysing the tense and narrative order, the correct value to be retrieved can be ascertained. For example, if the first two sentences are in present tense and the question is in past tense, the value in the first time step is retrieved. The reason information such as "John buys 11 apples" is stored is because sometimes, a question may be how many John bought or how many John ate.

4.3 List of Schemas

In the schemas we have designed, no sentence is explicitly matched against a template. Whenever a keyword is encountered, this information is adjusted according to its corresponding procedure. If the schema requires some information which is not available, a variable is introduced. If the value that corresponds to that variable is seen later, it is replaced in all the expressions that contain the variable. The list of schemas used is given in Table 2.

Name	Schema	Update
Change In	$Owner_1$ has X objects. $Owner_2$ has Y objects. Z objects were transferred from $Owner_2$ to $Owner_1$	$Owner_1$ has (X+Z) objects. $Owner_2$ has (X-Z) objects.
Change Out	$Owner_1$ has X objects. $Owner_2$ has Y objects. Z objects were transferred from $Owner_1$ to $Owner_2$	$Owner_1$ has (X-Z) objects. $Owner_2$ has (X+Z) objects.
Combine	$Owner_1$ had X objects. $Owner_2$ had Y objects. Together, they have Z objects.	$Z = X + Y$
Compare Plus	$Owner_1$ had X objects. $Owner_2$ had Y objects more than $Owner_1$.	$Owner_1$ has (X+Y) objects.
Compare Minus	$Owner_1$ had X objects. $Owner_2$ had Y objects less than $Owner_1$.	$Owner_1$ has (X-Y) objects.
Increase	$Owner_1$ had X objects. $Owner_1$ got Y objects more.	$Owner_1$ has (X+Y) objects.
Reduction	$Owner_1$ had X objects. $Owner_1$ lost Y objects.	$Owner_1$ has (X-Y) objects.

Table 1: List of Schemas

4.4 Common Sense Law of Inertia

When the number of discrete time steps increase, unaffected owners and entities are assumed to retain their value as per the common sense law of inertia (Shanahan, 1999). For example, "John has 3 apples. Mary gave 4 apples to Tom" implies that at the second time step also John has 3 apples.

5 Natural Language Processing

The natural language processing is done during the simplification and the analysis phase. The aim of the simplification phase is to make the text as unambiguous as possible and to make it amenable for analysis. After the analysis is completed, the relevant information needed for knowledge representation would have been extracted. These tasks, which are described below, extensively used the Stanford CoreNLP suite (Manning et al., 2014).

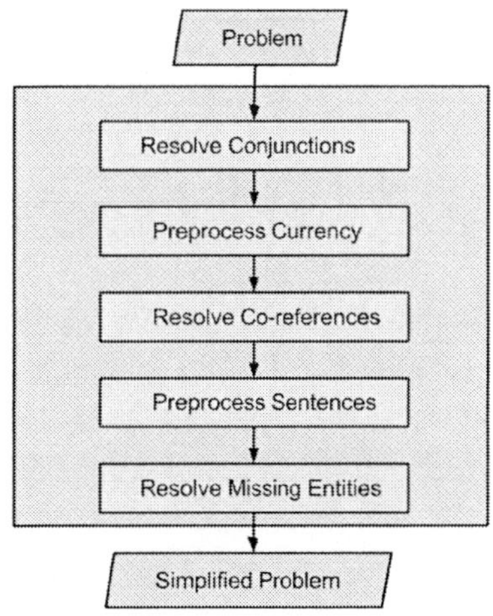

Figure 3: Simplifying the Problem

5.1 Problem Simplification

The steps involved in simplifying the problem is described in Figure 3.

5.1.1 Resolving Conjunctions

The first step of simplification is to deal with sentences that contain "and", "but", "if", and "then". To illustrate, take the example "John had 5 apples and ate 2 of them". The fact that "John" is the person who ate 2 apples can be made clearer if this sentence was split into the following sentences - "John had 5 apples. John ate 2 apples."
Algorithm:

- Separate the sentence into two parts, Part1 and Part2, by splitting at the conjunction.

- If the first part has no verb, then no processing is required. This is to handle situations like "Ram and Sita have 13 apples altogether". It does not make sense to split this sentence as "Ram has 13 apples. Sita has 13 apples.".

- Split each part into four strings, pre-verb (P), verb (V), after-verb (A), preposition- phrase (PrP). Some of these strings may be empty.

- Whenever a string of Part2 is empty, copy the corresponding string from that of Part1.

- Concatenate these four strings into a single sentence and return the two sentences.

This is depicted for a typical example in Figure

4

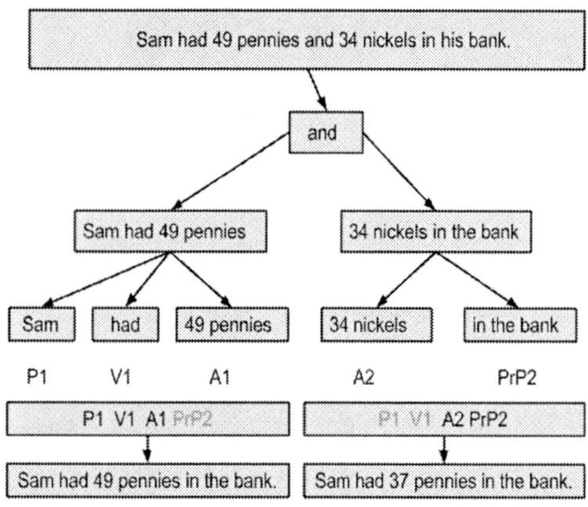

Figure 4: Resolving Conjunctions

5.1.2 Preprocessing Currency

The dependency parser provided by (Manning et al., 2014) links numbers to their corresponding entities using the "num" edge or the "number" edge. To maintain this consistency, "$5.5" is replaced by "5.5 dollars".

5.1.3 Resolving Co-references

The task of resolving co-references was described in the introduction. To reiterate, it has been used to map pronouns to the referring entity. The system uses the resolver provided by (Manning et al., 2014). Some heuristics are used to improve its current performance. These are listed below.

- If a pronoun refers to another pronoun, it is not considered. This is to avoid recursive computations.

- "They" and "their" are ignored. This is because the mapping found for these pronouns are often wrong. For example, the input "Ram has 6 apples. Sita has 7 apples. How many apples do they have in all?" results in "apples" being mapped to "they".

- A inherent ambiguity is exemplified by "Sam has 13 dimes. His dad gave him 3 dimes". Here, "him" is always mapped to the "dad" instead of "Sam". In word problems, such a pronoun mostly refers to someone else and the program uses this knowledge and maps it to "Sam" instead.

5.1.4 Preprocessing sentences

The sentences are simplified such that each sentence has exactly one verb. For example the sentence "John had 5 apples and Mary gave John 3 apples." is parsed by the Stanford Core NLP Suite(Manning et al., 2014) as follows:

Parser output (Stanford Core NLP) :

ROOT (S (S (NP (NNP John)) (VP *(VBD had)* (NP (CD 5) (NNS apples))))) (CC and) (S (NP (NNP Mary)) (VP *(VBD gave)* (NP (NNP John)) (NP (CD 3) (NNS apples)))) (. .)))

The corresponding phrase is extracted and converted into two sentences.

John had 5 apples. Mary gave John 3 apples.

Sometimes the verb phrase encompasses another verb phrase, hence this process is done recursively until every sentence has exactly one verb. Sometimes it is not possible to split sentences such as "How many apples did he have?". Here, both "did" and "have" are identified as verbs. Thus, such sentences are not simplified further.

5.1.5 Resolving Entities

This step is to address problems of the type "John has 5 apples. He gave 3 to Mary". Here, 3 is not explicitly specified as 3 apples. So, all plural entities are stored as potential entities and every time a number is not followed by a noun or an adjective, one of them is chosen. Their adjectives are also retained such that a typical entity list may have (balloons, red balloons, green balloons). The most suitable entity is chosen based on the sentence order. Most problems deal with just one type of entity.

5.2 Analysis of Simplified Problem

At the end of this phase, the following information would be available for representation.

- A list of all owners such as "John" and "basket".

- A list of all entities like "green balloons" and "red balloons".

- A list of processed sentences.

Each processed sentence would in turn have the following information.

Procedure	Keywords
Change Out	put, place, plant, add, sell, distribute, load, give
Change In	take from, get, pick, buy, borrow, steal
Increase	more, carry, find
Reduction	eat, destroy, spend, remove, decrease
Compare Plus	more than, taller than, longer than, etc.
Compare Minus	less than, fewer than, shorter than, etc.
Combine	together, in all, combined

Table 2: Schemas and their Keywords

- isAggregator - whether the sentence contains any aggregating phrases such as "altogether", "in all" etc.

- isComparator - whether the sentence contains any phrase such as "more than", "less than", "fewer", "taller" etc.

- isDifference - whether the sentence contains any phrase such as "left", "remaining" etc.

- isQuestion - whether the sentence denotes a question such as "Find the number of apples John has".

- keyword - whether the sentence contains any of the keywords listed in Table 2.

- schema - if there is a keyword, the schema linked with it

- $owner_1$ - the first owner in the sentence - "John gave 3 apples to Mary" would set $owner_1$ to "John" and $owner_2$ to "Mary".

- $owner_2$ - the second owner in the sentence

- entityName - the name of the entity in the sentence such as "apples".

- entityValue - the value connected to the entity - such as 3 in the previous example.

- tense - this is derived from the POS tag of the verb and is used for ordering the sentences in the representation.

To get this information, the dependency parser has been extensively used. Consider "Mary gave 3 apples to John."
Dependency Parser output (Stanford Core NLP) :
- gave/VBD (root)
- Mary/NNP (nsubj)
  - apples/NNS (dobj)
  - 3/CD (num)
- John/NNP (prep-to)

From this tree, the two owners Mary and John are identified as well as the entity "3 apples". As a general rule, the subject is identified as the first owner and the noun associated with a preposition is taken as the second owner. Every number is identified as "num" and that is taken as the value of the entity with the corresponding node of the edge being taken as the entity name. The verb is identified from the Part-Of-Speech (POS) tag "VBD" and stored.

If the sentence contains "some" or "few", the value of that entity is set to some variable. Sometimes, especially for word problems that involve decimals, the parse may not correctly map the entity name to the entity value. Hence, there is a check if there is any number in the sentence that has not been assigned an entity and if so, the nearest plural noun is set as the entity's name.

For a question, the entity's value is not available. Hence, the sentence is examined and checked against the list of existing entities and owners to ascertain what the question is about.

6 Some Heuristics

A list of heuristics are used to increase the performance. However, like all heuristics, they are not precise.

- Consider, "Sam grew 41 watermelons but the rabbits ate 5 watermelons". Usually, "eat" would denote that there is a reduction in one's own entities, i.e., the rabbits should have had some watermelons. In such a situation, if that information is not available, it is mapped to a reduction in the watermelons possessed by "Sam".

- As mentioned before, if there are two possible answers due to ambiguity in the question, then the answer which involved some calculation or which has no unknown terms is preferred. Consider, "There are 2 pencils in the drawer. Tim placed 3 pencils in the drawer. How many pencils are now there in total?". So the system would correctly display "drawer has 5 pencils" instead of "Tim has unknown pencils".

- If the final answer that the system derived is simply an entity mentioned in the question

395

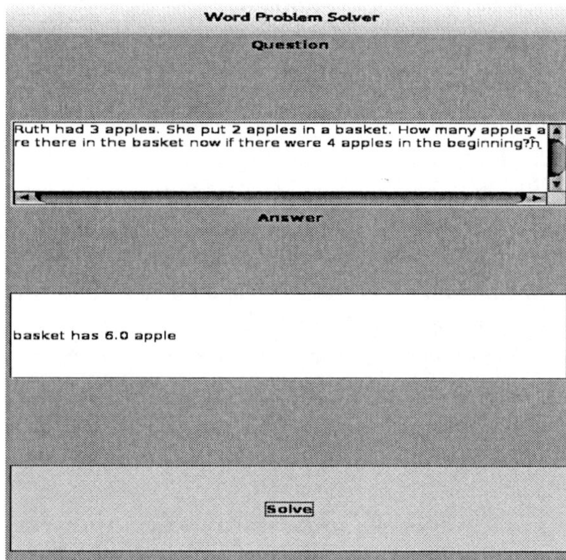

Figure 5: Screenshot of the System

and if it is known that the question has an aggregator like "altogether", then the system bypasses the representation and returns the sum of all entities.

7 Illustration

A screenshot of the system is available in Figure 5.

8 Experiments

The experiments are similar to the ones performed by (Hosseini et al., 2014). They had 3 datasets (DS1, DS2, DS3) with increasing difficulty in terms of natural language and irrelevant information. Our system's performance is compared against ARIS proposed by (Hosseini et al., 2014), ROBUST proposed by (Bakman, 2007) and the online mathematical query system (WolframAlpha, 2015). Also, as we are not learning the verb categorization, that is the keyword to schema mapping, the appropriate comparison is with "Gold ARIS" which is ARIS with perfect categorization.

	DS1	DS2	DS3	Avg
Our System	**96.27**	**80.00**	**90.08**	**88.64**
Gold ARIS	94.0	77.1	81.0	84.0
ROBUST	12.69	0.71	0	4.56
WolframAlpha	5.97	2.14	0.83	3.03

Table 3: Comparison with Existing Systems

ROBUST fails almost completely with the two complex datasets as its NLP is quite weak. WolframAlpha also does not scale well. However, they generate an answer in natural language. ARIS does not present the answer in natural language though it has the means to do so. The representation used by ARIS and our system is similar but there is more reasoning involved in our system by exploiting non-verb keywords and with some heuristics. Also, ARIS exploited only one type of schema, that is "Change" schema and did not address "Combine" and "Compare" schemas completely. (Hosseini et al., 2014) analysed the errors and classified them into five types - set completion, parser issues, irrelevant information, implicit knowledge and others. Our system was able to reduce errors in these areas. The only category of errors that remains unaffected is set completion. The system is not able to solve problems such as "Sara 's high school played 12 basketball games this year. The team won most of their games. They were defeated during 4 games. How many games did they win?". By using recognizing antonyms, these error can also be reduced in a future version. The errors involving parser issues, irrelevant information and implicit knowledge are reduced by the use of heuristics. Other issues are resolved significantly because of more information available about comparisons and combinations. For example, "In March it rained 0.81 inches. It rained 0.35 inches less in April than in March. How much did it rain in April?" can be solved by our system because of the keyword "less". ARIS fails because the verb "has" does not signify any operation.

9 Discussion

With the availability of sophisticated parsers, we are able to revisit age-old language understanding problems and get much better results. While traditional knowledge based approaches gave a good base for representation, their NLP was quite limited due to the limitations in technology at that time. On the other hand, the recent empirical systems performed much better language processing but were semantically limited in comparison by not exploiting all types of word problems.

Our system also offers the answer in natural language and in real time. Though the performance of WolframAlpha is poor, it provides visually pleasing explanations for the problems it can solve and presents the answer in natural language as well. It is also capable of analysing phrases such as "two times" that involve multiplication. One sure direction of future work is to generate good explanations with our proposed system.

10 Conclusion and Future Work

We developed a system that solves addition/subtraction word problems with considerable accuracy over the existing systems. It takes a problem, simplifies it and then extracts information such as owners, entities and keywords from every sentence. This extracted information is represented in a temporal representation and then presents the answer in natural language.

The system was developed in Java and the code is available at `https://github.com/Sowms/AdditionSolver/tree/KRexperiment`. The semantics can be improved greatly by using a more complex representation method such as Event Calculus described in (Shanahan, 1999) which is natural choice for temporal reasoning. Also, the semantics for units is not well defined. For example, consider "Marta picked 2 pumpkins. The first pumpkin weighed 4 pounds, and the second pumpkin weighed 8.7 pounds. How much did the 2 pumpkins weigh all together?". The question can refer to two entities, "pound" or "watermelon". It arbitrarily chooses "watermelon" and initially reports the answer as "Marta picked 2 watermelon". At this point, the system recognizes that this fact is already present in the problem and that there is an aggregator "altogether" and uses a heuristic to report the answer as "Altogether 14.7" instead of "12.7".

Also, more work can be done to improve the problem simplification, especially for the longer word problems that involve decimals.

To conclude, a system for solving addition/subtraction problems has been presented. It will hopefully be one of the many steps forward on a long journey towards representing knowledge that can lead to better question answering systems and can help teach the eager student.

References

WolframAlpha. Wolfram Research, Inc., Mathematica, Version 10.2, Champaign, IL (2015). `http://blog.wolframalpha.com/2012/10/04/solving-word-problems-with-wolframalpha/`

Princeton University "About WordNet." WordNet. Princeton University. 2010. `http://wordnet.princeton.edu`

Mohammad Javad Hosseini, Hannaneh Hajishirzi, Oren Etzioni, and Nate Kushman 2014. *Learning to Solve Arithmetic Word Problems with Verb Categorization*. Proceedings of the Conference on Empirical Methods in Natural Language Processing.

Nate Kushman, Yoav Artzi, Luke Zettlemoyer, and Regina Barzilay 2014. *Learning to Automatically Solve Algebra Word Problems*. Proceedings of the Conference of the Association for Computational Linguistics (ACL).

Christopher D. Manning, Surdeanu, Mihai, Bauer, John, Finkel, Jenny, Bethard, Steven J., and David McClosky. 2014. *The Stanford CoreNLP Natural Language Processing Toolkit*. Proceedings of 52nd Annual Meeting of the Association for Computational Linguistics: System Demonstrations, pp. 55-60

Anirban Mukherjee and Utpal Garain 2009. *A review of methods for automatic understanding of natural language mathematical problems* . Artificial Intelligence Review, Volume 29, Issue 2, pp 93-122

Y. Bakman. 2007. *Robust understanding of Word Problems with Extraneous Information*, `http://lanl.arxiv.org/abs/math.GM/0701393`

Shanahan, M. 1999. *The event calculus explained*, Wooldridge, M., & Veloso, M.(Eds.), Artificial Intelligence Today, pp. 409430. Springer Lecture Notes in Artificial Intelligence no. 1600.

D. Dellarosa. 1986. *A computer simulation of childrens arithmetic word-problem solving*, Behavior Research Methods, Instruments, and Computers Volume 18, Issue 2, pp 147-154

Charles R. Fletcher *Understanding and solving arithmetic word problems: A computer simulation.*, Behavior Research Methods, Instruments, and Computers, 17, pp 565-571.

Daniel Bobrow. 1964. *A question-answering system for high school algebra word problems.*. AFIPS 64 (Fall, part I) Proceedings of the October 27-29, 1964, fall joint computer conference, part I, pp 591-614

Analysis of Influence of L2 English Speakers' Fluency on Occurrence and Duration of Sentence-medial Pauses in English Readout Speech

Shambhu Nath Saha
Centre for Educational Technology
Indian Institute of Technology
Kharagpur, India
shambhuju@gmail.com

Shyamal Kr. Das Mandal
Centre for Educational Technology
Indian Institute of Technology
Kharagpur, India
sdasmandal@cet.iitkgp.ernet.in

Abstract

Pause plays important roles for the intelligibility, naturalness and fluency of speech. This paper reported the effect of native (L1) Bengali speakers' fluency of English on occurrence probability and duration of sentence-medial pauses with respect to three factors: phrase type, phrase length (l), distance (d). In this analysis, 40 nonnative (L2) English (L1 Bengali) speakers' data was divided into five different groups (poor, average, good, very good and excellent) based on their English fluency level. From result of this comparative study, it is seen that occurrence probability and duration of sentence-medial pauses for each phrase type, each l value and each d value increase as L2 English speakers' fluency decreases. Moreover like L1 English speakers, occurrence probability and duration of sentence-medial pauses are almost linearly dependent on l and d respectively for L2 English speakers regardless of their fluency. Furthermore effect of three factors on sentence-medial pauses of fluent L2 English speakers is more close to that of L1 English speakers compared to less fluent L2 English speakers.

1 Introduction

English is used as a language for international communication throughout the world today. English is also being studied and spoken as a second language in more countries than ever before. Thus, a comprehensive understanding of variations present in the dialects of English spoken in the world today is a fundamental issue for the development of English language education as well as spoken language science and technology. Asia is home to the largest number of English learners and speakers in the world (Nunan, 2003), and it is important to learn about Asian language speakers' English and identify their features. In India, combining native (L1) and nonnative (L2) speakers, more people speak or understand English than any other country in the world (Visceglia *et al.*, 2009). Thus research on spoken English of Indian speakers from a multidisciplinary perspective is urgently needed. Therefore it is necessary to collect L2 English speech from as many regions of India as possible and compare with L1 English speech based on segmental and supra segmental aspects in order to derive a set of core properties common to all varieties of English spoken by Indian speakers (Miller,1978). From the theory of second language acquisition, it is suggested that proper acquisition involves in correct production and perception of phonetic and prosodic features of English. One of the most important suprasegmental features in English is pause (Meng *et al.*, 2009), where proper positioning of pauses in speech of second language is necessary for the L2 speaker to understand in order to acquire the proficiency on that language.

During the act of generating spontaneous speech, pause is a highly variable phenomenon and is an outcome of processing activity (Fant et al., 2003). The pauses occur in speech generally at syntactic boundaries. Pauses in text reading (readout speech) can be divided into three categories:

D S Sharma, R Sangal and E Sherly. Proc. of the 12th Intl. Conference on Natural Language Processing, pages 403–412,
Trivandrum, India. December 2015. ©2015 NLP Association of India (NLPAI)

(1) pauses between paragraphs, (2) pauses between sentences in a paragraph, (3) pauses within a sentence (sentence-medial pauses). The occurrence of pauses is unconditional at sentence boundaries and paragraph boundaries, but is conditional at minor syntactic boundaries within sentences such as phrase boundaries, word boundaries (Fujisaki and Omura, 1971). Since sentence medial pause is conditional and based on syntactic structure of the text, so the aim of the current study is limited to the prediction of sentence medial pauses in English readout speech without specific foci and emotions. Their duration tends to be longer at the end of larger syntactic units, but have statistical variations. A speaker may choose to insert a pause at a location necessary to disambiguate a syntactic ambiguity, or if the preceding uninterrupted sentence segment is too long, or if he/she is simply out of breath. For instance, if there is no pause or if the pauses in a sentence are wrongly placed, then the meaning of the sentence will change. Control of pause occurrence and duration is an important issue for naturalness and correct meaning of the sentence.

There are few studies on analysis of occurrence probability and duration of sentence-medial pauses in readout speech. Fujisaki et al. (1999) investigated the occurrence probability and duration of sentence-medial pauses in Japanese readout speech. The results of this investigation showed that the occurrence probability and duration of sentence-medial pauses in Japanese readout speech increase almost linearly with phrase length and distance. Das Mandal et al. (2010) analyzed sentence-medial pauses for Bangla readout speech. This analysis also showed that occurrence probability and duration of sentence-medial pauses in Bengali readout speech are linearly dependent on phrase length and distance. In a study, Acharya and Das Mandal (2012) conducted a detailed investigation for sentence-medial pauses for readout speech of Bangla for different speech rates. The results of this study revealed that occurrence probability and duration of sentence-medial pauses in Bengali readout speech are linearly dependent on phrase length and distance in case of all speech rates; that means occurrence probability and duration of pause in case of fast speech is much lesser than the normal and slow. Moreover Saha and Das Mandal (2013) performed a comparative study of occurrence probability and duration of sentence-medial pauses in English readout speech between L1

American English and L1 Bengali speakers and reported that, although the occurrence probability and duration of sentence-medial pause are linearly dependent on phrase length and distance for both speaker groups, but the occurrence probability and duration of sentence-medial pause of L1 Bengali speakers are much higher than L1 English speakers. The results from these previous studies support the view that one of the key issues for speech prosody is control of pause occurrence and duration; that means occurrence probability and duration play important roles in prediction of intra-sentential pause insertion in readout speech. It is necessary for a speaker to put pauses at appropriate place in order to get the fluency on target language. Pause controls the fluency of speakers on a language, where fluency is defined as a level of language proficiency and depends on naturalness, intelligibility, accent placement, lexical stress, segmental correctness (Kondo and Tsubaki, 2012). But there is no such significant study on effect of L2 speakers' fluency over pause occurrence and duration. This paper deals with that issue. The objective of present study is to analyze the effect of L1 Bengali speakers' fluency of English on occurrence probability and duration of sentence-medial pauses in English readout speech compared to L1 English speakers.

2 Speech Material

The material used for the present study was the Aesop's fable "The North Wind and the Sun", which produces a large range of segmental and suprasegmental characteristics in English (Mondonedo, 1999). The material was read by 10 (5 male, 5 female) L1 American English speakers and 40 (20 male, 20 female) L1 Bengali speakers whose native language was Standard Colloquial Bengali (SCB) (Bhattacharya, 1988). All speakers were in the age group between 20 to 40 years and L1 Bengali speakers had studied English as a second language for a minimum of ten years. In order to let the speakers decided where and how long they inserted pause, sentence-medial punctuation marks were removed from the text. The speech was recorded in quiet room with 16 bit16 kHz digitization format. Pauses were detected and their duration was measured manually. To examine the effect of fluency of English on occurrence probability and duration of sentence-medial pauses in English readout speech, 40 L1 Bengali speakers' data was divided into five fluency groups. 10 English teachers evaluated 40 L1 Bengali speakers' English fluency level on a 5-point MOS scale based on naturalness, accent placement, lexical stress and segmental correctness. Figure 1 shows the distribution of average MOS score of the 40 L1 Bengali speakers' English fluency level. Average scores were grouped as follows: 1.5-2.49 (Poor), 2.5-3.2 (Average), 3.21-3.59 (Good), 3.6-4.19 (Very Good), 4.2-5 (Excellent). It is observed that the English fluency level of the majority of speakers was evenly distributed between 3 and 4.5.

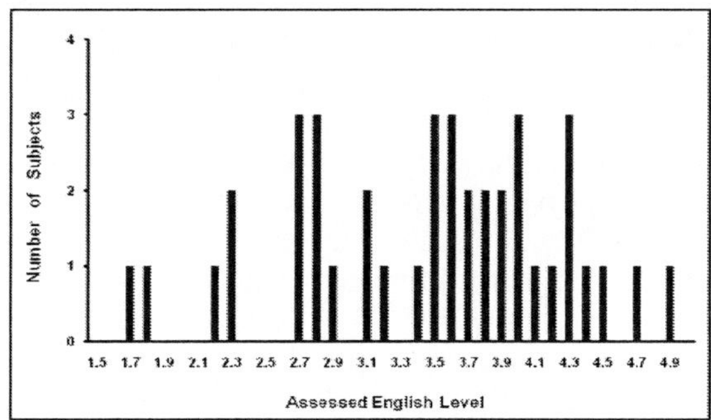

Figure 1. Distribution of average MOS score of L1 Bengali speakers' English fluency.

3 Factors Affecting the Occurrence and Duration of Sentence-Medial Pauses

Based on previous studies (Fujisaki et al., 1999; Das Mandal et al., 2010; Acharya and Das Mandal, 2012; Saha and Das Mandal, 2013), it is noted that the occurrence and duration of sentence-medial pauses in English mainly depends on the following three factors:

3.1 Phrase Type

In English, phrases are categorized into noun phrase (NP), verb phrase (VP), adjective phrase (AJP), adverb phrase (ADVP), prepositional phrase (PP) and conjunction phrase (CP). These types of phrases were considered in current study except prepositional phrase (PP), because there was only one prepositional phrase in the training corpus and it was at sentence final position.

3.2 Phrase Length

Phrase length is the length l of the phrase in terms of number of syllables. The phrase length is cumu-

lative if a pause does not occur at the end of the phrase. Figure 2 defines the cumulative phrase length.

S: ph$_1$ (no pause) ph2 (no pause) ph3 (pause) ph4 (end)

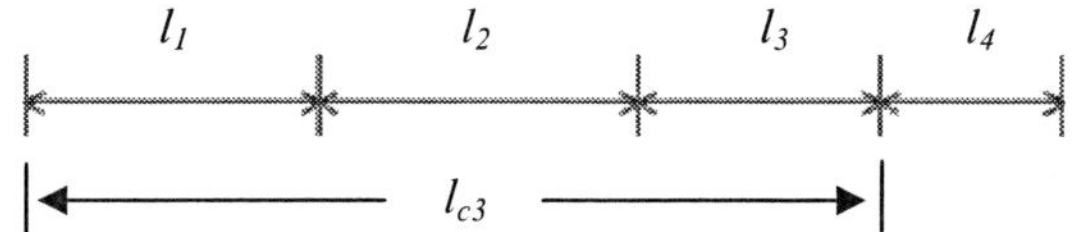

Figure 2. Illustration of the cumulative phrase length.

In Figure 2, Ph$_i$ represents the ith phrase of the sentence S and l_i represents the length of the corresponding phrase. So the cumulative length will be sum of the length of ph$_1$, ph$_2$ and ph$_3$, i.e. $l_{c3}=l_1 + l_2 + l_3$ if a pause occurs after ph$_3$.

3.3 Distance between the Current Phrase and its Dependent Counter Part

A dependency is an asymmetrical syntactic relation between a pair of constituents in a sentence known as the head and the dependent; the head of each dependency is then the dependent of another constituent, forming a recursive structure which connects the entire sentence. A constituent is right branching if it is to the right of the external head to which it connects; left branching if it is to the left. English is mainly right branching, but has left branching structure in certain situation. In English, major constituent types (NP, ADVP, PP, CP) are dependent on verb phrase (VP), that means English is mainly verb dependent language (Temperley, 2007). Adjective phrase (AJP) and prepositional phrase (PP) are dependent on noun phrase (NP) also. The distance d between the current phrase and its dependent phrase is the number of words between head of the current phrase and head of its dependent phrase (Temperley, 2005). For the extraction of the parameter d, the text is manually tagged with Parts of Speech (POS) and phrase information. Figure 3 illustrates the calculation of d for a given English sentence.

	NP	VP	ADVP	CC	ADVP	NP	VP	NP
	Then the sun	shone out	warmly	and	immediately	the traveler	took off	his cloak
Word No.	3 4	6	7	8		10	11	14
Related Word No.	4 11	4	11	11		11		11
Distance d	1 7	2	4	3		1		3

Figure 3. Illustration of the distance parameter calculation for an English sentence.

4 Results and Discussions

4.1 Effect of Fluency upon Pause Occurrence Probability

For each of the five phrase types (NP, VP, AJP, ADVP, CP), the pause occurrence probability is defined as the number of phrase boundaries which are followed by a pause divided by the total number of phrase boundaries having a given set of values of l and d. In this section, the effect of L2 English (L1 Bengali) speakers' fluency on occurrence probability of sentence-medial pause was examined with respect to each individual factor: phrase type, phrase length (l), distance (d). In order to examine the effect of fluency on occurrence probability of sentence-medial pause, one way ANOVA was performed with fluency as between group variable for each individual factor (phrase type, l, and d). After that, a series of bonferroni corrected post-hoc t-test was performed to determine which L2 English speaker groups differ significantly from each other for each individual factor, where bonferroni corrected p value was 0.04.

Phrase Type: Figure 4 shows the average occurrence probability of sentence-medial pauses of L1 and five L2 English speaker groups for different phrase types. The result of one way ANOVA (fluency as a between group variable) over five groups of L2 English speakers for each phrase type was shown in Table 1. The result of one way ANOVA shows that, there was a statistically significant effect ($p < 0.05$) of L2 English speakers' fluency for each phrase type.

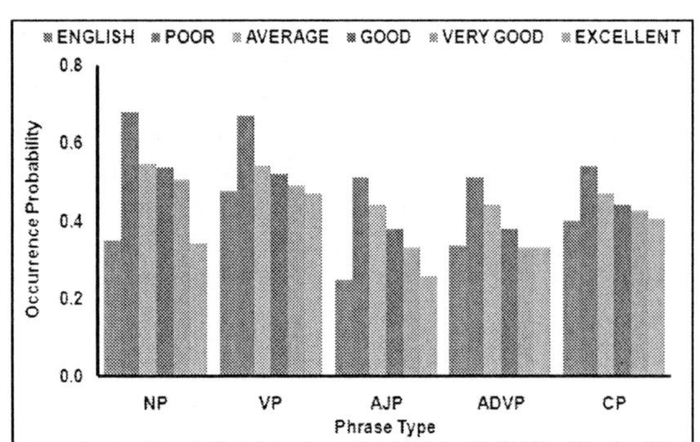

Figure 4. Effect of phrase type upon occurrence probability of sentence medial pauses at different fluency level.

Phrase Type	Result of One Way ANOVA
NP	F(4,35) = 6.2361,p = 0.0067, p<0.05
VP	F(4,35) = 3.2591,p = 0.023,p < 0.05
AJP	F(4,35) = 3.1053, p =0.027, p < 0.05
ADVP	F(4,35) = 2.9656,p = 0.033, p < 0.05
CP	F(4,35) = 2.4755, p =0.046,p < 0.05

Table 1: The result of one way ANOVA for each phrase type.

In case of NP, Bonferroni corrected post-hoc t-test revealed that there were statistically significant differences ($p < 0.04$) in occurrence probability between every pair of L2 English speaker groups; only exception was pair of average and good L2 English speaker groups, where no statistical significant difference exist ($p > 0.04$); that means occurrence probability after NP for average and good L2 English speaker groups was almost equal. In case of VP, AJP and CP, Bonferroni corrected post-hoc t-test revealed that there were statistically significant differences ($p < 0.04$) in occurrence probability between every pair of L2 English speaker groups after VP, AJP and CP. For ADVP, Bonferroni corrected post-hoc t-test revealed that there were statistically significant differences ($p < 0.04$) in occurrence probability after ADVP between every pair of L2 English speaker groups except pair of very good and excellent L2 English speaker group ($p > 0.04$); that means occurrence probability after ADVP for very good and excellent L2 English speaker groups was almost equal. These findings and Figure 4 imply that occurrence probability of sentence-medial pause after each phrase was decreased as fluency of L2 English speakers was increased. In addition, a series of t-test was carried out to determine which group of L2 English speakers differed significantly from the L1 English speaker group for each phrase type. Result of t-test revealed that every group except excellent L2 English speaker group was differed significantly ($p < 0.05$) from L1 English speakers for each phrase type. From this result and Figure 4, it is observed that each L2 English speaker group, except excellent L2 English speaker group, produced more sentence-medial pause after each phrase compared to that of L1 English speakers; but probability of excellent L2 English speaker group to insert pause after each phrase was almost equal with L1 English speakers. From this result of analysis, it is revealed that occurrence probability of sentence-medial pause after each phrase type for fluent L2 English speakers was lower than that of less fluent L2 English speakers, and occurrence probability of sentence-medial pause for each phrase type was almost equal for both L1 English speakers and excellent L2 English speaker groups.

Phrase Length (l): Figure 5 shows the average occurrence probability of sentence-medial pauses of L1 and five L2 English speaker groups for different phrase length (l).

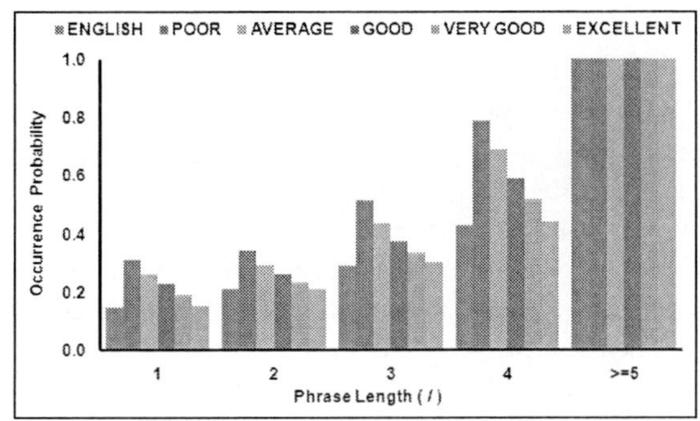

Figure 5.   Effect of phrase length (l) upon occurrence probability of sentence medial pauses at different fluency level.

Table 2 shows the result of one way ANOVA (fluency as a between group variable) over five groups of L2 English speakers for each l (except phrase length 5).

l	Result of One Way ANOVA
1	$F(4,35) = 3.3115$, $p = 0.021$, $p < 0.05$
2	$F(4,35) = 3.7361$, $p = 0.012$, $p < 0.05$
3	$F(4,35) = 3.3672$, $p = 0.019$, $p < 0.05$
4	$F(4,35) = 4.8442$, $p = 0.0032$, $p < 0.05$

Table 2:   The result of one way ANOVA for each phrase length (l).

The result indicates that there was a significant effect ($p < 0.05$) of fluency on occurrence probability of sentence-medial pause for each l. Bonferroni corrected post-hoc t-tests revealed that there were statistically significant differences ($p < 0.04$) in occurrence probability of sentence-medial pause between every pair of L2 English speaker groups for each level of l. From these results and Figure 5, it is observed that occurrence probability of sentence-medial pause was decreased as fluency level of L2 English speakers was increased for each l value.

Furthermore, one way ANOVA was performed on each L2 English speaker group with l as between group variable. Table 3 shows result of ANOVA for each L2 English speaker group.

Speaker Group	Result of One Way ANOVA
Poor	$F(4,20) = 5.8464$,$p =0.0028$,$p< 0.05$
Average	$F(4,30) = 5.0135$,$p = 0.0032$,$p<0.05$
Good	$F(4,35) = 7.3465$,$p=0.00021$,$p<0.05$
Very Good	$F(4,60) = 9.9866$,$p=0.00003$,$p<0.05$
Excellent	$F(4,30) = 9.8869$,$p=0.00092$,$p<0.05$

Table 3:   The result of one way ANOVA for each L2 English speaker group.

The result from Table 3 indicates that there was significant effect ($p < 0.05$) of l on occurrence probability of sentence-medial pause for each L2 English speaker group. Post-hoc tests using Tukey's HSD procedure were performed to determine which phrase length (l) type differs significantly from each other for each L2 English speaker group. Tukey's HSD procedure revealed that mean difference between every pair of l was statistically significant (mean difference > HSD value, $p < 0.05$) for each L2 English speaker group. From this result and Figure 5, it is observed that mean occurrence probability of sentence-medial pause for each L2 English speaker group was almost linearly dependent on l like L1 English speakers and probability to insert pause was maximum (1.0) after phrases with length five or more for each L2 English speaker group.

Distance (d) between Current Phrase and its Dependent Counter Part: Figure 6 shows the average occurrence probability of sentence-medial pauses of L1 and five L2 English speaker groups for different d. Table 4 shows the result of one way ANOVA (fluency as a between group variable) over five groups of L2 English speakers for each d (except distance 7).

The result indicates that there was significant effect ($p < 0.05$) of fluency on occurrence probability of sentence-medial pause for each d. Series of Bonferroni corrected post-hoc t-test revealed that there were statistically significant differences ($p < 0.04$) between every pair of L2 English speaker groups for each d. From these results and Figure 6, it is observed that occurrence probability of sentence-medial pause for fluent L2 English speakers was lower than that of less fluent L2 English speakers for each d.

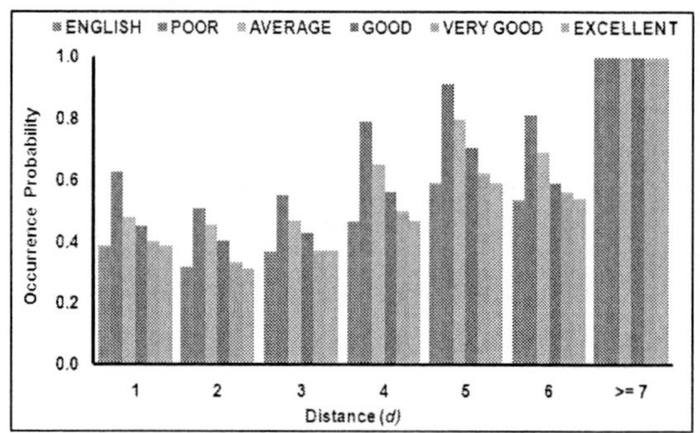

Figure 6. Effect of distance (d) upon occurrence probability of sentence medial pauses at different fluency level.

d	Result of One Way ANOVA
1	$F(4,35) = 6.7649$, $p = 0.00038$, $p < 0.05$
2	$F(4,35) = 2.6646$, $p = 0.0485$, $p < 0.05$
3	$F(4,35) = 4.4509$, $p = 0.0052$, $p < 0.05$
4	$F(4,35) = 6.7222$, $p = 0.0004$, $p < 0.05$
5	$F(4,35) = 3.4047$, $p = 0.019$, $p < 0.05$
6	$F(4,35) = 2.7127$, $p = 0.0456$, $p < 0.05$

Table 4: The result of one way ANOVA for each distance (d).

In addition, one way ANOVA was performed on each L2 English speaker group with d as between group variable. Table 5 shows the result of ANOVA for each L2 English speaker group.

Speaker Group	Result of One Way ANOVA
Poor	$F(6,28)=4.7073$, $p = 0.0019$, $p < 0.05$
Average	$F(6,42) = 3.8736$, $p = 0.0036$, $p < 0.05$
Good	$F(6,49) = 4.8918$, $p = 0.00055$, $p < 0.05$
Very Good	$F(6,84)=7.6766$, $p = 0.000014$, $p < 0.05$
Excellent	$F(4,30) = 6.9191$, $p = 0.00004$, $p < 0.05$

Table 5: The result of one way ANOVA for each L2 English speaker group.

The result indicates that there was significant effect ($p < 0.05$) of d on duration of sentence-medial pause for each L2 English speaker group. Post-hoc tests using Tukey's HSD procedure were performed to determine which distance (d) type differs significantly from each other for each L2 English speaker group. The result of series of Tukey's HSD procedure revealed that group mean difference between every pair of d was statistically significant (mean difference > HSD value, $p < 0.05$) for each L2 English speaker group. From this result and Figure 6, it is observed that mean occurrence probability of sentence-medial pause for each L2 English speaker group was almost linearly dependent on d like L1 English speakers. It is seen from Figure 6 that probability to insert pause was maximum (1.0) after phrases with d seven or more for each L2 English speaker group.

4.2 Effect of Fluency upon Pause Duration

For each of the five phrase types (NP, VP, AJP, ADVP, CP), the pause duration is defined as the amount of pause measured in millisecond (ms) at the phrase boundary. In this section, effect of L2 English (L1 Bengali) speakers' fluency on duration of sentence-medial pause was examined with respect to each individual factor (phrase type, l, d). For each factor, one way ANOVA was performed with fluency as between group variable to find out effect of fluency on pause duration. After that, a series of bonferroni corrected post-hoc t-test was performed to determine which L2 English speaker groups differ significantly from each other for each individual factor, where bonferroni corrected p value was 0.04.

Phrase Type: Figure 7 shows the average duration of sentence-medial pauses of L1 and five L2 English speaker groups for different phrase types.

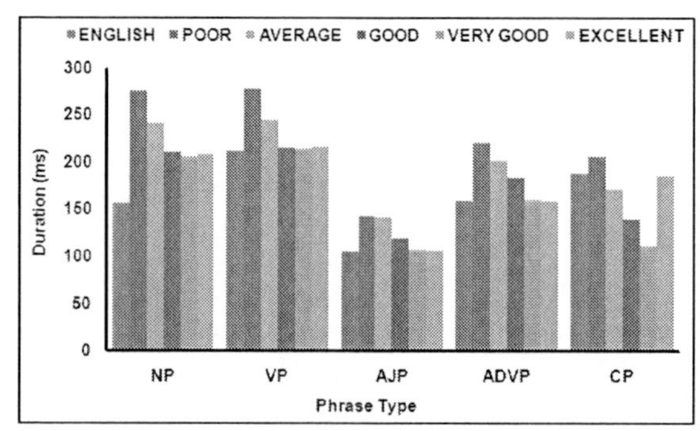

Figure 7. Effect of phrase type upon duration of sentence medial pauses at different fluency level.

The result of one way ANOVA (fluency as a between group variable) over five groups of L2 English speakers for each phrase type was shown in Table 6. The result shows that, there was a statistically significant effect ($p < 0.05$) of fluency for each phrase type.

Phrase Type	Result of One Way ANOVA
NP	F(4,35)=8.9039,p= 0.0045,p < 0.05
VP	F(4,35)=3.6386, p = 0.014,p < 0.05
AJP	F(4,35)= 3.5406, p = 0.016,p<0.05
ADVP	F(4,35)=5.3151,p = 0.0019,p <0.05
CP	F(4,35)=3.5309, p= 0.016, p < 0.05

Table 6: The result of one way ANOVA for each phrase type.

In case of NP and VP, there were statistically significant differences (p < 0.04) in pause duration between every pair of L2 English speaker groups, except good-very good, good-excellent, very good-excellent pairs where no statistical significant difference exist (p > 0.04). This finding and Figure 7 imply that duration of sentence-medial pause after phrase NP and VP was almost equal for good, very good, excellent L2 English speaker groups; otherwise duration of sentence-medial pause after phrase NP and VP was decreased as fluency of L2 English speakers was increased. In case of AJP, there were statistically significant differences (p < 0.04) in occurrence probability between every pair of L2 English speaker groups except poor-average pair. This finding and Figure 7 reveal that duration of sentence-medial pause after phrase AJP was almost equal for poor and average L2 English speaker groups; on an average duration of sentence-medial pause after phrase AJP was decreased as fluency of L2 English speakers was increased. For ADVP, bonferroni corrected post-hoc t-test revealed that there were statistically significant differences (p < 0.04) in pause duration between every pair of L2 English speaker groups except pair of very good and excellent L2 group (p > 0.04); that means pause duration after ADVP for very good and excellent L2 English speaker groups was almost equal. This finding and Figure 7 imply that duration of sentence-medial pause after phrase ADVP was decreases as fluency of L2 English speaker was increased. For CP, bonferroni corrected post-hoc t-test revealed that there were statistically significant differences (p < 0.04) in occurrence probability between every pair of L2 English speaker groups, which implies that duration of sentence-medial pause after phrase CP was decreased as fluency of L2 English speakers was increased (as shown in Figure 7). In addition, a series of t-test was carried out to determine which

group of L2 English speakers differed significantly from the L1 English speakers for each phrase type. Result of t-test revealed that every group except excellent L2 English speaker group was differed significantly (p < 0.05) from L1 English speakers for each phrase type. From this result and Figure 7, it is observed that duration of sentence-medial pause after each phrase for each L2 English speaker group except excellent L2 English speaker group was comparatively higher than that of L1 English speakers; but duration of pause after each phrase (except NP) for excellent L2 English speaker group was almost equal with L1 English speakers. From this result of analysis, it is revealed that duration of sentence-medial pause after each phrase type for fluent L2 English speakers was lower than that of less fluent L2 English speakers, and duration of sentence-medial pause for each phrase type was almost equal for both L1 English speaker and excellent L2 English speaker groups.

Phrase Length (l): Figure 8 shows the average duration of sentence-medial pauses of L1 and five L2 English speaker groups for different phrase length.

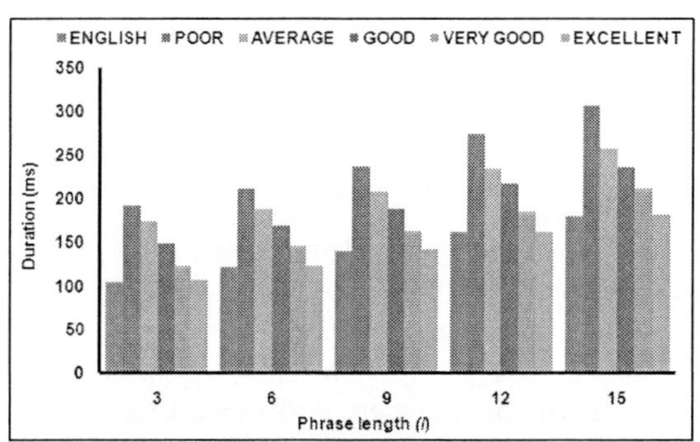

Figure 8. Effect of phrase length (l) upon duration of sentence medial pauses at different fluency level.

Table 7 shows result of one way ANOVA (fluency as a between group variable) over five groups of L2 English speakers for each l. The result indicates that there was significant effect (p < 0.05) of fluency on duration of sentence-medial pause for each l. Bonferroni corrected post-hoc t-tests revealed that there were statistically significant differences (p < 0.04) in duration of sentence-medial pause between every pair of L2 English speaker groups for each level of l. From these results and Figure 8, it is observed that duration of sentence-medial pause was inversely proportional to fluency level of L2 English speakers for each l.

l	Result of One Way ANOVA
3	F(4,35) = 2.7402, p = 0.044, p < 0.05
6	F(4,35) = 2.9548, p = 0.033, p < 0.05
9	F(4,35) = 3.8137, p = 0.011, p < 0.05
12	F(4,35) = 3.4439, p = 0.018, p < 0.05
15	F(4,35) = 3.5634, p = 0.015, p < 0.05
18	F(3,31) = 3.9202, p = 0.018, p < 0.05
21	F(1,18) = 6.0181, p = 0.025, p < 0.05

Table 7: The result of one way ANOVA for each phrase length (l).

On the other hand, one way ANOVA was performed on each L2 English speaker group with l as between group variable. Table 8 shows result of ANOVA for each L2 English speaker group.

Speaker Group	Result of One Way ANOVA
Poor	F(4,20)=9.3092,p = 0.00021,p < 0.05
Average	F(5,36)=13.4473,p=0.00002,p < 0.05
Good	F(5,42)=16.0595,p=0.000008,p<0.05
Very Good	F(6,84)=16.9523,p=0.000099,p<0.05
Excellent	F(6,42)=12.9145,p=0.000033,p<0.05

Table 8: The result of one way ANOVA for each L2 English speaker group.

The result from Table 8 indicates that there was significant effect (p< 0.05) of l on occurrence probability of sentence-medial pause for each L2 English speaker group. Post-hoc tests using Tukey's HSD procedure were performed to determine which phrase length (l) type differs significantly from each other for each L2 English speaker group. From the results of post-hoc Tukey's HSD procedure, it is observed that mean difference in pause duration between every pair of l was statistically significant (mean difference > HSD value, p < 0.05) except 3-6, 6-9 pairs of each L2 English speaker group. From result of this investigation and Figure 7, it is seen that mean duration of sentence-medial pause was almost linearly dependent on l for each L2 English speaker group like L1 English speakers.

Distance (d) between Current Phrase and its Dependent Counter Part: Figure 9 shows the average occurrence probability of sentence-medial pauses of L1 and five L2 English speaker groups for different distance. Table 9 shows result of one way ANOVA (fluency as a between group variable) over five groups of L2 English speakers for each d. The result indicates that there was significant effect (p < 0.05) of fluency on duration of sentence-medial pause for each d.

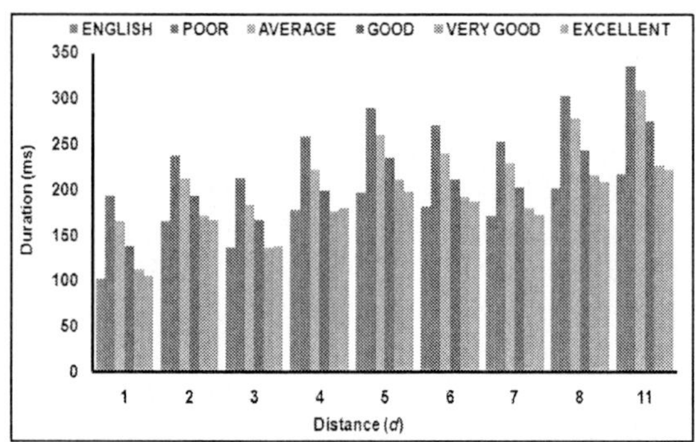

Figure 9. Effect of distance (d) upon duration of sentence medial pauses at different fluency level.

d	Result of One Way ANOVA
1	F(4,35) = 8.1601, p = 0.0093, p < 0.05
2	F(4,35) = 3.0539, p = 0.029, p < 0.05
3	F(4,35) = 2.9908, p = 0.032, p < 0.05
4	F(4,35) = 2.8627, p = 0.038, p < 0.05
5	F(4,35) = 3.0933, p = 0.028, p < 0.05
6	F(4,35) = 3.7137, p = 0.013, p < 0.05
7	F(4,35) = 4.4027, p = 0.0055, p < 0.05
8	F(4,35) = 2.8347, p = 0.039, p < 0.05
11	F(4,35) = 3.5055, p = 0.017, p < 0.05

Table 9: The result of one way ANOVA for each distance (d).

Bonferroni corrected post-hoc t-test revealed that there were statistically significant differences (p < 0.04) in pause duration between every pair of L2 English speaker groups except very good-excellent pair for each d. From these results and Figure 9, it is observed that duration of sentence-medial pause was almost equal between very good and excellent L2 English speaker groups for each d and duration of sentence-medial pause of fluent L2 English speakers was comparatively lower than that of less fluent L2 English speakers for each d.

In addition, one way ANOVA was performed on each L2 English speaker group with d as between group variable. Table 10 shows result of ANOVA for each L2 English speaker group.

Speaker Group	Result of One Way ANOVA
Poor	F(6,42)= 5.2162,p =0.00023,p < 0.05
Average	F(8,54)= 4.9018, p=0.00014,p < 0.05
Good	F(8,63)= 6.1464,p=0.000076,p< 0.05
Very Good	F(8,99)=3.4713, p = 0.0014, p < 0.05
Excellent	F(8,54)= 2.6484, p = 0.016, p < 0.05

Table 10: The result of one way ANOVA for each L2 English speaker group.

The result indicates that there was significant effect ($p < 0.05$) of distance on duration of sentence-medial pause for each L2 English speaker group. Post-hoc tests using Tukey's HSD procedure were performed to determine which distance (d) types differ significantly from each other for each L2 English speaker group. Tukey's HSD procedure reveals that mean difference between every pair of phrases (except some pairs of phrases) of each L2 English speaker group was statistically significant (mean difference > HSD value, $p < 0.05$).From Figure 9 and result of Tukey's HSD procedure, it is seen that average duration of sentence-medial pauses for each L2 English speaker group was almost linearly dependent on distance (d) like L1 English speaker group.

5 Conclusions

From this study, it is seen that there was significant effect of L2 English (L1 Bengali) speakers' fluency on occurrence probability as well as duration of sentence-medial pause. Result of this comparative study reveals that, for each phrase type, each phrase length level, and each distance level, occurrence probability and duration of sentence-medial pause were increased as fluency level of L2 English speakers was decreased. In particular, occurrence probability and duration of sentence-medial pause of every L2 English speaker group except excellent L2 English speaker group for each phrase type, each phrase length level, each distance level, were higher than L1 English speaker group, but occurrence probability and duration of pause after each respective phrase type, each phrase length level, and each distance level for excellent L2 English speaker group were almost equal to that of L1 English speakers. Moreover, occurrence probability and duration of sentence-medial pause were increased almost linearly with phrase length as well

as distance for every L2 English speaker group respectively. From this detailed comparative study, it may seem to suggest that occurrence probability as well as duration of sentence-medial pauses in English readout speech of fluent L2 English speakers are lower than that of less fluent L2 English speakers at every phrase length and distance values respectively. In addition, occurrence probability and duration of sentence-medial pauses in English readout speech are linearly dependent on phrase length and distance respectively for fluent as well as less fluent L2 English speakers.

References

David Nunan.2003. The Impact of English as a Global Language on Educational Policies and Practices in the Asia-Pacific Region. *TESOL quarterly*, 37(4): 589-613.

David Temperley. 2007. Minimization of dependency length in written English. *Cognition*, 105(2): 300-333.

David Temperley.2005. The dependency structure of coordinate phrases: A corpus approach. *Journal of psycholinguistic research*, 34(6): 577-601.

Gunnar Fant, Anita Kruckenberg, and Joana Barbosa Ferreira. 2003. *Individual variations in pausing. A study of read speech*, Proc. of Fonetik, Lovanger, 193-196.

Helen Meng, Chiu-yu Tseng, Mariko Kondo, Alissa M. Harrison, and Tanya Visceglia. 2009. *Studying L2 Suprasegmental Features in Asian Englishes: A Position Paper*, Proc. of Interspeech, Brighton, UK, 1715-1718.

Hiroya Fujisaki and T. Omura. 1971. *Characteristics of durations of pauses and speech segments in connected speech.* Annual Report, Engineering Research Institute, Faculty of Engineering, University of Tokyo, 30: 69-74.

Hiroya Fujisaki, Sumio Ohno, and Seiji Yamada. 1999. *Factors Affecting the occurrence and Duration of Sentence-medial Pauses in Japanese Text Reading*, Proc. of ICPhS, San Francisco, 99: 659-662.

Joanne L Miller.1978. Interactions in processing segmental and suprasegmental features of speech. *Perception & Psychophysics,* 24(2):175-180.

Krishna Bhattacharya. 1988. *Bengali phonetic reader*, volume 28. Central Institute of Indian Languages, Mysore.

Mariko Kondo and Hajime Tsubaki. 2012. *Fluency and L1 phonology interference on L2 English analysis OF Japanese AESOP corpus Speech Database and Assessments*, Oriental COCOSDA, Macau, China,123-128.

Miguel Rodríguez Mondonedo. 1999. IPA. Handbook of the International Phonetic Association. A Guide to the Use of the International Phonetic Alphabet. *LEXIS-LIMA*, 23(2): 451-462.

Shambhu Nath Saha and Shyamal Kr Das Mandal. 2013. *Analysis of occurrence probability and duration of sentence-medial pauses in English readout speech for L2 English speakers compared to L1 English speakers,* Oriental COCOSDA, Delhi, India, 1-6.

Shyamal Kr Das Mandal, Arup Saha, Tulika Basu, Keikichi Hirose, and Hiroya Fujisak. 2010. *Modeling of Sentence-medial Pauses in Bangla Readout Speech: Occurrence and Duration*, Proc. of Interspeech, Makuhari, Japan, 26-30.

Sudipta Acharya and Shyamal Kr Das Mandal. 2012. *Occurrence and Duration Modeling of Sentence Medial Pause for Bangla Text Reading at Different Speech Rate*, Oriental COCOSDA, Macau, China, 62-67.

Tanya Viscelgia, Chiu-yu Tseng, Mariko Kondo, Helen Meng, and Yoshinori Sagisaka. 2009. *Phonetic Aspects of Content Design in AESOP (Asian English Speech cOrpus Project*, Oriental COCOSDA,Beijing, China,60-65.

Acoustic Correlates of Voicing and Gemination in Bangla

Aanusha Ghosh
Center for Linguistics
Jawaharlal Nehru University
New Delhi
aanusha.ghosh@gmail.com

Abstract

The goal of this paper is to conduct an acoustic phonetic investigation of both primary and secondary cues that aid in the distinction between voiced and voiceless geminates in Bangla. Results of the statistical analyses examining both duration and non-durational correlates show that besides closure duration secondary cues such as the amplitude of the stop release burst and the fundamental frequencies of the vowels immediately preceding and following the obstruent are acoustically significant in the distinction between voiced and voiceless geminates and singletons. Voiced stops have significantly greater burst amplitudes than voiceless ones, and geminates are flanked by vowels with significantly higher F0's than those flanking corresponding singletons.

We also briefly explore the effects of gemination on V-to-V coarticulation. The assumption is that longer consonantal duration will act as a more effective barrier to V-to-V coarticulation in the case of geminates as opposed to singletons. Particularly, in the case of dental geminates, we hypothesize that longer consonantal duration contributes to lingual fronting, which manifests itself as greater resistance to V-to-V coarticulation.

1 Introduction

Maintaining voicing in obstruents is articulatorily challenging. Sufficient transglottal air pressure drop is required to maintain voicing. This becomes harder for obstruents, which require rapid increase in intraoral air pressure. The difficulty increases in geminate obstruents as they have longer closure. (Ohala, 1983) Hence, crosslinguistically, voiced geminates are rarer than their voiceless counterparts (Hayes and Steriade, 2004). Bangla, an Eastern Indo-Aryan language spoken in Bangladesh and the Indian states of West Bengal, Tripura and Assam, and the fifth most spoken language in the world[1] with nearly 300 million speakers is one of the few languages which have both voiced and voiceless geminates in their inventory.

Work on gemination in Bangla has been sparse. The only existing study on Bangla geminates focuses on voiceless stops and does not take voiced geminates into account (Lahiri and Hankamer, 1988; Hankamer et al., 1989). This paper aims to fill that gap by taking voiced geminates and the effects they might have on acoustic cues into consideration. It also takes a look at how vowel to vowel coarticulation might be affected because of gemination, especially in the case of dental stops. The articulatory motivation is that there should be some lingual fronting in the case of dental geminates, in order to maintain air pressure for a longer duration, and this fronting should then pose higher resistance to V-to-V coarticulation.

The rest of the paper is organised as follows: In Section 2, we cover a brief overview of work done on geminates and outline the aims and motivations of the current study. Section 3 presents the materials and methods used for the study, while Section 4 discusses the parameters measured in the study. Section 5 elucidates the statistical analysis employed for drawing inferences from the data. Section 6 deals with the F2 locus equations fitted for investigating the variation of the degree of coarticulatory resistance. Section 7 collates the results, and Section 8 concludes the work with a discussion on the inferences drawn from analysis and explores issues that need further work.

2 Related work

Lahiri and Hankamer (1988) investigated various acoustic cues and their perceptual relevance on the distinction between geminates and non-geminates in Bangla and Turkish. Their study, which focused only on voiceless stops, confirmed that closure duration was a perceptually salient cue for distinguishing between geminates and singletons in Bangla and Turkish, but discounted the fact that V1 duration was a secondary cue that could be used to identify geminates. In a subsequent paper (Hankamer et al., 1989), they concurred that secondary cues do contribute information about the distinction between geminates and singletons when the primary cues are ambiguous. However, they never explicitly stated exactly what these

D S Sharma, R Sangal and E Sherly. Proc. of the 12th Intl. Conference on Natural Language Processing, pages 413–418,
Trivandrum, India. December 2015. ©2015 NLP Association of India (NLPAI)

---

[1]https://en.wikipedia.org/wiki/Bengali_

secondary acoustic cues might be, proposing instead that the set of secondary features that biased subjects when the primary cue of consonant duration was ambiguous, was possibly due to a combination of cues, each by itself too subtle for their measurements to detect.

The cues that have been found to be consistently significant in the geminate-singleton distinction include stop closure duration and the length of the preceding vowel (V1 duration). Geminates have been found to have longer stop closure duration and shorter V1 duration (Esposito and Di Benedetto, 1999; Stevens and Hajek, 2004). Shortening of V2 duration in the case of geminates has also been observed. However, it has not been significantly different from that of singletons (Esposito and Di Benedetto, 1999).

Voicing has also been observed to have an effect on stop closure duration in obstruents. Stevens and Hajek (2004) found voiceless geminates to be substantially longer than voiced ones in Sienese Italian.

Studies of word-initial voiceless geminates in languages like Pattani Malay (Abramson, 1986; Abramson, 1987; Abramson, 1992; Abramson, 1999) and Kelantan Malay (Hamzah, 2013; Hamzah et al., 2013; Hamzah et al., 2012) show that when listeners do not have the advantage of relying on consonant duration as an acoustic cue for gemination, they make use of secondary cues which help in disambiguation. In particular, amplitude and fundamental frequency (Abramson, 1992; Abramson, 1999) were found to be significant cues to word-initial consonant length. Stevens and Hajek (2004) found that long voiced stops are often partially devoiced. Moreover, he revealed that in the case of Sienese Italian, voiceless geminates were preaspirated and their voiced counterparts were devoiced, so that the phonetic contrast between voiced and voiceless stops no longer manifested in a difference in the presence or absence of closure voicing, but rather in the absence or presence of aspiration before the geminated consonant.

F2 locus equations, which are a source of relational invariance that determine place of articulation, are also signifiers of the degree of coarticulatory resistance for a given consonant. Fowler and Brancazio (2000) showed that the more highly resistant a consonant is, the lower its locus equation slope. High coarticulation resistance, measured as a low standard deviation of F2 at the consonant normalized by variability of F2 across vowels, directly leads to a low locus equation slope. Low coarticulation resistance would, by the same logic, directly lead to a locus equation slope close to 1, since the variability of F2 measured at consonant release would be nearly the variability measured at the midpoint of the vowel.(Iskarous et al., 2010)

Esposito and Di Benedetto (1999) observed that

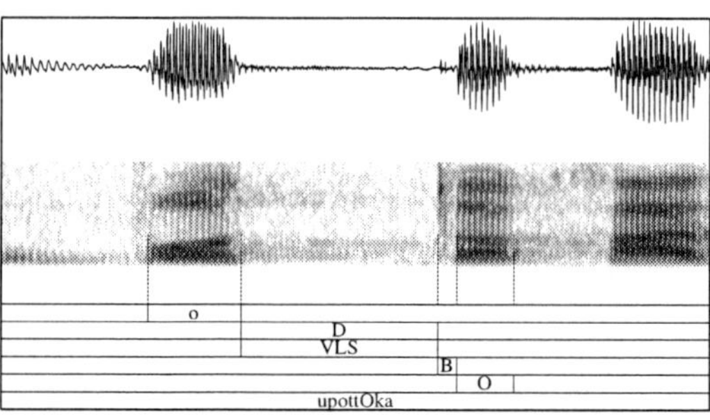

Figure 1: Waveform display of the word /upoṭːɔka/ ('valley')

V1 formant frequencies showed no relationship with gemination, suggesting that this showed that no extra vocal effort was required for articulating geminates. They made no comment about formant transitions, however, or cast any light on the question of the variance of coarticulatory resistance in the presence of geminates.

In a study of the effect of consonant duration on V-to-V coarticulation in Japanese, Löfqvist (2009) found no significant effect of consonant closure duration on the degree of vowel-to-vowel coarticulation.

The aim of this paper is to answer the following questions:

- What are the major acoustic cues that set voiced geminates apart from voiceless ones?

- Are the secondary cues employed by word-medial geminates identical to those employed by word-initial geminates (in languages that do have them)?

- If voicing does indeed shorten the duration of stop closure, and gemination leads to partial devoicing (Stevens and Hajek, 2004), how are voiced geminates differentiated from voiceless singletons?

- Does gemination affect V-to-V coarticulation?

3 Materials and methods

The Shruti corpus, a Bangla corpus of read speech, built and maintained by Indian Institute Of Technology, Kharagpur (IITKGP) was used as the source of data for this study. The corpus consists of 7383 unique sentences. There are 34 speakers with ages varying from 20 to 40 years. 26 of the speakers are male, and 8 female. The speaker age in the corpus varies from 20 to 40 yrs. 700 words containing geminate and singleton stop consonant sequences from the

Shruti corpus were hand annotated for word, place and manner of articulation, consonant burst, and preceding and following vowels using Praat [2]. Each annotation file had six tiers of information: the vowel preceding the consonant, V1, the place of articulation of the stop, POA, the manner of articulation of the stop, MOA, the release burst, the following vowel, V2 and the word in which the geminate/singletons sequence appears.

The distribution of the data is given in Table 1.

	Singleton		Geminate	
Place of Articulation	Voiced	Voiceless	Voiced	Voiceless
Bilabial	32	20	44	10
Dental	44	149	36	165
Retroflex	—	48	18	25
Velar	11	59	17	20

Table 1: Distribution of singleton and geminate tokens across places of articulation

There are no voiced retroflex singleton tokens because the voiced retroflex ɖ does not appear as a singleton word-medially in Bangla.

4 Measurements

The following parameters were examined:

- Consonant duration

- Duration of the preceding vowel (V1)

- Duration of the following vowel (V2)

- Duration of the stop release burst

- RMS amplitude of the stop release burst

- Fundamental frequency of the preceding vowel

- Fundemental frequency of the following vowel

These measurements were taken for both voiced and voiceless geminates as well as voiced and voiceless singletons corresponding to four places of articulation: bilabial, dental, retroflex and velar.

5 Analysis

Three-way ANOVAs were done to test the significance of place of articulation, voicing and gemination on the duration of stop closure and length of the preceding and following vowels (V1 and V2). The interaction effects of all three factors on each of the parameters are given in Figures 2 and 3. In carrying out all of the following tests, the probability of type I error, α was fixed at 0.01 (1%).

[2]Boersma, Paul & Weenink, David (2015). Praat: doing phonetics by computer [Computer program]. Version 5.4.08, retrieved 24 March 2015 from http://www.praat.org/

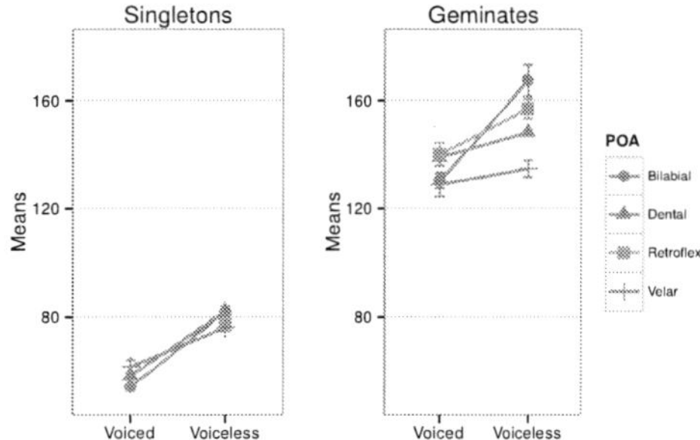

Figure 2: Effect of place of articulation, voicing and gemination on consonant duration

The ANOVA showed that gemination [F(1,806)=1146.749, p<0.0001], place of articulation [F(1,806)=6.242, p<0.001] and voicing [F(1,806)= 43.146, p<0.001] are all significant contributors towards variation of consonant duration.

In the case of V1 duration, gemination [F(1,810)=21.86, p<0.01], place of articulation [F(1,810)=24.109, p<0.00001], and voicing [F(1,810)=77.33, p<0.00001] are all highly significant factors.

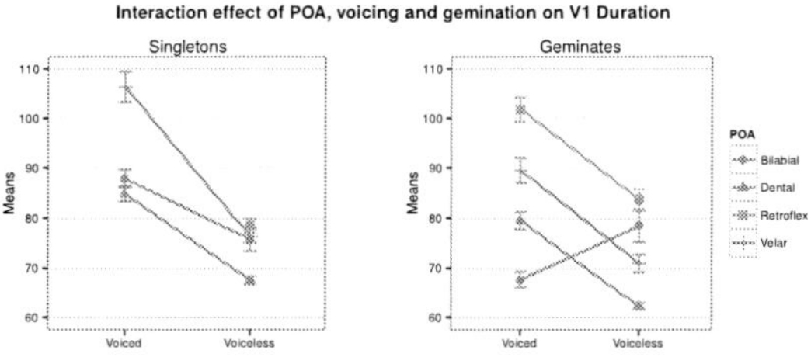

Figure 3: Effect of place of articulation, voicing and gemination on duration of preceding vowel

A three-way ANOVA carried out on V2 duration revealed that none of the factors appear to have any effect whatsoever of the duration of the V2.

Two-way ANOVAs were carried out to test the significance of voicing and gemination on duration and amplitude of the stop release burst, as well as the fundamental frequency (F0) of both the preceding and the following vowels. The effects of gemination [F(1,817)=19.102, p<0.01] and voicing [F(1,817)=71.13, p<0.0001] were found to be extremely significant contributors towards the variance of burst duration.

It was also found that voicing [F(1,817)=93.661, p< 0.0001] plays a very significant role in determining the burst amplitude.

The effect of gemination [F(1,817)=10.273, p<0.01] was found to be significant on the variation exhibited by F0 values of the preceding vowel.

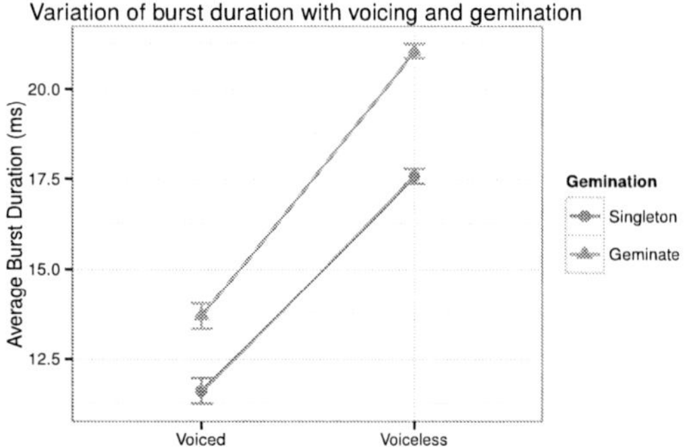

Figure 4: Effect of voicing and gemination on duration of stop release burst

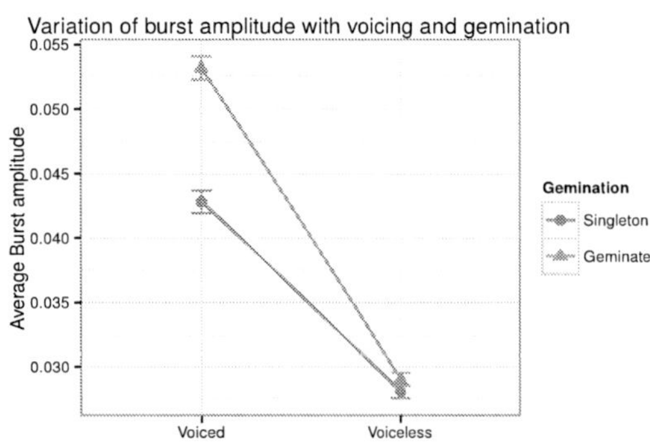

Figure 5: Effect of voicing and gemination on amplitude of stop release burst

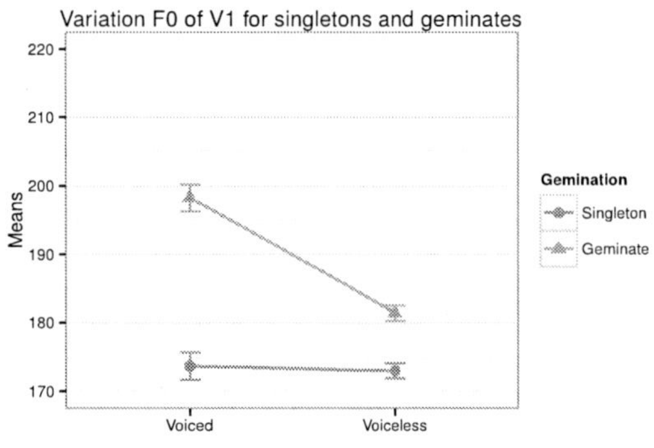

Figure 6: Effect of voicing and gemination on fundamental frequency of the preceding vowel

Voicing [$F(1,817)=4.613$, $p>0.01$] did not appear to have any effects on V1 duration.

Much like the preceding vowel, F0 of the following vowel is affected significantly by gemination [$F(1,817)=13.860$, $p<0.001$] but not by voicing [$F(1,817)=5.149$, $p>0.01$].

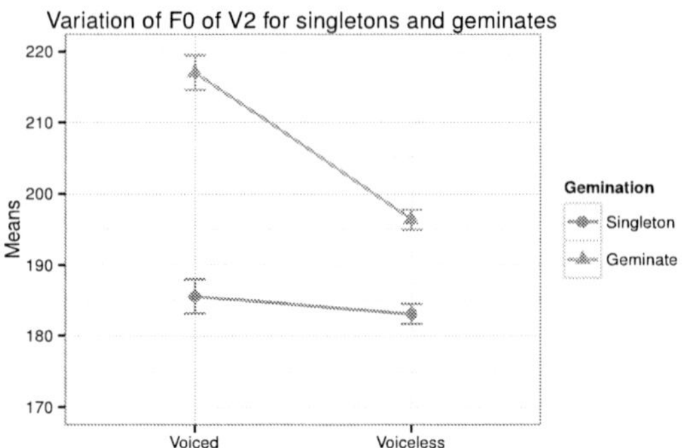

Figure 7: Effect of voicing and gemination on fundamental frequency of the following vowel

6 F2 Locus Equations

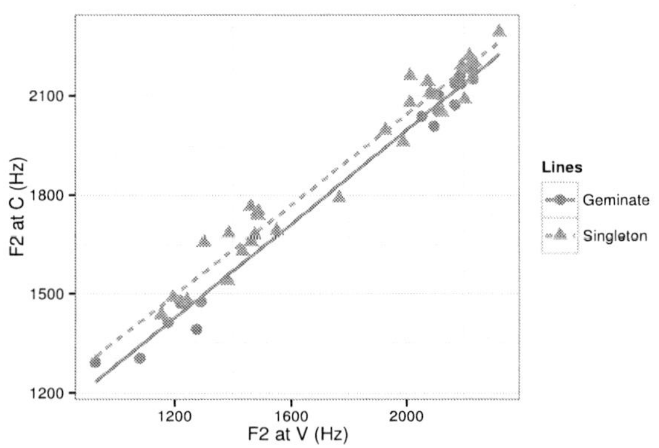

Figure 8: F2 Locus Equations for voiceless dental geminate and singleton

For modelling the variation of the degree of coarticulatory resistance of obstruents with gemination, locus equations of $F2_{onset}$ against $F2_{mid}$ of the vowel following the obstruent were plotted for both singleton and geminate tokens. Due to the sparsity of both inter and intra-speaker data, tokens from a single speaker, "Chan", was chosen for the study. The preceding vowel was fixed as the high front vowel /i/ and the obstruent was fixed as the voiceless dental /t̪/. 47 tokens were analysed, 18 of which were geminates and the others singletons. The unequal sample size is due to the fact that the data was taken from pre-existing corpus, and was thus subject to corpus-specific idiosyncrasies.

The second formant measures for the following vowel (V2) were taken as described in the previous chapter, with two measures for each formant - one at the 5% mark of the vowel for $F2_{onset}$ and another at the 50% mark of the vowel for $F2_{mid}$. The values were plotted and a regression line fitted through the data. The regression equation relating $F2_{onset}$ and $F2_{mid}$ is given by:

$$F2_{onset} = \beta + \alpha F2_{mid}$$

where α is the slope of the regression line, and β is the intercept.

The fitted regression lines for singletons and geminates (Figure 8) show no significant differences in their slopes. This implies that, at least for the given vocalic and consonantal environment, gemination does not affect the degree of coarticulation. However, more data from other speakers including different preceding vowels and obstruents is required to draw stronger conclusions in this regard.

7   Results

Burst Amplitude	F0 of surrounding vowels	
	High	Low
High	Voiced Geminate	Voiced Singleton
Low	Voiceless Geminate	Voiceless Singleton

Table 2: The roles of fundamental frequency and burst amplitude in the voiced-voiceless geminate-singleton distinction

Voicing has a significant effect on consonant duration, with both voiced singletons and voiced geminates having significantly shorter closure durations than their voiceless counterparts.

The duration of the preceding vowel is strongly affected by gemination. Geminates have shorter V1 duration. V1 duration is significantly affected by voicing as well — voiced obstruents are preceded by longer vowels. V1 duration is also contingent on the place of articulation, and displays interaction effects of place of articulation with both voicing and gemination.

Both gemination and voicing affect the duration of the stop release burst - burst duration is greater for geminates. Burst amplitude is significantly affected by voicing but not gemination — voiced stops have greater burst amplitude.

Fundamental frequencies of both vowels are affected by gemination. Vowels flanking geminates have higher fundamental frequency than those flanking singletons. Table 2 shows the variation of burst amplitude and fundamental frequency of surrounding vowels with voicing and gemination. Together, these two cues help in disambiguating voiced and voiceless singletons and geminates.

The F2 locus equations plotted for voiceless dental geminates and singletons with V1 fixed as /i/ show no appreciable difference in their slopes, indicating that geminates do not, after all, affect V-to-V coarticulation, at least as far as this particular vocalic and consonantal context is concerned.

8   Conclusion and further work

The perceptual experiments on voiceless geminate stops carried out by (Lahiri and Hankamer, 1988) and (Hankamer et al., 1989) focused exclusively on durational correlates. The presence of secondary acoustic cues, while acknowledged by them, were not credited with enough perceptual significance other than serving to bias listeners only when the primary cue of stop closure duration was ambiguous. However, the issue of voicing, the consequent perturbation of closure duration and its effects on the perception of geminates was left unaddressed in their work.

The results of this study clearly show that burst amplitude and fundamental frequency, both non-durational correlates, are significant contributors towards the distinction between voiced and voiceless geminates. Burst amplitude serves to disambiguate between voiced and voiceless stops, with the former having much greater burst amplitude than the latter. Fundamental frequency, on the other hand, is a key parameter in distinguishing geminates from non-geminates - F0 of vowels surrounding geminate consonants is consistently higher than for singletons. Burst duration is also a significant indicator for both gemination and voicing, with voiceless obstruents and geminates having longer burst duration than voiced stops and singletons respectively.

These results corroborate the findings of (Abramson, 1992; Abramson, 1999) and (Hamzah et al., 2012; Hamzah et al., 2013) regarding word-initial geminates in Pattani Malay and Kelantan Malay respectively. Thus, we can safely conclude that amplitude and F0 are powerful secondary cues that affect both word-initial and word-medial geminates.

We can also conclude that despite voicing shortening the duration of stop closure, geminates and singletons are still distinguishable by the fundamental frequencies of the surrounding vowels, which are significantly higher in the case of geminates.

From the preliminary study of the locus equations of the second formant of the following vowel, no difference was found between the slopes of the equations for geminates and singletons, indicating that geminates do no affect V-to-V coarticulation appreciably, at least as far as the voiceless dental /t̪/ is concerned. However, more data for other places of articulation and different vocalic contexts is required in this regard to draw a stronger conclusion.

One of the avenues of investigation that was left unexplored in this study, and which definitely merits further research, is a comparison of the degree of devoicing (a phenomenon noted in Sienese Italian and Japanese by Stevens and Hajek (2004) and Kawahara (2005) respectively) that occurs in voiced geminates and singletons in Bangla.

413

References

Arthur S Abramson. 1986. The perception of word-initial consonant length: Pattani malay. *Journal of the International Phonetic Association*, 16(01):8–16.

Arthur S Abramson. 1987. Word-initial consonant length in pattani malay. *Haskins Laboratories Status Report on Speech Research*, pages 143–147.

Arthur Abramson. 1992. Amplitude as a cue to word-initial consonant length: Pattani malay. *Haskins Laboratories Status Report on Speech Research*, pages 251–254.

Arthur S Abramson. 1999. Fundamental frequency as a cue to word-initial consonant length: Pattani malay. In *Proceedings of the 14th International Congress of Phonetic Sciences*, pages 591–594.

Anna Esposito and Maria Gabriella Di Benedetto. 1999. Acoustical and perceptual study of gemination in italian stops. *The Journal of the Acoustical Society of America*, 106(4):2051–2062.

Carol A Fowler and Lawrence Brancazio. 2000. Coarticulation resistance of american english consonants and its effects on transconsonantal vowel-to-vowel coarticulation. *Language and Speech*, 43(1):1–41.

Hilmi Hamzah, Janet Fletcher, and John Hajek. 2012. An acoustic analysis of release burst amplitude in the kelantan malay singleton/geminate stop contrast. In *Proceedings of the 14th Australasian International Conference on Speech Science and Technology*, pages 85–88.

Hilmi Hamzah, Janet Fletcher, and John Hajek. 2013. Amplitude and f0 as acoustic correlates of kelantan malay word-initial geminates.

Hilmi Hamzah. 2013. *The acoustics and perception of the word-initial singleton/geminate contrast in Kelantan Malay*. Ph.D. thesis.

Jorge Hankamer, Aditi Lahiri, and Jacques Koreman. 1989. Perception of consonant length: Voiceless stops in turkish and bengali. *Journal of Phonetics*, 17(4):283–298.

Bruce Hayes and Donca Steriade. 2004. The phonetic bases of phonological markedness. In B. Hayes, R. Kirchner, and D. Steriade, editors, *Phonetically Based Phonology*. Cambridge University Press.

Khalil Iskarous, Carol A Fowler, and Douglas H Whalen. 2010. Locus equations are an acoustic expression of articulator synergy. *The Journal of the Acoustical Society of America*, 128(4):2021–2032.

Shigeto Kawahara. 2005. Voicing and geminacy in Japanese: An acoustic and perceptual study. In K. Flack and S. Kawahara, editors, *University of Massachusetts Occasional Papers in Linguistics 31: Papers in Experimental Phonetics and Phonology*, pages 87–120.

A. Lahiri and J Hankamer. 1988. The timing of geminate consonants. *Journal of Phonetics*, 16:327–338.

Anders Löfqvist. 2009. Vowel-to-vowel coarticulation in japanese: the effect of consonant duration. *The Journal of the Acoustical Society of America*, 125(2):636–639.

John J Ohala. 1983. The origin of sound patterns in vocal tract constraints. In *The production of speech*, pages 189–216. Springer.

Mary Stevens and John Hajek. 2004. Comparing voiced and voiceless geminates in sienese italian: what role does preaspiration play? In *Proceedings of the 10th Australian International Conference on Speech Science and Technology. Sydney: S*, volume 340, pages 340–345.

Author Index

Association for Computational Linguistics
209 N. Eighth Street
Stroudsburg, Pennsylvania 18360

ISBN 978-1-5108-3787-4